Data Localization Laws and Policy

Data Localization Laws and Policy

The EU Data Protection International Transfers Restriction Through a Cloud Computing Lens

W Kuan Hon

Solicitor; Editor, Encyclopedia of Data Protection and Privacy*; Fellow, Open Data Institute*

Edward Elgar
PUBLISHING

Cheltenham, UK • Northampton, MA, USA

Published by
Edward Elgar Publishing Limited
The Lypiatts
15 Lansdown Road
Cheltenham
Glos GL50 2JA
UK

Edward Elgar Publishing, Inc.
William Pratt House
9 Dewey Court
Northampton
Massachusetts 01060
USA

A catalogue record for this book
is available from the British Library

Library of Congress Control Number: 2017931739

This book is available electronically in the **Elgar**online
Law subject collection
DOI 10.4337/9781786431974

ISBN 978 1 78643 196 7 (cased)
ISBN 978 1 78643 197 4 (eBook)

Typeset by Columns Design XML Ltd, Reading
Printed and bound by CPI Group (UK) Ltd, Croydon, CR0 4YY

Contents

Foreword

This new text marks a significant step in the analysis and understanding of the challenges of cloud computing and the protection of personal data. Kuan Hon is particularly well qualified to provide this guide to the issues, having a background in law, technology and the commercial world.

Importantly any work by Kuan is always readable, accessible and lively. These are important features in helping to bridge the gap which can sometimes exist between the academic and the practical work. The range of her experience helps Kuan to bring a broad perspective to the topic.

At the same time of course it examines in real depth the technology and the real, as opposed to the presumed, risks cloud computing can bring and how these can be addressed. Those of us who are weathered practitioners in this area have watched the doctrine that personal data is at risk once it has left the European Union and must be tightly constrained to prevent this risk assume increased importance over the years. There was no such presumption under the Council of Europe Convention (Treaty 108) which led to the UK's first data protection law in 1984. On the contrary, transfers of personal data were permitted but could be stopped if the regulator considered that the data would be at risk in the receiving jurisdiction.

The impulse and justification for Directive 95/46/EC was the need to establish a single market in the Union; the erection of a corresponding barrier to the free interchange of personal data with the rest of the world was something of a sideways consequence. Yet over the years it has become an aim in its own right; the barriers to free interchange have become more and more like an article of faith. Kuan shows how inappropriate those barriers are in today's environment and how little they are associated with real risk.

This text addresses what may seem to be academic issues, but in reality they are far from academic in nature. They impact on every facet of our commercial and social environment. It is a text which skilfully examines the issues and should make us focus on the real issues. It should be read by every data protection supervisory authority and lawmaker in Europe. Let us hope that it will.

Rosemary Jay
October 2016

Foreword

Kuan Hon's new book deals with a crucial question, namely how to protect personal data that are processed and transferred on the global Internet. Her dual background as a computer scientist and a lawyer allows her to analyse the relevant issues from both the technical and legal perspectives.

There is currently a debate in academia, business and politics about how data protection law should be applied to protect personal data that are processed and transferred across national borders. One set of views has been variously called data localization, data nationalism or informational sovereignty, and refers to the creation of incentives or requirements to localize data processing and storage. The other side rejects such initiatives as incompatible with a free and borderless Internet.

Discussions about data localization have become highly politicized in recent years. Data processing has attained great importance in economic, social and technological terms, and it is not surprising that this is reflected in the political debate. But the politics of the discussion often obscure the important questions that this phenomenon raises. It is the accomplishment of this book to illuminate the substantive legal and technical issues that are at stake in the debate about data localization.

Applicable law and jurisdiction have often been viewed as narrow technical areas of the law of interest only to specialists. As this book demonstrates, they are actually key topics of the information society, since they determine what rights individuals will have in the processing of their personal data, and how these rights can be enforced.

Data localization is not just a short-term phenomenon, but reflects a profound unease with increasing globalization, and a lack of certainty as to whether we want national borders carried over onto the online space. This book helps illuminate the choices that we face as a society in deciding where we want those boundaries to be set.

Christopher Kuner
Brussels, October 2016

About the author

Dr W Kuan Hon MA (Cantab), LLM (UPenn), MSc (Imperial), LLM (QMUL), PhD (QMUL) is an Editor of the *Encyclopedia of Data Protection and Privacy*, a Fellow of the Open Data Institute, a solicitor specializing in data protection law and cloud computing in the City of London and Adjunct Research Director at International Data Corporation (IDC). Formerly a Senior Researcher investigating cloud legal issues at Queen Mary University of London, she devised and taught its first cloud computing law LLM module.

An English solicitor and a (non-practising) New York attorney, Kuan has degrees in law and computing science and a joint law/computer science doctorate. Lead author of eight chapters in *Cloud Computing Law* (OUP 2013, Millard ed.) including four on data protection, she has also published numerous articles.

Formerly a member of the British Computer Society's Information Privacy Expert Panel, Kuan participates in the EU PRISMACLOUD project's user advisory board, and she is an invited observer of the Code of Conduct Task Force of CISPE (Cloud Infrastructure Services Providers in Europe). A UK Cloud Awards judge (2016–17), she was awarded a lifetime professional membership of the Cloud Industry Forum in 2017.

Kuan is a regular presenter at events, including for CERN, the Cloud Security Alliance and ENISA, and has been quoted and interviewed in the media.

Preface

Across the world, countries are introducing more – and more stringent – data localization laws, requiring certain digital data to be kept within equipment physically located on national soil, with limited exceptions. This increasing trend threatens digital globalization. Data localization laws are major barriers holding organizations back from using cloud computing, despite cloud's acknowledged benefits. Data localization is touted in the name of preserving individuals' privacy, which is of course an important goal. However, better ways exist to safeguard privacy and protect individuals' personal data from both corporations and governments, whether of individuals' own countries or other countries. These better ways should be developed further, instead of always focusing on data localization, which I argue is the wrong solution for privacy.

Calls for further and tighter data localization laws were spurred particularly by contractor Edward Snowden's revelations in 2013 ('Snowden's revelations') of mass collection and interception, by the US National Security Agency (NSA), the UK intelligence agency (GCHQ) and other authorities, of the digital data of many countries' citizens. Underlying these calls is the understandable aim of protecting a country's residents from excessive surveillance by other countries' authorities. However, far from data localization laws achieving their purported aim of preserving privacy and preventing bulk surveillance, the constant emphasis on data localization as the 'one true way' in fact primarily serves to cause other, better ways to be overlooked and, the cynical might suggest, diverts attention away from countries' mass surveillance of their *own* citizens (Ferracane 2015), enabling them to maintain and enhance their ability to surveil (Sargsyan 2016) – and control (Chander and Lê 2015) – their citizens by keeping citizens' data within easier reach (Kuner 2013a).

Taking a multidisciplinary approach, this book demonstrates data localization's dangers by using, as a case study, the EU restriction on international transfers of personal data in the context of cloud computing, as the most pertinent exemplar. However, most of its arguments apply equally to other countries' data localization laws, i.e. cross-border transfers from *non*-EU countries, partly because many non-EU countries have adopted very similar data protection laws. While I analyse the impact on cloud computing of the international transfers restriction under the Data Protection Directive and General Data Protection Regulation, many of my arguments also apply to cross-border transfers of *non*-personal digital data, and to cross-border transfers in technology sourcing, outsourcing or other transactions *not* involving cloud computing.

This book outlines cloud computing; explains the reasons for its scope, delineating it more precisely; and provides an overview of the DPD and the Restriction. Then, it discusses the Restriction's historical background and objective; analyses the meaning of 'transfer' 'to' third countries; unpicks assumptions underlying the Restriction, showing their inapplicability today; discusses uncertainties and practical problems with the Restriction's 'adequate protection' and 'adequate safeguards' concepts; and highlights compliance and enforcement problems. It then suggests how, given such issues, a different approach would better achieve the Restriction's avowed legislative objective, while being more technology-neutral: notably, focusing on control of access to personal data, particularly intelligible personal data, through emphasizing security and accountability regardless of data location. Where relevant, I also discuss other privacy-related policy objectives that may now underlie the Restriction's invocation, showing how they, too, are not necessarily advanced by restricting data location.

This book reflects the position as at October 2016. Developments thereafter are not covered unless stated, but updates (and links to many references cited here) are available from www.e-elgar.com/data-localization-laws-and-policy-companion-site.

W Kuan Hon, http://www.kuan0.com
London, October 2016

Acknowledgements

I dedicate this book to Erica Wells and Siobhan Ward, who have enriched my life immeasurably. I wouldn't be anywhere without you. Thank you so much for your unstinting love, friendship and support throughout the years. I thank Grace Yeoh, too, for her constant friendship since our schooldays.

This book is also dedicated to my inspirational early career mentors, Richard Bethell-Jones and Richard Newton-Price. To me, they set the standard in legal expertise and professionalism, in focus and clarity of thought. In particular, I have always sought to emulate Richard Bethell-Jones's uniquely transparent and accessible writing style. I am also very fortunate to have had the privilege of working with Robin Parsons, Jonathan Rushworth and Jenifer Williams in my past finance/insolvency life, whose leadership and support I very much appreciated.

In writing this book I stand on the shoulders of giants, and I must mention Christopher Kuner's seminal writings on international data transfers. I also learned much about practical data protection from the works of Rosemary Jay. I am honoured that they are contributing Forewords.

I am also grateful to Chris Reed, Hamed Haddadi, Chris Marsden and Toktam Mahmoodi for their invaluable guidance and insight, Christopher Millard and Ian Walden for the opportunity to participate in Queen Mary University of London cloud projects, Robin Callendar-Smith, Marc Dautlich and Sarah Cameron for their continuing encouragement, and Louise Townsend for her thoughts regarding security measures in adequacy criteria.

Finally, I thank the European Commission, Council and Parliament, EU Fundamental Rights Agency, Datainspektionen (Sweden), Datatilsynet (Denmark), the Information Commissioner's Office (UK) and Gartner for their helpful responses to my queries.

Abbreviations/glossary

1990-Proposal	1990 DPD draft, COM(90)314 final – SYN 287
1992-Proposal	1992 DPD draft, COM(92)422 final – SYN 287
2010 Decision	Commission Decision 2010/87/EU
2010 SCCs	SCCs under 2010 Decision
AEPD	Agencia Española de Protección de Datos, Spain's DPA
APEC	Asia-Pacific Economic Cooperation, comprising 21 countries
Authority, authorities	governmental authority(ies), whether law enforcement or intelligence/security
AWS	Amazon Web Services, Amazon's cloud services arm
BayLDA	Bayerisches Landesamt für Datenschutzaufsich, Bavaria's DPA
BCRs	binding corporate rules
CAHDATA	the Ad hoc Committee on data protection, established by the CoE's Committee of Ministers
CBP	College bescherming persoonsgegevens, Netherlands' DPA (former name)
CDN	content delivery or distribution network – p. 105
Ch.	chapter of this book
chap.	chapter of a cited reference
Charter	the EU Charter of Fundamental Rights
CIA	confidentiality, integrity and availability – 7.1.2
CIDPR	Community institutions' data protection regulation, Regulation (EC) 45/2001
CJEU	the Court of Justice of the European Union, formerly the ECJ

CNIL	Commission nationale de l'informatique et des libertés, France's DPA
CoE	Council of Europe
Commission	European Commission
Community	European Communities, the EU's predecessor
Controller	data controller within the DPD's Art.2(d)
Convention108	Convention for the Protection of Individuals with regard to Automatic Processing of Personal Data (ETS No.108)
Convention108-AP	Additional Protocol to Convention108
Convention108-APER	Convention108-AP's Explanatory Report
Convention108-ER	Convention108's Explanatory Report
Council	EU Council of Ministers
Council [number/year]	Pre-legislative Council document, under the heading Official documents – EU, sub-heading Council, in the Table of Legislation
CP	the Council's common position on the draft DPD, 1995/1/EC
CP-SR	the CP's statement of reasons
CPVP	Commission for the Protection of Privacy (Commission de la protection de la vie privée), Belgium's DPA
Data protection	data protection under the DPD/DPD Laws
Data subject(s)	individuals whose personal data are regulated under the DPD/DPD Laws
Datainspektionen	Sweden's DPA
Datatilsynet	Denmark's DPA
DoC	US Department of Commerce
DPA(s)	EEA data protection authority (national supervisory authority overseeing regulation of its DPD Laws). This may include, at EEA level, WP29
DPD	Data Protection Directive 95/46/EC
DPD Laws	national laws implementing the DPD, e.g. the UK Data Protection Act 1998

ECHR	European Convention for the Protection of Human Rights and Fundamental Freedoms
ECJ	the European Court of Justice, now the CJEU
EDPB	European Data Protection Board
EDPS	European Data Protection Supervisor
EEA	European Economic Area
EEA controller	controller incorporated in a Member State – p.9, n.20
Effective jurisdiction	a country's claimed jurisdiction to apply its laws to situations, which is enforceable in practice – p.7–8
ENISA	the EU's Agency for Network and Information Security
EU	European Union
Export	transmitting data to third country-located infrastructure
FISA	US Foreign Intelligence Surveillance Act
fn(n).	footnote(s) in cited reference
FRA	EU Fundamental Rights Agency
FTC	US Federal Trade Commission
Garante	Garante per la protezione dei dati personali, Italy's DPA
GATS	General Agreement on Trade in Services 1994
GCHQ	Government Communications Headquarters, the UK's security/intelligence agency
GDPR	General Data Protection Regulation (EU) 2016/679
GDPR's Restriction	GDPR provisions (primarily in its Chapter V) restricting international transfers (1.6.3), which will replace the Restriction
GPEN	Global Privacy Enforcement Network, whose members include many DPAs and other authorities internationally
Harborite	organization self-certified under Safe Harbour

Hardware	physical media and/or equipment housing/transmitting data: servers, storage appliances, portable drives, laptops, cables, etc.
IaaS	Infrastructure-as-a-Service
IAPP	International Association of Privacy Professionals
ICC	International Chamber of Commerce
ICO	Information Commissioner's Office, UK's DPA
Infrastructure	infrastructure for processing data, including datacentres and hardware
Intelligible access	access to personal data in intelligible form, i.e. to information contained in personal data – p.7
Mechanism	Mechanism for allowing transfers under adequate protection or adequate safeguards e.g. the Shield, SCCs (DPD), or adequate protection or appropriate safeguards (GDPR), as the context requires
Member State(s)	EEA Member State(s)
Microsoft warrant case	case against Microsoft in the US – p.93
n(n).	footnote(s) of this book
NIST	US National Institute of Standards and Technology
NSA	US National Security Agency
OECD-ExplanMem	Explanatory Memorandum to the OECD Guidelines
OECD Guidelines	OECD Guidelines on the Protection of Privacy and Transborder Flows of Personal Data, 1980
OECD Guidelines-2	OECD Guidelines governing the Protection of Privacy and Transborder Flows of Personal Data, 2013
Onward transfer(s)	transmission of transferred personal data from a third country 'to' another third country; sometimes, to others in the same third country
OPC	Office of the Privacy Commissioner of Canada, Canada's federal DPA
PaaS	Platform-as-a-Service
Parliament	European Parliament

Participant	Member State under DPD/CIDPR, party under Convention108/Convention108-AP, member country under the OECD Guidelines
PCPD	Office of the Privacy Commissioner for Personal Data, Hong Kong's DPA
PDPC	Personal Data Protection Commission, Singapore's DPA
PIPEDA	Canada's Personal Information Protection and Electronic Documents Act
Principles	substantive principles aimed at protecting personal data, stipulated under DPD and DPD Laws (excluding the Restriction and security requirements, not considered herein to be substantive principles)
Processing	processing of personal data within DPD Art.2(b); includes storage, transmission
Processor	processor within DPD Art.2(e)
Processor agreement	controller-processor agreement/contract under Art.17 DPD
Rec.	Recital
Restriction	the restriction on 'transfer' of personal data 'to' 'third countries', under Arts.25–6 DPD
SaaS	Software-as-a-Service
Safe Harbour	EU–US Safe Harbour scheme, under the Safe Harbour Decision
Safe Harbour Decision	Commission Decision 2000/520/EC
SCCs	standard contractual clauses (model clauses) in Commission Decisions promulgated under DPD Art.26(4)
Sensitive data	'special category' personal data under DPD Art.8, e.g. health data
Shield	EU–US Privacy Shield, under the Shield Decision
Shield Decision	Commission Decision (EU) 2016/1250, approving the Shield
Shield participant	organization self-certified under the Shield
SLAs	service level agreements (p.270, n.22)

SMEs	small/medium-sized enterprises
Snowden('s) (revelations)	former NSA contractor Edward Snowden's revelations in 2013 of mass acquisition, interception and surveillance of data by the NSA, GCHQ and other governmental intelligence/security authorities, widely reported since Greenwald and MacAskill (2013)
SSRN	Social Science Research Network
Strongly encrypted	secure against decryption for most practical purposes most of the time in the real world; in particular, encrypted, and keys secured, to recognized industry standards and best practices – 7.2.3.3.5, p.286
TBDF	transborder data flows
Third country	non-Member State country
TPB	The Pirate Bay file-sharing service (7.5.1.1)
Transfer	'transfer' of personal data within DPD Arts.25–6
Transmission	data conveyance, intra- *or* extra-EEA
VM	virtual machine (p.105 n.57)
Whitelisted country(ies)	country(ies) found 'adequate' under a DPD Art.25(4) Commission decision
WP29	Article 29 Data Protection Working Party, established under Art.29 DPD
WP[number]	WP29 working paper (opinion), see References – e.g. *WP196*

Table of cases

COURT OF JUSTICE FOR THE EUROPEAN UNION

NATIONAL COURT CASES

Ireland

United Kingdom

United States

DPA DECISIONS

Canada

EEA DPA CLOUD DECISIONS

Denmark

Norway

Sweden

Table of legislation

EU LEGISLATION

Decisions

Directives

EU POLICY DOCUMENTS

EU Council

EU Parliament

EU Pre-Legislative Documents

WP29 Opinions

NATIONAL LEGISLATION

Australia

Canada

Germany

INTERNATIONAL CONVENTIONS, AGREEMENTS AND TREATIES

OECD

MISCELLANEOUS DOCUMENTS

APEC

1. Background

1.1 INTRODUCTION

To show the fallacies underlying restrictions on the cross-border transfer of digital data, and the dangers they pose to personal data as well as to international trade, I dissect the restriction (Restriction), under Arts.25–6 of the EU Data Protection Directive (Directive 95/46/EC) (DPD), on 'transfer' of personal data 'to' so-called 'third countries' outside the European Economic Area (EEA),[1] as a barrier to EEA controllers'[2] processing of digital personal data using public cloud computing.[3]

I focus particularly on the interpretation of the Restriction by EEA data protection authorities (DPAs) as requiring personal data's physical location to be confined to the EEA. This approach is usually taken by authorities elsewhere also. As well as the DPD, I will address the position under the General Data Protection Regulation (EU) 2016/679 (GDPR), which applies directly in all EU Member States (Member States) from 25 May 2018.

I dub the Restriction a 'Frankenrule',[4] because it has taken on a life of its own. Often, DPAs insist upon compliance with (their interpretation of) the Restriction, and/or organizations devote time and costs attempting to comply with it, quite independently of compliance with the *substantive* data protection principles that it was intended to enforce. I will argue that that approach is wrong.

By way of background, I start by outlining cloud computing, EU data protection principles and the Restriction.

---

[1] Originally, the DPD applied only to EU Member States. EEA Joint Committee Decision 83/1999 extended it to Iceland, Liechtenstein and Norway, which are EEA but not EU members.

[2] Explained in 1.5.2.

[3] This book develops ideas first proposed in Hon and Millard (2012), updated in Hon and Millard (2013c) and Hon et al. (2016). I have published certain other ideas elsewhere – see http://www.kuan0.com/publications. Not every similar paragraph here will specifically cross-refer to those publications.

[4] After Frankenstein's unnaturally created monster (Shelley 1831).

1.2 CLOUD COMPUTING

1.2.1 Cloud Models

Essentially, cloud computing involves the self-service use of information technology (IT) resources over a network, typically the Internet, scalable up and down with demand or need (Hon and Millard 2013a: pp.32, 26). Cloud's service models are commonly categorized as 'Infrastructure as a Service' (IaaS), 'Platform as a Service' (PaaS) or 'Software as a Service' (SaaS)[5] (Mell and Grance 2011). The service model is termed SaaS when the scalable, self-service IT resources in question are software applications, installed on the provider's infrastructure and used over a network by the customer, instead of being installed locally by the customer. Where those resources are 'raw' IT resources or infrastructure (for what are called 'compute', 'storage' and/or 'networking' functions), the service model is termed IaaS. Where they comprise platforms for developing, hosting and deploying software applications of the cloud customer's choice, the service model is PaaS. These services are not necessarily discrete, but fall on a spectrum from IaaS to SaaS; the IaaS/PaaS boundary in particular is blurring. IaaS is the least user-friendly, requiring the most IT expertise and management on the part of the customer, but it offers customers the most flexibility. SaaS is the least flexible but most user-friendly, requiring relatively little customer expertise or management.

'As a service' emphasizes that cloud involves renting resources as services, more than using fixed technologies (Hon and Millard 2013a: p.4). Generally, providers utilize infrastructure in multiple locations, often simultaneously.[6] Resources are dynamically allocated to customers and dynamically deallocated, scaling with demand while optimizing the use of available capacity[7] (in whatever location). Generally, customers

---

[5]   SaaS for individuals includes social networking services (e.g. Facebook) and Webmail. SaaS for organizations includes Microsoft Office 365, Google Apps (now termed G-Suite) office applications and Salesforce's customer relationship management service. IaaS services include Amazon Web Services, Microsoft's Azure and Google Compute Engine (now part of Google Cloud Platform). PaaS services include Azure and Google Cloud Platform's App Engine.

[6]   E.g. Google replicates data to secondary datacentres to protect against datacentre failures – p.276, n.37.

[7]   Or to save energy (Quan et al. 2012), including shifting workloads to more energy-efficient datacentres elsewhere (Mahmoodi 2011: p.32).

pay only for services used: 'pay-as-you-go'.[8] Cloud is location-independent. Customers may use cloud from anywhere where they have Internet/network connectivity, whatever the location of the infrastructure used to deliver their services. Essentially, cloud is a *model* for accessing and delivering IT resources remotely. Hence, usages vary with customers' actions and choices, particularly with IaaS/PaaS. Popular IaaS/PaaS uses include website hosting and file storage/sharing as well as application hosting.

Cloud deployment models may be public, private, hybrid or community (Mell and Grance 2011).[9] Public cloud services are available to all; private, only to one user (or related users, e.g. corporate group members). Hybrid involves a mix: private cloud 'bursting' to public cloud during times of peak demand, or processing more sensitive data in-house but other data in-cloud. Community cloud is used by organizations with common interests, e.g. NYSE Euronext's community cloud for capital markets institutions. With public and community clouds, and even some private clouds, customers ('tenants') share the use of the underlying infrastructure (hence the term 'multitenanted'), enabling efficient utilization and economies of scale.

'Shadow cloud' must be mentioned, where organizations' employees subscribe to cloud services directly, often simply with credit cards, unbeknownst to the organization's IT or legal/risk/compliance functions, or IT departments take cloud services without involving legal/risk/compliance (Hon, Millard and Walden 2013a). This occurs even with highly regulated organizations like banks (Hon and Millard 2016).

Cloud contracts are generally offered on the provider's standard terms (Bradshaw et al. 2013). Large IaaS/PaaS providers are unlikely to negotiate their standard contract terms except in rare cases (Hon et al. 2013a), and rarely with customers who are small SaaS/PaaS providers.

1.2.2 Layered Cloud Services

Cloud often involves complex supply chains. Services may be 'layered'. An SaaS service may be built on another cloud provider's PaaS/IaaS service, or PaaS on top of IaaS: e.g. Netflix's consumer video SaaS service is built on Amazon Web Services (AWS) IaaS. Providers of

---

[8] Some cloud services, particularly those targeting individuals, are free, often advertising-supported.

[9] Cloud services may be hosted on-premise (e.g. private clouds) or, typically, off customers' premises. Even private clouds may be off-premise, if provided by third parties on their infrastructure (Hon and Millard 2013a: pp.5–6).

underlying IaaS/PaaS service(s) are thus the cloud provider's *sub*-providers. Multiple layers are possible, e.g. SaaS on PaaS on IaaS. Furthermore, even with unlayered services, elements may be sourced from and/or be owned or operated by third parties. Datacentre providers like Equinix may own buildings housing the hardware used by cloud providers to offer their services. Third parties may make or supply such hardware (servers, storage appliances, cables, etc.). Telecommunications service providers may provide connectivity services to datacentres. Utility service providers may pipe in electricity to power equipment, or water to help keep datacentres cool. Only the largest providers are likely to own all these supply chain elements. Even those providers may, in certain countries, use third party datacentres rather than building their own.

1.2.3   Infrastructure Cloud Services

It is important to note that, with many types of cloud services, providers simply provide IT infrastructure for remote direct self-service use by *customers* (but not by providers 'on behalf of' their customers). Providers of what I term 'infrastructure cloud services' (typically IaaS, PaaS and certain SaaS, e.g. pure storage) offer raw IT resources which customers may use for storage, compute and/or networking functions as the customer chooses.

Such infrastructure providers may be unaware of the nature of the data processed via their infrastructure by their customers, or their customers' customers – unless and until they 'look'. Logically, infrastructure cloud providers should not be considered 'processors' (1.5.2). They merely provide IT resources for customers' self-service use, rather than *actively* processing (as per controllers' instructions) personal data to which they always have intelligible access; but nevertheless, if their infrastructure is used to store or transmit personal data, even momentarily, they are considered 'processors' for DPD purposes because 'processing' includes storage and transmission (1.4) regardless of knowledge regarding whether the data are personal data (Hon, Millard and Walden 2013c, secs.4.3–4.4). Even if they 'look', infrastructure providers may not have *intelligible* access to data that were encrypted pre-upload by their customers (or customers' customers). Providers may use software to automatically access customer data to monitor usage (storage capacity used, volume of data traffic) for billing, support/troubleshooting, security or liability purposes, without disclosing or using intelligible personal data for other purposes, but other types of 'looking' may breach their contracts with customers and/or data protection law.[10]

Using infrastructure cloud services is more like renting IT infrastructure for the controller's own self-service use (Hon and Millard 2013b, secs.5.1–5.2), than engaging computer services bureaus to process personal data actively for controllers. Similarly, with layered cloud, subproviders of cloud infrastructure services rent out infrastructure resources, rather than actively processing personal data, and they do not generally 'look' or wish to look at what data are being processed using their services.

1.2.4 EU Cloud Use and Data Protection Laws

Cloud services from Salesforce, AWS, Microsoft, Google, Oracle and IBM, all US providers, were most popular in Western Europe, one study found (IDC 2014: p.65). Similarly with more recent worldwide research (Synergy Research Group 2016). In Europe, the Middle East and Africa (EMEA), cloud seems most used for marketing, collaboration, productivity and finance/accounting; and Microsoft, Facebook, Twitter, Google, Apple, Webex and Dropbox (all US) topped that list (Netskope 2016).

More efficient utilization of resources and economies of scale through using shared, standardized infrastructure to provide commoditized services make cloud efficient and cost-effective. Cloud has great potential to improve productivity and innovation[11] by affording customers cost-savings, flexibility/agility (including speed to market), greater convenience, process simplification[12] and, increasingly, strategic[13] and competitive[14] advantage – hence initiatives like the EU's cloud strategy (COM(2012)529 final), and the emphasis on the importance of exploiting cloud, e.g. in COM(2014)442 final, COM(2015)192 final.

---

[10] Providers may reserve contractual rights to scan content automatically, e.g. for security (checking for malware), to minimize their liability for illegal content, protecting their own interests (e.g. Kelly 2014), or (with SaaS providers) because of their business models, e.g. scanning emails for advertising purposes (Johnston 2014). However, under DPD Laws, explicit *contractual* access rights, even for highly restricted purposes, cannot legitimize such access – e.g. p.127, n.4. See also 4.5.1.2.

[11] Start-ups may avoid upfront capital investment in IT infrastructure and reduce time-to-market by using free or 'pay-as-you-go' cloud.

[12] E.g. Goulart (2014).

[13] E.g. Kroes (2013).

[14] E.g. Cloud Industry Forum (2014: p.10).

However, EU data protection laws may unnecessarily deter cloud use or provision, depriving potential customers of associated benefits. In particular, uncertainty regarding laws governing international data transfers is a major challenge for cloud (Civic Consulting 2012: p.45). Thirty-three percent of EU companies that do not use cloud reported that this was due to uncertainty about data location,[15] with 32 percent reporting uncertainty about applicable law as their reason (SWD(2015)100: p.59).

1.3 OUTLINE, SCOPE AND REASONS

The core of the problem is data 'location'. Regulations restricting data location and/or flow, notably the Restriction, are widely considered to impede cloud adoption (Commission 2012d; Graux 2014): 'indirect barriers' to cloud's use or promotion,[16] that unnecessarily increase the costs of cloud in Europe,[17] even using up resources (3.7.8) that would be better deployed elsewhere. Indeed, 'local data storage' was the form of regulation companies considered 'most intrusive' (Kommerskollegium 2014: p.2). Not just data localization regulations, but legal uncertainty about their requirements (1.2.4), lead some customers to insist on data localization for caution's sake. Some providers attempt to facilitate customers' compliance with the Restriction by offering 'regional clouds', enabling customers to choose geographic 'regions', e.g. the EEA, for

---

[15] Such uncertainty is one factor limiting cloud use by large organizations *already* using cloud (Giannakouris and Smihily 2014).

[16] Data localization requirements (storage/processing employing local hardware) were considered the 'most serious impediment' to cloud use, effectively rendering it 'impossible' (Kommerskollegium 2014: para.5.2.2). Given cloud deployments' complexity and the need to balance data flows across global infrastructure to optimize efficiency, geographical data segregation has been called 'not possible' and 'anathema to cloud' (Roberts 2014). Put another way, from a technical perspective, data localization is 'absolutely impossible' in cloud, although providers have been 'very lax' in how they communicate this; to truly localize data processing in cloud would require individual 'pipes' for all accesses to cloud data from all devices, no caching, and deletion after every session – which would make costs prohibitively expensive, and performance unacceptably slow (Finnegan 2015).

[17] One analysis found cloud was cheaper in the US; European users pay a 'protection premium' to comply with local data regulations (Sullivan 2016).

their data's 'location'.[18] The resulting costs are likely to fall on customers, EEA and/or global (n.17).

As commonly interpreted (Ch.3), the Restriction requires personal data's physical location to be confined to the EEA, with certain exceptions. Thus, the Commission considers cloud problematic for data protection because (SEC(2012)72 final, Ann.1, p.18):

> It is often difficult to determine the location of personal data, which is frequently replicated on all continents in order to improve its accessibility, and to enforce data protection rules particularly in situations where the controller targets services to EU residents but has no establishment or representative in the EU. This may involve the loss of individuals' control over their potentially sensitive information when they store their data with programs hosted on someone else's hardware.

I will show that this data location-centric approach derives from outdated assumptions (Ch.4) regarding physical access to data, jurisdiction and data movement. I argue that laws and regulations should concentrate, not on personal data location, but on:

- which persons have access to personal data (including remotely) – particularly access to personal data in intelligible form, i.e. access to the *information* contained in personal data (termed 'intelligible access', for brevity), and
- to which jurisdiction(s)' laws such persons may be effectively subject ('effective jurisdiction').

By effective jurisdiction, I mean a country's claimed jurisdiction to apply its laws in circumstances where it not only asserts such jurisdiction, but can enforce it effectively in practice. Notably, a country may claim to apply its laws to persons in other countries, but if those persons are not in or connected to it, it may not have effective jurisdiction over them. Ensuring effective jurisdiction over the processing of digital data is problematic (7.5.1.1), because digital data are relatively easily copied or

---

[18] Many providers are opening or using EEA datacentres because of the Restriction and/or similar governmental data localization policies (IDC 2014: p.75), such as Facebook (Mlot 2016), Salesforce and Oracle (MacIver 2013); see e.g. https://azure.microsoft.com/en-gb/regions/services/ and http://o365datacenter map.azurewebsites.net/. Yet even 'regions' are oversimplistic (3.7.3).

'moved';[19] or, a country may have effective jurisdiction to obtain encrypted data, but not the associated decryption keys, if controlled only by persons not under its effective jurisdiction. I argue that countries' jurisdiction over data processing should rely on better bases than data location. Also, countries ought to recognize that persons may be subject to multiple countries' jurisdictions simultaneously, resulting in risks of conflicts between their laws.

Furthermore, as regards the Restriction's professed anticircumvention objective (Ch.2), i.e. ensuring continuing compliance with substantive data protection principles, I will show that the Restriction is positively harmful rather than beneficial. Many DPAs require compliance with both substantive data protection principles and the Restriction (Ch.5). Costly efforts to implement box-ticking mechanisms for compliance with DPAs' interpretation of the Restriction divert resources away from important matters like information security improvements. The Restriction is rarely enforced; when it is, the focus is (rightly) on substantive data protection principles, not data location per se (Ch.6). Therefore, the Restriction does not achieve its avowed aim of preventing circumvention of data protection laws. It seems the Restriction, and other data localization laws, are now invoked more to serve other policy objectives, particularly preventing third country authorities from accessing personal data of EU citizens/residents. However, its practical efficacy to prevent such access has not been properly evaluated or proven. I suggest that imposing opposing laws on private actors cannot settle such issues; agreement between countries is needed. Finally, I will argue (Ch.7) that data protection laws do not, but should, properly recognize the role that technical measures like encryption or backups can play in protecting personal data, rather than insisting that only legal measures like contract can provide 'adequate' protection or safeguards for 'exported' personal data.

This book focuses on 'public' cloud. Private cloud customers generally have greater control over providers and data location, more akin to traditional outsourcing, so compliance with the Restriction is less problematic for them. Similarly with community cloud customers, who have collective bargaining power. Hybrid cloud customers, for the public element, face similar issues as public cloud customers.

I discuss the Restriction as a barrier to EEA controllers' use of public cloud for processing personal data. However, much of my analysis applies to the broader Internet, and to data localization laws beyond data

---

[19]   Strictly, 'moving' digital data involves copying data elsewhere, then deleting the data from the original media or equipment.

protection laws. The EU has at least 70 data localization regulations, particularly in finance/health but also regarding company records, accounting/tax data, telecommunications and government data (Commission 2016e). Many of the arguments in this book apply equally to cross-border personal data transfers from *non*-European countries, or cross-border transfers (from any country) not involving personal data. However, I will not specifically address such other transfers/flows. For brevity, my case study focuses mainly on transfers where *EEA organizations* use cloud, i.e. controllers incorporated in EU Member States ('EEA controllers'). If the Restriction is problematic for such controllers, it will also be problematic for non-EEA-incorporated controllers caught by the DPD,[20] and most of my arguments will apply equally to them.

Current data protection regulation targets controllers, and organizations are the main class of controller. Individuals may use cloud directly, e.g. social media/networking services, but whether they are controllers is not straightforward (*WP163*, para.3.1) and, if they are, they will encounter similar problems as organizational controllers (or worse, due to their relative lack of expertise/resources), so my arguments will apply equally there too.

Similarly, I focus mainly on the position of cloud customers using cloud providers *as processors*. Cloud providers are normally considered processors, but may be or become controllers[21] – including, it seems, by making transfers without the controller's authorization (3.6.3.2). If so, again my main analyses will apply to them. For space reasons, transfers by EU authorities direct to third country authorities, e.g. for crime investigation purposes, are not generally discussed; this book concentrates on private sector transfers, but may mention authorities' transfers where relevant.

---

[20] Many more non-EEA controllers may be caught, following Case C-131/12 *Google Spain* (*Google Spain*). This broadened EU jurisdictional reach, in certain circumstances, to controllers incorporated in *non*-EEA countries but having EEA-incorporated subsidiaries (p.52, n.46). Even an EEA agent or datacentre might be treated as an 'establishment' of a controller with no other EEA presence (Hon, Millard and Hörnle 2013: sec.2.1). On the GDPR position, see 1.5.2.

[21] Some providers, particularly providers of SaaS services to individuals, must know that data processed using their services probably include personal data, e.g. social networking or photo-sharing services. Such providers may be controllers, not just processors (Hon, Millard and Walden 2013c: sec.3.2, 4.4; *WP169*). The boundary is particularly unclear with modern complex outsourcing chains, e.g. Blume 2013.

I discuss only data protection under DPD and its forthcoming replacement, the GDPR, discussing certain national laws for illustrative purposes. The DPD emphasizes the protection of individuals' rights and freedoms regarding the processing of their personal data, notably rights to privacy under Art.8 of the Convention for the Protection of Human Rights and Fundamental Freedoms (ECHR) and general principles of European Communities (now EU) law.[22] However, with limited exceptions, I will not generally discuss laws regarding privacy rights under the ECHR, rights to private and family life or personal data protection under the EU Charter of Fundamental Rights (Charter),[23] or under the ePrivacy Directive 2002/58/EC on the privacy of electronic communications (currently undergoing review by the Commission, with a view to its modernization (Commission 2016b)).

1.4 TERMINOLOGY AND REFERENCES

DPD Art.2(a) defines 'personal data' as 'any information relating to an identified or identifiable natural person (a 'data subject'). An identifiable person is one who can be identified, directly or indirectly, in particular 'by reference to an identification number or to one or more factors specific to his physical, physiological, mental, economic, cultural or social identity'. The 'personal data' concept is critical under DPD Laws. While this definition is broad and difficult to apply, the DPD only covers information categorized as 'personal data'. Information *not* classed as 'personal data', 'anonymous data', escapes DPD regulation. To determine whether a person is identifiable, 'account should be taken of all the means likely reasonably to be used either by the controller or by any other person to identify the said person', and '... the principles of protection shall not apply to data rendered anonymous in such a way that the data subject is no longer identifiable ...' (Rec.26). The difficulty lies in how attempted anonymization measures can effectively render personal data sufficiently anonymous, given advances in reidentification techniques and the ability to combine data from different sources (Hon, Millard and Walden 2013b: sec.3; *WP216*). Although in practice the

---

[22] DPD Recs.1, 10–11.
[23] The Charter has greatly influenced EU policy and EU laws' interpretation. Its specific provision on data protection underlines the EU's view of data protection as a fundamental human right. However, I will argue that, while substantive data protection principles are indeed fundamental to human rights, the Restriction itself is not.

DPD's definition of 'personal data' has been interpreted broadly, the GDPR's definition (Art.4(1)) is broader, explicitly including, among identifiers such as identification numbers and names, location data and genetic factors (although it still exempts anonymous information 'which does not relate to an identified or identifiable natural person', and personal data 'rendered anonymous' – Rec.26).

'Processing' under the DPD (Art.2(b)) is broader than what technologists think of as 'processing'. Often, by 'processing', technologists mean 'actively operating on data or working on data': 'compute', in IaaS terms.[24] I use 'operations' (or 'compute') to mean 'working on data'. However, it is important to note that, for DPD purposes, the 'processing' of personal data also includes the storage and/or networking of personal data (the other main IaaS functions). 'Processing of personal data' effectively includes *everything* that can be done to or with digital personal data – including storing, displaying/viewing, accessing as well as transmitting, disclosing or using personal data. This book uses 'processing' in the broader DPD sense.

'Data protection', under data protection law, also differs from 'data protection' as used in IT. There is some overlap. However, IT 'data protection' may extend beyond DPD data protection, e.g. the protection of data not qualifying as 'personal data'; and vice versa, e.g. purpose limitation (1.5.6). Data protection in the IT sense, except where relevant under data protection *laws*, is not discussed in this book.

Cross-border personal data transfers are often termed 'international transfers', 'international data transfers', 'cross-border data flows', 'cross-border flows', 'cross-frontier data flows', 'transborder data flows' (TBDF) or transfrontier data flows. 'Transfer' is sometimes used, including by DPAs or courts, to mean the *transmission* or disclosure of personal data to third parties, even when it is only within the EEA. It is often unclear whether they mean mere transmission, an Art.25 transfer, or both. Hence, the references to 'transfers' in DPAs' reports etc. may be ambiguous. In this book, 'transfers' is used to mean only personal data 'transfers' regulated under Arts.25–6 DPD. I will use 'transmit' for data transmission/conveyance, intra- or extra-EEA; 'exports' for data transmissions (strictly, copying, for digital data) to hardware located outside

---

[24] In discussing 'processing, storage and networking' in the cloud, one industry standard seemingly equates 'processing' with 'compute' (ISO/IEC 2014a). However, in another standard, 'data processing' is defined to mean *operations* on data, with 'information processing' including data communication (ISO/IEC 1993).

relevant borders, and 'personal data exports' similarly – in each case, whether or not involving 'transfer' in the strict DPD sense.

Unless otherwise stated, 'provider(s)' means 'cloud service provider(s)', including subproviders where the context requires, and 'customer(s)' or controller(s) means 'EEA controller(s) who use cloud services to process personal data'. 'Infrastructure' generally means physical infrastructure used for processing personal data including hardware, e.g. servers and storage appliances, and datacentres housing such hardware, and infrastructure services and providers refer to cloud services and providers who offer infrastructure for customers' use (1.2.3). References to Articles (Arts.), Recitals (Recs.) section (sec.)/paragraph (para.) numbers are to the Articles, Recitals and sections/paragraphs of the DPD, GDPR or Shield principles (Shield Decision Annex II) etc., as the context requires, unless otherwise stated.

Opinions of the Article 29 Working Party (discussed shortly) are referenced by working paper number, e.g. *WP196*, listed under 'WP29 opinions' in the Table of Legislation. DPA cloud decisions are cited by controller name, Member State (if unclear from the context), then year, e.g. *Narvik 2012b* (Norway). They are listed in the Table of Cases under 'EEA DPA cloud decisions', alphabetically by country. Online automated translations were used where English translations of decisions or guidance were unavailable. Canadian DPA decisions are also listed in the Table of Cases under 'DPA decisions'.

1.5 DPD AND GDPR: SUMMARY

1.5.1 Objectives

The DPD aimed to encourage free movement of personal data within the EU (and now the EEA), by setting minimum standards for data protection laws aimed at protecting the rights and freedoms of individuals when their personal data are 'processed' 'wholly or partly by automatic means' (e.g. Recs.3, 9). The DPD only applies to 'personal data' (1.4).

The GDPR was adopted in 2016 alongside a separate Directive (EU) 2016/680 (not discussed further in this book) on authorities' processing of personal data for law enforcement and crime-related purposes. The GDPR was intended to modernize the DPD and harmonize still-disparate national DPD Laws. A Regulation, not a Directive, was chosen in hopes of better achieving cross-EU harmonization.[25] A Regulation becomes law directly in all Member States from the relevant effective date, without requiring any national implementing legislation. Accordingly, the GDPR applies directly in all Member States from 25 May 2018.[26] Its policy objectives include: 'To address globalisation and simplify and clarify the conditions for international transfers' and 'To simplify formalities for international transfers' (SEC(2012)72 final, p.43).

The GDPR emphasizes 'accountability': not only being responsible for compliance, but being able to demonstrate or prove compliance (Art.5(2)). Note the GDPR's specific, narrow view of 'accountability' as the ability to evidence compliance, which differs from other legislation or instruments (2.2.8) that view 'accountability' as having primary responsibility and liability for data regardless of location or any use of third party processors/contractors. Generally, the GDPR is more prescriptive and less flexible than the DPD. Despite its aim of simplifying transfers, the GDPR is (with one exception) in fact more restrictive regarding transfers, as I will discuss.

1.5.2 Controllers, Processors and Processing

The DPD requires EEA Member States to impose certain obligations on each 'controller' (who determines the purposes and means of processing personal data) in relation to its personal data processing, where it has the requisite EEA connection. This covers all personal data, not just that of EEA citizens;[27] so does the GDPR (Recs.2, 14).

A controller may use a 'processor' to process personal data on its behalf (Art.2(e)). When controllers use cloud to process personal data, the cloud providers are 'processors', and in this book I will assume providers are processors (p.9). Member States need not impose obligations directly on processors. Therefore, except in the few Member States

---

[25]   I use 'hopes' and 'better', not 'guarantee'. A Regulation cannot ensure harmonization if, like the GDPR, it specifically permits Member States to provide for differences in certain areas (EDRi et al. 2016), and/or is unclear/ ambiguous, enabling different Member States to interpret it differently.

[26]   'Brexit', the UK's proposed exit from the EU, is unlikely to be effective before 2019, so the GDPR will probably apply in the UK for a few months at least.

[27]   *WP56*, p.7. The Convention on which the DPD was based (2.2.4) requires parties to apply its protections to 'every individual regardless of nationality or residence' (Convention108, Art.1; Convention108-ER, para.26). The Shield Decision (5.3.3) re-emphasized this point: many references in the February 2016 drafts to 'EU citizens' were changed to 'EU individuals'.

which imposed such obligations, processors are regulated only indirectly, through obligations imposed on *controllers* regarding their use of processors, such as ensuring contracts on certain terms with processors. The DPD does not explicitly address *sub*processors, but cloud subproviders are generally treated as subprocessors. Processors who use any subprocessors nevertheless remain liable to controllers under their contracts with their controllers, including liability for subprocessors' actions/inactions. The Restriction applies to all qualifying 'transfers', whether made to controllers, processors, subprocessors, or even within the same organization (Ch.3).

GDPR Art.3(1) applies EU data protection rules, including GDPR's transfers restriction ('GDPR's Restriction'), to both controllers *and processors*[28] who process personal data in the context of activities of an 'establishment' of the controller or processor 'in the Union'. Art.3(2) GDPR has extraterritorial reach, catching non-EEA-established processors where the processing activities are 'related to' the 'offering' of goods or services to data subjects 'in the Union' or the monitoring of their behaviour taking place in the EU, which seems overbroad (Hon 2015a; Hon 2016c). Accordingly, the discussion in this book regarding controllers' obligations under GDPR's Restriction applies equally to processors, e.g. requirements for 'appropriate safeguards' (5.4.1.2).

Apart from GDPR's Restriction, the GDPR imposes certain other obligations directly on processors, including technical and organizational security obligations (Art.32), notification of 'personal data breaches' to their controllers 'without undue delay' (Art.33(2)), appointment of a data protection officer in some circumstances (Art.37) and record-keeping obligations (Art.30(2)), including in relation to transfers to a third country or international organization 'where applicable' (Art.30(2)(c)). More obligations apply to controllers, but processors are exposed to compensation claims under the GDPR even if controllers or others in the supply chain were more at fault, as the aim is to ensure that data subjects are made whole (Art.82).

---

[28] The GDPR's regulation of processors will not depend on personal data location, with one caveat. It is unclear whether, if processing personal data using EEA datacentres or EEA (sub)providers, non-EEA controllers could be deemed to have EEA 'establishments', and accordingly become subject to DPD Laws (Hon, Millard and Hörnle 2013: sec.2.1). Under the GDPR, similar uncertainties would afflict non-EEA *processors* who use EEA datacentres or subproviders, which may disincentivize non-EEA providers (not just controllers – p.14, n.28) from processing personal data using EEA infrastructure/providers.

1.5.3 Exemptions

Member States may provide for exemptions from various DPD obligations in certain areas (Art.3(2)) – e.g. processing operations concerning public security, defence, Member State security (including Member State economic well-being where the processing relates to Member State security matters), which I will collectively term 'national security', and Member State activities in areas of criminal law. Such exemptions only apply to the national security of Member States, not of third countries (*WP215*: p.7). Similarly, GDPR's Art.3(2) excludes processing in the course of activities falling outside the scope of EU law (effectively, national security), common foreign and security policy activities, e.g. defence, and (addressed in a separate Directive) competent authorities' processing for law enforcement purposes. These exemptions are obviously important when considering EU authorities' surveillance.

Art.3(2) DPD also exempts processing by a natural person (individual) in the course of a purely personal or household activity. GDPR Art.3(2)(c) maintains this exemption.

1.5.4 National Implementations

The DPD is a Directive, not a Regulation. Thus, it became law in Member States only when individual Member States enacted national implementing legislation, which I term 'DPD Laws'. I do not comprehensively examine national implementations, although I mention some examples, notably various EEA DPA cloud decisions.

Important differences in DPD Laws exist, e.g. on civil liability and penalties for non-compliance. These differences arose partly because the DPD gave Member States some 'margin of manoeuvre' to implement or apply certain provisions differently (Rec.9). Also, some Member States have failed to implement (or their DPAs have failed to interpret) the DPD correctly, with limited action having been taken against them regarding such failures.[29] Therefore, data protection laws are not fully harmonized cross-EEA.[30] Differing national approaches to enforcement magnify the problem.[31]

---

[29] Korff and Brown (2010: p.16); COM(2003)265 final, pp.11, 24; see p.241.

[30] E.g. applicable law rules on non-contractual obligations regarding data protection and privacy rights are unharmonized – Kuner (2013b: p.108) citing MainStrat (2009: p.5).

[31] Ch.6 discusses enforcement further.

A key objective of the GDPR was to improve cross-EU harmonization of data protection laws. However, many changes were made during its legislative passage, and its final version, as enacted, arguably gives Member States more flexibility in many areas than the DPD does (n.25).

1.5.5 Supervision

The DPD requires Member States to appoint independent DPAs with jurisdiction to supervise compliance nationally, who are responsible for monitoring and enforcing application 'within its territory' (and only its territory) of relevant national DPD Laws.[32] The UK's DPA is the Information Commissioner (ICO).

By Art.29, all national DPAs, with the European Data Protection Supervisor (EDPS) (2.2.6), participate in the Article 29 Data Protection Working Party (WP29). The WP29 independently advises on the level of data protection in the EU and 'third countries', harmonization of DPD Laws, and certain other DPD issues. It has published many opinions, including on cloud (*WP196*). Strictly, the WP29's opinions do not bind Member States, DPAs or courts. Because it makes decisions by a simple majority, not all DPAs may concur with its opinions or abide by its interpretations. However, its opinions are obviously authoritative and influential. Therefore, relevant WP29 opinions are discussed, as generally representing DPAs' collective views and indicating how they apply DPD Laws in practice.

Under Art.68 GDPR, the WP29 will become the European Data Protection Board (EDPB), with separate legal personality and enhanced powers, particularly to promote cross-EU consistency and harmonization. A new 'consistency mechanism' seeks to promote consistent approaches and cooperation/mutual assistance/joint operations between national DPAs, involving an EDPB opinion and dispute resolution procedure, with specific timetables and majorities (Arts.63–7). The EDPB may, on DPA or Commission request or on its own initiative, issue guidelines, recommendations and best practices to encourage consistent application of the GDPR on any question regarding its application (Art.70(1)(e)), which would include issues regarding GDPR's Restriction.

DPAs' harmonized, expanded powers under the GDPR include audit rights (Art.58(1)(a)–(b)), power to suspend 'data flows' (presumably only personal data flows) to a recipient in a third country or international organization (Art.58(2)(j)), and power to levy administrative sanctions or

---

[32]   Recs.62–4; Chapter VI DPD particularly Art.28.

fines in two tiers (depending on the provision infringed): up to 4 percent of total worldwide annual turnover or €20 million if higher (Art.83(5)); and up to 2 percent of total worldwide annual turnover or €10 million if higher (Art.83(4)).

1.5.6 Principles

The DPD requires Member States to oblige controllers to comply with certain principles regarding their processing of personal data, summarized as follows (mainly from Art.6):

1. often termed 'data quality' – personal data must be processed fairly and lawfully ('fair processing') ('lawfulness, fairness and transparency' under GDPR Art.5(1)(a), which explicitly requires transparency in relation to the data subject as well as lawfulness and fairness); collected only for specified, explicit and legitimate purposes (and further processing that is incompatible with those purposes must not be permitted) (termed 'purpose limitation' in GDPR Art.5(1)(b)); processing must be adequate, relevant and not excessive in relation to those purposes ('data minimization' under GDPR Art.5(1)(c)); sometimes termed 'proportionality'[33]); data must be accurate and, where necessary, kept up to date (alone sometimes termed 'data quality'; 'accuracy' under GDPR Art.5(1)(d)); and data must be kept in a form permitting identification of the relevant data subjects for no longer than is necessary for those purposes ('storage limitation' under GDPR Art.5(1)(e));
2. legal basis – personal data can be processed only under a specified legal basis, e.g. unambiguous consent, or necessity in the legitimate interests of the controller or disclosee (unless overridden by data subjects' fundamental rights e.g. privacy, e.g. because the processing would be too privacy-intrusive);
3. information to data subject (transparency) – certain information must be provided to data subjects regarding the controller, the processing etc.;
4. data subject rights – data subjects must have rights (sometimes termed 'intervenability' (*WP196*: p.16)) to: access their personal data; be given certain information in certain circumstances regarding the processing of their personal data; require rectification, erasure or blocking of their data if processed non-compliantly with

---

[33] E.g. *WP12*, p.6.

the DPD; object to the processing of their personal data in certain situations (e.g. direct marketing); and not be subjected to certain automated decisions;

5. security and processors – Art.17 (p.265) contains requirements regarding confidentiality and security of processing, including the implementation of appropriate technical and organizational measures to protect personal data against unauthorized access, loss, etc. and other unlawful processing; and requirements regarding controllers' use of processors (Art.17(2)–(3)), when the controller must:

    *   choose a processor that provides 'sufficient guarantees' regarding technical security and organizational measures,
    *   ensure compliance with those measures, and
    *   obtain written contractual obligations from the processor ('processor agreement') to implement such measures and to 'act only on instructions from the controller';

6. transfers restriction – i.e. the Restriction; and
7. 'special category' personal data ('sensitive data') – additional rules apply to the processing of personal data under the DPD (Art.8) regarded as particularly sensitive, such as personal data revealing race, political opinions, religious beliefs or regarding health or sex life – but not financial data – e.g., they cannot be processed unless exceptions apply, such as data subjects' *explicit* consent. The GDPR tightens up on 'special category' processing, and processing of criminal convictions data – not discussed further here.

The above all involve obligations on controllers, rights for data subjects (notably to seek remedies for breaches) and both supervisory obligations and rights for DPAs.

I argue that rules 1–4 and 7 above represent the DPD's core substantive principles (Principles): the 'what' of data protection. The DPD addresses data subject rights separately, but I consider data subject rights to be part of the Principles. As Ch.7 will discuss, I further argue that security and transfer requirements are the 'how' of data protection, designed to *facilitate and ensure* compliance with the core Principles – but are not substantive principles in their own right (although under GDPR Art.5(1)(f), 'integrity and confidentiality' is a core principle, infringement of which exposes controllers to a higher-tier fine). For example, *WP211* (para.5.0) considers data protection's 'key' principles to be fair and lawful processing, purpose limitation, data minimization and storage limitation. The basic Principles broadly reflect those under e.g. the Organisation for Economic Co-operation and Development (OECD) Guidelines (2.2.3), as also reflected in the Asia-Pacific Economic

Co-operation (APEC) Privacy Framework (2.2.8), the US Fair Information Practice Principles (FIPPS) and various national laws.

Any 'transfer' also constitutes a 'processing' (e.g. *Schrems*, para.45 (5.3.2)). Therefore, every transfer must comply with the Principles, including a legal basis being required for the transfer.[34] However, DPAs generally regulate 'transfer' in its own right, separately from and additionally to the Principles. This is a major problem with the Restriction, as Ch.5 will discuss.

Generally, the GDPR's processing rules are broadly similar, but wider in scope, extending in some cases to processors (1.5.2), and tougher, particularly GDPR's Restriction – discussed later.

1.6 THE RESTRICTION – OVERVIEW

1.6.1 Introduction

Chapter IV DPD provides:

CHAPTER IV TRANSFER OF PERSONAL DATA TO THIRD COUNTRIES

Article 25

Principles

1. The Member States shall provide that the transfer to a third country of personal data which are undergoing processing or are intended for processing after transfer may take place only if, without prejudice to compliance with the national provisions adopted pursuant to the other provisions of this Directive, the third country in question ensures an adequate level of protection.
2. The adequacy of the level of protection afforded by a third country shall be assessed in the light of all the circumstances surrounding a data transfer operation or set of data transfer operations; particular consideration shall be given to the nature of the data, the purpose and duration of the proposed processing operation or operations, the country of origin and country of final destination, the rules of law, both general and sectoral, in force in the third country in question and the professional rules and security measures which are complied with in that country.

---

[34] Art.25(1) is 'without prejudice to compliance with the national provisions adopted' under other DPD provisions. See also *WP114*, p.8, Kuner (2007a: pp.59–61) citing e.g. Rec.60 DPD, Commission (2009: p.28).

3. The Member States and the Commission shall inform each other of cases where they consider that a third country does not ensure an adequate level of protection within the meaning of paragraph 2.

4. Where the Commission finds, under the procedure provided for in Article 31(2), that a third country does not ensure an adequate level of protection within the meaning of paragraph 2 of this Article, Member States shall take the measures necessary to prevent any transfer of data of the same type to the third country in question.

5. At the appropriate time, the Commission shall enter into negotiations with a view to remedying the situation resulting from the finding made pursuant to paragraph 4.

6. The Commission may find, in accordance with the procedure referred to in Article 31(2), that a third country ensures an adequate level of protection within the meaning of paragraph 2 of this Article, by reason of its domestic law or of the international commitments it has entered into, particularly upon conclusion of the negotiations referred to in paragraph 5, for the protection of the private lives and basic freedoms and rights of individuals.

Member States shall take the measures necessary to comply with the Commission's decision.

Article 26

Derogations

1. By way of derogation from Article 25 and save where otherwise provided by domestic law governing particular cases, Member States shall provide that a transfer or a set of transfers of personal data to a third country which does not ensure an adequate level of protection within the meaning of Article 25(2) may take place on condition that:
    (a) the data subject has given his consent unambiguously to the proposed transfer; or
    (b) the transfer is necessary for the performance of a contract between the data subject and the controller or the implementation of precontractual measures taken in response to the data subject's request; or
    (c) the transfer is necessary for the conclusion or performance of a contract concluded in the interest of the data subject between the controller and a third party; or
    (d) the transfer is necessary or legally required on important public interest grounds, or for the establishment, exercise or defence of legal claims; or
    (e) the transfer is necessary in order to protect the vital interests of the data subject; or
    (f) the transfer is made from a register which according to laws or regulations is intended to provide information to the public and which is open to consultation either by the public in general or by any person who can demonstrate legitimate interest, to the extent that

the conditions laid down in law for consultation are fulfilled in the particular case.

2. Without prejudice to paragraph 1, a Member State may authorize a transfer or a set of transfers of personal data to a third country which does not ensure an adequate level of protection within the meaning of Article 25(2), where the controller adduces adequate safeguards with respect to the protection of the privacy and fundamental rights and freedoms of individuals and as regards the exercise of the corresponding rights; such safeguards may in particular result from appropriate contractual clauses.

3. The Member State shall inform the Commission and the other Member States of the authorizations it grants pursuant to paragraph 2.

   If a Member State or the Commission objects on justified grounds involving the protection of the privacy and fundamental rights and freedoms of individuals, the Commission shall take appropriate measures in accordance with the procedure laid down in Article 31(2).

   Member States shall take the necessary measures to comply with the Commission's decision.

4. Where the Commission decides, in accordance with the procedure referred to in Article 31(2), that certain standard contractual clauses offer sufficient safeguards as required by paragraph 2, Member States shall take the necessary measures to comply with the Commission's decision.

1.6.2 Adequate Protection, Adequate Safeguards, Derogations

Accordingly, any 'transfer' 'to a third country' of personal data 'which are undergoing processing or are intended for processing after transfer' may occur only if:

- Adequate protection: 'the third country in question ensures' adequate protection (Art.25(1)), assessed in light of all circumstances surrounding the transfer (Art.25(2)). The Commission may make decisions that certain third countries do (or do not) ensure adequate protection by reason of its domestic law or international commitments (Art.25(3)–(6)), often known as 'whitelisting' decisions; or
- Adequate safeguards: a Member State authorizes transfer to a third country which 'does not ensure' adequate protection, based on the controller adducing 'adequate safeguards' (Art.26(2)); or
- Other derogation: an Art.26(1) derogation applies. Notwithstanding lack of adequate protection or safeguards, Member States must permit transfers under certain derogations, with exceptions (Art.26(1)).

Without 'adequate protection', 'appropriate safeguards' or a derogation, transfers are impermissible (Rec.60). Ch.5 discusses the mechanisms recognized as enabling adequate protection or safeguards (Mechanisms), e.g. the now-defunct Safe Harbour, its replacement the EU–US Privacy Shield (Shield), standard contractual clauses or 'model clauses' (SCCs), and certain derogations.

1.6.3 GDPR's Restriction

Ch.V contains the main provisions regarding the GDPR's Restriction. The basic transfer restriction under Art.44 GDPR provides:

> Any transfer of personal data which are undergoing processing or are intended for processing after transfer to a third country or to an international organisation shall take place only if, subject to the other provisions of this Regulation, the conditions laid down in this Chapter are complied with by the controller and processor, including for onward transfers of personal data from the third country or an international organisation to another third country or to another international organisation. All provisions in this Chapter shall be applied in order to ensure that the level of protection of natural persons guaranteed by this Regulation is not undermined.

The rest of Chapter V GDPR sets out requirements regarding GDPR's Restriction. For a table setting out and comparing the key provisions of DPD's Restriction and GDPR's Restriction, please see the Appendix. Generally, GDPR's Restriction is tighter and more prescriptive (a comparative table is online (Hon 2016d)) – with higher-tier fines for infringement (1.5.5). Details will be discussed later, but, in brief, its requirements catch processors, not just controllers, and transfers to international organizations, not just third countries; it extends to any 'onward transfers' of transferred personal data; it restricts who will be entitled to assess 'adequate protection'; 'adequate safeguards' will become 'appropriate safeguards', with some important differences; and derogations are also amended. This means that providers, as processors, will be treated as transferring personal data if they use subproviders' non-EEA infrastructure. It permits transfers under international agreements between the EU and third countries with 'appropriate safeguards', provided they do not 'affect' the GDPR and include 'appropriate' protections (Art.96, Rec.102).

Under the GDPR, the 'instructions' restriction in controller-processor contracts explicitly extends to transfers (p.129). Also, under increased transparency and accountability obligations, controllers must notify data subjects of proposed transfers, adequacy decisions or safeguards and how to obtain a 'copy'[35] of any appropriate or 'suitable' (5.5.2) safeguards (Arts.13(1)(f), 14(1)(f), 15(2)). Both controllers' and processors' new record-keeping obligations include recording certain information regarding transfers (Arts.30(1)(d)-(e), 30(2)(c)).

The Commission must, by 25 May 2020 and every four years thereafter, evaluate and report on the GDPR to the Parliament and Council, making such reports public, including regarding the application and functioning of GDPR's Restriction, particularly GDPR adequacy decisions and 'grandfathered' DPD adequacy decisions (including whitelisting decisions under the DPD) (Arts.97(1), 97(2)(a)).

1.7 SUMMARY

The Restriction forbids 'transfer' of 'personal data' 'to' third countries unless 'adequate protection' or 'adequate safeguards' can be assured, or a derogation applies. GDPR's Restriction will be even tighter. I discuss the Restriction's legislative background and objectives next, before considering various difficulties with applying the 'transfer' concept in the Internet age.

---

[35] Copies of exactly what is unclear, for some safeguards: entire instruments between public authorities (5.4.1.2)? All documents supporting a certification application, or just the certificate (5.4.5)? Generally, for security reasons, providers are unwilling to share full security certification documentation with customers, only summaries (Hon, Millard and Walden 2013a), so sharing full documentation with data subjects may be problematic for them.

2. Legislative history and objectives

2.1 INTRODUCTION

To investigate whether the Restriction has achieved its legislative objectives and whether better alternatives are possible, we must first understand
those objectives more fully.

The DPD was intended (Rec.11) to build on an existing international
treaty, the Convention for the Protection of Individuals with regard to
Automatic Processing of Personal Data (ETS No.108). The Convention
was adopted in 1981 by the Council of Europe (CoE), with an explanatory
report (Convention108-ER), and amended by Amendments to the Convention for the Protection of Individuals with regard to Automatic Processing
of Personal Data (as amended, Convention108). Convention108 was produced in close collaboration (Convention108-ER, paras.14–16) with the
Organisation for Economic Co-operation and Development (OECD),
whose Council adopted Guidelines on the Protection of Privacy and
Transborder Flows of Personal Data (OECD Guidelines) in 1980, also
with an explanatory memorandum (OECD-ExplanMem).

Therefore, when considering the policy objectives underlying the
Restriction and Principles, it is important to consider the legislative
history of Convention108 and the OECD Guidelines also.

2.2 HISTORICAL OVERVIEW: EXPORT CONTROLS

2.2.1 Policy Objectives

For any law, there seem to be three main kinds of policy objectives.
Firstly, there are the lawmakers' original objectives, which could themselves either be explicit, or unexpressed or hidden. Secondly, there are
objectives, possibly different and again often unexpressed, that implicitly
drive why and how regulators, courts and policymakers have since
interpreted, and currently apply, that law. Thirdly, there are policy
objectives, which could be different again, that in practice may be met by

the law and its application, which may have their own, perhaps unintended, consequences (Reed 2007).

Kuner (2011: pp.22–4) identified[1] four main policies, often unarticulated, that motivate the regulation of TBDF of personal data generally, based on the perceived risks of transferring personal data across national borders:

- preventing circumvention of national data protection/privacy laws;
- guarding against processing risks elsewhere, e.g. US authorities accessing non-US citizens' data;
- difficulties asserting data protection/privacy rights abroad;[2] and
- enhancing consumers' and individuals' confidence in the processing of their personal data (and in ecommerce (Brown and Marsden 2013: p.51)).

Anticircumvention is cited most frequently as the reason for restricting TBDF of personal data, and was the original justification for the Restriction itself.[3] Accordingly, one main issue discussed by this book is: does the Restriction in fact effectively prevent circumvention of DPD Laws, and is it even necessary to achieve that purpose?

The Restriction put pressure on many non-EEA countries to pass 'adequate' laws[4] (Kuner 2007a: chap.4.51; Greenleaf 2012; Bygrave 2010: p.163; Makulilo 2012: p.172), and many countries have indeed adopted DPD-like laws (Greenleaf 2011b: pp.8, 13), e.g. South Africa and Kazakhstan, while Australia has amended its privacy legislation. To some extent that motivation may be an original, partly articulated one; the DPD mentions negotiating for 'inadequate' third countries to adopt adequately data-protective laws (Rec.59, Art.25(5)–(6)). That objective, strictly separate, is not my core focus, but may be discussed where relevant.

---

[1] Also Hoyle (1992); Robinson (1986).

[2] *WP47*, para.2 considers that data location in third countries makes the enforcement of contracts or DPA decisions 'considerably more difficult'.

[3] Arguably this policy goal is no longer valid except as 'an aggravating factor in particular cases', because its effective application requires examining whether a transfer *has* circumvented TBDF regulation's purpose, then whether parties benefited from that – which is impractical, hence, e.g., anticircumvention is no longer cited as an objective of New Zealand's data protection law (Kuner 2013b: pp.109–10).

[4] Although few countries have been found 'adequate' – 5.2.3. See also SEC(2012)72 final, Ann.2, para.10.11.1.

To the four policies listed above could be added a possible fifth policy: namely, preserving the ability of a country to access, some may say surveil, its own citizens' personal data (Kuner 2013a), which is obviously related to a country's desire to maintain control over its citizens. This seems to be an emerging, although very much unexpressed, motivation behind many countries' continued insistence on TBDF restrictions, and/or requiring storage of their citizens' data in equipment located within their territories. It was suggested, e.g. by Hawes (2014), as the main motivation behind the Russian Federation's relatively recent law (Hon et al. 2016) requiring data on its citizens to be located in Russia, even if copies may also be stored elsewhere.[5]

Another policy concern, much mentioned in the media and elsewhere, is preserving 'sovereignty'[6] over data. However, definitions of 'data sovereignty' differ. Below are a few examples:

- 'cloud providers storing data in the country of origin' (Ring 2013) or 'the coupling of stored data authenticity and geographical location in the cloud ... establishing data location at a granularity sufficient for placing it within the borders of a particular nation-state' (Gondree and Peterson 2013),
- (regarding governmental cloud use) 'Government's exclusive authority and control over all virtual public assets, which are not in the public domain, irrespective whether they are stored on their own or third parties' facilities and premises' (Irion 2012),
- 'many governments (including Singapore) consider certain data to be of such importance that it should not leave the country, or, in

---

[5] To offer services in China, AWS had to use local datacentres and communications infrastructure run by Chinese datacentre providers (Smolaks 2013). While Google refused to build Chinese datacentres due to censorship and privacy concerns (instead using Hong Kong servers), Apple moved to using a Chinese datacentre provider, China Telecom, to store the personal data of 'some' Chinese users, citing the aim of performance improvements (p.108, n.65); reportedly that data are stored encrypted with keys held outside China and unavailable to China Telecom, but some were sceptical regarding whether Apple could withhold user data requested by the Chinese government (Shih and Carsten 2014) – underlining my point regarding effective jurisdiction over providers who hold decryption keys (p.305). Microsoft licensed Azure and Office 365 to a Chinese datacentre services company, 21Vianet, which offers the services from its Chinese datacentres (Finley 2012).

[6] One early definition is 'loss of control of information; dependency on technology and/or information; and perceived impact on culture' (Bender 1988).

some cases, the custody of the data controller' (Singapore Parliament Debates 2012).

I consider the best definition is that of the Asia Cloud Computing Association (ACCA) (ACCA 2014: p.6), although I suggest clarifications (square-bracketed):

> Traditionally, data sovereignty is the respect for the rights associated with data – based on where the entity that has control of the data resides. However, with the globalization of data flows, the picture is less clear. A government's claim of legal jurisdiction over data may be based on the law of the country where the [entity having] control over that data resides, based on jurisdiction over that same entity in another country where it does business, or by virtue of jurisdiction over a third party that may have access to or control of the data. Each country may have laws that impact the determination of which country has a claim of jurisdiction over data.

ACCA's definition has become more sophisticated over time, in my view rightly. Initially, it mentioned only data location/movement: 'Data Sovereignty and Data Privacy are two aspects of data protection: the first to allow/restrict the movement of data and take advantage of offshore services; the second serves to protect the confidentiality and integrity of personal data' (ACCA 2012: p.7). I quote ACCA's current full definition because, while this book concentrates on legislators' avowed anti-circumvention objective, it seems not unlikely that unspoken policies regarding 'data sovereignty', notably countries' jurisdictional clashes, may underlie the continued insistence on the Restriction by EU courts, DPAs and policymakers, and the GDPR Restriction's narrower, more prescriptive requirements. The term 'data residency' is also often employed.[7] Its meaning seems clearer (physical data location in a particular country),[8] although it is also sometimes used more broadly.

I do not favour using the phrase 'data sovereignty', because it has emotional and/or political connotations (perhaps deliberately so), yet, as can be seen from the above, it lacks a generally accepted definition. Many references to 'data sovereignty' do not clarify what is meant, and exactly whose 'sovereignty' is under consideration: controllers', data subjects' (Mosch 2011: p.1) or governments'? Those are, of course, entirely different: your country having 'sovereignty' over your data is not

---

[7]   E.g. analyst Gartner's narrow formulation: 'to prevent access by government authorities and agencies while data resides in or is passing through other jurisdictions' (Perspecsys 2013).

[8]   E.g. Winstead (2011).

the same as *you* having sovereignty over your data, indeed that might be considered to negatively affect your own sovereignty over your data. In particular, constraining the location of digital data, controlling 'data residency', is not the same thing as controlling intelligible access to that data; rather, it is sometimes, but not always, a subset of the latter. This is a major point, to which I will return.

Whether relating to anticircumvention or 'data sovereignty', I argue that one major reason behind the Restriction's problematic nature is that EU policymakers, DPAs and others have failed to distinguish clearly between physical data location, jurisdiction and applicable law[9] – including the differences between theoretical and *effective* jurisdiction, 'jurisdiction' to enact laws, 'jurisdiction' in the strict sense of national courts' jurisdiction to hear cases, and national DPAs' supervisory 'jurisdiction'. Indeed, often, TBDF regulation and rules on applicable law serve the same function, effectively extending a country's data protection laws extraterritorially (Kuner 2013b: chap.6.B),[10] presaging wider global problems if not resolved. Another, related, issue is the failure to distinguish between physical location and intelligible access, which I will address in detail later.

But first, I discuss the Restriction's background, starting with a historical overview of key instruments preceding the DPD.

2.2.2   Data Export Controls

With ever-increasing automated processing of personal data facilitated by scientific and technological developments, privacy protection concerns mounted steadily from the late 1960s – e.g. OECD-ExplanMem, sec.I. West German state Hesse enacted the first data protection law (1970), and Sweden the first national data protection legislation (1973) (Blume

---

[9]   Strictly, 'jurisdiction' and 'applicable law' are different concepts. Conflicts of laws raise questions regarding 'which courts should have jurisdiction over specific issues (choice of jurisdiction) and which system of law should govern specific issues (choice of law)' (OECD-ExplanMem, para.74). A court with jurisdiction to hear certain claims might apply *another* country's laws, e.g. in contract-related claims where the parties' contract has validly chosen the application of another country's laws.

[10]   E.g. using rules on applicable law to apply their laws to data transferred to *other* countries (Kuner 2013b: chap.6.C; Kuner et al. 2013). An article on Australian and New Zealand privacy laws also considers that extraterritoriality is unlikely to solve cross-border issues, particularly given possible conflicts (Gunasekara 2007: p.382).

1992: p.401). Hesse's law did not regulate personal data export. However, several other countries' data protection laws did so, e.g. Sweden (Svantesson 2011: p.180), although seemingly exceptionally rather than routinely, and motivated mainly by anticircumvention concerns.

National laws regulated data exports in different ways, categorized as follows (Kuner 2011: p.14):

- requiring explicit DPA authorization or licence before export, e.g. Austria;
- adopting Convention108 Art.12 (2.2.4), e.g. Ireland;
- requiring the relevant individual's consent to export; or
- requiring the importing country to have data protection laws with similar protection levels, e.g. Finland.[11]

The focus was on controlling data exports, which was assumed to be the best way to prevent circumvention of laws regulating personal data processing – discussed shortly and in Ch.4. This is termed the 'geographical' approach (Kuner 2013b: chap.3.B.2). In contrast, the 'organizational', 'accountability' approach, taken e.g. by certain Canadian legislation and APEC's Privacy Framework (2.2.8), focuses on the measures taken by data exporters and importers, who remain 'accountable' for their personal data processing regardless of data location.[12]

As countries attempted to deal with increasing privacy concerns by introducing data export controls, this triggered other concerns regarding the impact of these controls on trade, the world economy and the free flow of data globally. As a result, the OECD adopted the OECD Guidelines, and the Council of Europe adopted Convention108. These instruments are similar, having been developed in parallel. Convention108-ER, para.9 noted some countries' introduction of data export controls due to fears that their data protection laws could be

---

[11] Council 8651/91, paras.3–9 summarizes Member States' data export rules as they were in 1991.

[12] Also see Weber (2013: p.123). I support a 'mixed' approach (Kuner 2013b: chap.3.B.2). With digital data, the geographical approach may be ineffective, even harmful, as this book shows. Location is only one factor. I believe the organizational accountability approach, where controllers remain responsible and liable for compliance with Principles irrespective of data location, should have primacy. Unfortunately, while industry advocated extending accountability to transfers by imposing obligations on controllers and processors to safeguard personal data adequately regardless of location (SEC(2012)72 final, Ann.4, p.86), the GDPR's Restriction does not take this approach, and indeed will generally be narrower and more inflexible – Ch.5.

avoided or evaded by moving 'operations' outside their borders to 'data havens' with lesser or no data protection laws – note the assumption that the locations of operations and data must coincide.

2.2.3 The OECD Guidelines

The OECD Guidelines aimed at 'economic efficiency and ... the generally free sharing of information essential to the proper operation of democratic governance and free market economies' (Kirby 2011: p.8). Recognizing that TBDF of personal data contribute to economic and social development, the OECD feared that, to protect privacy, European nations and institutions might erect legal and economic barriers against such flows, resulting in inefficiencies or 'serious disruption' in important sectors like banking and insurance (OECD Guidelines: Preface, Recitals). Rather than promulgate an international treaty, it favoured non-binding guidelines recommending general principles regarding personal data protection which, if introduced domestically, would hopefully help to reduce such barriers, as countries could have confidence that countries to which personal data were transferred, if they had adopted the OECD Guidelines, would apply similar protections. It felt that international consensus on fundamental principles for protecting individuals would 'obviate or diminish' reasons for regulating data export and 'facilitate resolving' conflict of laws problems; they could constitute a first step towards 'more detailed, binding international agreements' (OECD-ExplanMem, para.8). Many EEA Member States are OECD members.

The OECD Guidelines' Recitals (and Convention108 and the DPD) recognized a common interest in 'reconciling fundamental but competing values such as privacy and the free flow of information', and recommended that 'Member countries endeavour to remove or avoid creating, in the name of privacy protection, unjustified obstacles to transborder flows'. The emphasis was thus on *not* obstructing TBDF unnecessarily in the name of privacy protection, while attempting to balance the conflicting interests. To encourage international personal data flows was not 'an undisputed goal in itself' (OECD-ExplanMem, para.66); such flows between members should be permitted once the OECD Guidelines' requirements for protecting privacy and individual liberties had been 'substantially, i.e. effectively, fulfilled' (OECD-ExplanMem, para.63).

Explicitly not addressing 'other possible bases' of restricting TBDF (OECD-ExplanMem, para.63), the OECD Guidelines were not meant to limit members' rights to regulate TBDF in relation to 'free trade, tariffs, employment, and related economic conditions for intentional [*sic*: international] data traffic' (OECD-ExplanMem, para.68), although admittedly 'interests in privacy protection may be difficult to distinguish from other interests relating to trade, culture, national sovereignty ...' (OECD-ExplanMem, para.19(h)).

Accordingly, the OECD Guidelines provided:

PART THREE. BASIC PRINCIPLES OF INTERNATIONAL APPLI-CATION: FREE FLOW AND LEGITIMATE RESTRICTIONS

15. Member countries should take into consideration the implications for other Member countries of domestic processing and re-export of personal data.
16. Member countries should take all reasonable and appropriate steps to ensure that transborder flows of personal data, including transit through a Member country, are uninterrupted and secure.
17. A Member country should refrain from restricting transborder flows of personal data between itself and another Member country except where the latter does not yet substantially observe these Guidelines or where the re-export of such data would circumvent its domestic privacy legislation. A Member country may also impose restrictions in respect of certain categories of personal data for which its domestic privacy legislation includes specific regulations in view of the nature of those data and for which the other Member country provides no equivalent protection.
18. Member countries should avoid developing laws, policies and practices in the name of the protection of privacy and individual liberties, which would create obstacles to transborder flows of personal data that would exceed requirements for such protection.

Thus, the OECD Guidelines permitted flows to be restricted for 'certain categories' of personal data which are specifically regulated by national laws because of the data's nature, where the destination Member 'provides no equivalent protection': meaning, protection 'substantially similar in effect to that of the exporting country, but which need not be identical in form or in all respects' (OECD-ExplanMem, para.67).

The OECD Guidelines specifically defined 'transborder flows' of personal data as 'movements' of personal data 'across national borders' (para.1(c)). This was clearly derived from 1970s/1980s definitions of TBDF, e.g. 'electronic transmission of data across political boundaries for processing and/or storage in computer files' (Bender 1988), and 'movement across national boundaries of computerized, machine-readable data for processing, storage or retrieval' (UN 1982). While undefined, 'movement' implies *changes* in personal data's location, from one country's territory to another's. Being 'neutral with regard to the particular technology used' (OECD-ExplanMem, para.38), it was noted that data movements 'will often take place through electronic transmission but other means of data communication may also be involved', including satellite (OECD-ExplanMem, para.42). In restricting flows territorially, the OECD Guidelines' fundamental unspoken assumption, which I will return to, is that countries must have jurisdiction to apply their laws to data physically 'located' in their territories, and will apply their laws accordingly. As I discuss later (4.4.1), this reflected the technologies of the time, and nowadays such assumed jurisdiction may not be effective in practice (7.5.1.1). It may be 'nearly impossible' to avoid reference to territoriality in provisions regulating TBDF, since TBDF's 'very notion' presupposes that data have changed location (Kuner 2013b: p.139). However, this book argues that the 'locations' of (or more precisely, jurisdiction over) the transferors/recipients is more important than the *data's* location.

While not providing guidelines on applicable law, the OECD Guidelines (para.22) exhorted member countries to 'work towards' developing domestic and international principles to govern applicable law regarding TBDF. Identifying 'one or more connecting factors which, at best, indicate one applicable law' was acknowledged as 'particularly difficult' for 'international computer networks where, because of dispersed location and rapid movement of data, and geographically dispersed data-processing activities, several connecting factors could occur in a complex manner involving elements of legal novelty' (OECD-ExplanMem, para.75). Nevertheless, the OECD Guidelines must assume that member countries have 'jurisdiction' to apply their own laws effectively to regulate personal data processing occurring 'in' their territories.

2.2.4 Convention108

Convention108 took effect in 1985. Fifty contracting parties (countries) have ratified it, including all EEA Member States and some non-European countries.[13]

Convention108 aimed to strengthen individuals' legal protection regarding the automatic processing of their personal data (Convention108-ER, para.1). Sharing the OECD Guidelines' rationale, Convention108 banned restrictions on transfers to parties as unnecessary because 'all Contracting States, having subscribed to the common core of data protection provisions ... offer a certain minimum level of protection' (Convention108-ER, paras.20, 67).

---

[13] For overlaps and differences between EU, EEA and Convention108 participants, see http://www.kuan0.com/doc/europe-eea-eu-efta-council-of-europe-venn.html.

Convention108's Art.12 sought to balance effective data protection against, not economic efficiency, but rather ECHR Art.10's principle of free information flow regardless of frontiers (Convention108-ER, para.62), aiming for free flows of TBDF between parties (Convention108-ER, para.21, 67):

Article 12 – Transborder flows of personal data and domestic law

1. The following provisions shall apply to the transfer across national borders, by whatever medium, of personal data undergoing automatic processing or collected with a view to their being automatically processed.
2. A Party shall not, for the sole purpose of the protection of privacy, prohibit or subject to special authorisation transborder flows of personal data going to the territory of another Party.
3. Nevertheless, each Party shall be entitled to derogate from the provisions of paragraph 2:
    a. insofar as its legislation includes specific regulations for certain categories of personal data or of automated personal data files, because of the nature of those data or those files, except where the regulations of the other Party provide an equivalent protection;
    b. when the transfer is made from its territory to the territory of a non-Contracting State through the intermediary of the territory of another Party, in order to avoid such transfers resulting in circumvention of the legislation of the Party referred to at the beginning of this paragraph.

The concept of data 'recipient' mainly referred to countries as 'recipients' (Convention108-ER, para.69). Nevertheless, Convention108 recognized that *organizations* may receive data, with references to 'sender and recipient (within[14] one organization or different organizations)' (Convention108-ER, para.63). As with the OECD Guidelines, parties may restrict flows of 'certain categories' of personal data, unless 'regulations' of the recipient party provide 'equivalent protection'. However, unlike the OECD Guidelines, neither Convention108 nor Convention108-ER defined 'transborder data flows', 'transfer' or 'equivalent protection'.

Like the OECD Guidelines, Convention108 prevents parties from *restricting* flows 'going to the territory' of other parties. Clearly, by 'transfer', Art.12 Convention108 must have envisaged physical data 'movements' between territories (e.g. 'transfer across national borders'

---

[14] A controller may 'move' personal data to third country-located infrastructure without making any 'transfer' to a *third party* there, if the controller owns the third country-located datacentre or infrastructure concerned.

and 'from its territory to the territory ...') – even within the same organization (n.14). Art.24 Convention108 allowed parties to specify or extend 'a territory or territories to which' Convention108 applies. Also, Convention108-ER, para.91 noted the 'practical importance' of applying Convention108 to 'remote territories under the jurisdiction of Parties or on whose behalf a Party can make undertakings', 'in view of the use that is made of distant countries for data processing operations either for reasons of cost and manpower or in view of the utilization of alternating night and daytime data processing capability' – presaging such uses in cloud computing. Again, Convention108 must assume that countries exercise territorial jurisdiction based on physical location of data, or at least of data-processing operations, because Art.1, regarding its scope, states that Convention108's purpose is to secure, 'in the territory of each Party', privacy rights for individuals in relation to automated processing of their personal data.

Recognizing the complexities of applicable law issues in the TBDF context, Convention108-ER, para.23 acknowledged that applicable law problems might arise 'when data processing operations are carried out on the territory of two or more States (contracting or non-contracting) or when parties concerned by data processing, particularly the data subjects and the data users, reside in different countries'; however, it was considered 'premature' to include specific rules on applicable law, on the basis that a 'common core' of substantive law, which partly harmonizes procedure, would help reduce risks of conflict of laws or legal lacunae. However, as with the OECD Guidelines, for Convention108's Art.12 to make sense it must assume that parties have effective 'jurisdiction' over, and will apply their Convention108-compliant laws to, personal data physically located 'in' their territories.

2.2.5   The DPD

Despite exhortations[15] to Member States to ratify Convention108, by 1990 few had done so. Fewer had passed laws nationally regarding automated personal data processing. Even those took different approaches. Furthermore, Convention108 left certain implementation options open. Therefore, the Commission proposed a draft Directive (COM(90)314 final) (1990-Proposal), which culminated in the DPD and

---

[15]   E.g. Resolution on the protection of the rights of the individual in the face of technical developments in data processing, OJ C87/39, 5.4.1982.

related legislation. Many objections were raised, including by the European Parliament following Parliamentary committees' scrutiny. Accordingly, after consultation, the Commission proposed a modified draft Directive (COM(92)422 final) (1992-Proposal). The Council adopted Council Common Position 1995/1/EC (CP) in 1995, including 'Statement of the Council's Reasons' (CP-SR). After considering the Commission's opinion on the CP, the Parliament suggested changes, which the Council agreed, with the DPD finally being adopted in 1995.[16]

The DPD's objectives include not only personal data protection but free exchange of personal data within the European Communities (Community).[17] This was recognized as important for and inevitable as a result of achieving the internal market, and important for international trade. Therefore, like Convention108, the DPD attempted to balance free flow of personal data with privacy protection. Differing protection levels for personal data processing could obstruct flows because Member States might invoke the protection of rights, particularly privacy, to inhibit free movement of personal data between them, by arguing that other Member States' protection levels were insufficiently high. Therefore, the DPD aimed to facilitate free personal data movement, *intra*-Community, by affording individuals certain minimum, high protection levels for their personal data processing, harmonized cross-Community. Harmonization was considered necessary because national laws diverged widely, and cross-border personal data flow needed consistent regulation consonant with the internal market objective. This approach and rationale echoed OECD Guidelines' and Convention108's. The DPD became effective in 1995, requiring national Member State implementation by December 1998. I will discuss the Restriction's detailed legislative evolution specifically (2.3), after concluding my chronological overview of relevant instruments.

2.2.6   The CIDPR

In 2000, the Community adopted Regulation (EC) 45/2001 (CIDPR, for Community institutions' data protection regulation). Similar to, and intended to be consistent with,[18] the DPD, the CIDPR regulates personal data processing by Community institutions and bodies. The European

---

[16]   On Member States' DPD negotiations see Pearce and Platten (1998) and Bignami (2004: pp.839–40). On the DPD's background and legislative progress, including how Member States reached various compromises, see Simitis (1994).

[17]   And now EEA – p.1, n.1.

[18]   CIDPR Art.12.

Data Protection Supervisor (EDPS) is their DPA. The CIDPR's equivalent of the Restriction (Art.9) differs slightly, referring to transfers to recipients rather than to countries or territories (emphasis added): 'Personal data shall only be transferred to *recipients*, other than Community institutions and bodies, *which are not subject to national law adopted pursuant to Directive 95/46/EC*, if an adequate level of protection is ensured *in the country of the recipient* or within the recipient international organisation ...' (Art.9(1)).[19]

Art.2(g) CIDPR[20] defines 'recipient' as 'a natural or legal person, public authority, agency or any other body to whom data are disclosed', whether third party[21] or not; and 'authorities which may receive data in the framework of a particular inquiry shall not be regarded as recipients'. Accordingly, if a recipient is subject to DPD Laws, Art.9 permits transfers to it; if it is not, transfers are prohibited in the absence of adequate protection 'in the country of the recipient', adequate safeguards or a derogation. Also, if a 'recipient' is subject to DPD Laws but is *also* subject to third country laws, Art.9 would permit transfers to it. Thus, the CIDPR seems to assume that a recipient is only subject to *one* country's jurisdiction, which cannot be assumed with multinational organizations.

Note the references to disclosure, and to recipients not being subject to DPD Laws. The Restriction does not refer to 'recipients'. However, lawmakers apparently considered it implicit in the DPD that any 'transfer' must be to *recipients* subject, or not subject, to relevant laws. For example, regarding the then draft CIDPR, the Commission commented (emphasis added): 'Article 9 *reproduces* Articles 25 and 26 of the Directive and deals with the transfer of personal data *to a recipient who is neither subject to this Regulation nor to Directive 95/46/EC*' (COM(1999)337 final).

2.2.7 Convention108 Additional Protocol

The DPD triggered proposals for an Additional Protocol to Convention108 (Convention108-AP), with explanatory report (Convention108-APER). Opened for signature in 2001, it became effective in 2004. It

---

[19] The remainder of Art.9 is not quoted; its provisions are similar to those of Arts.25–6 DPD.

[20] Same as Art.2(g) DPD.

[21] '[A] natural or legal person, public authority, agency or body other than the data subject, the controller, the processor and the persons who, under the direct authority of the controller or the processor, are authorised to process the data' (Art.2(f) CIDPR).

added two substantive provisions (Convention108-APER, para.1): on parties establishing supervisory authorities, and on TBDF to countries or organizations *not* party to Convention108. The latter was intended to clarify the position on TBDF to non-parties, given the increase in cross-border personal data exchanges between parties and non-parties and the resulting need to improve effective protection of rights by internationally harmonizing data protection principles and implementation (Convention108-APER, paras.3–6, 21–33).

Following the DPD (CoE 2000b, sec.II.7–8), Convention108-AP aimed to balance privacy protection with the free flow of data from parties to non-parties based on 'adequate protection'[22] or adequate safeguards, and it adopted many of the DPD criteria (Convention108-APER, paras.25–33) (emphasis added):

Article 2 – Transborder flows of personal data to a recipient which is not subject to the jurisdiction of a Party to the Convention

1. Each Party shall provide for the transfer of personal data to a *recipient that is subject to the jurisdiction of a State* or organisation that is not Party to the Convention only if *that State or organisation ensures an adequate level of protection* for the intended data transfer.
2. By way of derogation from paragraph 1 of Article 2 of this Protocol, each Party may allow for the transfer of personal data:
    a. if domestic law provides for it because of:
       – specific interests of the data subject, or
       – legitimate prevailing interests, especially important public interests, or
    b. if safeguards, which can in particular result from contractual clauses, are provided *by the controller responsible for the transfer* and are found adequate by the competent authorities according to domestic law.

Like the CIDPR, Convention108-AP refers to transfers to recipients[23] (subject to the jurisdiction[24] of non-parties), rather than transfers 'to'

---

[22] Criteria for appraising adequate protection were deliberately made not 'too specific'; 'Case-law should develop', and criteria 'gradually established' (CoE 2000a: para.36).

[23] Convention108-AP's drafters must have considered 'recipient' implicit in Convention108 itself. This is because they interpreted Convention108's Art.12(3)(b) anticircumvention derogation, which allows transfers 'from its territory to the territory of a non-Contracting State through the intermediary of the territory of another Party', as a derogation from (emphasis added) 'the principle of the free circulation of data between its territory *and a recipient*

non-parties' territories. Again, it assumes (see 4.6–4.8) that a recipient can be subject to only one country's jurisdiction, so that if it is subject to a non-party's jurisdiction it cannot be subject to a party's jurisdiction, and vice versa.[25] No doubt because of that assumption, under Convention108-AP the question is whether the recipient is subject to a non-party's jurisdiction; whereas, under the CIDPR, the question is whether it is *not* subject to DPD Laws. This difference matters. If a recipient is subject to jurisdictions of both a Participant[26] and non-Participant, CIDPR would permit transfers to it, but seemingly Convention108-AP would not (unless there is adequate protection etc.). The inconsistency in their approaches when a recipient is subject to multiple jurisdictions highlights one of the key problems with current TBDF restrictions.

2.2.8 Non-EEA Countries

I now outline some issues regarding the position in non-EEA countries (space does not permit detailed dissection of non-EEA privacy laws).

This book will cite some examples under Canada's Personal Information Protection and Electronic Documents Act 2000 (as amended) (PIPEDA), because I consider the EEA's geographic data localization approach inferior to an organizational, accountability-based approach (2.2.2) like PIPEDA's. PIPEDA's regime is accountability-based (OPC 2012): not in the narrow GDPR sense (1.5.1), but in the sense that an organization is held *responsible* for personal information under its control and must implement policies and practices to comply with PIPEDA's information-protective principles – even if using a third party processor,

---

which is not subject to the jurisdiction of a Party via another Party' (Convention108-APER, para.22).

[24] Convention108 seemingly assumed that Parties would apply their (Convention108-compliant) laws to data under their jurisdiction (2.2.4). In Convention108-AP, 'subject to the jurisdiction' similarly assumes that the relevant party/non-party would apply its laws to recipients under its jurisdiction.

[25] Convention108-AP's Art.2 title/heading and Convention108-APER, paras.22–3, 25, 32, refer to transfers to 'a recipient which is not subject to the jurisdiction of a Party'. However, Art.2(1) Convention108-AP mentions 'a recipient that is subject to the jurisdiction of' a non-party. This indicates that Convention108-AP equates the two.

[26] Used here to mean a Member State under the DPD/CIDPR, a party under Convention108/Convention108-AP, or a member country under the OECD Guidelines, as the context may require.

when it must employ 'contractual or other means to provide a comparable level of protection' (principle 4.1.3).

A multilateral instrument that also emphasizes the organizational approach is the Asia-Pacific Economic Co-operation (APEC) Privacy Framework (APEC 2005),[27] endorsed by APEC ministers to promote 'a flexible approach to information privacy protection across APEC member economies, while avoiding the creation of unnecessary barriers to information flows'. It contains information privacy principles 'intended to provide clear guidance and direction to businesses in APEC economies on common privacy issues and the impact of privacy issues upon the way legitimate businesses are conducted' (APEC 2005: p.8). Thus, like previous instruments, it aims to facilitate free flow of data *intra*-region by encouraging consistent high standards of privacy protection among members. Its information privacy principles relate to preventing harm, notice, collection limitation, use, choice, integrity, security safeguards, access and correction, and accountability (based on the OECD Guidelines). Accountability here means that the controller is accountable for complying with measures implementing the Framework's principles, and when transmitting personal information must obtain consent or 'exercise due diligence and take reasonable steps' to ensure the recipient protects the information consistently with the Framework's principles, with the controller remaining accountable for such protection (APEC 2005). An associated framework, the APEC Cross-Border Privacy Enforcement Arrangement (CPEA), provides for regional cooperation in enforcing privacy laws (APEC 2009), effective from 2010. This aims to facilitate DPA information-sharing, provide mechanisms for cross-border cooperation in enforcement, and encourage information-sharing and cooperation on privacy investigation and enforcement with *non*-APEC DPAs. Currently, 25 DPAs participate (APEC n.d.).

The APEC Cross-Border Privacy Rules (CBPR) system was developed in 2011 (APEC 2011) to operationalize the APEC Privacy Framework, with a dedicated website (CBPRs). All 21 APEC countries initially committed to implement CBPR, but to date only the US, Mexico, Japan and Canada have done so. Voluntarily participating organizations must implement legally enforceable privacy policies consistent with Framework and CBPR requirements, with independent, CBPR-recognized, public or private sector 'accountability agents' that assess and certify

---

[27] Agreed between countries participating in the APEC trade group (certain Asian and South American countries, Australia, Canada, New Zealand, Russia and the USA).

their compliance with such policies and practices.[28] The WP29 has produced a checklist for organizations applying for both binding corporate rules (BCRs) (5.4.3) and CBPR certification, not for mutual recognition but as a basis for double certification (*WP212*). As the APEC Privacy Framework only applies to controllers, in late 2015 APEC endorsed the Privacy Recognition for Processors (PRP) system for certifying data processors' privacy programmes as effective to implement controllers' own obligations, and allow controllers to identify qualified and accountable processors (US International Trade Administration 2015).

This book covers PIPEDA in more detail than CBPR, mainly because there is more to discuss under PIPEDA. Currently there are only two accountability agents, one US (TRUSTe) and one Japanese (JIPDEC), and 17 participating organizations, all US, including on the cloud front Adaptive Insights (SaaS), Apple, Box (SaaS), Hewlett Packard Enterprise, HP, IBM and Workday (SaaS). Clearly, US organizations are adopting CBPR to facilitate doing business in the Asia-Pacific region. In 2016, the US Federal Trade Commission (FTC) took enforcement action against 28 US companies falsely claiming CBPR certification on their websites (FTC 2016b), settling one so far (FTC 2016a). There are no PRP certifications to date, but PRP may well suit cloud providers – space does not permit detailed discussion of PRP.

Although not required by the APEC Framework or OECD Guidelines, both the DPD and Convention108-AP restrict personal data exports to countries without 'adequate' privacy protection – i.e., data export controls. This European approach of imposing 'border controls' on personal data was followed in 28 of 33 subsequent non-European national privacy laws examined by Greenleaf (2012). Perhaps some countries did so for unarticulated policy reasons unrelated to preventing circumvention of their privacy laws – e.g., European countries have personal data export controls, so joining them in introducing such controls might level the playing field and/or improve their future negotiating positions with European countries on personal data exports/imports. Whatever their reasons, where countries have introduced privacy laws, personal data export controls are more the norm than the exception, and countries keep incorporating them.[29]

---

[28] The CBPR programme requirements (CBPRs 2012b) and CBPR intake questionnaire (CBPRs 2012a) are used in accountability agents' compliance assessments.

[29] E.g. Singapore's Personal Data Protection Act 2012, effective 2014.

2.2.9 OECD Guidelines Updated

The OECD Guidelines were updated in 2013 (OECD Guidelines-2), in particular:

PART FOUR. BASIC PRINCIPLES OF INTERNATIONAL APPLICATION: FREE FLOW AND LEGITIMATE RESTRICTIONS

16. A data controller remains accountable for personal data under its control without regard to the location of the data.
17. A Member country should refrain from restricting transborder flows of personal data between itself and another country where (a) the other country substantially observes these OECD Guidelines or (b) sufficient safeguards exist, including effective enforcement mechanisms and appropriate measures put in place by the data controller, to ensure a continuing level of protection consistent with these OECD Guidelines.
18. Any restrictions to transborder flows of personal data should be proportionate to the risks presented, taking into account the sensitivity of the data, and the purpose and context of the processing.

The definition of 'transborder data flows' was unchanged. Accordingly, unlike with the CIDPR and Convention108-AP, OECD Guidelines-2 perpetuates the concept of flows 'between' countries. Reversing the OECD Guidelines' approach of allowing flows generally except in certain situations (OECD Guidelines-2, p.29), and reducing the OECD Guidelines' emphasis on ensuring uninterrupted flows (p.45), the OECD Guidelines-2 p.30 exhort member countries to refrain from restricting flows where 'sufficient safeguards' exist, including measures taken by the controller, e.g. technical and organizational security safeguards, contracts, complaint-handling processes, audits, etc.; but such measures 'need to be sufficient and supplemented by mechanisms that can ensure effective enforcement in the event these measures prove ineffective'.

While jurisdiction over 'recipients' is not mentioned, the OECD Guidelines-2 explicitly stress a controller's continued responsibility to ensure that personal data are processed in accordance with OECD Guidelines-2's principles regardless of data location (para.16),[30] i.e. some accountability emphasis.

2.2.10 Convention108 Reform

Plans are afoot to modernize Convention108 (CoE 2010). This is a moving target, one might even say a yoyo, as certain provisions in one

---

[30] Also p.30, OECD Guidelines-2.

draft seem to be deleted from the next, restored in the next, etc. However, following a public consultation and various drafts and meetings, a consolidated draft of September 2016 is available (CoE 2016c), with draft amending protocol (CAHDATA 2016b). As with the GDPR, there is pressure to conclude the process simply because it has already spanned over five years. The position as at the date of writing is that the Ad hoc Committee on data protection (CAHDATA), established by the CoE's Committee of Ministers, will discuss outstanding reservations by the EU and Russian Federation (CAHDATA 2016d); update the draft explanatory report (CoE 2016b); modify the draft amending protocol based on CAHDATA discussions; and submit the modified draft protocol and draft explanatory report to the Committee of Ministers, which will consult the CoE's Parliament Assembly before examining and adopting the protocol and report (CAHDATA 2016c). The current draft Article 12(1)–(2) on transborder data flows provides (CoE 2016c):

1. A Party shall not, for the sole purpose of the protection of personal data, prohibit or subject to special authorisation the transfer of such data to a recipient who is subject to the jurisdiction of another Party to the Convention. Such a Party may however do so if bound by harmonised rules of protection shared by States belonging to a regional international organisation.
2. When the recipient is subject to the jurisdiction of a State or international organisation which is not Party to this Convention, the transfer of personal data may only take place where an appropriate level of protection based on the provisions of this Convention is secured ...

Note the explicit use of 'subject to the jurisdiction', following some (but not all) of certain recommendations made to take better account of jurisdictional issues (Moiny 2012). These aspects are discussed later (2.4.5, 3.8). Also note the new provision allowing parties to prohibit or require special authorization for transfers, even to a party, if 'bound by harmonised rules of protection' of a regional international organization – notably the EU (CoE 2016b: para.102). Somewhat surprisingly, only one party, the Russian Federation, objected to this provision on the basis that it 'diffuses and weakens the legal regime' of Convention108 and 'de facto creates a "privileged" group of states with a lesser scope of obligations [to allow data flows] within the framework of the Convention' (CAHDATA 2016d: p.6). The latter is important. Put more informally, this new provision would allow any group of parties (not just the EU) to get together, form an exclusive club with 'harmonised rules of protection' (not even 'more protective' rules, just *harmonized* rules), and then create 'additional regional binding harmonised rules governing data flows' (CoE 2016a: para.102) that ban transfers outside the club. But how can free flow of information be ensured between all parties to achieve the overarching goal of Convention108, if a subset of parties can prevent transfers to other parties outside their club? To what extent can the GDPR be said to create 'harmonised' rules anyway, when it allows so much Member State flexibility (EDRi et al. 2016)?

The provisions on derogations are unclear. Derogations permitting transfers are only allowed for 'explicit, specific and free' informed data subject consent; if required in the 'specific interests' of the data subject; under 'prevailing legitimate interests, in particular important public interests, are provided for by law and such transfer constitutes a necessary and proportionate measure in a democratic society'; or if the transfer constitutes a necessary and proportionate measure in a democratic society for freedom of expression (CoE 2016c: p.5).[31] While it is understandable why any laws permitting transfers by way of derogation should be necessary and proportionate in a democratic society, it is unclear why (as the draft seems to suggest) any *transfers* under such laws should be necessary and proportionate 'measures', and hopefully this will be clarified before the update is adopted.

The draft also includes new and expanded substantive processing principles, effectively reflecting the GDPR – e.g. data subjects' right to object to processing, breach notification obligations, enhanced DPA powers including on accountability (demonstrating compliance), improved cooperation between parties' DPAs, and criteria to evaluate compliance with its principles.

2.3 OBJECTIVE: COMPLIANCE WITH SUBSTANTIVE PRINCIPLES

I now trace the evolution of specific key aspects of the instruments outlined above. First, I discuss in detail the anticircumvention policy objective of TBDF restrictions, including how lawmakers intended it to be achieved. Then, I discuss the evolution of approaches to responsibility for compliance.

---

[31] Explained by the draft explanatory report as 'Such derogations are permitted in limited situations only: with the data subject's consent or specific interest and/or where there are prevailing legitimate interests provided by law and/or the transfer constitutes a necessary and proportionate measure in a democratic society for freedom of expression' (CoE 2016b: para.107).

2.3.1 The Anticircumvention Goal

2.3.1.1 The OECD Guidelines and Convention108

As previously discussed (2.2.2), many countries adopted data export controls in the 1970s because they wanted to prevent circumvention of their national privacy laws through physically moving data outside the country. This widespread adoption of data export controls spurred the OECD Guidelines and Convention108. Both instruments envisaged that circumvention might be possible through:

- directly transferring personal data to a non-Participant (n.26); or
- exporting personal data to a Participant, and thence to a non-Participant – often termed 'onward transfer', e.g. *WP4*, sec.3(i)(6), *WP12*, p.6.

The OECD Guidelines' focus on data's territorial location as enabling circumvention, or conversely protection, is evident from references to (emphasis added) 'attempts to circumvent national legislation by processing data *in* a Member country which does not yet substantially observe the OECD Guidelines' (OECD-ExplanMem, para.67), and to countries' common interest in 'preventing the creation of *locations* where national regulations on data processing can easily be circumvented' (OECD-ExplanMem, para.9). Similarly: 'In practice, however, protection of persons grows weaker when the geographic area is widened', and concerns were noted that 'data users might seek to avoid data protection controls by moving their operations, in whole or in part, to "data havens"', i.e. countries with lesser or no data protection laws (Convention108-ER, para.9). Problems were envisaged upon 're-import of data processed abroad in violation of certain provisions of the law of the country of origin Party to the convention', but it was for the country of origin to take, before export, the necessary measures (Convention108-ER, para.66).

Both instruments allowed Participants to derogate from the principle of not restricting TBDF, in order to prevent circumvention of national privacy laws through 're-export of such data' (OECD Guidelines, para.17; OECD-ExplanMem, para.67) or transfers 'through the intermediary of the territory of another Party' (Convention108, Art.12(3)(b) (2.2.4)), i.e. through onward transfers. Participants were reminded to consider the 'implications for other Member countries of domestic processing *and re-export*' of personal data,[32] both to respect other countries' interests in protecting personal data and their nationals'/ residents' privacy and liberties, and to permit processing of 'foreign data and data on non-nationals', e.g. providing data on foreign nationals living abroad to their country of nationality (OECD Guidelines, para.15; OECD-ExplanMem, para.64). Re-export was explicitly mentioned to emphasize the importance of ensuring that personal data were not deprived of protection 'as a result of their transfer to territories and facilities for the processing of data where control is slack or non-existent' (OECD-ExplanMem, para.64).

Concerned, however, that Participants might use the anticircumventory derogation to restrict transfers unduly, Convention108-ER, para.70 stressed that it could be invoked only when it was 'clearly established that the data transferred are actually only passing through' the Participant – not on the 'mere presumption or expectation' that data transferred to another Participant might 'eventually' pass to a non-Participant. Transborder data flow may occur by transferring data directly between the countries of origin and destination – or 'via one or more countries of transit' (Convention108-ER, para.63), as is common with Internet communications. 'Transit', i.e. passing through a member country 'without being used or stored with a view to usage in that country' (OECD-ExplanMem, para.66), is *not* considered to be a circumventory 'transfer'. OECD Guidelines, para.16 exhorted[33] members to 'take all reasonable and appropriate steps' to ensure that TBDF, including 'transit through a Member country', are 'uninterrupted and secure' against unauthorized access, loss and similar risks.[34]

---

[32]　This was tactfully worded, but sought to address 'liberal policies' contrary to the OECD Guidelines' 'spirit', which may 'facilitate attempts to circumvent or violate' other Participants' protective legislation. Such circumvention/violation was not specifically mentioned, as several countries considered it unacceptable to require Participants directly or indirectly to enforce, extraterritorially, other Participants' laws (OECD-ExplanMem, para.64).

[33]　The OECD Guidelines-2 omitted this exhortation, for 'clarity and to avoid repetition', because members' commitment to global free flow of information and security was 'underlined elsewhere' (OECD Guidelines-2, p.35).

[34]　This indicates concerns, even in the 1970s, that countries could intercept data in transit.

2.3.1.2   DPD – the Restriction

The DPD's text does not mention the Restriction's legislative objective.[35] However, in relation to the 1992-Proposal, this objective was clearly stated to be anticircumvention (COM(92)422 final, pp.4, 34):

> 4. Third countries
>
> The rule intended to prevent the Community rules from being circumvented in the course of transfers of data to non-community countries takes the form of a ban on the transfer of data to countries which do not provide an adequate level of protection; this has now been clarified in order to remove any ambiguity as to the purpose pursued. Tests by which adequacy is to be measured have been added. Exceptions to the principle have also been laid down in a limited number of cases where particular circumstances appear to justify this … Without such a provision the Community's efforts to guarantee a high level of protection for individuals could be nullified by transfers to other countries in which the protection provided is inadequate. There is also the fact that free movement of data between Member States, which the proposal seeks to establish, will mean that there will have to be common rules on transfer to non-Community countries.[36]

The Council also emphasized anticircumvention. Denying any 'trade barrier' objective, it asserted that Arts.25–6 were merely 'corollary' to other DPD provisions 'of which they formed an integral part', designed to 'make the system "water-tight"' by avoiding any 'laxity' regarding transfers to third countries (CP-SR, sec.III.A). Subsequently, EU DPAs reiterated the aim of preventing European data protection legislation being circumvented by transferring personal data to third countries (*WP114*, p.7).[37] The CJEU in *Schrems* (5.3.2), paras.72–3 confirmed that the Restriction was 'intended to ensure that the high level of that protection continues where personal data is transferred to a third country', which in its view 'could easily be circumvented by transfers' to third countries unless the third country ensured adequate protection through its domestic laws or international commitments (see also 5.3.4.2). GDPR's

---

[35]   E.g. Reed (2012: pp.175–6).

[36]   The second paragraph quoted suggests another objective: harmonizing national rules, here regarding transfers to non-EEA countries. As I will show, the Restriction, and GDPR's Restriction, fails in that objective also (Ch.5).

[37]   *WP114*, pp.6–7 also considers that Art.26's 'adequate protection' rationale is intended to ensure that individuals 'continue to benefit from the fundamental rights and freedoms which they are granted in relation to the processing of their data in the European Union once these data have been transferred to a third country'. This seemingly envisages continuance of DPD rights, rather than adequate or even equivalent rights.

Restriction similarly aims to ensure continued protection of individuals' rights when personal data are 'transferred from the EU to third countries' (COM(2012)011 final, p.10), going further by explicitly restricting 'onward transfers' (1.6.3).

I now discuss the evolution in how that anticircumvention goal was intended to be achieved, largely reflecting the evolution in DPD's jurisdictional grounds. It is with some lawmakers' and regulators' narrow and rigid view of *how* adequate protection can be ensured that I disagree. As I will show, it should not be assumed that only countries' laws or international commitments can provide adequate protection.

2.3.2   Preventing Circumvention – Data Location and Jurisdiction

Art.4 DPD stipulates the circumstances when Member States must apply their DPD Laws to personal data processing, including when:

● processing is carried out in the context of the activities of an establishment[38] of the controller on the territory of the Member State (Art.4(1)(a)), or

● a controller (not established on Community territory), for personal data-processing purposes, makes use of equipment situated on the Member State's territory (Art.4(1)(c)).[39]

Art.4 is often considered to give jurisdiction to DPAs and courts,[40] so applicable law and DPAs' jurisdiction usually coincide (*WP179*, p.10).

---

[38]   Which need not be a branch or subsidiary of the controller, as long it conducts 'real and effective' activity –even a minimal one – through stable arrangements: Case C-230/14 *Weltimmo*. See also p.9, n.20.

[39]   See also p.73, n.5.

[40]   Arguably Art.4 (headed 'Law applicable' and, since 1992-Proposal, 'National law applicable') provides for choice of law, rather than entitling Member States to assert jurisdiction over controllers (Kuner 2007a: paras.3.06– 3.11). Art.28 DPD allocates jurisdiction as between national *DPAs* on a territorial basis. However, many DPAs base jurisdiction over controllers on Art.4 (Kuner 2007a: para.3.08). *Google Spain* (p.9, n.20) did not discuss the applicable law/jurisdiction distinction, but clearly assumed that Art.4 gave Spanish courts direct jurisdiction over US corporation Google. In Case C-230/14 *Weltimmo*, the CJEU stated that if a DPA concluded that the applicable law, by virtue of Art.4, was another Member State's, not its own, it cannot exercise its powers outside its Member State territory or impose penalties based on its own law on a controller not established in its territory, but must seek the cooperation of the DPA of the Member State whose law *is* applicable.

Generally, in this book I use 'jurisdiction' and 'applicable law' inter-changeably, because 'determination of applicable law and jurisdiction often go hand in hand' in the TBDF (Kuner 2013b: p.122),[41] and indeed broader data protection, context.

Initially, Art.4(1)(a), 1990-Proposal founded jurisdiction on the phys-ical location of 'data files': Member States were to apply the DPD's requirements to the processing of data files 'located' in their territories. Art.4(1)(b), 1990-Proposal also required Member States to apply DPD to 'the controller of a file resident in its territory who uses from its territory a file located in a third country whose law does not provide an adequate level of protection', unless such use was 'only sporadic'. Art.4(2), 1990-Proposal required certain DPD provisions to be applied to a user 'consulting a file located in a third country from a terminal located in the territory of a Member State'. Art.4(3) addressed temporary moves of files between Member States, prohibiting the recipient Member State from placing 'obstacles' or requiring formalities beyond those in the Member State where the file was 'normally located'. Those provisions arose from concerns that:

- Member State-resident controllers could move files to a country without adequate protection and then, from Community territory, 'use' a file in ways incompatible with the DPD; and that
- users, seemingly whether Member State-resident or not, could remotely 'consult' files 'located' in a third country via 'terminals' sited on Community territory.

Such file moves would have been rare in 1990, given the technologies available at that time (4.4.1). Again reflecting then-current technologies, 1990-Proposal's Art.4(3) assumed that a file must have a 'primary' location (remaining as the primary location even if files were 'temporar-ily' removed, e.g. through 'removal of data storage media' (COM(90)314 final, p.22)). Accordingly, it sought to ensure that only the laws of the country of a file's 'primary' location should apply to it.

As regards controllers avoiding compliance with EU data protection laws through 'relocating' a data file outside the Community and then 'consulting' it from within the Community, the Commission noted (COM(90)314 final, pp.21–2) (emphasis added):

---

[41] Cf. p.29. In practice, DPAs are 'often reluctant to apply any law but their own' (Kuner 2013b: p.122).

This article specifies the connecting factors which determine the application in each Member State of the Directive's provisions. The choice of factors in paragraph 1 is motivated by the desire to avoid a situation in which the data subject is completely unprotected owing, mainly, to the law being circumvented. The factual criterion of the *place in which the file is located* has therefore been adopted. In this connection, each part of a file which is geographically dispersed or divided among several Member States must be treated as a separate file.

The desire to *protect the data subject in the event of relocation* is at the root of a provision which requires a user *consulting a file located in a third country* from a terminal located in a Member State to comply with the Directive's provisions on the lawfulness of processing, the informing of the data subject in the event of the communication of data, sensitive data, data security and liability. This requirement is imposed where such use is not simply sporadic … This article is also designed to avoid any overlapping of applicable laws.

Clearly, remote access from the Community to personal data located outside was envisaged, but remote access *from* third countries *to* Community-located personal data was not (Reed 2012: pp.175–6). Arguably, this failure partly underlies DPAs' subsequent broad interpretations of Art.4 DPD (p.53), aiming to prevent undesired processing of EEA data subjects' personal data by non-EEA controllers.

Art.24 1990-Proposal, which became Art.25 DPD, bolstered Art.4's anticircumvention provisions by banning 'transfer' of personal data to third countries without adequate protection, save in the circumstances stated. Obviously, jurisdiction founded on a file's location may be circumvented by moving the file to another country, so logically circumvention may be prevented by restricting such 'transfer'. On that basis, Art.24 1990-Proposal was understandable. Nevertheless, it might seem unnecessary. 1990-Proposal's Arts.4(1)(b) and 4(2) clearly caught 'use' by Community-resident controllers and 'consultation' by users via Community-located terminals, respectively, of files located in (or moved to) third countries, implicitly through remote access. Because the 1990-Proposal explicitly regulated such use or consultation, controllers could not circumvent it by remotely accessing files located in third countries.

However, when the interrelationship between 1990-Proposal's Art.24 and Art.4(1)(b) was queried, the Commission stated that 'both provisions were necessary in order to embrace the obligations of a sub-contracter [*sic*] (for example, Article 22 [processors]) operating outside an EC country' (Council 8651/91, para.21). This indicates that the purpose of 1990-Proposal's Art.24 was to prevent circumvention through a controller transferring a file to a third party acting on its behalf, i.e. its third country processor, having the processor process the data in undesired ways and then, presumably, receiving 'back' the data and/or processing results from the processor. This Commission statement shows very clearly that the Restriction was originally intended to prevent the circumvention of substantive Principles through controllers making transfers of personal data *to processors in third countries*, while Art.4 separately addressed *direct* controller use or consultation of personal data located in third countries. Unfortunately, that original specific purpose has been forgotten, or is generally ignored.

The Parliament sought to generalize 'data files' to 'data', deleting the reference to 'sporadic' use of 'files' located in a third country as too vague (COM(92)422 final, p.13). Significantly, the 1992-Proposal recognized that EU data protection laws should not be applied based on data location, due to practical difficulties with determining data location and possible distributed processing locations (COM(92)422 final, p.13; emphasis added):

> Under the original proposal the place where the file was located was to determine territorial jurisdiction, but this criterion has not been retained in the amended proposal, *on the ground that the location of a file or of a processing operation will often be impossible to determine: processing operations may have more than one location and take place in several Member States,*[42] particularly in the case of data bases connected to networks, which are becoming increasingly frequent.

> Under the amended proposal, therefore, the law applicable is defined by reference to the place of establishment of the controller … The reference to the place of establishment of the controller means that the temporary removal of a file does not affect the law applicable. Article 4(3) of the initial proposal has accordingly been dropped.

Instead, the first alternative jurisdictional ground proposed by the 1992-Proposal related to the controller's 'establishment' in a Member State's territory or within its jurisdiction, consistently with 'usual internal market criterion' (CP-SR, sec.III.B.2(iii)).[43] This combined and developed the 1990-Proposal's grounds regarding 'files located in' Member States, and

---

[42] Convention108 recognized distributed processing: 'not only data files consisting of compact sets of data, but also sets of data which are geographically distributed and are brought together via computer links for purposes of processing' (Convention108-ER, paras.8, 30). Even the concept of bringing together distributed data for processing is not necessarily true anymore, as with Hadoop (p.132) where, conversely, 'processing' may be brought to distributed data.

[43] See also *WP179*, p.7.

Member State-resident controllers 'using third country files from its territory'. The Council then made 'useful clarifications' to the concept of 'establishment of the controller' (CP-SR, sec.III.B.2(iii)).

Accordingly, if a controller is 'established' in Member State X, X's national DPD Laws apply to its *worldwide* processing of its personal data, including personal data located in third countries, even if it uses personal data otherwise than 'from' Community territory. Therefore, 1990-Proposal's reference to Community-resident controllers' use of files located in third countries became unnecessary. Furthermore, Art.4(3) (temporary movement of files) was dropped as unnecessary.

The 1992-Proposal also changed the jurisdictional ground regarding a 'user' consulting third country-located data from a Member State-located 'terminal'. That became what is now DPD's second main jurisdictional basis: namely, where a controller (*not* being Community-established) 'makes use of means, whether or not automatic (terminals, questionnaires etc.), which are located in the territory of a Member State', to process personal data; the law applicable is then that of the Member State 'on whose territory those means are located' (COM(92)422 final, p.13). This jurisdictional basis, which generalized 'terminals' from 1990-Proposal's Art.4(2) to 'means', carried through to the DPD, although the Council changed 'means' to 'equipment' (seemingly narrower) without any explanation beyond a general comment (CP-SR, sec.III.A) that some amendments were for clarification, simplification or greater flexibility. However, the broader 'means' wording still appears in DPD Rec.20 and in some language versions of the DPD, and certain Member States and WP29 interpret 'equipment' as 'means'.[44]

The 1990-Proposal Art.4(2)'s purpose was clear: 'The desire to protect the data subject in the event of [data file] relocation' (COM(90)314 final, p.21). 1992-Proposal Art.4's general purpose was explained as follows (COM(92)422 final, p.13):

> This Article lays down the connecting factors which determine which national law is applicable to processing within the scope of the Directive, in order to avoid two possibilities:
>
> – that the data subject might find himself outside any system of protection, and particularly that the law might be circumvented in order to achieve this;
> – that the same processing operation might be governed by the laws of more than one country.

Thus, Art.4 1992-Proposal had two purposes:

---

[44]   E.g. *WP179*, p.8; n.45; p.249, n.39.

- anticircumvention (as with Art.4 1990-Proposal), and
- determining the national law applicable (unlike the OECD Guidelines and Convention108, which deliberately omitted applicable law rules).

When the 1992-Proposal replaced 'terminal' with 'means', its Rec.20 stated that processing by a third country-established person 'must not stand in the way of the protection of individuals' provided by EU data protection laws; the processing 'should be governed by the law of the Member State in which the means used are located', with guarantees to ensure that data subjects' rights and obligations are 'respected in practice'. It was not explained why 'means' applied only to *non*-EEA-established controllers, whereas 1990-Proposal's Art.4(2) had applied to any 'users' of Community-located terminals. Perhaps it was thought sufficient to confine the 'means' ground to non-EEA-established controllers because the amended Art.4(1)(a) would cover EEA-established controllers in relation to their worldwide personal data processing.

However, the DPD failed to consider possible remote access by *non-EEA* controllers *to* EEA residents' personal data located in EEA territory. Policy concerns regarding non-EEA controllers' collection/use of EEA residents' personal data have undoubtedly influenced EU DPAs' and the CJEU's subsequent broad interpretations of the DPD's 'equipment'[45] and 'establishment' grounds (n.45),[46] even though 'relocation for circumvention' by EEA controllers is irrelevant in such situations. An overbroad approach to 'equipment' is problematic for several reasons. It may catch non-EEA controllers having no relationship with EEA controllers, but e.g. merely using EEA datacentres remotely (Hon, Millard and Hörnle 2013: sec.2.3). There are issues of comity and the practical

---

[45] E.g. applying DPD Laws to third country controllers who save or read cookies in EEA users' computers, not just controllers' own EEA-located equipment (*WP56*, p.11; *WP148*, p.11). While primarily deciding that Google's Italian subsidiary was Google's Italian 'establishment', an Italian appeal court also considered that the subsidiary was Google's non-electronic 'means' (n.45) in Italy (Hon, Millard and Hörnle 2013: pp.224–5; *WP179*, p.20).

[46] See generally Hon, Millard and Hörnle (2013). *Google Spain* (p.9, n.20) held that Art.4(1)(a) applies when a search engine operator 'sets up in a Member State a branch or subsidiary which is intended to promote and sell advertising space offered by that engine and which orientates its activity towards the inhabitants of that Member State'. Because US search engine Google Inc. had a Spanish subsidiary which sold such advertising, Google Inc. was held to have an 'establishment' (its subsidiary) within the meaning of Art.4(1)(a), so that DPD Laws applied directly to Google Inc. (and not just to its subsidiary).

enforceability of EU laws in third countries. Furthermore, 'a possible universal application of EU law' carries undesirable consequences, as EU data protection regulators recognized (*WP179*, p.31).

Unfortunately, it seems that none of the 1992-Proposal, CP or DPD properly considered these jurisdictional changes' 'knock-on effects' on the Restriction, especially the 'transfer' concept. The difficulty of pinpointing digital data's physical location certainly motivated the move away from the initially proposed jurisdictional basis of 'data file' location. Therefore I argue that, logically, with the same objective of anticircumvention, it should have been recognized that difficulties with physically locating data would be equally problematic for the Restriction too. I submit that, when the jurisdictional bases were changed in the 1992-Proposal, the Restriction should also have been deleted, or at least amended consequentially for the same reasons – but it was not.

While the Restriction made sense in the 1990-Proposal when jurisdiction was based on data location, with the 1992-Proposal's change in its jurisdictional bases to catch worldwide processing by EEA-established controllers, arguably the Restriction became unnecessary for jurisdictional purposes. The purpose of Art.24 (the 1990-Proposal's version of the Restriction) was to prevent circumvention through controllers transferring personal data *to third party processors* in third countries. Therefore, the Restriction should now be unnecessary for anticircumvention purposes because, under the 1992-Proposal and Art.4(1)(a) DPD, EEA-established controllers must comply with, and remain liable under, DPD Laws when they process personal data – wherever located, whether they use processing infrastructure located in the EEA or outside, and whether they process personal data directly or through third party processors. They cannot avoid their obligation to comply with DPD Laws simply by using third country processors; they retain decision-making control and liability (pp.64, 184).

As controllers cannot avoid being subject to DPD Laws simply by transferring personal data physically to third countries (internally or to processors), the Restriction should be unnecessary where EU law applies under Art.4 (Kuner 2007a: chap.4.33).[47] Even when non-EEA controllers use EEA-located equipment under Art.4(1)(c) (p.52), it is arguable that, under an overly broad interpretation of Art.4(1)(c), the rules restricting

---

[47] It seems 'equally unjust and politically incorrect' to exercise Art.4 jurisdiction regarding a country deemed to offer 'adequate protection' e.g. under Safe Harbour (Maier 2010: p.162).

transfer of personal data to third countries 'would be rendered super-fluous, since the Directive would apply fully to every controller from the moment the information is collected over the Internet' (Kuner 2007a: para.4.33, citing Bergkamp and Dhont 2000). In short, surely even non-EEA-established controllers who become subject to DPD Laws through using EEA-located 'equipment' need not be subject to the Restriction, because Art.4(1)(c) DPD subjects them *directly* to DPD Laws, including the requirement to comply with the Principles. The real practical issue is how to enforce DPD Laws effectively against such controllers (Ch.6 discusses enforcement). Therefore, because controllers subject to DPD Laws must apply them to their personal data processing wherever conducted, and cannot avoid DPD Laws simply by 'moving' personal data to, or using processors located in, third countries, I submit that there are compelling logical reasons for arguing that there is no longer any justification *on antiavoidance grounds* for restricting data location, certainly with EEA controllers.

GDPR Art.3(2) addresses policy concerns regarding non-EEA control-lers more clearly and directly, by replacing 'equipment' use with the 'offering' of goods or services to data subjects in the EU or monitoring their behaviour. However, it still risks being overbroad as regards non-EEA processors (p.14). 'Offering' seems less helpful than the recognized 'targeting' concept (Hon, Millard and Hörnle 2013: sec.5); the law applicable to personal data transferred to non-EEA-established controllers seems unclear (Council 9788/15, fn.450) although GDPR's Restriction purports to apply its requirements to 'onward transfers' by recipients of transfers (1.6.3); and issues of comity and practical enforce-ability remain unaddressed. Most importantly, the argument above applies with even greater force here – if the GDPR directly subjects non-EEA controllers and processors to its requirements, it should be unnecessary to restrict transfers to them *for anticircumvention reasons.* The hidden reason for retaining the Restriction in such circumstances may be concerns about the practical enforceability of EU data protection laws against such non-EEA controllers and processors. But, as I discuss in this book, neither the Restriction nor GDPR's Restriction are neces-sary or sufficient to ensure enforceability against non-EEA organizations – nor are they sufficient to prevent third countries from exercising effective jurisdiction even over EEA organizations.

2.3.3 Summary

Although the Restriction's normative aim was not made sufficiently explicit or understandable in the DPD's text, its legislative history shows that the Restriction was intended as a metarestriction: an overarching rule that, in itself, does not in fact directly relate to substantive personal data protection. It was intended to ensure compliance with the core Principles regulating data protection (1.5.6), by preventing controllers from avoiding DPD Laws through moving personal data outside Community territory. When the jurisdictional bases under the 1990-Proposal were changed so that controllers could not circumvent EU data protection laws by moving personal data to third countries or using third country processors, logically the Restriction should have been amended or deleted correspondingly – but it was not, and much of this book is devoted to discussing the unfortunate consequences.

It is generally considered, I believe correctly, that any 'transfer' constitutes a 'processing' which must comply with the Principles (p.19). If transfers can be effected compliantly with the Principles, and the transferred personal data can continue to be processed compliantly, I argue that the Restriction's anticircumvention aim can be satisfied without *also* restricting data location as such. Many countries now have data protection laws, often DPD-based (2.2.8). Thus it is possible, even probable, that the Restriction is being invoked to serve unstated policy purposes other than circumvention of DPD Laws by controllers,[48] e.g. trade protectionism (O'Quinn 1998: p.692; Cate 1998: p.35),[49] or concerns regarding non-EEA controllers' use of EEA citizens' personal data (p.52) and/or other countries' authorities, notably US authorities, accessing EEA residents/citizens' personal data (7.5). At least the policy concerns underlying the GDPR's Restriction are clear – e.g., the so-called 'anti-FISA' clause (after the US Foreign Intelligence Surveillance Act) seeks to restrict third country authorities' access to EEA citizens'/residents' personal data (p.119), rather than to prevent EEA controllers' circumvention of DPD Laws through making transfers.

Nevertheless, I consider it is justifiable to address the Restriction's *original* aim of anticircumvention, because that was its objective as stated by the DPD's legislators and reiterated in relation to GDPR's Restriction. If the DPD's lawmakers had other policy aims, they should have made them explicit, and properly considered the Restriction's effectiveness to

---

[48] E.g. Weber (2013: p.121).

[49] Bygrave (2010: p.187) states, 'While there is perhaps more evidence linking the origins of the Directive to protectionist concerns, the linkage is still tenuous', considering that there is more evidence that DPD's adequacy criterion reflects its emphasis on safeguarding privacy. Nonetheless, protectionism allegations continue, e.g. regarding suggestions for EU or national-only networks (Office of the United States Trade Representative 2014: p.5).

achieve those aims. Accordingly, one of the main questions this book addresses is: is the Restriction (as currently interpreted) necessary or indeed sufficient to prevent circumvention of, and thereby achieve continued compliance with, the Principles – or are there better ways? I will further consider: are measures such as the Restriction or GDPR's Restriction effective to prevent third countries' intelligible access to EU individuals' personal data?

2.4 PROTECTION – COUNTRIES VS CONTROLLERS/RECIPIENTS?

Having shown that the Restriction was originally intended to prevent the circumvention of DPD Laws, i.e. ensure continued compliance by controllers with the Principles, I now discuss the legislative evolution regarding *who* should ensure data protection, and how. This is another important theme of the DPD, its predecessor instruments and earlier national data export laws.

2.4.1 Pre-DPD Methods

Several points emerge from an analysis of key pre-DPD cases[50] involving requested transfers between Member States and/or third countries (Vassilaki 1993), many of which seem to have been reflected in the DPD.

Firstly, the existence or not of data protection laws in the recipient country was a major factor; lack of such laws was sometimes used to justify refusing transfers (see cases cited in Vassilaki 1993: sec.A). Even when the recipient country had data protection laws, but different ones, some transfers were prohibited (Vassilaki 1993: sec.B). This illustrates the importance that was, and is, placed on recipient countries' legal regimes. That in turn illustrates a fundamental assumption underlying such refusals, and more generally data export controls (discussed further in 4.6–4.8): namely, that the country where data are physically located has jurisdiction to regulate the data's processing and, also, that no other country does.

Secondly, relatively few cases covered by Vassilaki involved absolute transfer prohibitions. Transfers were blocked mainly to prevent breach of data protection rules, particularly unlawful processing, with direct marketing being a notable bête noire especially in Austria. Often, transfer

---

[50]   Not directly cited here as they are numerous and only peripherally relevant – please see Vassilaki (1993) for her primary sources/citations.

was eventually permitted, subject to requirements aimed at ensuring data protection in the recipient country.

Thirdly, most often the main precondition for permitting transfer was a contract containing undertakings by the recipient regarding data protection, data subject rights and/or security guarantees, particularly purpose limitation and non-disclosure. Another common requirement was notification to affected data subjects and/or obtaining their informed consent. However, contract was not the only accepted solution. In a case involving Spanish civil war prisoners, data were anonymized before transfer from France to Spain (Vassilaki 1993: fn.4). Similarly, clinical testing data from Sweden were anonymized, or consent obtained, before their transfer (Vassilaki 1993: para. containing fn.25). To transfer medical data from France to Belgium, as well as a contract[51] France's DPA CNIL required 'security measures that the software should be altered so that transmission of patients' names would be impossible', and keycoding of the data (identifying patients not by name but by alphanumeric codes). Sweden's DPA permitted transfer of a telephone directories file to Israel based on security measures during processing, and destruction of data thereafter (Vassilaki 1993: fn.21). Another solution involving a multinational technology organization may have been the first use of an arrangement similar to binding corporate rules (5.4.3) (Vassilaki 1993: fn.35). Thus, safeguards such as contracts, security measures and anonymization were all considered acceptable to permit transfers.

2.4.2 Countries' Laws and Evolution

As summarized above, before the DPD's adoption, countries prioritized the existence of adequate data protection laws in recipient countries. This was consistent with the assumption in both the OECD Guidelines and Convention108 that substantial observation of their provisions by the recipient country, 'to' whose territory data were transferred, was the most important protection for personal data.[52] Unsurprisingly, the DPD also assumes that countries are primarily responsible for protecting personal data, particularly through their laws and regulations, and indeed perhaps

---

[51] With non-disclosure and purpose limitation guarantees (Kraus 1993: fn.66).

[52] E.g. a Contracting State that requires special authorization for TBDF may not deny such authorization on the grounds of protecting privacy, if the recipient *country* provides equivalent protection (Convention108-ER, paras.69–70).

that *only* countries are capable of protecting fundamental rights.[53] This approach is clear in the Restriction's specific references (preserved in the GDPR) to transfers to a third *country* or countries.[54]

Reflecting its focus on the country 'to' which a 'transfer' is made, the DPD empowers the Commission to find that a third country 'ensures' an adequate level of protection 'by reason of its domestic law or of the international commitments it has entered into ... for the protection of the private lives and basic freedoms and rights of individuals' – e.g. through ratifying treaties such as Convention108 (Art.25(6)). No other grounds are stated in the DPD based on which the Commission may find adequate protection. Similarly, the WP29 must provide the Commission with opinions and annual reports on the level of protection in the Community and third countries (Arts.30(1)(b), 30(6)), and Commission negotiations are envisaged with third countries that do not ensure adequate protection (p.25). So the focus was mainly on the adequacy of protection 'afforded by a third country' through recipient countries' laws or international commitments, rather than any protections implemented by the transferor or transferee, e.g. through technical security measures.

However, any assessment of the adequacy of protection 'afforded by a third country' must take into account 'all the circumstances surrounding a data transfer operation', including the data's nature, purpose and duration of proposed processing, and professional rules and security measures complied with in that country, as well as rules of law in force there (Art.25(2)). This move away from considering only third countries' domestic laws or international commitments, to a risk-based approach involving contextual evaluation of risks, was initiated by the 1992-Proposal (COM(92)422 final, p.35), reflecting what some countries had previously permitted nationally (2.4.1). The 1992-Proposal introduced detailed adequacy assessment factors partly because the 1990-Proposal was criticized as being 'excessively ambiguous'; were 'adequacy' interpreted as 'equivalent', it would, in particular, have 'threatened data transfers to countries such as the United States which have favoured a sectoral approach to the problems of data processing rather than the omnibus model adopted within Europe' (Lloyd 1996: para.2.9).[55]

---

[53]   A more European, than US, approach, for historical and cultural reasons (Cate 1998: p.17). Data protection is considered a fundamental human right in Europe – p.10, n.23.

[54]   Also see DPD Recs.56–7, 59 (lack of protection 'in a third country'), Art.19(1)(e); COM(90)314 final, p.41, COM(92)422 final, pp.34–6.

[55]   As Ch.5 will discuss, it is insufficiently clear exactly what other matters might suffice to provide adequate protection (if a country's laws do not), what

The CP added, to Art.25(2)'s list of adequacy factors, the country of origin (not just destination) and the security measures complied with in 'those countries' – thus recognizing that measures other than laws or rules, i.e. 'code' in the form of technical security measures,[56] could facilitate adequate protection. Accordingly, under Art.25(2), third country laws may suffice to conclude that it ensures adequate protection, but they are not necessary to find adequate protection. Art.25(2) recognizes explicitly that adequacy should be determined in light of all the circumstances (including the specified factors) in the context of the *individual* transfer or series of transfers, rather than only the country's laws – i.e., that adequacy of protection should be assessed case-by-case for individual transfers, so that, even if a country's laws are considered inadequate for one transfer operation, e.g. involving sensitive data, it might be adequate for other transfers.

Even the 1990-Proposal's Art.25(1) envisaged that exceptions might be needed to allow transfers in certain situations. Individual Member States could authorize a derogation for 'a given export', if the controller could 'guarantee' and submit 'sufficient proof' of adequate protection for 'that export' (COM(90)314 final, pp.41–2), i.e. case-by-case derogations. The 1990-Proposal required prior notification of each such authorization to be given to the Commission and Member States, who could object individually to proposed transfers. However, following stakeholder consultation, representations to the Commission and the Parliament's opinion, the Commission recognized that *general* exceptions were needed, 'compatible with' protection for individuals (COM(92)422 final, p.35). Accordingly, the 1992-Proposal allowed Member States to provide for derogations in the form of general exemptions for specified types of transfers, such as transfers necessary to protect the data subject's vital interests. In parallel, individually authorized derogations for 'given exports' morphed into another method whereby transfers might be permissible despite the lack of adequate protection or a general derogation: namely, 'adequate safeguards' (Art.26(2) DPD, discussed shortly).

---

level of protection is required, and how those matters overlap or interrelate with 'adequate safeguards'. This lack of clarity may partly be due to the relatively late introduction, during the DPD's legislative process, of the concept that adequate protection might be provided through ways other than a country's laws.

[56]   I.e. 'code as law' (Reidenberg 1997; Lessig 2006).

2.4.3 Controllers

As mentioned earlier (2.3.2), the 1990-Proposal regulated 'data files'. Accepting that a more modern, technologically neutral approach was needed, the 1992-Proposal shifted to regulating 'processing' by 'controllers' (COM(92)422 final, p.10). As the DPD was intended to regulate 'the use of data in the light of the object being pursued', 'automated files' was replaced by 'automatic processing of data' (COM(92)422 final, p.27). The 1992-Proposal borrowed the 'controller' concept from Convention108; a controller is 'ultimately responsible' for choices governing the processing's design and operation (COM(92)422 final, p.10). Art.27(1) 1992-Proposal referred to the controller adducing 'sufficient justification' guaranteeing the 'effective exercise of data subjects' rights' (COM(92)422 final, p.36), which the CP changed to 'sufficient guarantees' regarding the protection of privacy, fundamental rights and freedoms and their exercise.

The basic Art.25 Restriction was not amended to refer to 'controllers' instead of (or as well as) countries. However, Art.25(2) DPD explicitly recognizes that other methods, notably security measures, may provide adequate protection. Controllers may offer 'appropriate safeguards',[57] taking 'particular measures' to compensate for lack of protection in a third country (Rec.59). Art.26(2) allows Member States to 'authorize' transfers to a third country without adequate protection if the controller 'adduces adequate safeguards' for protecting individuals' privacy and fundamental rights (a separate concept from adequate protection), in particular through 'appropriate contractual clauses' as permitted under some pre-DPD national laws (2.4.1) – e.g., obliging third country *recipients* to implement adequate safeguards.[58] The Commission is empowered to issue decisions, binding Member States, on standard clauses providing sufficient safeguards (Art.26(4)).

Thus, the DPD envisages adequate protection not just via third country laws but also through measures taken by controllers, e.g. security measures 'complied with in that country', and adequate safeguards, e.g. through appropriate contractual commitments obtained by controllers from recipients. However, transfers based on adequate safeguards require Member State authorization, and approaches to authorizations (and indeed adequate protection) vary significantly between Member States, as Ch.5 will discuss.

---

[57] Changed from 'appropriate assurances' between the CP and the DPD.

[58] E.g. *WP114*, p.5 discusses adequate safeguards adduced by controllers under Art.26(2), but is headed 'Adequate safeguards put in place by *recipient*'.

GDPR's Restriction applies to processors as well as controllers, and transfers may be made under 'appropriate safeguards' (replacing 'adequate safeguards'), i.e. measures taken by transferring processors, not just controllers (Art.46).

2.4.4 Recipients

In the DPD, 'recipient' means entities to whom data are 'disclosed' (Art.2(g)). That term is not used in the context of the Restriction. However, the CIDPR and Convention108-AP mention transfers 'to recipients ... which are not subject to' DPD Laws, and a 'recipient that is subject to the jurisdiction' of a non-Participant (n.26), respectively (2.2.7). This suggests a further development from the OECD Guidelines, Convention108 and the DPD, which focuses, not on countries' laws, data physically flowing between territories, or even from transferors, but on the *organization receiving personal data*, and whether the recipient is subject to DPD Laws or non-Participants' laws.[59] Some DPD Laws also refer to the adequacy of protection offered by the 'recipient' in any 'third country', rather than the protection offered by third country laws (Commission 2003, p.31).

I argue that both transferors and recipients may play roles as significant to personal data protection as destination countries' laws, particularly in relation to security measures. Regarding the factors affecting adequate protection in a third country (including security measures 'complied with in that country'), Art.25(2) does not specify *who* 'complies with' such measures. It is not just transferring controllers, but also recipients, who may provide 'adequate protection' or 'adequate safeguards', e.g. by applying security measures to personal data. Indeed, the WP29's cloud guidance summarizes the Restriction as allowing (emphasis added) 'free flow of personal data to countries located outside the EEA only if that country *or the recipient*' provides adequate protection, or if 'specific safeguards' are implemented by the controller 'and its co-controllers and/or processors' (*WP196*, para.3.5). Recipients may take such measures voluntarily, or because they are required to do so to meet legal obligations under contracts with controllers, or under other legally binding arrangements[60] or laws applicable to them. Obviously, laws are relevant in regulating the actions that controllers, recipients or others

---

59 Here, 'X's jurisdiction' must mean 'applying X's laws' – pp.7, 48.
60 E.g. BCRs – 5.4.3.

must or must not (or can or cannot) take. However, it is the shift in approach that I highlight.

I suggest that the focus of CIDPR and Convention108-AP on whether the recipient is subject to DPD Laws or a non-Participant's laws (or indeed other jurisdictions' laws) was a move in the right direction: more realistic and effective than focusing on countries where data are located. I reiterate that the CIDPR restricts transfers to recipients not subject to DPD Laws, while Convention108-AP restricts transfers to recipients who *are* subject to a non-Participant's jurisdiction (2.2.7), but that this difference matters when recipients are subject to multiple jurisdictions. Unfortunately, the same problem arises with the proposed update to Convention108 (2.4.5).

In recognizing that adequate safeguards could be provided through contracts, albeit subject to Member State authorization (2.4.3), the DPD acknowledges that the processing of personal data by third country processors, who receive transferred personal data, may be controlled not only through the country's laws but also through contractual obligations. *WP12*, chap.4 also stressed the importance of an EEA-established entity exercising control over personal data by implementing an adequate processor contract. However, it did not consider controls through technical security measures, notably controller encryption and backups (see p.138 and Ch.7).

While recipients are often separate organizations from transferors, Convention108 (and therefore presumably the DPD) envisaged that data 'movement' to a third country internally within the controller's organization, without any third party recipient, would constitute TBDF (n.14). In such cases, the true underlying concern is clearly that of *multiple* applicable jurisdictions – the controller-'recipient' remains subject to DPD Laws regarding 'transferred' personal data, but should it obey its Member State's laws or the third country's if they conflict regarding how the transferred personal data may or must (not) be processed?[61] With today's complex supply chains, not just in cloud, a single 'transfer' may involve multiple 'recipients', so further jurisdictional conflicts could easily arise. The DPD and its predecessors did not properly address such situations. Such conflicts, particularly between one country's data protection laws and another's collection of data for national security purposes, have been brought to a head by events such as Snowden's revelations.

---

[61] The OECD Guidelines and Convention108 deliberately avoided addressing conflicts of laws (2.2.3–2.2.4). The *SWIFT* case, where such conflicts arose following data movement within the *same* organization, is discussed at pp.89–90, 92.

Unfortunately, GDPR's Art.44 does not refer to 'recipients', maintaining the DPD's wording on transfers 'to a third country', and extending it to international organizations (who are clearly organizational recipients). However, unlike the DPD, the GDPR does occasionally mention 'recipients' elsewhere in the international transfers context[62] – but again without defining 'transfers' or 'to' third countries – perpetuating problems that Ch.3 will discuss.

2.4.5 Jurisdiction, Applicable Law, Transferors and Recipients

The CIDPR and Convention108-AP, but not the DPD (2.2.6), explicitly refer to 'recipients' and 'jurisdiction'. One of my core arguments is that regulation should concentrate more on the jurisdiction(s) and laws to which transferors and recipients may be subject, rather than on data location. Interestingly, FRA and CoE (2014: p.130), in discussing both Convention108/Convention108-AP and the DPD, define 'transborder data flow' as the 'transfer' of personal data 'to a recipient who or which is subject to a foreign jurisdiction', again assuming that 'recipient' is implicit in the DPD's Restriction. Certain respondents to a Commission survey, who were concerned about 'data sovereignty' (2.2.1), suggested (emphasis added) that 'cloud service provider access to the market should be limited only to those *established in* the EU' (SWD(2014)214 final, p.6) – again reflecting a focus on jurisdiction over the provider rather than data location.

---

[62] Rec.101 on GDPR's Restriction generally; notifying data subjects 'where applicable, that the controller intends to transfer personal data to a recipient in a third country or international organisation ...' (Art.14(1)(f)); data subjects' access rights to information on 'in particular recipients in third countries or international organisations', to whom personal data would be 'disclosed' (Art.15(1)(c)); obligations on controllers to record 'categories of recipients' to whom personal data 'have been or will be disclosed including recipients in third countries or international organisations' (Art.30(1)(d)); a derogation for public registers (Art.49(2)); and DPA powers to order suspension of data flows to a 'recipient in a third country or to an international organisation' (Art.58(2)(j)) and/or to levy fines for infringing GDPR's provisions on 'transfers of personal data to a recipient in a third country or an international organisation' (Art.83(5)(c)). The GDPR seems to envisage that a third country recipient might be neither a controller nor processor (although what its status would be is unclear), given references to 'controllers, processors or recipients in third countries' (Rec.101), and DPA-approved contractual clauses between controller/processor and 'the controller, processor or the recipient of the personal data in the third country or international organisation' (Art.46(3)(a)).

The WP29 recognized the importance of jurisdiction in *WP9* (p.11) and *WP12* (p.16), which noted that any contractual basis for transfer to a third country recipient must provide additional safeguards for data subjects 'made necessary by the fact that the recipient in the third country *is not subject to*' an 'enforceable' set of data protection rules providing adequate protection (emphasis added). Also, even pre-Snowden, *WP47* (para.2) reiterated the possibility of processors 'in' third countries 'being subject to public interventions which might go beyond what is necessary in a democratic society'.

Specifically regarding third country processors, the WP29 emphasized the continued application of DPD Laws to personal data transferred by an EEA-established controller to such a processor, and the controller's continued liability under Member State law for damage from the processing, if the contract sufficiently constrained the recipient's autonomy, retaining the controller's control correspondingly even if data were physically transferred to a third country (*WP9*, pp.6–7; *WP12*, pp.18–19, 23; *WP179*, p.25). On that approach, provided controllers' contracts with their processor-recipients are 'adequate', an EEA-established entity retains control over the data and relevant Member State law still applies.[63] *WP56*, fn.17 reiterated that where processing 'involves elements going beyond' EU borders, the DPD's applicability is 'not affected by the fact that a controller in the EU has a processor operating outside the EU. In that case the directive still applies to the whole of the processing operations'. These statements support my argument that the Restriction became unnecessary for anticircumvention purposes following the 1992 change in Art.4's jurisdictional bases, even when EEA controllers use third country processors (p.53), because the controller remains subject to, and liable under, DPD Laws, and can retain control of transferred personal data through 'adequate' processor contracts. Indeed, controllers remain liable under DPD Laws even if they have *not* entered into any processor contracts, although implementing such contracts obviously facilitates compliance with their DPD Law obligations. Accordingly, I argue that if continued compliance with relevant DPD

---

[63]   However, for transfers to *controllers*, the WP29 considers it impossible to rely on continued applicability of Member State law and transferors' continued liability; accordingly, the aim of continued legal redress for data subjects cannot be met, it considers, unless they have third party beneficiary rights (e.g. supported by binding arbitration, as under industry codes); or transferors contractually accept liability to data subjects for recipients' data protection failures; or Member States impose such liability on transferors (*WP9*, pp.7–8; *WP12*, pp.19–20). Cf. p.185.

Laws can be assured when controllers use cloud computing, including effective remedies for data subjects, whether that be through legal (e.g. contract) or technical measures applied by such controllers and/or their recipient providers, then personal data's physical location need not be restricted to EEA territory.

There is some support for a jurisdictional, over data location-based, approach. Proposals to update Convention108 (2.2.10) emphasized the goal of protecting 'every individual regardless of nationality or residence, subject to the jurisdiction of the Parties' (CoE 2016b: para.14). The jurisdiction concept was deliberately employed for 'better standing the test of time and accommodating continual technological developments' (CoE 2016b: para.25).[64] Each party must apply the proposed requirements to 'data processing subject to its jurisdiction' (CoE 2016c: p.2). Private sector controllers' processing falls within a party's jurisdiction only where there is 'sufficient connection' with its territory, e.g. if the controller is established on its territory or (emphasis added) 'activities involving data processing *are performed in that territory* or are related to the monitoring of a data subject's behaviour that takes place within that territory, or when the processing activities are related to the offer of services or goods to a data subject located in that territory ...' (CoE 2016b).

Referring to jurisdiction is more technology-neutral, but unfortunately, by mentioning processing 'performed in that territory' (as does the draft explanatory report, regarding data storage locations (CoE 2016b: para.100)), the focus is brought back to processing infrastructure and data location, whereas a previous draft did not refer to processing activities 'performed in that territory'. Also, the same problem recurs regarding whether the recipient is, or is not, subject to certain jurisdictions. The update (2.2.10) seeks to allow transfers to 'a recipient who is subject to the jurisdiction of another Party', while *restricting* transfers to a recipient who 'is subject to the jurisdiction of a State or international organisation which is not Party' – without recognizing that a recipient could well be subject to both a party's and non-party's jurisdictions, especially if it is a multinational. Indeed, in today's globalized world, this is more the norm than the exception for multinationals. So with such a recipient, are transfers to be allowed – or restricted? The proposed update creates a possible contradiction in terms, rather than providing a clear answer. It is

---

[64] The extension of Convention108's coverage from the 'territory' concept, to take account of territoriality's diminishing role, may show how countries are 'coming to terms with the reality that transborder data flows can no longer be defined solely in terms of territoriality' (Kuner 2013b: p.141).

unclear how conflicts may be resolved when a recipient is subject to both a party's and non-party's jurisdiction simultaneously. There is pressing need for international agreement (Hague Conference on Private International Law 2010, paras.14, 21), particularly as modern outsourcing chains, indeed modern international business operations, often involve multiple organizations who may each be subject to different, possibly multiple, jurisdictions.

2.4.6   Protection: Evolution – and Devolution?

While the primary focus of earlier multilateral instruments was on *countries* providing adequate protection for imported personal data through their laws or international commitments, the DPD's lawmakers eventually recognized that other ways are possible, focusing on context-specific protection and measures that controllers can take, such as contractual commitments from third country recipients. In many ways, this evolution reflected how individual countries' treatment of data exports evolved in the 1980s/early 1990s. Later instruments explicitly considered the role of recipients, recognizing that both transferors and/or transferees may help to protect personal data, e.g. by applying security measures.

However, as I discuss in detail later, the GDPR has reversed this evolution. Ignoring advances in technological protections, the GDPR's Restriction seems squarely based on the view that only countries' laws (and law-based protections, such as contract) are good enough to protect personal data. As this book argues, that approach is misconceived: all types of protections should be encouraged equally and in combination, including organizational and technical measures applied by controllers, processors and/or recipients. Technological protections can sometimes be more effective than law-based mechanisms, and should not be deprecated as the GDPR seems to do. Consider one concrete example. If you store your personal data in removable media (such as a memory stick) which you are handing to a stranger to hold for you temporarily, what would you rather do: give them the data stored in unencrypted media, asking them to sign a contract with you to keep the media securely and not view, use or disclose your data except on your instructions; or, hand them the data on encrypted media to which only you have the decryption key?

Worryingly, the GDPR has also influenced a similar reversal in Convention108's proposed update (2.2.10). Like the DPD and GDPR, the proposed update's Art.12(3) is prescriptive regarding *how* 'an appropriate level of protection' may be achieved; this 'can' be by laws[65] including international treaties/agreements, or safeguards 'provided by legally binding and enforceable instruments adopted and implemented by the persons involved in the transfer and further processing' (CoE 2016c: p.5). As with GDPR's 'appropriate safeguards' (5.4.1.2), it is unclear whether these are meant to be exhaustive, or whether other ways of providing appropriate protection, notably technical measures like encryption, will be permitted. I fear they are meant to be exhaustive, given a reference to 'two mechanisms' (CoE 2016b: para.103). If technical protections are disallowed, that would be retrograde rather than modernizing.

2.5 SUMMARY

From the 1970s, national laws and multilateral instruments were adopted based on the assumption that data export controls were necessary, or at least important, to maintain privacy protections. The clear regulatory aim was that data subjects should not lose their privacy protections upon their data being exported, and particularly that data protection laws should not be circumventable by exporting personal data elsewhere. However, it should be remembered that those instruments sought to *balance* privacy with other societal interests such as free trade and free data flows, e.g. the DPD itself; even a resolution on cloud computing by data protection regulators did not advocate restricting data exports, but rather that lawmakers should 'assess the adequacy and interoperability of existing legal frameworks to facilitate cross-border transfer of data and consider additional necessary privacy safeguards' (International Conference of Data Protection and Privacy Commissioners 2012: p.2).

To reduce export controls and enable free data flows, there were initiatives to harmonize data protection levels across Participants, whether under the OECD Guidelines, Convention108 or the DPD. The DPD envisaged, as did the OECD Guidelines and Convention108, that it should be primarily for the receiving third country, rather than the exporting controller, to ensure adequate protection for exported personal data. The 'importing' or 'receiving' third country's laws and/or international commitments relating to personal data were considered one, even *the*, major factor in ensuring adequate protection. There was then recognition that controllers and/or recipients could take measures to

---

[65] Whose required content (CoE 2016a: paras.104–6) seems to reflect the GDPR's 'adequate protection' assessment factors, although (no doubt inadvertently) duration of processing remains a factor, unlike under the GDPR – 3.7.3.

protect personal data (including technical measures), and a realization that it was necessary to consider the jurisdictions to which recipients may be subject. However, in a globalized society, multiple organizations may be involved in one 'transfer', and multiple jurisdictions may claim to apply their laws to the same data simultaneously, which none of these instruments address properly. Even worse, there is a worrying devolution, starting with the GDPR, back towards equating jurisdiction with data location, and allowing only legal rather than technical protections. It is possible that the proposed update to Convention108 may circumscribe transfers even more narrowly than the GDPR, and the voting procedure is such that the EU could push through most decisions, as the Russian Federation noted (CAHDATA 2016a: p.6).

I will return to these issues later but first, with the Restriction's professed anticircumvention objective in mind, I will consider in detail how DPAs and courts have interpreted the central 'transfer' concept, and the assumptions that underlie such interpretations (and the DPD and GDPR). Then, I will discuss Mechanisms for compliance with the Restriction and its enforcement, to demonstrate the Restriction's (in)effectiveness in achieving the anticircumvention objective.

3. The 'transfer' concept

3.1 INTRODUCTION

Against the background of related instruments, Ch.2 discussed the Restriction's aim, unstated in the DPD itself, of anticircumvention: preventing controllers from making transfers to avoid compliance with the Principles. It noted the conflation of physical data location, jurisdiction and applicable law, and some unspoken assumptions which may underlie how lawmakers felt the anticircumvention objective should be achieved, i.e. through the Restriction.

This chapter analyses various difficulties with the meanings of 'transfer', 'transfer to a third country' and 'transit', which were left undefined by the DPD and are interpreted differently by the WP29 and others. It is unclear to what extent 'transfer' occurs on making personal data available for remote 'pull' access (compared with 'push', e.g. email), notably via public websites potentially accessible to unknown third country persons. More complications arise where processing involves multiple stages and/or entities, e.g. websites hosted using third party services, or public cloud. Many 'recipients' of 'transfers' are possible, with different permutations of countries where data may be located and/or which may have effective jurisdiction over (sub)providers.

I will first discuss how the European Court of Justice (ECJ) interpreted 'transfer' in C-101/01 *Bodil Lindqvist* (*Lindqvist*), and *Lindqvist*'s later interpretation by DPAs and others. *Lindqvist* clearly held that a controller's upload of publicly available webpages, containing personal data, to the servers of an *EEA-established* hosting provider was not a 'transfer'. It shed light on little else in the transfers context. In particular, does a 'transfer' occur upon actual access of those webpages by website visitors, or only if the uploader intended personal data to be accessed in a third country (or, perhaps, can be presumed to have so intended, based on the likelihood of such access)? It also did not clarify whether 'transfer' occurs only when specific (limited) recipients/countries are intended to have access, or if 'transfer' occurs when potentially anyone has access, i.e. 'making available' personal data to the world.

Generally, DPAs consider 'transfer' to involve the physical movement of personal data between geographical territories. This interpretation's historical origin is clear, as previously discussed (2.2.3–2.2.4), but it assumes that:

- the 'location' of personal data in a third country must necessarily entail the 'disclosure' or 'communication' of that data to a recipient located in that country, and that
- the recipient, through being also located in that country, is subject to, and perhaps only to, that country's jurisdiction (as flagged in Ch.2's discussion of earlier instruments).

However, 'transfer' may not always give the recipients access to intelligible personal data, because controllers may apply technical measures such as encryption (p.138). Accordingly, countries' assertion of jurisdiction to regulate personal data 'located' in their territories may not afford them *effective* jurisdiction to regulate persons controlling intelligible access to personal data. The failure to spell out these assumptions and their consequences has resulted in problems in interpreting the meaning of 'transfer' in light of technological advances, particularly the Internet and cloud computing. The emergence of widespread capabilities to access data remotely over the Internet together with the availability of encryption mean that personal data may be located in a third country without the controller necessarily ceding control (or allowing intelligible access) to anyone else. Conversely, a person subject to a third country's jurisdiction may have the technical capability to access intelligible personal data remotely, even if the data are physically located in the EEA.

When a controller uses a third party provider, several countries' jurisdictions may be relevant: countries with jurisdiction over the provider, e.g. because it is incorporated or has operations there; and countries where the physical infrastructure (datacentre, servers, etc.) used by the provider is located – possibly several countries, if it uses datacentres in multiple countries. A country with jurisdiction over a provider may seek to compel it to deliver customer data, including by remotely accessing data located in another country.[1] Therefore, when considering 'transfer', I argue that it is necessary to consider all countries

---

[1]   E.g. the *Microsoft warrant case* (p.93); and Brazil (4.5.1.2). However, to guarantee intelligible access to *encrypted* data, a country needs effective jurisdiction over decryption key holders, not just persons with access to encrypted data (7.2.3.1).

with jurisdiction over the provider, and not just countries where infra-structure used by providers is located. The countries having effective jurisdiction over a provider may well correspond with the countries where such infrastructure is located, but equally they may not – especially with large providers who use multiple datacentres globally, possibly including third party-owned infrastructure. Even *EEA* providers (or EEA controllers) may use third country datacentres or (sub)providers. Similarly, subproviders' countries of incorporation or establishment may differ from the countries where the datacentres they use are located. Yet seemingly DPAs consider only personal data location when determining whether a 'transfer' has occurred, as I discuss further below.

This chapter and Ch.5 will discuss uncertainties regarding what 'transfer' means and what Mechanisms controllers must use to comply with the Restriction, with Ch.4 analysing key assumptions behind the Restriction that influenced and exacerbated these uncertainties.

3.2 THE MEANING OF 'TRANSFER'

The 'transfer' concept is central, because the Restriction restricts 'transfers' of personal data 'to' a 'third country'. However, the DPD does not define 'transfer',[2] or provide guidance on data 'location', even though Internet use was growing when it was drafted.[3] Presumably the DPD's drafters assumed that 'transfer' was self-explanatory, but that is not necessarily so, as this chapter and Ch.4 will show.

Data 'movement' has been suggested as a starting point, consistently with the OECD Guidelines (2.2.3) (EDPS 2014b: p.6). On another approach, 'transfer' involves 'sending' personal data outside the EEA (ICO 2016b: p.83); the 'ordinary meaning' of transfer is 'transmission from one place, person, etc. to another' (ICO 2010: para.1.3.2), i.e. by the transferor's active act. Examples of 'transfers' include use of a multi-national's intranet by its third country-located employees; forwarding an email containing customer details to a third country; and (rather circu-larly) 'transfer' of a database to a third country following an acquisition, or of customer information to third country call centres (Carey 2010: p.12), in each case if including personal data.

Clearly, the DPD envisaged that personal data could be 'transferred' by physically transporting, to a third country, the physical equipment or media (collectively termed 'hardware' in this book) 'holding' the patterns

---

[2] Some national laws do – 3.8.
[3] E.g. Rec.47 mentions email.

of bits (p.105) representing the personal data. Transportation by non-electronic means constitutes 'transfer' if the transported personal data are 'intended for processing [in the third country] after transfer' (Art.25(1)). Thus, 'transfer' may include posting, to a third country, floppy disks containing personal data; or an employee travelling outside the EEA with a laptop containing personal data (6.4.3.1).[4] As a non-digital example, Iceland's DPA held that sending blood samples to the US was a transfer of personal data to which its TBDF rules applied (OECD 2006: p.19).

However, what constitutes a 'transfer' via the Internet? Internet use involves 'moving', not hardware, but *patterns of bits* representing digital personal data. These patterns are transmitted, or strictly copied, through stationary hardware (e.g. undersea cables), probably routing through multiple pieces of hardware physically situated in numerous countries, including third countries, before reaching hardware in the final destination country. Convention108 contemplated cross-border personal data transmissions via 'circuit-switched or packet-switched telecommunications link' (Convention108-ER, para.63), and even the DPD's lawmakers envisaged remote access *by* Community users to personal data located elsewhere (2.3.2). Unfortunately, the DPD did not properly take account of Internet transmissions, certainly not at current scales, or at the level of 'pull' rather than 'push', particularly 'pulling' from third countries – discussed further below. Originally, TBDF involved 'the explicit intent to transfer data internationally (e.g. when a computer file was deliberately sent to a specific location in another country)' (Kuner 2013b: p.3). However, given the Internet's architecture, sending data over the Internet to someone in the same country may well involve that data transiting other countries, including third countries, without the sender's knowledge or intention.

Personal data may be 'transferred' to a third country without there being a third party recipient, as in the 'travelling with laptop' example above. However, many transfers do involve third party recipients. In such cases, 'transfer' has been equated with 'communication', which implies the transmission of *intelligible* personal data, where three types of 'transfer' were envisaged involving communication of personal data by, respectively:

---

[4] Nevertheless, the employer may reasonably decide adequate protection exists if security etc. risks are addressed (ICO 2016b: p.91). See also p.33, n.14; 6.4.3.1.

1. a Community-based controller to another, third country-based, controller;
2. a Community-based controller to a third country-based processor processing on behalf of the controller;
3. a Community-based data subject to a third country-based controller (*WP4*, sec.4(ii)).

Similarly, a case study regarding a UK credit reference agency's transfer of creditworthiness data referred to 'communication' (*WP12*, p.31). In Sweden, 'transfer' involves disclosure (Datainspektionen 2011). Where personal data are 'disclosed' to third countries, Datainspektionen considered whether Swedish DPD Laws permitted this 'transfer' (*Enköpings* (Sweden), p.3).

'Transfer' has been explained as 'any procedure whereby data will be transferred outside the European Union', whoever transfers the data, including a transfer 'made to persons responsible for Internet Web sites of the transferor', and when data are 'submitted out of the territory of the European Union', but not a transfer to an embassy in a third country, as the relevant national law applies to embassies under international law (Zinser 2002: p.549). While equating transfer with 'transfer' or 'submitted out' seems tautological, note the focus on territories to which laws apply, including embassies.[5] I return to this, and Zinser's comment regarding websites, later (p.77).

As illustrated above, 'transfer' is used to mean many things, from the 'movement' of personal data, so as to be physically located in a third country (i.e. export), to the *communication* of personal data to a third country-'based' third party, and to (it seems) personal data ceasing to be subject to relevant DPD Laws through being 'submitted out' of EU territory. These may involve all or some of the elements of personal data location, jurisdiction and applicable law.

The first meaning is prevalent. Hence, many consider that the Restriction compels what is often termed 'data localization', particularly when using cloud computing. I argue that, if the aim is to protect

---

[5] Under Art.4(1)(b) DPD, DPD Laws must apply to controllers 'not established on' the Member State's territory but 'in a place where its national law applies by virtue of international public law' – i.e. embassies or consulates (Council 7695/93, p.11, fn.2). I do not dissect Art.4(1)(b), but note that Estonia backs up its data to its embassies worldwide, and is exploring possible diplomatic recognition of 'virtual data embassies' for public cloud backups (Estonian Ministry of Economic Affairs and Communication and Microsoft 2015).

personal data from being processed inconsistently with DPD Laws, i.e. anticircumvention, the data localization approach is misguided and indeed counterproductive.

3.3 TRANSIT

Before analysing 'transfer' further, I consider 'transit'. The routing of data traffic over the Internet, whether email or Web data, etc., is complex. It involves considerations not only of technology but also of time, costs, efficiency and commercial relationships. Much has been written on this subject, e.g. Halabi (2000). Detailed discussion of Internet routing is out of scope. The key point is that data transmitted over the Internet are generally split up into parts or 'packets', different parts taking different routes, possibly though different countries, before reaching their final destination for reassembly. Crucially, how this happens, and which countries packets are routed through, are usually not within the sender's control. The paths taken by different packets, from source to destination, depend on Internet routing protocols and autonomous systems' routing policies; communications service providers could constrain Internet traffic routes, if appropriate technical and commercial changes are made, but generally *end-users* cannot control routing (Singh et al. 2014: p.7; Hon, Millard, et al. 2014: p.4).

Illustrating the DPD's failure to take into proper consideration the Internet's architecture and operation, the DPD does not exclude from the Restriction 'transit' of personal data through a third country. It only addresses the converse: external data transiting through Community territory. Where non-EEA-established controllers use 'equipment' on Member State territory, the DPD does not apply to such use if it is 'only for the purposes of transit through' Community territory (Art.4(1)(c)).[6] An example is the use of 'telecommunication networks (cables) or postal services which only ensure that communications transit through the Union in order to reach third countries', i.e. simple 'point-to-point' cable transmission (*WP179*, p.23). That opinion did not define 'transit'. It interprets the transit exception narrowly; seemingly, telecommunications services that 'merge pure transit and added value service', like spam filtering, would exceed mere 'transit'. This suggests that non-EEA service providers should conduct spam filtering using non-EEA hardware or risk being considered controllers with attendant obligations/liabilities.

---

[6] Because mere transit does not affect EU citizens' rights or freedoms (Kuner 2013b: p.16).

This seems counterproductive as spam and anti-malware filtering is beneficial and should be incentivized, not discouraged.

Both the OECD Guidelines and Convention108 consider countries of transit irrelevant to 'transfer' (2.3.1.1). This implies that, under the DPD (which was based on Convention108), 'transit' should also be irrelevant when considering whether 'transfer' occurs (see also p.106). Interpreting 'transfer' to include mere routing through third countries would severely restrict Internet use by EEA-located persons. Thus, 'transfer' and 'transmission' have been distinguished, with the routers used being considered irrelevant: an email between two parties both having adequate protection is thought 'acceptable' even if routed through countries not having adequate protection (Blume 2000: p.82).[7] Similarly, Art.25 should arguably not encompass transit, given Art.4(1)(c)'s exclusion of transit (Kuner 2007a: chap.4.09).[8] The fact that 'electronic transfer' of personal data 'may be routed through a third country on its way from the UK to another EEA country does not bring such transfer within the scope of the [Restriction]' (ICO 2010: para.1.3.2). For data 'only in transit through a non-EEA country', there is no transfer outside the EEA (ICO 2016b: p.83), and if personal data are transferred via a server in country C 'which does not access or manipulate the information' while in C, there is no transfer to C (ICO 2016b: p.86). Accordingly, generally, transit is not considered 'transfer' under the DPD.

Respondents to the Commission's consultation on DPD reform had requested clarification of 'transfer', arguing that not every 'travel' of personal data between physical locations is a 'transfer', and also sought explicit provision for 'transit' where 'data is only physically moved from one place to another without any further access or manipulation' (Commission 2010b: p.6).[9] Views might be affected by Snowden's revelations

---

[7] Email involves at least two servers: the sender's and the recipient's. These servers could be in different countries from the sender, the recipient, indeed their email providers. Emails may be stored on the email providers' servers. Intermediate routers would also be involved. However, only the recipient's country is normally considered.

[8] I agree, although some could argue that because Art.25, unlike Art.4, did not *expressly* exclude transit, the Restriction was intended to cover transit.

[9] Cf. the definition of 'transit' through Singapore, in Singapore's Personal Data Protection Regulations 2014, Reg.8, reflecting OECD-ExplanMemo, para.66 (p.45) (emphasis added):

'data in transit' means personal data transferred through Singapore in the course of onward transportation to a country or territory outside Singapore, *without the personal data being accessed or used by, or disclosed to,* any

of US and other intelligence authorities' tapping of certain fibre-optic cables routing Internet traffic, and sharing data with other countries' intelligence authorities (7.5.2.1). Even in 1989, it was considered that transit could affect privacy, 'when data are piped through communication lines which traverse countries where little or no attention is accorded to issues of data protection' (CoE 1989: para.9), perhaps presaging Snowden's revelations. Nevertheless, it seems unrealistic to prohibit Internet traffic's transit through third countries generally, given the realities of Internet routing, still less to prohibit EU organizations from using the Internet, and such prohibitions alone would not prevent third country authorities' access (5.3.3.5, 7.5.2.1). Proposals for EU-only routing or EU-only cloud are problematic for many reasons (Hon et al. 2016).

Therefore, I argue that transit should be explicitly defined, and excluded from 'transfer'. Unfortunately, the GDPR does not mention transit, even in its applicable law provisions. This is retrograde: if physical location of digital personal data in a third country, even transitorily, is considered 'transfer', then, strictly speaking, much Internet use would involve unlawful transfers – and turning most organizational Internet users into lawbreakers surely cannot be the intention, and would engender disrespect for data protection laws. Hopefully the next iteration of EU data protection laws, perhaps in another 20 years, will address the issue of transit properly. Meanwhile, organizations must rely on the WP29 and national DPAs taking a sensible approach to Internet routing and 'transfers'.

3.4 WEBSITES: MECHANICS

Personal data may be 'transferred' via 'push' (e.g. email) or 'pull' (providing access rights or making data available on websites) (Malcolm 2012: p.327). The DPD contemplated only 'push'. The treatment of 'pull' transfers was unaddressed – indeed perhaps even unenvisaged, judging by lawmakers' apparent failure to consider non-EEA controllers' remote access to Community-located data (p.49). Websites represent a significant area where the DPD did not properly take account of Internet models and adoption: notably, that personal data on public webpages are available for

---

organization (other than the transferring organization or an employee of the transferring organization acting in the course of the employee's employment with the transferring organization) while the personal data is in Singapore, except for the purpose of such transportation.

remote 'pull' access at unknown times by unknown persons from unknown countries.

When using third party[10] webhosting providers, cloud or otherwise, at least three separate stages are involved:

1. uploading data[11] to servers, usually effected by the website owner after logging into their account with the hosting provider;
2. storing data on the provider's (or its subprovider's) servers, usually passively after upload without any action by the provider or subprovider; and
3. accessing data, occurring when someone visits the relevant web-page (thereby downloading the website file(s) to their local device, to be displayed, run or stored there), or clicks to download data.

Such website data are accessible via the Internet to anyone.[12] Generally, hosting providers also have the technical means to access any personal data uploaded to their services' servers, including underlying databases (7.4.2.2). Presumably this is why Zinser stated that websites involve transfer 'to persons responsible for Internet Web sites of the transferor' (p.73).

With webhosting, several locations may be relevant. Consider an EEA controller uploading personal data to a webhosting provider's server. Could this involve a 'transfer'; if so, at what stage, by whom, and why? There are several main permutations, applying equally to cloud:[13]

---

[10] Websites may be self-hosted, i.e. storing and serving webpage files and associated data from servers owned/operated by the controller. However, *third party*-hosted websites better parallel public cloud, which is my main focus.

[11] Website data, i.e. HTML files with associated data, e.g. image files and scripts. Webpages served to website visitors may be created programmatically, dynamically (often using data from associated databases), but I do not discuss the distinction between static and dynamic webpages further – the 'transfer' analysis applies equally to both types. The locations of any underlying databases containing personal data may be relevant, but similar issues will arise regarding uploading personal data to those databases, downloading the data, etc.

[12] With public, non-password-protected websites.

[13] Other locations may also be involved (3.7). Providers may have operations outside their countries of establishment. Particularly with cloud, providers may use subproviders, who may be third country-established, and/or use datacentres in yet further countries. Controllers may be physically located in a third country when conducting the uploading process (although Art.4(1)(a) applies the DPD to all EEA-established controllers, regardless of the physical locations of controllers or the equipment they use – p.53). Downloaders of personal data may, when

EEA-established provider using infrastructure located in:

(A) the EEA,
(B) a third country, or
(C) both the EEA and a third country; or

Non-EEA-established provider using infrastructure located in:

(D) the EEA,
(E) a third country, or
(F) both.

As I discuss shortly, based on DPAs' general view, using EEA-located infrastructure (A and D) would not involve 'transfers', and similarly with mixed locations (C and F) to the extent personal data are processed in EEA-located infrastructure; but using third country infrastructure (B and E) would, and using mixed locations (C and F) would to the extent personal data are processed in non-EEA-located infrastructure. This approach seems to contradict *Lindqvist* which held that, in A–C at least (EEA-established provider), *uploading* personal data to the provider's infrastructure is not 'transfer'. I analyse *Lindqvist* in detail next. While *Lindqvist* was about webhosting, the analysis applies equally to online storage/sharing and webmail, via cloud or otherwise.

3.5 WEBSITES: *LINDQVIST*

Church volunteer Mrs Lindqvist created and uploaded webpages to assist parishioners, also containing information about her and some colleagues, including full names or first names, describing her colleagues' jobs, hobbies, family circumstances and telephone numbers, also mentioning that one colleague was on 'halftime' on medical grounds having injured her foot.

Mrs Lindqvist did not obtain her colleagues' consent, or notify the Swedish DPA (Datainspektionen). On discovering that her webpages were 'not appreciated' by some colleagues she removed them, reporting herself to the police (*WP54*, pt.II, p.57). She was prosecuted, convicted and fined for breaches of Swedish DPD Laws. On appeal, Göta hovrätt (a

---

downloading, be located outside their country of citizenship/residence or incorporation/establishment.

Swedish court) referred certain questions to the ECJ for preliminary rulings, including regarding the Restriction.[14]

Before dissecting the ECJ's statements regarding webhosting and the Restriction, I summarize various submissions made to the court which illustrate the uncertainties with interpreting 'transfer' in light of websites' multiple stages (*Lindqvist*, paras.53–5):

- Uploading personal data to websites accessible to third country nationals constitutes 'transfer' – irrespective of whether any third country person actually accesses data, and regardless of server location (Commission and Sweden).
- 'Transfer' means 'intentionally transferring' personal data 'from the territory' of a Member State to a third country; how data are made accessible to third parties is irrelevant, so uploading cannot be 'transfer' (Netherlands).
- Art.25 relates to transfer to third countries, not their *accessibility from* third countries, i.e. 'transfer' means active 'transmission' of personal data 'from one place and person to another place and person' (UK).

The first submission effectively considers 'transfer' to include 'making available for pull'; the others consider 'transfer' to involve 'push' only, not 'pull'.

The ECJ felt it necessary to take account 'both of the technical nature of the operations thus carried out and of the purpose and structure of Chapter IV [containing the Restriction]' (para.57). Highlighting the uploading/downloading distinction, it stated (para.60):

> in order to obtain the information appearing on the Internet pages on which Mrs Lindqvist had included information about her colleagues, an Internet user would not only have to connect to the Internet but also personally carry out the necessary actions to consult those pages. In other words, Mrs Lindqvist's Internet pages did not contain the technical means to send that information automatically to people who did not intentionally seek access to those pages.

It further stated, seemingly treating 'transfer' as requiring *direct* transmission:

> 61. It follows that, in circumstances such as those in the case in the main proceedings, personal data which appear on the computer of a person in a third country, coming from a person who has loaded them onto an Internet

---

[14]   I only discuss the Restriction. Garcia (2004) covers *Lindqvist* in detail, including other questions raised.

site, were not directly transferred between those two people but through the computer infrastructure of the hosting provider where the page is stored.

62. It is in that light that it must be examined whether the Community legislature intended, for the purposes of the application of Chapter IV of Directive 95/46, to include within the expression transfer [of data] to a third country within the meaning of Article 25 of that directive activities such as those carried out by Mrs Lindqvist. It must be stressed that the fifth question asked by the referring court concerns only those activities and not those carried out by the hosting providers.

63. Chapter IV of Directive 95/46, in which Article 25 appears, sets up a special regime, with specific rules, intended to allow the Member States to monitor transfers of personal data to third countries. That Chapter sets up a complementary regime to the general regime set up by Chapter II of that directive concerning the lawfulness of processing of personal data.

Thus, *Lindqvist's* application was explicitly limited to activities 'such as those carried out by Mrs Lindqvist', i.e. uploading. The court was not asked to opine on any activities conducted by the *provider* on her behalf, i.e. storing uploaded data on, and making such data available from, its server wherever located. Deliberately not ruling on, and leaving open, issues regarding the 'location' of hosting providers' activities, the ECJ noted that the DPD 'contains no provision concerning use of the Internet', and that it 'does not lay down criteria for deciding whether operations carried out by hosting providers should be deemed to occur in the place of establishment of the service provider or at its business address or in the place where the computer or computers constituting the service's infrastructure are located' (para.67).

Lindqvist's main ruling regarding transfers was (paras.69–71):

> there is no 'transfer [of personal data] to a third country' … where an individual in a Member State loads personal data onto an Internet page which is stored with his hosting provider which is established in that State or in another Member State [i.e. established in the EEA], thereby making those data accessible to anyone who connects to the Internet, including people in a third country.

I reiterate *Lindqvist's* focus on uploading,[15] not downloading, when holding that uploading to an EEA-established provider was not 'transfer' *by the uploader*. The ECJ considered that, given the state of the Internet's development when the DPD was drafted and the 'absence of criteria applicable to use of the Internet in Chapter IV', lawmakers could not be

---

[15] Also stressed in EDPS (2014b: p.6).

presumed to have intended 'transfer' to include uploading 'by an individual in Mrs Lindqvist's position' – even if the uploaded personal data thereby became accessible to third country persons with Internet access (para.68). Unfortunately, the ECJ considered it 'unnecessary to investigate whether an individual from a third country has accessed the Internet page concerned or whether the server of that hosting service is physically in a third country' (para.70). Although acknowledging that providers' infrastructure might be located in other countries unknown to uploaders (para.59), the court confined its decision to the position of someone uploading data to a provider 'established in' a Member State, declining to address downloading or the provider's position. Note again the focus on the *provider's establishment* rather than server location, i.e. scenarios A–C above (p.78).

Policy considerations undoubtedly influenced the ECJ's pragmatic view that treating the uploading of personal data to Web servers as 'transfers' would produce impracticable, unrealistic results (para.69):

> If Article 25 of Directive 95/46 were interpreted to mean that there is 'transfer [of personal data] to a third country' every time that personal data are loaded onto an Internet page, that transfer would necessarily be a transfer to all the third countries where there are the technical means needed to access the Internet. The special regime provided for by Chapter IV of the directive would thus necessarily become a regime of general application, as regards operations on the Internet. Thus, if the Commission found, pursuant to Article 25(4) of Directive 95/46, that even one third country did not ensure adequate protection, the Member States would be obliged to prevent any personal data being placed on the Internet ...[16]

A contrary ruling could have hobbled EEA controllers' digital businesses by preventing their websites from incorporating any personal data, and controllers would probably have ignored it.[17] Also significant is that *Lindqvist* focused on the uploading of personal data to an *EEA-established* provider, i.e. one subject to the jurisdiction of its Member State of establishment. This supports one of my key points, that jurisdiction over controllers/processors should be more important than data location.

---

[16] This seems a 'logical and necessary consequence' of EU territorial limitations; it means European data subjects would lack full protection in a networked society involving ubiquitous information, but 'the jurisdiction of the European legislator is not ubiquitous' (EDPS 2007b: paras.41–2).

[17] Ch.6 discusses low compliance with the Restriction, and low enforcement.

3.6 *LINDQVIST* – UNANSWERED QUESTIONS

Several questions were not answered, or answered fully, in *Lindqvist*.

3.6.1 'Transfer' on Downloading?

Even with an EEA-established provider, is there a 'transfer' when a third country user *downloads* uploaded data? If so, who 'makes' that 'transfer'? *Lindqvist* only held that no 'transfer' occurs upon uploading to EEA-established providers; it did not state that websites could never involve 'transfer'. Four main options seem possible:

a.   No 'transfer' even upon downloading, because 'transfer' means direct transmission, thus excluding websites with their indirect, multiple-stage use.
b.   'Transfer' upon downloading – from the uploading controller to the downloading third country user.
c.   'Transfer' upon downloading – from the provider to such a user.
d.   'Transfer' upon downloading – effected by such a user direct.

Neither (c) nor (d) has been suggested for websites.[18] Option (a) seems supported by the ECJ's statement that uploading did not constitute a 'transfer' regardless of whether data were thereby made accessible to third country persons (p.81). However, *Lindqvist* only addressed uploading, not downloading. Conflating the two ignores the ECJ's deliberate restriction of its ruling to Mrs Lindqvist's uploading, without discussing downloading, and its emphasis on the provider being EEA-established when holding that no 'transfer' occurred upon uploading personal data to such a provider.

Option (a), no 'transfer' occurring even when third country users access uploaded data, is sometimes favoured, at least when personal data are uploaded to an *EEA-established* provider's servers (Brownsdon 2004).[19] Thus, consistently with *Lindqvist,* no 'transfer' occurs when publishing personal data to a website 'stored with an Internet provider

---

[18]   The Commission stated, seemingly ruling out option (d), that 'the [*Lindqvist*] Court clarified that the information appearing on a computer in a third country does not constitute a transfer of data by the users themselves' (SEC(2012)72 final, Ann.2, p.21) – but without explaining *who* then was responsible for making the information 'appear'.
[19]   Similarly, uploading is arguably not 'transfer' because 'substantive processing by an external party would be needed to access it' (Baker 2006: p.7).

established within the EU' (Datainspektionen n.d.: para.3). Accordingly, where a school's chairman, without consent, published an employee's personal data on its website, based on *Lindqvist* Sweden's Supreme Court rejected the 'transfer' aspect of the employee's claim (WP29 2006: p.110).

Option (a) has been espoused in relation to Art.9 CIDPR's transfer provisions (EDPS 2007a: p.2), which should be interpreted consistently with the DPD (2.2.6) and *Lindqvist*. The EDPS initially considered that, under *Lindqvist*, Art.9 CIDPR does not apply to worldwide publication of personal data 'through a public website' (EDPS 2007a: para.2). This approach, shared, e.g. by Reed (2012: p.161), is related to the ECJ's view of the Restriction as creating a special regime for transfers to *specific* third countries (p.80), as opposed to 'making available' personal data to potentially all third countries (see also CBP 2007: p.50). Furthermore, Art.9 CIDPR was considered to apply to any 'closed website' or intranet accessible only to a defined group, because 'special regime' problems do not apply in that situation (EDPS 2007a: p.3) – presumably because a private intranet would not involve 'indefinite' third countries, but limited end-users from known countries. This reasoning could also extend to password-protected webpages, and cloud services where only specific authorized users have access. However, more recent EDPS guidance has moved on from this 'closed/restricted circle' approach, as discussed later (p.118).

Option (a) could apply more broadly, beyond websites (FRA and CoE 2014: p.138) (emphasis added):

> The principle that mere publication of (personal) data is not to be considered as transborder data flow applies also to *online public registers or to mass media, such as (electronic) newspapers and television.* Only communication which is *directed at specific recipients* is eligible for the concept of 'transborder data flow'.

The view that only direct transfer constitutes 'transfer' relies on the ECJ's discussion (p.79) regarding the indirectness of access to webpages (Davidson et al. 1999: para.111.43). *Lindqvist*'s justification by reference to relevant technology has been criticized as weak (Svantesson 2011: p.185): it is 'no different than the fact that a TV station cannot provide TV programmes to somebody who does not turn on their TV, or who does not select the station's particular channel'. Acknowledging the technical difference that TV stations actively send signals receivable in other countries, Svantesson considers that, unless someone *receives* the signal, no 'transfer' occurs. This suggests he espouses option (b), i.e. that uploading a webpage containing personal data constitutes a 'transfer', but only if a third country person accesses it. However, he does not clarify who he thinks would make that transfer – presumably the original uploader?

On another interpretation of *Lindqvist*, a 'transfer' only occurs 'where the Internet page was actually accessed by a person located in a third country' (ICO 2010: para.1.3.4; ICO 2016b: p.87), i.e. option (b). However, the view that transfer involves actual access in a third country seems inconsistent with *Lindqvist*'s statement that actual access is irrelevant (p.81), although that statement related to the uploading (not downloading) of the data. Another issue with focusing on actual access is that the 'access' concept may be problematic: e.g., if a third country search engine provider's automated crawler/bot accesses a webpage containing personal data, is that a 'transfer'?[20]

Interpretation (a), that website use never involves 'transfer', could result in the Restriction never applying to websites, or at least public websites. However, arguably *Lindqvist* was motivated by factors inapplicable to most organizational controllers (Kuner 2007a: chap.4.08): there was no evidence of actual access from third countries; Mrs Lindqvist's webpages were in Swedish, clearly targeting EU citizens only, and were 'designed to be accessed on limited scale', i.e., her town's church community.[21] Accordingly, Kuner suggests the safest interpretation is that making personal data available on the Internet *can* indeed be viewed as 'transfer' if it involves granting large-scale access to others' data (e.g. employees, customers) for business purposes. Effectively, he considers that the ECJ was influenced by the knowledge that Mrs Lindqvist had not *intended* to make data available to third country persons. If considerations of intention influenced its decision, unfortunately the ECJ did not state this. However, some DPAs have considered the role of 'intention'.

3.6.2   Intention to Provide Access to Personal Data

The ICO focuses on the uploader's intention that personal data be accessed in a third country, although Art.25 does not mention such

---

[20]   Controllers publishing personal data on websites were advised that they can block search engine indexing (through robots.txt), or design for data subject consent e.g. with Web communities (CBP 2007: p.33).

[21]   The ECJ may have sympathized with Mrs Lindqvist (Kuner 2007a: para.2.48) – the classic 'hard case'. However, while finding in her favour regarding 'transfer', it did not do so on other questions referred to it.

'intention':[22] 'In practice, data are often loaded onto the Internet with the intention that the data be accessed in a third country, and, as this will usually lead to a transfer, the principle in the *Lindqvist* case will not apply in such circumstances' (ICO 2010: para.1.3.4).

On that basis, uploading personal data to public websites would indeed constitute 'transfer', at least when such data are accessed by third country visitors (ICO 2016b: p.87):

> Putting personal data on a website will often result in transfers to countries outside the EEA. The transfers will take place when someone outside the EEA accesses the website. If you load information onto a server based in the UK so that it can be accessed through a website, you should consider the likelihood that a transfer may take place and whether that would be fair for the individuals concerned. If you intend information on the website to be accessed outside the EEA, then this is a transfer.

The use of 'likelihood' suggests that the ICO may go beyond actual intention, to presumed or inferred intention based on probability of actual access – i.e., knowledge or 'recklessness' regarding possible third country access. Similarly with the Netherlands' argument in *Lindqvist* (p.79). The Netherlands' DPA reiterated the view that 'transfer' involves the transferor's *intention* to make personal data available to specific persons in a third country (CBP 2007: p.50). Regarding 'onward transfer' from the US to another third country, if 'known by the EU data Controller' even before transfer to the US, or if the EU controller is 'jointly responsible' for the onward transfer decision, the onward transfer should be considered a *direct* transfer to that country, to which the Restriction applies (WP29 2014c: p.6).

UK and Dutch views differ regarding what classes of recipients the transferor must have intended, for website publication of personal data to be considered a 'transfer': persons in any/all third countries, versus persons in specific third countries only? Nevertheless, both focus on the intention to make transfers to such recipients. Similarly, arguably only communications 'directed' at specific recipients can constitute transfers to them: 'directing' clearly connotes intention (FRA and CoE 2014: p.131). However, it seems untenable that situations where personal data

---

[22]   Art.25(1) restricts the transfer of personal data 'intended' for processing after transfer. However, strictly, intention to 'process' transferred personal data in a third country is not the same as *intention to allow intelligible access* by persons there. 'Processing' is very broad (p.11), so personal data could be 'processed' (e.g. stored in encrypted form) in a country, without someone there having intelligible access – 3.7.1.

are not being actively 'transmitted' to other countries should not constitute 'transfers', because an intention to make data available to third countries may equally exist when data are merely made accessible to persons from those countries (Kuner 2013b: pp.43–5).

I agree that if, for policy reasons, it is considered necessary to regulate acts of controllers that make personal data accessible to persons subject to third country jurisdiction, then *intention* to enable such access, which may be inferred, seems a better test than 'transfer'. I also submit that the issue should not be whether personal data are intended to be accessible in specific third countries, or any/all of them. It cannot be right that personal data may be published freely if the intention was to make the data available to anyone anywhere, yet adequate protection/safeguards must be implemented if the intention was to make the data available only to people in limited third countries (see 3.8). However, knowledge and intention may be difficult to determine or infer, and it is interesting that, in its cloud guidance, Slovenia's DPA explicitly considers 'transfer' to include the 'enabling' of remote access by third country persons to EEA-located personal data, without mentioning intention (Information Commissioner (Slovenia) 2012: sec.3.4).

3.6.3 The Provider's Status

I now consider certain questions that *Lindqvist* did not address regarding the provider:

1. Is there a 'transfer' by the uploader if the provider is not EEA-established (scenarios D–F, p.78)? *Lindqvist* implies this is possible, but in exactly what circumstances would there be a 'transfer'?
2. Is there a 'transfer' by the EEA-established provider to whose service personal data were uploaded, if it chooses to use non-EEA servers?[23]

3.6.3.1 Upload to non-EEA-established provider

Under *Lindqvist,* if an EEA controller uploads a webpage with personal data to an EEA-established provider's server, thereby rendering personal

---

[23] On one view, the Restriction applies to hosting providers who 'permit a website containing personal data to be accessed from a third country' (Brownsdon 2004). I disagree. It is for the *website owner/uploader*, as controller of the personal data it uploaded to its website, to 'permit' or otherwise control such access; the hosting provider is merely its processor. Brownsdon did not discuss the (different) issue of choice of server location.

data potentially accessible to third country persons, that uploading alone is not a 'transfer' by the controller.[24] Most other commentators do not discuss the ECJ's qualification regarding the provider being EEA-established. That qualification raises an important question: could such an upload constitute a 'transfer' if the provider is *not* EEA-established?

Generally, a provider can access personal data uploaded to its service, so it could be considered a 'recipient' to whom personal data are 'disclosed' (7.4.2.2).[25] Unfortunately, the ECJ did not explain the reason for its 'EEA-established provider' qualification, possibly because the provider there was EEA-established, so the alternative position did not require consideration. However, I suggest that the most likely and logical basis for this qualification is that an EEA-established provider-recipient, whether controller or processor, would be subject to the jurisdiction and DPD Laws of its Member State.[26] This qualification may reflect (perhaps was influenced by?) Art.9 CIDPR, which explicitly restricts 'transfers' to 'recipients' not subject to Member State jurisdiction, implicitly permitting transmissions to recipients who *are* so subject (2.2.6):[27] such as, here, EEA-established providers.

If that is *Lindqvist*'s unspoken rationale, could the uploading of personal data to non-EEA-established providers' servers constitute 'transfer'? I suggest this should depend on whether the provider is subject to EEA jurisdiction regarding the uploaded personal data.[28] If it is, the uploading alone may not be a 'transfer', based on a logical extension of *Lindqvist*'s 'EEA-established provider' qualification. If it is not, the

---

[24] Regardless of subsequent access by website visitors, considered strictly a separate issue – 3.5–3.6.1.

[25] 2.2.6. However, why should personal data that were strongly encrypted before upload be considered 'disclosed' to providers who cannot access the decryption key (7.2.3.2)? Transmissions to processors are considered 'use', not 'disclosure', in Canada – p.262, n.1.

[26] The DPD does not require direct regulation of processors, but the GDPR will (1.5.2).

[27] Seemingly 'recipient subject to Member State jurisdiction' was considered implicit in the Restriction (2.2.6).

[28] The CIDPR (2.2.6) does not specifically mention recipients being subject to EEA jurisdiction *in relation to the received personal data*, but logically any upload of personal data to such providers should escape being considered a 'transfer' only if they are so subject. While *Lindqvist* did not state such an additional qualification, it seems implicit.

uploading could well be a 'transfer'. However, whether providers are subject to EEA jurisdiction is complex and fact-dependent.[29]

There is another nuance. Webhosting and cloud providers are generally processors, but could be or become controllers (p.9). The DPD only requires Member States to regulate controllers, so most do not regulate providers as processors, although this will change under the GDPR (1.5.2). Nevertheless, non-EEA-established providers may be subject to EEA data protection jurisdiction under Art.4(1)(c) DPD (equipment use), if they are or become controllers and use EEA-located servers[30] to process the uploaded personal data (p.52). Even if non-EEA providers use only non-EEA servers, they might nevertheless be subject to EEA data protection jurisdiction regarding the uploaded personal data, indeed EEA jurisdiction generally, depending on the circumstances and Member State laws. Under *Google Spain*,[31] more providers might be considered controllers (not processors), and directly subject to EEA data protection jurisdiction as such. If such non-EEA-established providers are only processors, then relevant Member State law determines whether they are subject to EEA data protection jurisdiction as processors, because Art.4(1)(c) only addresses controllers.

As regards uploads to processors, I reiterate the point (p.53) that, because controllers must comply with DPD Laws when using processors, any personal data transmitted to such processors (EEA-established or not) would remain subject to DPD Laws. The true problem, which remains unaddressed, is that such personal data are *also* exposed to third country laws if third countries have effective jurisdiction over the relevant provider (EEA-established or not), i.e. the risk is that of multiple simultaneous jurisdictions applying (pp.38, 62, 119 (anti-FISA), 146, 314). However, even controllers who only process personal data *in-house* may be exposed to third country jurisdiction, if they have any operations or assets located in third countries (as with SWIFT – 3.7.1).

---

[29] Under the DPD and GDPR (1.5.2), non-EEA providers could become directly subject to EEA jurisdiction and DPD Laws if they have EEA 'establishments', e.g. branches or subsidiaries, perhaps even if the establishment's operations are unrelated or only indirectly related to the processing of the uploaded personal data – *Google Spain* (p.52). Later cases have confirmed an expansive, flexible interpretation of 'establishment' and 'context of activities', e.g. C-230/14 *Weltimmo* (p.47, n.40): 'in the context of' is broader than 'by'.

[30] Even third party-owned servers.

[31] P.9, n.20; p.52, n.46. The CJEU held that Google was a controller regarding its search engine operations, not a mere processor.

I have argued that *Lindqvist*, although difficult to interpret, supports a jurisdictional approach to 'transfer'. Yet, notwithstanding *Lindqvist*, generally DPAs still take a personal data location-centric approach (3.7.1). In their view, seemingly any uploads to *EEA-located servers* (scenarios A and D, p.78) are not 'transfers', apparently regardless of the provider's status (as controller or processor) or its country of establishment/ incorporation; while, conversely, transmissions from EEA to non-EEA-located servers (scenarios B and E, p.78) are considered 'transfers', regardless of whether the transferors and/or recipients are or remain subject to EEA jurisdiction. Focusing purely on infrastructure location seems narrower in some ways, yet broader in other ways, than *Lindqvist*'s 'EEA-established provider' qualification. That is unsatisfactory. I argue that 'transfer' should be ascertained, not by considering personal data location, but by considering whether recipients are or are not subject to particular countries' jurisdictions, as in the CIDPR and Convention108's Additional Protocol (Convention108-AP) (2.2.7). However, where recipients are subject to *both* Participant (p.38, n.26) and non-Participant jurisdictions, it seems the CIDPR would permit transfers, but Convention108-AP would not, which is also unsatisfactory (pp.13, 62), and requires clarification. Situations involving multiple jurisdictions require proper consideration and reconciliation. In today's globalized economy, cloud and webhosting providers, and even controllers, are often subject to both EEA and third country jurisdictions simultaneously. EEA incorporation will not save controllers or providers from being also subject to third countries' jurisdiction if they have operations/assets in those countries, i.e. they may be subject to multiple jurisdictions, including non-EEA jurisdictions, simultaneously. These uncertainties highlight that one core problem underlying the 'transfer' issue is that of conflicts between jurisdictions, which only countries, not private organizations, can resolve (7.5.3).

3.6.3.2   EEA-established provider using non-EEA servers

I now consider the second unanswered question regarding the position of providers. Under the DPAs' location-centric approach, an EEA-established provider (or indeed non-EEA provider) would 'transfer' personal data simply by using non-EEA-located infrastructure.

Post-*Lindqvist*, the WP29 considered that a Belgian processor, SWIFT, could become a controller through taking 'critical' decisions regarding processing that exceeded a processor's prerogative, including choosing to 'mirror' (automatically replicate) personal data stored on its EEA servers to third country locations (*WP128*, p.11).[32] The WP29 considered that such mirroring was a 'transfer' (3.7.1.2).[33] This suggests that, in *Lindqvist*-type situations, EEA-established providers who choose to use third country-located servers would thereby become controllers, responsible as such under the Restriction.

However, the WP29's opinions are non-binding (1.5.5), *WP128* inexplicably failed altogether to discuss *Lindqvist*, and *Lindqvist* itself explicitly refused to consider the provider's position (p.80; Harris 2006: fn.234) or server location. Indeed, ultimately Belgium's DPA took no enforcement action against SWIFT, finding it only 'marginally' a controller (CPVP 2008: para.247; see p.98). Certainly, nothing in *Lindqvist* itself justifies DPAs' insistence on infrastructure location as the chief determinant of 'transfer'. I discuss *WP128* further shortly (3.7.1).

3.6.4 Summary

'Transfer' includes direct transmission. However, multistage, indirect access to personal data, e.g. on webpages, is problematic. While views differ, the better view seems to be that, upon third country persons accessing such personal data, 'transfer' occurs, but only if the uploader intended (or must reasonably be presumed to have intended) such access, although inferring 'intention' may itself be problematic.

Under *Lindqvist*, no 'transfer' occurs on uploading personal data to EEA-established providers. It is unclear whether uploads to *non*-EEA-established providers are 'transfers'. From a jurisdictional viewpoint, such providers would be subject to DPD Laws if they are controllers and use EEA infrastructure or, perhaps, have EEA subsidiaries. Even when focusing on jurisdiction rather than personal data location, the issue of multiple applicable jurisdictions still causes difficulties, and the core problem remains that DPAs focus only on personal data location, as I will show next.

---

[32] 'Data processors ... can export personal data only if the data controller has given such instructions' (Dhont et al. 2004: p.23).

[33] The main reason the WP29 decided to treat SWIFT as a controller was, as the WP29 stated (emphasis added), that 'SWIFT *decided to comply with* the US subpoenas ... Indeed, the control mechanisms obtained and operated by SWIFT affected the *purpose and scope* of the transfer of data to [US authorities]' (Kuner 2007b: para.2.25).

3.7 'TRANSFERS' IN CLOUD COMPUTING

3.7.1 Personal Data Location, Jurisdiction and Intelligible Access

3.7.1.1 Location fixation

This section discusses the DPAs' fixation on personal data location (or strictly, infrastructure location), when assessing whether 'transfer' has occurred. One unspoken assumption seemingly underlying this 'location fixation' is that persons present where personal data-processing infrastructure is located, e.g. the owners of datacentres housing personal data-processing servers, must necessarily have access to that personal data, particularly intelligible access; and, conversely, that persons not physically there have no access to the data. I debunk this assumption later (4.5), but first I demonstrate the prevalence among DPAs of the 'personal data location-centric' approach and the absurdity of related assumptions (4.5.1), which support my argument that laws and regulations should focus on who has intelligible access to personal data (and which countries have effective jurisdiction over such persons), rather than only or mainly on personal data 'location'.

Lindqvist might suggest that controllers may use cloud to process personal data compliantly with the Restriction by using EEA-established providers, regardless of infrastructure location (3.5). Indeed, when using EEA-established providers, it is even more arguable with cloud than with webhosting that no 'transfer' occurs. Third country visitors may access personal data on public websites, whereupon 'transfers' may result. However, many cloud uses[34] do not contemplate any third party recipient accessing or monitoring uploaded data (except perhaps the provider, for billing etc. purposes – 7.4.2.2). Rather, only the EEA controller/customer and its authorized users are intended to store and/or operate on data.[35] Furthermore, where personal data are strongly encrypted (pp.138, 286)

---

[34] Except services used for hosting public websites, public sharing of photos/documents, etc.

[35] True, if in-cloud personal data are intended for access by a restricted circle (the customer's authorized staff), that resembles an intranet where, under the EDPS's initial view (p.83), the Restriction applies. However, as argued previously, intention to allow third country persons access seems a better test than 'restricted circle' (3.6.2; and see the EDPS's newer view – p.118). With many cloud uses, EEA controllers do not intend any intelligible access by third country persons (on the provider's potential access, see 7.4.2).

and the provider cannot access the decryption key, arguably there may not even be 'transfer' to the provider, because it has no intelligible access (7.2.3.2).

3.7.1.2   EU DPAs' location-centric approach

No WP29 opinion specifically analysed *Lindqvist*'s interpretation of 'transfer'. However, 'transfer' included SWIFT (p.90) mirroring personal data to servers in its own US datacentre (*WP128*, p.21) and (emphasis added) 'if the data is transferred outside the EU, for example, *to servers located in third countries*, ad network providers must ensure compliance' with the Restriction (*WP171*, para.5.4). Despite *Lindqvist*, the WP29 has consistently considered infrastructure location to be the main or sole determinant, so that a 'transfer' occurs whenever personal data, un-encrypted or encrypted, are 'processed' using third country-located servers or other hardware – even if no third party 'recipient' exists, e.g. data remain under the controller's control in its own infrastructure, and even if the 'recipient' is subject to DPD Laws. The WP29 considers that the location(s) of servers or other hardware used for processing personal data, i.e. infrastructure location, must be known before it can be ascertained whether a 'transfer' occurs. However, I submit that it is oversimplistic to consider that 'transfer' occurs whenever personal data are 'moved' to third country-located infrastructure regardless of who *controls* access to personal data there. In the Internet age, a more nuanced approach is needed to 'transfer' than data location alone.

3.7.1.3   Location and country risk

With SWIFT, the real issue was that SWIFT had agreed to give US authorities access to personal data stored in its US datacentre (n.33) – i.e., unauthorized disclosure of personal data to third parties in breach of DPD Laws. SWIFT's use of a US datacentre gave US authorities effective jurisdiction to subject SWIFT to subpoenas requiring disclosure. Under US law, SWIFT had to comply. The true mischief was the disclosure, but SWIFT's use of infrastructure located in US territory to process personal data gave US authorities power against SWIFT to demand access. 'Transfer' of personal data location to the US created a 'foreseeable' *risk* of access by US authorities or under a US court order (*WP128*, sec.4.1.2). SWIFT, as a Belgian entity, remained subject to Belgian DPD Laws. Its use of US infrastructure for processing personal data was not in itself a 'disclosure' to third parties, but it *exposed* SWIFT to the risk of being subject to US as well as Belgian laws. Perhaps that risk is the true rationale behind the WP29's focus on personal data location, epitomized by *WP196*; in that sense, the WP29 may consider geography fundamental to maintaining compliance. This harks back to the data movements 'to' other countries' territories, envisaged by the OECD Guidelines and Convention108 (Ch.2), and makes the same assumption: that location of data in a country gives that country effective jurisdiction to regulate that data's processing. However, two aspects regarding digital data undermine that assumption, as Ch.4 and Ch.7 will detail: the relative ease of moving/copying digital data, and the availability of technical measures to restrict intelligible access regardless of location, notably encryption.

3.7.1.4 The *Microsoft warrant case* and US extraterritoriality

A US case involving Microsoft (*Microsoft warrant case*)[36] highlights the problem of multiple jurisdictions. It also shows that EEA location may not prevent a third country, which has effective jurisdiction over a provider, seeking intelligible access to personal data located elsewhere. In a US drug trafficking/money laundering investigation, a warrant was issued to 'search' the email account of a Microsoft customer, stored in an Irish datacentre operated by Microsoft's wholly owned subsidiary – i.e., requiring Microsoft to remotely access and disclose EEA-located data to US authorities. Microsoft had the technical ability to access the requested data remotely; the issue was, could the US Stored Communications Act (SCA) compel it to do so? Microsoft argued the warrant was invalid: the SCA did not permit warrants for information stored outside the US, the government should seek the information from Irish authorities under the US–Ireland mutual legal assistance treaty (MLAT), and there were international comity issues. A New York magistrate judge upheld the warrant, stating that Microsoft in the US had 'possession, custody, or control' over the Dublin-located data, so must produce the content sought, regardless of location. On appeal, the district judge upheld the magistrate judge, reportedly stating, 'It is a question of control, not a question of the location of that information' (Ax 2014); the relevant law regulated *providers* not data (Kerr 2014); and her ruling did not involve applying US law extraterritorially (Palazzolo and Ovide 2014): Microsoft could produce the information in the US without intruding on Ireland's sovereignty (AP 2014b).

On Microsoft's appeal, a three-judge panel of the Second Circuit Court of Appeals unanimously reversed the district judge, holding that the US Congress had *not* intended the SCA's warrant provisions to apply extraterritorially. The US Justice Department asked a full panel of

---

[36] For citations, see the Table of Cases.

appeals judges to review that decision, stressing that US criminal/national security investigations could be thwarted by locating data outside the US (because seeking data through the US–Ireland MLAT is cumbersome, indeed impossible with organizations like Google where only US-based employees can access customer email accounts wherever stored) (Nakashima 2016). It also argued that extraterritoriality was irrelevant because Microsoft is US based, controls its servers and would disclose data to US authorities in the US (ibid.). The court was split four–four on granting a full panel hearing so the previous decision stands; the matter may ultimately reach the US Supreme Court.

Whether the targeted account-holder is a US or Irish citizen/resident was unstated. The latter would more obviously engage Ireland's sovereign interests. However, the battle is over whether the SCA was *intended* to apply extraterritorially. My point is that US laws *can* have extra-territorial reach, where that is clearly intended (as mentioned in the *Microsoft warrant case* itself). Indeed, even EU laws, like the GDPR (1.5.2), may have explicit extraterritorial reach.

Triggered by the *Microsoft warrant case*, US lawmakers introduced bills to amend the US Electronic Communications Privacy Act, in 2015 (Law Enforcement Access to Data Stored Abroad Act or LEADS Act) and 2016 (International Communications Privacy Act (ICPA)). They were intended to entitle US law enforcement authorities to seek court-issued warrants for disclosure of the contents of electronic communications held by providers of electronic communication or remote computing services (including cloud providers), *regardless* of storage location – but only if there were reasonable grounds to believe the relevant subscriber/customer was (under ICPA):

1.   a US citizen or lawful permanent resident,
2.   physically located in the US,
3.   a national (including organization) of a country having an MLAT or similar executive agreement/treaty with the US, where the country agreed, or did not object to disclosure within 60 days after a formal request, or
4.   a national of a country without such an agreement.

If the subscriber/customer's nationality or location could not reasonably be ascertained (to address situations where that might be impossible), a warrant could also be issued.

While these bills failed to pass, they clearly sought a balanced and practicable approach, focusing on jurisdiction over the relevant *person* rather than data location. That would not resolve all conflicts, as the contents of a US person's account could relate to non-US persons, e.g. emails from EEA individuals, and allowing warrants where locations are unknown carries its own problems, because innocent persons could conceal their locations for privacy rather than criminal reasons. However, I argue that a person-centric approach is superior to data location-centric approaches: the Restriction certainly does not prevent or resolve such conflicts.

3.7.1.5 Cloud and infrastructure location

Returning to EEA controllers' use of cloud computing to process personal data, at least two locations seem relevant: the provider's 'location', and the location of the infrastructure it uses to process its customers' personal data. A provider may have multiple 'locations': the country of its incorporation or 'establishment', any country where it has operations or conducts business (e.g. branch), perhaps even a country where it merely has (or uses) a datacentre. I suggest that the main significance of a provider's 'location' is *jurisdiction*: which countries have jurisdiction to subject it to their laws and effectively compel, or even just persuade, it to disclose customer data? Multiple countries may, simultaneously, have jurisdiction over multinational organizations that operate internationally, whether they are incorporated in the USA or the EEA. Such overlapping jurisdiction is one of the biggest problems.

WP196 (pp.12, 25) clearly recognized some aspects of cloud, e.g. noting that personal data 'may be kept redundantly on different servers at different locations', and that often 'large-sized providers with complex infrastructures come into play; this is why the cloud might span several locations and customers might ignore where exactly their data are being stored'. However, *WP196* does not explain what it means by 'location' for the purposes of the Restriction. Do *WP196*'s references to 'locations' of providers or subproviders (*WP196*, para.3.2; p.18) include their countries of establishment – or merely their infrastructure locations?[37] It

---

[37] '[I]f a cloud client is established outside the EEA', but 'commissions' a 'cloud provider located in the EEA', 'the provider exports the data protection legislation to the client' (*WP196*, p.7). There, 'located in the EEA' must mean EEA infrastructure location, use of which subjects non-EEA cloud customers to DPD Laws under Art.4(1)(c) (equipment/means) (*WP179*, p.20), because EEA-established providers could use non-EEA infrastructure, e.g. of US subproviders. Alternatively, that statement may treat 'commissioned' EEA-'located' providers as EEA-located 'means' used by non-EEA controllers (p.52, n.45).

does seem clear, from references to locations of servers/datacentres, storage/processing locations, and locations 'in which' services may be provided (*WP196*, pp.4, 6, 11, 12, 13, 17, 20, 21), even within the EEA,[38] that by 'transfer' the WP29 means, or at least includes, personal data movement to a third country processing location – i.e., third country *infrastructure* location.[39] Other regulatory opinions also consider infrastructure location paramount, e.g. (Konferenz der Datenschutzbeauftragten des Bundes und der Länder and Düsseldorfer Kreises 2014).

National DPAs' cloud decisions again illustrate the 'location-centric' approach and resulting emphasis on data localization. Denmark's DPA (Datatilsynet) opined on Odense municipality's proposed use of Google Apps (now termed G-Suite) SaaS for certain schools-related purposes, including personal data processing (*Odense*). The processor was to be Google Ireland Ltd, but data would be 'at' Google Inc.'s datacentres 'located in the USA and Europe', although European customers 'primarily get their data from data centres in Europe'. However, 'Europe' is broader than the 'EEA'. Some European countries are not Member States; 'Europe' could include third countries outside both the EEA and the US (p.32, n.13). Therefore, Datatilsynet considered it insufficient that Google Inc. was a 'harborite' participating in the (then still valid) US Safe Harbour scheme (5.3.1). Personal data transmissions to datacentres located in EU or EEA countries would not constitute 'transfers'. Personal data transmissions to Google Inc.'s US datacentres *were* transfers, but were permissible because such datacentres 'must be presumed' to have adequate protection under Safe Harbour. However, Datatilsynet considered that transmission of data to datacentres 'in other insecure third countries than the USA' required a legal basis, e.g. SCCs (5.4.2) – even if Google Inc., which was bound by Safe Harbour principles, owned those

---

Subjecting all non-EEA customers to DPD Laws simply because they use services from (unaffiliated) EEA-'located' providers seems to overreach, and may disincentivize use of EEA providers. Thus, to encourage use of French providers (considered as French 'means' – p.51, n.44), CNIL exempted from various French DPD Laws, in some circumstances, non-EEA controllers who use French service providers to process certain non-EEA personal data (Hon, Millard and Hörnle 2013: pp.238–9).

[38] Location in a particular Member State *within* the EEA affects laws applicable to data protection disputes between customers and providers and to non-EEA controllers using EEA-located equipment for personal data processing (*WP196*, pp.6–7).

[39] Also nn.46, 49.

datacentres.[40] Without evidence of SCCs 'with' those datacentres or other DPA authorization, exports 'to' third country datacentres were impermissible.

Datacentres are buildings, not legal entities. You cannot contract 'with' a datacentre: only with whoever owns or uses it (Google Inc. being both the owner and user in *Odense*). This is problematic, because Google cannot contract with itself (CBI 2002: p.2). A provider or datacentre provider that signed up to Safe Harbour was required to comply with Safe Harbour obligations, which applied if they were 'established in' the US (5.3.1); those obligations were not restricted to situations where it used US-located infrastructure to process personal data, just as DPD Laws apply to EEA-established controllers whatever the location of their personal data-processing infrastructure.[41] Perhaps DPAs' true concern is the *risk* of a non-US third country's laws applying to a harborite through its use of infrastructure in that country, as with SWIFT and US laws.[42] However, SCCs cannot prevent such laws from applying, or stop organizations signing SCCs (harborites or not) from complying with such laws, just as SWIFT becoming a harborite (discussed shortly) could not prevent US laws from applying to SWIFT or stop SWIFT from obeying them (5.3.4.3 (Safe Harbour), 5.4.2.6 (SCCs); also p.116, n.79).[43] Therefore, it is unclear how requiring SCCs to be implemented would have addressed this risk in *Odense*.[44]

Establishing a separate entity to own any non-US third country datacentre and sign SCCs is possible – but involves an artificial extra step. A discussion paper for the Commission's cloud contracts expert

---

[40] *Narvik 2012b* (Norway), p.10 also implies that transfers to a harborite are adequate only if the transferred personal data are US-located.

[41] P.53.

[42] P.92.

[43] Norwegian DPD Laws prevented Google from disclosing data to others without controller approval, but Google Apps' terms permitted Google to disclose confidential information 'when required by law after giving reasonable notice'. Disclosure based on orders from US law enforcement authorities could, however, be considered permissible if legally binding on the provider and not contrary to other Norwegian legislation (*Narvik 2012b* (Norway), p.9; *Moss* (Norway), p.3).

[44] Some harborite-providers offer SCCs. Seemingly this seeks to address both DPAs' concerns regarding Safe Harbour's adequacy (and provide a Mechanism for US transfers following Safe Harbour's invalidation – 5.3.2), and DPAs' insistence on SCCs whenever a datacentre located outside both the US and EEA is used for personal data processing, even if the datacentre is provider-owned – p.200.

group[45] shared the 'one entity per datacentre' view (Bartoli 2014: p.8), suggesting that an EU-located provider, with 2500 EU-located customers but 4 non-EU-located datacentres, would (if using SCCs) have to sign 10 000 contracts (2500 × 4): 'One can really question the legal interest of such an exercises [*sic*] as well as the added value.' In that example, four separate affiliates would be required ('4 ... datacentres'). However, practitioners generally take this approach. One provider signed over *8000* SCCs with customers (Vincens 2012: p.25). But beyond tick-box 'compliance' and make-work for lawyers, do SCCs truly improve data subjects' protection against third country authorities' access?

The SWIFT incident (3.6.3.2) exemplified the location-centric approach. Belgium's DPA ultimately took no enforcement action against SWIFT (p.90), but one measure that SWIFT took, to provide adequate protection compliantly with Belgian law, was to subscribe to Safe Harbour '[a]s an organization with a fixed establishment in the U.S., recipient of personal data transferred from the European Union' (CPVP 2008: paras.216–17). Again, it seems artificial and unnecessary that SWIFT – a Belgian-incorporated entity, clearly subject to Belgian DPA jurisdiction and DPD Laws – had to subscribe to Safe Harbour additionally.

Safe Harbour membership would not enable it to avoid compliance with US laws compelling disclosure. Thus, Canada's DPA recognized that PIPEDA 'cannot prevent U.S. authorities from lawfully accessing the personal information of Canadians held by organizations in Canada or in the United States, nor can it force Canadian companies to stop outsourcing to foreign-based service providers' – however, it required transparency about personal information-handling practices, and protection of customer personal information held by non-Canadian third party providers to the extent possible (emphasis added): 'The measures by which personal information is protected by a foreign-based firm must be formalized with the organization by using contractual *or other means. No contract or contractual provision can override the laws of a country to which the information could be subject once the information has been transferred* ...' (PIPEDA Case Summary #2008-394). The OPC acknowledged that the risk of US-based providers being ordered to disclose information to US authorities was not unique to US organizations; for national security/antiterrorism purposes, Canadian organizations were subject to similar orders to disclose Canadians' personal information to *Canadian* authorities. Accordingly, a Canadian bank who used a US

---

[45] Established under Commission Decision 2013/C174/04/EU.

processor, having notified customers that their information was accessible by US authorities under the US PATRIOT Act, was considered compliant with PIPEDA (PIPEDA Case Summary #2005-313). Also contrast Canada's approach to complaints against Canadian banks following SWIFT's disclosures to US authorities (p.218).

Again illustrating EU DPAs' location-centric focus, in another Google Apps decision Sweden's DPA highlighted personal data location, stating that personal data movement to US-located datacentres was 'transfer' (*Salems 2011* (Sweden), p.17). It considered a list of subproviders inadequate without knowing their 'locations': there were insufficient guarantees that the controller always knew where personal data were processed, particularly as a webpage giving Google's datacentre locations was not guaranteed to be accurate (*Salems 2013* (Sweden), para.3.3) – upheld by a court on appeal (including for insufficiency regarding processing purposes and data deletion – pp.127, 203; 7.4.2.4) (Datainspektionen 2014).

The WP29 (*WP196*, pp.4, 11, 20; see p.96) and DPAs' national cloud guidance or decisions have consistently focused on personal data location, i.e. the geographical location of infrastructure used for processing personal data, although some also mention locations of (sub)-providers without always clarifying whether they mean their jurisdictions of incorporation and/or the locations of their personal data-processing infrastructure.[46] The WP29 considers that 'cloud computing is most

---

[46] Some examples – Czech Republic: references to data storage/processing locations (UOOU 2013: pp.1, 4, 9). Denmark: to ensure processor security measures are met, controller must know data locations (*Odense*, para.3.3; 5.3.2); possible remote access by Microsoft US to data in Ireland (*KL*, para.2.6), including locations of backup datacentres (*KL*, para.3.4.2; *Office 365*, paras.2, 3.4.1.1). France: mentioning server location (p.16), although seemingly equating 'location' with country of establishment, for subproviders (p.13) (CNIL 2012: pp.9, 13, 15, 16, 17). Ireland: stating data location is 'a particular aspect of data security' (Data Protection Commissioner of Ireland 2012). Italy: Garante (2012: pp.22, 28) mentioning server location. Netherlands: reiterating *WP196*, para.3.5 (Autoriteit Persoonsgegevens (formerly CBP) 2012: p.9). Norway: *Moss*, p.8; *Narvik 2012b*, pp.1, 11, 10; Datatilsynet (2012). Slovenia: considering data location to be an aspect of security (Information Commissioner (Slovenia) 2012: pp.10, 14, 20). Spain: stating that locations of the provider and physical resources used are relevant (AEPD 2013: pp.9, 10, 15). Sweden: the Restriction applies if personal data 'comes to be processed by processors in a country outside the EU/EEA ...' (Datainspektionen 2011); Azure data, stored in Ireland/Holland, was stated never to be transferred to or accessible from third countries: not questioned by the DPA (*Brevo 2011*, p.5). UK: mentioning location of 'computing resources', countries 'where' data are likely to be processed, and

frequently based on a complete lack of any stable location of data within the cloud provider's network. Data can be in one data centre at 2pm and on the other side of the world at 4pm' (*WP196*, p.17),[47] and that therefore controllers rarely know their data's real-time locations. DPAs consider such knowledge necessary for compliance with DPD Laws, notably regarding security[48] and data subject rights.[49] I suggest these views are misguided, as Ch.4 will show, particularly where subproviders are involved. Knowing all relevant datacentre locations may indeed be necessary *if* the location of personal data outside the EEA must always

---

'when data will be transferred to these locations' (ICO 2012a: paras.82, 84), although para.85 also mentions subprocessors' 'locations'. See n.48.

[47] However, cloud data do not continuously fly around the globe. While large volumes of data can indeed be transmitted quickly (Laoutaris et al. 2009), most often data or operations are *replicated or synchronized* to multiple locations in real time or near-real time (p.276, n.37), rather than constantly whirling around.

[48] E.g. Denmark, Ireland, Slovenia (n.46). Spain: 'data location must be known to obtain accurate information on what happens to data' (AEPD 2013: p.10). Sweden: 'If a cloud provider without the user's knowledge can move data not only between different subcontractors but also between different countries, [it] will reduce the controller's ability to monitor and ensure that processors have really taken the actions they committed to' (*Enköpings*, p.9; *Salems 2011*, p.16; *Brevo 2011*, pp.8–9).

Norway's DPA considers that data location affects security:

> As the processor does not wish to release information concerning the countries in which their IT centres are located, this presents challenges with regard to the requirements in a processor agreement … The local authority will not be able to adequately clarify the level of security in the solution without knowing that the States to which information is transferred have an adequate level of protection for personal data … (*Narvik 2012a* (Norway), pp.5, 6).

I suggest that is the 'wrong way round' – knowledge of the country of location is unnecessary for adequate protection, so long as appropriate *security measures* are implemented by the controller and/or processor to provide adequate protection whatever the data's location – p.139, n.21; p.274, n.35; 7.1.2, 7.4.2.5, 7.5.1.1.

[49] *Salems 2013* (Sweden), para.3.3:

> For the controller to be able to ensure that data subjects can exercise their rights, the [controller] [must have] knowledge of the subcontractors who process their personal data and where such suppliers are located … The list of suppliers provided by the cloud service provider is inadequate in that it does not specify where each company is located. The list does not constitute a sufficient guarantee that the person responsible at all times shall have knowledge of where personal data are processed.

This echoes CNIL and CoE (4.5.1); cf. 4.5.1, 4.5.1.2, 7.4.2.5.

involve 'transfer'. However, I argue that it makes little sense to consider personal data location without also considering the extent to which third countries have effective jurisdiction over a (sub)provider with intelligible access, without which such jurisdiction is irrelevant. The location of personal data in a third country does not necessarily afford that country effective jurisdiction over *intelligible* personal data, although DPAs seemingly assume that it does.

DPAs' insistence on SCCs 'with' 'datacentres' also highlights their assumption that datacentre providers must necessarily have intelligible access to all personal data processed using their infrastructure. In *Odense* (Denmark), the same provider group owned and used the datacentres concerned. However, with many cloud services, indeed Internet services such as webhosting, providers may not own the datacentres they use. They rent (use of) servers and/or space within datacentres owned/operated by third party datacentre providers or cloud subproviders. Datatilsynet's approach in *Odense* (Denmark) implies that, had the third country datacentres used by Google been owned by unrelated parties, SCCs would have been required from the *datacentre providers* also. That approach must assume that 'transfer' occurs to datacentre providers as 'subprocessors' (see p.97).[50] Indeed, there seems to be a general assumption that cloud providers and subproviders (including presumably datacentre providers) must always have intelligible access to data processed using their infrastructure,[51] ignoring the availability of technologies such as encryption (4.5.1.1). It may indicate DPAs' mistrust of encryption (not justified or elaborated, but anecdotally shared by many non-technologists), despite its being relied on routinely every day, e.g. to secure online payments. However, that oversimplistic approach fails to take proper account of modern technologies or commercial relationships.

---

[50] With layered services (1.2.2), are there 'transfers' to IaaS/PaaS subproviders, particularly if they are not EEA-established but the *infrastructure* they use is EEA-located?

[51] E.g., 'Due to the current limitations of encryption technologies, it is expected that the cloud provider will very often have full access to most personal data controlled by its customers' (SEC(2012)72 final, Ann.2, p.18). Many providers have intelligible access, not because encryption does not work (it guards against most risks if implemented properly – p.271; 7.2.3.1), but because, under current business practices, generally controllers do not *apply* encryption properly and/or often enough, or because some cloud uses require operations to be conducted on unencrypted data (7.2.3.3).

3.7.2   Cloud Supply Chain, Intelligible Access and Jurisdiction

To dissect the assumed correspondence between location, access and physical control/ownership, consider an office building. Its owner may lease out space, reserving rights to enter lessees' areas in emergencies. That does not mean it can access personal data stored in lessees' filing cabinets, locked or unlocked, or that lessees can access personal data stored on other lessees' floors. Nor need the owner assume any obligations to controllers who entrust personal data to lessees to store or analyse for them.

Similarly, datacentre providers may rent out space: racks, cages, rooms, floors. Renters contract with datacentre providers for the supply of power, heating, cooling as well as space. Renters can and do physically secure their spaces against datacentre providers and others, e.g. with biometric locks. They may encrypt data stored on the servers they use (self-owned or rented from third parties), to protect their data from intelligible access by unauthorized persons. They may encrypt communication channels to/from such datacentres.[52] Accordingly, datacentre providers do *not* necessarily have intelligible access to their customers' data. Such access is restricted, physically/technically and/or contractually. Therefore, when personal data are processed using cloud, it cannot be assumed that every subcontractor of a provider always has intelligible access.[53] Even *providers* may lack intelligible access, where controllers have strongly encrypted their data (pp.138, 286; 7.2.3.1) before upload to the cloud (analogy: deliver only a safe containing files for storage, without the key).

The building analogy highlights related but separate issues: control over intelligible access, and responsibility for compliance with Principles regarding personal data. Responsibility should be based on control. Under the Restriction's anticircumvention objective, I submit that the key issue is whether EEA controllers (who remain subject to EEA jurisdiction) can be enforceably required to, and can, comply with the Principles, despite the risks associated with data location. If so, e.g. because their processors who use third country datacentres are subject to SCCs or the Shield (5.3.4.2), the Restriction's objective can be satisfied without necessarily requiring contracts 'with' any datacentre providers also. I argue that it is inappropriate and unfair to impose data protection obligations or liability (effectively, regardless of knowledge) on those

---

[52]   Ch.7 discusses encryption further.
[53]   E.g. AWS – p.177.

who do not control intelligible access and are only intermediaries –
except explicitly, for good policy reasons, after proper, evidence-based
consideration of the implications (Hon, Kosta, et al. 2014: p.19). For
example, for public safety reasons, Directive 85/374/EEC imposes strict
liability for defective products regardless of fault. However, it is unrealistic to impose data protection obligations on every organization in a
processing service's supply chain, when controllers remain subject to
EEA jurisdiction including DPD Laws.

Controllers are legally responsible for the Principles-compliant processing of their personal data, even when using processors. Controllers
cannot circumvent any Principles, including Art.17's requirements
regarding use of processors, simply by using non-EEA processors (1.5.2;
p.18). However, Member State implementations and DPA interpretations
of the Restriction and Mechanisms (Ch.5) result in tighter restrictions
when processing personal data using non-EEA infrastructure. These
tighter restrictions apply regardless of whether non-EEA persons have
legal or technical means to gain or control intelligible access, even
though EEA controllers remain subject to EEA jurisdiction and liable to
data subjects under DPD Laws irrespective of infrastructure location, and
processors remain liable to controllers under their processor agreements.

DPAs' focus on personal data location, rather than on which countries
have effective jurisdiction over controllers or providers, is misguided
partly because they assume that physical 'possession' necessarily affords
access (and control over access) to data.[54] This assumption is undermined
by the availability of remote access and technical, contractual and/or
commercial constraints on access by datacentre providers and other
subcontractors. Physical access/control is but one element among others,
and may or may not afford intelligible access. *Logical* control of data
through systems and software, including through remote access to cloud
data and the use of encryption, is more important in practice – but is
given insufficient weight, or disregarded entirely.

Thus, third country support staff/subcontractors could remotely access
EEA-located personal data, which practitioners generally treat as 'transfer'.[55] 'Making available' is also relevant (3.5, 3.6.3, 3.8). Furthermore,

---

[54]   4.5.1.1: discusses to what extent physical access to hardware may afford
intelligible access.

[55]   Therefore recommending e.g. SCCs as precautionary best practice in such
situations. Unlike with persistent storage, DPAs seem more persuadable regarding remote support, where interception risks are lower (Hon and Millard 2016:
para.9.1.3), underlining the relevance of considering 'duration' – unfortunately
impossible post-GDPR (p.106).

EEA individuals travelling in third countries could remotely access their organizations' EEA-located data, thereby making 'transfers' under the location-centric approach; yet no Mechanism allows this (within the same organization), except self-assessment of adequacy, based e.g. on security measures – which the GDPR will disallow (5.2.4). Taking laptops containing personal data out of the EEA is also 'transfer' (p.72). Surely, lawmakers and regulators cannot intend to prevent EEA organizations' employees from working during trips outside the EEA and whitelisted countries, or to turn EEA organizations into lawbreakers (with large fines – 6.4.3.4) if they allow such trips. Border checks for personal data in laptops, tablets, mobiles, etc. to be 'exported' from the EEA by business travellers are impracticable as well as arguably unlawful. However, that is the consequence of a data location-centric approach once self-assessment becomes impossible, and a rule that many organizations cannot help but break can only engender disrespect for laws. The GDPR is retrograde in prohibiting self-assessment of adequacy based on technical protections. This example shows the illogicality of location-centricity. Codes/certifications are possible under the GDPR (5.4.5), but fining organizations for allowing business travel without obtaining such codes/certifications again makes no sense.

I submit that if personal data in cloud computing can be adequately secured through technological measures taken by the controller and/or provider (e.g. by the controller applying strong encryption (7.2.3.3.5) before upload, implementing backups elsewhere, and using secure communication channels), then data location should be of less concern, whatever the content of the third country's laws – and without requiring contracts with datacentre providers etc. too. Ch.7 discusses this further. Next, I consider other problems arising from a data location-centric approach to 'transfer'.

3.7.3   Many Possible Data 'Locations'

Many DPAs seemingly only consider the locations of persistent storage for data. Other possible locations are ignored or overlooked, particularly locations where data are operated upon. But if one data location is relevant, then surely *all* possible data 'locations' must be relevant. Yet it would be complicated, impracticable, even impossible to apply the Restriction (and Mechanisms) to all such locations.

Digital data are represented by patterns of bits, 0s or 1s, whose representations[56] are recordable in hardware, and transmissible over cables, by satellite, etc. Digital data may be moved (strictly, copied) far more readily than physical objects, so tying jurisdiction to digital data location seems misconceived – as lawmakers realized during the DPD's legislative passage (2.3.2). Digital data's 'location' seems as metaphysical as intangible information's 'location'. The best that can be said is that digital personal data are 'located' in whatever *hardware* stores or transmits the relevant patterns – including cables transmitting personal data, and, in IaaS, hardware where 'virtual machines' (VMs)[57] run to operate on data (which I term 'working personal data'[58]). Multiple locations are possible: not just of permanent, persistent storage ('stored personal data'), but also backups (duplicates of data stored within other hardware in the same or, often, a different datacentre[59]), and temporary storage in caches or content delivery networks (CDNs) located closer to customers to improve performance ('cached personal data').

3.7.3.1 Stored personal data

On DPAs' interpretation, clearly personal data are 'transferred' to a third country if stored in persistent storage within infrastructure located in that country, as already discussed, including third country locations to which personal data are copied for backup purposes (7.2.2.2), e.g. *Office 365* (Denmark), para.2.

---

[56] In any way that clearly distinguishes two separate states/values, e.g. off/on, north/south, low/high voltage, transition from low to high/high to low voltage, transition from pit to flat/flat to pit surface, direction that a DNA section points, etc.

[57] In IaaS, multiple VMs, each with its separate operating system, applications, etc., may be 'instantiated' within one physical machine, sharing its resources, which improves efficiency and deployment speed. VM 'images' or snapshots may be saved, stored and transmitted, enabling quick deployment and 'migration' to other servers, even in different locations. Cloud technology continues evolving, e.g. the emergence of Docker containers, more lightweight than VMs and sharing the operating system not just hardware (Merkel 2014; Bernstein 2014).

[58] Not a term of art, defined for convenience.

[59] Implemented for business continuity, to protect availability and integrity – p.2, n.6; 7.2.2.2.

3.7.3.2 Cached personal data

If stored data locations are important, then CDN locations would be relevant too. For example, end-users were concerned that file-sharing service The Pirate Bay's temporary use of US-incorporated CDN service CloudFlare would allow US authorities to 'spy on' them (Ernesto 2015). Here, I suggest that it is effective US jurisdiction over CloudFlare, rather than its globally distributed CDN locations, that might facilitate US 'spying'.

Caching duration is also relevant. In *Narvik 2012a* (Norway, p.11), regarding Google Apps, Norway's DPA held that caching during Internet transmissions did not involve 'transfer' because 'data will be buffered along the way in the transport network'; it could not be ruled out that 'data will be stored temporarily (cached) [treated as temporary storage or buffering] during transfer in Google's data centres outside the EU/EEA or the USA or by other ISPs [Internet service providers] depending on how the traffic is routed in the network'. Under Norway's DPD Laws, 'information sent electronically to an addressee in Norway [but] actually transported via another country' is not necessarily 'transfer', i.e., may involve only 'transit' (3.3). Similarly with information 'stored temporarily abroad without the controller being aware of this in advance'. So, if the controller was aware that information could be stored in third countries, even temporarily, would that make it a 'transfer'? A US provider Shield subscriber could use CDNs to cache personal data (e.g. videos) in locations outside both the EEA and the US. Must controllers check all possible CDN server locations? Are they better off *not* knowing that their provider uses CDNs? Should cached data always be considered to be 'in transit'? In assessing adequacy of protection, the proposed operation's 'duration' is one factor (Art.25(2) DPD), so perhaps operations using non-EEA infrastructure may be considered adequately protected if they are sufficiently transient.

Unfortunately, the GDPR does not provide for transit (3.3) or allow consideration of processing duration when assessing adequacy of protection (Art.45), so the physical locations of caches, however temporary, must seemingly be taken into account for 'transfer' purposes under GDPR's Restriction. In practice the Restriction may well be ignored in this context for reasons of impossibility. It is unsatisfactory to have a law that is likely to be breached on a large scale, and regrettable that the GDPR failed to cater for either transit or temporary caching.

3.7.3.3 Working personal data

Cloud systems may automatically 'instantiate' (n.57) VMs in locations with spare capacity[60] or better energy-efficiency (p.2, n.7). Working personal data would probably be 'transferred' if personal data are stored in the EEA but VMs or other servers operating on personal data (to which relevant personal data must be copied first) are in third countries. Virtualization software provider VMWare now allows 'live' VMs to be migrated between datacentres 'as far as 3,000 miles apart' without interrupting workloads (Babcock 2015). However, as with cached data, perhaps adequate protection is currently possible when operations on working data are only transient.

3.7.3.4 Metadata

Metadata, data about data, may relate to or be produced during operations on cloud data, such as indexes of data automatically produced by a provider's service to enable customers to search, e.g., their webmail, contacts or documents. Some metadata may include personal data, e.g. individual customers' account information, or usage/access logs (*WP196*, p.12). Similarly, indexes may contain personal data.[61] On a location-centric approach, storing metadata containing personal data in third country infrastructure would involve 'transfer'. Providers are increasingly providing information about where specific metadata could be stored, e.g. Microsoft[62] and AWS.[63]

---

[60] To operate on data, data must be copied from persistent storage to the server(s) that will perform the operations. Locating such servers near the data's permanent storage location is more efficient, in IaaS by 'instantiating' VMs in the same datacentre. Theoretically, such servers could be in different locations from that of permanently stored data – but data must be copied to the servers' locations, or VMs 'brought' to the persistent storage locations (p.50, n.42).

[61] So Norway's DPA stated in *Narvik 2012b* (Norway), p.11, noting that personal data could be 'processed' even if indexes contained only fragments 'structured in a logical manner that is only recognizable for machine reading'. However, interestingly, it *assumed* that Google Apps' indexing did not entail personal data processing, noting that it was the customer's responsibility to ensure that was the case. This could be difficult as emails etc. often include personal data, so indexes of them may contain personal data.

[62] E.g. Microsoft n.d.

[63] AWS's terms as at October 2016, Section 3.3, make clear that, to provide billing and administration services, it may process account usage data (e.g. resource identifiers, metadata tags, security and access roles, permissions and usage policies, statistics and analytics) in both the customer's selected AWS region(s) and AWS's US regions (AWS 2016).

3.7.3.5 Regions

Given DPAs' focus on personal data location and EEA customers' pressure for EEA data localization,[64] providers are increasingly building or using EEA-located datacentres in order to offer regional clouds, enabling customers to choose 'regions' for their data processing (p.6, n.18). Providers hope thereby to gain business from EEA customers,[65] particularly public sector organizations who (as with DPAs) often wish their data to be processed using only infrastructure located in their country.[66] Thus, AWS opened a Frankfurt datacentre for German customers (AWS 2014b). Providers are also offering more visibility regarding their datacentres; e.g. Google initially refused to provide customers with datacentre information for security reasons (*Narvik 2012a* (Norway), p.6), but in late 2012 it introduced virtual tours (Hölzle 2012) and a map (Google 2012).

Data location may depend on service type as well as customers' choices because, for certain services to function globally, operationally providers may need to store certain data across multiple datacentres, including outside the EEA. Thus, customers can select regions for persistent storage or 'compute' when using certain services, typically IaaS or PaaS; however, to preserve scalability and availability, not many SaaS providers allow customers to choose regions (Hon 2016d). Even with IaaS/PaaS, customers cannot select regions for services designed to operate globally (p.108), or choose locations for metadata, caches, etc. (Microsoft n.d.). Google as yet provides no information on metadata or other locations. In *KL*, involving Microsoft Azure, Danish DPA Datatilsynet noted that, even if the customer (KL) chose to use Microsoft's

---

[64] Perhaps *trust* matters as much as compliance – EEA customers may simply feel more comfortable using EEA 'regions'. Thus, 86 percent of a survey's respondents considered it important to ensure that their business-critical data 'is stored with a UK-based cloud service provider', which might mean establishment – or datacentre location (Venkatraman 2014).

[65] Although some providers use EEA datacentres for latency, not regulatory, reasons, i.e. better customer service, because using datacentres physically closer to customers improves response speeds and performance for customers. This motivated PaaS provider Heroku's introduction of a 'Europe' region (Meyer 2013).

[66] AWS's cloud services for US government use US-only datacentres and vetted US personnel (Barr 2013). However, UK government policy notes that location even in 'geopolitically appropriate' countries does not guarantee security, while 'technical security controls around a service may mean that the solution is appropriate despite hosting data in countries not recognised as generally acceptable' (Cabinet Office 2015).

Irish datacentre, Azure's operation might necessitate availability or transfer of specific data to the US to some extent. While *KL* itself contained few details, Microsoft's website indicates that, for certain services, software deployment packages are backed up to the US, while European users' Azure Active Directory data is stored 'in Europe and the United States' (Microsoft n.d.). Providers who offer regions may not clarify whether all relevant customer data are kept in the customer-chosen region, e.g. backups, caches, metadata. For instance, customers may select 'regions' for storing 'objects' in AWS S3 'buckets', but it is unclear where associated metadata are located. Similarly, AWS's EC2 virtual servers may be instantiated in customer-chosen regions, but hardware used for persistent storage, caches, etc. could be located elsewhere.

The *Microsoft warrant case* illustrates the many possible locations involved for cloud email, including metadata. As described in that case, when a customer registers for an email account, partly for latency reasons (p.108, n.65) Microsoft migrates account data to the datacentre *geographically closest* to the customer based on the customer's entered country code, deleting from its US servers all content and most 'non-content information' associated with the account (metadata such as sender address, recipient address, transmission date/time). Nevertheless, some data are retained in the US: certain non-content information (in a US-located data warehouse) for testing and quality control; some 'address book' information (in a central 'address book clearing house'); and basic non-content account information, including customers' names and countries (in a US-located database).

Because many non-EEA locations are possible beyond locations of persistent storage, and some providers do not offer a choice of regions even for stored personal data, many providers are offering SCCs (p.200).

3.7.3.6 All locations?

Taking DPAs' interpretation to its logical conclusion, to know whether the Restriction applies and how to comply, customers would need to know every possible location where their personal data could be processed, including indexes, CDNs/caches and working data locations – which is not easy with possibly multiple, changeable, locations. Location-centricity favours large providers, who are better placed to control infrastructure locations and subproviders as tightly as DPAs require (e.g. 5.4.2.9), but this consequence may be unintended and the implications for competition, innovation and consumer protection seem not to have been fully considered.

3.7.4   Contractual Commitments Regarding Location?

'Regions' provide no guarantees. Not all providers will contractually commit to confine customers' data to their chosen regions, even stored personal data. Any such commitments will be qualified, e.g. AWS's terms as at October 2016: 'We will not (a) disclose Your Content to any government or third party or (b) subject to Section 3.3, move Your Content from the AWS regions selected by you; except in each case as necessary to comply with the law or a binding order of a governmental body' (AWS 2016). Accordingly, AWS's terms entitle it to move customers' data outside their selected regions, including to the US, if required by law or governmental order – supporting my point about effective jurisdiction trumping personal data location. In specifically mentioning non-disclosure (no doubt to address customer concerns regarding governmental requests) and explaining in Section 3.3 (n.63) that metadata may be processed in the US, these terms seek to be more nuanced and transparent than a previous version, which simply provided (AWS 2015: para.3.2): 'We will not move Your Content from your selected AWS regions without notifying you, unless required to comply with the law or requests of governmental entities.'

From providers' viewpoint, such qualifications are needed for their own protection, so they can avoid breaching their customer contracts should they be legally compelled to disclose customer data to third country authorities. However, reserving rights to disclose data merely on 'request' (cf. legal compulsion) is less likely to be considered reasonable by customers or DPAs. Indeed, given increased concerns following Snowden's revelations (e.g. Taieb and Cohen 2013), which drove GDPR's Art.48 (p.119), providers (or controllers) who are subject to conflicting legal obligations may be placed in an impossible position (pp.116, 314; 7.5.3) if they receive court orders in third countries with effective jurisdiction over them, but with whom there is no applicable treaty, or where an MLAT exists but the third country authority insists on compliance with the order because the MLAT procedure is considered too slow (as in the *Microsoft warrant case* – p.93).

3.7.5   Locations Outside Any Country's Jurisdiction

A location-centric approach to the Restriction also fails to address servers on floating datacentres[67] moored in international waters, drones in international airspace[68] or satellites in outer space. If data location is the main determinant, such servers are not 'in' third countries. Therefore, transfers 'to' them would escape the Restriction.

In the *Microsoft warrant case*, the magistrate judge specifically noted reports of Google exploring offshore server farms in international waters, 'beyond the territorial jurisdiction of any nation'. If US authorities could access data in a non-US country only under an MLAT with that country, data in offshore servers would be unavailable to them even if a *US* person controlled those servers. On that basis (and others), he upheld the search warrant, noting that focusing on data's location in Ireland rather than the provider's control over access could permit circumvention of US law (contrast the DPD's assumption that requiring personal data location in the EEA is necessary to prevent circumvention of EEA law). This was one argument made by the US Department of Justice, in seeking review of the appeals court decision reversing the lower courts (p.93). The failed ICPA sought to address this problem by focusing on the targeted person, rather than the data's location (p.94).

3.7.6   Possible Service Layers: Subproviders

Many cloud services are 'layered'. SaaS services may be built on IaaS/PaaS, or PaaS on IaaS (1.2.2). In such situations, the *provider* may have a choice of regions. However, again its subprovider may have backups, caches, metadata, etc. in other locations, not necessarily known to the provider – subproviders may not offer location transparency to their customers, let alone their customers' end-users. So even providers may lack knowledge and/or control over the locations of infrastructure used for their services (p.134), particularly small/medium sized enterprise (SME) providers who lack negotiating power against large IaaS/PaaS subproviders.

---

[67] Patented by Google employees (Clidaras et al. 2009). Proposals for floating cities include Seasteading – http://www.seasteading.org/.

[68] Authorities wishing to intercept satellite signals could position drones *above* airspace regulated by EEA or other countries.

3.7.7   Data Localization – Disadvantages[69]

Data localization also carries many disadvantages for countries and their residents, as this section summarizes.

3.7.7.1   Costs

Location-independence is one of the benefits of Internet and cloud (1.2). Customers need not be concerned about data location, and increasingly consider it irrelevant,[70] except to the extent laws such as the Restriction require them to be concerned. Data location requirements were recognized as posing 'a barrier to a single market for cloud computing and big data' (COM(2014)442 final, p.12), limiting economies of scale (Commission 2015c: p.1) and competitive choice (SWD(2015)100, p.61).

Forced data localization, under the Restriction or otherwise, raises costs by making organizations 'build expensive local infrastructures (datacentres) in each region or country' (COM(2015)192 final, p.14) (p.6, nn.17, 18; p.108). Conversely, increased scale and preventing 'unnecessary duplication of infrastructure' also carry energy-efficiency and environmental benefits (Commission 2016e).

Recognizing the benefits of free data flow, the Commission proposes to tackle restrictions on free movement of data within the EU 'for reasons other than' data protection (COM(2015)192 final, p.15); a Communication is expected in 2016 (Commission 2016e). Arguably data protection should not be excluded, from a logical perspective, but the DPD and GDPR already emphasize the free flow of personal data within the EU.

3.7.7.2   Resilience and business continuity

Data localization cannot guarantee to protect personal data against remote access by persons in third countries (3.7.9, 7.5.2.2). Yet it has a negative impact on availability, depriving users of the benefits of using geographically distributed datacentres (Dekker and Liveri 2015: p.6) to back up data or replicate operations for improved resilience and 'redundancy' – i.e. preserving availability and integrity[71] against natural or

---

[69]   Studies on data localization's disadvantages, not necessarily in cloud or data protection, include Bauer et al. 2014.

[70]   In one cloud study, participants who wanted control over their data valued control over 'who will be able to see your data' (52.9 percent), i.e. control of intelligible access, over 'where your data is stored and the laws that apply' (23.5 percent) (Angulo et al. 2013: p.41).

[71]   On availability (Hon et al. 2016) and integrity, see 7.1.2.

other disasters affecting one geographical region,[72] even against seizures by one country's authorities (7.5.1.1). 'Geographic spread' in cloud facilitates resiliency, not just against natural disasters but also denial of service attacks, while offering customers performance improvements (Dekker and Liveri 2015). Even EU financial services regulators consider business continuity an important incentive for financial services institutions to adopt cloud (Naydenov et al. 2015: p.20). Indeed, Estonia backs up its data to geographically dispersed embassies, datacentres, even cloud (p.73, n.5), to protect against risks of Russian invasion or cyberattack (Reynolds 2016).

3.7.7.3 Global trade/business

All types of operations involve personal data, so data localization in the name of privacy may affect global trade and business, even for goods (Kommerskollegium 2015), or prevent organizations from offering global services e.g. banking (du Preez 2014). There is much material on the negative impact of data localization on trade, and therefore economies, e.g. ECIPE (2013); on one estimate, without a mechanism for EU–US transfers, Europe's gross domestic product (GDP) could reduce by up to 1.3 percent and EU services exports to the US could fall by 6.7 percent (AmCham EU 2016). Trade concerns indeed motivated the OECD Guidelines (2.2.3), and allowing free trade *within* the EU by promoting high harmonized standards of data protection was one of the DPD's objectives (1.5.1).

Illustrating the tension between free trade and privacy protection, proposals to limit data localization requirements have appeared in leaked drafts of the Trade in Services Agreement (TISA) – an international agreement to remove barriers to trade in services, being negotiated between countries including the USA and EU. In a leaked draft of TISA's annex on electronic commerce, the USA and others suggested prohibitions on requiring service suppliers to use or locate computing facilities in a party's territory as a condition for supplying a service, and on preventing suppliers from 'transferring, accessing, processing or storing information, including personal information', within or outside the party's territory where conducted in connection with the supplier's business; indeed, Switzerland proposed a provision banning parties from requiring

---

[72] E.g. lightning, floods, earthquakes, cable damage, etc. causing datacentre failures (Leviathan Security Group 2015b). In one survey, 50 percent of participating companies had suffered datacentre disruptions from natural disasters in the last decade, averaging one every other year (Zenium 2015).

'suppliers of electronic commerce' to use or establish any local infra-structure as a condition for the supply of services (Anon 2015). It is unknown to what extent TISA will, like the World Trade Organization's General Agreement on Trade in Services 1994 (GATS),[73] allow excep-tions to protect personal data; in the leaked draft, some countries want to allow parties to require use of local infrastructure to achieve a 'legitimate public objective' if not for 'arbitrary or unjustifiable discrimination' or as disguised trade restrictions. More recently, 'a clause guaranteeing inter-national data flows' may be included in TISA but without affecting EU data protection laws (Stupp 2016); further analysis is impossible without TISA's full text.

There are concerns regarding TISA's privacy impact (Woollacott 2015). Other free trade initiatives are criticized for privacy risks, e.g. the proposed EU–Canada free trade agreement (CETA), for mass surveil-lance in Canada without sufficient accountability (Vrijschrift Foundation 2016). Some fear that the proposed Transatlantic Trade and Investment Partnership (TTIP) could be used to weaken privacy rights and allow personal data flows outside the EEA (BEUC 2015) – leading to, e.g., Commission assurances in Parliament against 'any rule in TTIP or TISA' that could compromise EU data protection laws (Commission 2015a).

However, free trade agreements' provisions against data localization may seek to prevent 'data protectionism' rather than erode privacy (Ezell 2015); trade negotiations could equally be used to improve privacy protections in other countries. The Commission seemingly takes a 'have cake and eat it' approach to trade and data protection, emphasizing that EU data protection rules are non-negotiable in trade agreements while stating that its (one-way) adequacy decisions 'can ease' trade negotiations and reduce risks of *third countries* invoking data protection to 'impose unjustified data localisation' requirements, and that it will use trade agreements to 'tackle new forms of digital protectionism' (COM(2017)7 final, pp.8–9).

---

[73] While not targeting data flows or data protection, GATS allows members exceptionally to adopt measures 'necessary to secure compliance with laws or regulations which are not inconsistent with' GATS – including measures to protect individuals' privacy regarding 'the processing and dissemination of personal data', and confidentiality of 'individual records and accounts' – pro-vided such measures are not 'a means of arbitrary or unjustifiable discrimination between countries where like conditions prevail, or a disguised restriction on trade in services' (GATS, Art.XIV(c)(ii)). Measures must not be more trade-restrictive than necessary to fulfil such objectives (WTO 1999: para.14).

Privacy should not be sacrificed on the altar of free trade; but equally, privacy should not trump free trade (or freedom of expression). A balance should be struck in the relevant context, rather than absolutism one way or another. Trade issues are not analysed further as I am not arguing that free trade should override privacy, or vice versa. Rather, I aim to show that data localization is not the only or even the best way to ensure privacy protection, yet (as in the trade arena) it carries many disadvantages. The twofold objective should be to facilitate free trade and access to information globally while protecting privacy. Arguably, data localization cannot achieve either: EEA location does not guarantee privacy protection, while data may flow outside the EEA without compromising privacy. In working towards this twofold objective, the distinction between data/infrastructure location and law/jurisdiction is critical; location in 'safe' countries should not be conflated with effective protection of data or privacy.

3.7.8 Location Knowledge and Verification

While ignorance of the law is no excuse, some organizations, particularly SMEs, do not even realize that using cloud services may involve transferring personal data, let alone know the data's location. Seventeen percent of companies asked by a German DPA were unaware that, by using cloud services like Google Analytics, Microsoft's Office 365 or Facebook for data like names, addresses and telephone numbers, they may effect US transfers that engage data protection obligations; they claimed not to make US transfers despite using cloud (Rheinland-Pfälzische Landesdatenschutzbeauftragte 2015b). Shadow cloud (1.2.1) compounds this problem.

Another difficulty with location-centricity is: how can customers verify providers' claimed data locations? Providers' mechanisms for achieving regional clouds differ. For commercial secrecy and security reasons, providers may not wish others to scrutinize the source code of any software they use to determine/control data location (let alone code for general 'processing'), even under non-disclosure agreements – although there is precedent for independent certifications of, e.g., hardware or service security.[74]

Some providers allow customers to check their data's location, e.g. via a webpage.[75] Nevertheless, customers must still trust the accuracy of

---

[74] Which may include code review – p.281, n.470; p.286, n.62. See also 5.4.5.

[75] E.g. Salesforce (Hon, Millard and Walden 2013a: p.87).

providers' webpages or other information given. Laws or national policies restricting data location have triggered much research on data location verification and/or location constraint mechanisms.[76] However, for costs, technical integration and efficiency reasons, providers may not rush to implement them. Generally, many providers' systems do not log audit trails of all data locations, which has performance and costs implications particularly if each fragment is logged separately. I query how knowing all locations at all times of all data fragments (including any copies) helps to protect data confidentiality, integrity or availability,[77] as opposed to just 'proving' tick-box compliance with (DPAs' interpretation of) the Restriction. Again, I suggest that the real underlying concern is jurisdiction over *control* of data processing, which may, and should be, addressed in ways other than constraining data location (see Ch.7).

3.7.9 Physical Location vs Jurisdiction and Access

Further illustrating location-centricity's problems, consider third country-established providers who use EEA datacentres. Personal data transmission to such providers might constitute 'transfer', under *Lindqvist* (3.6.3.1), but seemingly not under DPAs' approach (3.7.1). This reasoning must underlie non-EEA providers' decisions to offer regional EEA clouds (p.7, n.18; p.108; 3.7.7).

Yet EEA location alone cannot protect personal data; EU data localization 'does not solve the problem of foreign governments extending extraterritorial reach into EU data centres' (BBA 2016). Third countries may access EEA-located data with EEA authorities' cooperation under MLATs, or directly under certain international agreements,[78] or even through hacking (4.5.1.2). Where a provider (or indeed a controller) is effectively subject to third country jurisdiction, it may face third country court orders or other legal compulsion to retrieve and disclose data to which it has access, *wherever* located. Legally, it must comply, even if it thereby becomes a 'controller'.[79] Where providers have intelligible

---

[76] E.g. Bartock et al. (2015). See also Hon et al. (2016), Hon, Millard, et al. (2014), Smart, Rijmen, Stam, et al. (2014: pp.21–2). On information flow control techniques, see Singh et al. (2014: para.7.2).

[77] On confidentiality, integrity and availability, see 7.1.2.

[78] E.g. the Cybercrime Convention 2001 (Walden 2013) – although cloud raises new challenges (CoE 2015; CoE 2016a).

[79] As with SWIFT (*WP128*, p.11; cf. Belgium's DPA – p.90). The ICO indicated it would not necessarily take enforcement action (ICO 2012b):

access, unauthorized disclosure of personal data to third country persons may result. Complying with one country's laws may involve breaching another's, because their requirements conflict. Microsoft (Whittaker 2011) and Google (Constantin 2011) had previously acknowledged that they might have to provide EEA-located data to US authorities if required under the US PATRIOT Act[80] (and see Van Hoboken et al. (2012)), although data was more likely to be sought from controllers under that Act (Determann 2013: p.18). The *Microsoft warrant case* (3.7.1.4) illustrates the ongoing battle on this front.

Furthermore, EEA location alone will not protect data's confidentiality, integrity or availability (7.1.2). Implementing adequate technical and organizational security measures is more important in that regard. However, controllers' and/or providers' security measures, logical or physical (Ch.7), depend on their actions and inactions, not on data location (p.139, n.21; p.274, n.35; 7.4.2.5, 7.5.1.1.).

3.8 THE WAY FORWARD?

Many argue that 'transfer' should be defined, to resolve current uncertainties, and/or that 'transit' through third countries should be defined and addressed specifically.[81] The UK's Data Protection *Bill* originally defined 'transfer' (inexplicably omitted when it was passed) (Malcolm 2012: p.327):

Regulatory action against the client [*cloud customer*] is unnecessary because the client has not acted wrongly simply because it has chosen a provider which is subject to foreign law enforcement agency requests. Regulatory action against a provider, in its role as a data controller, is unlikely because it is responding to a request it is legally obliged to comply with. However if the request comes from a country which has questionable rule of law – then we would have to consider the issue on the facts of the matter.

However, those statements pre-dated the ICO's cloud guidance (ICO 2012a) and Snowden's revelations (resulting in possible questions regarding whether the US has 'questionable rule of law'!). See also p.97, n.43; 7.5.3.

[80] Since expired in part, but renewed under the USA Freedom Act 2015, which terminated or restricts certain bulk collection and introduced more transparency.

[81] E.g. submissions to the Commission's 2009 consultation on data protection laws (Rackspace 2009: p.2; Copyright Task Force 2011: p.5; Konarski et al. 2012: sec.4.5; EESC 2012: para.4.6.2).

A person who:

a)   discloses data to a person a country or territory; or
b)   otherwise makes the information contained in the data available to a
     person in a country or territory,

is taken to transfer the data to that country or territory.

Switzerland's Federal Act on Data Protection 1992, Art.6 refers to cross-border 'disclosure', not 'transfer'. Australian Privacy Principle 8 (under Australia's updated Privacy Act 1988) refers to 'disclose' (formerly 'transfer'), and to persons not 'in Australia'. Germany's Federal Data Protection Act, sec.3(4)(3) also defines 'transfer' (in the 'transmission' rather than 'export' sense) as 'disclosure of personal data recorded or obtained by data processing to a third party either (a) through transfer of the data to a third party, or (b) by the third party inspecting or retrieving data available for inspection or retrieval'. Other references to 'communication' and/or 'disclosure' were discussed previously (3.2). Similarly, regarding DPD reform proposals and 'transfer' (EDPS 2012a: para.109):

> The fact that it is aimed at communicating data to identified recipients (rather than making data openly available), could be taken into account, as it justifies the assessment of the level of protection guaranteed by the (country of the) recipient, as well as possible measures to be taken in order to ensure the protection of the data. Other elements to take into consideration are whether the data has been made freely available with the aim of giving access to it and whether the transfer is likely to have actually reached one or more recipients abroad.

Again, 'transfer' would normally imply 'communication, disclosure or otherwise making available of personal data, conducted with the knowledge or intention of a sender subject to the [CIDPR] that the recipient(s) will have access to it' (EDPS 2014b: p.7). This view is close to the UK and College bescherming persoonsgegevens (CBP; Netherlands' then DPA) interpretations (3.6.2), particularly regarding intention to give access, and the likelihood of reaching third country recipients. Retreating from previous EDPS views regarding the Restriction's inapplicability to public websites (p.83), the EDPS now refers to a deliberate intention or objective to make information available, including to the public in third countries (EDPS 2014b: p.6).

Jan-Philippe Albrecht was the rapporteur for Parliament's lead committee on the GDPR (the Civil Liberties, Justice and Home Affairs Committee (LIBE)). His draft report (PE 501.927v04-00), amendment 86, new

Art.4(3a), defined 'transfer' as 'any communication of personal data, actively made available to a limited number of identified parties, with the knowledge or intention of the sender to give the recipient access to the personal data'. Unfortunately, that definition was omitted from the version of the GDPR submitted to and approved by Parliament in 2014 (A7-0402/2013), and the final adopted text of the GDPR. Illustrating the uncertainties, two Member States had queried whether 'transfer' in the cloud context or 'disclosure of personal data on the internet' constituted 'transfer' under the GDPR (Council 9788/15, fn.448). The GDPR does not define 'transfer', but maintains the reference to transfers 'to' third countries, which perpetuates and indeed seems to entrench the 'physical location' approach. Confusingly, its 'anti-FISA'[82] Art.48 ('Transfers or disclosures not authorised by Union law') denies recognition or enforcement of third country judgments or administrative decisions requiring 'transfer or disclosure' of personal data, unless based on an MLAT or other international agreement. This implies that, at least in that Article (and its related Rec.115) if not elsewhere in the GDPR, 'transfer' is intended to mean something *other* than 'disclosure'. Furthermore, the GDPR contains some explicit references to 'recipients'[83] 'in third countries' (p.63, n.62). The continued uncertainty is highly unsatisfactory.

Draft updates to Convention108 initially referred to 'disclosure' or 'making available' of data to a recipient who is not subject to the jurisdiction of a party, e.g. CoE (2012). Unfortunately, the latest draft only refers to 'transfer' (2.2.10), although the draft explanatory report states, 'A transborder data transfer occurs when personal data is disclosed or made available to a recipient subject to the jurisdiction of another State or international organisation' (CoE 2016b: para.99).

It is a major problem that, under the data location-centric interpretation, personal data could be transferred 'to' third countries (e.g. the transferor's own datacentre), and therefore caught by the Restriction's requirements, without being 'disclosed' to any 'recipient' there. It is accordingly very important for DPAs, and indeed laws, to be clear as to the distinction between 'transfer' and 'disclosure' or 'communication'. Even 'making available' is very broad, as unencrypted data stored on a provider's infrastructure could be said to be 'made available' to the provider, but it seems unlikely that the update will distinguish between this and 'making available' in the sense of uploading personal data to a

---

[82] The US Foreign Intelligence Surveillance Act, authorizing NSA surveillance of non-US persons outside US territory.

[83] Entities to which personal data are 'disclosed', whether 'third party or not' (Art.4(9) GDPR).

public website. Nevertheless, I argue that locating data in a third country, where persons there have no intelligible access (e.g. because of strong encryption), does not involve, and should not be treated as involving, any disclosure/communication, 'making available' or 'transfer' to them.

The influential sources cited above suggest key elements for a 'transfer', whether 'push' or 'pull':

1. *disclosure/communication or making available*: the recipient must be afforded *intelligible* access, otherwise data cannot be 'communicated' or 'disclosed' to it, i.e. it cannot understand the data; and similarly with 'making available';
2. *transferor*: the transferor must *intend* to disclose, or *know* that the recipient would have access (which must mean *intelligible* access); and
3. *recipient*: the recipient must be subject (or not subject) to the relevant jurisdiction.

However, further uncertainties arise. Are 'disclose' and 'making available' clear enough (Kuner 2013b: p.141)? Would 'transfer' occur only if the intention was to disclose to limited identified recipients in third countries? What about intention to disclose to potentially indefinite numbers of unknown third country recipients (such as when publishing personal data on public websites)? How can knowledge or intention be proved? When can it be inferred, e.g. knowledge that the recipient would (more likely than not) have intelligible access? Can 'recklessness' be inferred, e.g. from storing personal data in a weakly secured Internet-accessible database, and how strong must security measures be to prevent such inferences? Must knowledge be objective ('reasonable persons ought to have known'), or must it involve actual knowledge? Is the issue whether the recipient is, or is not, subject to certain jurisdictions, and how can multiple simultaneous jurisdictions be addressed and any conflicts resolved?

These difficulties suggest that focusing on compliance with Principles, without any Restriction, seems more practicable and sensible than retaining the Restriction, even in improved form with full definitions.[84] Here, it is instructive to examine the ICO's and initial EDPS approaches

---

[84] The concepts of disclosure/communication and availability/access, rather than data location, are *enablers* for compliance with Principles – see Ch.7.

to personal data published on websites where, because of their interpretations of 'transfer', such publication risked escaping the Restriction (3.6.1–3.6.2). If 'transfer' requires intention and actual access, what if no intention to transfer to a third country can be inferred, or no access from a third country can be proved? If neither uploading nor downloading constitutes 'transfer', for public websites, could EU institutions publish personal data freely on public sites? The solution that both adopted was to stress that, irrespective of whether the Restriction applies to websites, the Principles apply to website publication, and accordingly must be complied with, particularly fair processing (p.17). Thus (ICO 2010: para.1.3.4):

> in situations where there is no intention to transfer the data to a third country and no transfer is deemed to have taken place as the information has not been accessed in a third country (i.e. the eighth principle [Restriction] does not apply), data controllers will still need to ensure that the processing complies with all of the other principles. In particular, data controllers must consider the requirement in the first data protection principle that the processing must be fair which may be contravened by making the data so widely accessible.

Denmark's Datatilsynet apparently shared this view, as it allowed Internet disclosure of personal data when legally disclosable in another manner, so that the method used, i.e. Internet publication, 'has no specific importance' (Blume 2000: p.83). Blume (2000) considered that this approach, while sensible and pragmatic, 'in reality neglects the problem'. I submit that this approach does not neglect the problem – it solves it.

A similar approach was taken where a Swedish municipality stored, on free SaaS service Dropbox, documents (containing personal data) that were also published on its website after assessing requirements under confidentiality rules and Sweden's DPD Laws (*Enköpings*, p.7). Datainspektionen considered that any Dropbox security deficiencies should not reasonably give rise to significant privacy risks: the post-assessment website publication could be presumed lawful,[85] and the personal data were publicly available there, so a processor agreement with Dropbox would add no value. Thus, where the website publication was lawful under the Principles, Datainspektionen did not insist on compliance with the Restriction also, or even require a processor agreement. However, Datainspektionen required Enköpings to consider whether Sweden's DPD Laws permitted its employees to use Dropbox for processing personal data other than for the purpose of storing records lawfully posted on its

---

[85] Translation from Svantesson (2012: p.479).

website, after conducting risk assessments (including reviewing Dropbox's contract terms), and to develop clear instructions to employees on Dropbox use accordingly. Risks included whether Dropbox might process personal data for other purposes, or disclose personal data to third countries.[86]

If it is fair and lawful to publish personal data on a website (and other Principles are satisfied regarding the publication), it should not matter whether the hosting provider is EEA-established or not, and whether EEA or third country persons can or do access the personal data. If the website publication would not be fair and lawful, bearing in mind who may access the data (e.g. third country authorities), or would otherwise not comply with the Principles (e.g., with sensitive data, if explicit consent was not obtained), then it should not be published, regardless of the provider's or data's location. In such a situation and, I argue, other similar situations, the Restriction is unnecessary, and even diverts attention from the Principles.

These DPA interpretations and decisions support my argument that compliance with the Principles should be the key issue, not personal data location. That approach is both logical and practical, and furthermore consistent with the Restriction's professed objective: to prevent controllers from circumventing Principles through transfers. It would also make it unnecessary to consider difficult questions of knowledge or intention to 'transfer'. Thus, provided that the Principles can continue to be complied with, I suggest that the Restriction (however interpreted) should be irrelevant, indeed unnecessary. In short, I submit that the focus should be on meeting the Principles' requirements, not splitting hairs analysing whether any 'transfer' has occurred. Furthermore, that would, in my view rightly, mean that locations of servers, or indeed providers, could be ignored; their location should be immaterial so long as the controller can comply with the Principles in relation to any transferred personal data.

3.9 SUMMARY

As this chapter has shown, the meaning of 'transfer to a third country', undefined in the DPD, has been interpreted differently by WP29, national DPAs and others. 'Transit' for the purposes of the Restriction was also undefined, exacerbating the uncertainties. 'Transfer', particularly in cloud

---

[86] Assessing Dropbox's standard contract terms and drawing up procedures for using Dropbox, including deletion, was also emphasized in *Rudolf Steinerskolen* (Norway).

computing, is generally taken to mean the physical location of personal data in a third country, without considering to what extent anyone located there or otherwise subject to its jurisdiction has intelligible access to that data. I argue that data protection laws should regulate those with intelligible access, instead of conflating personal data location with intelligible access and jurisdiction/applicable law, and restricting personal data's 'location' in third countries on the assumption (mistaken, as Ch.4 will show) that such restrictions will prevent intelligible access by persons in third countries and prevent third countries from exercising jurisdiction over or applying their laws to such data.

I recommend, based on *Lindqvist* and business/technological realities, that the primary focus should be, not on country(ies) of personal data location, but rather on countries that have effective jurisdiction over those with intelligible access to personal data – which may, or may not, include cloud (sub)provider(s). In cloud DPA decisions or guidance to date, countries of data location and countries having effective jurisdiction over those with intelligible access to data have largely coincided, which may have confused the issue. DPA cloud opinions and decisions have focused primarily on countries of data location, which I suggest is the wrong issue. Basing regulation on data location is problematic, particularly if developments such as datacentres in international waters or outer space eventuate. I argue that data location is relevant only to the extent that location of a datacentre in a country may give that country jurisdiction over the provider and/or its customers and, nevertheless, use of a datacentre in country X does not necessarily give X *effective* jurisdiction over end-customers[87] or even provider(s) who use that datacentre, particularly third party datacentres (7.5.1.1). In short, cloud's complex supply chain may actually result in the country of datacentre location not having effective jurisdiction over those using (but not owning) that datacentre, if the service's supply chain and use are structured appropriately, as the availability of technologies like encryption means X may not always have intelligible access to personal data processed in datacentres located in X's territory, where neither the provider nor the datacentre provider has intelligible access, as Ch.7 will discuss.

DPAs' focus on infrastructure location has caused the Restriction to become a 'Frankenrule' (p.1, n.4), with an unnatural life of its own. As

---

[87]   Cf. Art.4(1)(c) DPD, applying the DPD to third country controllers using EEA 'equipment' including datacentres (p.47). There seems some recognition that such jurisdictional claims may be overbroad, difficult to enforce and even disincentivize non-EEA controllers from using EEA providers or datacentres – hence CNIL's action to counter such disincentives (p.96, n.37).

Ch.5 will show, many DPAs insist on compliance with the Restriction as a stand-alone rule for its own sake, requiring personal data location to be restricted to the EEA, or Mechanisms to be implemented, even if the Principles could otherwise be complied with (e.g. because the controller retains control over intelligible access to encrypted personal data).

Conversely, DPAs distrust the adequacy of Mechanisms promulgated to secure adequate protection or adequate safeguards for personal data exports, insisting on further measures under national DPD Laws. The location-centric interpretation of the Restriction is positively counter-productive, creating bureaucracy to no good purpose and obscuring its objective of ensuring compliance with Principles. Hence, most radically, I suggest that the Restriction should be abolished. Unfortunately, this seems very unlikely, partly because of political 'inertia' (Greenleaf 2011a: p.18): it would entail changing not only EU DPD Laws and the GDPR, but also Convention108 (2.2.4), its proposed update (2.2.10) and numerous non-EEA laws that followed the DPD in adopting data 'border controls' (2.2.8). However, I argue that, at the very least, 'transfer' should be defined or interpreted by reference to intention to disclose intelligible personal data, and 'transit' should be defined and excluded (3.3).

Having discussed problems with the 'transfer' concept, in Ch.4 I will unpack assumptions underlying the DPD and its precursors which explain (but cannot justify) many of these difficulties.

4. Assumptions

4.1 INTRODUCTION

Ch.3 discussed difficulties with applying the Restriction, given the uncertainties regarding the meaning of 'transfer', and suggested that implicit (sometimes, explicit) assumptions behind the Restriction and its precursors may underlie those difficulties and uncertainties. This chapter draws together and summarizes the main such assumptions, explaining why they no longer hold true and should not form the basis for regulation.

One major dual assumption is that when personal data are 'transferred' to a third country, so that they are 'located' there, the third country can, through its legislation, regulation and/or other action, affect the level of protection afforded to that personal data; and, conversely, that those located outside that country, including other countries' legislature/authorities, cannot, or at least will be less able to, affect such protection.

Underlying that assumption is a more basic dual assumption: that entities (individuals, organizations or governments) who are physically present where personal data are 'located' can:

- obtain access to the physical infrastructure processing the personal data, and
- thereby gain access to the data in order to use intelligible personal data for their own purposes, or to disclose data to others (such as authorities); modify, destroy or otherwise interfere with personal data; and control such access, use or modification by others, e.g. by preventing others' access.

Intelligible access to data is a prerequisite to unauthorized disclosure or misuse of that data. Indeed, surely the DPD's legislative aim (except for the Restriction, if its aim is truly different) is to protect the *information* contained in personal data against unauthorized disclosure or misuse. 'Disclosure' of unintelligible personal data is not true disclosure, as it does not reveal any meaningful information or enable any misuse of information. That is why the DPD and GDPR do not need to apply to anonymous data (1.4).

As discussed previously, I argue that focusing on personal data location, and consequent attempts to control personal data flows, diverts attention away from what should be the core issue that I believe requires consideration at a more fundamental and nuanced level: namely, effective jurisdiction over whoever controls access to personal data, particularly intelligible access, and accordingly effective jurisdiction over what they can do with or to the information contained in personal data. In short, I argue that the true underlying data protection concerns are intelligible access to personal data and any resulting disclosure or use of that data, along with data integrity (7.1.1).

Firstly, I discuss assumptions arising from 1970s outsourcing models regarding processor use, which have affected the application of DPD Laws generally to cloud and are unfortunately perpetuated by the GDPR. Then, I discuss assumptions underlying the Restriction that arose from 1970s mainframe models and which explain the focus on data location.

4.2 ASSUMPTIONS REGARDING PROCESSOR USE

DPD Art.17's provisions on processor use (1.5.2; p.18) assumed 1970s/ 1980s outsourcing models, whereby controllers delivered to their processors media containing personal data, such as magnetic tapes or punched cards, and the processors actively processed that data as instructed by their controllers. Often, under that model, controllers relinquished 'possession' and processors gained both exclusive possession of, and intelligible access to, the relevant personal data. Such outsourcing could involve a 'transfer' to processors, if they processed the data in third countries. In such cases, controllers had to 'go through' their processors to access their personal data, and relied on their processors to process the personal data as instructed.

However, cloud involves controllers' remote, *self-service* use of IT resources supplied by providers as a service. Customers retain direct remote access to their cloud data, without having to go through any providers: i.e., providers' access to customers' data is not exclusive. Some cloud providers may well have intelligible access to users' data, but others may not (7.2.3.2, 7.4.2.2). This means that Art.17 is problematic for cloud. With traditional outsourcing, it made sense to require processors to follow controllers' 'instructions' on processing personal data. Similarly, requiring processors to apply security measures made sense where processors had exclusive 'possession' of, and intelligible access to, personal data, because in such cases *only* processors (and not controllers) can secure and use the data. However, those requirements make little sense in cloud, particularly infrastructure cloud (1.2.3).

Thus, Art.17's 'instructions' requirement is difficult to apply in cloud (4.2).[1] Also, cloud security involves 'shared responsibility' between customer and provider (p.273). With classic outsourcing, processors need intelligible access to the data in order to provide their services. But cloud processors may not always have intelligible access, even though it is generally assumed that they do.[2] Art.17(3), regarding security measures required of processors, fails to consider that controllers may themselves encrypt personal data (retaining exclusive control of keys) before transferring the data to any processors, thus preventing *intelligible* access by providers (4.5.1.1). Thus, a provider commented that, when hosting encrypted data from which individuals could not be identified, it was difficult for data importers to determine whether data protection laws would apply to such processing operations and whether they needed to sign SCCs (Rackspace 2009: p.5).

Even when providers have potential intelligible access to unencrypted personal data, they may not actually access personal data themselves unless they 'look' for billing or support reasons (1.2.3) – or decide to use/disclose the data for 'unauthorized' purposes, e.g. to meet court or authorities' orders or requests, whereupon they would become controllers in their own right (Hon et al. 2013c: secs.3.2, 4.4).[3] As the true intention of the 'instructions' requirement was to prevent processors from using or disclosing personal data for *unauthorized purposes*,[4] arguably Art.17 and similar provisions in the GDPR (Arts.28(3), 29, 32(4), 82(2)) should have stated this explicitly to achieve their objective in a more technology-neutral way, instead of requiring contractual provisions on 'instructions' (Hon, Kosta, et al. 2014: pp.16–17). Thus, in *Salems 2013* (Sweden), para.1.3, Google Apps' terms were rejected, partly because they gave

---

[1] E.g., are computerized requests, automatically sent when customers use cloud software, 'instructions' (Hon, Millard and Walden 2013c: p.199)? If so, effectively this may impose strict liability on SaaS providers for the functioning of their software, which would not be imposed if the same software was installed on-premise. This does not seem right. The 'instructions' requirement is difficult to apply even outside cloud, with arguments in practice about what 'instructions' contracts must contain (e.g. n.4), can 'instructions' be given outside the contract, etc.

[2] Pp.101, 285; 7.4.2.2–7.4.2.3; *WP196*, para.3.4.1.2, quoted in *Salems 2013* (Sweden), p.5; *WP196*, pp.4, 11, 20.

[3] As in *SWIFT* – p.90. See further 7.4.2.

[4] E.g. p.122. See further p.196; 7.1.1, particularly n.1.

Google too much room to process personal data for its own purposes. Similarly, Norway's DPA felt that a Google Apps for Education agreement failed to ensure clearly that Google did not use users' personal data (staff or students) for its own purposes; it stressed that the issue was not whether Google processed personal data otherwise than as contractually agreed, as the contract might permit Google to use personal data for marketing purposes; the 'instructions' must also cover the controller's processing *purpose*, and the contract must not allow the processor to process personal data in a way the controller would not itself be permitted to do (*Randaberg* (Norway)) (see also 7.4.2.3). Cloud providers with intelligible access may remain mere 'processors' if, contractually, they have 'no scope' to use personal data for their own purposes, and do not themselves collect information (although usage logs could constitute individual users' personal data – p.107) (ICO 2014b: paras.48–9). See 7.4.2.4 on 'instructions' regarding data deletion.

With traditional outsourcing, controllers may require all subprocessors to be identified and approved by them first. But requiring identification and approval of cloud subproviders (*WP196*, para.3.3.2), particularly with infrastructure services and layered cloud (1.2.2–1.2.3), is like requiring identification and approval of processors' (indeed, controllers') hardware procurement. Even when controllers process personal data internally using purchased hardware, hardware suppliers could install, or allow, 'backdoors' enabling them or others to access data[5] or to secretly transmit to suppliers (or others) copies of data processed using their hardware. In those situations, clearly EU location of data is irrelevant to preventing such access. If potential intelligible access by third parties is the concern, then logically DPAs should require scrutiny of all hardware used for personal data processing (including controllers' in-house processing), not just of cloud use. Yet DPAs do not require controllers to identify all suppliers of any hardware used for personal data processing, or compel controllers to obtain rights to approve their processors' hardware procurement. These inconsistencies in DPAs' approach may reflect their general mistrust of cloud (see also p.291, n.75). Furthermore, cloud involves a 'reverse direction of travel' compared with traditional outsourcing (Hon and Millard 2013b: sec.5.2). Cloud providers do not engage subproviders after having been engaged by controllers; providers have already chosen their subservices, based on which they then offer their own services as a prebuilt package; therefore, requiring controllers'

---

[5] Reportedly the NSA requires or secretes backdoors into hardware, e.g. routers (Appelbaum et al. 2013) or computers (Sanger and Shanker 2014).

'prior' consent to existing subproviders is problematic, and indeed meaningless.[6]

Illustrating the perpetuation and unthinking application to cloud of unarticulated assumptions deriving from 1970s outsourcing models, the Commission stated, when proposing the GDPR, that 'concrete implementation' of data subject rights, e.g. to modify or delete personal data, is 'frequently operated by the cloud provider's subcontractors' (SEC(2012)72 final, Ann.2, para.10.1.2). That view seems misconceived. Cloud customers may *directly* modify or delete data remotely themselves through using self-service cloud software, without having to 'instruct' providers (or subproviders) to do so 'for' them. At most, providers or subproviders may be better placed than controllers to ensure that data are 'completely' deleted from hardware where necessary.[7] The quoted statement is rather like saying that, when you exercise your right to modify data on your Dell computer's Western Digital (WD) hard drive, the right is 'operated by' WD, so you need contractual rights against Dell, who must ensure contractual rights against WD.

GDPR Art.28 (replacing Art.17 DPD), rather than making data protection laws truly technology-neutral, unfortunately makes matters worse by expanding the DPD's provisions on processors to cover *subprocessors* explicitly, effectively 'hardcoding' *WP196* requirements (p.128; 7.4.2.3). Art.28(3)(a) also requires a contract term obliging processors to process personal data only on 'documented' controller instructions, 'including with regard to transfers …' unless otherwise required by EU or Member State law to which the processor is subject. Art.28's restrictions on the use of subprocessors and its numerous prescriptive contractual requirements, including obligatory 'flowdown' of the required contractual terms to subprocessors, subsubprocessors, etc., whether transfers are involved or not, will be difficult or impossible to achieve in cloud (5.3.4.2) – except for large providers who can comply because they own or have sufficient control over the entire relevant supply chain (Hon 2015a). This change, driving business towards the largest organizations, will hit not only cloud computing, but also other modern technology sourcing/ outsourcing arrangements with complex supply chains.

In summary, the DPD's processor provisions are neither technology-neutral nor cloud-appropriate, and the GDPR exacerbates the resulting problems.

---

[6] See pp.201–2 on changing subproviders; Hon, Kosta, et al. (2014: pp.17–18).
[7] On deletion, see 7.4.2.4.

4.3 ASSUMPTIONS BEHIND THE RESTRICTION

I now discuss the train of thought that seems to underlie the Restriction and its conflation of data location with physical access, intelligible access and effective jurisdiction. Mainly arising from pre-Internet 1970s 'mainframe' technological and business models[8] prevalent when the DPD and its precursors were conceived, this seems to run as follows:

- *Data location.* A dataset has a clear, known, usually single and central (rather than multiple), physical 'location'; location 'moves' only rarely, and any movement involves a 'one-off movement of data between Point A and Point B, between two entities only' (EPOF 2011: p.2), usually via EDI (electronic data interchange) (DIGITALEUROPE 2009: p.3).
- *Access to data.* Data are 'located', only or primarily, in hardware 'holding' the data, and accordingly:
  - whoever has physical access to such hardware will inevitably have intelligible access, can compromise the data's integrity/ availability,[9] and also block others' access to the data; and
  - *only* those with such physical access can have intelligible access; those without such 'possession' cannot have intelligible access.
- *Countries' effective jurisdiction.* When hardware holding personal data are located in a country, only (or mainly) that country has effective jurisdiction over whoever has physical access to such hardware – including jurisdiction to regulate the processing of that personal data, and therefore to ensure that such personal data are protected (or not).
- *Who can protect data.* Thus, *countries* should be solely or primarily responsible for protecting personal data; indeed, perhaps only countries are capable of protecting fundamental rights; and countries can only, or primarily, ensure such protection through their laws regulating personal data processing.
- *Export restrictions.* Therefore, to ensure protection of personal data in compliance with data protection principles, and prevent circumvention of data protection laws, it is necessary (and sufficient) to confine data 'location' to the relevant geographical territory, and

---

[8] In the wide sense of activity, rather than commercial uses of cyberspace (Reed 2012: p.156).

[9] On integrity and availability, see 7.1.2.

restrict transfers to other countries: hence the 'border control' approach to personal data, as exemplified by the Restriction.

I now discuss these assumptions in turn.

4.4 DATA LOCATION

4.4.1 Assumption: Mainframe Model

Table 4.1 compares key elements of the mainframe model that the DPD and its precursors assumed, against modern 'information society' technological realities:

Table 4.1

Mainframe model (based mainly on Reed (2007))	Modern position
Limited number of computers, usually only one, and only in large organizations. Accordingly, the DPD was designed for large-scale data collection and processing in a few mainframe computers (O'Quinn (1998: p.690) citing Swire and Litan (1998: pp.52–8))	An 'explosion' in the number of computers, increases in computing power, cost reductions and increased availability of computers in homes, enterprises and public administrations (CoE 1989: para.1.1)
Datasets held in a single, centralized[A] location (usually one set of punched cards, magnetic tapes or disks, mainframe disk packs, even compact discs),[B] meaning that datasets were processed under centralized control.[C]	Decentralized systems (CoE 1989: para.1.1) with distributed processing, both for storage and operations.[D] Digital data may not necessarily have one fixed, central or even fully known location,[E] particularly in cloud, so it is difficult to apply the Restriction to remote computing (Alcatel-Lucent 2009: p.10); 'where numerous computers physically located in multiple jurisdictions, randomly process personal data to optimize server capacity, technology may have made the term "national border" an obsolete notion' (Axciom 2009: p.2)

Table 4.1 (continued)

Mainframe model (based mainly on Reed (2007))	Modern position
Only a few core technical staff had direct access to the organization's computer and datasets	Near-ubiquitous remote access over the Internet or other network for multiple, often mobile, employees and others (e.g. malicious hackers), enabling copying of data as well as access, and use of remote IT infrastructure including cloud. Web/ Internet servers and cloud storage enable indirect, 'anytime', multistage, location-independent access
Limited or no connectivity to other computers	Widespread 'always-on' connectivity of computers and other devices
Infrequent data transmissions between networked computers, typically over private networks. 'Transfers' were discrete events, exceptional and large, with data travelling in bulk (Tene 2011b: p.26) between identified parties, e.g. in large batches via physical media such as tapes,[F] flowing directly, linearly, point-to-point (Microsoft 2009: p.5). This is partly because bandwidth (data transfer rate) in the 1980s was so low (56Kbps),[G] that storing data in one place and processing them in another (requiring the relevant data to be copied across networks) was usually very inefficient	Frequent data movements in huge volumes (6.2): continuous and multipoint (OECD 2011: p.15) within and between organizations, cross-border, in multiple directions (Microsoft 2009: p.5); particularly in cloud (EDPS 2010: p.4).[H] Data may be replicated to hardware in other locations (pp.105, 112–13, 271, 276), possibly other countries, and/or deleted, much more easily and quickly than with paper files. The deployment of optical technologies in the late 1990s/early 2000s enabled broadband connectivity at reasonable prices (Minoli 2004: p.45). For instance, in 1998 the UK academic network JANET increased its transatlantic link to 90MBps (Coffman and Odlyzko 2003: p.5). Improved bandwidth availability at increasingly lower costs fostered cloud growth; by 2011, data transfer rates had reached 300Mbps (wireless networks) and 1Gbps (wired networks) (KPMG 2011: p.3)

Notes:

A. Thus the 1990-Proposal envisaged that 'data files' had a primary location – p.48.
B. Compact discs were introduced in 1982 (Europe, Japan) and 1983 (USA), CD-ROM computer drives in 1985 (Pohlmann 1989: p.12). On the media envisaged by Convention108, see p.33, n.14.
C. Although Convention108 did contemplate distributed processing – p.50, n.42.
D. 'It may be, however, that the notion of a file, as used in [Convention108], suggests centralized storage and processing and is not in keeping with the new reality of distributed processing and networks which allow data to be dispersed and yet linked up at will through the possibility of computer-to-computer, or terminal-to-computer, dialogue' (CoE 1989: p.25).

   Network File System (NFS), the first widely used Internet Protocol-based network filesystem for distributed storage, was developed only in the 1980s (Henderson 2009: pp.335, 261). The open source Hadoop framework for efficient large-scale distributed computations was developed by Doug Cutting and others (White 2009: p.9) in the last decade, based on Google's distributed filesystem GFS (p.137) and Google's MapReduce for distributed computations (Dean and Ghemawat 2008).

E. Noted long ago e.g. by de Terwangne and Louveaux (1997: p.238): 'the Internet is made up of information which is not easily located geographically'.

F. OECD (2006: p.6): 'International data banks were just emerging, and the Internet was still in its infancy with commercial usages prohibited'; see ibid., pp.7–8 generally.

G. E.g. the NSFnet network, connecting the US National Science Foundation's supercomputer centres, in the mid-1980s. By 2004, its bandwidth had increased nearly 42 *million* times, to 40Gbps; 155 Mbps for some corporate Wide-Area Networks (WANs) (Minoli 2004: p.45).

H. Cloud makes 'cross-border transfers of data ubiquitous and instantaneous' (Bigo et al. 2012: p.12).

The DPD, while not overtly based on the mainframe model, plainly embeds (Reed 2012: chap.9) its assumptions. DPAs' approach to 'transfer' in particular focuses primarily on personal data's location, which has resulted in many problems (Ch.3). During the DPD's passage, various amendments were made attempting to accommodate technological changes, but arguably they were incomplete and inadequate. By 1992, the Commission had recognized difficulties with determining the location of electronic data or processing, and acknowledged that multiple data locations and distributed processing are possible in a networked world (2.3.2). However, the failure to consider these developments and their implications fully,[10] notably in relation to the Restriction, means that pre-Internet models regarding control over physical files, albeit movable and possibly distributed, have infected the Restriction. A more fundamental, holistic reformulation was needed, but did not occur. Indeed, the same could be said of the GDPR. Unfortunately, the GDPR's Restriction has spread this infection further, rather than excising it, as I argue any truly modernizing law should and would have done.

These pre-Internet assumptions, and therefore the Restriction's justification, have been undermined by technological,[11] social and business developments, whose existence and scale the DPD did not properly anticipate. Typical modern data flows are complex; there have been 'dramatic' changes from previous paradigms, with the 'continuous, multipoint nature of modern international data flows'; transmissions not

---

[10]   'Organizations were sharing data cross-border via proprietary networks rather than physically transferring datasets between those countries'; articulating this fact would have raised questions whether such sharing constituted 'transfer', and avoided embedding in the DPD the assumption that cross-border use involves physically transferring copies of datasets (Reed 2012: p.174). Also see p.50, n.42.

[11]   Technological changes even between 1990 and 1995 were massive (Charlesworth 2002: p.932).

point-to-point, but part of a networked series of processes to deliver a business result; and management changes including shifts to process-oriented management (Schwartz 2009: p.4). Note in particular the huge increases in distributed processing and automation of processing across different hardware in different locations, and another major development: technical measures to protect data (Ch.7), particularly access controls and encryption/tokenization (7.2.3.2).

4.4.2   Reality: Data 'Location'

Paper files have clear physical locations. However, digital data can only be 'located' in the physical infrastructure that stores, operates on or transmits the data. Distributed storage is common, and data may be replicated to infrastructure in different locations, even in other countries. Such distribution and replication are automated. This means that even providers using their own datacentres, while usually knowing which datacentre(s) hold a particular customer's data, may not necessarily know in which *hardware* units that data are stored or otherwise processed, or be able to track all copies of a given dataset, e.g. McKenty (2013). It is harder still for customers to verify their data's exact locations (3.7.8). Accordingly cloud creates 'special problems' for regulation of cross-border data transfers, 'which is basically based on protecting data in a given physical infrastructure in a defined location' (Konarski et al. 2012: p.12). Similarly, the DPD's 'presumption' that personal data have 'a particular location' is no longer true, e.g. with cloud, and reconsideration was urged regarding whether personal data location is still an appropriate legal criterion (Air Berlin 2011: p.4).

I argue that it is not. If regulation continues to be based on personal data location, the current difficulties will be exacerbated should servers be located neither in the EEA nor any third country, e.g. international waters (3.7.5). Another problem with regulating digital data based on infrastructure location is that it seemingly equates physical 'possession' with intelligible access, which is incorrect, as I discuss next.

4.5   ACCESS TO DATA

4.5.1   Assumption: Physical Possession and Intelligible Access

A major implicit assumption behind the Restriction is that whoever has physical *access* to infrastructure that houses data has intelligible access to that data (and, conversely, that whoever does not, has not). Effectively, such physical access is assumed to be both necessary and sufficient to enable access, notably intelligible access, to the data housed. On that basis, when personal data are transferred 'to' a third country, that country and any recipient there would have intelligible access to the data. However, that is not necessarily so.

With digital data what matters is, not physical access to bits, but access *in a way that extracts meaningful information.* Yet many lawmakers and regulators assume, apparently without further analysis, that, as with paper files, physical access to infrastructure 'containing' digital personal data is both necessary and sufficient for intelligible access to that data, i.e. access to the information contained in personal data. This key dual assumption fed the further assumption that 'physically transferring [hardware holding] copies of datasets' was 'the only way' cross-border use would occur (n.10).

Illustrating the transposition of this assumption to cloud, Datainspektionen stated that, to ensure that data subjects can exercise their rights ('intervenability'), controllers must know who any subproviders are, and where (*Salems 2013* (Sweden), para.3.3). This is a common view, e.g. EDPS (2012b: para.104). Similarly CNIL (2012: fn.7):

> The fact that data may be spread across servers located in different countries can make it more complicated for data subjects to exercise their rights. It is therefore necessary to ensure that the service provider and the customer are providing the necessary safeguards to enable the data subjects to exercise their rights of access, correction, alteration, updating or deletion.

This view is not new (CoE 1989: p.25):

> If a data file is divided into several subsets of data, an unacceptable burden is imposed on the data subject who is obliged to piece together the various pieces of the puzzle, including the unravelling of the network, before it may truly be said that he has had access to his data. Effective exercise of subject access, in reality, breaks down, individual control over data processing is weakened and transparency is diminished.

However, even in 1989, this view was untrue. It is even more misconceived today. It ignores remote logical access, seeming to assume that a dataset is accessible only by physically visiting all constituent fragments' locations to physically collect and reassemble them, so that complex outsourcing chains prejudice intervenability. However, given cloud's abstraction and location-independence (1.2), customers and data subjects would never attempt *physical* retrieval or reassembly. Internet use is of course also location-independent. To obtain data from an Australian website, you do not have to fly to Australia. Although Australia is geographically distant from the EEA, you can access that data as easily as you can obtain data from a UK, or French, or US, website. Similarly, personal data in the cloud are accessed remotely and, where data are stored in distributed form, the *software* that customers or data subjects directly use (a browser, for websites) will, seamlessly and invisibly to the end-user, automatically retrieve and reassemble the constituent fragments and deliver the full dataset to the customer or data subject, without their needing to physically visit or even know the underlying storage locations, whether at geographic or hardware unit level. As controllers who process personal data in cloud have direct self-service access to their data (4.2), they can retrieve and edit such data remotely to meet any data subject requests, without needing to 'instruct' providers or subproviders to do anything. In self-service cloud, intervenability can be assured through maintaining the personal data's availability and integrity (7.1.2), and ideally providing an indexing feature enabling customers to search their data.[12]

The emphasis on physical access is thus misconceived. Yet some jurists,[13] and regulators other than DPAs such as the UK's Financial Conduct Authority (Financial Conduct Authority 2016), still seemingly assume that control of data *location* is necessary to maintain control over data. However, physical access does not necessarily afford intelligible access. Conversely, intelligible access is possible without physical access, as digital data may be accessed logically through software (often remotely), as highlighted above. A DPA can supervise compliance by a controller established in its Member State even if the controller's data are stored outside that Member State, provided the controller controls intelligible access to that data, including via remote access and implementing backups. Also, physical access does not necessarily prevent others' intelligible access. I discuss these in more detail next.

---

[12]   Although indexes may themselves contain personal data – p.107.
[13]   In Joined cases C-293/12 and C-594/12 *Digital Rights Ireland Ltd*, para.68, the CJEU stated:

> that directive [2006/24] does not require the data in question to be retained within the European Union, with the result that it cannot be held that the control, explicitly required by Art.8(3) of the Charter, by an independent authority of compliance with the requirements of protection and security, as referred to in the two previous paragraphs, is fully ensured ...

That statement's interpretation is contested (Hon, Millard, et al. 2014: fn.135), but it clearly illustrates the 'physical access' assumption.

4.5.1.1 Physical access without intelligible access

Physical access to infrastructure does not always afford intelligible access, because of two main factors: distributed storage, and techniques to restrict intelligible access such as encryption or tokenization (7.2.3.2).

4.5.1.1.1 Distributed storage Physically accessed hardware may hold only part of a dataset. For intelligible access to the full dataset, all hardware holding the constituent fragments must be found.[14] To identify all related fragments in different (or even the same) hardware, e.g. where one fragment starts/ends, and then reassemble them correctly, requires knowledge of the filesystem used. That may be proprietary or unknown (e.g. Google's GFS[15]). Therefore, it may be difficult, with only physical

---

[14] A fragment may include personal data, and even be readable if it contains ASCII-encoded text (e.g. 1001000 represents 'H'). However, technical measures like encryption may be employed to mitigate this risk.

[15] GFS (Ghemawat et al. 2003), since succeeded by Google's Colossus file system (Corbet et al. 2013), is:

> a distributed file system designed to store large amounts of data across large numbers of computers. Structured data is then stored in a large distributed database built on top of the file system. Data is chunked and replicated over multiple systems such that no one system is a single point of failure. Data chunks are given random file names and are not stored in clear text so they are not humanly readable' (Google 2011: p.4).

Google's Central/Northern Europe cloud services head, Kai Gutzeit, reportedly stated, 'if anyone ever did break into Google's top-secret computer center ... the intruder would find "absolutely nothing" usable, only "meaningless bits and bytes" because Google uses a proprietary file system' (Weichert 2011: sec.10). See also 4.5.1.

Weichert (ibid.) considers 'security by obscurity' (e.g. proprietary filesystems) inadequate, advocating 'security by transparency': state-of-the-art technical measures to restrict access to customer-authorized parties – with the possible exception of administrative rights. 'This could be achieved with a multi-level access regime, encryption capabilities and possibly aliasing tools.' I agree. Proprietary formats may provide one 'layer' of security that helps protect confidentiality, but that is their possible consequence or side-effect, rather than purpose. Further 'layers' are best, particularly encryption. That does not mean, however, that the first 'layer' is entirely ineffective.

Despite 'raw' bits generally not being human-readable, software can extract meaningful information from unencrypted data (n.14). Nonetheless, it is not straightforward to retrieve the correct fragments from different hardware, physically reassemble them and then discern meaningful information from them, without knowing the filesystem and representation format. Authorities could require providers to divulge information regarding their filesystems etc., but it seems much easier simply to compel providers to use any means they may have

access to hardware, to access full datasets in intelligible form, although some fragments may be intelligible (n.14). Accordingly, usually intelligible access to the full dataset is most easily obtained through logical remote access, via software.

4.5.1.1.2 Encryption   Data may be encrypted, i.e. scrambled via cryptography, using a mathematical algorithm to render data unintelligible unless unscrambled with the correct decryption 'key' (7.2.3.1). Even if providers have logical or physical access to encrypted data, only those with the correct decryption key (e.g. the customer who applied the encryption) can be certain to have intelligible access. Similarly, subproviders with physical or indeed remote access to encrypted data may not have intelligible access without the key (held by the encrypting customer and/or provider).[16] Physical access to hardware holding encrypted data cannot guarantee intelligible access to the full target dataset. However, intelligible access may be gained by acquiring the encrypted data (remotely or physically) *and* the decryption key, or breaking the encryption (7.2.3.3). Other measures to protect intelligible access exist, e.g. tokenization (p.279, n.44).

Datacentres' physical security is undoubtedly important (p.272; 7.2.2.2). Physical access to datacentres or communications links allows access to hardware, and may also enable installation of other hardware designed to access, monitor or intercept[17] unencrypted data within or moving to or from that datacentre, with or without the providers' cooperation or knowledge. Outsider thefts are rare, targeting hardware more than data (e.g. King 2011), and affecting availability more than confidentiality.[18] Insider threats are more likely (Harris Poll and Ovum 2015), including through deceiving datacentre employees (Miller 2014).[19] However, physical security (locks, guards, etc.), personnel vetting and training (as organizational (p.268, n.16) rather than physical measures),

---

to access the full dataset remotely through software, i.e. direct logical (p.103) rather than physical access.

[16]   Dropbox emphasized that the customer data which it stored were encrypted, but had to clarify that, as it applied the encryption, it held the keys; its employees could access customer data (Singel 2011) but were prohibited from doing so (Dropbox 2011).

[17]   E.g., in a non-cloud context, physical access to banks' IT systems enabling data theft (Cluley 2014).

[18]   On confidentiality and availability, see 7.1.2.

[19]   Even physical access by insiders, e.g. datacentre provider and staff, may not afford intelligible access. Again, datacentre users' practices are relevant, particularly encryption.

restricting physical access to different areas, and ideally encrypting data on servers, all depend on the security policies and practices of datacentre providers[20] and their users (e.g. cloud providers), rather than on the *countries* of datacentre location.[21] Threats from remote access greatly exceed those from physical access.[22]

Authorities may legally compel physical access to infrastructure located in their country. Post-Snowden, this risk looms larger. Hardware seizure by authorities in the country of datacentre location poses greater risks to confidentiality than hardware theft, as nation-states are more likely to have the resources to gain intelligible access, e.g. by breaking encryption. But, while not unheard-of, again such seizures are relatively rare. Authorities' datacentre hardware seizures fall into two main categories: firstly, crime-related: investigating suspected criminal activities (Zetter 2012), and taking action against cybercriminals, e.g. taking down botnets (Constantin 2015; Rashid 2011); and secondly, taking down claimed copyright-infringing content (Gibbs 2014) or other illegal content. Cloud customers could be specifically targeted, particularly if in breach of that country's laws.

Also, colocation risk arises for those whose applications, websites and/or data are hosted using the same hardware or datacentre as a

---

[20] Datacentre providers may be certified to recognized standards covering physical and/or logical security. Datacentre-specific standards and best practices exist, e.g. the Uptime Institute's Tier Standard for datacentres, (ANSI/TIA 2005; CPNI 2010).

[21] A country's laws could require minimum measures, e.g. physical security at datacentres, or conversely (and more worryingly) compel datacentre providers to allow authorities physical access to install interception hardware, read or delete data, etc. However, whether countries can *effectively* compel cloud customers or providers to comply with such laws depends on many factors. Data location in a country may or may not afford it effective jurisdiction to access intelligible data of the datacentre's customers/providers – Ch.7, particularly 7.5.1.1.

[22] Risks to personal data from unauthorized remote access (i.e. hacking), insiders, indeed portable hardware thefts from offices or vehicles, far outweigh risks through physical theft from datacentres, which most surveys do not even mention. E.g. Trustwave (2014: p.33) noted, regarding attackers' intrusion methods, that only 4 percent involved 'Remote file inclusion, physical access or directory traversal' (the first and third are remote, so physical access must involve under 4 percent, and physical access to datacentres even less). During 2011–13, physical theft/loss (many of which must be of devices from offices/ vehicles, not datacentres) comprised just 1 percent of all security incidents (Verizon 2014: p.14).

targeted person's, affecting their availability and possibly even confidentiality. Innocent parties have suffered loss of service, data and/or hardware from seizures, particularly in the US, if authorities do not prioritize minimizing collateral damage to third parties (e.g. by taking only minimum relevant hardware, copying data rather than seizing hardware, and/or returning hardware after copying data or performing analyses).[23] Certainly, some such incidents have triggered fears regarding cloud (Schwartz 2011), criticisms of US authorities' apparent lack of concern about collateral damage (Chernicoff 2011), and even decisions to site servers in Canada instead of the USA (Berkens 2011). These risks are not cloud-specific. They arise from shared infrastructure, where different customers' data use the same hardware, e.g. shared webhosting, or where hardware used is in the same vicinity as targeted hardware in the same datacentre. But again, remote access by US or other authorities is the greater confidentiality threat, whether through providers' cooperation or direct hacking (4.5.1.2). Risks to availability and integrity (7.1.2) may be mitigated through backups, as I will discuss (7.1.3). As for risks to confidentiality through physical access, technical measures like encryption by users or providers may delay or stymie thieves' or authorities' intelligible access (7.5).

4.5.1.2 Intelligible access without physical access

Physical access to infrastructure is unnecessary for intelligible access, because cloud customers, providers or others may have direct *remote* logical access to data over the Internet or other networks.

4.5.1.2.1 Customers Customers may gain intelligible access to unencrypted data remotely, via software that automatically retrieves and reassembles dataset fragments, wherever located within the provider's distributed filesystem/database (p.136). With some services, multiple users may access the same data concurrently.

4.5.1.2.2 Providers For support or related purposes (1.2.3), many providers' systems have 'backdoors' enabling employees (if assigned appropriate administrative rights by the provider) to login remotely as customers or to bypass customer logins. Such employees could, remotely, obtain intelligible access to data stored by the provider that have not been

---

[23] One commentator noted, regarding one such incident, that seizure could not prevent usage, as the server could be copied and replaced 'overnight'; the FBI could have copied the data, or installed surveillance software to monitor traffic; 'Instead, they decide to take the server' (McGinn 2011).

encrypted by customers or higher-level providers.[24] This means that countries with effective jurisdiction over such providers could gain intelligible access and otherwise control that data's processing, including remotely, e.g. Brazilian courts have ordered Google to access and disclose data from US-located hardware (Koman 2006) and to intercept emails (AP 2014a). In other words, where providers have intelligible access, data location is 'moot' (Finnegan 2015) – it is effective jurisdiction over providers that is more important.

It is possible to prevent or tightly control intelligible access even by providers' employees. Microsoft's Office 365 Customer Lockbox, apparently using its VC3 technology (Ziadeh 2015; Schuster et al. 2015), enables customers, inevitably at a higher price, to explicitly approve or reject access requests by Microsoft's engineers (Kumar and Dani 2015) – including access following authorities' requests (Gallagher 2015). Encrypted stored data are retrieved from storage to special hardware which its employees cannot access/monitor, decrypted and operated upon only within that hardware, and re-encrypted within such hardware before storage elsewhere.

4.5.1.2.3 Others Unauthorized intelligible access to personal data, even if located in the EEA, may occur through remote access by persons outside or indeed within the EEA, including third country authorities – e.g. US authorities seeking data from US providers under the US PATRIOT Act (p.117) or otherwise,[25] or by hacking the target directly[26] or tapping communications links. Again, encryption helps to reduce the risks of unauthorized intelligible access, physical or remote, as may other technical measures to protect the network or prevent or detect unauthorized intrusions (7.1.3).

---

[24] If customers encrypt data pre-upload (pp.102, 138; 7.2.3.1), providers can only access encrypted data. Some providers' software encrypts the data on users' machines, with keys that only customers can access, e.g. storage service Spideroak. Where providers have 'backdoor' access (4.5.1.2), their control of which employees have full administrative rights is obviously important, together with proper vetting, etc. (p.268, n.16). Providers, e.g. Dropbox (n.16), may encrypt data to prevent intelligible access by subproviders or unauthorized third parties.

[25] E.g. the *Microsoft warrant case* (p.93); Brazil (4.5.1.2).

[26] NSA's dedicated 'TAO' (Tailored Access Operations) hacking unit (SPIEGEL Staff 2013) infiltrated the networks of EU institutions (Poitras et al. 2013) and organizations (Scahill and Begley 2015).

4.5.1.3   Physical access does not preclude others' access

Physical access to infrastructure does not necessarily guarantee *exclusive* access to data held within that infrastructure. Remote concurrent access to the same data by multiple users is possible, as mentioned previously. Also, because digital data may be replicated relatively easily, gaining physical control of infrastructure that holds one copy, e.g. by seizing particular hardware, may not prevent others from accessing copies held in other hardware (or even remotely accessing the 'seized' hardware, if not disconnected). Protecting service and data availability against seizures, or simply against problems affecting one datacentre, is one reason why customers implement, and should implement, backups to other geographical locations (7.1.3).

4.5.1.4   Summary

The assumption that physical access necessarily enables intelligible access ignores the possible use of distributed storage, proprietary formats, encryption and/or backups to control access regardless of location. With digital data, physical access to infrastructure used for processing data may not always afford intelligible access. Conversely, such physical access is not necessary to enable remote access to the data, including intelligible access, perhaps by multiple users simultaneously. With increasing globalization, 'external borders become less relevant for data flows'; the economy is increasingly dependent on global networks and, generally, 'the physical place of a processing operation is less relevant' (EDPS 2007b: para.6).

4.5.2   'Access' and Intelligible Access

Particularly significant to cloud is another related assumption: that any access to data, whether physical or logical, affords intelligible access. For instance, Snowden's revelations were thought to show that cloud providers 'present an avenue for those who want to access data' (Reding 2013). EU DPAs also tend to assume that all providers and subproviders have intelligible access (*WP196*, p.21) (p.103), which may partly underlie the WP29's insistence that controllers must know all subproviders' identities and locations. Again, this ignores the availability of access controls, encryption and other technical measures to restrict intelligible access.

4.6 COUNTRIES' EFFECTIVE JURISDICTION

Many DPAs view the country of data location as the main source of personal data protection, e.g. AEPD (2013: p.15): 'The location of the data is important because the guarantees required for their protection are different depending on the country in which they are located' (also see p.100, nn.48, 49). This seems based on the assumption that a country has effective jurisdiction over whoever has physical access to or control of hardware, located on its territory, that is used to process data (2.2.2, 2.3.2). However, a person with such physical access may not necessarily have intelligible access, or even exclusive access, to such data (4.5). If that person has neither, then even a country's jurisdiction over that person will not enable that country to regulate the data's processing effectively. The assumption that physical access to infrastructure affords access to intelligible data may explain why many countries seek to base their regulation on data location. Just as countries regulate copying as a *proxy* for regulating the use of intellectual property (Reed 2012: pp.152–6), so they treat data location as a proxy for both access to intelligible data (controlled through security, see Ch.7), and effective jurisdiction to regulate the data processing. I first mentioned the concept of data location as a proxy for access, security, etc. in unpublished work, which this book updates. The Commission asked to see that work and my email of 1 December 2015, responding with a copy, also summarizes the 'data localisation as proxy' concept. The 'proxy' formulation appears without attribution in COM(2017)9 final. Readers may note the timeline.

As previously discussed (Ch.2, 3.1, 3.7.2), a one-to-one correspondence also seems to be assumed between a country's protection of data, and the data's location:

- if data are 'located' in country X, then X (and *only* X) can protect that data;[27] conversely,
- if data are 'located' outside X's borders, then X has no say in or control over the data's protection.

---

[27] E.g. Convention108-ER, para.66 noted that data import (emphasis added): 'presents no problems because *imported data are in any case covered by the data protection regime of the importing State*'. References to transfer to non-Parties' territories within the same organization (Convention108-ER, para.63) imply an assumption that the laws applicable to data depend on the data's location. The 1992-Proposal's Art.4 was amended because the DPD's legislators recognized the difficulties with this assumption (2.3.2), but unfortunately it still lives on in relation to the Restriction, and in many lawmakers' and regulators' minds.

This dual assumption rests on another assumption: that a country has jurisdiction to apply its laws effectively to data located 'in' its territory, but not to data located outside.[28] This was implicit in the 1990-Proposal's jurisdictional and anticircumvention provisions which, reflecting traditional 'territorial jurisdiction' approaches, based countries' jurisdiction to regulate data solely on data location (see n.27).

Similarly, it was thought that data users could avoid data protection laws by moving 'operations' to data havens (2.3.1.1). This implies another assumption: that 'operations' (rather than just data) would be subject to, but seemingly only to, the jurisdiction of the country where the operations were located. Another implicit assumption is that the data processed by certain 'operations' are always located in the same country as the 'operations'. That is not necessarily true, with cloud or the Internet: an organization's business operations and the datacentres it uses (directly or through providers) may be in different countries. However, certainly effective jurisdiction over 'operations' can afford practical control over the data processed by those 'operations', wherever the data are located.

Traditional jurisdiction is founded on physical territoriality, so the dual assumption is unsurprising. With direct transfers to recipients 'in' a third country, e.g. by email, the country's jurisdiction over the recipient seems straightforward.[29] However, when data 'lands' in a datacentre during cloud or Internet use, the position is more complicated. Many countries claim jurisdiction over data (and/or infrastructure) located in their territories: one reason for the 'location fixation'. In a sense, this seems illogical because data can be moved/copied to other countries relatively easily; the same data (as regards informational content) could be subject to different laws at different times, even simultaneously if replicated. Nevertheless, countries may claim such jurisdiction, at least over infrastructure sited within their territories, for several reasons (4.5.1.1). Firstly, they may wish to access data stored within that infrastructure, for national security or crime-fighting purposes; indeed, overbroad access to the personal data of other countries' residents is a main concern post-Snowden (7.5.3). Secondly, they may wish to prevent 'undesirable' data

---

[28] E.g., OECD-ExplanMem, para.65 recognized a country's interest in accessing data on its nationals living abroad, such as their addresses, seemingly assuming that the country of residence would have jurisdiction over such data. The latter may be more likely to have *access* to that data, so this may reflect a conflation of access with jurisdiction.

[29] Non-citizens and non-residents of a country, while travelling there, could also be subject to its jurisdiction – but not exclusively, as their country of nationality may also claim jurisdiction over them.

from being hosted in their territories, e.g. terminating the availability of copyright-infringing or other illegal material by claiming jurisdiction over data 'in' infrastructure there. So, in another sense, from countries' viewpoint it seems logical to claim such jurisdiction, even if they would lose jurisdiction 'over' such data if it were moved to infrastructure elsewhere (unless they have effective jurisdiction over whoever can access the data remotely). Nevertheless, few countries claim data protection law jurisdiction over personal data located 'in' their territories *as such*. Countries assert jurisdiction to regulate data processing on many possible bases: location of establishment, operations or assets of controllers, processors, recipients or others who control access to data; location of infrastructure for data processing (which could be multiple, as copies could exist in different hardware, even different countries), e.g. DPD's 'equipment' ground or Malaysia's law;[30] even 'targeting' or monitoring data subjects in the relevant territory, as under the GDPR (1.5.2).

Undoubtedly, a country can secure physical control of infrastructure located 'in' its territory, and exercise effective jurisdiction over such infrastructure or, strictly, over the infrastructure's owner/operator, i.e. the datacentre provider. Similarly with owners/operators of hardware located in that datacentre, and even connectivity providers who run cables there. The location of infrastructure in a country facilitates its effective jurisdiction over that infrastructure, which I argue is the main significance of location. However, a country will not necessarily have effective jurisdiction over *data* transferred to that infrastructure, or even over the data's recipients (if in another country). Given the ease of moving/duplicating digital data, the availability of measures like encryption, and cloud and Internet service supply chains' complexity, effective jurisdiction over a datacentre provider (or other infrastructure providers) does not necessarily guarantee its effective jurisdiction over that provider's customers, or those customers' users, or even data processed in that infrastructure. As a US court noted, 'Typically, states' jurisdictional limits are related to geography; geography, however, is a virtually meaningless construct on the Internet' – *American Libraries Ass'n v Pataki*, 969 F.Supp.160, 168-69 (1997).

To expand on the supply chain issue, different parties may, and often do, own and/or operate different components of a cloud or Internet service: multi-intermediation, in short. Multiple recipients and data locations are possible, perhaps in separate countries, because some cloud

---

[30] Personal Data Protection Act 2010, s.2(2)(b) – which excludes transit.

providers use third party subproviders and/or datacentres. If an organization owns a datacentre in a particular country, that country's authorities could force it to deliver (perhaps even decrypt) its data, as occurred with SWIFT (p.92). If a cloud provider owns the datacentre, then the country's authorities may have effective jurisdiction to gain intelligible access to any cloud data to which the *provider* has intelligible access, whether in that datacentre or elsewhere. However, if neither the cloud provider nor customer owns the datacentre or any hardware in the datacentre, then those authorities can gain intelligible access to cloud data processed in that datacentre only if the datacentre provider or hardware owner itself has intelligible access to that data. Thus, a country may have effective jurisdiction over those with a sufficient physical nexus there, e.g. the owners of infrastructure located there. However, it may not have effective jurisdiction over any users of the datacentre, or their users, if those users have no tangible connection with that country other than their data being processed in that datacentre. A country could claim jurisdiction and attempt to apply its laws to such data/processing, but, in some circumstances, such users may be able to prevent that attempt from being *effective* (7.5.1.1).

A single 'processing' may involve multiple physical locations and jurisdictions, even when 'transfers' are made within the same organization. Belgian processor SWIFT was forced under US laws to disclose data to US authorities. Because it owned and used a US datacentre, US authorities could assert effective jurisdiction over SWIFT (p.92). This incident also underlines that organizations operating multinationally, even if EEA-incorporated, may be subject to conflicting laws. Again, this risk arises not so much from *data* location, particularly as data may be 'moved' out relatively quickly, as from tangible connections to the country concerned – branch, subsidiary, datacentre or other physical assets or employees in the country – that enable it to assert its jurisdiction effectively.[31] In addition, countries are increasingly attempting to extend their jurisdiction over data processing beyond their own geographical borders,[32] despite convincing arguments that, to engender respect for and compliance with their laws,

---

[31]   ICC (2012: p.1) mentions an increasingly common situation: authorities of country A, where organization X does business, ask X for data on individuals stored in X's database in country B, failing which A threatens criminal proceedings against the board of X's subsidiary in A. Because X has a subsidiary in A, A can make enforceable threats against X and effectively access X's data located in B.

[32]   E.g. Kuner et al. (2013); the WP29's approach to cookies (p.52, n.45); *Google Spain* (p.9, n.20); the GDPR (1.5.2).

countries should endeavour to restrain their laws' application to cyberspace, particularly extraterritorially (Reed 2012: chap.3). This means that the problem of multiple jurisdictions is increasing: different countries claim jurisdiction to regulate the processing of the same data, based on jurisdiction over controllers and/or recipient(s), or otherwise. In cases of conflict, which country's laws should apply; would a country choose another country's laws to govern (Swire 1998: p.992)? Both the OECD and CoE decided not to address such conflicts (2.2.3–2.2.4). Arguably, resolving such conflicts in favour of DPD Laws is one of the unstated policy drivers behind EU DPAs' current insistence on the Restriction.

To summarize, in today's globalized world it cannot be assumed that only the country of the recipient's or datacentre's location has jurisdiction over the processing of transferred personal data. Many organizations, including datacentre providers, cloud providers and customers, may operate multinationally, being subject to several countries' jurisdictions simultaneously, regarding their operations in the relevant country and possibly beyond. Different countries' laws may conflict. Cloud brings such conflicts to the fore. Furthermore, the assumption that the country of data location always has effective jurisdiction over the data's processing has been undermined by data's movability and duplicability; the availability of technical measures like encryption, so that effective jurisdiction to retrieve encrypted data may be futile without effective jurisdiction over whoever holds the decryption key; supply chain multi-intermediation; and, again, globalization. The restriction of data location is no longer necessary or sufficient to ensure that only countries with 'adequate' data protection laws have effective jurisdiction over data processing. Yet the geographical approach to data persists: e.g., for Canada's consolidated government email systems, its federal government cited national security to require data storage in Canadian processing facilities, while two Canadian provinces compel public bodies to store and access personal information only in Canada, with limited exceptions (Office of the United States Trade Representative 2016).

4.7 POWER/RESPONSIBILITY OF COUNTRIES TO ENSURE ADEQUACY

I showed above that physical access to data does not always afford intelligible access, and countries with effective jurisdiction over those having such physical access may not necessarily be able to gain intelligible access, or to regulate the processing of such data exclusively or effectively. However, the DPD and its precursors seemingly assumed that the country of data location can and will so regulate.

It was eventually recognized that it cannot be assumed that only countries have responsibility for data protection (2.4); controllers' actions (particularly in relation to the intended recipient) can achieve the desired objective. However, even more fundamentally, the assumption that adequacy of protection derives primarily from countries' laws seems misguided. The existence of 'adequate' laws, even enforcement systems, cannot guarantee transferees' practical compliance. Even if the destination country has been found 'adequate', a transferring controller should (morally or normatively) assess the appropriateness of protection for the transferred data in the context of the particular transfer (2.4.2). Yet under the Restriction and the GDPR, it need not do so for any transfers to 'adequate' countries – which seems the wrong approach (5.2.2.2).

Whether the laws of the country where personal data are located are 'adequate' is obviously relevant to the overall risk assessment. However, it does not determine the level of protection of personal data transferred to that country (Kuner 2013b: p.171). The 'adequacy' of a country's laws should be but one factor, among others,[33] just as physical security should be part (but not the only part) of the package of security measures that should be implemented. For example, personal data may be better protected if a customer processes the data itself using third country datacentres, than if it used a third party processor in its own country (Kuner 2013b: p.171). Some DPAs and even other governmental authorities (Financial Conduct Authority 2016; Federal Office for Information Security (Germany) 2016) claim that the country of location affects data security (p.100, n.48), but that view assumes that persons in that country always have intelligible access, and that the country's laws (and *only* that country's laws) determine the level of protection afforded to personal data there. Those assumptions are wrong, as discussed above: the true issue is the risk of that country having effective jurisdiction, which may or may not be the case. Furthermore, security measures by controllers

---

[33] E.g. under Canada's PIPEDA, organizations must 'take into consideration all of the elements surrounding the transaction. The result may well be that some transfers are unwise because of the uncertain nature of the foreign regime or that in some cases information is so sensitive that it should not be sent to any foreign jurisdiction' (OPC 2009). Effectively, the issue is country risk – economic, social and political conditions and events in a foreign country that could adversely affect the organization if they prevent the service provider from complying with its contract with the organization (MAS 2016: para.5.10.1). See also p.185.

and/or providers may restrict access, protect integrity, etc., regardless of data location (Ch.7).

4.8 EXPORT RESTRICTIONS

Although lawmakers' proposed jurisdictional grounds eventually took account of distributed storage and the difficulty of determining data location (2.3.2), the Restriction assumed that geographically restricting personal data's location was the only or best way to prevent circumvention of substantive data protection rules.[34] This assumption itself derived from assumptions, dating from Convention108, that control of data depends on 'possession' of physical data files, and that the country where data are located would regulate that data's processing; so that if data were allowed to move to another country, exported data could 'escape' application of the exporting country's laws, be processed abroad unlawfully and then perhaps reimported, and data subject protections might be lost.

That reasoning resulted in some countries' imposition of export controls (Convention108-ER, para.9), and the DPD's similar 'border control' approach. The DPD's legislators assumed, but seemingly did not analyse, whether such geographical restriction was the most appropriate way to achieve their policy objectives, or was even likely to be effective in practice. However, in today's environment, a border control approach to data is 'plainly unreasonable and ineffective' for an 'inherently borderless technology' (LeSieur 2012: p.104).[35]

Nevertheless, those assumptions remain prevalent today, and permeate many lawmakers' and regulators' approach to data protection and the Restriction. For example, a report for the European Parliament noted that the Restriction 'implicitly acknowledge[s] that transfers to third countries lacking equivalent provisions lead to reduced data protection' (Cave et al. 2012 p.18). As this chapter has shown, the assumptions behind the Restriction no longer hold true. Ch.7 will discuss how compliance with

---

[34] A related motivation may have been to pressurize third countries to adopt DPD-like laws (Art.25(5) DPD); this seems to have succeeded – p.25.

[35] Conversely Svantesson (2011: p.191) considers 'data crossing borders represent a loss of control for the data subject ... some form of border control is a necessary element of any sound model for the regulation of cross-border data'. I disagree. *Any* collection, disclosure or use of personal data involves loss of data subject control. That 'data crossing borders' was singled out indicates that outdated 1970s assumptions still hold too much sway.

Principles may be maintained (and circumvention prevented), even if personal data exports are not restricted geographically.

4.9 SUMMARY

This chapter showed that the assumptions underlying the Restriction have been undermined. Those assumptions partly explain current problems with the Restriction, particularly the DPAs' interpretation of it as restricting personal data's physical location per se. Unintended consequences may arise when laws are made or interpreted based on unstated assumptions belied by subsequent developments, so that they no longer match the realities of everyday Internet usage (Reed 2007). At worst, regulation based on such assumptions may produce results contrary to the original objective – which I argue has transpired with the Restriction, and continued with GDPR's Restriction. Such Restrictions therefore remain in urgent need of re-evaluation, in the cloud and broader Internet context.

Physical data location is relevant, but only as one factor among many factors that require consideration. Location should not be the be-all and end-all. EEA location of personal data does not guarantee protection, as data may be accessed remotely from outside the EEA, e.g. by hackers, or by providers (or controllers) under third country court orders (4.5.1.2). Conversely, data in a third country may be more secure against unauthorized access than unencrypted data in the EEA, e.g. because strong encryption is applied, the data are stored in distributed form and/or proprietary formats used (4.5.1.1), and the customer or provider (perhaps at the customer's behest) has implemented measures to maintain the data's availability and integrity (to be discussed in Ch.7). I argue that the real issues are:

- control of access to data, particularly intelligible access, regardless of data location; and
- countries' jurisdiction to apply their laws effectively to persons having such control, and thereby effectively regulate the processing of that data (including requiring disclosure) (4.6). Here, the main relevance of location is that the location of infrastructure in a particular country enables it to assert jurisdiction over any data processing that uses that infrastructure. However, that assertion may not always be enforceable in practice against cloud providers and/or customers, i.e. such claimed jurisdiction may not be effective.

Ch.7 will discuss control of access to data, and how such control underlies and enables compliance with the Principles without the Restriction being necessary. But first, I will discuss uncertainties and complexities regarding the Mechanisms that were designed to enable compliance with the Restriction, which support my view that the Restriction should be abolished or at least significantly altered. I will also consider enforcement and compliance problems with the Restriction, resulting at least in part from difficulties with the meaning of 'transfer' and issues with the Mechanisms.

5. Mechanisms and derogations

5.1 INTRODUCTION

Data localization laws generally permit transfer of personal data in limited circumstances. The DPD's Restriction provides for Mechanisms to enable transfer of personal data. The WP29's favoured hierarchy of Mechanisms puts adequate protection ahead of adequate safeguards, with transfer under certain derogations only as a last resort (*WP114*, p.9). The GDPR's Restriction maintains this hierarchy, but narrows how adequate protection may be found, renames 'adequate safeguards' to 'appropriate safeguards', and makes certain other changes, resulting in Mechanisms generally being more prescriptive.

As I will discuss below, the conditions and requirements for using Mechanisms are insufficiently clear, particularly in cloud, and Member States' approaches differ. The Mechanisms are generally complex, cumbersome, unnecessarily expensive and time-consuming for both DPAs and controllers, particularly multinationals, causing practical compliance difficulties. This may have discouraged their use, resulting in poor compliance. Uncertainties arising from overcomplexity must also weaken the Restriction's normative effect (Reed 2012: chap.8). Enforcement is low (Ch.6).

Yet, as I will show, the Mechanisms do not necessarily achieve the Restriction's anticircumvention objective, with some DPAs insisting on *further* measures to comply with national DPD Laws even when a Mechanism is used (p.19). This approach underlines the Restriction's status as a separate Frankenrule which positively causes harm, wasting time and money that ought to be spent elsewhere if the true goal is better privacy protection. In particular, Mechanisms are too inflexible for modern supply chains that employ (possibly multiple) subprocessors. Also, I will show that, in assessing adequacy, DPAs generally do not allow technological protections to be taken into account sufficiently or at all, which I argue is mistaken.

I will analyse Mechanisms for adequate protection: who assesses adequate protection and how it is assessed. Then I cover Mechanisms for adequate safeguards. Finally, I consider certain derogations. Although

Safe Harbour has been invalidated (5.3.2), this book still discusses aspects of it, partly because many cloud providers were harborites, but mainly because DPAs' approach to Safe Harbour exemplifies problems, not exclusive to Safe Harbour, with attempting to apply the Restriction and Mechanisms to cloud. Unfortunately, the GDPR exacerbates many of these problems, rather than solving them.

5.2 ASSESSING 'ADEQUATE PROTECTION'

5.2.1 Who Assesses Adequacy?

It is important to clarify who assesses adequacy, consistently across Member States (Commission 2003: p.51). Uncertainties and inconsistencies increase compliance complexities, particularly for controllers operating in multiple Member States.

Member States' approaches differ (COM(2003)265 final, sec.4.4.5; Commission 2003: p.32). Some delegate this assessment to their DPA or government. A few (Marchini et al. 2007: p.24), like the UK (ICO 2010: para.2.3.1), allow controllers to self-assess: i.e., conclude adequate protection for a transfer based on technical measures addressing security and other risks (ICO 2016b: p.91), e.g. through encryption (ICO 2015a: p.4). Self-assessment may be risky for controllers because DPAs may disagree with self-assessments and take enforcement action; it might also allow circumvention through transfers to a 'less strict' Member State and thence to third countries (Korff 2002b: p.211).[1]

The Commission disfavours self-assessment, because it could result in differing Member States' views of the protection levels in the same third country (COM(2010)609 final, para.2.4.1). However, its approach very much centres on the *laws* of the third country, without considering that technical means may provide adequate protection even in countries with 'bad' laws (cf. p.108, n.66). GDPR Art.45 implicitly prohibits self-assessment, as it permits 'adequate protection'-based transfers only under Commission decisions that the relevant third country or international organization affords adequate protection (although transfers are still possible under appropriate safeguards or derogations, discussed later).

---

[1] Apparently, self-assessment in the UK was one trigger for the Commission's action against the UK claiming defective DPD implementation (Ministry of Justice 2011: p.4; Commission 2010a) – since dropped following UK 'clarifications' (Commission 2012a: p.41).

Nevertheless I first cover the position under the DPD, to enable comparison with the GDPR's changed approach and to illustrate issues arising with cloud that will persist under the GDPR. As will become evident, many of the GDPR's changes reflect the WP29's views on certain aspects of the Restriction and Mechanisms.

5.2.2   How Is Adequacy Assessed?

Under the DPD, adequacy is assessed (emphasis added) (Art.25(2)):

> in the light of all the circumstances surrounding *a data transfer operation or set of data transfer operations*; particular consideration shall be given to the nature of the data, the purpose and duration of the proposed processing operation or operations, the country of origin and country of final destination, *the rules of law, both general and sectoral, in force in the third country in question* and the professional rules *and security measures* which are complied with in that country.

Thus, third country rules of law are relevant. Under Art.25(6), if the Commission decides a third country does (or does not) ensure adequate protection by reason of its domestic law or international commitments, Member States must allow transfers to countries thus found adequate, and prevent transfers to those found inadequate. But how should adequate protection be assessed:[2]

- for an individual transfer operation or set of transfer operations, or
- in a particular third country, for the Commission's adequacy decisions?

It might be that the same criteria should apply to both. However, they do not, partly because who assesses adequacy may differ – discussed next.

5.2.2.1   Individual transfers or sets of transfers

Art.25(2) clearly intended adequacy assessments to be contextual, and that protection may be based on security measures, not just legal/ professional rules (2.4.2). The WP29's opinions on adequacy assessment (consolidated in *WP12*) recommend, for specific transfers, a risk-based analysis to determine what would be 'adequate protection' for that

---

[2]   E.g. a study for the Commission: 'conceptual problems remain, concerning the meaning of adequacy, sensitivity and risk' (Bennett et al. 1998: p.206).

transfer[3] and to help target policing/enforcement resources towards transfers involving greater privacy risks (*WP4*, sec.2(ii)).

It might seem consistent with the Restriction and a risk-based approach to conclude that encrypting personal data before 'transfer' may provide adequate protection (ICO 2010: para.2.4.1.4). Yet WP29's opinions do not discuss how adequate protection may be provided through security measures, notably technological measures such as encryption or technical access controls. This is a critical omission,[4] given Art.25(2)'s reference to security and the efficacy of technical measures to restrict access to personal data regardless of location. The failure of lawmakers and DPAs to give due weight to technological protections, indeed technology's role generally, is one of this book's major themes.

Transactions are considered particularly 'risky' if they involve sensitive data; risk of financial loss, serious embarrassment or reputational damage; are effected in order to make a decision 'which significantly affects the individual'; and, significantly for cloud, involve 'repetitive transfers involving massive volumes of data (such as ... the Internet)' (*WP12*, p.28). Sheer volume alone, indeed mere Internet use, was clearly considered to increase risks when *WP12* was written (1998). However, huge volumes of data are now routinely transmitted over the Internet (6.2). True, with larger volumes, the privacy of more people is threatened if adequate protection is not provided. But that is different from saying (as the WP29 implies) that volume alone makes adequate protection difficult or impossible. For example, numerous secure online payments involving personal data transfers occur frequently everyday – protected by encrypted browser connections. A truly risk-based approach should recognize risk-mitigation measures. Yet the GDPR entrenches, indeed extends, DPAs' assumption that large-volume or frequent transfers cannot be adequately protected (5.5.2). I argue that adequacy should require case-by-case consideration, including of *technical* measures applied. It is too rigid, and wrong given modern technological protections, to assume that personal data can never be adequately protected when volumes are large or transfers frequent. More significantly, that assumption misses the point, and undermines the supposed context-dependent nature of 'adequacy' under the DPD.

---

[3] Similarly, service type is relevant: protection may be adequate for one kind of service, but not another, 'although the data may be exactly the same' (Home Office 1996: para.7.7).

[4] E.g. 'Technical standards and configurations can offer valuable protections, but these are not clearly recognized' (Reidenberg 2002: p.2).

5.2.2.2 Third countries

Personal data may be transferred 'to' countries (whitelisted countries) found adequate by the Commission (Art.25(6)). The WP29 has opined on several countries' 'adequacy', based on its recommended approach to considering third countries' protection (*WP12*, ch.2). Both the content of rules applicable to personal data transferred to a country and procedural/ enforcement means to ensure their effectiveness require evaluation (*WP12*, p.5). For that purpose, it indicated 'core principles' and requirements as a starting point, emphasized not to be set in stone but dependent on individual privacy risks (*WP12*, pp.6–7).

5.2.2.2.1 Content   Third country laws should embody 'core principles' reflecting the Principles: purpose limitation; 'data quality'[5] and proportionality; 'transparency';[6] security; and data subject rights (*WP12*, p.6; *WP4*, sec.3(i)).[7] Further principles may be needed for specific processing – e.g. explicit consent for sensitive data, and rights regarding automated decisions.

Significantly, the WP29's core principles include restricting 'onward transfers' to other third countries (*WP12,* p.6), i.e. 'further transfers' by recipients, without any exceptions other than Art.26(1) derogations – although the DPD itself does *not* restrict onward transfers. This was because the WP29 wanted to prevent any possible use of the initial ('adequate') third country as a 'staging post' for transfers to another,

---

[5]   Although Art.6 DPD, headed 'Data quality', encompasses all the Principles except data subject rights – 1.5.6.

[6]   Meaning that individuals should be given information regarding the processing purpose and the third country data controller's identity, and other information insofar as necessary to ensure fairness (*WP12*, p.6), reflecting Rec.38, Art.10, Art.11(1). The DPD Principles do not cite 'transparency' as such, but the GDPR's Principles do (1.5.6).

[7]   *WP12*'s 'core principles' are not stated to include Art.6(1)(a)'s fair processing. Its 'transparency' principle (n.6) implies that 'fairness' involves notifying individuals. I disagree. Fairness is a broader concept, which should be a core principle separate from 'transparency'. Sometimes, transparency is required for fairness; other times, fairness may require additional or alternative elements beyond transparency, e.g. fair treatment of data subjects regardless of notifications to them. Art.7's criteria for legitimizing processing, e.g. consent, are necessary, but not sufficient, for fair processing. The GDPR's first Principle requires lawfulness, fairness *and* transparency (1.5.6).

inadequate, third country.[8] GDPR's Art.5 list of core principles (5.6) does not include GDPR's Restriction, but its Art.44 explicitly extends GDPR's Restriction to 'onward transfers' (1.6.3), although without defining them.

Furthermore, under *WP12*, p.17, fn.10, controller-recipient contracts, signed to provide adequate safeguards, should prohibit onward transfers in the absence of means to bind onward transferees contractually to data protection guarantees. The 2010 SCCs (5.4.2.1) and the Shield (5.3.4.2) reflect this approach, but insisting on contractually binding means again ignores technical protections. (5.6 revisits onward transfers.)

5.2.2.2.2 Procedure   For adequacy, the WP29 requires supervision by an independent regulatory authority. A country's procedural mechanisms, judicial or non-judicial, should be assessed for their ability to meet certain objectives which, the WP29 considers, a data protection procedural system should aim to provide (*WP4*, sec.4; *WP12*, p.7):[9]

- 'a good level of compliance' (acknowledging that no system can guarantee complete compliance) – characterized by a 'high degree of awareness' among controllers of their obligations, and data subjects of their rights and their exercise. To ensure respect for laws, the WP29 emphasizes 'effective and dissuasive sanctions' and systems for direct verification by DPAs and/or auditors under audit rights etc. (*WP9*, pp.10–12; *WP12*, pp.7, 12–13, 20–21);
- support/help for data subjects' exercise of their rights, rapidly, effectively and without 'prohibitive cost', i.e. institutional mechanisms for independent complaints investigation; and
- 'appropriate redress' for breaches, which 'must' involve an independent arbitration system with compensation and sanctions.

Arguably, the existence of a third country legal order which appears to match the DPD is insufficient in itself to ensure that transferring controllers will actually take adequate measures to protect personal data and can be held accountable if problems arise (Robinson et al. 2009: p.34). Third country laws and procedural mechanisms are relevant, but I argue that protection should not rely solely on laws and legal mechanisms. The measures *actually* implemented are critical. The role of technical protective mechanisms should be recognized appropriately,

---

[8]   Stated when commenting on Convention108's 'inadequacy' due to its lack of 'substantive rules' restricting transfers to *non*-parties (*WP4*, sec.4(i); *WP12*, p.8) – since addressed by Convention108-AP (2.2.7). See also 2.3.1.2, 5.3.4.2.

[9]   One might query how well *EEA* systems meet those objectives!

when considering compliance with the Principles for individual transfers or sets of transfers.

In short, all transfers to whitelisted countries are considered 'adequately protected' under the Restriction without more (e.g. without needing to apply any technical measures). However, I argue that third country (and EEA) laws alone are neither necessary nor sufficient to prevent circumvention of the Principles. The transferor should consider what specific protective legal, organizational and/or technical measures are appropriate in the individual circumstances, and implement them as necessary.

5.2.3 Commission Adequacy Decisions

How third countries' adequacy has been assessed under the DPD has been questioned, including whether the requirements for Commission adequacy decisions are sufficiently specified (COM(2010)609 final, para.2.4.1); the practical efficacy of the assessment system (Robinson et al. 2009: p.43); and the slowness of Commission decisions (Council 9788/15, fn.452). Also, arguably only third countries that follow the DPD strictly have been considered adequate; the adequacy rule has been called 'highly restrictive and polarizing' (Robinson et al. 2009: p.33), suggesting that the test applied was not adequacy but equivalence. Following *Schrems* (5.3.2), the test for Commission adequacy decisions is now 'essential equivalence' of protection under the country's legal order – different from 'equivalent' or 'identical' (*Schrems*, para.73; 5.2.2.2). Unfortunately for legal certainty, the meaning of 'essentially equivalent' is unclear.

The practical efficacy of whitelisting as a Mechanism for transfers is low, because few countries have been found 'adequate' – mostly small European countries. Few Member States accord Commission adequacy decisions 'direct effect' without further national legislative/administrative formalities, causing inconsistencies meanwhile (SEC(2012)72 final, Ann.2 para.10.11.1). One quasi-'sectoral' decision exists (Commission Decision 2002/2/EC), focusing on *recipients* more than territory: Canada is considered to provide adequate protection for transfers to recipients subject to Canada's PIPEDA (2.2.8). The WP29 has considered 'inadequate' only one third country, Australia (*WP40*),[10] and one province, Quebec (*WP219*: p.218). However, no Art.25(4) Commission

---

[10] The Principles were not considered fully implemented in Australia. Notably, its export restriction protected only Australians. If Australia was found to be 'adequate', Australian companies could import European citizens' personal

'inadequacy' decisions have been issued to date. A 'blacklist' of 'inadequate' countries, even for guidance purposes, would be politically sensitive (*WP4*, sec.2(i); *WP12*, p.27). Nonetheless, the adequacy requirement has caused many countries to adopt DPD-like laws (including TBDF restrictions), in hopes of fostering personal data flows from, and therefore trade with, the EEA (p.25).

Transfers to cloud providers are permissible where the datacentres they use are in whitelisted countries (3.7, 5.3.4.1).[11] The USA is not whitelisted. To comply with the Restriction when using US datacentres of US providers, who are currently most popular with cloud customers (1.2.4), other Mechanisms are necessary. A significant Art.25(6) decision for transfers to US providers was the Safe Harbour Decision, discussed shortly.

Current whitelisting decisions risked being invalidated for restricting DPAs' powers to terminate/suspend data flows, as they used the Safe Harbour Decision wording struck down in *Schrems* (5.3.2). To 'cure' that issue in extant whitelisting and SCCs decisions respectively, the Commission issued Commission Implementing Decision (EU) 2016/2295 and Commission Implementing Decision (EU) 2016/2297, removing such restrictions; it must still be notified if a national DPA bans or suspends flows to third countries. Despite these decisions, whitelisting decisions could still be challenged, e.g. if the recipient country conducts mass surveillance.

5.2.4 Adequacy under the GDPR

The Council was divided on GDPR's Restriction (Council 9788/15, fn.448): some Member States considered 'the public interest exception would in many cases be the main ground' for transfers, querying whether the 'old' adequacy test should be maintained and detailed 'as it would in practice not be applied in that many cases'. One thought 'the manifold exceptions emptied the adequacy rule of its meaning'. Some doubted whether the adequacy principle was the right way to protect personal data

data, then export that data (i.e. onward transfers) to countries without privacy laws *without* Australia's export restriction applying – circumventing the DPD.

[11] Based on DPAs' data location-centric approach, personal data may be 'transferred' to datacentres in whitelisted countries, even when the provider is third country-established. However, with *recipients* subject to PIPEDA (5.2.3), would DPAs still require EEA data localization? This question illustrates the difficulties arising from not distinguishing clearly between personal data location and jurisdiction over providers.

in the transfers context, given 'the many practical and political difficulties'. Seven including France, Germany, Italy and the UK queried the feasibility of maintaining an adequacy test 'with reference to the massive flows of personal data in the context of cloud computing'. Several raised its impact on existing Member State agreements. However, ultimately, GDPR's Restriction maintained the adequacy requirement.

The GDPR deliberately prevents Member States from allowing controllers to self-assess adequacy (5.2.1). Art.45(1) permits transfers, without further authorization, by both controllers and processors to third countries found adequate under the Commission decisions, based on amended adequacy factors applying only to the Commission's adequacy assessments (Art.45(2)). I discuss these factors shortly, but the fundamental test for adequacy under the GDPR is 'essential equivalence' of the third country's *legal order* with the EU's data protection regime (Rec.104; 5.2.3). One extension is that the Commission may find adequate protection for, not just a third country, but also a territory or specified sector(s) within that country, or an international organization (Art.45(1)).

Because only the Commission may assess the adequacy of third countries or international organizations, context-specific assessments in 'all the circumstances' of individual transfers no longer factor. Accordingly, the data's nature and processing purpose and duration are irrelevant to GDPR adequacy assessments (Art.45(2)). Under the GDPR, 'security measures' must mean measures applied, not by controllers, processors or recipients for particular transfers, but by international organizations; or, minimum security standards applied by a third country's sector or territory. New explicit factors include respect for human rights and public authorities' access to personal data, indicating post-Snowden concerns (Art.45(2)(a), Rec.104); and, reflecting previous WP29 opinions (5.2.2.2), data protection rules, onward transfer rules, effective data subject rights and redress, and effective independent supervisory authorities in the third country (Art.45(2)(a)–(b)), which 'should' provide cooperation mechanisms with Member States' DPAs (Rec.104).

The EDPB should be consulted for its opinion on the adequacy of the proposed third country, sector, etc. (Rec.105, Art.70(1)(s)). As with the DPD, its opinion is not decisive; that power lies with a committee (Art.93(2)),[12] whose 'comitology' procedure mirrors DPD Art.31's (5.3.3.1). Significantly, Commission GDPR adequacy decisions must be

---

[12] For all GDPR provisions requiring the Art.93(2) procedure, with flow-chart, see Hon (2016b).

reviewed in light of all relevant information at least every four years (Art.45(3)), in consultation with the relevant third country and others (Rec.106), and reports publicized (Art.97(1)). It must evaluate the functioning of adequacy decisions, reporting relevant findings to the Art.93(2) committee, Parliament and the Council (Rec.106 GDPR). The Commission must generally monitor for third country developments that could affect any such decisions (Art.45(4)), and promulgate decisions as necessary to repeal, amend or suspend the relevant decision, but without retroactive effect (Art.45(5)). The comitology procedure applies to such decisions, except that the Commission is empowered to take immediate action 'on duly justified imperative grounds of urgency', when it must commence negotiations with the country or organization concerned to remedy the situation (Art.45(6)). National DPAs or others could still challenge GDPR adequacy decisions, ultimately before the CJEU (5.3.2).

Pre-existing Art.25(6) DPD whitelisting decisions, including the Shield Decision (discussed shortly) remain effective, i.e. are 'grandfathered', unless and until amended, replaced or repealed by a Commission GDPR adequacy decision (Art.45(9) GDPR). However, the Commission must monitor and evaluate the functioning of such pre-existing decisions (by 25 May 2020 and every four years thereafter – Art.97).

A cut-down version of self-assessment has been retained as a very limited derogation, which is impracticable and unlikely to be used (5.5.2). In my view, prohibiting self-assessment by controllers and processors is retrograde, increasing prescriptiveness and inflexibility rather than contextualizing risk, and removing incentives for them to deploy important technical protective tools. It could make data protection laws less, not more, able to address new technologies.

There is another important point. EU or Member State law may, for 'important reasons of public interest', 'expressly set limits' to transfers of 'specific categories of personal data' to third countries or international organizations for which no Commission adequacy decision has yet been issued (Art.49(5)). This could lead to further fragmentation rather than harmonization, contrary to the GDPR's claimed objective.[13] Uncertainties

---

[13] Another fragmentation risk arises because Member States must promulgate exemptions or derogations from GDPR's Restriction as necessary to reconcile data protection rights with freedom of expression and information (Art.85(2)). Also, fragmentation may result because the GDPR allows Member States to require 'specific' safeguards for 'transfers' in the employment context within a group of undertakings or joint enterprises, unfortunately without clarifying whether this means international 'transfers', or disclosure – Art.88(2).

also arise. If a Commission adequacy decision regarding a particular third country exists under the *DPD* but not yet the GDPR (like the Shield Decision), are such national restrictions permitted? If a Member State imposes limitations regarding a third country but the Commission then adopts a GDPR adequacy decision regarding that country, would the national limitations automatically cease to be effective? What 'public interests' may be invoked, what does 'important' mean here, what kinds of 'specific categories' are envisaged, what sorts of limits can be set, and how far can they extend? Transparency is also a concern: any such Member State laws must be notified to the Commission, but seemingly notifications need not be published.

5.3 SAFE HARBOUR AND PRIVACY SHIELD

5.3.1 Overview

I now discuss Mechanisms for transfers to the USA: Safe Harbour and the Privacy Shield. The USA could not be whitelisted under the DPD, having a 'patchwork of narrowly-focussed sectoral laws and voluntary self-regulation' regarding privacy (*WP15*, p.2). The Safe Harbour scheme was accordingly proposed as a Mechanism to facilitate US transfers, given the high volumes of EU–US trade.

Although Safe Harbour has been invalidated by the *Schrems* case (covered shortly), I nevertheless discuss it, partly to facilitate my later comparison of certain aspects of Safe Harbour with its replacement, the EU–US Privacy Shield (Shield), and partly to illustrate certain problems with transfers and Mechanisms particularly relevant to cloud, which could continue under the Shield and furthermore apply to other Mechanisms too.

The Safe Harbour framework was a largely self-regulatory scheme created under a 2000 EU–US agreement. Promulgated under the Commission's powers under Art.25(6) to find that a third country ensures adequate protection, Commission Decision 2000/520/EC (Safe Harbour Decision) was intended to permit transfers to organizations 'established in the United States' that were validly self-certified under Safe Harbour and subject to US Federal Trade Commission (FTC) or (as air carriers and ticket agents) US Department of Transportation jurisdiction. Telecommunications common carriers (some of which are cloud providers) and financial institutions (e.g. banking, insurance) were ineligible, not being so subject. This coverage gap (Bigo et al. 2012: p.43) continues under the Shield.

The US Department of Commerce (DoC) issued US Safe Harbor Privacy Principles with Frequently Asked Questions (DoC 2000), whose text was negotiated with the Commission. These principles approximated the Principles, representing a political compromise to bridge the gap between EEA data protection and US privacy laws, rather than requiring US persons to comply with Principles in full force. Participating US organizations (harborites) had to comply with Safe Harbour principles covering: notice, choice, onward transfer, security, data integrity, access for individuals (data subjects), and enforcement (including an accessible alternative dispute resolution (ADR) mechanism). They had to recertify annually. Data subjects had direct rights against harborites, enforceable through ADR mechanisms. Transfers to harborites required no prior detailed authorizations or should have been approved automatically (Safe Harbour Decision, Rec.2), but some DPAs still required notifications or filings (Dhont et al. 2004: p.82).

Safe Harbour's adequacy was controversial. Harborites' compliance with Safe Harbour principles, and accordingly Safe Harbour's efficacy to protect data subjects, had been doubted.[14] German DPAs even required German controllers, before using Safe Harbour, to conduct and document certain checks and, if any doubts arose regarding compliance, recommended using SCCs (5.4.2) or BCRs (5.4.3) instead (Düsseldorfer Kreis 2010).[15]

I will outline *Schrems* and the invalidation of the Safe Harbour Decision, before discussing certain cloud issues under Safe Harbour and the Shield.

5.3.2 Safe Harbour's Invalidation – *Schrems*

Following Snowden's revelations, the Commission made 13 recommendations to strengthen Safe Harbour (COM(2013)847 final, pp.18–19), noting that large-scale access by intelligence agencies to data transferred to the US 'by' (*sic*: 'to') harborites raised 'serious questions' regarding the continuity of data protection rights of Europeans whose personal data were thus transferred. It commenced discussions with the US to revise Safe Harbour. The WP29 published its own views on how Safe Harbour should be improved (WP29 2014c). The Commission's

---

[14] E.g. *WP27*, p.14; Parliament's resolution P7_TA(2014)0230; SEC(2004)1323 p.13; Connolly 2008; Palekar 2007; *WP196*, para.3.5.1.

[15] Düsseldorfer Kreis comprises the 16 German federal and state DPAs.

negotiations were accelerated by the invalidation of the Safe Harbour Decision in case C362-14, *Schrems v Data Protection Commissioner* (*Schrems*).

In that case, Austrian lawyer Max Schrems complained to the Irish DPA regarding transfers of personal data by (Irish-incorporated) Facebook Ireland Ltd to the US-located servers of its parent, US-incorporated Facebook Inc., which was a harborite. He argued that US law and practice did not ensure adequate protection against US authorities' surveillance activities, given Snowden's revelations. The Irish DPA considered itself bound by the Safe Harbour Decision's finding that Safe Harbour provided adequate protection for transfers to harborites. Schrems commenced litigation for judicial review of the DPA's decision in the Irish court, which considered the real issue was the legality of Safe Harbour, and referred the matter to the CJEU accordingly.

The CJEU ruled the Safe Harbour Decision invalid, for two main reasons. Firstly, the Decision's Art.1, which stated that Safe Harbour principles were considered to ensure adequate protection, did not comply with Art.25(6) DPD and the EU Charter of Fundamental Rights (*Schrems*, paras.79–98). This was because it did not find, duly stating reasons, that the US in fact 'ensures' an adequate level of protection by reason of its domestic law or its international commitments; it contained no finding regarding the existence, in the US, of rules intended to limit any interference by US authorities (in pursuit of legitimate objectives such as national security) with the fundamental rights of persons whose data are transferred to the US, or of effective legal protection against such interference (paras.88–9). So, Art.1 was invalid for what might be considered a technical defect, without the CJEU needing to consider the *content* of Safe Harbour principles (para.98). Secondly, the Decision's Art.3(1) constrained national DPAs' powers 'under restrictive conditions establishing a high threshold for intervention', which the Commission had no legislative competence to do because, under Art.28 DPD (regarding DPAs) and the Charter's Art.8 (on data protection), national DPAs must have 'complete independence' to review 'any claim concerning the protection of a person's rights and freedoms in regard to the processing of [their] personal data' (para.99). Therefore, Art.3 was invalid. As Arts.1 and 3 were inseparable from the Decision's other provisions, their invalidity tainted and invalidated the entire Decision (para.105).

The CJEU emphasized that no Commission adequacy decision could prevent national DPAs from examining individuals' claims regarding the inadequate protection of their personal data transferred to a third country: indeed, they should investigate such claims with 'all due diligence' (para.63). However, neither national courts nor DPAs are empowered to declare Commission decisions invalid; only the CJEU can do so (para.62). National courts must refer such matters to the CJEU, while national laws must enable DPAs to seek referrals to the CJEU from their national courts (paras.64–5).

It also ruled that, when considering 'adequacy' of protection in a third country for the purposes of a Commission Art.25(6) decision, the test is whether the country's legal regime provides 'essentially equivalent' protection (5.2.3). Strictly, it addressed only the conditions under which the *Commission* can determine that a third country affords adequate protection under Art.25(6) (Commission 2015b), rather than controllers' self-assessment of adequacy under Art.25(2), but its observations should be considered in that context also. The GDPR abolishes such self-assessment altogether (5.2.4).

Technically, the CJEU's decision rested on the two points summarized above, so it did not need to consider Safe Harbour principles' substantive content. Nevertheless, it made various influential statements on mass surveillance (paras.91–5).[16] The elephant in the room is Art.3(2) DPD's exemption for Member States' national security (1.5.3), not stated to be restricted in any way as State security remains the sole responsibility of individual Member States under Art.4(2) Treaty on European Union and Art.346(1)(a) Treaty on the Functioning of the European Union (which is why some CJEU opinions (e.g. n.23) refer to terrorism as serious crime, which *is* within the EU's competence). Many Member States have mass surveillance legislation (or may conduct mass surveillance outside any specific authorizing legislation) but, in most Member States, DPAs have no or very limited competence to oversee national intelligence agencies (FRA 2015: sec.2.3.2). The GDPR similarly excludes such agencies' processing from its scope (1.5.3).

---

[16] Reaffirming that constraints and limitations apply to EU legislation interfering with Charter rights (private life and data protection). The WP29 set out four 'European essential guarantees' that must apply to state surveillance whether EU or third country *(WP237)*, clearly influenced by the Charter, *Schrems* and ECHR cases, as follows:

- clear, precise, accessible rules for processing, to give individuals reasonable foreknowledge of what might happen to their transferred personal data;
- demonstrating necessity and proportionality regarding the legitimate objectives pursued (generally national security);
- an independent, effective oversight mechanism; and
- effective remedies for individuals before an independent body.

As EU authorities indicated that SCCs and BCRs could still be used for US transfers pending further analysis (WP29 2015b; Commission 2015b), with the WP29 effectively offering a 'grace period' from enforcement until 31 January 2016, Safe Harbour's invalidation motivated a scramble towards SCCs (5.4.2)[17] and/or moving personal data physically back to the EEA. Indeed, on its post-*Schrems* webpage (since changed following the Shield's approval), Austria's DPA initially suggested to organizations previously relying on Safe Harbour for US transfers that they could retrieve their personal data from the US to a server in the EU or another country with adequate protection (Arbeit der DSB 2016). Anecdotally, from my practitioner experience, some UK organizations have indeed 'retrieved' their data to the EU. That solution, while exemplifying the location-centric approach, seems futile. Moving personal data back to the EEA does not necessarily stop US authorities from accessing the data (as I will discuss), and indeed, if they had already accessed the data, it would make no difference – so the main purpose of such a move would be formal compliance with the Restriction as a data location-constraining rule.

Following *Schrems*, some DPAs threatened, indeed took (6.4.3.3), enforcement action against organizations that previously relied on Safe Harbour for transfers to harborites but failed to implement alternative Mechanisms like SCCs post-*Schrems*. Cloud providers were quick to stress their SCCs offerings, e.g. Microsoft (Smith 2015a), or to introduce SCCs (Salesforce 2015). Oracle stated that its customers could choose to store their data in Europe, but clarified that 'Certain cloud operations may require access from engineering resources in other regions [see 3.7.3]. Those resources are subject to EU data transfer requirements without reliance on the Safe Harbor Framework' (Lillington 2015) – presumably SCCs?

Schrems also hastened the adoption of the EU–US Privacy Shield, designed to allow US transfers in place of Safe Harbour. I will discuss and compare specific data localization issues under Safe Harbour and the Shield after outlining the Shield framework.

---

[17] Over 80 percent of companies use SCCs for US transfers, one survey found; BCRs (5.4.3.2) were considered too expensive and/or slow, especially for SMEs (IAPP and EY 2016).

5.3.3 Privacy Shield

5.3.3.1 Overview

The process leading to the Shield was not straightforward (Hon 2016f). Draft documents of February 2016 were changed to:

- address criticisms, notably from the WP29 (*WP238*), echoed by the EDPS (EDPS 2016a) and a Parliament resolution (2016/2727(RSP); P8_TA(2016)0233), and
- make changes requested (Commission 2016a) by the 'Art.31 Committee', comprising Member State representatives, which under Art.31 DPD has the chief decision-making power regarding proposed DPD adequacy decisions.[18]

The Commission adopted a decision on the Shield (Shield Decision)[19] in July 2016 (Commission 2016d), finding that the US ensures adequate protection for transfers under the Shield 'from the Union' to what was described as 'organisations in the United States' (cf. 'organisations established in' the US, under Safe Harbour – 5.3.1; Shield Decision Rec.6). If this change suggests a *SWIFT*-like approach (p.90), whereby even EEA-established organizations 'in' the US must participate in the Shield to host personal data in their own US datacentres, that would reach the heights of absurdity. The different wording may simply result from the continuing conflation of location and jurisdiction, but this issue would benefit from clarification.

The Shield Decision's Annexes include Shield privacy principles (Annex II), a new arbitral model for individuals' 'last resort' redress before a 'Privacy Shield Panel' (cf. 5.2.2.2), and various US authorities' letters including regarding US law enforcement access to commercial data, US 'signals intelligence' oversight and transparency, and bulk collection of signals intelligence.

The changes from Safe Harbour reflect concerns regarding not only mass surveillance, but also circumvention through onward transfers (discussed shortly). The Shield framework retains the structure of Safe

---

[18]   Four Member States abstained during the committee vote (Baker 2016a). An online flowchart of the Art.31 process is available (Hon 2016a).

[19]   Commission Implementing Decision (EU) 2016/1250 of 12 July 2016 pursuant to Directive 95/46/EC of the European Parliament and of the Council on the adequacy of the protection provided by the EU–U.S. Privacy Shield (notified under document C(2016) 4176) (Text with EEA relevance), OJ L207/1, 1.8.2016.

Harbour's framework and principles (5.3.1), with 'onward transfer' becoming 'accountability for onward transfer', 'data integrity' becoming 'data integrity and purpose limitation' and 'enforcement' becoming 'recourse, enforcement and liability'. It includes further and tighter protections for data subjects, such as improved disclosures, transparency and dispute resolution avenues, and (addressing one of *WP238*'s concerns) a new explicit data retention principle. It clarifies certain rights and obligations (although perhaps implicit in Safe Harbour), adding definitions of 'controller' and 'processing' (but, inexplicably, not 'processor', although the term is used in relation to data-processing contracts: Shield principles III.10.a), and provides for a US Ombudsperson to hear complaints regarding US national security access (generally, not just for transfers made under the Shield). Detailed discussion is out of scope; I only highlight issues most relevant to this book. However, there are clarity, consistency and substantive issues. The first joint annual review in 2017, which will inevitably take account of the GDPR, affords an opportunity to address these issues.

5.3.3.2 Annual reviews

The Shield became effective from 1 August 2016,[20] when the US Department of Commerce began accepting self-certifications; Safe Harbour renewals ceased to be accepted from 31 October 2016.[21] Even after the GDPR becomes effective, the Shield Decision remains in force until amended, replaced or repealed by a Commission Decision under GDPR Art.45 (GDPR Art.45(9)) – or invalidated by the CJEU.

Presaging the GDPR (5.2.4), Shield Decision Art.4(4) requires annual Commission re-evaluations of its adequacy finding, following annual joint reviews between the Commission and US authorities (including intelligence representatives and the new Ombudsperson established to deal with EU individuals' requests/complaints regarding any US signals intelligence issues, not just under the Privacy Shield), where EU DPAs and the WP29 can be involved (Shield Decision Recs.124, 146–9, 152).[22]

5.3.3.3 DPA concerns

While welcoming the Shield's improvements over Safe Harbour, the WP29 noted the continuing lack of 'specific rules on automated decisions and of a general right to object', lack of clarity regarding how the

---

[20] Privacy Shield Framework, 81 Fed. Reg. 51052 (2 Aug. 2016).

[21] According to https://safeharbor.export.gov/list.aspx.

[22] This goes further than the GDPR, which requires adequacy decisions under it to be reviewed only every *four* years (Art.45(3)).

Shield's principles apply to processors, guarantees regarding the Ombudsperson being less strict than 'expected', and lack of 'concrete assurances' that US authorities do not engage in mass indiscriminate data collection (despite the US Office of the Director of National Intelligence committing not to do so) (WP29 2016). Significantly, the WP29 stated, 'The results of the first joint review regarding access by U.S. public authorities to data transferred under the Privacy Shield may also impact transfer tools such as Binding Corporate Rules and Standard Contractual Clauses', implying that, at least collectively, DPAs might not take action regarding BCRs or SCCs for US transfers before then.

5.3.3.4 Invalidation risk

Following an annual review, or indeed anytime, the Shield Decision could be amended, suspended or revoked (Art.4(6)). It seems the WP29 collectively will await the first joint review's assessment of the Shield's robustness and efficiency, but meanwhile DPAs will 'proactively and independently' assist data subjects to exercise their Shield rights (WP29 2016).

More significantly, this decision is being challenged, in T-670/16 *Digital Rights Ireland v Commission* and T-738/16 *La Quadrature du Net and Others v Commission*, by among others the privacy advocacy group whose challenge resulted in the CJEU invalidating the Data Retention Directive 2006/24/EC (Joined cases C-293/12 and C-594/12 *Digital Rights Ireland Ltd*). Hopefully the CJEU will expedite the hearing to avoid prolonging the legal uncertainty. Unlike the Safe Harbour Decision, the Shield Decision contains extensive recitals finding adequate protection (Recs.136–41), detailing its grounds based on Shield privacy principles protections (5.3.4.3). It does not purport to restrict DPA powers as the Safe Harbour Decision did. These differences clearly attempt to address *Schrems*'s criticisms of Safe Harbour and seek to make the Shield Decision more able to resist challenge. Much will depend on whether the CJEU considers the US's safeguards and limitations sufficient, and its important ruling is awaited.[23]

---

[23] On the ePrivacy Directive, Advocate-General Saugmandsgaard Øe opined (although the CJEU could ultimately disagree) that Member States may legislate for electronic communications services providers to retain users' communications data to fight serious crime particularly terrorism, subject to strict safeguards and conditions (Joined Cases C-203/15 and C-698/15, *Tele2 Sverige AB*). On the legality of a draft agreement between the EU and Canada for exchange of Passenger Name Record (PNR) data, Advocate-General Mengozzi suggested (Opinion 1/15) that, for automated comparisons of PNR data against scenarios or

5.3.3.5 Data localization misconceptions

Efforts to address government surveillance by restricting commercial data flows through data protection laws, e.g. suspending or terminating the Shield Decision, seem misconceived and could adversely affect EEA and US users' access to EEA, US and other organizations' services. More importantly, such restrictions alone cannot improve EEA citizens' protection against government access to data for national security purposes (Boué 2013).

Terminating or suspending the Shield would not protect EEA citizens better against government surveillance, without more. It would not stop EEA residents from using US websites or cloud providers, particularly SaaS, for personal purposes – such use is generally outside the scope of EU data protection laws (1.5.3), yet may involve much personal data being uploaded to such providers.[24] Furthermore, it cannot stop EEA intelligence agencies from collecting/intercepting and passing personal data to the NSA (7.5.2.1); that requires enforcing appropriate rules regarding state surveillance, as a human rights matter,[25] against *EEA* not just third country authorities. EEA authorities' mass surveillance has not necessarily been conducted lawfully, e.g. in the UK (Travis 2016).

5.3.4 Safe Harbour, Privacy Shield and Cloud

Many US cloud providers were Safe Harbour-certified before its invalidation, including Apple, AWS, Facebook, Google, Microsoft and Twitter.[26] However, whether controllers could use their services compliantly with the Restriction was complicated – particularly when services were provided wholly or partly using datacentres *not* located in the US or EEA (p.96).

I now discuss aspects of Safe Harbour and the Shield particularly relevant to data localization and cloud:

---

predetermined risk assessment criteria or databases to identify 'targets' for further checks, principles and rules should be included regarding the scenarios and criteria/databases, which should not be based on race, religion or other sensitive data.

[24] The NSA has collected private webmail users' address books (Gellman and Soltani 2013a).

[25] Noted as applicable to EU, not just third country, authorities in *WP237* – n.16.

[26] Denmark's DPA banned use of US provider Dropbox's SaaS service because Dropbox was not a harborite (*Dropbox* (Denmark)). Perhaps not coincidentally, Dropbox subscribed to Safe Harbour soon afterwards.

- the Restriction as a Frankenrule on data location;
- onward transfers and processors, particularly with layered services; and
- law enforcement etc. access.

5.3.4.1 The Restriction as a Frankenrule

As discussed earlier (p.96), Denmark's DPA, Datatilsynet, insisted that personal data transferred to a harborite (Google) must be processed *only* in Google's US or EEA datacentres; otherwise, standard contractual clauses (SCCs) or another Mechanism must be used. However, the Safe Harbour Decision/principles contained no conditions or qualifications regarding data location. Under Safe Harbour Decision Art.1(1), adequate protection was deemed for transfers 'to organizations established in the United States', focusing on transferees' *US establishment* (undefined), not data location. Datatilsynet's approach illustrates DPAs' treatment of the Restriction as a rule regarding physical location of personal data. Recall also that when personal data were mirrored to SWIFT's US datacentre, SWIFT (a Belgian entity) ended up having to subscribe to Safe Harbour to regularize its personal data location in the US – which seems artificial and absurd (p.98). SWIFT remained subject to Belgian data protection jurisdiction. Subscribing to Safe Harbour did not affect the Belgian DPA's jurisdiction over SWIFT. Neither did it affect SWIFT's ability to resist US subpoenas, indeed arguably Safe Harbour subscription exposed SWIFT further to US authorities' action. SWIFT being required to subscribe to Safe Harbour merely ticked a box to satisfy a separate Frankenrule that physical data location in the US requires Safe Harbour subscription or SCCs etc., without considering the underlying Principles.

Similarly illustrating the Restriction's Frankenrule status and also DPAs' concerns regarding cloud security, the WP29 echoed German DPAs' doubts about Safe Harbour's adequacy (5.3.1), further stating that, given cloud-specific risks, Safe Harbour self-certification alone might not be sufficient without 'robust enforcement' of data protection principles in the cloud, and that Safe Harbour principles 'by themselves' might not 'guarantee' that US cloud providers apply appropriate security measures; therefore, *additional* safeguards might be advisable, e.g. independent certifications of providers' systems (*WP196*, pp.17–18).[27] In considering Dutch controllers' use of a US provider's cloud service, the Netherlands'

---

[27] See pp.186, 286; 5.7 particularly p.211; 5.4.5.

DPA (CBP) interpreted Safe Harbour Decision Art.2[28] as signifying that compliance with Safe Harbour principles meant 'solely that personal data may be transferred to the US', without guaranteeing that the US processing met all requirements under the DPD or applicable DPD Laws (Autoriteit Persoonsgegevens (formerly CBP) 2012: p.4). This epitomizes many DPAs' view of the Restriction as a stand-alone rule regarding personal data location *only*. Reflecting DPAs' continuing dissatisfaction with Safe Harbour's adequacy generally (not just in cloud), the CBP's opinion considered, consistently with *WP196*, that Safe Harbour alone offered no 'certainty' that personal data processed in cloud were adequately protected or that processing in the US met national law or security requirements; processor agreements would need to include additional provisions in that regard (Autoriteit Persoonsgegevens (formerly CBP) 2012: pp.4–5). Similarly, Hungary's DPA 'opposed' 'transfer' 'to the "cloud"' by a political association which wished to process supporters' personal data using a cloud service (US parent, Irish subsidiary); although the provider was a harborite, the DPA had doubts about cloud's security, given the sensitive nature of political data (WP29 2015a: p.62). The underlying concern there was clearly compliance with security requirements, where the DPA did not consider Safe Harbour sufficient to ensure such compliance.

Note the inconsistency and disconnect. The Restriction/Mechanisms were designed to prevent circumvention of, and accordingly ensure continued compliance with, DPD Laws. However, some DPAs clearly considered that Safe Harbour was insufficient for that purpose, insisting on further measures for compliance (particularly regarding security) by interpreting the Restriction as a separate rule regulating only 'transfer', interpreted as the physical 'movement' of personal data to third country territory (Ch.3).[29]

In emphasizing Safe Harbour's 'inadequacy' and requiring continued compliance with national DPD Laws, it might seem that DPAs were veering towards requiring equivalence rather than adequacy: equivalence with individual national implementations, at that. However, controllers must comply with relevant national DPD Laws anyway, including when using processors (pp.53, 64, 103), so arguably Safe Harbour (and indeed

---

[28]   'This Decision concerns only the adequacy of protection provided in the United States under the Principles … and does not affect the application of other provisions of that Directive that pertain to the processing of personal data within the Member States …'

[29]   Also Korff (2010: pp.44, 47, 79–80, 99).

the Restriction) added nothing as regards controllers' US 'transfers'. The US response (DoC 2013) to *WP196* stressed:

- Harborites' 'fully enforceable'[30] commitment to Safe Harbour principles provided the adequate protection guarantee: 'Additional requirements cannot be imposed exclusively on US service providers ... simply because they satisfy the "adequacy" requirement' through Safe Harbour.[31]
- Safe Harbour's principles-based framework allowed controller and processor to define specific security requirements, and Safe Harbour's 'reasonable precautions' security requirement echoed Art.17's requirements (security measures, choosing processors, etc.).

DoC's statements were strictly correct regarding US providers particularly as, independently of the Restriction, controllers who use processors must comply with Art.17(2)–(3) DPD. Indeed, regarding use of US providers, DPAs' and DoC's views may not conflict. Art.17(2)–(3) requires controllers to choose providers providing sufficient guarantees regarding security measures, implement required contracts with such providers and ensure compliance with those measures, which must include cloud-appropriate measures if using cloud. Thus, arguably the Restriction (and Mechanisms such as Safe Harbour or the Shield) in fact diverts attention away from core compliance with DPD Laws, notably national requirements regarding security measures, including when using non-EEA cloud providers (p.172). A recipient using non-US third country infrastructure risks being subjected to that country's laws, so DPAs' concerns regarding those risks may underlie such insistence.[32] However, given technological developments and supply chains' complexity, particularly in cloud, using infrastructure in a country does not necessarily give it effective jurisdiction to apply its laws to personal data processed there (Ch.4), and risk-mitigating steps are possible (7.5.1.1).

The Privacy Shield seems set to continue the misconceived focus on data location, and the confusion between data location and jurisdiction. Its Rec.15 states that the Shield does not affect the application of Union legislation governing the processing of personal data 'in' the Member

---

[30]   On Safe Harbour enforcement, see 6.4.4.3.

[31]   Art.25(6) DPD adequacy decisions and their enforcement should not 'arbitrarily or unjustifiably discriminate' between third countries or constitute a disguised trade barrier (Safe Harbour Decision, Rec.4).

[32]   See SWIFT – p.92.

States (rather than by controllers subject to Member State jurisdiction); a footnote emphasizes the equipment ground but overlooks the fact that EEA controllers must comply with their DPD Laws when processing personal data, *wherever* the processing facilities are located (2.3.2).

Shield participants certified at October 2016 include cloud providers such as Amazon, Dropbox, Facebook, Google, Microsoft, Oracle, Salesforce and Workday – but not Apple, IBM or Twitter. It seems likely that DPAs will, as with Safe Harbour, treat the Shield as only enabling US location of personal data, and insist on further requirements for compliance with the Principles. The Shield's security principle (II.4) follows DPD Art.17 more closely than Safe Harbour did, in referring not to 'reasonable precautions' but 'reasonable and appropriate' security measures taking due account of the risks and nature of the personal data. Whether it would satisfy DPAs concerned about cloud security is unknown. However, large cloud providers offer large customers summaries or copies of independent third party experts' security certifications (Hon, Millard and Walden 2013a), and cloud security may exceed internal security measures (7.3.).

5.3.4.2 Onward transfers and processors

Safe Harbour's onward transfer requirements varied with the onward transferee's status – as a 'third party'[33] (separate legal entity) or the harborite's 'agent' (a third party that 'performs tasks on behalf of and under the instructions of the organization') (DoC 2000: endnotes 1–2). These concepts corresponded approximately, but not precisely, with DPD concepts of 'controller' and 'processor'.[34] The Shield's principles (I.8) define 'controller' and 'processing', and the Shield Decision emphasizes (Rec.14) that processors may be Shield participants,[35] but in several respects the Shield framework still does not deal appropriately with processors or even distinguish properly between the roles of controller and processor (5.3.3.1). It still refers to 'third party', with occasional references to a 'third party' acting as a controller or 'agent' (II.3).

---

[33] Perhaps analogous to 'third party' for DPD purposes, although the position is uncertain – 'third party' under the DPD *excludes* controller and processor (Dhont et al. 2004: fn.28).

[34] Dhont et al. (2004: fnn.27–8; p.24). The 'controller'/'processor' boundary is blurred – p.9. The 'third party'/'agent' boundary is difficult also.

[35] Some queried whether processors (not just controllers) could be harborites. The better view is, they could (Kuner 2007a: p.182; Determann 2013: p.19).

There are particular issues with 'onward transfers'. How Safe Harbour dealt with onward transfers was unsatisfactory, but the Shield, while clarifying and improving some issues, has exacerbated others. At least the purpose of the Shield's onward transfer rules, termed the 'Accountability for Onward Transfer Principle', is explicitly anticircumvention: 'to ensure that the protections guaranteed to the personal data of EU data subjects will not be undermined, and cannot be circumvented, by passing them on to third parties' (Rec.27) – i.e., concern that personal data could be disclosed or transmitted by a Shield participant to a US or other third country controller who might then process personal data against data subjects' interests free of the Principles or Shield principles.[36] However, as I will discuss, the Shield framework does not implement the best or even most appropriate way to prevent circumvention and maintain data protection.

Under Safe Harbour, the 'onward transfer' principle applied if a harborite 'discloses information to a third party', US or otherwise.[37] So, 'onward transfer' was effectively equated with 'disclosure', suggesting *active revelation* of intelligible personal data to another person who would thereby gain knowledge of its content, without another third country necessarily being involved. The Shield Decision changed 'discloses' to 'transfers', defining 'onward transfers' as 'transfers of personal data from an organisation to a third party controller or processor, irrespective of whether the latter is located in the United States or a third country outside the United States (and the Union)' (Rec.27). Unfortunately, it does not define 'transfer', which is problematic (3.7.6), or what 'location' is intended: the location of the third party's physical operations, or its jurisdiction of incorporation?

The terminology change to 'transfers' was presumably for consistency with the DPD. However, the 'disclosure' phraseology is retained elsewhere. For example, the Shield's Choice principle (II.2), applicable when making onward transfers to a controller (II.3.a), refers to individuals' right to 'opt out' of their 'personal information' being 'disclosed to a third party' or used for 'materially different' purposes (or, for sensitive information, express consent is needed). Similarly, the Notice principle (II.1) requires notice before such use or disclosure (not 'transfer') to a

---

[36] Some considered that Safe Harbour's onward transfer principles were 'less stringent' than the DPD: 'advantageous' for transferors, but possibly resulting in the USA being used as a 'staging post' to circumvent EU law (Dhont et al. 2004: p.106; Kuner 2009: sec.III.B).

[37] Safe Harbour's notice and choice principles both referred to 'disclosure' (DoC 2000).

third party. A paragraph regarding retention of information in identifiable form mentions, regarding identifiability, whether an individual could reasonably be identified by 'a third party if it would have access to the data' (II.5.b, fn.3), which I argue must imply *intelligible* access by the third party is required for 'onward transfer'. Hopefully the Shield's first review (5.3.3.2) will clarify these inconsistencies.

I now consider onward transfers under the Shield. Clearly, Shield participants (and, previously, harborites) may be controllers or processors, even both for different transfers. Therefore, onward transfers may be made by a controller, to a controller or processor; or by a processor, to a controller or a processor – e.g. a subprocessor, as with layered cloud services (1.2.2). In this context, two major issues arise with the Shield, as with Safe Harbour before it. Firstly, it generally assumes that the US participant is a controller, rather than processor (e.g. Shield Decision, fn.31). Secondly, it focuses mainly on the onward transferee's status, rather than whether the *Shield participant* is a controller or processor. As a result, neither framework caters adequately for onward transfers by processor participants to other (sub)processors. The Shield envisages onward transfers *to* processors, who could transfer personal data further to a subprocessor (Rec.20, Shield Decision), but it does not properly address onward transfers *by* processor Shield participants to subprocessors (see also Rec.29).

These issues pose difficulties for onward transfers in layered cloud. Suppose that an EEA controller uses, as its processor, a US SaaS/PaaS provider which is a Shield participant. If that processor's service was built on the service (typically IaaS/PaaS) of another provider, the IaaS/PaaS subprovider (as the processor's subprocessor or 'agent') would generally be considered the processor's onward transferee. However, neither Safe Harbour nor the Shield deals appropriately with the role of infrastructure cloud, or IaaS/PaaS providers in layered cloud. The nature of layered cloud services, rather than any explicit intention of an SaaS/PaaS processor to 'disclose' or 'transfer' data to its IaaS/PaaS subprocessor, means that subprocessors typically have the technical ability to access data processed via their infrastructure/service by their customers, or perhaps their customers' customers (whether processors or controllers). Subprocessors may be restricted or prevented from exercising intelligible access through legal means, e.g. their contracts with the processors (or direct contracts with controllers), or, crucially, through technical means, e.g. when controllers or processors apply strong encryption to render data unintelligible to processors and/or subprocessor(s) respectively. But technical protections are generally overlooked by lawmakers and regulators (discussed further in Ch.7). For example, SaaS provider Dropbox, which originally[38] used AWS IaaS, encrypted its customer data; therefore, Dropbox's employees potentially had intelligible access.[39] However, Dropbox's then-subprovider AWS had no intelligible access, without Dropbox sharing its decryption keys with AWS.

This again exemplifies the difficulties with applying laws based on outdated assumptions to modern technologies. Particularly given references to 'disclosure' in both Safe Harbour and Shield frameworks, and despite one terminology change in the Shield to 'transfer', I argue that no 'onward transfer' occurs if 'onward transferees' (as opposed to Shield participants) have no *intelligible* access. Clarification is much needed. However, the discussion below assumes, conservatively, that 'disclosure' or 'transfer' does include mere use of another provider's infrastructure/ service to process personal data, i.e. that there is always 'onward transfer' to the IaaS/PaaS subprovider or 'third party agent' used by a Shield-participating SaaS/PaaS processor engaged by an EEA controller, even when the data involved are encrypted and the subprovider cannot access the decryption keys.

Safe Harbour offered several options (including contract, and the onward transferee's Safe Harbour subscription) allowing onward transfer to third party agents. It did not require contracts for transfers to controllers. However, the Shield generally requires contracts for onward transfers,[40] whether by and/or to controllers or processors (Recs.14, 28, fn.14, Shield Decision; Shield principles II.3) – with limited exceptions,

---

[38] In early 2016, Dropbox announced its move away from AWS, having grown so large that using its own infrastructure became more efficient – contrary to most cloud customers' experiences (Hansen 2016). However, because of data localization issues, it will still 'partner with Amazon where it makes sense for our users, particularly globally ... we'll expand our relationship with AWS to store data in Germany for European business customers that request it' (Gupta 2016). Such German storage has since transpired (Lacor 2016).

[39] P.138, n.16. If Dropbox's *customers* encrypt data pre-upload, retaining sole access to the decryption keys, even Dropbox employees should not have intelligible access.

[40] Acknowledging that implementing compliant contracts with pre-existing third party commercial partners would take time, a 'grace period' (transitional provisions) permitted participants who certified by 30 September 2016 to bring those relationships into conformity with Shield rules as soon as possible but within nine months after self-certification – prompting a rush to certify by that deadline. Meanwhile they must apply the Notice *and Choice* principles and, for onward transfers to agents, ensure agents provide at least the same level of protection (Rec.17, Shield Decision; Shield principle III.6.e).

e.g. for controller–controller onward transfers[41] under 'instruments' to ensure continued protection such as BCRs or 'other intra-group instruments' (Shield Decision, fn.29; Shield principles, III.10.b[42]). The Shield's insistence on contracts for most onward transfers exceeds the DPD's requirements, but follows the 2010 SCCs (discussed shortly). It illustrates the prioritization of legal over technical means of protection (such as encryption to prevent intelligible access by onward transferees like IaaS/PaaS providers), and again puts prescriptive requirements ahead of fundamental compliance with the Principles.

Like the GDPR, the Shield requires contracts for processor–subprocessor onward transfers, seemingly even if they both subscribe to a BCR (n.42). For onward transfers to processors (agents), participants must:

- transfer only for limited and specified purposes;
- 'ascertain that the agent is obligated' to provide at least the same level of privacy protection required by the Shield's principles;
- take reasonable and appropriate steps to ensure the agent effectively processes transferred personal information consistently with the participant's Shield obligations;
- require the agent to notify the participant if it determines it can no longer meet its obligation to provide the same level of protection;
- upon notice, including after such determination, take reasonable and appropriate steps to stop and remediate unauthorized processing; and
- provide a summary or representative copy of the relevant privacy provisions of its contract with that agent to DoC upon request (II.3.b).[43]

---

[41]   Onward transfers to controllers also require applying the Choice principle (II.2) – not discussed further here.

[42]   This 'instruments' exception unfortunately does not include transfers involving processors (e.g. processor–subprocessor transfers under BCRs), again illustrating the Shield's failure to consider processors' position properly.

[43]   III.10.a's requirements, regarding contracts when EEA controllers transfer to Shield processors, were intended to reflect Art.17 DPD but, confusingly, sit under a higher-level heading 'Obligatory contracts for onward transfers', implying that they apply to *onward* transfers by such processors to subprocessors. They were not *intended* to apply to onward transfers contracts, despite that higher-level heading (DoC 2016, pers. comm., 30 September). However, clarification during the Shield's review would be helpful, e.g. by moving that section away from that higher-level heading.

These requirements are direct obligations on participants, but to comply with some of them they should include appropriate terms in their contracts with onward transferee 'agents' (II.3.b): i.e. specific purposes, obligations to maintain privacy protection levels and notify any inability to comply, and obligation to remediate (DoC 2016, pers. comm., 30 September). These requirements are similar to Art.17 DPD's requirements when a controller uses a processor, echoing and broadening the 2010 SCCs. Tending towards the GDPR, like Safe Harbour they require not only security measures but 'at least the same' (exceeding 'essentially equivalent') level of privacy protection, and notification/remediation commitments. However, the terms that processor–subprocessor contracts must include for onward transfers are inappropriate and unworkable in layered cloud, where EU controllers directly control their personal data processing on a self-service basis and subprocessors (even processors) may not know what controllers do with or to that data using the service, or even what data controllers are processing.

The focus on contracts with onward transferees also overlooks the issue of jurisdiction over transferees. Safe Harbour allowed onward transfer to 'agents' (i.e. processors) if the onward transferee subscribed to Safe Harbour principles, was subject to the DPD or another adequacy decision, or agreed to provide at least the level of protection required by 'relevant' Safe Harbour principles. That was the 'wrong way round'. Those conditions made sense for onward transfers to *controllers*,[44] but not to processors: the DPD requires no obligations to be imposed on processors (1.5.2) and processors, as agents, must follow harborites' instructions. The Shield requires contracts for onward transfers even to controllers who are Shield participants or subject to DPD jurisdiction or another adequacy decision (e.g. EEA controllers or controllers in whitelisted countries). That also goes beyond the DPD. It seems absurd to require contracts for onward transfers to controllers subject to EEA or other 'adequate' laws, when *direct* transfers by EEA controllers to such controllers would not require contracts. The onward transfer definition (Rec.27) covers third parties in the US or 'a third country outside the United States (and the Union)', suggesting that further transfers to *EEA* third parties might not be 'onward transfers', but clarification is needed.

---

[44] An EEA controller may disclose personal data to another controller if there is a legal basis for the disclosure and the disclosure otherwise complies with the Principles (disclosure is 'processing'). Generally, it would not be liable for subsequent data protection breaches by the recipient controller (p.122). Relinquishing control to another controller has been likened to true alienation or disposal (Gunasekara 2007).

Another problem with Safe Harbour's onward transfer principle was that a harborite who onward transferred to an agent, compliantly with one of the conditions above, was not liable for the onward transferee's 'contrary' processing unless it knew or should have known about the contrary processing and had not taken reasonable steps to prevent or stop it. Again, this is appropriate if a controller-harborite compliantly onward transferred to another controller, but not with onward transfers to 'agents', as surely harborites should remain liable for their agent's defaults.[45] Addressing this point, the Shield clarifies that a participant making onward transfers to a 'third party' agent remains liable under Shield principles if the agent processes the transferred information inconsistently with the Principles, unless the participant proves it is 'not responsible for the event[46] giving rise to the damage' (II.7.d).[47] That phrase, while mirroring GDPR's Arts.82(3), 47(2)(f) liability provisions, is unfortunately both too broad and too narrow. Like GDPR Art.82(3), it is too broad because it refers to responsibility for the 'event', not responsibility for the 'damage' (whereas GDPR Rec.146 refers to the latter). In a complex supply chain, if all subservice components are needed to effect a processing operation, all processors and subprocessors could be considered to contribute to the 'event', if not necessarily the 'damage'; so all could be exposed to liability even where the damage was

---

[45] The WP29 considered Safe Harbour's liability exclusion inconsistent with general rules for guaranteeing enforcement and harborite liability (*WP27*, p.7). However, that exclusion seemed a fair substitute for the position on EEA controller-*to-controller* disclosures/transmissions (n.44; p.185), although, problematically, it might have allowed processor-harborites to escape liability following onward transfers to other harborites etc. Of course, an EEA controller transferring personal data to a harborite *processor* remained liable for any onward transferee's breaches.

The WP29 felt data subject consent should be required for onward transfers to non-harborite third parties (*WP32*, para.3.3). Such consents are arguably irrelevant with controller–processor or processor–subprocessor onward transfers (or transfers). Indeed, Shield principle II.2.b confirmed the inapplicability of the 'Choice' principle on 'disclosure' to a third party 'agent'. Even for controller–controller onward transfers, I suggest only the Principles (or equivalent) should apply, without always requiring contracts or data subject consent.

[46] 'Responsible for the event' is undefined – does it target causation, or legal responsibility? If the latter, controllers and processors are legally 'responsible', so the phrase seems superfluous. If the former, controllers and processors might escape liability for breaches caused by their (sub)processors.

[47] Shield Decision Rec.29 only notes the liability of a participant 'acting as the controller'; Shield principle II.7.d is broader. The latter is preferable: surely processors should be liable for their subprocessors' breaches.

not their fault (Hon 2015b). It is too narrow because, as a normative data protection policy issue, controllers should remain liable for their processors' breaches, and processors' for their subprocessors' breaches, even if a controller (or processor respectively) was not itself 'responsible' for the 'event' giving rise to the damage.

Furthermore, as processors have obligations under their Art.17 contracts with their EEA controllers (as III.10.a makes clear), why should contracts for onward transfers by processor participants to subprocessors always be necessary? Such contracts may be sensible from processors' viewpoint, to help them comply with their contractual obligations to their controllers, as they remain liable to their controllers for subprocessor breaches. However, equally, in some situations strong encryption by processors, where subprocessors cannot access the decryption keys (as in the Dropbox/AWS example), could protect data as well if not better than contracts with subprocessors. Unfortunately, the prescriptive requirement for onward transfer contracts ignores the possible use of technical protections.

IaaS/PaaS subproviders' standard terms normally govern their provision of services to SaaS/PaaS providers and other customers (1.2). It remains to be seen whether IaaS/PaaS providers are willing to change their standard terms to offer the obligations required for processor–subprocessor 'onward transfer' contracts; if not, that may preclude SaaS/PaaS providers from accessing infrastructure services and/or from offering their services to EEA customers. It is not just layered cloud where these issues arise. A *non*-cloud US processor engaged by an EEA controller might wish to use third party cloud services for more efficient, flexible, cost-effective processing, but may be unable to if subproviders will not offer the required processor–subprocessor terms because they are inappropriate for infrastructure cloud.

These difficulties regarding onward transfers illustrate how the Restriction, Safe Harbour and the Shield have increased confusion, and increasingly prescriptive requirements have exacerbated the unsatisfactory position. I argue that the focus should instead be on fundamental Principles – compliance with Art.17[48] and other substantive Principles should suffice when using cloud or other providers as processors, whether US or not, whether harborite/Shield participant or not, and whether using subprocessors or not – regardless of physical data location, and without also requiring the Restriction.

---

[48]   Provided Art.17 is made more technology-neutral – 4.2.

5.3.4.3   Law enforcement, national security, etc.

Under Safe Harbour's 'escape clause':

> Adherence to these Principles may be limited: (a) to the extent necessary to meet national security, public interest, or law enforcement requirements; (b) by statute, government regulation, or case law that create conflicting obligations or explicit authorizations, provided that, in exercising any such authorization, an organization can demonstrate that its non-compliance with the Principles is limited to the extent necessary to meet the overriding legitimate interests furthered by such authorization;[49] or (c) if the effect of the Directive of Member State law is to allow exceptions or derogations, provided such exceptions or derogations are applied in comparable contexts.

A study for the Commission on Safe Harbour's functioning noted that US PATRIOT Act provisions expressly authorized disclosures to government agencies without data subject choice, for purposes outside those of the original data collection (Dhont et al. 2004: p.101) – but considered Safe Harbour's derogations justified on law enforcement/security grounds. Three respondents had never 'put restrictions' on their Safe Harbour adherence to meet national security, public interest or law enforcement requirements 'under any statute, government regulation, or case law that creates conflicting obligations or explicit authorizations' (Dhont et al. 2004: p.78).[50] Accordingly, the PATRIOT Act's 'controversial provisions' were considered 'essentially irrelevant' to Safe Harbour data flows (Dhont et al. 2004: p.104).

Subsequent studies noted issues with Safe Harbour.[51] Norway's DPA remarked that the US PATRIOT Act represented a 'challenge' to privacy protection, even with Safe Harbour.[52] The US attempted to dispel disquiet regarding US authorities' access to data held with US providers and 'myths' regarding access to personal information in the EU and US (US State Department 2012). Snowden's revelations of US authorities' wholesale surveillance, including apparent 'direct' access to data held

---

[49]   Exception (b) only applied where 'explicit authorisation' existed, i.e. where the relevant statute, regulation or court decision 'affirmatively' authorized the particular harborite conduct (not where it was silent) and such authorization conflicted with Safe Harbour (DoC 2000: Ann.IV pt.B).

[50]   However, US law may have prohibited revealing such disclosures.

[51]   Notably Connolly (2008).

[52]   *Narvik 2012a* (Norway), p.6.

with US providers through the 'Prism' programme,[53] marked the beginning of the end for Safe Harbour. *Schrems* delivered the killing blow.

The Shield principles include a provision (I.5) containing wording identical to the Safe Harbour 'escape clause' quoted above, which is said to show that adherence to Shield principles 'is limited to the extent necessary to meet national security, public interest or law enforcement requirements' (Rec.64). However, unlike with Safe Harbour, the Shield Decision then details the Commission's assessment of US laws' limitations and safeguards regarding access and use by US authorities of personal data transferred under the Shield for national security, law enforcement, etc. purposes (Recs.64–135), concluding, based on 'the available information about the U.S. legal order' including US governmental representations and commitments, that, for data transferred under the Shield, any interference with fundamental rights by US public authorities for such purposes, and the ensuing restrictions imposed on self-certified organizations regarding Shield principles, would be 'limited to what is strictly necessary to achieve the legitimate objective in question', and that there was 'effective legal protection against such interference' meeting the *Schrems* standard (Recs.140–41).[54]

Exceptions to Safe Harbour (and now the Shield) should be interpreted restrictively (specific cases/investigations only, to the extent necessary and proportionate); they cannot allow transfers for third country authorities' indiscriminate, 'massive' surveillance (*WP215*, p.7; *WP227*, para.10; *WP228*). However, assuming that providers' denials of authorities' direct access are true (n.53), the issue there seems to be, not transfer for the purposes of indiscriminate surveillance, but rather direct covert collection by authorities unbeknownst to the providers, e.g. through cable taps (7.5.2.1). That the legality of such authorities' secret direct collection (without providers' knowledge or control) may be questionable, should not affect the legality of the initial transfers *to the providers*. 'Transfers' to US providers may increase exposure to US

---

[53] Several providers denied giving any US authorities direct 'backdoor' access (Ingram 2013; Gidda 2013), stating that they delivered data only upon court order – specific 'push', rather than general 'pull' (Efrati 2013).

[54] Unsurprisingly post-Snowden and *Schrems*, the Shield Decision emphasizes collection of 'signals intelligence' only as authorized by applicable laws, executive orders or presidential directives; only for 'legitimate and authorized national security purposes', with retention or dissemination as 'foreign intelligence' only for 'authorized' intelligence requirements; safeguards against unauthorized access, use and disclosure; and oversight, with a supplemental letter regarding bulk collection of signals intelligence (Ann.IV).

authorities, who could issue disclosure requests or orders to those providers, but that should only be one factor affecting the overall risk. This point applies to all Mechanisms, not just Safe Harbour or the Shield. Larger issues are at stake, and focusing only on preventing or restricting transfers risks missing the true target (5.3.3.5).

5.3.5 'Transfers' to Processors

The preceding analysis of certain Safe Harbour and Shield issues supports my argument that the Restriction is superfluous, at least where EEA controllers 'transfer' personal data to processors. In such cases, controllers must comply with Art.17 (1.5.6) or its GDPR replacement, Art.28 (4.2). EEA controllers are legally obliged to process personal data compliantly with DPD Laws (or the GDPR when applicable), and are liable to data subjects and accountable to DPAs, including for breaches of DPD Laws caused by their processors (or their subprocessors) – whether they process personal data internally or via processors, whether they use processing infrastructure located in the EEA or outside, and irrespective of the processor's country of establishment (p.172). Initially, the ICO's precursor espoused this view in early guidance on the Restriction (Data Protection Commissioner 1999: para.12.1), although those statements inexplicably disappeared from later versions:

> a presumption of adequacy can be made in most, if not all, instances of transfers outside the EEA made by exporting controllers to overseas processors. This presumption is based on the fact that the exporting controller in such circumstances necessarily remains, in law, the data controller in the UK for the purposes of the Act, remaining subject to the Act and the Commissioner's powers of enforcement and individuals' rights thereunder. Subject to overall compliance with the requirements of the Act, in particular the seventh data protection principle [security] and the requirement of that principle that there should be a written contract between the controller and processor, the Commissioner acknowledges that such transfers can ensure adequacy subject to there being no particular risks clearly apparent in the third country in question.

The GDPR imposes certain obligations directly on processors, including cloud providers (1.5.2), against whom data subjects may generally, in their countries of residence, complain or take proceedings (Art.79(2)). However, even where processors are *also* directly liable under the GDPR, controllers remain liable for the personal data they control. EEA controllers cannot circumvent their obligations under the DPD or GDPR by

transferring personal data to non-EEA processors. True, if EEA controllers use non-EEA processors who are not subject to GDPR obligations,
data subjects may be worse off than if controllers used EEA processors.
However, data subjects can still exercise their rights against the controllers, and if direct rights against processors were that critical GDPR could
have prohibited controllers from using non-EEA processors altogether –
but it does not. Controllers who remain liable for their (EEA or
non-EEA) processors' breaches are unlikely to choose non-EEA processors simply to deprive data subjects of their direct GDPR rights against
processors!

The GDPR's imposition of certain obligations on processors subject to
EEA data protection jurisdiction, e.g. EEA-established processors (1.5.2),
aims to improve data subjects' rights and protection, rather than against
circumvention by controllers. Also, personal data location is a different
issue from processor establishment. Non-EEA processors can, and do,
use EEA datacentres. Accordingly, if restricting personal data location to
the EEA is the goal (as many DPAs hold), using non-EEA processors
may not always entail 'transfer'; conversely, EEA processors using
non-EEA datacentres for personal data will be treated as making
transfers.

The adequacy of protection under third country laws (4.7, 5.2.3) seems
most relevant if an EEA controller relinquishes control to or shares
control of personal data with another *controller* who is subject to third
country laws. If those laws permit or require that the other controller uses
personal data inconsistently with the Principles, arguably the EEA
controller would, by relinquishing or sharing control, breach the Principles – unless it takes contractual or technical measures to prevent such
misuse. However, even with *intra*-EEA personal data transmissions/
disclosures, if the controller knows or has reason to believe the recipient
would breach Principles regarding the received personal data, it should
take preventative measures there too, to render the transmission/
disclosure 'fair' (despite the recipient being subject to DPD Laws);
otherwise, it should not transmit/disclose the personal data.[55]

In those situations, data location is irrelevant. The Principles should
have primacy over data location. Similarly, if controllers use *processors*
who are subject to third country laws permitting or requiring processor
'misuse', then preventative measures should be implemented also. However, Art.17 (and Art.28 GDPR) already requires such measures. Thus, I

---

[55] Attempting to reflect this, Safe Harbour imposed liability if such preventative measures were not taken – p.179.

argue that the adequacy of protection under third country laws should simply be one factor when considering compliance with the Principles; the Restriction per se should be unnecessary. As a normative matter, controllers' transfers to processors should only need to engage Art.17 (Data Protection Commissioner 1999: para.12.1) – and, I argue, not even that, if the data are unintelligible to processors (7.2.3.2, 7.4.2.2) or are legitimately available publicly (p.121; 7.4.2.2.).[56]

Granted, many controllers, e.g. SMEs, lack expertise or resources to evaluate the adequacy of third countries' laws (effectively, country risk) or technical measures' efficacy (p.285). Accordingly, use of standardized mechanisms like whitelisting, the Shield, SCCs, and independent certifications, codes or seals, should be encouraged,[57] as the GDPR intends (5.4.5). I argue that their use should allow transfers, but not as the *only* way to allow transfers. Their role would need clarification, following fully considered policy assessments. Would their use mean protection is likely, but not guaranteed, to be considered 'adequate'? Could their use provide some defence or liability reduction?[58] Compliance with Principles for individual processing operations should be the aim, without imposing the Restriction also. In particular cases, this might require additional measures, appropriate to specific risks – i.e., a contextual, risk-based approach.[59] That would be consistent with the Restriction's objective and DPAs' concerns that Safe Harbour alone might be insufficient especially in cloud: the focus should be on compliance with the Principles.

---

[56] See also p.148, n.33.

[57] Along with awareness-raising, educating potential cloud customers, and guidance/tools like ENISA's SME cloud security risk assessment tool (ENISA 2015).

[58] E.g. recipients in whitelisted countries could be presumed to comply with the Principles, disprovable if the transferor knew or ought reasonably to have known otherwise (Reed 2012: p.231, fn.35). An alternative to whitelists or blacklists is a three-tiered system, as used by the US State Department to assess countries' human trafficking protection levels, placing countries with partial or sectoral adequacy in the middle tier (Kamarinou 2013: p.51).

[59] Emphasized in Council 9788/15, e.g. fnn.233, 483, 615. The WP29 supports a risk-based approach 'as a scalable and proportionate approach to compliance', not as an 'alternative' to established data protection rights and principles (*WP218*). My argument of course is that the Restriction is not itself a Principle, but was intended to prevent circumvention of, and maintain compliance with, substantive Principles.

5.4 ADEQUATE SAFEGUARDS AND AUTHORIZATIONS

5.4.1 Overview

5.4.1.1 Current position

Having covered transfers using Mechanisms deemed to provide adequate protection, I now discuss transfers without adequate protection, using Mechanisms that provide adequate safeguards. After an overview of the current position I outline the GDPR's Mechanisms for 'appropriate safeguards' (replacing 'adequate safeguards'), then discuss Mechanisms for adequate safeguards, including under the GDPR.

Member States may authorize 'a transfer or set of transfers' if the controller adduces 'adequate safeguards' (Art.26(2) DPD), in particular through appropriate contractual clauses, e.g. with third country recipients (*WP114*, p.5; 2.4.3). Uncertainties and inconsistencies have arisen from differing Member States' authorization requirements: to what extent are authorizations required, what safeguards do different Member States consider adequate? This has caused complexities and compliance difficulties, particularly in cloud.

If DPAs must individually authorize all transfers without adequate protection, or conduct *ex post facto* checks, 'the shear [*sic*] volume of transfers involved may mean that a system to prioritize the efforts of the supervisory authority will need to be envisaged' (*WP12*, p.27).[60] Thus, the Commission, Member States and WP29 all thought it desirable to develop 'block authorizations' under Arts.25(6) and 26(4) to reduce requirements for individual *ex ante* authorizations or notifications, given their 'considerable administrative burden' for both transferors and DPAs; 'More work' was considered necessary to simplify conditions for transfers (COM(2003)265 final, p.19).

Even in 1997, when transfer volumes were much lower, it was argued that attempting to control transfers through prior notification/ authorization would be 'bureaucratic and costly': 'If all of these TDF [transborder data flows] were notified the authorities could not cope with collecting the information let alone have time to make an informed decision about whether or not to consent to the TDF' (White 1997: p.237). Similarly, the WP29 acknowledged that, given the 'huge number of transfers', no Member State could subject every case to detailed

---

[60] While regarding Art.25's implementation, this applies equally to Art.26 authorizations.

examination, so mechanisms were needed to 'rationalise the decision-making process for large numbers of cases, allowing decisions, or at least provisional decisions, to be made without undue delay or excessive resource implications' (*WP4*, sec.2; *WP12*, p.26), such as SCCs. I discuss SCCs after outlining the GDPR's position on 'appropriate safeguards'.

5.4.1.2 GDPR's 'appropriate safeguards'

In the absence of adequate protection via Commission decision (5.2.4), the GDPR permits transfers only under 'appropriate safeguards' or a derogation. 'Appropriate safeguards' (Art.46) are based on the DPD's 'adequate safeguards', with some important differences. Appropriate safeguards 'may' be provided:

- without requiring specific DPA authorization, using (Art.46(2)):
  - (new) binding instruments between public authorities/bodies;
  - (new) GDPR-compliant BCRs;
  - standard data protection clauses adopted by the Commission and approved by the Art.93(2) committee (5.2.4) – effectively, new forms of SCCs;
  - (new) standard data protection clauses adopted by a national DPA and approved by the Commission and Art.93(2) committee; or
  - (new) GDPR-approved codes of conduct or GDPR-approved certifications (5.4.5); or
- *with* DPA authorization, 'in particular' in one of two ways (Art.46(3)), subject to the new consistency mechanism (1.5.5; Art.46(4)):
  - contractual clauses between 'the controller or processor and the controller, processor or the recipient of the personal data in the third country or international organisation' (i.e. ad hoc clauses), subject to the new consistency mechanism; or
  - (new) provisions in administrative arrangements between public authorities/bodies which include enforceable and effective data subject rights.

To date, no GDPR-compliant SCCs or other such Mechanisms have been adopted (or proposed in draft) by the Commission.

Illustrating that the GDPR's Restriction is generally more prescriptive and retrograde, transfers under 'appropriate safeguards' are permitted *only* if 'enforceable data subject rights and effective legal remedies for data subjects are available' (Art.46(1)). Now, it might seem that, when

EEA controllers transfer to non-EEA processors, effective and enforceable rights and remedies remain available for data subjects against the controllers, suggesting that this requirement could be satisfied for controller–processor transfers, but this is unclear. It seems that even GDPR-approved codes or certifications require 'binding and enforceable commitments' of the third country controller or processor to apply the appropriate safeguards including regarding data subjects' rights (Art.46(2)(e)–(f)). This again demonstrates the GDPR's undue and illogical prioritization of legal/contractual over technical means of protection. Ignoring technology's invaluable role in protecting personal data, and trusting only laws/contracts, seems retrograde and counterproductive (Hon, Kosta, et al. 2014: pp.32–6).

Art.46's wording creates further uncertainties. Under Art.46(2)–(3), appropriate safeguards 'may' be provided in one of the enumerated ways; the draft GDPR, as originally proposed by the Commission, used 'shall'. The Council changed 'shall' to 'may' and deleted draft Art.42(5) (requiring that prior DPA authorization 'shall' be obtained for transfers not provided by 'appropriate safeguards' in a legally binding instrument); instead, with DPA authorization, appropriate safeguards 'may' be provided by contractual clauses (e.g. ad hoc agreements such as intra-group agreements (5.4.4)) or public authorities' administrative arrangements (Council 10680/15). Does that change mean that appropriate safeguards 'may' be provided in ways *other than* those specifically listed, e.g. through strong encryption or, more generally, even controllers' or processors' self-assessment of appropriate safeguards? Or are the GDPR's lists of appropriate safeguards meant to be exhaustive? Similarly, for appropriate safeguards authorized by DPAs (Art.46(3)), does the use of 'may' and 'in particular' mean that DPAs could authorize safeguards *other than* the two listed, and if so could they 'block authorize' appropriate technical safeguards (e.g. use of strong encryption); or are only the two listed ways eligible for DPA authorization? Given the GDPR's general approach, my suspicion is that the Mechanisms listed in Art.46 are intended to be the *only* ones recognizable for appropriate safeguards, but the change from 'shall' to 'may' suggests otherwise, and clarification is much needed.

Also, as individual DPAs have complete independence following *Schrems* (5.3.2), and DPAs or others could challenge the adequacy of 'appropriate safeguards' such as GDPR-approved clauses, codes or certifications, the GDPR's attempt at harmonizing these and other aspects of data protection law might seem doomed to failure.

5.4.2 Standard Contractual Clauses (SCCs)

5.4.2.1 Background

I now discuss Art.26(4) DPD block authorizations for adequate safeguards, starting with SCCs. Transfers are permitted under contracts between the transferor and third country recipient incorporating standard contractual clauses (SCCs), adopted by Commission decisions under Art.26(4), with Art.31 committee approval (5.3.3.1), as offering 'sufficient safeguards' for Art.26(2) purposes. Following Safe Harbour's demise under *Schrems* (5.3.2), in practice SCCs became the most popular Mechanism for regularizing US transfers, being quicker and cheaper to implement than BCRs (p.166). However, the SCCs decisions are being challenged (5.4.2.7).

Currently, three sets of SCCs exist: two for controller–controller transfers, under 2001 and 2004 Commission decisions (2001 SCCs and 2004 SCCs respectively),[61] with either being usable; and one for controller–processor transfers (2010 SCCs) under Commission Decision 2010/87/EU (2010 Decision), replacing another (revoked) set. All define 'data importer' as one who 'agrees to receive' personal data from the 'data exporter'. The 2001 SCCs involve joint and several liability of importers and exporters, with indemnification. The 2004 SCCs, negotiated with industry associations, are considered more business-friendly, e.g. fault-based liability allocation, while maintaining protection levels and giving DPAs more powers (Commission 2005a).[62]

The 2010 SCCs are most relevant to EEA controllers' cloud use. They allow processor transfers to subprocessors (even subsubprocessors etc.) under certain conditions. However, they apply only to 'recipients established outside the territory of the European Union who act only as processors', i.e. third country-established processors (2010 Decision, Arts.2, 3(d), Rec.18), and to subprocessing using subprocessors 'established in third countries' (Rec.17, 2010 Decision). This means that *EEA*-established processors cannot use the 2010 SCCs (2010 Decision, Rec.23; *WP176*, p.3). SCCs might seem unnecessary when controllers transmit personal data to EEA-established processors.[63] However, some EEA processors utilize third country *sub*processors, particularly in cloud,

---

[61]   One set under Commission Decision 2002/16/EC; another under Commission Decision 2004/915/EC, amending the earlier Decision.

[62]   The Commission began negotiating the 2004 SCCs, incorporating industry input, after realizing that the 2001 SCCs were 'not massively used' (SEC(2006)95, p.7).

[63]   *Lindqvist* (3.5).

where EEA SaaS/PaaS providers' services may be layered on US providers' IaaS/PaaS. DPAs generally consider this to involve 'transfer', if non-EEA personal data locations are involved, i.e. storage in US datacentres (3.7.1).[64] SCCs' unavailability when EEA-established processors make transfers to non-EEA subprocessors may disadvantage and discourage the use of EEA, over third country, processors (*WP161*, p.3).[65]

Consistently with the Restriction's anticircumvention objective, the SCCs aim to ensure continued compliance with DPD Laws following transfer. Unlike the two controller–controller SCCs, the 2010 SCCs do not oblige importer-processors to comply with the Principles, because such recipients are processors, not controllers (Commission Decision 2002/16/EC, Rec.8).[66] Instead, importing processors must process personal data only on the exporter's behalf, compliantly with its instructions (as per Art.17(3)) and the SCCs, and must implement the security measures required by SCCs' Appendix 2 (tailored to individual contracts).

To assist controllers to 'ensure compliance' with security measures under Art.17(2) and the Principles generally, audit rights are stressed (see pp.157, 196). Cl.8(2), 2010 SCCs explicitly entitles exporters and DPAs to audit the 'data processing facilities' of importers (and any subprocessors). The SCCs also give data subjects certain direct rights[67] against exporters and, in some circumstances, importers and subprocessors.

---

[64] Accordingly, *WP176* (p.4) suggests: the controller and *each* non-EEA subprocessor sign 2010 SCCs; the controller contractually mandates its EEA processor to sign 2010 SCCs with each subprocessor on the controller's behalf; or ad hoc contracts under national DPA authorization, echoing 2010 SCCs (obliging subprocessors to comply with the controller's national law security requirements). These entail further contractual and procedural complexities, which may be impossible to implement with every subprovider involved.

[65] This also suggested that SCCs (or DPA authorizations) could be based on ad hoc clauses between EEA processors and third country subprocessor(s). *WP214* proposed such draft clauses, but no adopting Commission decision has been issued to date. However, those 'highly uncommercial' (Kupczyk 2014) clauses inherit 2010 SCCs' problems (5.4.2.9); can EEA processors persuade non-EEA subprocessors to agree them? Large non-EEA IaaS/PaaS providers who already offer 2010 SCCs may be willing, although ad hoc clauses would be more time-consuming and expensive than 2010 SCCs.

[66] Contrast Safe Harbour, where onward transfers to agents were permitted only if the *agents* subscribed to Safe Harbour principles – p.179.

[67] Third party beneficiary rights – which not all Member States recognize, so such Mechanisms are unavailable in those Member States.

Therefore, unsurprisingly, DPAs generally considered that SCCs' protection exceeded Safe Harbour's, and they favoured SCCs (p.163) including when subprocessors were used.[68] Controllers' awareness of SCCs was however low,[69] although undoubtedly it has increased post-*Schrems*.

Under GDPR Art.46(5), pre-existing SCCs decisions remain valid until amended, repealed or replaced by Commission decisions on new forms of SCCs (5.4.1.2) – unless they are invalidated sooner by the CJEU, at least for US transfers (5.4.2.7). For practical workability, I hope that any Commission GDPR decision revoking or replacing pre-existing SCCs decisions will provide an appropriately long grace period. As some organizations have hundreds or even thousands of SCCs, it will inevitably take time to implement new GDPR-adopted SCCs.

Next, I discuss SCCs issues particularly relevant to cloud.

5.4.2.2 Transfer, location and/or law/jurisdiction?

The 2010 SCCs focus on 'law to which the data importer or a subprocessor is subject' (Art.4(1)(a), Cl.5, fn.1), not personal data location as such. Yet, confusingly, they define 'data importer' as one '*not* subject to a third country's system ensuring adequate protection' (Art.3(d), Cl.1(c)). As for subprocessors, Art.3(e) defines 'subprocessor' without mentioning locations but clearly targets subprocessors 'established in' third countries (2010 Decision, Recs.17, 23; *WP176*, p.3).

All this raises similar uncertainties as with CIDPR and Convention108's Additional Protocol (2.2.7): is the question whether a provider is, or is *not*, subject to certain countries' laws, and how can conflicting laws be resolved? Hopefully new SCCs adopted under the GDPR will clarify these issues.

5.4.2.3 Subprocessors

SaaS/PaaS providers who use IaaS/PaaS providers would be considered to 'onward transfer' to subprocessors, as previously discussed (5.3.4.2).

The 2010 SCCs address 'onwards transfers' from processors to subprocessors (2010 Decision, Rec.16). Exporting controllers accept liability

---

[68] E.g. *Office 365* (Denmark). Cf. the WP29's hierarchy of Mechanisms (5.1) which strictly prefers 'adequate protection' (e.g. whitelisting) over 'adequate safeguards' (e.g. SCCs).

[69] When asked whether they were aware of SCCs, 65 percent of controllers surveyed replied negatively (Gallup 2008b: pp.28, 32). However, only those who indicated that their companies exported personal data were asked that question – p.229.

to data subjects for ensuring that any *sub*processing provides at least the level of protection required of importer-processors (2010 Decision, Cl.4(i)).[70]

Subprocessing requires (2010 Decision, Cl.11):

- the exporter's prior written consent;
- a written agreement imposing, on subprocessors, importers' SCCs obligations; and
- direct rights for data subjects against subprocessors (limited to their own processing operations) in certain circumstances.

Contractual structures and procedures to comply with these requirements can be complex, particularly with multiple subprocessors. Controllers may consent generally to processors' use of subprocessors, or require consent to each subprocessor (*WP176*, p.5). However, subprocessors such as IaaS/PaaS providers may be reluctant to undertake SCCs' importer obligations or accept liability to data subjects.

The Shield echoes but broadens the 2010 SCCs in requiring contracts for onward transfers, not only to subprocessors but also controllers (5.3.4.2). The GDPR's detailed requirements for controller–processor contracts (whether transfers are involved or not), including mandatory 'flowdown' of the required terms to subprocessors, subsubprocessors, etc. (4.2), will undoubtedly be reflected in any new forms of SCCs for processor use adopted under the GDPR by the Commission or national DPAs (5.4.1.2).

5.4.2.4 Bipartite vs same organization, and multipartite arrangements

An organization cannot contract with itself, so SCCs are unavailable when controllers 'move' personal data (or copy personal data) outside the EEA within the *same* organization (Henderson 2014), e.g. by using its private cloud, or taking backups to its own third country datacentre.[71] However, establishing separate entities in controllers' groups, just to own/operate third country datacentres and sign SCCs, seems cumbersome and artificial (p.97). Again, I stress that EEA controllers must comply

---

[70] Although controllers remain liable to data subjects under DPD Laws, even without SCCs (p.172).

[71] As SWIFT did – p.92.

with the Principles when processing personal data, wherever the process-ing location, so that arguably the real underlying problem is that of conflicting third country laws.[72]

SCCs envisaged simple, one-off bilateral arrangements involving 'point to point' transfers from controller to identified recipients, whether controller(s), processor(s) and/or subprocessor(s), in identified locations (4.4.1). Requiring a 'web of rigid, individual contracts' (IPPC 2009: p.2), sometimes thousands of them (ICC 2004: p.8),[73] SCCs are impractical for modern outsourcing transactions, like cloud, that typically involve globally provided services with dynamic data flows and chains of multiple providers and subproviders, datacentres and countries.[74] Uncer-tainties have arisen regarding even which organizations should sign which contracts (Rackspace 2009: sec.2.5). Practitioners have long viewed SCCs as ill-suited to modern cross-border (out-)sourcing,[75] 'hardly keeping up with the evolving increase, complexity and speed of today's transborder data flows' (Commission 2010b: p.8). Many feel that SCCs only involve 'box-ticking'. Overly rigid, cumbersome, time-consuming and bureaucratic,[76] SCCs (and BCRs) impose high adminis-trative burdens and costs on controllers (Commission 2010b: p.8) without necessarily improving compliance or data protection.[77] As SCCs are inflexible, ongoing updating for the 'slightest' change[78] is time-consuming and costly (Robinson et al. 2009: paras.3.3.6, 3.3.4). Further-more, generally SMEs lack resources[79] to deploy and maintain SCCs.

---

[72] On third country authorities' access to personal data transferred under SCCs, see 5.4.2.6.

[73] See p.98.

[74] E.g. Orange (2009: p.3); Verizon (2010: p.2).

[75] Hoskins (2014) summarizes practitioners' views on SCCs' use(lessness), except as make-work for lawyers and a 'cost of doing business in the EU' rather than improving data protection.

[76] E.g. Robinson et al. (2009: sec.3.3.6).

[77] Wojtan (2011: p.80) bemoaned 'a mindless mechanical game played out by legions of lawyers and privacy and security professionals', noting consider-ably increased administrative burdens without 'discernable [sic] benefit' to data subjects or evidence of better or more efficient compliance with substantive data protection requirements; '[d]ata subjects have so far ignored [SCCs] completely …'.

[78] E.g. changes in corporate group members, or data categories (Axciom 2009: p.3).

[79] On data protection compliance disproportionately affecting SMEs, see Kommerskollegium (2014: p.19), ECIPE (2013: pp.9, 13), Christensen et al. (2013).

Although the 2010 SCCs attempted to acknowledge modern multiple-processor models, they remain impracticable as numerous contracts may still be needed (Wojtan 2011: p.79). Accordingly, 'organizations involved in multiple and complex international transfers are prone to either ignore their compliance obligations or put in place a version of the [SCCs] which becomes rapidly out of date' (Verizon 2010: p.3).

Unfortunately, any new forms of SCCs promulgated under the GDPR will inherit all these problems.

5.4.2.5 Differing national procedures

By Art.26(4), Member States must comply with Commission SCCs decisions, and cannot refuse transfers under SCCs. However, national requirements/procedures for approval/notification differ. Some require prior filings (*Office 365* (Denmark), para.3.4.1.1) or prior authorizations (*WP226*, p.2). Many are cumbersome and costly (Rambøll Management 2005: p.59; SEC(2006)95, p.6). Where prior authorization is required (to check that SCCs match the prescribed form),[80] approvals may take months (Axciom 2009: p.3), even years (EPOF 2011: p.2), reflecting high transfer volumes and DPAs' limited resources, with no guarantee of approval.[81] Recognizing problems with Member States' divergent approaches, *WP226* proposed cooperation procedures (e.g. lead DPA) for assessing the compliance of company-submitted clauses with SCCs, to avoid different DPAs reaching different conclusions.

The burden is compounded when subprocessors or onward transferees are involved, requiring signing, filing and approval of 'innumerable'[82] SCCs, and reauthorizations for changes (n.78). Controllers operating

---

[80] E.g. Commission (2009: p.26); Dhont et al. (2004: p.83).

[81] E.g. Austria's DPA rejected an application to transfer personal data from an Austrian subsidiary to its US parent under SCCs, finding them 'invalid' for the stated purpose ('worldwide statistic reports and editing'). The applicant claimed no editing would occur in the US. However, the contract allowed the importer considerably broader use of data than the exporter requested. Also, the DPA felt that enforcement against the importer would not succeed, 'since the data importer as the superior parent entity has decisional powers over the Austrian entity' – which, if that is truly a valid ground for refusing authorization, might disallow the vast numbers of SCCs signed with importing parent entities! Finally, the transfer was considered 'serious' because so much human resources data was involved, 'as well as the potential of breach' (Kuner 2008: para.4.98).

[82] Orange (2009: p.3); IAPP (2013); 5.4.2.4.

cross-EEA may need multiple language versions.[83] Insufficient information and guidance on completing SCCs' schedules/appendices has also resulted in different Member State approaches.[84]

The GDPR attempts to address this fragmentation, and reduce associated bureaucracy and time/costs, by providing that certain 'appropriate safeguards' will not require 'specific' DPA authorization (5.4.1.2), to prevent DPAs from insisting on pre-transfer authorizations. However, GDPR's wording does not explicitly prevent them from requiring post-transfer filings/notifications (although that was the Commission's intention – COM(2017)7 final, p.5), and individual DPAs could well challenge adopted 'appropriate safeguards' (*Schrems*, 5.3.2).

5.4.2.6 Law enforcement etc. access

Some DPAs insisted on SCCs not Safe Harbour (even before its invalidation), but SCCs cannot prevent importers from disclosing personal data to third country authorities (p.97). Cl.5, 2010 SCCs requires importers to *notify* exporters of 'any legally binding request for disclosure' by law enforcement authorities, unless otherwise prevented, e.g. by 'a prohibition under criminal law to preserve the confidentiality of a law enforcement investigation'. Those SCCs do not expressly forbid disclosure; a footnote to Cl.5 simply states that mandatory national law requirements applicable to the importer, 'which do not go beyond what is necessary in a democratic society' on the basis of certain interests (necessary measure to safeguard national security etc.), are 'not in contradiction with' SCCs.

Accordingly, SCCs allow importers to accede to disclosure requests, at least where not disproportionate. However, as with Safe Harbour, the WP29 considers that SCCs cannot allow 'indiscriminate', 'massive' access, under third country authorities' surveillance programmes, to personal data transferred under SCCs (*WP215*, p.7; *WP228*, para.5.2.2).[85]

---

[83] E.g. SEC(2006)95, p.8.

[84] E.g. Orange (2009: p.3); Cisco (2009: p.6). Also, 'fill-in-the-blanks' provisions ill suit the standard 'click-to-accept' clauses common with websites and cloud. Google's and Microsoft's SCCs were slightly modified for online use, incorporating standard appendices. DPAs' subsequent cloud decisions/guidance did not query those changes (e.g. *Office 365* (Denmark), *Moss* (Norway), *Narvik* (Norway), *Salems* (Sweden)); but clarification that such minor changes do not invalidate SCCs would be helpful.

[85] But again these indicate problems with third country authorities' direct access, not necessarily importers' disclosure to them – p.183.

Unfortunately, even if SCCs contractually prohibit disclosure by importers, contractual provisions cannot override laws to which a party is subject, as Canada's DPA acknowledged (p.98). Any such prohibition would simply put importers in the impossible position of having to break laws – or contracts. In that sense, contractual solutions can never provide 'adequacy'; such conflicts cannot be resolved through contract. It is unknown how new forms of SCCs adopted under the GDPR will address third country authorities' access, but clearly contractual requirements alone cannot solve the conflicts problem.

5.4.2.7 SCCs' adequacy

Some DPAs doubted whether SCCs' 'adequate safeguards' ensured compliance with the Principles, notably (even pre-Snowden) German DPAs (Kuner 2007b: para.4.28). For example, Sweden's Datainspektionen considered that SCCs may not satisfy Art.17 DPD (Tung 2013) because they do not specify the controller's instructions (Datainspektionen 2013, pers. comm., 26 November).[86]

German DPAs also took unilateral action regarding Safe Harbour (6.4.3.3). Such actions may seem inconsistent with EU harmonization aims and Member States' Art.26(4) obligations to comply with Commission decisions, exacerbating complexities arising from the fragmentation of EU laws. However, *Schrems* (5.3.2) enshrined national DPAs' absolute independence, which EU legislation cannot restrict.

SCCs Decisions Art.4(1) allowed Member State authorities to ban or suspend transfers made under SCCs in certain circumstances, informing the Commission accordingly (Commission 2005b). By 2006, it had received no such notifications (SEC(2006)95, fn.8). None have been reported since. Following Snowden's revelations, German DPAs considered suspending transfers under SCCs, not just Safe Harbour (German Conference of Federal and State Data Protection Commissioners 2013).[87] Also, post-Snowden, US importers might feel unable to sign SCCs given

---

[86] However, Art.17 (1.5.6) does not require the contract to specify the instructions, only the processor's contractual obligation to *follow* instructions, and 2010 SCCs do require the importer to comply with the exporter's instructions (Cl.5); so perhaps a more likely reason was that, in *Salems* (Sweden), the SCCs were with Google Inc. but the processor agreement was with a different entity, Google Ireland (5.4.2.9). Datainspektionen has since required narrow 'instructions' limiting the purposes for which the processor can use the data – n.96.

[87] However, arguably the stated grounds for such suspension/prohibition do not include wholesale data collection without *importers'* knowledge/cooperation

the standard warranties regarding local laws or legislation with a substantial adverse effect on their model clauses obligations.

This Art.4(1) effectively mirrored Safe Harbour Decision Art.3, which was invalidated in *Schrems*, so the Commission amended it (5.2.3). However, those decisions still risk invalidation, at least for transfers to the US or other third countries that conduct mass surveillance. Thus, post-*Schrems*, some German DPAs questioned SCCs' validity for US transfers (Pinsent Masons 2015). For US transfers at least, DPAs may yet invalidate SCCs and/or BCRs during (but hopefully not before) the first joint review of the Shield in mid-2017 (5.3.3.3), prolonging the legal uncertainty.

Following *Schrems*, while DPAs 'may not refuse' transfers 'on the sole basis' that SCCs do not offer sufficient safeguards, they are still empowered to examine those clauses in light of *Schrems*'s requirements (Commission 2015b: p.6), particularly upon data subjects' complaints, although only the CJEU may invalidate Commission adequacy decisions (5.3.2). Accordingly, Ireland's Data Protection Commissioner investigated Schrems's complaints regarding Facebook's US transfers, issuing a draft decision in May 2016. She asked the Irish court to refer the matter to the CJEU for a preliminary ruling on the validity of the SCCs decisions for US transfers (Data Protection Commissioner of Ireland 2016). The court joined the US government, US Electronic Privacy Information Centre, BSA Business Software Alliance and Digital Europe as *amici curiae* as, if a reference was made, they could not be heard before the CJEU unless involved before the court of first instance (para.16, *Data Protection Commissioner v Facebook Ireland Limited & Anor* [2016] IEHC 414). Developments are awaited, but such a reference seems likely. Given SCCs' important role for legalizing US transfers post-*Schrems*, the CJEU's decision will be critical in determining the fate of US transfers.

5.4.2.8   Other difficulties

SCCs must be used unchanged. Additional business-related terms (not conflicting with SCCs) are permissible: SCCs may form part of a larger commercial contract (2010 Decision, Rec.4, Annex Cl.10). However, drafting to avoid conflicts is not straightforward.[88]

– highlighting possible lacunae in SCCs Decisions, and the nature of the underlying problem.

[88]   E.g. *Salems 2013* (Sweden), para.4.2. See n.84 on modifications for online acceptance.

The relationship between SCCs and Art.17 processor agreements remains unclear. Arguably SCCs could satisfy Art.17 (cf. n.86.); indeed, processor agreements could benefit from incorporating certain SCCs terms for 'clarity' (2010 Decision, Rec.10). Initially, the WP29 considered that draft SCC clauses for controller–processor transfers 'to a certain extent' overlapped with Art.17(3)'s processor agreement requirements (*WP46*, p.20). However, despite arguments that processor SCCs are unnecessary for controller–processor transfers because the controller-exporter remains liable, including for implementing processor agreements, processor SCCs were still required because the WP29 felt that, with transfers, it was more difficult for data subjects to be aware of processor breaches or obtain redress (Poullet et al. 2001: p.174). Compliance with Art.17(2) (choosing a processor providing sufficient security measures and ensuring compliance) was considered not, per se, to adduce adequate safeguards allowing Art.26(2) authorization of transfers, because 'these contracts [i.e. SCCs] need to supply for the lack of adequate protection in the country of destination which is not the purpose of Article 17' (*WP47*, para.2).

This view, illustrating again the Restriction's status as a Frankenrule, is too narrow. If technical measures (e.g. security measures required under processor agreements) can ensure compliance with the Principles and protection of personal data despite the data being located in a third country, as Ch.7 will discuss, then Mechanisms such as SCCs should be unnecessary. Furthermore, it can be difficult for data subjects to become aware of processor (or indeed controller) breaches even *in* the EEA (6.4.1), and, as previously emphasized, they retain redress rights against EEA controllers wherever their data are located.

Transfers risk being considered invalid if the 'wrong' SCCs are used. Different SCCs are required for transfers to controllers or processors, but the controller/processor[89] boundary is unclear. Hence, sometimes both controller–controller and controller–processor SCCs are signed (Hon and Millard 2013c: p.273). But can the Shield be combined with 2010 SCCs? The better answer is 'Yes'. While Shield participants' eligibility to sign 2010 SCCs is unclear,[90] *WP196* p.18 encouraged Safe Harbour transfers

---

[89] Or processor, or 'neither' – 1.3.

[90] Art.3(d), 2010 Decision defines 'data importer' as a third country processor 'not subject to a third country's system ensuring adequate protection' within Art.25(1) DPD. But harborites were so subject (5.2.4); similarly with Shield participants. Art.3(d) implies that they cannot be 'data importers'. However, it seems more likely that this possible problem is due to unconsidered drafting, than any intention to disallow harborites etc., from signing SCCs.

to be bolstered with SCCs or BCRs, and DPA cloud decisions involving harborites have recommended SCCs without querying harborites' eligibility.[91] Providers, including harborites, have increasingly offered SCCs as 'additional means' of meeting DPD requirements, e.g. Microsoft (Smith 2012) and Google (Google n.d.; Hon and Millard 2013c: p.271). This trend accelerated significantly post-*Schrems*, with Salesforce offering SCCs on the day of the judgment (Salesforce 2015).

5.4.2.9 SCCs and cloud

Using SCCs for cloud computing can be particularly problematic, 'where data may be continuously transferred across a long chain of recipients' (EDPS 2012b: para.81).

Firstly, consider supply chain structures. For Microsoft Office 365 and G-Suite SaaS, both providers offer processor agreements with their Irish-incorporated subsidiaries, but SCCs with the US parent (which presumably owns the datacentres used in the USA and elsewhere). Those parents were harborites, and are now Shield participants. Presumably *direct* SCCs with the US parents were offered[92] because SCCs are unavailable when EEA processors (Irish subsidiaries) use non-EEA subprocessors (US corporations owning datacentres) (5.4.2.1). This un-availability is a problem, preventing many EEA processors from using US IaaS/PaaS.

Now, large providers can employ structures involving SCCs between EEA customers and affiliated non-EEA subproviders.[93] However, with layered cloud, smaller providers, e.g. SaaS providers (EEA-incorporated or not) who build services on large providers' IaaS/PaaS, may be unable to persuade third country subproviders, i.e. 'lower layer' cloud or datacentre providers, to assume SCCs obligations (5.4.2.3). Subproviders' services (or chains of subservices) form the *pre-existing* foundation for layered cloud services, a 'reverse direction of travel' compared with traditional

---

Again, this highlights the importance of clarifying whether the issue is that a recipient is, or is *not*, subject to certain jurisdictions etc. (p.45).

[91]   E.g. *Salems* (Sweden); *Sollentuna* (Sweden); *Office 365* (Denmark).

[92]   *WP176*'s first suggested option – n.64. The 2010 SCCs may be signed for reasons other than use of US datacentres, e.g. because third country staff have (remote) access to customers' personal data, or US parents may actively process transferred personal data – which seem better reasons than personal data location alone.

[93]   Although providers could make SCCs' availability clearer (*Office 365* (Denmark), para.3.4.1.2); also, many providers' Art.17 agreement and SCCs are 'opt-in' only.

outsourcing (4.2). Providers may be unable to renegotiate existing sub-provider contracts; subproviders may decline onerous SCCs obligations and liabilities, and indeed in practice many IaaS/PaaS providers do refuse, especially given the bargaining power differential between small customers, small SaaS/PaaS providers and large IaaS/PaaS subproviders. Furthermore, if DPAs consider affiliated owners of third country data-centres to be subprocessors, they would consider *un*related datacentre providers to be subprocessors too,[94] and unaffiliated subproviders may be even more unwilling to assume obligations to providers' customers.

Therefore, SCCs are impracticable for cloud, except for large providers who control all or most of the supply chain, and can secure the required subprocessor obligations. Even then, arrangements are likely to be complicated, e.g. contracts with every subprocessor, subsubprocessor, etc. (5.4.2.3–5.4.2.4; p.98). Given cloud supply chains' complexity, cloud's 'reverse direction' (4.2), and large subproviders' negotiating power, the 2010 SCCs' subprocessing requirements may be difficult or impossible to implement, except for large providers who have more control over their supply chains including subproviders. Again, this favours large providers (p.109). Subproviders might conceivably accept the required obligations if they were paid higher fees. However, if providers pass those costs on to customers, cloud services would become less cost-effective. Alternatively, some controllers may deliberately proceed without such subprocessor obligations, considering enforcement risks to be acceptably low (6.3.4.3, 6.4.2) – perhaps after assessing the likelihood of DPAs discovering and enforcing the breach, and/or mitigating potential privacy problems e.g. through encryption. A major issue is that, as with processor SCCs, the GDPR requires flowdown of mandatory processing agreement obligations to subprocessors, with many new prescriptive requirements – even intra-EEA when no transfers are involved (Art.28(3)–(4)) – extending the problems for cloud use posed by SCCs to *all* cloud use, possibly rendering cloud use by EEA controllers impossible except with the largest providers (4.2).

Group procurement of cloud can be particularly difficult, with multiple due diligence and audit rights requirements – e.g., a German subsidiary may need rights to approve the supply chain, unlimited liability for security breaches, etc. Such increased administrative burdens seem incompatible with the group's goal of centralizing and streamlining global procurement of cheap commoditized IT services. Internally,

---

[94] However, the position is unclear – Google and Microsoft's US entities may do more than own or run datacentres – n.92.

groups address these requirements differently, e.g. with terms of reference regarding each affiliate's level of control over subprocessors, centralized audits that affiliates must rely on, etc. Organizations seem to take risk-based commercial decisions; some consider compliance unrealistic, others do not wish to risk breaches, expending resources accordingly (IAPP 2013).

Regarding controllers' consent to subprocessors, providers could require controllers to approve the provider's pre-existing (and, strictly, identified – p.296) cloud subprocessors when controllers subscribe to their services, or at least to SCCs, so that controllers must either accept the existing subprocessors, or not subscribe. Some DPAs consider it unacceptable for providers to require blanket advance consent, but some controllers may choose to agree, accepting the enforcement risk. Demonstrating some flexibility and pragmatism in this context, the WP29, after being approached by Microsoft regarding its terms, announced that it considered that Microsoft's Enterprise Enrollment Addendum Microsoft Online Services Data Processing Agreement and Annex 1 'Standard Contractual Clauses (processors)' were 'in line with' SCCs, rather than being ad hoc clauses requiring specific DPA authorization (WP29 2014d). Microsoft's two key amendments that facilitated the WP29's approval were (Harrison 2014):

- prior notice to customers before appointing new subprocessors, with early termination rights for objecting customers (addressing the consent issue), and
- obligation to delete personal data within a maximum period after termination.[95]

Those periods appear to be 14 days (subprocessors) and 180 days (deletion) (Microsoft 2014: p.10). Soon afterwards, Google changed its 'data processing amendment' (processing agreement) for enterprise customers, committing to delete customer-deleted data as soon as practicable

---

[95] The deletion *standard* was unstated, beyond 'Component Disposal. Microsoft uses industry standard processes to delete Customer Data when it is no longer needed' (Microsoft 2014: p.12), more relevant to end-of-life hardware disposal than data deletion. GDPR Art.28(3)(g), which replaces Art.17 DPD, explicitly requires the controller–processor contract (processor agreement) to oblige the processor 'at the choice of the controller' to delete or return all personal data after service termination and delete 'existing copies' unless retention is required by EU or Member State law, but without specifying a maximum period. On 'deletion' of digital data see 7.4.2.4.

and within 180 days maximum (Google 2014), partly to address criticisms by Sweden's DPA that Google's terms were inadequate regarding data deletion (*Simrishamn*).[96]

France's CNIL emphasized that the WP29 letter only enabled transfers, and did *not* find 'that Microsoft's contractual arrangements overall comply with all EU data protection requirements, neither that Microsoft comply in practice with EU data protection rules. It is only acknowledged that Microsoft has taken the sufficient contractual commitments to legally frame international data flows, in accordance with Article 26 of Directive 95/46/EC' (CNIL 2014). This clearly illustrates, in the SCCs context, DPAs' treatment of the Restriction as a separate Frankenrule on data location alone.

Advance controller consent is required for *all* subprocessing under Art.28(1) GDPR (echoing requirements for onward transfers under SCCs (5.4.2.3) and BCRs (5.4.3.1)), not only where transfers are involved. It is helpful that the GDPR, although entailing increased box-ticking in other ways, explicitly allows such consent to be 'general'. Where consent is general, again reflecting the WP29's approach to Microsoft's terms, notice is required of intended changes to subprocessors, to give the controller 'the opportunity to object' (but not, it seems, to prevent the change, so presumably termination is the controller's only solution unless its contract provides otherwise).

---

[96] Another concern was that 'instructions' must prevent Google from processing personal data for its own purposes – pp.128–9. Datainspektionen was also satisfied with Office 365 terms regarding deletion, restricting 'own purposes' use, and security requirements, but not the lack of information on countries where Microsoft's subcontractors operated (*Ale* (Sweden)). The amended 2014 Google terms that Datainspektionen found satisfactory, regarding 'instructions' and purposes as well as deletion, were quoted in *Simrishamn* (Sweden) as follows:

5.2. Scope of Processing. Google will process Customer Data in accordance with Customer's Instructions. Customer instructs Google to process Customer Data to: (i) provide the Services (which may include the detection, prevention and resolution of security and technical issues) and (ii) respond to customer support requests.

5.3. Processing Restrictions. Google will only process Customer Data in accordance with this Agreement and will not process Customer Data for any other purpose. For clarity, and notwithstanding any other term in the Agreement, Google will not serve Advertising in the Services or use Customer Data for Advertising purposes …

7.2. Deletion on Termination. On expiry or termination of the Google Apps Agreement, Google will delete all Customer-Deleted Data from its systems as soon as reasonably practicable and within a maximum period of 180 days …

Others have noted problems with using SCCs in cloud: 'the requirement to sign a contract and notify data protection authorities for all the parties involved (and in cloud computing this can be a lot) reduces [SCCs'] applicability' (Buttarelli 2012: p.4). The SCCs regime also needs updating to address 'processor-to-processor transfers originating from the EU, constant multijurisdiction transfers and the lack of precise identification of where the data may be located at a given time, as well as information/notice and accountability mechanisms', and to specify conditions for law enforcement access (EDPS 2012b: para.84). I agree with parts of that statement, but, as this book argues, lack of location information should not be as important as proper control of intelligible access through technical and/or contractual means.

5.4.2.10 Summary

In summary, SCCs are difficult and cumbersome to use, particularly in cloud, supporting my argument that the Restriction and Mechanisms are more harmful than beneficial; there are far better ways to meet the Restriction's anticircumvention objective. While the Commission or national DPAs may adopt new forms of SCCs under the GDPR, as explained previously they are unlikely to solve the current problems and may make matters worse.

5.4.3 Binding Corporate Rules (BCRs)[97]

5.4.3.1 Overview

BCRs, not explicitly envisaged by the DPD, represent another method to provide adequate safeguards. Originally developed (with industry input) by the WP29 on 'an extensive interpretation'[98] of Art.26(2), BCRs are authorized by relevant national DPAs, with a 'lead authority'.[99] Other Member States may accept lead DPA-approved BCRs under a mutual recognition procedure. However, not all Member States participate (Commission 2016i), so applications to non-participating Member States for authorization are needed, including translations into their languages and re-scrutiny under their laws.

BCRs enable transfers within a corporate group, particularly multinationals. Members in 'non-adequate' third countries agree to a legally

---

[97] Moerel (2012a) analyses BCRs comprehensively.

[98] SEC(2012)72 final, Ann.2, fn.175, which cites Art.25(2) (*sic*).

[99] Organizations with approved BCRs are listed at http://ec.europa.eu/ newsroom/document.cfm?doc_id=40100

binding corporate code of practice tailored for the group and transfers concerned, including certain minimum requirements regarding privacy principles and tools to ensure practical effectiveness (Commission 2016f). The EU-based headquarters (if none, delegated EU member) accepts liability for third country members' acts, including compensation for damages, affording data subjects local recourse (*WP74*, para.5.5.2). Each member subscribes once; contrast multiple intra-group webs of SCCs. The WP29 has issued numerous documents on BCRs for controllers, e.g. requirements, checklists and forms.[100]

BCRs' requirements are similar to SCCs', e.g. obligations regarding Principles and cooperation with DPAs (*WP74*, paras.4, 5.4; *WP153*; *WP154*); restrictions on 'onward transfers' to non-group members except under SCCs (*WP74*, para.3.2;[101] *WP153*, sec.6.1; *WP154*, sec.12); and direct DPA audit rights (*WP74*, paras.5.2, 5.4; *WP153*, paras.2.3, 3.1; *WP154*, para.14). DPAs may accept that BCR obligations are subject to mandatory national laws requiring disclosure, as with SCCs (5.4.2.6; IAPP 2013).[102] BCRs go beyond SCCs in several respects, e.g. systems/procedures for compliance/complaints-handling including independent data protection officers, staff training and programmes for regular internal audits; also, controversially, the EU headquarters/member must disprove claimed breaches (*WP74*, p.19).[103] Unsurprisingly, DPAs favour BCRs.[104] BCRs have become popular because SCCs are inflexible and do not suit data sharing. Some controllers prefer BCRs to 'drowning in' SCCs (IAPP 2013).

5.4.3.2 BCRs: issues

While more flexible than SCCs, BCRs are time-consuming, taking months, even years, to approve,[105] involving many internal departments

---

[100] *WP74*; *WP107*; *WP108*; *WP133*; *WP153*; *WP154*; *WP155*. On processor BCRs see 5.4.3.3.

[101] Contracts must be available to DPAs on request, and to data subjects on certain conditions.

[102] Unless 'prohibited by a law enforcement authority', the EU member must be notified and 'should take a responsible decision and have to consult' competent DPAs (*WP74*, para.3.3.3; *WP228*, para.5.2.3).

[103] DPAs have accepted a precondition: data subjects must demonstrate damage, and plausibility that it was caused by the BCR breach (Moerel 2012a: p.104, fn.27). Processor BCRs may employ similar wording (p.207).

[104] E.g. *WP168*, paras.37–9; IAPP (2013).

[105] At October 2013, according to practitioners (IAPP 2013), approvals took approximately 5 months with CNIL, or 18 months with the ICO, as lead DPA. WP29 (2013b: p.2) reports an average of 5 months (lead DPA and reviewer),

and external lawyers in multiple Member States, lead and secondary DPAs, and approvals or filings/notifications for Member States not participating in mutual recognition (IAPP 2013), with differing and opaque substantive/procedural national requirements.[106] DPAs may, and have, altered their requirements, e.g. with staff changes (IAPP 2013). Reviews and refreshes, sometimes more often than annually, increase administrative burdens, e.g. as members join or leave; large groups may have hundreds or thousands of members.[107]

Accordingly, BCRs are expensive[108] and high-maintenance. Some controllers even have staff dedicated to managing BCRs. The time, costs and expertise required[109] render BCRs effectively unavailable to SMEs, e.g. startups (IAPP and EY 2016; Cave et al. 2012: p.61). Fewer than 90 BCRs have been authorized (n.109), although the pace is accelerating (WP29 2013b: p.2), particularly post-*Schrems*. (On BCRs post-*Schrems*, see p.198; 6.4.3.3). A multinational, Merck, broke new ground by having its BCR approved based on its APEC CBPR certification (2.2.8), saving time and costs on its BCR, implying that obtaining CBPR first is the better strategy (Carson 2016; Wandall and Cooper 2016). However, smaller organizations may still face difficulties.

5.4.3.3 BCRs and cloud

The use of BCRs in cloud is problematic. Some query whether BCRs allow transfers to processor members, as strictly Art.17 requires processor agreements with them. This again highlights difficulties caused by separating the Restriction from the Principles. However, in practice many consider BCRs acceptable for transfers to processors (Allen & Overy 2013: p.10). But BCRs still do not allow controllers to process personal data in third country datacentres owned by the controller. Creating affiliates to own datacentres and subscribe to BCRs is as artificial as creating affiliates to sign SCCs (p.97).

3–3.5 months (mutual recognition and cooperation), and 7.5 months (applicant to submit amendment incorporating DPA comments).

[106]   E.g. AmCham (2010: p.10).

[107]   E.g. Intel has updated its BCR several times since 2011, v.4.1 being in December 2015 (Intel 2015).

[108]   SEC(2012)72 final, Ann.4, fn.177: €20 000 (average) but – for large companies with many subsidiaries – even €1 million; p.17, n.38.

[109]   Robinson et al. (2009: secs.3.3.4, 4.2); Kuner (2007a: para.4.122); and generally Commission (2010b) including ICC (2009: pp.7–8), GDV (2009: p.6).

BCRs are available if third country members own/operate the relevant datacentres, or employ staff who remotely access EEA-located personal data. However, BCRs only allow intra-group transfers. Transfers to non-group providers or subproviders require processor agreements and, if 'located' in 'inadequate' third countries, Mechanisms like SCCs, which unaffiliated transferees may decline to sign (5.4.2.9). Therefore, BCRs enable the use of private cloud where a subscribing affiliate owns the relevant datacentre(s), but not public cloud, particularly layered services, or even private cloud where unaffiliated third parties own the datacentres used.

Recognizing existing Mechanisms' unsuitability for outsourcing and cloud (CNIL 2013), the WP29 issued requirements for processor BCRs (BCR-P) (*WP195*; *WP204*). These allow processors to transfer to group subprocessors. Like controller BCRs, BCR-P benefit from limited mutual recognition, but they must be legally binding and enforceable by data subjects and controllers against group processors and any third party non-EU subprocessors, with similar DPA audit rights; reversed burden of proof; and notification of law enforcement authorities' requests for personal data disclosure (*WP195*, paras.1.3, 1.4, 2.3, 1.7, 6.3; *WP204*, paras.2.3.3, 4.2, 4.6, 2.3.4), including to the controller and its DPA, as with controller BCRs (*WP228*, para.5.2.3; p.205). The processor's EU headquarters, EU exporter-processor or delegated EU-based member must assume liability for other members. Unlike with controller BCRs, if no EU-established member exists then the third country headquarters must assume liability; controllers and data subjects are entitled to complain to DPAs or courts in their countries of residence/establishment (*WP195*, para.1.5). 'Onward transfers' outside the BCR group require prior information to the controller, its prior written consent,[110] and, for transfers to external subproviders, processor agreements incorporating certain BCR obligations incumbent on group members; also, the Restriction must be complied with where relevant, e.g. SCCs with any external non-EU subprocessors (*WP195*, p.10; *WP204*, para.2.2.2).

'Transfers' (here meaning disclosures) to authorities must be based on legal grounds under applicable law, as BCR-P requirements 'only create an information process' (*WP204*, para.2.3.4). Interestingly, *WP204* (pp.12–13) was modified in 2015 to require processors to seek prior DPA approval for law enforcement/security requests, but it recognizes possible conflicts: if, despite 'best efforts', the processor cannot notify competent

---

[110] General consent is possible, with notification and the opportunity to object/terminate.

DPAs, 'it must commit in the BCR to annually providing general information on the requests it received to the competent DPAs'. This seems a sensible approach, but unfortunately is not followed in the GDPR's Art.48 (p.119).

BCR-P could enable EEA subsidiaries of large third country providers such as AWS, Google, IBM and Microsoft to transfer personal data to the datacentres of third country affiliates. The only large cloud provider to have implemented BCR-P so far is Salesforce, in 2015 (CNIL 2016c: p.52). However, controllers cannot rely on BCR-P for transfers. They must still seek DPA authorization *based on* their intended processors' BCR-P (*WP204*, p.6). Hopefully such authorizations would be auto-matic,[111] but BCR-P's practical operation remains unclear. If DPAs impose additional requirements for BCR-P authorizations, as with con-troller BCRs currently, BCR-P may not prove particularly useful for cloud. Furthermore, smaller providers are unlikely to be able to afford BCR-P, and BCR-P cannot be used for layered services involving unrelated subproviders, which again require SCCs or other Mechanisms or contractual obligations mirroring BCRs – and which again external subproviders may refuse (5.4.2.9).

Restricting BCRs to transfers within a corporate group limits their scope and utility (Vodafone 2011: p.12; ICO 2013b: p.59), so BCRs are not useful for cloud (Robinson et al. 2009: p.59). Allowing transfers to external BCR-P subprocessors without further authorization could assist, but might drive providers further towards large subproviders who have the resources to implement BCR-Ps; again, is that the policy intention? Furthermore, difficulties would remain regarding non-group members, particularly cloud subproviders.

5.4.3.4   BCRs under the GDPR

Acknowledging BCRs' slowness, bureaucracy, complexity and cost, the Commission accepted[112] the merit of calls by DPAs[113] and controllers[114] to recognize explicitly, clarify, simplify and harmonize BCRs' role and requirements, including mandatory mutual recognition. Controller or processor BCRs meeting GDPR Art.47 criteria must be recognized as providing 'appropriate safeguards' allowing transfers without 'specific authorization' (Art.46(2)(b)), once approved by the relevant DPA: the

---

[111]   E.g. CNIL (2013).
[112]   COM(2010)609 final, para.2.4.1; Commission (2010b: para.2.2.10); COM(2012)011 final, p.11; COM(2012)9 final, p.11.
[113]   E.g. *WP168*, pp.37–8; Buttarelli (2012: p.5).
[114]   E.g. Air Berlin (2011: p.4); Orange (2009: p.3).

GDPR's main simplification in relation to transfers. The EDPB is empowered to issue guidelines, recommendations and best practices to further specify criteria and requirements for transfers based on BCRs 'and on further necessary requirements' to ensure data protection (Art.70(1)(i)). However, when approving BCRs, DPAs must apply the new consistency mechanism (1.5.5), intended to improve cross-EU harmonization. This could increase complexity and delays (and therefore affect affordability for SMEs), or even result in rejection of BCR applications.

Also, unfortunately for sourcing/outsourcing, easier or automatic authorizations for controllers based on approved BCR-P are still not clearly mandated, so that (as now) BCR-P can enable a processor to transfer to its group members, but will not regularize third party *controllers'* transfers to that processor or its group. Furthermore, Art.47(2)(f) requires assumption of liability by a controller or processor 'established on the territory of a Member State' for breaches by non-EU-established members – ruling out BCR-P for groups with no EU-established member whereas, currently, a processor's third country headquarters may assume liability (ICO 2013b: pp.60–61).

The GDPR incorporates a Council proposal (Council 9565/2015) to allow BCRs to be used for transfers within a 'group of undertakings or group of enterprises engaged in a joint economic activity' (Art.47(1)(a), Rec.110). This could include third party processors, even subprocessors. The structure required seems unclear – a 'group of enterprises' would apparently have a 'board' (Art.47(2)(j)), but how does 'group of enter-prises' (undefined) differ from 'group of undertakings' (defined in Art.4(19))? Notwithstanding this option, BCRs' utility for cloud would remain low. Even if a 'group of enterprises' could encompass cloud providers and unrelated subproviders, their relationship would presumably have to be close, and intended to be longer-term, for them to wish to undertake a long BCR procedure whereby the (possibly unaffiliated) EU member assumes liability (Hon 2016d).

GDPR Art.46(5) 'grandfathers' existing DPA authorizations of BCRs, so they remain valid until amended, replaced or repealed by the author-izing DPA. This suggests that any processor groups with no EU members who nevertheless want to implement BCRs should seek authorization before the GDPR takes effect.

5.4.4 Ad Hoc Agreements

Ad hoc contracts for transfers merit mention, e.g. intra-group agreements (IGAs) for transfers. Often based on SCCs and/or Safe Harbour terms, in some ways IGAs presaged BCRs. IGAs are more flexible than SCCs: they may be multipartite, may include more business-friendly provisions, and each entity need only sign one agreement once. IGAs are generally enforceable by DPAs and third parties, although less transparent than BCRs.

IGAs require prior individual DPA authorization or filing in many Member States (Art.26(2)), but some controllers do not seek approvals where the regime 'is just too much of a compliance challenge' (Jones 2012: p.9). Individually negotiated contracts are inefficient, and procedural requirements (apart from authorizations/filings) may include translations into relevant languages (Weber 2013: p.9). Because IGAs are only usable for intra-group transfers, they are unlikely to assist cloud services involving external providers or subproviders. Specific ad hoc agreements for transfers outside a group, e.g. unaffiliated cloud providers, involve time and expense, outweighing the benefits of commoditized public cloud, and some DPAs may not entertain them.

Under the GDPR, IGAs and other ad hoc contracts may be authorized by DPAs as providing appropriate safeguards (5.4.1.2). As with BCRs, IGAs authorized under the DPD remain valid until the relevant DPA amends, repeals or replaces its authorization (Art.46(5)).

5.4.5   GDPR's Codes and Certifications

GDPR's new 'appropriate safeguards' that may allow transfers (5.4.1.2) include GDPR-approved codes of conduct (Arts.46(2)(e), 40–41) or GDPR-approved data protection certifications and seals or marks (Arts.46(2)(f), 42–3), in each case 'with binding and enforceable commitments of the controller or processor in the third country to apply the appropriate safeguards, including as regards data subjects' rights' (Art.46(2)(e)–(f)). Certifications issued under criteria approved by the EDPB may constitute a 'common certification', the European Data Protection Seal (Art.42(5)).

Despite binding commitments being additionally required for transfers, GDPR-approved codes of conduct or certifications seem attractive. As well as enabling transfers, such codes/certifications may be used as 'an element' to demonstrate compliance with data protection obligations (Art.24(3)) in line with the accountability concept (1.5.1) – notably, controllers' obligations when using processors (Art.28(5)), and controllers' and processors' security obligations (Art.32(3)). Significantly, they affect whether DPAs impose fines, and how much (Art.83(2)(j)) – e.g., as a mitigating factor to reduce a fine. Codes (but not certifications) adhered to by controllers or processors are relevant when controllers conduct data protection impact assessments (Art.35(8)), newly required by the GDPR in certain circumstances. Certifications (but not codes) can help demonstrate compliance with controllers' new obligation of data protection by design and default (Art.25(3)). Certifications may incorporate GDPR-adopted SCCs (Art.28(6)), although it is unclear how.

Some DPA cloud decisions have considered industry-standard security certifications, obtained e.g. by Azure (*Brevo 2011* (Sweden), pp.4, 9) and Google Apps (now G-Suite) (*Narvik 2012b* (Norway), p.13; *Moss* (Norway), pp.5, 7). Third party audits 'can be relevant' to controllers' obligations to ensure continued compliance (*Office 365* (Denmark), para.3.4.2.2.3). Independent, reputable third party verification or certification can be a 'credible means' for cloud providers to demonstrate compliance (*WP196*, p.22). Regarding Dutch controllers' use of a US provider's cloud services, certifications of the provider to industry standards 'can be a means for the controller to ascertain' whether the processor actually took the required measures (Autoriteit Persoonsgegevens (formerly CBP) 2012: p.6). The Commission's planned European Cloud initiative would include cloud services certification (COM(2015)192 final, p.15). A Cloud Select Industry Group (C-SIG) on cloud certification schemes, with EU security agency ENISA, produced a list of voluntary cloud certification schemes for transparency and the Cloud Certification Schemes Metaframework (CCSM).[115] The latter aims to assist potential cloud customers by providing a neutral, high-level mapping of their security requirements against the security objectives in existing certification schemes.

The WP29 commented on drafts of an industry-standard cloud code of practice (ISO/IEC 2014b), since adopted e.g. by Dropbox (Baesman 2015) and others, but my requests for the WP29's comments were rejected. A Commission working group under (COM(2012)529 final, p.3) drafted a cloud code of conduct, but the WP29 recommended changes (WP29 2014a: p.1). The status of a redrafted version of June 2016 is currently unclear (Graux 2016). In September 2016, CISPE (Cloud Infrastructure Services Providers in Europe) proposed a code for IaaS providers, intended to be submitted for GDPR approval (Hon 2016g).

Industry-standard codes/certifications, e.g. ISO 27017/27018 for cloud, will *not* qualify for GDPR purposes unless formally approved under GDPR-mandated criteria and processes (with separate requirements for codes and certifications) – hence my references to 'GDPR-approved'. Indeed, DPAs have stressed (*WP196*; BayLDA 2016) that

---

[115] At https://resilience.enisa.europa.eu/cloud-computing-certification.

codes/certifications must centre on data protection obligations (not just security), so many current codes/certifications may be insufficient without substantial amendment. Guidance on codes/certifications is promised from the WP29 during 2017; helpfully CNIL, whose head chairs the WP29, already issues data protection certifications, so current French criteria/procedures could form a good starting point (Gardner 2016). DPD Art.27 sought to encourage the use of codes nationally and at cross-EU level, but has barely seen any WP29 approvals, possibly because their benefits for controllers were unclear. Accordingly, the workability and take-up of GDPR codes and certifications remains to be seen. While the GDPR clearly states that approved codes/certifications will help demonstrate compliance, legal uncertainty about when fines can be imposed in relation to codes/certifications may impede adoption.[116] Even if the EDPB clarifies the fines position, unfortunately the GDPR's requirement for binding commitments rules out the use of technical protections *alone*, even under industry-standard certifications, to enable transfers. We await clarification of exactly what binding commitments will be considered sufficient to allow use of codes or certifications for transfers, and of other uncertainties regarding GDPR's provisions on codes/certifications.

Although, with both codes (Art.40(1)) and certifications, the 'specific needs' of SMEs must be considered (Art.42(1)), adhering to a code and, especially, a certification, may still involve considerable time and costs. For example, Portuguese location-tracking startup Movvo took *two years* to obtain a privacy seal from German certification organization EuroPriSe (Mizroch 2014). Accordingly, simple, direct application of technical protections like encryption (even without adherence to codes/certifications) should be encouraged, not ignored or disallowed. Perhaps EU institutions' approach to GDPR stems from (misconceived) mistrust of technology. If appropriate safeguards cannot be provided, or authorized by DPAs, through technological/organizational measures alone (5.4.1.2), and only contractual/statutory measures are deemed 'good enough', then the GDPR would restrict data transfers further – which may result in even more breaches, and engender disrespect for data protection laws rather than adapting those laws to modern technological and social realities.

---

[116] Lower-tier fines are possible for infringing the obligations of the controller, processor and certification body 'pursuant to' the certification articles, Arts.42–3 (Art.83(4)). However, what those obligations are is insufficiently clear (Hon 2016e).

5.5 DEROGATIONS

5.5.1 Consent Etc.

Controllers transferring personal data under Art.26 DPD derogations need not ensure adequate protection or obtain DPA authorization. Personal data transferred under derogation may have 'total lack of protection' in the recipient country, where recipients need not comply with DPD Laws (*WP114*, p.6).[117] Derogations are effectively 'exemptions, which are tightly drawn'; accordingly, the WP29 urges their use only where the risks to data subjects 'are relatively small' or other interests (public interest or the data subject's) override privacy rights (*WP12*, p.24; *WP114*, p.7), recommending derogations only as a last resort (*WP114*, p.9). Nevertheless, many controllers may use derogations as their first option (*WP114*, p.9).[118]

Most derogations, being restrictively interpreted by DPAs, will not assist cloud use. Art.26(1)(b)–(c) allows transfers 'necessary' for the performance of a contract between data subject and controller or for implementing precontractual measures taken in response to data subject request, or for concluding or performing a contract between the controller and third party concluded in the data subject's interest.[119] However, cost-efficiency is not 'necessity' (ICO 2010: para.4.3.2). Cloud's efficiencies cannot 'necessitate' transfer to countries without adequate protection. Art.26(1)(d) allows transfers 'necessary or legally required on important public interest grounds', but public interests under third country, rather than EU/Member State, laws are considered insufficient here (*WP114*, p.15; *WP228*, p.39) – see p.119 (Art.48 GDPR), cf. 7.5.1.

Art.26(1)(a)'s derogation for 'unambiguous' data subject consent to proposed transfers merits further consideration. 'Consent' (Art.2(h)) requires a freely given, specific, informed (plus, here, unambiguous) indication of the data subject's wishes; the WP29 interprets these strictly.[120] For one-off transfers, it considers that a data subject may

---

[117] Again, overlooking that EEA controllers remain subject to applicable DPD Laws wherever they process personal data – p.52.

[118] The UK suggested that controllers would 'probably find it most convenient' to consider derogations before adequacy (Home Office 1996: para.7.1). See 5.5.2.

[119] E.g., when individuals book third country hotels, travel agents must send their personal data to those hotels (*WP114*, p.13).

[120] The WP29's prerequisites for valid 'consent' to transfers include 'properly informing' data subjects of the risk that their personal data are to be transferred

consent specifically to 'the particular transfer or a particular category of transfers in question'. But for 'repeated or structural' transfers, consent cannot provide a satisfactory practical long-term framework (*WP114*, p.11):

> particularly if the transfer forms an intrinsic part of the main processing (e.g. centralisation of a world database of human resources, which needs to be fed by continual and systematic data transfers to be operational), the data controllers could find themselves in insoluble situations if just one data subject subsequently decided to withdraw his consent.

The WP29 deprecates consent for transfers where the parties have unequal bargaining power; e.g. employees' consent to employers may not reflect 'free' choice (*WP48*, p.3). Furthermore, to be 'free', consent must be revocable. Any doubt regarding a consent's unambiguity may also disapply the exemption (*WP12*, p.24). If consents are obtained to transfer the personal data of all but one employee, or one employee revokes consent, that might jeopardize the other consents' validity (Kuner 2007a: para.4.105). Other practical difficulties are that consent must be given before the transfer (Kuner 2007a: chap.4.105), and, for advance consent to be valid, future transfers' details must be 'predetermined, notably in terms of purpose and categories of recipients' and notified,[121] again subject to the consent being revocable anytime, requiring isolation of the data concerned and preventing its transfer.

Therefore, while 'consent' could be sought via website forms when collecting personal data online, for regular or repeated transfers in commercial relationships (e.g. cloud use), a basis other than consent seems safer for controllers. Also, where organizations use cloud to process their individual customers' data, e.g. orders, the consent required is that of data subjects who are the organization's customers. Thus, for cloud processing of personal data, it may be problematic to obtain data subjects' consents and prove that they were freely given, specific, informed and unambiguous. Due to the practical difficulties with managing consents, and DPAs' negative view of using consent for transfers, many controllers may prefer Mechanisms, particularly for human resources data.

---

to a country lacking adequate protection (*WP12*, p.24; *WP114*, pp.10–12). *Implied* consent, e.g. notification of transfer and failure to object, is unlikely to be considered sufficient. On 'consent' generally, see *WP187*.

[121] Arguably consent cannot be 'informed' unless data subjects are aware, at inception, of all possible 'downstream' uses (Gunasekara 2007: p.381).

Another issue with consent is that inconsistent or erroneous national DPD Laws[122] may nevertheless require data subject consent before DPAs may authorize transfers under adequate safeguards (Kuner 2007a: para.4.86, fn.193), or even prohibit transfers despite consent being given.[123]

5.5.2 GDPR's Derogations

Several Member States had considered that the GDPR should acknowledge that, in reality, 'derogations' would be the 'main basis' for transfers (Council 9788/15, fn.480). However, that has not transpired.

GDPR's Art.49(1)(a) derogation for data subject consent only applies if consent is 'explicitly' given after the data subject has been informed about the possible risks due to absence of an adequacy decision or appropriate safeguards. This tighter provision, introduced by the Parliament, makes consent more difficult to use for transfers.

Clearly influenced by the pre-21st century *WP12* (5.2.2.1), the original draft GDPR (COM/2012/011 final) proposed a derogation for transfers necessary in the legitimate interests of the controller or processor, 'which cannot be qualified as frequent or massive', where 'appropriate safeguards' had been adduced where necessary – originally intended to increase flexibility by effectively allowing controller or processor self-assessment in limited circumstances.[124] The final GDPR changed 'frequent or massive' to 'repetitive', but this derogation (Art.49(1) final paragraph) has become an 'absolute last resort' derogation, usable only in the absence of adequate protection, appropriate safeguards or any other derogation. Its conditions are so restrictive that it seems unlikely to be usable in practice – transfers must be not repetitive (which rules out most cloud use), concern only a limited number of data subjects, be necessary for the purposes of 'compelling' legitimate interests pursued by the controller which are not overridden by data subjects' interests, 'suitable safeguards' must be provided, and the transfer must be notified to the DPA and (along with information about the 'compelling legitimate interests' pursued) to data subjects. This derogation is unavailable to processors. Uncertainties also arise. How many transfers must be made to

---

[122] E.g. in Spain (Kuner 2007a: pp.160–61).

[123] Hungary's DPA could not legally authorize transfers to third countries not found adequate by the Commission, *even if* data subjects consented, 'practically inviting' controllers to transfer personal data without notifying the DPA (Kuner 2007a: para.4.30).

[124] SEC(2012)72 final, Ann.5, p.102; Weber (2013: p.129).

qualify as 'repetitive'? Many Internet transfers, not just cloud, might be considered 'repetitive'. Also, what is the difference between 'appropriate' (5.4.1.2) and 'suitable' safeguards, and 'compelling' versus non-compelling legitimate interests?

Asymmetric treatment of transfers by size and frequency may result in 'adverse competition and innovation impacts' (although ultimately size was omitted as a factor), and 'artificially tilts the playing field but does not correspond to current and evolving market behaviour' (Cave et al. 2012: p.66). Furthermore, 'legitimate interests' needs clearer definition[125] – e.g., does this include transfers necessary for efficient data management and explicitly agreed in contracts? As location-independent processing and demands for ubiquitous access increase, data subjects may not be able to control or verify whether transfers are repetitive, or prevent '[non-repetitive] but potentially damaging transfers' (ibid.). As previously argued, qualification by frequency or volume (or repetitiveness), although welcomed by *WP222* p.7, is misguided – the focus should be on adequate (or 'appropriate' or 'suitable') safeguards, which could be provided by technical measures, even for repetitive 'structural' transfers (5.2.2.1).

GDPR Art.49(4) confirms that the DPD's 'public interest' derogation, recast as a derogation for transfers 'necessary for important reasons of public interest', only applies to public interests recognized in EU law or the law of the Member State to which the controller is subject, also implying that *processors* cannot use this derogation.

Generally, the EDPB is empowered to issue guidelines, recommendations and best practices to further specify criteria and requirements for transfers based on derogations (Art.70(1)(j)).

5.6 ONWARD TRANSFERS: ISSUES

I now discuss onward transfers more broadly. Recall that, in the cloud context, if a customer transfers personal data to a provider as its processor, and the provider uses subprocessors, generally the provider will be considered to make 'onward transfers' to the subprocessor, and subsubprocessors may also be involved in some cases (5.3.4.2).

Onward transfers 'could require complicated mechanisms to enforce adequate guarantees' (*WP38*, para.4.2), and initially the WP29 felt that SCCs should prohibit onward transfers altogether. It considers that a third

---

[125]   Although *WP217* offers guidance.

country provides 'adequate protection' only if (among other requirements) its laws restrict onward transfers to further countries without
'adequate protection' – i.e., the WP29's onward transfer principle
(5.2.2.2). This approach is reflected in the GDPR: the factors that the
Commission must consider in assessing third countries' adequacy of
protection explicitly include 'rules for the onward transfer of personal
data to another third country or international organisation' (Art.45(2)(a)).
However, could those further countries be considered to provide adequate
protection if *their* laws lack similar restrictions? Surely this approach,
taken to its logical conclusion, would effectively require 'adequate
protection' in all countries in the possible onward chain, to prevent
circumvention through staging post(s).

In practice, the WP29 has not required third countries' own export
restriction laws to prohibit onward transfers from their importer countries. For instance, the WP29 issued a positive adequacy opinion (*WP22*)
on Switzerland. However, Switzerland's laws simply restrict personal
data from being 'disclosed' abroad if data subjects' privacy would be
seriously endangered thereby, in particular due to the absence of legislation guaranteeing adequate protection[126] – without requiring such legislation to restrict further exports/onward transfers. More significantly, the
WP29 noted that New Zealand's laws do not provide protections when
personal data are transferred to third countries – but New Zealand
agencies holding personal data in a third country, directly or through
processors, remain responsible for harm or loss from use or disclosure in
the third country, 'so it is in their interests to minimize the risk and
ensure appropriate safeguards are in place' (*WP182*, p.9). Accordingly,
while New Zealand's laws did not comply fully with the WP29's onward
transfer principle, this was not considered a 'major shortfall' blocking an
adequacy finding for New Zealand (*WP182*, pp.9–10). Surely the same
reasoning applies equally to EEA controllers who use cloud providers or
other processors, or process personal data in third country locations. Such
controllers remain responsible under DPD Laws (p.172); it is in their
interests too to ensure appropriate safeguards in such situations.

Requirements for 'onward transfers' (particularly to subprocessors)
under Safe Harbour, the Shield, SCCs and BCRs differ, as discussed
previously. Also, if an onward transferee transfers to another party,
another contract or measure may be necessary (Gunasekara 2007: p.385).
However, using contracts to protect data under onward transfers may be
problematic, e.g. privity; so one possible solution is to empower national

---

[126] Art.6(1), Federal Act on Data Protection.

DPAs to enforce relevant contracts, or to treat contractual breaches as privacy rule breaches (Gunasekara 2007: p.387).

More fundamentally, 'onward transfer' suffers from similar problems as 'transfer' (Ch.2). Requirements regarding adequate protection, Mechanisms and particularly onward transfers, all seemingly assume that personal data 'location' in a third country inevitably involves 'transfer' there, and that subproviders (including datacentre providers) are always onward transferees with intelligible access. That is not necessarily true, and disregards technical measures' role in protecting personal data, as Ch.7 will discuss. For example, the WP29 opined favourably (*WP39*) on Canada's PIPEDA, taking its principle 4.1.3 (2.2.8) to mean that data transfer outside Canada requires 'contractual or other binding provisions' capable of providing comparable protection (*WP39*, p.6). Its narrow view of 'other means' ignores technological means, and contradicts Canadian DPAs' own broader approach. For example, following complaints that a security system provider shared customer information with its US parent (by routing alarm signals to a US monitoring centre if a catastrophe befell the Canadian centre), Canada's OPC held, despite no contract existing between the affiliates, that 'other means' provided comparable protection: the US company had a closed private network and comprehensive strategy/techniques to safeguard customers' personal information. These practices satisfied PIPEDA's principle 4.1.3 (2.2.8; PIPEDA Case Summary #2006-333). Similarly, upon complaints against Canadian banks following SWIFT's disclosures of data to US authorities, the OPC ruled that those banks satisfied principle 4.1.3 because they had 'other means' to ensure comparable protection including cooperative oversight, technical oversight groups and auditing mechanisms, contractual language and various security measures (PIPEDA Case Summary #2007-365).

In a qualified negative opinion on Quebec, the WP29 reiterated its narrow view that only *legally binding* protections are sufficient, noting that 'the Quebec Act does not specify the means to this end. Although [Quebec's DPA] recommends to use contractual means it is not a mandatory requirement' (*WP219*, p.9). This implies that the WP29 considers that only mandatory contractual means are 'adequate'. As this book makes clear, arguably that view is outmoded.

The GDPR explicitly restricts onward transfers. It states that transfers, including onward transfers, should not undermine data subjects' protection (Rec.101), i.e. the aim is anticircumvention. GDPR's Restriction also catches 'onward transfers' 'from the third country' 'to another third country or to another international organisation' (Art.44). However, unfortunately, the GDPR does not define 'onward transfers'. Confusingly, 'onward transfers' apparently involves, variously (emphasis added), onward transfers 'from the third country or international organisation to controllers, processors *in the same or another* third country or international organisation' (Rec.101), but 'to' another third country or international organization (Arts.44, 45(2)(a)), and 'to bodies not bound by' BCRs (Art.47(2)(d)). In practice, DPAs are likely to treat as 'onward transfers' any transmission by the third country recipient to another person, whether in the same or another third country (even the EEA?). Uncertainties regarding onward transfers in the Shield context have already been discussed (5.3.4.2).

Unfortunately, the GDPR does not explain exactly how restrictions on onward transfers should operate and how onward transfers may be effected by *third country* controllers or processors in practice (GDPR SCCs?). Its onward transfers restriction extends the GDPR extraterritorially, apparently indefinitely, wherever the relevant data may flow and keep flowing. While the anticircumvention aim is understandable, this wide extraterritoriality is likely to increase conflicts with third country laws in future, and the failure to distinguish between onward transfers by/to controllers and processors may cause practical problems, particularly where processors use subprocessors, subsubprocessors, etc. For transfers by controllers to processors, Art.28 GDPR already contains detailed requirements on the use of processor, subprocessors, etc.; my argument that controller–processor transfers should not require anything beyond compliance with Art.17 DPD applies equally to processor–subprocessor 'onward transfers', so that the onward transfers restriction should be unnecessary. At least for controller–processor transfers, compliance with Art.28 should suffice and GDPR SCCs should be unnecessary (although Art.28 is not without its own problems – 4.2). To modernize data protection laws properly, the position regarding disclosures/transmissions by controllers to other controllers requires careful analysis, separately from the very different position regarding controller-to-processor 'disclosures' (see my illustrative discussion in the Safe Harbour context, p.179).

The 'onward transfers' position is highly unsatisfactory. The possibility of onward transfers, and further transfers, shows that the Restriction's anticircumvention objective may be bypassed. However, as with transfers themselves (Ch.6), onward transfers may be impossible to monitor or control. Yet the GDPR seems intent on restricting them even more narrowly (and unclearly), thereby turning more actors into lawbreakers and threatening international comity, while disregarding or deprecating, rather than encouraging, technical means that *could* be used to control onward transfers effectively.

5.7 GDPR, MECHANISMS AND CLOUD

As shown above, despite the DPD's harmonizing objective, costs and burdens arise from Member States' differing approaches to implementing or interpreting the DPD and relevant Commission decisions – particularly the Restriction[127] and Mechanisms (COM(2003)265 final, sec.4.4.5; Commission 2003: p.50). One of the GDPR's major drivers was the need to address issues arising from lack of harmonization.

The DPD's transfer provisions are 'additionally challenged' by the increasingly globalized nature of data flows, 'i.e. the fact that personal data are being transferred across a large number of virtual and geographical borders, such as in the framework of cloud computing' (SEC(2012)72 final, p.16). Simplification and harmonization could make DPD implementation more cost-effective, notably facilitating transfers by multinationals operating cross-EEA, through harmonizing national transfer rules (Rambøll Management 2005: pp.69–70). Uniform Member State implementation of transfer grounds was considered important to avoid forum shopping (*WP114*, p.3) or 'havens' *within* the EU (White 1997: p.239). Accordingly, one GDPR objective was to simplify rules and procedures for transfers 'by giving the Commission exclusive competence for adequacy decisions, introducing more flexibility' and extending BCRs to include processors, while eliminating prior authorizations 'in the large majority of cases' (SEC(2012)72 final, p.47). The Commission considered that these proposals would significantly reduce administrative burdens (SEC(2012)72 final, Ann.2, para.10.11.1).

The GDPR intended to address cloud issues by clarifying applicable law issues 'directly and uniformly' across Member States, levelling the playing field and reducing businesses' administrative burden and compliance costs while ensuring 'a high level of protection for individuals' and giving them more control, 'increasing transparency' of processing to help increase consumer trust, and facilitating transfers while ensuring continuity of protection for individuals, particularly by improving tools like BCRS 'which is essential to regulate issues such as cloud computing' (Commission 2012c: para.4; COM(2012)529 final, p.8).

Despite such hopes, the GDPR will be problematic for cloud, particularly providers, in many ways – including aspects beyond this book's scope (see Hon, Kosta, et al. 2014). More generally, by making transfers

---

[127] The 'broadly divergent and, in many cases, inconsistent' implementations of the Restriction are considered to affect the DPD's international credibility (Bygrave 2010: p.197).

'more cumbersome and costly', the GDPR would 'significantly' increase overall average costs for organizations whose core operations include regular transfers (London Economics 2013: p.51).

Stakeholders' responses to the Commission's 2010 data protection consultation included (SEC(2012)72 final, Ann.2, p.86):

- Adequacy assessments should focus on outcomes, not the list of prescriptive provisions in the legal regime being analysed.
- The procedure should move from prescriptive rules to a risk-based model of accountability, focusing on adequacy of specific transfers rather than of a country. More attention should be paid to the competence and adequacy of the body handling data, rather than the territory where data is held – i.e., a recurring industry view was that adequacy should be replaced by extending the accountability principle to transfers, emphasizing that both controllers and processors should ensure that personal data are adequately safeguarded regardless of location.
- Academics also advocated greater flexibility, proposing a risk-based model built on a controller's obligation to evaluate all relevant factors (e.g. nature of data, how long data will be in the third country, whether data will remain under the controller's control, etc.). That might permit transfer 'even in situations where the general legal regime governing data protection is not similar to that as within the EU, but reasonably effective in protecting individuals' core rights and interests'.

I support these views. Unfortunately, the GDPR did not take the requested risk-based, accountability-based approach that would truly modernize data protection regulation, so the Commission's expectations regarding the GDPR's positive impact on cloud seem over-optimistic. As I have shown, the GDPR risks neither improving data protection nor facilitating cloud, particularly in the transfers context, and furthermore creates new uncertainties.

If transfers are permitted only under 'binding' and 'enforceable' measures, and even DPAs will be disempowered from authorizing technological protections, that would be highly retrograde. Contrast some other countries' laws that take a technologically neutral approach based on reasonableness of steps taken (legal, technical, procedural, and/or otherwise) to ensure continued compliance with their privacy/data protection laws. The APEC Privacy Framework's accountability principle requires, for 'transfer' of personal information to another, the individual's consent or due diligence and 'reasonable steps' (2.2.8), not necessarily contractual ones. In Canada, 'The critical question for institutions which have outsourced their operations across provincial or international borders is whether they have taken reasonable steps to protect the privacy and security of the records in their custody and control' (IPC 2012: p.6; see further p.217). Under Australia's updated Privacy Act 1988, before 'disclosing' personal information to a person 'not in Australia', steps 'reasonable in the circumstances' must be taken to ensure the recipient does not breach Australian Privacy Principles. Hong Kong's data export restriction (not yet effective), sec.33 Personal Data (Privacy) Ordinance 1995, would permit transfer of personal data outside Hong Kong if, inter alia, 'The data user has taken all reasonable precautions and exercised all due diligence to ensure that the data will not, in that place, be collected, held, processed, or used in any manner which, if that place were Hong Kong, would be a contravention of a requirement under the Ordinance.' This due diligence requirement can be satisfied through 'an enforceable contract' e.g. model clauses, but non-contractual oversight and auditing mechanisms are acceptable, including (non-exhaustively) transferees' sufficient technical and organizational measures, good data protection track record, robust policies/procedures including adequate training and effective security measures, data subjects' rights of access and correction not being affected by the transfer, and regularly exercised audit/inspection rights (PCPD 2014: p.7).

5.8 SUMMARY

Mechanisms for permitting transfers are complex (Cave et al. 2012: sec.3.3.4), impractical[128] and 'not related to commercial realities' (SEC(2012)72 final, Ann.4, p.85) – unnecessarily burdensome,[129] time-consuming (Robinson et al. 2009: p.32), inflexible, bureaucratic and costly as regards both time and resources.[130] Lack of harmonization or coordination regarding national implementations, requirements and practices (Robinson et al. 2009: p.32) mean that the Mechanisms are

---

[128] Practical problems with Mechanisms have been reported to the Commission (Commission 2010b: p.8). See also Kuner (2013b: chap.7.D).

[129] E.g. Robinson et al. (2009: p.26); Kamarinou (2013: p.50).

[130] Including dealing with third country transferees: 'transfers to and from other companies who may not be familiar with EU legislation is a major problem resulting in a lengthy educational process and protracted negotiations over contractual provisions' (VON Europe 2011: p.7).

available only to large organizations – leading to widespread non-compliance and/or unnecessary costs.[131]

Private sector controllers have emphasized the importance of improving intra-EU harmonization, in order to improve the practical application of the Principles (SEC(2012)72 final, p.10). The Mechanisms' complexity impedes their operations, including transfers. Mechanisms also burden *DPAs*. No Mechanism (except whitelisting certain countries) enables EEA controllers to 'transfer' personal data to their *own* third country datacentres without artificial structures, although DPD Laws require them to apply the Principles regardless of personal data location.

Furthermore, it is questionable to what extent the Mechanisms achieve the objective of maintaining compliance with Principles. This chapter discussed DPAs' insistence on additional measures they consider necessary to enable compliance with Principles, notwithstanding the use of Mechanisms. Compliance with the Restriction as such, to permit 'transfer', is treated separately from compliance with the Principles.[132] Mechanisms are used to enable the former, but the latter is the Restriction's true objective. Unfortunately, DPAs' tendency to treat the Restriction as a separate rule on personal data location, combined with uncertainties and inconsistencies in the Mechanisms' meaning and interpretation, renders compliance with the Principles confusing and/or difficult.

The Restriction is positively harmful because it fails to achieve its objective properly, yet many controllers waste time and costs attempting to comply via Mechanisms to which many DPAs take a 'box-ticking' rather than purposive approach. Thus a response to the Commission (Vodafone 2011: p.19), while supportive of protection following data 'wherever it travels' and accountability resting with the controlling organization, called for abolition of *ex ante* controls on transfers, querying to what extent current Mechanisms provided 'any real increase in privacy protection. They have certainly absorbed enormous resources in establishing formal legal arrangements intended to achieve that end, but in our view, at the expense of adequate attention to operational realities and effective global information governance'.

The position regarding processor use is particularly problematic. If measures, whether legal (e.g. processor agreements) and/or technical (e.g. encryption), can adequately restrict processors from using, disclosing or modifying personal data without the controller's authority, then logically why should SCCs or the like be required in addition, just because

---

[131]   Verizon (2010: p.3). Ch.6 covers enforcement.
[132]   E.g. *WP128*, para.4.6.

personal data are to be processed in non-EEA locations? I reiterate, EEA controllers remain liable for breaches by their processors (p.172).

All these suggest fundamental issues with interpreting and applying the DPD and Mechanisms, constraining unnecessarily not just cloud but, more broadly, legitimate business processes involving modern supply chains and Internet use (VON Europe 2011: p.7). The DPD and Mechanisms envisaged infrequent, linear, point-to-point data flows, and are too inflexible for today's continuous, multidirectional, cross-border data movements, both within and between organizations (4.4.1). The position has been further muddied by seemingly knee-jerk beliefs, following Snowden's revelations (and reflected e.g. in GDPR's anti-FISA clause – p.119), that restricting commercial transfers can prevent third country, specifically US, authorities from accessing EU citizens' personal data.

The Mechanisms need to be 'reviewed and streamlined so as to make transfers simpler and less burdensome' (COM(2010)609 final, para.2.4.1), to produce workable, flexible solutions particularly for multinationals. However, with the exception of mandatory recognition of controller BCRs, generally the GDPR fails to do so, instead exacerbating the uncertainties and restricting transfers further, as discussed above. I agree with a response to the Commission arguing that increasingly complex transfers need practical compliance mechanisms and organizational accountability cultures; transfers should not require 'complex, lengthy and costly administrative processes' as long as adequate protection and accountability are provided, focusing on meeting the core Principles (Intel 2009: p.4).

Ex ante DPA checks of transfers are already unworkable, given their volumes (5.4; Ch.6). Even 'block' Mechanisms are overly complex and rigid. Calls have been widespread to 'remove all ex-ante controls' in TBDFs and to make data exporters fully liable for all subsequent processing once personal data are transferred outside the EU, avoiding this liability only if 'compliance measures are taken' (Commission 2010b: p.8). I will argue (Ch.7) that, particularly for controller–processor transfers, the more sensible way to achieve the Restriction's objective in a globalized world, while better balancing data protection with practicality, is to focus on continued compliance with Principles (notably via technical measures), rather than on the location or movements of personal data per se, or requiring bureaucratic Mechanisms. Furthermore, the use of technical protections like encryption (even without adherence to codes etc.) should be encouraged, not ignored or disallowed.

But first, I will show how difficulties with using the Mechanisms, together with ubiquity of modern data flows, have led to widespread non-compliance with the Restriction in practice, with little enforcement – underlining the Restriction's futility.

6. Compliance and enforcement

6.1 INTRODUCTION

Ch.5 highlighted compliance complexities arising from the lack of cross-Member State harmonization and difficulties with using the Mechanisms. If a regulatory system is seen, not just by controllers but also by DPAs, as 'unduly bureaucratic' and not fulfilling its purpose, 'that system will not be effectively adhered to or enforced' – even if, theoretically, criminal sanctions apply to infringement (Korff 1998: p.62).

I will show that the total likely volumes of transfers occurring in practice must far exceed the (relatively low) numbers of compliant transfers through using Mechanisms, and that therefore there must be many non-compliant transfers. Yet, despite many non-compliant transfers, the Restriction is little enforced in practice. Its existence, indeed its enforcement, does not make compliance with the Principles more likely. The vast majority of enforcement actions for infringing the Restriction have focused on the Principles, rather than breach of the Restriction per se. This demonstrates the Restriction's ineffectiveness and suggests its pointlessness as a separate rule in its own right, indeed its harmfulness because of wasted time and costs attempting to comply.

I discuss the volumes of non-compliant transfers first, then the lack of enforcement. Direct evidence of negatives, i.e. non-compliance and non-enforcement, is impossible. However, they can be deduced from indirect evidence, as follows:

- Volumes of data exports are high.
- A substantial proportion must be personal data (although the exact proportion is unknown).
- Many of those transfers must be occurring otherwise than under Mechanisms or derogations.
- Therefore, there must be many non-compliant transfers.

6.2 UBIQUITY OF TRANSFERS

Volumes of data, and data exports, have increased dramatically since the DPD was drafted. A high proportion must be personal data, given technological, societal and business changes[1] such as the growth of cloud computing, mobile computing and 'Internet of things'; user-generated content and social media becoming commonplace; and personal data's increasing treatment as an asset class or 'new oil' (WEF 2011). Therefore, the amount and proportion of personal data transferred nowadays must be at least several times that when the DPD was adopted.

Today, continuous data exports and imports are the norm, rather than exception. Although both the OECD Guidelines and the DPD assumed the opposite (4.4.1), the exponential rise in Internet usage has fundamentally reversed that assumption. Even in 1997, a 'huge number of transfers' of personal data were 'leaving the Community on a daily basis', with a 'multitude of actors involved in such transfers' (*WP4*, sec.2). Some DPAs noted increased transfers in the early 2000s, e.g. Austria (*WP14*, p.8). In 2006, 'an acceleration of international data transfers' was mentioned, which national DPAs' 'daily practice' 'shows as obvious' (*WP114*, p.17). There was emerging 'an inter-connected world where information flows are fluid and decentralised, and cross-border data exchange is routine. Moving data around the world or across the corridor now requires the same "click"' (OECD 2006: p.7). Thus, 'In today's globalised world, occasional transborder transfers' of personal data have evolved into 'a continuous, multipoint data flow' (OECD 2011: p.15).

Given the volumes of international trade involving the EU, and Internet usage by EU businesses and individuals, there must now be huge, and increasing, data exports to third countries, many of which must involve personal data. In 1988, an estimated 2–5 percent of TBDF involved personal data (Briat 1988, cited in White 1997: p.233). Assuming conservatively that this proportion remains as low as 2 percent, given today's volumes of cross-border business and Internet usage, there must be vast numbers of personal data exports.

Statistics regarding the volumes and growth of trade between the EU and third countries, and regarding EU Internet use, help indicate the likely transfer volumes. In concrete terms, of the EU's ten biggest merchandize trading partners in 2015 (Commission 2016c), topped by

---

[1] E.g. Tene 2011b.

the US, only two countries were EEA (Norway) or whitelisted[2] (Switzerland). As regards Internet use, take the example of email traffic alone. In 2012 an estimated 22 percent of all email users were in Europe,[3] 75 percent being consumer accounts and 25 percent corporate accounts; most global email traffic originated from corporates, with 89 billion (thousand million) business emails being sent and received daily (The Radicati Group, Inc. 2012). Assuming 22 percent of that daily traffic involved Europe, that means 19.6 billion business emails were sent/received daily involving Europe. If half of those went from Europe (the other half to), that still indicates 9.8 billion business emails sent from Europe daily. On more recent statistics, over 112 000 million emails were sent per second on 4 September 2016.[4] Applying the same calculation (half of 22 percent), over 12 000 million emails were sent from European corporates per second. If only 2 percent of those contained personal data, that is still over 246 million email transmissions of personal data per second, or 21 million million emails daily (see also n.12).

I should address a survey for the Commission (Gallup 2008b: pp.6–7), where only 10 percent of EU companies indicated that they transferred personal data to third countries (78 percent of them by email), contradicting the general statistics. Ten percent seems 'far too low' given companies' widespread email/Internet use (Kuner 2013b: p.119). Several issues could explain the low proportion reported. Firstly, respondents were informed that the survey was for the Commission (Gallup 2013, pers. comm., 27 May). So if they were transferring personal data possibly in breach of the Restriction, they may not have wished to admit it.[5] Secondly, respondents may not have understood the term 'transfers', or been aware of their type or extent.[6] One question asked how a company

---

[2]   Whitelisted countries together have a low share of global services trade – 6 percent (Kommerskollegium 2014: p.18, citing ECIPE 2013: p.8).

[3]   Many statistics cover 'Europe' not the EEA (see http://www.kuan0.com/doc/europe-eea-eu-efta-council-of-europe-venn.html for the differences), and may therefore include Turkey and Russia. However, even discounting those countries, the figures must be substantial.

[4]   From http://www.internetlivestats.com/.

[5]   The Commission cannot directly enforce DPD Law breaches against controllers, but could have notified national DPAs.

[6]   Given difficulties with what 'transfers' means – Ch.3. Tellingly, when asked about difficulties experienced when needing to transfer personal data outside the EU, 58.2 percent of SMEs said 'Don't know/not applicable' (SEC(2012)72 final, Ann.8, p.135). Unfortunately, controllers were not asked whether they knew about the Restriction, or whether they used SCCs: only whether they were familiar with the expression 'standard contractual clauses'. Of

transferred personal data (enumerated as: telephone, fax, registered mail, courier, regular mail, email, private network, open Internet,[7] or other means) to 'other countries'. However, this question was asked only after the respondent answered 'Yes' when asked *whether* their company transferred personal data to third countries. Respondents were not informed, before being asked whether they 'transferred' personal data, that 'transfer' included the methods listed (Gallup 2013, pers. comm., 27 May). Thus, respondents may have interpreted 'transfer' more narrowly than telephone, fax, etc. In the same survey, inconsistently, 65 percent of respondents stated that their company transferred personal data via the Internet. Therefore, despite that survey, statistical evidence as well as the reported experiences of DPAs, the Commission and others indicate large volumes of transfers.

6.3 NON-COMPLIANT TRANSFERS?

Many transfers must breach the Restriction, because the overall transfers must exceed the transfers made under Mechanisms or derogations.[8] To support this, I show that the latter numbers are much lower than the former, based on available statistics. Exact figures are impossible as not all transfers under Mechanisms or derogations are monitored or recorded.

6.3.1 Whitelisted Countries

Transfers to whitelisted countries, while permitted, generally need not be reported or recorded. Whitelisted countries are few, and not top EU trading partners (p.228). This alone suggests there must be many more transfers to non-whitelisted third countries. 'Key economic trading partners are not covered by adequacy findings' so other Mechanisms play 'a crucial role in practice'; 'When these are not easily available, non-compliance is de facto encouraged' (Robinson et al. 2009: p.43).

---

those indicating that their company transferred data to non-EU countries, 34 percent were 'familiar' (Gallup 2008a: p.32).

[7] E.g. IP phone, FTP.

[8] Compliance with regulation of transborder data flows lags behind the amount of personal data being transferred internationally (Kuner 2013b: p.146).

6.3.2   Safe Harbour

The US was the EU's biggest merchandize trading partner in 2015 (Commission 2016c), and has been for years. Over half the EU–US cross-border trade in services depends on the Internet (Commission 2013a: fn.11). However, only 5478 organizations were Safe Harbour-certified on the date of the *Schrems* judgment, 6 October 2015.[9]

One certification may cover numerous transfers to that harborite, but under 6000 is still not large. Given the massive trade volumes with the US and relatively few harborites, I argue that there must have been many transfers to the USA that were not made under Safe Harbour, even pre-*Schrems*.

6.3.3   Adequate Safeguards: SCCs Etc.

Member States must notify the Commission (Art.26(3)) of transfer authorizations granted based on adequate safeguards (5.4). In practice, these mainly relate to ad hoc contracts e.g. IGAs (5.4.4) and BCRs. The Commission considers that SCCs authorizations need not be notified (SEC(2006)95, p.3), but many Member States were previously notifying them – discussed shortly. Art.26(3) notifications have been far fewer than probable transfer volumes suggest. These low numbers may reflect DPAs' reluctance or inability to handle authorization requests, enforce failures to request authorizations, or both, rather than few requests being *made* (6.3.4).

Most DPAs could not indicate how many processing operations involved transfers; '[w]here figures were available, they were insignificant' – 600 (France), 1352 (Spain), 150 (Denmark) (COM(2003)265 final, p.19). This number was considered 'derisory' compared with 'what might reasonably be expected'[10] (COM(2003)265 final, p.19), although transfers were permissible otherwise than under Art.26(2), e.g. under Safe Harbour, pre-*Schrems*. Even Member States who required DPA

---

[9]   Based on an Internet Archive snapshot on the date stated http://web.archive.org/web/20151006203614/https://safeharbor.export.gov/list.aspx.

[10]   Only five Member States enacted obligations to notify authorizations to the Commission; even those notified 'a rather low number ...'; three other Member States, although not so required by national laws, gave notifications (Commission 2003: p.34).

authorization for transfers based on Commission adequacy decisions or SCCs notified 'extremely low' numbers of authorization requests.[11]

From information obtained under my access to information requests, by 31 May 2007 only ten Member States had ever notified the Commission, of about 350 authorizations altogether (Commission 2013b).[12] Most involved SCCs (280), 38 involved BCRs,[13] 5 data subject consent (Greece), 20 were 'not identifiable' – perhaps ad hoc contracts or consent. Some Member States, e.g. the UK, had never notified authorizations. This is probably because many Member States do not require SCCs etc. to be reported to, authorized or checked by DPAs, before or after transfer; therefore, DPAs lack the information (SEC(2006)95, pp.3–4). Member States' absence of information on SCCs was felt to raise questions regarding whether they were 'properly implementing the obligation to monitor the transfer of personal data to [inadequate] third countries' and preventing such transfers unless based on Mechanisms or derogations, and whether transfers might be occurring 'systematically and without appropriate control' to 'inadequate' third countries (SEC(2006)95, p.6).

In 2007, the Commission asked Member States to cease notifying SCCs authorizations (Commission 2007). This seems to reflect its views on the necessity of notification, compared with associated burdens for Member States and the Commission, and accords with some Member States' moves to obviate or relax requirements for prior authorizations or notifications of transfers, e.g. Italy (WP29 2004: p.13) and Portugal (WP29 2006: p.95).[14] Between 1 June–31 December 2007, only three Member States notified (Commission 2013c). For 2008, only Spain notified (all SCCs) (Commission 2014b). Numbers of 'authorized' or notified transfers, from the WP29's latest published annual report, for 2012 (WP29 2015a), still seem miniscule compared with likely actual volumes: in 2012, Austria made 61 authorizations (not all for transfers),

---

[11] 'From zero ... to 11, with the authorization procedure taking two months on average' (Commission 2003: p.50). There must have been more than 11 transfers!

[12] Until 2007, the AEPD had received controller notifications regarding only 8 483 transfers; but telephone calls, emails, faxes, corporate data transfers, data transfers via the Internet, etc. between Spain and third countries must total millions, even billions per year (Kuner 2013b: p.146).

[13] Far fewer organizations have BCRs (5.4.3.2) than were Safe Harbour-certified. Most are multinationals, obviously responsible for large transfer volumes, but there must be many transfers not involving such organizations.

[14] Conversely, from 2007 France required notifications to data subjects regarding transfers (WP29 2008: p.41).

France authorized 950 transfers, Slovakia 25; Bulgaria considered 8 transfer requests, the Czech Republic 18, Poland 51; Italy authorized 3; Greece was notified of 57 transfers and renewed 81 permits (not all regarding transfers); Latvia conducted 234 'prior checks' (only some for transfers) and Slovenia 5 on transfers. Noting that Member States' notification obligations were satisfied 'only sporadically', the GDPR's lack of such notification obligations has been welcomed, given mass ubiquitous cross-border data flows: such obligations would be 'an unnecessary administrative burden', without attendant benefits; it was already 'quite evident' that they fail to work properly in practice (Konarski et al. 2012: p.73).

In summary, while notifications to the Commission may not reflect actual transfer volumes under SCCs, BCRs, etc., particularly post-2007 when it no longer required notification, two points seem clear. Firstly, the Commission and others consider that actual transfers must far exceed transfers under Mechanisms. Even if one Safe Harbour certification, SCC or BCR could cover numerous transfers by the relevant organization or group, the massive overall volumes of trade and Internet use, compared with the relatively low numbers reported for Mechanism usage, suggest that there must be many more organizations transferring personal data without using Mechanisms. Secondly, even *ex post* notifications of authorizations have proved over-burdensome; therefore, *ex ante* authorizations must be even more burdensome, so much so that some Member States which initially required such authorizations or notifications have reversed their approaches (p.231).

6.3.4 Breaches of the Restriction? – Why?

The 'extremely low number' of notifications to the Commission was thought to indicate that either Member States had failed to notify authorizations, or they were not granting authorizations (Commission 2003: para.13.6); 'either data are not transferred, or ... they are transferred without respecting the conditions set out in national legislation' (Commission 2003: pp.51–2). It seems unlikely that personal data were not being transferred at all, as shown above. More likely, controllers were not *seeking* authorizations for their transfers of personal data.

Why might controllers not seek authorizations? They may have been unaware of DPD Law requirements to obtain prior authorization. Alternatively, some Member States may not have required authorizations, e.g. where Mechanisms like Safe Harbour were used. Another possibility is that some controllers, although aware of the Restriction, chose to make transfers without seeking authorizations, i.e. deliberate breaches. I discuss these in turn.

6.3.4.1 Lack of awareness

Ignorance of the Restriction seems to have been widespread. A few years ago, only 17 percent of EU citizens 'had heard' that personal data could only be transferred to countries ensuring an adequate level of data protection (Gallup 2008a; Gallup 2008b). This proportion seems low for laws that, at that time, had been in force for a decade. One might hope that the proportion would be higher among controllers, but it seems not unlikely that a similar proportion of SMEs lack awareness of the Restriction, indeed DPD Laws generally. For example, a survey of 300 senior UK IT professionals found that 40 percent were unaware of the ICO's cloud guidance; under 27 percent of those who were aware of it considered their organizations compliant (CipherCloud 2012). However, large organizations must surely know of the Restriction and its requirements, particularly multinationals, as they generally take legal advice e.g. on outsourcing contracts. Media publicity around *Schrems* (5.3.2) has undoubtedly helped raise awareness of the Restriction.

6.3.4.2 No authorization required

Some transfers may not require authorization. Firstly, authorizations may be unnecessary because the nature of the information or processing may remove it from DPD Laws' scope, e.g. anonymous non-personal data (1.4), or may subject it to a lighter regime, e.g. pseudonymous data (where exports are sometimes permitted without authorization).[15] Other transfers may be exempt, e.g. for purely personal purposes (1.5.3). Such transfers need not be authorized or notified, and their volumes must be large, such as social networking SaaS users uploading personal data, but, given the huge total volumes of transfers, many transfers must be within the DPD's scope.

Secondly, derogations may cover some transfers. Most derogations are unusable for cloud and the WP29 deprecates consent as a legal basis for transfers (5.5.1). Nevertheless, particularly in the DPD's early years, multinationals used consent to address seemingly irreconcilable differences between national DPD Laws; typically, to transfer employee personal data to centralized human resources systems in third countries,

---

[15] E.g. in Austria, with keycoded pharmaceutical data, where names etc. are replaced with codes and the 'key' showing correspondences is kept separately (Hon, Millard and Walden 2013b: pp.171–2). See 7.2.3.2.

notably the USA (Rambøll Management 2005: p.59). Indeed, DPAs have advised or required consent for certain transfers.[16] In 2003, Italy's DPA asked 50 large multinationals active in Italy about their transfers: consent was reportedly the legal basis most relied on (48 percent) (Kuner 2007a: pp.496–7). However, this finding cannot necessarily be generalized – e.g. in Austria in 2006, SCCs were used most, preferred even by US-based corporations over Safe Harbour (they did not inform Austria's DPA why), with consent not even being mentioned (WP29 2007: p.19). Consent may not be the safest basis for controllers' transfers (5.5.1). Tellingly, in notifications of authorizations to the Commission cumulatively to 31 May 2007, consent only accounted for 1.5 percent (Commission 2013b). Also telling as regards current realities, Mechanisms including Safe Harbour, SCCs, BCRs, even ad hoc contracts, have been discussed by practitioners (IAPP 2013) – but not consent.

Thirdly, some controllers may not request DPA authorizations for proposed adequate safeguards, because their Member States allow controllers to self-assess adequacy (5.2.1). In such Member States, if the controller considers that adequate protection exists (e.g. from contractual arrangements or encryption), no authorization is needed, even for transfers to a third country whose *laws* do not provide adequate protection. The volumes of transfers based on controllers' self-assessment are unknown, and could be large. However, few Member States allow self-assessment, so there must be many transfers otherwise than under self-assessed adequacy.

Fourthly, controllers may use Mechanisms (Ch.5). However, transfers under whitelisting, Safe Harbour, and BCRs etc. must be relatively few, when compared with the huge volumes of trade and Internet use (6.3.1–6.3.3).

6.3.4.3 Deliberate failure to comply with Restriction

Finally, given the Restriction's incompatibility with modern business and technological practices (Ch.4) and the compliance complexities (Ch.5), seeking advance authorization is likely to involve many difficulties including delay and costs. Therefore, some controllers, even if aware of the Restriction, may take the calculated risk of making transfers without attempting to use Mechanisms, relying on their breach not being discovered or enforced (6.4.2). It was observed, regarding the Restriction but

---

[16]   E.g. Ireland, Portugal 1997, employee data or intra-group transfers to US parent (*WP14*, pp.16, 20); Sweden 1998, airline reservations (*WP14*, p.26); and Netherlands 2001, acquired company's consumer data (WP29 2003: p.56).

equally applicable to *ex ante* authorizations, that 'if properly implemented', the regime would probably 'collapse from the weight of its cumbersome, bureaucratic procedures' or else collapse from 'large-scale avoidance of its proper implementation due precisely to fears of such procedures' (Bygrave 2010: p.200).

The first Commission report on the DPD's transposition in the (then 15) Member States considered that many non-compliant transfers were indeed occurring, through ignorance or intention (COM(2003)265 final, p.19). A report for the Commission stated, 'the basic impression is that compliance with the legal rules on data transfers is generally very low', and 'Overall, in many Member States, whether strict or lax on paper, Art.26 therefore appears to be honoured more in the breach than through compliance' (Korff and Brown 2010: paras.76–9). Perhaps in practice there is no need for authorization, or no significant risk without it, so generally controllers have not sought authorization.

DPAs have acknowledged difficulties with handling massive transfer volumes. Even in 1994, the UK's then-DPA noted that the growth of a 'universal communications system' (i.e. the Internet), whose 'whole purpose is to facilitate the exchange of information', posed challenges in seeking to monitor and control so many users, querying such control's feasibility: 'Can transborder data flow be effectively regulated when so many millions of data users have a relatively simple method of exchanging personal data with other data users overseas?' (Data Protection Registrar 1994: p.29). Former UK Information Commissioner Richard Thomas has stated, '[The DPD's] international transfer rules are unrealistic against a backdrop of high-volume, globalised data flows' (Robinson et al. 2009: executive summary foreword, p.2). The Restriction's aim of protecting European citizens' data may be undermined by the 'sheer quantities' of transfers (Robinson et al. 2009: p.33).

A plaintive submission to the Commission (Austrian Bar 2009: p.4) highlighted the resource-intensive nature of notifications/authorizations, and DPAs' lack of resources:

> In particular as to international data transfers, only one (!) person is preparing the decisions of the commission. Even though this person is working already Saturdays and Sundays, this leads to long approval procedures with regard to international data transfers …

There is some evidence of deliberate breaches of the Restriction to avoid months of delays (n.11; p.195) which might slow, or even stymie, business transactions. Where a separate licence/permit was required for transfers, because the process took so long, 'some organizations do not wait for them to be issued ...' (Robinson et al. 2009: p.33). Thus, controllers may be reluctant to seek authorization, whether because of delays or risks of refusal, because their focus is on completing transactions.

To summarize, comparing the ability to send a message 'almost instantaneously' at the press of a button with the political process to persuade all EU Member States to approve a transfer, 'it is difficult to imagine most computer users doing anything other than pressing the button without any regard to the legal regime in which they operate' (Millard and Carolina 1995: p.282). In short, compliance with the Restriction seems so at odds with current (even 1995) environments and business practices, that many simply 'press the button'. Widespread disregard of the Restriction appears both to reflect, and reinforce, its perception as a bureaucratic 'box-ticking' rule that is unrealistic in modern global environments (Ch.5).

6.4   ENFORCEMENT OF THE RESTRICTION

I have shown that many transfers have been, and probably are being, made in breach of the Restriction, even deliberately so. However, enforcement action seems relatively lacking, whether to block transfers, require deletion of transferred personal data and/or impose monetary or criminal penalties.

The Restriction's practical incompatibility with the Internet's architecture and operation, and the near-impossibility of strictly complying with or enforcing it when 'technology allows the information to be whisked out of the jurisdiction' with a mouse click (Gunasekara 2007: p.382), have been noted often (Millard and Carolina 1995: p.282; Chissick 2000; Durie 2000: p.90; Reid 2004: para.3.3). 'Technology has made all aspects of personal data processing dramatically easier, from overseas transfers to archiving' (Ministry of Justice 2012: p.5). '[I]t is fairly impossible to enforce legal rules on the net' (Blume 2000: p.82). The TBDF definition is so wide that it extends to 'most acts of data processing on the Internet', but national laws can never be consistently enforced against such huge data-processing volumes globally (Kuner 2013b: p.155).

I first discuss enforcement by data subjects and DPAs of DPD Laws generally, then the Restriction specifically. Then, I consider the related issue of enforcement of breaches of Mechanisms, because analysis of the Restriction's enforcement would be incomplete without considering enforcement of the Mechanisms designed to ensure compliance with its requirements.

6.4.1   Data Subject Enforcement[17]

Arts.22–3 DPD require Member States to provide data subjects with judicial remedies and compensation for damage.[18] However, there are relatively few reports of successful data subject enforcement of DPD Laws. Data subject litigation is relatively rare and lacks 'serious impact on enforcement overall' perhaps because, for data subjects, the risks, costs and effort are often disproportionate to the uncertain compensation or other remedies obtainable (Korff 1998: p.58),[19] while controllers are often major corporations with the resources and motivation to defend lawsuits, to avoid disadvantageous precedents (Korff 2010: sec.5.1). Lack of litigation regarding TBDF laws may indicate that such law 'is so weak as to rarely be of significance' (Svantesson 2011: p.181): infringements are seldom noticed, victims are in no position to pursue infringements, DPAs have not prioritized transfers sufficiently and/or (which Svantesson dismisses) transfers are uncontroversial and thus unlikely to result in legal disputes.

Another reason for the relative lack of successful data subject enforcement action could be data subjects' ignorance regarding DPD Laws and their rights,[20] e.g. of the Restriction itself and/or of any transfers or breaches (White 1997: pp.234–5). It may be difficult to discover the root

---

[17]   See generally FRA (2014: chap.3); FRA (2010).

[18]   FRA (2010: pp.32, 36) summarizes data protection administrative, non-judicial and judicial remedies and compensation in different Member States.

[19]   'In cases with smaller impact, it is unlikely that the victims of a breach of data protection rules would bring individual actions against the controllers, given the costs, delays, uncertainties, risks and burdens they would be exposed to' (EDPS 2011: para.96). Enforcing the DPD can be difficult because 'it is difficult to assign a value to any damages, and determining responsibilities is complex' (Robinson et al. 2009: p.35). In ten Member States including the UK, it was found impracticable to seek compensation or damages from private entities for data protection violations because of the burden of proof, difficulties quantifying damage and 'infrequent support from the supervisory bodies, which are mainly engaged in promotional activities' (FRA 2010: sec.5.1.3).

[20]   The evidence suggests that individuals are unaware of regulations, rarely complain about perceived violations and sometimes misunderstand them (Kuner 2013b: p.119). See FRA (2010: secs.4.4, 5.1.4) on data subjects' awareness of rights generally, including some national survey results, and Wubben et al. (2012: pp.3–4).

causes of data protection breaches with transferred personal data (*WP9*, p.9; *WP12*, p.20), even *non*-transferred personal data, let alone success-fully obtain judgments against foreign defendants and enforce them abroad. Ignorance of DPD Laws among data subjects, even judges, seems prevalent (FRA 2014: p.3). This leads to reliance on DPAs for enforce-ment, unless specialized non-governmental organizations (NGOs) can assist data subjects. However, litigation may increase in future as GDPR Art.80 allows quasi-class actions – qualifying not-for-profit bodies may complain or sue on behalf of data subjects who authorize them or, in Member States that allow it, independently of data subjects' mandate.

Data subjects may find it harder to complain to foreign authorities. They may be unaware that a foreign organization was involved,[21] or to whom they may complain. Privacy and data protection authorities had not reported receiving cross-border complaints 'in significant number' (OECD 2006: p.9). This might indicate few breaches with cross-border dimensions, or simply lack of information about such breaches.[22] If third country organizations are involved, enforcing breaches of the Restriction may indeed require more time and expense (White 1997: p.242); cross-border enforcement is difficult (Moerel 2012a: chap.4.3). However, difficulties with asserting legal rights abroad are not unique to data protection and privacy law, resulting rather from the lack of a global legal framework for cross-border recognition and enforcement of judgments (Kuner 2013b: p.117). Practical enforcement even by DPAs is difficult without effective cross-border enforcement mechanisms (ICO 2012c: p.5): 'This means that, in reality, non-EU data controllers' compliance with [the GDPR] would be voluntary. [The GDPR] should be realistic about this and should not lead EU consumers to believe that the law offers them a degree of protection that, in reality, it cannot deliver'.

It is unclear whether cross-border complaints reported (OECD 2006) were about transfers as such, or whether individuals only complained if they felt that Principles (or their equivalent in other countries) had been breached. Perhaps that was because that study focused on substantive breaches, not unlawful transfers per se. For instance, spam was cited when discussing cross-border complaints. However, spam is not regulated by the Restriction, but under the Principles. Transfers are only likely to be discovered 'after the fact and only where there has been abuse of the

---

[21]   With Internet processing, it may be difficult for data subjects or DPAs to determine the controller's physical location, let alone where it is 'established' (Charlesworth 2002: p.931).

[22]   Obtaining good quantitative data regarding the volumes and nature of cross-border complaints is problematic (OECD 2011: p.5).

basic rules with consequent loss to the data subject', as data subjects only seek to exercise their rights, reactively, when something goes wrong (White 1997: pp.234–5). In short, consistently with the Restriction's anticircumvention objective, in practice data subjects may be concerned about transfers only if any Principles are breached following the transfer, and that breach and any resulting damage are likely to concern them more than transfer per se.

To summarize, enforcement of DPD Laws through data subject litigation has been rare. Complaining to local DPAs to request enforcement (Art.28(4)) may be more fruitful for data subjects, and some regulatory action has ensued, as I discuss next.

6.4.2 DPA Enforcement of DPD Laws Generally

There is relatively low compliance with, and enforcement of, data protection laws generally (COM(2003)265 final, p.12), and therefore probably the Restriction also. DPD enforcement is a 'sore issue'; it is 'an open secret that the framework is largely not enforced' (Tene 2011a). This perception seems widely held: in a 2008 survey for the Commission, citizens believed the level of protection in their *own* countries might be inadequate (Gallup 2008a: p.27). In another survey, 77 percent of employees in France, Germany and UK were 'not confident' about their organizations' compliance with DPD Laws generally (Sophos 2014). Another important point regarding DPD Laws' enforcement generally is that enforcement is uneven across Member States, with unclear rationales (to punish or affect behaviours), and differing criteria for sanctions (Robinson et al. 2009: p.26; FRA 2014; Bygrave 2010: p.197). This complexity also renders compliance more difficult, although the GDPR seeks to harmonize DPAs' powers better, cross-EEA (1.5.5).

Reports to the Commission on the DPD's implementation noted that DPAs' powers, as then exercised, were unable to counter 'continuing widespread disregard' of DPD Laws (Korff 2002a:[23] p.209; Korff 2010: p.108). Other studies confirm this (Robinson et al. 2009: p.35; FRA 2010). Difficulties were acknowledged with obtaining accurate, complete information about compliance with DPD Laws, '[g]iven (or despite) the ubiquitous character' of personal data processing; however, from anecdotal evidence and 'various elements of "hard" information available to

---

[23] On which the Commission based its first report on the DPD (COM(2003)265 final): (Commission 2003).

the Commission', three interrelated phenomena were observed (COM(2003)265 final, p.12):

- an under-resourced enforcement effort and DPAs with a wide range of tasks, where enforcement action had 'a rather low priority';
- 'very patchy' compliance by controllers, no doubt reluctant to change existing practices to comply with complex and burdensome rules when the risks of getting caught seemed low;
- data subjects' apparently low level of knowledge of their rights, 'which may be at the root of the previous phenomenon'.

Even in the EU/EEA, enforcement by DPAs 'is often weak and ineffective' (Korff and Brown 2010: para.104), citing an (unpublished) FRA report that DPAs were not effective in terms of policing or enforcement. The position seems not to have improved much since 1998 (Korff and Brown 2010: para.104). DPAs lack independence, powers and resources in certain Member States (FRA 2010). Enforcement is problematic, mainly due to DPAs' limited resources and non-prioritization of enforcement, and 'more vigorous and effective enforcement' was felt to be necessary to improve compliance (COM(2003)265 final, pp.12–13). Again, '[T]he situation has not really improved since then' (SEC(2012)72 final, p.17).

Why is DPA enforcement 'weak'? Inadequate resources is one issue, as mentioned. Generally, DPAs' resources remain unchanged, or are decreasing.[24] DPAs may also lack the right *types* of resources: e.g., regarding the Irish DPA's investigation of SaaS social networking service Facebook (whose European headquarters is in Ireland), it was noted that the DPA did not then have a technical expert or legally trained official, while facing 'a whole armada of lawyers' from Facebook (FRA 2012: p.110).[25]

Secondly, DPAs may not always have strong sanctions available.[26] Even when they do, formal sanctions may be applied only 'extremely

---

[24] E.g. FRA (2010: sec.4.2); FRA (2014: sec.5.1.1).

[25] Ireland's DPA recruited a technology adviser and in-house legal expert 'for the first time' in late 2012 (Campbell 2014).

[26] On differing DPA powers, see Robinson et al. (2009: pp.35–6); FRA (2010: p.34). Only in some Member States can DPAs levy economic sanctions; in others, DPAs 'may only negotiate amicable solutions' with those in breach, causing concern about the effectiveness of DPAs' administrative sanctions as 'the level of fines is seen as too low or fines are imposed too infrequently to have a

rarely' or at relatively low levels (Korff 2010: p.108). This means that the prospect of sanctions may not significantly deter breach (FRA 2010: sec.5.1.3). Indeed, Commission action[27] against the UK for deficient DPD implementation was initiated partly because ICO powers and judicial remedies are limited, including its inability to perform random checks on those processing personal data or to enforce penalties following checks; UK courts could refuse the right to have personal data rectified or erased; and UK legislation restricted rights to compensation for 'moral damage' when personal data are used inappropriately[28] (Commission 2010a). There is some evidence that low or zero awards of damages or administrative penalties against controllers, even those found in breach of DPD Laws, has led some controllers to treat data protection breaches as a business cost, especially when weighed against the financial benefits of breach – i.e., it is cheaper to pay any damages/fines if and when a breach is discovered and sanctioned, than to implement compliance measures (Moerel 2012a: p.66, fn.15).[29] If so, enforcement risks may have little deterrent effect: 'a low chance of enforcement' may cause controllers to regard data protection rules as 'a kind of bureaucratic nuisance' rather than 'law' (Kuner 2010: p.236).

Some consider that, to improve enforcement and compliance, DPAs' role needs strengthening – sanctions should be imposed more often, more stringent sanctions made available and compensation increased.[30] Since the ICO was granted certain fining powers in 2012, it has employed those powers more often (and at higher levels) than most EU DPAs, although mainly for security breaches rather than Principles such as purpose

---

dissuasive effect'; in other Member States, courts 'proved to lack a dissuasive effect', with criminal sanctions never having been imposed in some Member States (FRA 2010: p.35).

[27] Since dropped – p.153. The ICO cannot impose a monetary penalty exceeding £500 000. In contrast, the Financial Services Authority (as it then was) fined Zurich Insurance Plc's UK branch £2.75m for not implementing adequate systems and controls to prevent loss of customers' confidential information, i.e. personal data (Financial Services Authority 2010).

[28] A UK court has since disapplied that restriction as incompatible with the DPD. *Google Inc. v Vidal-Hall & Ors*, [2015] EWCA Civ 311, para.105.

[29] This may explain some media organizations' practice of invading celebrities' privacy, disregarding DPD Laws but increasing revenues.

[30] Of Europeans surveyed, 51 percent felt that companies who use people's personal data without their knowledge should be fined (TNS Opinion & Social 2011: p.3). 84 percent of surveyed UK consumers wanted fines imposed on organizations who fail to protect their data (Institute of Customer Service 2016). See also *WP168*, para.90; COM(2010)609 final, para.2.5.

limitation, perhaps because security breaches are easier to establish evidentially (Grant and Crowther 2016). The ICO uses monetary penalties for both sanction and deterrent purposes, with the overarching aim of promoting compliance and improving public confidence; research indicates (although from a relatively small sample size) that such penalties improved compliance in penalized organizations and, on becoming aware of such penalties, their 'peers', while ICO audits had also supported compliance (ICO 2014d). The GDPR would enhance DPAs' powers, including to impose fines of potentially huge amounts and to audit controller and processors (1.5.5). However, DPA actions such as audits and detailed investigation of potential infringements are resource-intensive. The GDPR does not compel Member States to increase or even maintain adequate DPA resources, which may exacerbate current enforcement issues (although DPAs 'should' be given resources to perform their tasks effectively – Rec.120).

There is another factor, arguably the most important, explaining the lack of enforcement: many DPAs' 'softer' approach of guiding controllers towards compliance. DPAs tend to have mixed roles, as guides/educators not just enforcers; many consider their roles to be more as 'advisers, facilitators and conciliators than as policemen: referees rather than Rambos' (Korff 1998: p.55). Many DPAs take a 'cautious', 'pragmatic' approach, rather than constant aggressive enforcement (Korff 2010: p.29). Often, they provide advice and guidance 'without actually even examining whether the law had been violated', even for 'quite manifest breaches', pursuing only cases that raise wider issues or indicate 'serious, persistent violations' (Korff 2010: p.101).[31] However, it should be noted that some DPAs are legally obliged to educate, not just enforce, e.g. the ICO has a statutory duty to promote good practice among data controllers (s.51 Data Protection Act 1998), so it is not a simple policy decision for them as to whether to educate or enforce.

This was considered a 'general problem, not limited to the UK' (Korff 2010: p.102): namely, that DPAs' approach to complaints may suggest 'soft' and negotiable enforcement, which is 'not conducive' to wider compliance and could partly explain 'widespread disregard' of laws in many countries (Robinson et al. 2009: p.36). Although complaints were investigated 'with some vigour', the 'vast majority' of investigations were

---

[31]   Although of 'little comfort' to data subjects whose complaints were not deemed 'serious enough' (Korff 2010: p.101). DPAs target 'particular issues or sectors ... in a given period', e.g. because of the importance of processing in that sector, sensitivity of data or operations in question, or level of complaints received about that sector (Korff 2010: p.106).

conducted and resolved in a conciliatory way, aiming to reach compromise (Korff 1998: pp.55, 40). This approach, along with 'lack of detailed reporting on individual cases and on the satisfaction level of the procedure', particularly from data subjects' perspectives, was taken to indicate that the complaints system had little effect on overall compliance (Korff 1998: p.40). That hard measures are rarely used does not prove that 'strict adherence to the legal requirements' is the result (Korff 2010: p.107).

However, that hard measures are rarely used does not prove that *increased* breaches result, either. Indeed, DPAs' conciliatory approach was considered 'largely effective' in obviating 'hard' enforcement measures (Korff 1998: p.64). Many DPAs' preferred approach of quiet resolution through 'backroom' negotiation, rather than public threats of punitive sanctions, pre-dates the DPD. They aim to *prevent* privacy invasions, as much as provide reactive remedies, but the former's impact is by definition difficult to measure (Bygrave 2010: p.195). Indeed, a cooperative regulatory approach to the DPD, with enforcement only against 'grievous offenders', was previously predicted ((O'Quinn 1998), fnn.26, 28 and accompanying text). Broad, strict laws may result in flexibility in practical enforcement. Contrast narrower laws, e.g. in the USA, which may be enforced more rigidly (O'Quinn 1998: pp.691–2, citing Swire and Litan 1998: pp.152–3, 162).[32] That said, in some respects DPAs do favour penalties for deterrence purposes, e.g. opining that contracts for enabling transfers should include 'dissuasive penalties' and audit rights (p.157). A more nuanced approach might suggest that the type of organization is relevant: public sector organizations may benefit more from practical guidance than fines that divert money from public services, while fines could be more effective against the private sector due to the possible impact of negative publicity on profits and customer trust; also, fines may be most effective for breaches where controllers have control over whatever led to the breach, rather than for breaches resulting from unawareness (Grant and Crowther 2016).

Underlying calls for tougher penalties is an assumption that enforcement produces compliance. That is not necessarily true. Despite criticism of the 'conciliatory' approach, it is arguable, based on regulatory theory (Black 1987), that 'conversational' regulation, continuing discussions between regulators and regulatees focused on guiding regulatees towards compliance, rather than enforcement, might be the most effective way to

---

[32] There is some evidence of strong US enforcement – e.g. high fines (Cline 2014).

maximize overall compliance with complex regulatory systems such as DPD Laws. Such discourse plays an important part in finding new points of equilibrium in what is termed the regulatory flux (Murray 2006), as conflicts between cyberspace norms and pre-Internet laws gradually change the 'regulatory settlement'. Put another way, because of the growing amounts of personal data being processed (let alone transferred) and limited DPA resources, DPAs require a 'strategic mindset', as *ex ante* process-orientated mechanisms 'are arguably no longer valid'; the regulatory system must be made to 'work for itself', only requiring DPA intervention where necessary to encourage positive practices in the use of personal data, enforcing only if 'significant risk of harm or actual harm exists' (Robinson et al. 2009: pp.40–41).

The GDPR (Arts.33–4) introduces mandatory notification of most 'personal data breaches' by controllers to DPAs and (in some situations) data subjects, and by processors to controllers. Along with potential fines for breaches, any failure to *notify* personal data breaches when required is subject to a (lower-tier) fine (Art.83(4)(a)). The impact of GDPR's higher fines and mandatory breach notification laws remains to be seen. It is out of scope to discuss the reputational or economic impact of publicity regarding data protection breaches or the extent to which laws regarding fines, publicity and other measures are effective in practice to improve data protection (including security) compliance generally. Although research in this area is increasing, more empirical research is clearly needed.

6.4.3 DPA Enforcement of the Restriction

Having discussed low enforcement of DPD Laws generally, I now consider DPA enforcement of the Restriction specifically.

Few reports of DPA enforcement regarding transfers have been published. Most did not state the resulting action (e.g. fine or inaction). In some cases, it was unclear whether the issue was 'transfer' under Art.25 or simply intra-EEA transmissions/communications, which DPAs sometimes term 'transfers' (1.4). Bearing these caveats in mind, I now summarize such reports.[33]

---

[33] Derived from publications in English, primarily Commission-published WP29 annual reports.

6.4.3.1 Transfers – DPA cases

Initially, DPAs took a strict approach to transfers as such. Thus, a laptop storing medical data was seized at an airport under Sweden's DPD Laws, presumably to prevent 'transfer' through flying it abroad (O'Quinn 1998: fn.27, citing Swire and Litan 1998: p.72). Following a data subject complaint, an Austrian hospital's transfer of personal data to a computer company abroad 'for technical service and debugging (service processing)' was ruled illegal for lack of a transfer licence (*WP35*, p.12).

A few cases involved Safe Harbour (or lack of Safe Harbour participation). Netherlands' DPA held that, while antipiracy association BREIN's collection of name, address, bank account number and IP address was legitimate, their transfer for antipiracy purposes to BREIN's US counterpart was impermissible, absent Safe Harbour participation or another method permitted under Dutch DPD Laws (CBP 2004). Rejecting a Greek legislator's complaint, the Commission stated that the transfer to Abbott Laboratories' US headquarters of personal data of its Greek subsidiary's employees did not violate data protection law, given Abbott's Safe Harbour participation (Kuner 2007b: para.4.66). Snowden's revelations triggered data subject complaints regarding transfers to US cloud providers under Safe Harbour, mostly dismissed on the basis that Safe Harbour provided adequate protection (Essers 2013) – until *Schrems* (5.3.2, 6.4.3.3).

Some DPAs emphasized data subjects' prior consent to transfers, notwithstanding the availability of Mechanisms and the WP29's deprecation of consent as a basis for transfers (5.5.1). Thus, German DPAs criticized AOL for allowing the export of users' online address books to AOL in the US via AOL's updated software, without users' knowledge or prior consent (Kuner 2007a: chap.4.105, fn.213).

However, most cases have focused on breaches of Principles (1.5.6). Spain's DPA, the AEPD, held that data transmission between enterprises in the same group constituted 'transfer' requiring 'consent of the party concerned or legal powers to take this course', confirmed judicially on appeal (*WP54*, pt.2, p.51).[34] Seemingly the primary focus was on a legal basis for the 'transfer'. The AEPD also received complaints regarding 'data transfers' in the direct marketing/advertising context (ibid.). Whether those involved Art.25 transfers or merely communications within Spain or the EEA, they must have involved direct marketing

---

[34] It is unclear if this involved 'communication' (cf. Art.25 'transfer'), but it seemed to emphasize the need for a legal basis (consent) for the communication/transfer.

(where data subjects have rights to object). Poland's DPA (GIODO) also considered complaints concerning direct marketing firms, where controllers tried to avoid Polish data protection laws by transferring '(at least formally)' processing to other countries (the US or Cyprus); 'because of limited access to direct marketing companies, the Inspector General notified the prosecution bodies of a crime' (WP29 2005: p.79). Assuming it was the Polish controllers who were prosecuted, this supports my point (p.64) that EEA controllers cannot avoid liability for breaches of Principles (here, regarding direct marketing) by using third country processors.

Under Spanish judgments, 'cession of data' occurs when data are communicated via the Internet, 'processing' when images are 'emitted on the Internet', and 'it is the liability of the person ceding the data to obtain consent, and due diligence can be demanded of him/her' (WP29 2004: p.74). A legal basis for processing and fair processing seemed to be the underlying concerns there. A German DPA ordered a multinational to delete an employee's personal data 'in its subsidiaries around the world', after the employee complained that his former employer had a US-hosted global human resources database system 'which resulted in his data being transferred around the world' without a legal basis for the database (Kuner 2007a: pp.494–5). Accordingly, that order concerned the legal basis and also enforced the data retention Principle.

Lloyds Bank's employee trade union complained about the outsourcing of personal data to India but the ICO, having found no evidence of violation of data protection laws, declined to pursue the matter (Kuner 2007a: chap.4.36, fn.72). The ICO has never taken any enforcement action regarding the Restriction (ICO 2013, pers. comm., 23 May), with one peripheral exception.[35] In considering 'Requests for authorization for transfer of data flows', Belgium's DPA, CPVP, noted that 'in pursuit of administrative simplification – but also, on occasion, as part of monitoring processes – various administrations increasingly intend to couple the data of a given citizen', and emphasized the Principles of 'legality and purpose, as well as to the right of the person concerned to be properly informed' (WP29 2007: p.20). Thus, its concerns related not to

---

[35]   E*Trade Securities' paper archives, containing Middle Eastern customers' personal data, were found to be missing from a UK storage facility. E*Trade signed an undertaking with the ICO, including to comply with the Restriction. That requirement was included because, during ICO investigation, it 'became apparent' that personal data had been processed outside the EEA, so guarantees of appropriate controls to ensure safe transfer were sought (ICO 2013, pers. comm., 15 July).

the Restriction per se, but to fair processing and purpose limitation. SWIFT's case has already been discussed, including CPVP's decision not to take enforcement action against SWIFT (p.90).

An Italian court ruled that a bank was liable to two customers for unauthorized bank transfers to a third country via its online banking service, which lacked security measures for adequate protection (WP29 2011: p.59). Thus the issue there was not transfer per se, but security (see also a Hungarian decision, p.172). Similarly, Slovenia's DPA, on a complaint regarding personal data of an online dating site's users being disclosed online, ordered the website operator to cease processing and notify users; while a transfer 'to third countries without a legal basis' was 'additionally established', primarily the issue was security: the website design, entrusted to an Indian contractor, did not include 'measures for traceability of processing', and poor programming enabled the perpetrator to obtain users' data; also, no data-processing agreement had been concluded (WP29 2014b: p.102). Norway's DPA discovered 'unauthorised disclosure of health information', suspecting 'transfer' of many patients' personal data from 11 Norwegian controllers to GE Healthcare Systems (GE) in the US, who had agreed to operate, monitor and maintain their equipment; here the issue was not location as such, but that GE could retrieve health information without any barriers, so it ruled that the controllers must establish adequate safeguards to secure confidentiality, and inform affected patients (WP29 2015a: p.141).

In summary, the dearth of reported cases suggests that there has been very little enforcement by DPAs or courts of the Restriction, despite probable high volumes of non-compliant transfers, and most enforcement has focused on Principles rather than data location as such.

6.4.3.2 Low DPA enforcement

Even under pre-DPD export restrictions, the practical effect of export restriction rules on TBDFs 'tends to have been, for the most part, negligible' (Bygrave 2010: p.186). Regarding 'many unauthorized and possibly illegal transfers', 'there is little or no sign of enforcement actions by the supervisory authorities' (COM(2003)265 final, p.19). Since then, the position seems to have changed little; indeed it is often doubted whether the Restriction is enforced (Weber 2013: p.124). Why might DPA enforcement of the Restriction, even following complaints, be so low, compared with probable volumes of transfers and breaches?

Firstly, DPAs may be unaware of transfers. Given the likely massive volumes of transfers through multiple possible means, DPAs lack the technical ability and/or resources to monitor all Internet activities by users in their countries to check whether they involve transfers, and (which would require verification of the Mechanisms used, e.g. whether SCCs have been signed) whether any may have breached the Restriction.[36] In short, realistically DPAs may not know about breaches unless they receive complaints, or breaches are publicized by the media or self-reported by controllers.

Secondly, even if DPAs know of breaches of the Restriction, they may not take formal enforcement action, for various possible reasons (6.4.1–6.4.2):

- Inadequate resources compared with volumes of breaches – DPAs 'are not sufficiently equipped to deal with the increasing flow' of personal data in cross-border business (Commission 2010b: p.7);
- DPAs may take a conversational (rather than confrontational) approach to enforcement, aimed at guiding future compliance rather than punishing past breaches;
- DPAs may decide not to pursue matters due to known difficulties with extraterritorial investigation and enforcement (OECD 2007; *WP56*, pp.14–15).[37] The WP29 noted 'significant doubts as to whether it is proper, practical, or indeed feasible from a resource point of view, for a supervisory authority of an EU Member State to take responsibility for investigation and inspection of data processing taking place in a third country' (*WP12*, p.21). Nevertheless, it felt that ways could be developed to achieve 'a reasonable degree of enforcement', remarking that many third countries will recognize and enforce EU judgments, but even if not, a foreign website (or other organization) might follow the judgment and adapt its data processing for good business practice and commercial reputational reasons (*WP56*, p.14); and/or
- DPAs may decide not to take extraterritorial enforcement action, to avoid perhaps absurd results which furthermore may risk breaching comity[38] and engendering disrespect for DPD Laws. Notably, where personal data are processed using 'equipment' in Member State territory, that Member State's DPD Laws apply under Art.4(1)(c) (2.3.2), including the Restriction (*WP179*, p.25) – even if personal data are processed by non-EEA controllers with no other EEA presence, relate only to non-EEA residents and are intended for

---

[36]	For DPAs to monitor processing outside national boundaries is 'far from easy ...' (Reidenberg and Schwartz 1998: p.45).

[37]	Cross-border recognition and enforcement of judgments is problematic, administrative sanctions perhaps even more so (OECD 2007: p.21).

[38]	E.g. Swire (1998: p.1010); Reed (2012: chap.3).

re-export to third countries after processing.[39] However, when a law's jurisdictional scope is far broader than its chances of enforcement, respect for the law risks being diminished (Kuner 2010: p.235).

Thirdly (related to the preceding point, because resource limitations force prioritization), arguably another reason exists. The Restriction's objective was to prevent avoidance of the Principles (2.3.1.2). Therefore, DPAs may focus investigation/enforcement resources on any breach of the Principles that follow, chronologically if not causally, any breach of the Restriction, rather than the latter alone. Indeed, most complaints have generally concerned any breaches of Principles following transfers, not transfers per se; this view is supported by actual enforcement action regarding the Restriction (6.4.3.1). In a survey of DPAs worldwide, 26 of 31 DPAs committed 10 percent or less of their investigative/enforcement work to 'transborder issues' (which may be broader than just the Restriction or its equivalent), with the EU 'at 50%', 'albeit having no enforcement powers' (IAPP 2010: p.32).[40] In the early 2000s, CNIL had 'never encountered a situation' where a transfer 'violated the provisions of the Directive' (Korff 2002a: p.179).[41] Similarly, 'we have not been presented with any evidence to suggest that international transfers from the UK, where there is currently no prior authorization mechanism, have resulted in data subjects being disadvantaged or personal data being misused' (ICO 2012c: p.19).

Fourthly, even if DPAs enforce breaches of the Restriction, there seems no uniform cross-Member State system for recording and reporting their

---

[39] *WP179* p.21. The UK's then-DPA considered that applying DPD Laws extraterritorially under the equipment ground made 'little sense', was 'very difficult if not impossible to enforce' and disincentivized businesses from locating processing operations in the EU (Korff 2002a: p.55). Indeed, CNIL promulgated exemptions from data protection rules precisely so as to not discourage non-EEA controllers from using French providers – p.96, n.37. See p.52; Korff (2010: secs.3.2–3.3); *WP56*, pp.9–12.

[40] A later survey noted a shift – 'many DPAs' indicated that 'they enforce laws protecting citizens from the misuse of their data not only by domestic organizations but by those that either transfer data outside the jurisdiction or, in some cases, are located entirely outside the DPA's country or jurisdiction' (IAPP 2011: p.24).

[41] Korff thought this statement seemed 'if not naive then indicative of a desire to "see, hear no evil, speak no evil"'. However, it could simply indicate that CNIL had not, by 2002, encountered breaches of Principles resulting from transfers.

enforcement action (Korff 2010: pp.102, 105). Therefore, some enforcement action may have gone unreported.

6.4.3.3   DPA enforcement of US transfers, post-*Schrems*

Schrems triggered significant changes. The WP29 declared that continued US transfers based on Safe Harbour were unlawful (5.3.2). The UK's ICO recognized that organizations might take 'some time' to implement another Mechanism for their US transfers (ICO 2015c), noting that Safe Harbour principles still provided 'a measure of protection' for personal data transferred to harborites, and 'We're certainly not rushing to use our enforcement powers'; but the automatic assurance of adequacy previously provided by using Safe Harbour was lost so controllers 'should make their own assessment of risk to compliance' (on self-assessment see 5.2.1). While US authorities were criticized for continuing to administer the Safe Harbour scheme post-*Schrems*, because that might imply the Safe Harbour Decision's continuing validity (Meyer 2016), the ICO's statement suggests the benefits for data subjects of that continuation. Under *US* law, the FTC could still take enforcement action against harborites who breached Safe Harbour principles post-*Schrems*, so from a data protection enforcement viewpoint the US's continued administration (and policing) of Safe Harbour made sense. From 11 October 2015 (based on an Internet Archive snapshot on that date[42]) if not earlier, the US Safe Harbour list webpage had clearly indicated Safe Harbour's invalidation under *Schrems*.

The ICO (Wood 2016) and CNIL (2016d) emphasized that other Mechanisms like SCCs and BCRs remained available for US transfers. However, German DPAs, who doubted Safe Harbour's adequacy even pre-*Schrems* (5.3.1), declared even SCCs and BCRs questionable for US transfers; for such transfers they would not approve BCRs or 'data export contracts' (presumably ad hoc contracts rather than SCCs), and would ban transfers based only on Safe Harbour (Conference of Data Protection Commissioners (DSK) 2015).

Post-*Schrems*, many controllers rushed to implement SCCs for US transfers or 'repatriate' personal data to the EU before the WP29's 31 January 2016 'grace period' deadline (p.166). Some chose to await adoption of Safe Harbour's replacement, which proved risky in Germany. In November 2015, Rhineland-Pfalz's DPA asked 122 large organizations about their US transfers; it felt 53 percent had answered satisfactorily

---

[42]   http://web.archive.org/web/20151011164718/http://safeharbor.export.gov/
list.aspx.

with privacy-protective 'no-cloud policies' or preference of EU providers (Rheinland-Pfälzische Landesdatenschutzbeauftragte 2015b) – evincing somewhat anti-cloud, anti-US provider views. It continued investigating 16 organizations thereafter (Leuthner 2016). In June 2016, having investigated some 35 international organizations with Hamburg operations, Hamburg's DPA fined three US multinationals for still using Safe Harbour (HmbBfDI 2016): reportedly Adobe (€8000), Punica (€9000) and Unilever (€11 000) (Gruber 2016); their fines were not 'significantly' bigger only because they implemented SCCs after the fining process commenced. Reportedly, it continued investigating further organizations; Schleswig-Holstein's DPA began investigating nine organizations in March 2016, mainly regarding employee data; and DPAs both within Germany and the WP29 were to discuss coordinated enforcement against organizations who were still using Safe Harbour, independently of the Shield's availability (5.3.3; Meyer 2016).

Shortly after *Schrems*, CNIL contacted controllers previously registered with it as using Safe Harbour, emphasizing that it should no longer be employed for US transfers but SCCs, BCRs or derogations were permissible (Umhoefer and Malafosse 2015). A group of DPAs from France, Belgium, the Netherlands, Spain and Hamburg reviewed US corporation Facebook's 2015 announcement on amending its privacy policy, including CNIL's on-site and online inspections and a documentary audit; in 2016, CNIL highlighted, to Facebook Inc. and Facebook Ireland, areas of perceived non-compliance by Facebook with French data protection laws, giving them three months to comply (CNIL 2016a). One such issue was that Facebook's website data policy stated, quoting CNIL's unofficial English translation (CNIL 2016a):

> Facebook, Inc. complies with the US–EU and US–Swiss Safe Harbor framework for the collection, use and retention of information from the European Union and Switzerland, as set out by the US Department of Commerce … The European Commission approved Standard Contractual Clauses and the Safe Harbor program (in the case of US based importers) are amongst the means by which Facebook Ireland ensures such exports are (i) lawful; and (ii) adequately protect the relevant data subjects.

CNIL stressed that, post-*Schrems*, Facebook could not transfer personal data to the US based on Safe Harbour in violation of French data protection law, and ordered it to stop such transfers. This notification seems odd as Facebook's policy made clear that it also used SCCs to legalize its US transfers, so perhaps CNIL's problem was that Facebook's French privacy policy gave the impression that Facebook was still relying on Safe Harbour (Lomas 2016). Reportedly, Facebook responded to

CNIL in August 2016, having requested an extension (Leloup 2016); developments are awaited.

CNIL also notified Microsoft in June 2016 of issues regarding the collection of data of users of Microsoft's Windows 10 operating system, including transferring[43] their data to the US based on Safe Harbour (as per its privacy statement); Microsoft was told not to do this, again within three months (CNIL 2016b). Developments are also awaited there, but both Microsoft and Facebook have since subscribed to the Shield (and Facebook's notice no longer refers to Safe Harbour).

The flurry of post-*Schrems* action suggests enforcement of the Restriction for its own sake, regardless of the Principles. However, the underlying concern was of course the access, retention and use of EU individuals' personal data by US intelligence authorities in a way and to an extent considered excessive and unfair, whereby data subjects could not access or correct such personal data, etc. – i.e., Principles – and none of this undermines my argument that data localization is not the best or only way to protect data subjects' rights. Even implementing SCCs would not prevent US or EU intelligence access (5.4.2.6, 7.5.2.1).

6.4.3.4   DPA enforcement under the GDPR

Potentially huge fines are possible under the GDPR (1.5.5). Significantly, infringement of GDPR's Restriction carries a *higher-tier* fine (GDPR Art.83(5)(c)) for both controllers and processors, as does non-compliance with any DPA order to suspend data flows to a recipient in a third country or international organization (GDPR Art.83(5)(e)). Otherwise, processors such as cloud providers are generally subject only to lower-tier fines. The prospect of such fines may well focus boardroom minds, but will the GDPR actually strengthen enforcement in practice, given Internet usage and globalized data processing (Kuner 2013b: p.154)? (And see generally 6.4.2.)

GDPR Art.53 would also empower DPAs to investigate and audit controllers and processors, obtain information and access their 'premises' and equipment/means, but I query whether physical DPA visits to datacentres (EEA or non-EEA) would be as helpful to verify compliance or security as audits by independent experts of the logical security of relevant software and systems (7.4.2.5; Hon and Millard 2016).

---

[43]   This illustrates simultaneous collection and 'transfer' of personal data, directly by a non-EEA controller from data subjects. SCCs are unavailable. They contemplate a controller signing SCCs with the recipient, but it cannot sign SCCs with itself, or with data subjects who are not controllers. However, it could use the Shield or before that Safe Harbour (5.3), or seek consent (5.5.1).

6.4.4 Enforcement of Mechanisms

Enforcement of breaches of the Restriction cannot be evaluated fully without considering breaches of the Mechanisms that were designed to ensure continued compliance with the Principles for personal data transferred thereunder. Accordingly, I now examine to what extent any breaches of Mechanisms have been enforced (a separate question from whether Mechanisms are adequate, discussed previously).

6.4.4.1 Contracts

Breaches resolved privately *inter partes* may not be reported publicly. I found no reported cases of controllers enforcing breaches of SCCs or ad hoc contracts. There are 'particular practical difficulties' with investigating non-compliance with a contract for extra-EU processing, where the third country in question has no supervisory body (*WP9*, p.11).

However, SCCs audit rights have been exercised.[44] SCCs are a relatively new development (in law years), so perhaps eventually litigation will arise. Regarding contracts as a control mechanism, an article pre-dating SCCs commented that it could be 'impossible' for DPAs to enforce compliance with contractual obligations; the 'only consequence' of breach of contract was the blocking of further transfers, which is 'of little help in respect to already transferred data' (Blume 2000: p.72).

This may explain pre-DPD regulatory reluctance to accept contracts as a foundation for transfers, the WP29's emphasis on contractual audit rights and 'dissuasive penalties' (p.157), and the GDPR explicitly empowering DPAs to suspend data flows (1.5.5).

6.4.4.2 BCRs

BCRs are an even newer development, but given the extensiveness of multinationals' global compliance programmes, 'continuous monitoring by the Lead DPAs is unrealistic to say the least' (Moerel 2012b: paras.40, 45, 65), although DPAs may obtain copies of internal audits and BCR members must cooperate with DPA investigations/audits. No lead DPA sanctions regarding BCRs have been reported publicly. BCR complaints information need not be publicized, even in generalized or aggregated form.[45] However, from Moerel's empirical research, BCR

---

[44] E.g. Spain's DPA has at least once audited a non-EEA processor (Colombia), under contractual clauses whereby the importer granted it audit rights (Kuner 2013b: p.152).

[45] Moerel (2012a: p.209) suggests they should be.

participants[46] reported no (or very few) data subject complaints, which had not (yet) increased after BCR implementation.

6.4.4.3 Safe Harbour

Initially, Safe Harbour complaints were 'very few' – by 2001, only one dispute resolution body (TRUSTe) had received complaints (27) against harborites, all resolved 'without enforcement action' (Commission 2002: p.7). TRUSTe reported 881 complaints in 2010; 3 were considered justified, where those harborites were required to change their privacy policies; in 2011, of 879 complaints, only one harborite was so required; indeed most complaints were requests, e.g. from users forgetting their passwords who could not obtain them from the service (COM(2013)847, fn.46). An FTC director stated that, for Safe Harbour, 'we had gotten only four referrals [from EU DPAs]' in total (Nielsen 2015).

I now consider complaints to the EU Data Protection Panel (Panel), comprising EU DPAs. Established under Safe Harbour Decision FAQ 5, it was competent to investigate complaints:

- regarding personal data collected in the employment context (51 percent of harborites processed such data in 2013 (COM(2013)847, fn.16)), or
- where harborites chose it for dispute resolution (some 53 percent of harborites, in 2013 (COM(2013)847, p.12)).

By 17 December 2013, the Panel had received only four complaints: two in 2010 (referred to Swiss and UK DPAs[47]), two in 2013 (COM(2013)847, para.5.2). The 2013 investigations were led by CNIL (regarding a US social networking service where users may send and read 'tweets') and Finland's DPA respectively (concerning a Finnish communications and IT multinational corporation) (Commission 2013, pers. comm., 17 December). Again, there seem to have been very few

---

[46] Fifteen organizations, among the first to implement BCRs. Within the required timeframe only ten completed all questions; one completed part (Moerel 2012b: p.2).

[47] Switzerland – regarding human resources data; UK – complaint that a major US social networking service had not granted access to all data the individual believed it held about him, which complaint, because it did not concern employee data, was referred to the ICO (Commission 2013d, pers. comm., 17 December). As the ICO generally deletes casework information after two years, it could find no record of that complaint when I requested further information (ICO 2015, pers. comm., 21 July).

complaints to the Panel, compared with likely transfer volumes, perhaps partly explained by lack of awareness – although Panel information was more visible on the Commission website from 2004 (COM(2013)847, fn.43).

A report to the Commission, on Safe Harbour's implementation, observed implementation deficiencies and 'lax compliance by US organizations', but very few or no complaints – attributed to data subjects' ignorance regarding Safe Harbour, e.g. privacy policies drafted only in English, rather than lack of breaches (Dhont et al. 2004: pp.112, 107–8). Conversely, that Safe Harbour complaints were 'quite rare, both from US and European citizens,' might suggest 'successful application of co-regulation' (Robinson et al. 2009: p.9).

Next, I consider FTC enforcement of Safe Harbour principles. Absent complaints during Safe Harbour's first decade, FTC decided to identify Safe Harbour violations in future privacy/security investigations (COM(2013)847, para.5.1). Between adoption of Safe Harbour and its invalidation in 2015, the FTC brought 39 enforcement actions alleging Safe Harbour violations, 29 of those after 2013; most were technical rather than regarding substantive principles: substantive Safe Harbour infringements were identified and enforced 'only when a company was investigated for other privacy-related consumer protection concerns' within the FTC's jurisdiction (Myers 2016: pp.5–6). From 2009, FTC took several enforcement actions,[48] mainly for false representations by non-renewing harborites claiming that their certifications remained current. Subsequently, FTC took action against SaaS providers Google (FTC 2011b), Facebook (FTC 2012a) and Myspace (FTC 2012b) for using or disclosing personal data for other purposes (to advertisers in Myspace's case), without notifying data subjects or giving them choice. All were settled with undertakings rather than monetary penalties,[49] some involving agreements to be subject to audits for 20 years. This suggests a guidance-focused approach, similar to many EEA DPAs' (6.4.2). Another 20-year order, against TES Franchising, included an allegation of deception regarding the nature of TES's dispute resolution policies, and required certain documents to be made available to the FTC for five years

---

[48] Although FTC had received 'very few referrals' from Member State authorities (Brill 2013: p.5).

[49] However, although not specifically regarding Safe Harbour, subsequently Google agreed to pay a record $22.5 million civil penalty to settle FTC charges that, in breach of its settlement, Google misrepresented to users of Apple's Safari Internet browser that Google would not place tracking cookies or serve them targeted ads (FTC 2011b).

(FTC 2015). While such enforcement might indicate that US cloud providers are breaching Safe Harbour, equally they could indicate that the FTC is able and willing to enforce Safe Harbour principles. The level of Safe Harbour membership and compliance among cloud providers was 'quite high'; with 'one or two important exceptions', cloud provider-harborites were 'compliant with the key provisions relating to dispute resolution and enforcement' with no major cloud providers making false membership claims 'at this time' (Connolly 2013: p.7).

In summary, there have been very few complaints or enforcement action for breach of Safe Harbour principles, although Safe Harbour's overall adequacy was questioned and the Safe Harbour Decision itself invalidated (5.3.2).

6.4.5   Compliance with Principles and Cross-Border Cooperation

As shown above, numerous breaches of the Restriction are probable, with little enforcement – partly because volumes involved far exceed DPAs' resources and many DPAs negotiate compliance for the future rather than imposing punishment while penalties imposed may be low (6.4.2), so that risks of enforcement may lack deterrent effect.

Enforcement action that has occurred has mainly targeted any breaches of the Principles following transfers, consistently with the Restriction's anticircumvention objective and data subjects' primary concerns (6.4.3.1). Although privacy breaches with cross-border elements may be increasing, again many problems stem not from breach of the Restriction as such, but breaches of the Principles – e.g. unfair, even criminal, use of personal data, lax IT security practices, or disclosures being unauthorized or unfair, regardless of geography (OECD 2006). Greater concerns arise regarding effective redress for data subjects against controllers responsible for breaches (Commission 2012b). This may be difficult with controllers having no presence in data subjects' Member States, but not with EEA controllers. I argue that concerns regarding personal data misuse would be better addressed through ways other than maintaining or broadening the Restriction.

One major way is to improve cross-border DPA cooperation, to promote compliance with and assist enforcement of the Principles. DPAs and data subjects may effectively seek redress against EEA controllers in the EEA (p.53) – including for breaches by the controller's processor, even if third country-'located'. Where controllers are subject to DPD Laws only through 'use' of EEA-located 'equipment' (or, under the GDPR, monitoring EEA data subjects' behaviour etc. – 1.5.2), then practical enforcement may be difficult or impossible; attempting to assert jurisdiction against them raises issues of comity and international relations, quite apart from the Restriction (pp.52, 248). In practice, securing cooperation from DPAs in third country controllers' countries, who may be more able and hopefully willing to take enforcement action, is more important. Such cooperation has been urged (OECD 2007), with growing awareness of the need for international cooperation rather than unilateral national procedures, given personal data exports' complexity and global nature (Hague Conference on Private International Law 2010: para.3).

Safe Harbour and the Shield illustrate EU–US cross-border cooperation, whereby US authorities enforce certain principles (similar to the Principles) in relation to personal data transferred to harborites. One FTC Safe Harbour enforcement action involved the (then-called) UK Office of Fair Trading's assistance (FTC 2011a). Indeed, Safe Harbour's development may have been one reason for the relative lack of extraterritorial enforcement previously (Swire 2004: p.1985). The APEC framework (2.2.8) provides for intra-regional DPA cooperation and encourages cooperating with non-APEC DPAs.

Within the EEA, DPAs are required to cooperate (Arts.28(6)–(7)), including on enforcement. Initially, cross-border cooperation was limited, even intra-EEA[50] – perhaps because of limitations or uncertainties regarding DPAs' authority/power to apply sanctions, cooperate and/or share information with foreign DPAs, and/or lack of resources/knowledge of foreign contact points (OECD 2011: pp.7, 11). However, informal cooperation outside traditional legal assistance channels has been increasing,[51] including coordinated privacy enforcement action on

---

[50] The 'progressive increase' in transfers and controllers operating across several Member States 'did not lead, by itself', to increased DPA cooperation, so it was considered that legal uncertainties arising from inconsistent, sometimes contradictory, DPA decisions would increase, with related costs, which would negatively affect the credibility of the EU data protection framework (SEC(2012)72 final, p.36); p.220, n.127.

The WP29 facilitates cross-DPA coordination and enforcement actions on major data protection issues with international implications, e.g. social networks and search engines, and coordinated inspections in different Member States on telecommunications and health insurance; however, WP29 enforcement actions are limited under current laws (EDPS 2011, paras.148–9).

[51] Many DPAs agreed a Global Cross Border Enforcement Cooperation Arrangement framework to improve cooperation on international enforcement when DPAs investigate data breaches (International Conference of Data Protection and Privacy Commissioners 2014).

a bilateral,[52] regional,[53] even global basis, partly to address difficulties asserting rights abroad due to lack of cross-border recognition of judgments (p.238), and partly to achieve common objectives more effectively by pooling limited resources (ICO 2015b: p.27). DPAs internationally recognize the importance of DPA cooperation (International Conference of Data Protection and Privacy Commissioners 2016). A notable example of such cooperation is GPEN (Global Privacy Enforcement Network). Members include many national DPAs, the US Federal Communications Commission and FTC (GPEN 2016). It has conducted coordinated international privacy 'sweeps' regarding websites (OPC 2013b), resulting in some organizations changing privacy policies (OPC 2013a), and regarding mobile apps (26 authorities from 19 countries (OPC 2014)), the latest 'sweep' being on Internet of Things devices (ICO 2016a). GPEN is focusing on information and knowledge-sharing also.

Art.50 GDPR requires the Commission and DPAs to develop international cooperation mechanisms and provide mutual assistance to facilitate enforcement of data protection laws, and promote knowledge exchange 'including on jurisdictional conflicts with third countries'. The proposed update to Convention108 (2.2.10) also contains provisions requiring DPA cooperation and mutual assistance, including coordinated investigations/actions. Improving and increasing cross-border DPA cooperation and coordination is more compatible with comity, and seems more achievable, near-term, than globally agreeing binding common standards on privacy,[54] applicable/law jurisdiction (Hague Conference on Private International Law 2010: para.28) or recognition of judgments. Such cooperation has great potential as a tool to enforce compliance with the Principles. It is important to ensure that countries internationally empower and authorize their DPAs to engage in cross-border cooperation, including legal powers to assist and exchange information with foreign DPAs.

---

[52] E.g. ICO–FTC memorandum of understanding (FTC 2014); Dutch–Canadian DPA investigation of Californian mobile app provider WhatsApp (CBP 2013).

[53] E.g. APEC 2005 Annex B.II and III. Regional action includes EEA DPAs' coordinated action regarding Google's privacy policy (CNIL et al. 2012).

[54] Although DPAs' Madrid Resolution (International Conference of Data Protection and Privacy Commissioners 2009) had proposed international standards.

6.5 SUMMARY

This chapter showed that, as commentators have highlighted since the DPD's inception, transfers abound in modern society, many probably in breach of the Restriction, with hardly any enforcement action. But trying to stop or further restrict transfers would be futile, as business and international trade are now 'totally dependent on data flows'; 'Data transfer is not confined to high-tech companies in the IT and communication sectors. Rather data is essential in all economic sectors'[55] (Kommerskollegium 2014: pp.1–2).

Low compliance and insufficient enforcement of TBDF may arise from uncertainties arising from regulatory complexity (Reed 2012: chaps.8, 10), lack of DPA resources, and above all the 'disproportionate relationship' between ever-expanding transfer volumes and the 'limited possibility' of enforcing TBDF regulation by 'traditional means such as injunctions and lawsuits' (Kuner 2013b: p.154). It is increasingly unrealistic to expect DPAs to police or enforce the Restriction, given limited regulatory resources and huge volumes of transfers that have continued increasing with the many global commercial, social and technological changes since 1990. It would also be impractical to ban altogether data flows to 'inadequate' third countries such as China, given their economic and social relationships with the EU (Chase et al. 2016) – yet Mechanisms are also impracticable, as the previous chapter showed.

A certain minimum level of successful enforcement of any law is necessary to engender compliance. This seems especially so in cyberspace where, generally, laws cannot be enforced at a scale large enough to make fear of enforcement a true deterrent against law-breaking, particularly cross-border; in cyberspace, compliance effectively depends on actors' *choice* to obey a country's law out of respect for it, and consistent failure to enforce a law suggests it is not expected to be obeyed, diminishing respect for it, while inability to enforce it consistently and effectively suggests the country's impotence, reducing respect for all its laws (Reed 2012: chap.4). Compliance need not be perfect. Any data protection system aims to deliver a 'good level of compliance', as no system can guarantee complete compliance (*WP12*, p.7). Granted, that TBDF restrictions are not always complied with is not, itself, a reason not to apply them (Blume 2000: p.82). However, enforcement of

---

[55] If BCRs, SCCs and Safe Harbour all cease to be recognized, EU GDP could reduce by an estimated 0.8–1.3 percent, and EU exports to the USA by 6.7 percent (services) or up to 11 percent (manufacturing) (ECIPE 2013: p.3).

infringements of the Restriction or Mechanisms has been minimal, focusing mainly on the Principles rather than preventing transfers or requiring deletion of transferred personal data (6.4.3.1). That approach, I suggest, is correct given the Restriction's anticircumvention objective. Forcing personal data to be 'reimported' to EEA territory or deleted would not remedy breaches of the Principles, e.g. from unauthorized disclosure or misuse.

All this again raises the question of whether the Restriction is needed as a separate requirement, and indeed may be pointless given that breaches of the Restriction are likely, yet mostly go unsanctioned. Where regulation is not enforced consistently, parties may query the need for compliance, while those against whom it is enforced may query their singling out: a large gap between regulatory scope and enforcement may corrode trust in the overall regulatory framework (Kuner 2013b: p.154).

Enforcement probably strategically targets large-scale violations with substantial chance of harm to significant numbers of individuals, but if so that should be stated openly,[56] and greater incentives provided for privacy by design and the like (Kuner 2013b: p.155). I argue that increasing informal international cooperation signals a significant new trend, which, with other aspects I will discuss shortly, may more effectively promote wider cross-border compliance with the Principles than maintaining or extending the Restriction. Enforcement of the Restriction per se is never likely to achieve such compliance. Even if it could, the real issue for data subjects is compliance with the Principles, which can be achieved in more effective ways as Ch.7 will discuss.

---

[56] As the ICO did regarding its targeted approach (ICO 2014a).

7. Access and security

Chapter 6 showed that enforcement of the Restriction is minimal. This, along with the problems discussed in preceding chapters, indicates that a different approach is needed to achieve the Restriction's aims. In this chapter, I show that the Restriction is unnecessary to maintain compliance with the Principles regarding transferred personal data. Instead, if appropriate measures can be implemented to control access (notably intelligible access) to personal data, particularly when using processors, then data location need not be restricted in order to prevent circumvention of DPD Laws. In short, controllers may protect personal data, even when using infrastructure located in third countries, through applying appropriate security measures (and, in some cases, contractual measures).

This chapter ends by discussing the special case of access by third country authorities, the role of security measures in preventing such access, and the need for international agreement to resolve any conflicts arising when controllers and/or processors are subject to multiple jurisdictions.

7.1 INTRODUCTION

7.1.1 DPD's Basic Objectives: Use, Disclosure, Condition

It is important first to consider the fundamental objectives and behaviours targeted by the DPD and the Restriction. It has been suggested that data protection laws are reducible to three general rules, regarding the collection, use or disclosure of personal data (Reed 2012: p.231). I recommend adding another: personal data's condition. The DPD regulates personal data 'processing'. While 'processing' is broad (1.4), it is clear, from 'first principles' common sense, and from the DPD and its history, that *what* the Principles aim to regulate, and the chief risks they intended to address,[1] relate to personal data's:

---

[1] When discussing compelled data retention, the CJEU stated that EU legislation must provide sufficient guarantees to protect personal data against

- *use* and the purposes of use, including for automated analyses;
- *disclosure* – including 'making available'; and
- *condition* – protecting integrity (including ensuring data accuracy as well as guarding against corruption or loss), and deleting personal data when appropriate.

In a sense, functionally 'disclosure' could be considered a subset of 'use', although it raises the risk of misuse by another person, the disclosee.[2] Furthermore, for proper use by controllers, personal data should be accurate (i.e. in the correct condition), so that, most fundamentally, it is personal data's *use* that data protection laws regulate.[3] However, I will discuss use, disclosure and condition separately.

'risk of abuse' and 'any unlawful access and use ...' (*Digital Rights Ireland Ltd*, para.54). Safe Harbour principles also concerned use and disclosure, e.g. 5.3.4.2. Similarly with other privacy laws. For example, the 'preventing harm' principle of the APEC Framework (2.2.8) focuses on preventing *misuse* of personal information. Canada's PIPEDA contains (sec.3):

> rules to govern the collection, use and disclosure of personal information in a manner that recognizes the right of privacy of individuals with respect to their personal information and the need of organizations to collect, use or disclose personal information for purposes that a reasonable person would consider appropriate in the circumstances.

Further indicating that the main privacy harm targeted is unauthorized use or disclosure, Canada's DPA considered, under PIPEDA, that contracts with non-Canadian recipients should prohibit 'use and disclosure ... except as required by the law of the country' where the recipient 'is situated' (OPC 2006). In Australia's updated Privacy Act 1988, Australian Privacy Principles cover 'collection, use, disclosure and storage of personal information'. Singapore's Personal Data Protection Act 2012 (preamble) is 'An Act to govern the collection, use and disclosure of personal data by organizations'. While those terms are undefined, under guidance from Singapore's DPA, 'collection', 'use' and 'disclosure' relate to 'obtains control over or possession' (PDPC 2014: para.7.2). See also, on 'transit', pp.45, 75; on the intention of the 'instructions' requirement, p.127; 7.1.2.

    2   Under PIPEDA, transmission to a third party for processing, e.g. when outsourcing, is considered mere 'use' (OPC 2009) – unlike 'disclosure' to a *third party for entirely new purposes*. Thus, sharing information with a payment processor and CDN was considered 'use', not a 'disclosure' requiring consent (PIPEDA Report of Findings #2012-001).

    3   Regarding the DPD (emphasis added), 'the Directive sets out to regulate the *use* of data in the light of the object being pursued ...' (COM(92)422 final, p.10). Requirements on controllers 'are due to the belief that misuse of such data can lead to infringements of privacy' (Blume 2000: p.66). On one view, the true objective of data protection standards – EEA, OECD, CoE, etc. – is not

I do not cover data collection,[4] as my discussion centres mainly on 'transfers' occurring when controllers of already-acquired personal data upload such data to cloud services. Personal data could be collected and transferred simultaneously, e.g. when third country websites (cloud or otherwise) automatically acquire personal data from EEA visitors. However, as previously discussed (1.3), I focus on EEA controllers' use of cloud for personal data processing, as issues affecting them will also affect non-EEA controllers; hence, I focus on 'transfer' of already-acquired personal data, rather than 'transfer-as-collection'. Many of my arguments apply equally to the latter, but further considerations would be relevant there also, which for space reasons are not discussed here. For example, SCCs are unavailable if a non-EEA controller collects personal data *directly* from EU individuals who visit its website or use its devices or software (p.252, n.43).

Disregarding collection then, even the DPD obligations to comply with data subject rights generally relate to personal data's use, disclosure and/or condition. Subject access rights entail controllers' disclosure to data subjects of their personal data, enabling data subjects to check their condition and/or use; correction or deletion involves changing personal data's condition; rights regarding objection, deleting or ceasing to use personal data, and judicial or administrative remedies for data subjects, again relate to controllers' use, disclosure and/or the condition of the data. The right to object to direct marketing relates to the undesired use of personal data to contact someone against their will, intruding on their 'right to be let alone'.

7.1.2   Access (the 'How') and Security (the 'How of the How')

For controllers to comply with laws regulating personal data's use, disclosure or condition, it goes without saying that they must be able to *control* such use, disclosure and condition.[5] Control of access to personal data enables controllers to use the data fairly, lawfully and for appropriate purposes, meet data subjects' access requests, and otherwise comply with the Principles (1.5.6). To exercise such control it seems obvious, but I justify it further below, that one multifaceted 'how' is necessary:

'privacy', but to control the obtaining, maintaining, processing and 'transferring' of personal data in order to avoid unauthorized *uses* (Baker 2006: p.24). See also DPD, Recs.30, 39; *WP12*, p.19 (excluding processor *use*).

[4]   When data subjects must be provided with certain information (Arts.10–11 DPD).

[5]   See Singapore's guidance, n.1.

namely, control of access[6] to personal data. Such control must include the ability, physically or remotely, both to read and modify (i.e. add to, delete or change all or part of the data) the personal data oneself, and also to allow others to read/modify the personal data or to disallow such actions.[7]

Control of access to *intelligible* personal data, which I abbreviated to 'intelligible access', is critical. For digital data, this means the ability both to retrieve and understand the pattern(s) of bits representing the informational content, as well as to restrict and change access to that pattern. Such control is necessary, but not sufficient,[8] to enable compliance with the Principles, because using or misusing personal data presupposes intelligible access. Unintelligible data may be transmitted or shared, but recipients cannot thereby acquire knowledge of the information contained in such data; unintelligible data are, by definition, devoid of informational content. Indeed I argue that, more generally, laws should only regulate those who control intelligible access (3.7.2, 3.9, 7.2.3.2), including making them responsible for maintaining that control, e.g. by taking backups even of data which they have encrypted. It is pointless to regulate processing of personal data by those to whom the personal data are unintelligible (e.g. those holding encrypted personal data where they have no access to relevant decryption keys), as that 'processing' involves no privacy risks. Someone who does not know the content of personal information cannot misuse or disclose it.

To control access to personal data, controllers need to implement security measures to protect confidentiality, integrity and availability (CIA). Security is the 'how' behind the 'how', the necessary facilitator

---

[6] Notably logical access – p.103 and 7.2.1. Regarding data subjects' 'access' to their personal data, Art.12(a) requires communication to them of data in 'intelligible form'. Generally, in the DPD, 'access' implicitly means *intelligible* access, e.g. definition of 'recipients' (Art.2(g) referring to 'disclosed'), Arts.28(3), 28(7), Recs.42–43 – although see p.167 on risks to the *condition* of unintelligible data from unauthorized access. Similarly with the GDPR, e.g. its definition of 'recipient' (Art.4(9)).

[7] '... [a data subject's] right to privacy is also jeopardized if his data are misused by third parties through unauthorized access to and use of the data' (COM(90)314 final, p.37).

[8] Because personal data could be used by someone with authorized access for unauthorized *purposes* – 7.4.1, 7.4.2.3.

for controlling access.[9] CIA are the widely recognized planks of information security,[10] an important part of information/data governance. The WP29 discussed CIA under the heading 'Lack of control' (*WP196*, p.5), implicitly acknowledging that CIA relate to control. While the DPD does not specifically mention CIA in terms, Table 7.1 compares some definitions.[11]

Availability is required for controllers' intelligible access. Controllers need to maintain personal data's availability, both for their own use and to enable them to meet data subjects' requests to access, delete or correct their data.[12] The DPD does not mention 'availability' in terms.[13] However, Art.17(1) (discussed shortly) effectively aims to maintain CIA, in requiring controllers to prevent unauthorized access or destruction/corruption/loss, i.e. protect confidentiality and integrity, bearing in mind that data corruption/loss affects the availability to controllers of accurate data. This is important whether during storage, operations or transmission (in IaaS terms, storage, compute or networking). If unauthorized persons obtain intelligible access, they could use or disclose personal data in breach of the Principles, compromising confidentiality. If unauthorized persons can access data, intelligible or not, they could corrupt or destroy the data, compromising integrity and availability, so controlling access even to encrypted data (and implementing backups, discussed below) is important for integrity and availability. In short, control of intelligible access protects confidentiality; control of access to personal data,

---

[9]   Rec.46 DPD: 'to maintain security and thereby to prevent any unauthorized processing ...'. I exclude security from the substantive Principles (1.5.6): it is the 'how of the how' rather than 'what' of compliance, as this chapter discusses, although the GDPR elevates security to a core Principle for controllers – p.269.

[10]   E.g. *WP196*, p.4. The US Federal Information Security Management Act (FISMA) of 2002, §3552(b)(3) defines 'information security' as 'protecting information and information systems from unauthorized access, use, disclosure, disruption, modification, or destruction in order to provide' CIA.

[11]   Including definitions from FISMA (n.10), Stine et al. (2008: para.3.1.2), NIST (2004: US Federal Information Processing Standard Publication (FIPPS) 199).

[12]   Cf. assumptions on intervenability and physical access – 4.5.1.

[13]   Perhaps because remote Internet access was relatively uncommon in the 1990s, when data were stored mainly on controllers' internal networks (4.4.1), so that threats to availability from distributed denial of service attacks, loss of controllers' Internet connectivity, etc. were minor.

Table 7.1

Objective	FISMA	FIPS 199	*WP196*	Commission 2013d
Confiden-tiality	Preserving authorized restrictions on [information]^A access and disclosure, including means for protecting personal privacy and proprietary information	A loss of confidentiality is the unauthorized disclosure of information	[Undefined, but *WP196* (p.9) cites cloud providers' duty of confidentiality, quotes Art.16 and mentions Art.17 (both discussed shortly) and providers' access to data]	Assurance that information is shared only among authorized persons or organizations
Integrity	Guarding against improper information modification or destruction, and includes ensuring information non-repudiation and authenticity	A loss of integrity is the unauthorized modification or destruction of information	The property that data is authentic and has not been maliciously or accidentally altered during processing, storage or transmission. The notion of integrity can be extended to IT systems and requires that the processing of personal data on these systems remains unaltered (*WP196*, para.3.4.3.2)	Assurance that the information is authentic and complete
Availability	Ensuring timely and reliable access to and use of information	A loss of availability is the disruption of access to or use of information or an information system	Ensuring timely and reliable access to personal data^B	Assurance that the systems responsible for delivering, storing and processing information are accessible when needed, by those who need them

Notes:
A Deleted by the US Federal Information Security Modernization Act of 2014.
B The WP29 refers to whether providers have 'backup internet network links, redundant storage and effective backup mechanisms' (WP196, para.3.4.3.1). Regarding breach notification, the WP29 defines 'availability breach' as 'accidental or unlawful destruction or loss' of personal data, and 'integrity breach' as 'alteration' of personal data (WP213, sec.1). However, destruction or loss (not just alteration) constitutes an integrity breach, which affects availability only if no backups were taken. Also, availability can be affected even when no personal data were destroyed or lost, notably if connectivity, enabling the retrieval of networked data, is disrupted through technical failure or denial of service attacks.

whether intelligible or unintelligible, protects integrity and availability. CIA's components are not necessarily separate but may be related; e.g. integrity problems (data loss/corruption) can affect availability if no backups were taken.[14]

With that in mind, we now consider the DPD's provisions on confidentiality and integrity. Art.16 provides:

Any person acting under the authority of the controller or of the processor, including the processor himself, who has access to personal data must not process them except on instructions from the controller, unless he is required to do so by law.

Art.16 is headed 'Confidentiality of processing', indicating that its aim is to restrict disclosure (CP-SR, III.B.2.ix). However, 'processing' is broader than disclosure or communication (1.4), so conceivably Art.16's wording could cover a person, authorized to *access* personal data (in intelligible *or* unintelligible form), modifying or deleting data without authorization, thus compromising integrity and/or availability.

Under Art.17(1):

the controller must implement appropriate technical and organizational measures to protect personal data against accidental or unlawful destruction or accidental loss, alteration [the foregoing affect integrity/availability], unauthorized disclosure [affecting confidentiality] or access [unauthorized access could threaten all CIA components], in particular where the processing involves the transmission of data over a network, and against all other unlawful forms of processing. Having regard to the state of the art and the cost of their implementation, such measures shall ensure a level of security appropriate to the risks represented by the processing and the nature of the data to be protected.

Essentially Art.17's objective is security (it is headed 'Security of processing'). It requires 'technical and organisational measures' to protect both CI, and implicitly A, with obligations regarding technical security aimed at preventing unauthorized intelligible access (CP-SR, sec.II) which could enable unauthorized *use* (COM(90)314 final,

---

[14] Hence backups are critical for integrity and availability – pp.228–9; n.B, p.266.

pp.37–9) or *disclosure* (COM(92)422 final, p.28).[15] Even Art.17(2)–(3), regarding processor use and processor agreements (1.5.6), targets security, aiming to protect CIA of personal data in the hands of a processor. I focus on technical more than organizational[16] measures, because one of my key arguments is that legislators and DPAs tend to undervalue technical measures compared with legal protections (notably contracts), despite technology-neutrality often being a policy aim. I discuss Art.17 further later (7.4).

Art.17's successor, GDPR Art.32, is broadly similar but expanded, imposing security obligations directly on processors not just controllers. While measures must still be implemented to ensure a level of security 'appropriate to the risk', factors to consider (along with the data's nature, state of the art, etc.) specifically include the scope, context and purposes of processing (Art.32(1)). The processing risks that must be considered include, rather than comprise, the above Art.17 list of risks (accidental destruction etc.), but 'against all other unlawful forms of processing' was omitted, it is unclear why. Measures to ensure appropriate security explicitly include, 'as appropriate', 'the ability' to ensure ongoing confidentiality, integrity, availability and resilience of processing systems and services and to restore availability and access to personal data in a timely manner upon any physical or technical incident – i.e., business continuity/disaster recovery – as well as 'pseudonymisation and encryption' of personal data, and 'a process for regularly testing, assessing and

---

[15] Similarly, Art.4(3) Directive 2002/58/EC requires notification of personal data breaches ('a breach of security leading to the accidental or unlawful destruction, loss, alteration, unauthorized disclosure of, or access to, personal data transmitted, stored or otherwise processed in connection with the provision of a publicly available electronic communications service in the Community' (Art.2(i)) – i.e., threats to CI and, implicitly, A.

[16] Organizational measures are vital for effective security (p.293). Over 95 percent of incidents investigated in one study involved 'human error', the top 'error' being double-clicking on infected attachments or unsafe URLs (IBM 2014). Organizational measures include vetting employees; ensuring employees are bound by contractual confidentiality obligations (*WP196*, p.13), given access only to data needed to perform their jobs (access control) and not to more data than they need (scope of authorizations, 'least privilege' (*WP196*, p.16)); and taking responsibility to understand, and ensure that employees understand, what relevant laws require of them, including formulating adequate strategies and policies/procedures, awareness-raising and staff training on appropriate data handling/use.

evaluating the effectiveness of technical and organisational measures for ensuring the security of the processing' (Art.32(1)). Adherence to a GDPR-approved code/certification (5.4.5) may help demonstrate compliance (Art.32(3)).

Oddly, perhaps reflecting 'drafting by committee', Art.32(4) partly duplicates GDPR Art.29 (which replaces Art.16 DPD). Both are substantively identical to Art.16 DPD, except that Art.32(4) explicitly places the obligation on the controller or processor,[17] and processing otherwise than under the controller's instructions is permitted only under EU or Member State (not third country) law.[18] Therefore, generally, the following discussion applies equally to the GDPR.

Another duplication is between GDPR Arts.32 and 5. GDPR's core Principles applicable to controllers (Art.5(2)) include ensuring that personal data are 'processed in a manner that ensures appropriate security of the personal data, including protection against unauthorised or unlawful processing and against accidental loss, destruction or damage, using appropriate technical or organisational measures ("integrity and confidentiality")' (Art.5(1)(f)). Presumably this is because security, the 'how' of the 'how', is critical for controlling access to personal data. Breach of this Principle carries a higher-tier fine (Art.83(4)(a)), whereas processors' breach of their Art.32 security obligations only carries a lower-tier fine (Art.83(5)(a)).

7.1.3   CIA in Practice

Normally treated as controller obligations under data protection law, implementing security measures in fact enables, indeed is essential for, control of access including intelligible access. In outline, CIA risks may be mitigated, even rendered negligible, through *controllers* taking risk-appropriate[19] technical measures to maintain their control of access, wherever the data's location.[20]

---

[17]   This explicit reference seems to make little effective difference – only controllers or processors may be fined for infringements of Arts.29 or 32 (Art.83(4) GDPR); perhaps others could be sued for compensation.

[18]   Cf. Art.16's intention to allow compliance with anti-money laundering requirements – p.304.

[19]   E.g. stronger security for sensitive data.

[20]   Space does not permit coverage of cloud-specific security issues or recommended cloud security measures generally; these are covered by numerous sources, e.g. Jensen et al. (2009), Carroll et al. (2011), Jansen and Grance (2011), Leviathan Security Group (2015c).

Availability may be protected by maintaining intelligible access for controllers and their authorized persons, including maintaining the availability of Internet or other network links where relevant,[21] and – a non-technological measure – ideally securing contractual obligations from providers regarding minimum availability, e.g. suitable service level agreements (SLAs);[22] and (both practical and legal) avoiding 'lock-in' by ensuring data portability.[23]

Confidentiality may be protected by preventing unauthorized access to the network, applications and data, and controlling access to intelligible data. The former includes installing and updating firewalls, anti-malware, application and other software, to prevent intrusions, and conducting penetration testing. The latter includes implementing access controls and identity management; taking and testing backups, i.e. making copies of data whether encrypted or unencrypted, ideally at another geographic location of the provider, the controller or another provider;[24] implementing 'failover' of running operations (at other locations or providers), to enable switching to replicated operations if the primary service or application becomes unavailable; and implementing and testing appropriate business continuity and disaster recovery procedures (mixed technical/organizational) (p.276).

---

[21] Including assurances regarding providers' network links or implementing 'backup' links (n.B, p.266). Where personal data are accessible only remotely, connectivity between a controller and its personal data requires particular protection, including ensuring availability of both controllers' and providers' communications links, e.g. Internet connectivity.

[22] Many providers offer contractual SLAs, which generally cover availability – e.g. Google (2015a) regarding a 'Monthly Uptime Percentage'. Remedies for SLA breaches are often limited to service credits (Hon, Millard and Walden 2013a: p.84), so backups are advisable. Availability relies not only on SLAs but also 'architectural engineering, business clarity, platform transparency' and, ultimately, what responsibility (and actions) a customer takes regarding its cloud-located data and applications (Bridgwater 2013).

[23] 'Lock-in' from lack of data portability (Hon and Millard 2013b: sec.4.2) affects availability (*WP196*, p.5).

[24] Some providers implement backups, assuming liability accordingly, only if higher prices are paid. Increasingly, third parties offer backup services for popular cloud services, e.g. Backupify for Google Apps and Salesforce SaaS data, with an API allowing SaaS services integration (Block 2014).

In more detail, access controls[25] and identity management controls are used to restrict who can access which data and what actions they can perform, so that only authorized persons can access relevant intelligible data. This includes user account management, controlling privileged user access (users with wide administrative authorizations), possibly even using granular and contextual access controls e.g. based on end-user physical location.[26] These essentially involve controls regarding:

- *authentication* – verifying that someone attempting to access certain data is who they claim to be (being someone authorized for such access) – typically this is through their logging in with the correct username/password, but more secure login methods may include two-factor authentication (2FA), a.k.a. two-step verification, or multifactor authentication (involving two or more factors[27]);
- *authorization* – limiting actions affecting accessed data only to the persons authorized to do them, e.g. only to access restricted data, or also to edit or delete that data (although decisions on *allocation* of authorizations and their individual extent involves organizational policies/procedures, not technical measures);
- *strong encryption*[28] (7.2.3.3), with proper key management[29] – to restrict intelligible access, including encrypting communications/ transmissions channels as well as stored data;

---

[25]   I.e. 'establishing authority levels with regard to access to the data' (COM(90)314 final, p.37).

[26]   Examples include role-based access controls (Ferraiolo and Kuhn 1992), attribute-based access controls (Hu et al. 2014; NIST 2016), and contextual team-based access controls (Georgiadis et al. 2001).

[27]   The classic factors are something you know (e.g. password), something you have (physical device) and something you are (biometrics) (Anderson 2008: p.31).

[28]   P.286. Encryption may 'significantly contribute' to the confidentiality of personal data, if implemented correctly (*WP196*, para.3.4.3.3). Strong encryption has long been recognized as a privacy-enhancing technology (Cave et al. 2011: p.85).

[29]   With encrypted data, decryption keys must be secured, both at rest and in transmission, to prevent unauthorized intelligible access. Authorities would need effective jurisdiction to obtain *both* encrypted data and decryption key, to guarantee intelligible access – 4.5.1.1, 4.6, 5.3.4.2, 7.2.3, 7.5.1. Some may have the resources to break encryption, but this is difficult at scale (and see 7.2.3.1).

- *appropriate 'deletion'* (7.4.2.4) of data when deleted by the customer/end-user, and following termination of the customer's relationship with the provider; and
- *physical access controls* regarding datacentres and hardware and other physical security measures (p.138; 7.2.2.2).

Accepting that complete prevention of all breaches is impossible (Bowen et al. 2006: p.124), best practices increasingly emphasize not just preventative measures but also *detecting* and *responding* appropriately to security breaches (Cichonski et al. 2012: pp.1, 6–7), particularly post-incident investigation (Dekker et al. 2013: p.36). Attackers continuously probe boundaries and will exploit even temporary lapses, inevitable in any organization; preventative measures such as intrusion detection, while important, are 'brittle', requiring careful monitoring of alerts (Leviathan Security Group 2015c: p.13) and taking appropriate action. Rec.17, Commission Regulation (EU) 611/2013,[30] emphasizes measures to 'prevent, detect and block' personal data breaches.[31] The WP29 suggests 'continuous monitoring of potential vulnerabilities' and keeping software updated (*WP213*, p.7). Thus, it is also important to implement usage logging and auditing for post-event tracking, checking and verification,[32] e.g. application auditing to identify who has accessed which

---

[30] Specifying measures applying to the notification of personal data breaches by providers of publicly available electronic communications services under Directive 2002/58/EC.

[31] While the DPD imposes no breach notification obligations, the GDPR does regarding 'personal data breaches' (6.4.2), although in terms only relating to breaches of confidentiality/integrity, not availability. However, integrity breaches can affect availability – p.265. 'Personal data breach' is a breach of security leading to the accidental or unlawful destruction, loss, alteration, unauthorized disclosure of, or access to, personal data transmitted, stored or otherwise processed – GDPR Art.4(12).

[32] Considered necessary to prevent processing for unauthorized purposes (*WP196*, para.3.4.1.2). Cloud providers increasingly offer monitoring and logging, with better integration, easier customer viewing/auditing, log-searching and API access for an increasing number of services – e.g. AWS's CloudWatch and CloudTrail, logging for CloudFront, AppStream, etc.; Google's Drive audit log, Cloud Logging and Cloud Monitoring; Microsoft's App Service monitoring in its Azure Portal, Azure Security Center and Office 365's unified audit log. Also, increasingly, third parties offer cloud monitoring services, e.g. Kusnetzky (2014). Frameworks for automated auditing of cloud integrity, availability, etc. have been proposed, e.g. the Cloud Security Alliance's CloudAudit.

data – together with organizational procedures to check logs regularly and address any issues detected.

CIA's objectives may themselves conflict, requiring appropriate balancing – e.g., implementing multiple backups may increase confidentiality risks by increasing 'attack surface', but it protects integrity and availability (p.289).[33] In particular, backups to different geographical locations (perhaps with different providers) help safeguard data against natural disasters affecting one location (3.7.7.2), so transfers for backup purposes positively assist integrity and availability. Similarly, duplicating operations (failover) to different countries protects availability, integrity and (if encryption is applied) confidentiality, should authorities attempt to access data or block operations in one location (7.5.1.1).

In cloud, security involves 'shared responsibility', where the elements for which the provider and customer are separately responsible differ with the service model (AWS 2014a: pp.5–6; Ryan et al. 2013: p.56; Simorjay 2016). A table clearly illustrating shared responsibility in IaaS, PaaS and SaaS separately is available online (Swain et al. 2011). Some security aspects are only within customers' control, particularly with IaaS/PaaS. There, customers must take appropriate technical/organizational security measures. Other aspects are only within providers' control, as with many SaaS services. There, customers can control the situation only by contractually requiring providers to take appropriate security measures. Still other aspects involve a mixture. For instance, application security measures (including code review/testing), to eliminate vulnerabilities that might enable unauthorized access, are important to protect both SaaS providers' applications, and applications installed in cloud by IaaS/PaaS customers. There, providers and customers respectively must check their application code.[34] Thus, with cloud, a one-size-fits-all approach cannot be taken.

---

[33] Encrypting backups where feasible should reduce confidentiality risks.

[34] Using cloud may actually assist security, e.g. the Amazon Inspector service automatically assesses applications deployed on AWS for security vulnerabilities and deviance from best practices, Google's Cloud Security Scanner automatically checks App Engine (PaaS) web applications for common vulnerabilities, and similarly with Microsoft's Tinfoil Security for Azure. Cloud security may exceed in-house security measures particularly with SMEs (p.290).

7.2   SECURITY FOR COMPLIANCE

Even with third country-located personal data, I argue that the Principles can be complied with, including when using processors, by controlling access through security measures that protect CIA. Indeed, a report to the Commission noted, 'it is often possible and advisable to replace formal legal requirements (such as geographic location of the data) by the corresponding functional requirements (such as ensuring the accessibility and security of the data)' (Graux 2014: p.19). Through security measures, controllers can control access, the 'how' of data protection, and therefore comply with the 'what' of the Principles. With digital data, what matters more for compliance is not where data are processed, but how well data are secured[35] to control access. I discuss both logical and physical security measures next, then encryption specifically.

7.2.1   Logical Security

7.2.1.1   Relevance

Logical security is critical. Logical access through software, e.g. after an authorized person logs in to a system using the correct username/password, enables the automated retrieval and reassembly of a dataset's constituent parts. This provides intelligible access to data wherever the person or constituent parts are located, if the data were unencrypted or if the person has access to the decryption key (which may be automatically retrieved by software when a person with sufficient privileges logs in, invisibly to that person). Logical access often occurs remotely over a network. Difficulties with determining the physical location of data do

---

[35]   E.g. 'while certain laws may impose minimum security standards' (p.139, n.21), security is not dependent on where data are stored, 'only on the measures used to store it securely' (Castro 2013: p.1). An Austrian official was quoted as stating that 'fostering a functioning single market for cloud computing' did not necessarily mean 'putting walls around where data can be stored'; the question is not where the bits are stored (which may be 'anywhere'), but 'how are they secured' (Hakim 2013). Similarly, 'Data are no more likely to be secure or insecure' in different countries; breaches and rogue employees can be anywhere; indeed, just as money is more secure in banks, data are more likely to be secure in large established global cloud providers (Ezell et al. 2013: p.21) – see also 7.3.

not necessarily equate to losing control over the data, as long as control of *logical* access to the data can be maintained.

7.2.1.2 Risks and mitigation

Detailed discussion of logical security is out of scope, but key logical security threats include unauthorized persons hacking into systems. Protective technical measures include encryption, isolation of customer applications, data and networks through software, firewalls, anti-malware, intrusion prevention/detection systems, and secure access controls including authentication and (partly organizational) maintaining and updating software (7.1.3).

Notwithstanding access controls, hackers may acquire or guess the usernames/passwords of authorized end-users (or even controllers' or providers' administrators), e.g. through phishing attacks. This is a major risk, so organizational measures regarding customer/end-user education and training are vital (n.16), as are appropriate systems/procedures for usernames/passwords, e.g. minimum password length, secure password storage, and appropriate use of multifactor authentication. Again, all these depend on the measures applied – not data location. Confining personal data location to the EEA under the Restriction cannot guarantee logical security, while third country-located data may be well secured.

7.2.2 Physical Security

7.2.2.1 Relevance

Unauthorized physical access to part of a dataset, e.g. through physical hardware access, enables data corruption/destruction or disruption of connectivity, thus depriving controllers of continued access to accurate data. Such physical threats to availability and integrity may arise from thefts or seizures, including colocation risk when the hardware used are located in countries whose authorities make overbroad hardware seizures (p.140). Attackers might even discern intelligible fragments (p.137, n.14), or install hardware to intercept data although, as highlighted previously (4.5.1), physical access to hardware does not necessarily afford intelligible access.

Accordingly, securing data locations against unauthorized physical access is important.[36] However, the strength of that security depends on

---

[36] '[S]afety measures for access to data processing and storage locations' (COM(90)314 final, p.37). See p.138.

the measures taken – not on the country of location (p.139, n.21; p.274, n.35). Data location is one factor affecting security, but it should not be a separate all-encompassing requirement, as it is under common interpretations of the Restriction (Ch.3). Risks to CIA are far greater from unauthorized persons obtaining *logical* access to all or part of a dataset, because remote unauthorized access to Internet-accessible data is much easier to gain than unauthorized physical access, underlining the importance of logical security. The main relevance of infrastructure location in a country is that it may allow its authorities to gain intelligible access through lawful or unlawful physical access, e.g. to install interception hardware (p.138), and/or may enable them to assert jurisdiction over the infrastructure owner/user and require it to disclose data, *wherever* located, to which it has intelligible access (4.5.1.2). However, implementing encryption and backups to other locations would mitigate this risk (and see 7.5.1.1).

7.2.2.2   Risks and mitigation

Regarding confidentiality, as discussed previously, physical access will not necessarily afford intelligible access, and confidentiality may be protected against unauthorized physical access – even unauthorized logical access – by a cloud customer, or (sub)provider, implementing encryption or other technical measures to restrict intelligible access.

To protect integrity and availability, cloud systems may be designed and managed to back up/synchronize data to datacentres in different places/countries and/or to replicate operations or shift operations execution elsewhere if interrupted in one datacentre (p.270). Some providers implement such approaches as best practice.[37] Such designs and practices help to protect service and data availability and integrity, perhaps even against authorities' demands (7.5.1.1).

Physical measures for uninterrupted, efficient hardware functioning – power continuity, fire-proofing, temperature controls, etc. – also help to protect integrity (hardware failure may corrupt data) and availability (access may be lost upon hardware failure). Again, such protections depend on the measures taken in a datacentre, not its country of location.

---

[37]   E.g. Google (Ghemawat et al. 2003) and Microsoft (Calder et al. 2011). Google's globally distributed, resource-balancing Spanner database system automatically replicates data in near real-time (Corbett et al. 2013).

7.2.3 Relevance of Encryption

Encryption[38] may be applied to protect personal data's confidentiality, regardless of data location. However, I argue that encryption is also relevant to whether data protection *obligations* should be imposed, on whom and to what extent, and that policymakers should consider specifically its role in this regard, and laws' approach to encrypted data.

7.2.3.1 Overview

To protect confidentiality, encryption may be applied to data stored in hardware, i.e. 'at rest', and in communications channels, i.e. data 'in motion' (a.k.a. 'in flight', 'in transit') – ideally, both. Intelligible access to encrypted data requires access to both the encrypted data and the decryption key; keys are usually stored and accessed automatically through software (7.2.1.1). Alternatively, attackers could intercept or steal keys, or 'crack' the encryption algorithm or (most commonly) the system implementation.

Hence, the security of the algorithm, key, key management and implementation are all critical. 'Key residency' is as important as 'data residency' (p.27), if not more so: if a person or country can access both encrypted data and the associated decryption key, it will gain intelligible access. Conversely, if encrypted data are stored in a country, its authorities may not have intelligible access if they cannot access the key, which may be stored where it has no effective jurisdiction (Stackpole 2013).

Encryption may, and ideally should, be applied to data at rest (in servers or storage appliances) by cloud providers, subproviders and/or customers. Despite DPAs' wariness regarding US cloud providers, a German DPA acknowledged, 'If a US provider offers encrypted means of storing [data] in a cloud, that would be a technical alternative to increase security', and it would consider those measures in deciding whether to allow a transfer (Bhatti 2013).

Providers with intelligible access could be compelled by authorities to disclose data. However, depending on the system/service design, cloud providers may – or may not – have access to the decryption keys for data encrypted pre-upload, e.g. using provider software on customers' local devices. Accordingly, to prevent providers' intelligible access, customers may encrypt data themselves with keys only they control (e.g. stored only in their local devices). Some Dropbox customers store files in encrypted 'containers' on local drives, created using software like TrueCrypt (which

---

[38]   4.5.1.1; p.271; Hon and Millard 2013b: sec.2.1.

has defeated even the FBI, e.g. Leyden (2010)), uploading only the encrypted containers. Certain cloud services claim to encrypt data, without provider access to customers' keys, e.g. Spideroak (Soghoian 2011) – recommended by Snowden (Kiss 2014). Strong customer encryption and secure key management should minimize or prevent unauthorized intelligible access, perhaps even by nation-states – even if all providers and subproviders cooperate with authorities or each other. It also mitigates risks to confidentiality from remote access by unauthorized persons, i.e. risks of unauthorized logical, not just physical, access. Similarly, providers may apply encryption, e.g. Microsoft's Azure Storage Service Encryption, restricting intelligible access by subproviders and others. Thus, encryption's value has been noted, particularly in cloud (Commission 2013d):

> It is true however that cyphers can be broken, or the keys can be accessed. But solutions can be developed to make encryption as safe as can be. Once again the critical point of weakness is likely to be the human and procedural failings. Security authentication could for instance remain only in the hands of the data owner using the cloud.

For data in flight, providers (and IaaS/PaaS customers) may enable, even enforce, encryption of channels to cloud services, to protect transmissions of encrypted or unencrypted data against interception. Transmissions between browsers and cloud servers may be encrypted using SSL/TLS (https). Post-Snowden, cloud providers are increasingly enforcing communications encryption[39] as well as strengthening encryption generally, e.g. by using stronger algorithms,[40] longer keys,[41] and un-reusable keys.[42] In 2013, Google began encrypting internal flows between its own datacentres (Timberg 2013), and Microsoft announced plans to expand encryption across its services (Smith 2013). Also, emails between servers of senders' and recipients' email providers are often unencrypted in transit. Initiatives have commenced to improve email

---

[39] E.g. Facebook made communications https by default (Renfro 2013), offered users 'end-to-end' encryption of notification emails (Weis et al. 2015) and is testing end-to-end encryption for instant messaging (Facebook 2016).

[40] E.g. Microsoft disallowed use of the SHA-1 algorithm from 2016, preferring SHA-2 (Microsoft 2013a).

[41] E.g. Google moved from 1024-bit to 2048-bit keys for SSL (Dulay 2013). See p.286.

[42] 'Perfect forward secrecy', using different keys for different secure browser sessions, so that key thieves cannot intercept other sessions (IEEE 2000: para.D.5.1.7); implemented e.g. by Twitter (Hoffmann-Andrews 2013).

security and promote end-to-end secure email systems[43] (including non-disclosure of metadata), e.g. better usage of STARTTLS for email encryption and perfect forward secrecy (n.42), and work on a proposed draft SMTP Strict Transport Security (STS) standard to prevent interception (Margolis et al. 2016).

7.2.3.2 Intelligible access and legal obligations

Arts.16–17 assume that processors have intelligible access. That is not necessarily true (p.127), particularly where *controllers* apply measures to restrict processors' intelligible access, such as encryption or tokenization.[44] Laws should consider whether processors or subprocessors have intelligible access (3.7.2, 3.9, 4.2): i.e., for encrypted data, access to both the data and decryption key. If not, arguably they should not even be considered 'processors' who are required to sign Art.17(3) (or Art.28 GDPR) processor agreements, or regarding whom information must be given to data subjects.[45]

Recognizing that technical measures may restrict data's intelligibility, breach notification is not required for data encrypted to qualifying standards under many US states' laws (Schwartz and Solove 2013: p.12; Burdon et al. 2010) and the US Health Insurance Portability and Accountability Act (King and Raja 2013: pp.445–6). Similarly, Art.4(3) Directive 2002/58/EC exempts providers of publicly available electronic communications services from notifying breaches on showing that they had implemented appropriate technological measures to render data 'unintelligible'[46] to unauthorized persons. Art.34(3)(a) GDPR similarly

---

[43] Certain mobile apps offer end-to-end secure messaging, not involving email (Munson 2014; Osborne 2015).

[44] Tokenization involves replacing values with other, randomly generated but individually unique, substitute values (obfuscating tokens), i.e. effectively a form of pseudonymization; under the PCI-DSS security standard for organizations handling payment cards, tokenization is often used to protect payment card data like credit card numbers (PCI SSC 2011: para.1.3). A 'key' shows correspondences between the original data and substitutes, stored in a token 'vault' or mapping. Vaults may be stored on-premise, or with another provider. Unlike with encryption, no mathematical correlation is necessary between the original value and token which could allow one to be calculated from the other, so tokenization proponents consider it more secure.

[45] P.121 (Dropbox); 1.2.3; p.127. Cf. p.127, n.2.

[46] More technology-neutral formulations are possible, but under Art.4(2) Commission Regulation (EU) 611/2013 (p.272), data are 'unintelligible' if (a) it has been securely encrypted with a standardized algorithm, the key used to decrypt the data has not been compromised in any security breach, and the key

exempts, from the requirement to notify personal data breaches to data subjects (but not to DPAs), data rendered unintelligible to unauthorized persons by measures such as encryption.

Unintelligible data carry reduced or no privacy risks. Indeed, surely that is why 'anonymous' data are exempted from DPD and GDPR obligations (1.4). Therefore, I suggest that the unintelligibility of data should be considered in contexts beyond data breaches, to relax or even obviate data protection obligations.[47] It seems unfair to impose data protection obligations on mere intermediaries who are unaware that encrypted data stored using their infrastructure are (when decrypted) personal data (3.7.2). Suppose that, in the street, you find a memory stick storing encrypted personal data. You cannot decrypt the data, so you are unaware that the data are personal data. Should you nevertheless be considered that data's 'controller', with associated obligations (and liability)? I argue not, but the WP29 considers otherwise (p.283). The GDPR perpetuates this unfairness, or at least uncertainty. Under Rec.21, the GDPR is 'without prejudice' to Directive 2000/31/EC ('notice and takedown' defences for neutral intermediaries who lack knowledge or control over the data concerned); however, as that Directive explicitly excludes data protection matters from its scope (Hon 2016g), the position is far from clear.

A controller with access to both encrypted personal data and the decryption key must certainly comply with the Principles in relation to the encrypted personal data, which clearly remain personal data as far as that controller is concerned. However, should encrypted personal data remain subject to the Restriction? Given the Restriction's objective, I argue that exports of encrypted personal data should be permitted,[48] e.g.

---

used to decrypt the data has been generated so that it cannot be ascertained by available technological means by any person who is not authorized to access the key; or (b) it has been replaced by its hashed value calculated with a standardized cryptographic keyed hash function, the key used to hash the data has not been compromised in any security breach, and the key used to hash the data has been generated in a way that it cannot be ascertained by available technological means by any person who is not authorized to access the key. (On hashing see Hon and Millard 2013b: sec.2.1).

[47] This would require regulators and governments to agree, e.g. on the qualifying types of encryption, how to verify its use, etc., which may not be easy – but while technology increases data protection risks, 'it can provide new solutions as well, and these have not been sufficiently explored' (Kuner 2013b: p.175).

[48] E.g., creating 'safe harbours' to facilitate regulatory approval of TBDF of encrypted data (Kuner 2013b: p.99).

storing such data in third country-located hardware – provided the controller-exporter can still comply with the Principles, e.g. by maintaining its ability to retrieve data to meet data subject access/correction requests, and implementing mechanisms to back up/replicate the data to protect availability and integrity. Compliance with the Principles should have primacy over data location.

Encryption may address 'data residency' issues (p.27), and was reportedly the solution used by a German-headquartered multinational group deploying SaaS service Salesforce globally (Lowans et al. 2012: fn.6). Storing 'sensitive' customer data using Salesforce might conflict with German federal data protection laws; therefore, it used CipherCloud's 'cloud encryption gateway',[49] 'including Web-to-case and email-to-case functionality, and encrypted key fields, comments, notes and attachments', while preserving Salesforce functionality, e.g. searching and sorting.[50] It is unclear whether that arrangement was approved by any German DPA, or simply enabled the controller to 'take a view' regarding compliance without approaching DPAs. Similarly, for PIPEDA compliance, a top Canadian bank reportedly used CipherCloud's solution to share sensitive merger and acquisitions (M&A), initial public offering (IPO) and other data on US servers using Salesforce's services, applying granular AES 256-bit encryption 'down to individual data fields and characters ... including ... text and search fields', impacting performance by under 3 percent (CipherCloud 2014). Gateway providers, unsurprisingly, advocate this approach, whether using encryption or tokenization (n.44). Many gateways integrate with popular SaaS services such as Office 365, even IaaS services like AWS, and their popularity has escalated post-Snowden (Pearce 2013).

---

[49] Defined as a 'cloud security proxy (typically at the application level)' (Gartner 2013), applying format-preserving encryption (Bellare et al. 2009), tokenization (n.44) or both 'on an item-by-item basis as data flows through the proxy', storing only obfuscated (encrypted or tokenized) data in the SaaS application. Typically, gateways offer a choice of encryption and tokenization algorithms, depending on the protection strength needed and to what extent format preservation is necessary, e.g. to preserve sorting. Thus, they enable real-time processing of only encrypted or tokenized data in cloud, while preserving search etc. functionality and seamless end-user usage.

[50] Customers of gateway providers must trust that gateways have no 'backdoors' sending providers (or allowing them to access or decrypt) intelligible data, keys, etc. The absence of backdoors cannot be guaranteed unless security experts review the source code, and only applications compiled from the reviewed code are used. Hence, some providers allow code inspection by large customers under confidentiality/non-disclosure agreements – e.g. n.62.

A non-binding advisory opinion by the US State Department's Directorate of Defense Trade Controls (US DDTC 2014b) to gateway provider Perspecsys (since acquired by security company Blue Coat) stated that, for US International Traffic In Arms Regulations (ITAR) purposes, tokenization could enable cloud processing of export-controlled technical data without a licence, 'even if the cloud computing provider moved tokenized data to servers located outside the US' – provided 'sufficient means' were taken to ensure only US persons, employed by the US government or a US corporation (not a foreign subsidiary), could receive and use data 'throughout all phases of the transfer' including transmission, storage and receipt. Subsequently, DDTC stressed that its opinions were not general guidance or precedents and that its Perspecsys opinion was 'not intended to imply that "sufficient means" to accomplish the requisite assurance levels exists today technologically' or to suggest that tokenization alone could provide the requisite assurances (US DDTC 2014a). Nevertheless, the opinion is interesting in emphasizing access over location.

Gateway providers argue that, at least where fields like 'name' or message body are tokenized, tokenized data contain no personal data and should be capable of being processed in cloud free of data protection law restrictions.[51] However, the WP29 considers that encrypted personal data are 'personal data' (*WP196*, para.3.4.3.3) – effectively, pseudonymous data (*WP216*, sec.4), even when held by providers with no access to relevant decryption keys. Previously, it took a more nuanced view regarding keycoded clinical data (*WP136*, p.20): keycoded data might be personal data as regards those who could identify individuals, but not as regards others for whom the scheme excluded reidentification and where appropriate technical measures had been taken to that end – even if, in unforeseen circumstances, reidentification might occur (whereupon the data would be personal data for whoever had effectively accessed identifiable information). That approach suggested, sensibly, that encrypted/tokenized personal data would not be personal data when held by those without decryption keys, unless they obtained the key or broke the encryption (Hon, Millard and Walden 2013b: sec.3.3). However, contradicting and not even referencing this aspect of *WP136*, *WP216* instead takes a rigid, extreme approach, despite acknowledging that encryption can render personal data unintelligible to those without

---

[51] E.g. 'Tokenization meets data residency requirements because the actual data never goes outside the customer's firewall, only the random tokens do' (Gould 2013).

decryption keys. Extrapolating from its view that aggregated statistics are considered anonymous only if the original data are deleted (*WP216*, p.9), seemingly the WP29 considers that encrypted/tokenized data remain personal data if *anyone* in the world has the key or the original data (*WP216*, p.29).[52] This approach, which disregards who can access which data, seems overbroad. In contrast, an English court stated: 'although the Agency held the information as to the identities of the children to whom the requested information related, it did not follow from that that the information, sufficiently anonymized, would still be personal data when publicly disclosed' – *Department of Health, R (on the application of) v Information Commissioner* [2011] EWHC 1430 (Admin), para.51. Similarly, Singapore's financial services authority generally does not treat strongly encrypted customer information as 'customer information' (Hon and Millard 2016: para.8.3.5.3).

I advocate the English and Singaporean approach. I argue that encrypted personal data, where a 'recipient' (e.g. provider) cannot access the decryption key, are not 'personal data' in the recipient's hands, and therefore the recipient should not be subject to data protection rules (Hon, Millard and Walden 2013b: pp.177–8). Such providers should not be 'processors', because they have no intelligible access (ibid.). Similarly, a Düsseldorfer Kreis (p.163, n.15) opinion on German DPD Laws stated: 'if the German data processor cannot access data submitted by the client (because the data processing occurs in the closed system or is encrypted, without the data processor having access to the key)', then encrypted data are not 'personal data' in the recipient's hands, and data protection rules – including the Restriction – need not apply to them (Kuner 2013b, p.98). Indeed, Bavaria's DPA itself stores encrypted personal data with external providers, considering that there is no 'processing' by the archivist, although the controller must maintain contractual controls to retrieve data and prevent subcontractor use (BayLDA 2015: sec.5.2). Some other national DPAs might be willing to accept that, where the controller has encrypted/tokenized personal data, a provider with no intelligible access cannot reasonably be considered a 'processor' (Van Eecke 2015: p.8). It is interesting that, even post-*Schrems* (5.3.2, 6.4.3.3), Rhineland-Pfalz's DPA stated its willingness, for US transfers, to consider technical solutions such as encryption or pseudonymization in the overall context (Rheinland-Pfälzische Landes-datenschutzbeauftragte 2015a).

---

[52] Also stating that encryption's aim is to protect communications channels, without mentioning that it can also protect *stored* data.

In summary, where providers have no intelligible access because of controller measures such as encryption/tokenization, no processor agreement should be necessary and the Restriction and data location are irrelevant.[53] Similarly, data protection laws should not need to require identification of, or information regarding, providers or subproviders who lack intelligible access (p.127; 7.4.2.2), e.g. because of controller or provider encryption.

7.2.3.3 Encryption – issues

I have argued that security should be emphasized over data location. In many situations, the Restriction should be unnecessary if appropriate security measures are applied. Use of measures like encryption, as appropriate to the particular personal data and processing activity, should be encouraged. However, I acknowledge that encryption is no panacea and, where providers do have intelligible access, then contractual measures may be needed (7.4.2.3). Several other issues require analysis.

7.2.3.3.1 Costs/performance Encryption increases costs[54] and decreases performance. That trade-off seems inevitable, for improved security. Costs may decrease, and performance improve, as technology develops and (particularly post-Snowden) more resources target encryption products/services.

7.2.3.3.2 Operations Encryption is possible for stored data[55] or transmissions (7.2.3.1), but not if more functionality is needed. The potential benefits of cheap, flexible cloud services for useful operations on data – sorting, analytics, deduplication, searching, etc. – are realizable only with unencrypted data.[56] But upon decryption, even momentarily, whether in

---

[53] The controller remains responsible for ensuring integrity and availability. Accordingly, cloud customers may implement backups, e.g. to another provider's cloud service, or internally. Some controllers can impose backup obligations (and SLAs) on providers, including liability for data loss/corruption. However, even damages may not compensate for irretrievably lost data. Therefore, customers may, and should, implement backups or failover procedures (p.270), using that provider's infrastructure or another's, notwithstanding the extra cost.

[54] For a large SaaS implementation, 'best-in-class security' was estimated to increase costs by 15–20 percent (Brewster 2014).

[55] E.g. encrypted data uploaded to the cloud for backup/restore or file-sharing (7.5.1.1) purposes.

[56] Encrypting data in cloud 'robs businesses of much of the cloud's utility' while searchable encryption involves 'trade-offs between security, functionality, and efficiency' (GTISC and GTRI 2013: p.3).

cloud or locally, 'cleartext' data could theoretically be accessed or intercepted, even if the data are re-encrypted after the operations.[57] Homomorphic encryption (Smart and Vercauteren 2010), allowing operations on encrypted data *without* decryption, was too slow for practicable use (Catteddu and Hogben 2009: p.55), but work continues on that and other efforts to enable useful operations on encrypted data/databases.[58]

Therefore, particularly sensitive or risky data could be kept, and operated upon, in-house only, i.e. hybrid cloud. Alternatively, use of cloud encryption/tokenization gateways may be feasible (p.281). Other methods are being developed to prevent providers' intelligible access, even to 'working personal data'. German government-funded 'Sealed Cloud' combines encryption with special hardware/software to protect data and applications (Jäger et al. 2013)). 'Shielded execution' protects the confidentiality/integrity of applications/data from the *platform* (cloud provider's operating system, VM and firmware) (Baumann et al. 2014). Microsoft's Office 365 Customer Lockbox (p.141) is now available, storing encrypted data and allowing operations on data decrypted only within secure servers to which its employees have no access unless specifically authorized by the customer.

Finally, much enterprise cloud usage,[59] particularly in markets starting to adopt cloud, involves data storage/backup/sharing,[60] where encryption should be possible; and public web/media hosting, where encryption should be unnecessary.[61] Therefore, even if some other cloud uses are incompatible with encryption, it is not irrelevant to emphasize encryption in the cloud.

7.2.3.3.3 'Snake oil'   Non-technical, even technical, people often cannot differentiate true security from 'snake oil' (Schneier 1999). How can customers verify the security of algorithms/implementations and the lack of key access/backdoors, particularly when providers refuse access to

---

[57]   If an encrypted filesystem is used, stored data would be undecipherable after powering down servers. However, the operating system decrypts files for applications' use, so authorities could obtain intelligible access by entering a datacentre, keeping servers running and accessing VMs (through the provider's network, e.g. using an available connected terminal). But this could be achieved remotely, without physical access (4.5.1.2).

[58]   Cloud-relevant initiatives exist, e.g. Smart, Rijmen, Stam, et al. (2014: sec.5), Zyskind, Nathan and Pentland (2015).

[59]   Under surveys like 451 Research (2014).

[60]   In 2014, 53 percent of EU enterprises used cloud for file storage (Giannakouris and Smihily 2014).

[61]   *Enköpings* (Sweden), p.121.

their source code?[62] Many services' privacy-protectiveness or security claims have been proved false, e.g. WhatsApp's messaging app (Ring 2014). Hence, independent expert certifications and the like should be encouraged and incentivized, as the GDPR aims to do (5.4.5).

7.2.3.3.4 'Breakable', so useless? Encryption may become breakable over time, as computing resources for 'cracking' increase, or vulnerabilities are discovered. Important factors include algorithm strength, key length (longer keys are more secure) and secure key management[63] including restricting key access (Hon and Millard 2013b: sec.2.1). However, best practices and standards address that issue. Assuming that adversaries could retain encrypted data until they have the technical means to decrypt the data, cryptographic protection using a given algorithm and key size should not be applied if the relevant data's 'security life', the period for which the data needs to be secured, exceeds the 'algorithm security lifetime', i.e. into the timeframe when the relevant algorithm or key size is disallowed (Barker 2016, p.58).[64]

7.2.3.3.5 Poor implementation Encryption may be implemented badly, rendering encrypted data vulnerable. I term data 'strongly encrypted' if the data are secured against decryption for most practical purposes most of the time in the real world; in particular, if data are encrypted, and the decryption keys secured, to recognized industry standards and best practices (Hon and Millard 2013b: sec.2.1). This includes re-encrypting data to stronger standards if the algorithms used are cracked or become vulnerable over time (Barker and Roginsky 2015: p.18), and, within a reasonable time, substituting stronger implementations for any implementations found to be vulnerable.[65] (Generally in this

---

[62] N.50. Accordingly, Microsoft opened 'Transparency Centres' allowing government customers to review its source code for application security and lack of backdoors (Thomlinson 2014).

[63] Recommendations and standards on keys and key management exist, e.g. from NIST, ISO and ENISA.

[64] Thus 80-bit encryption may suffice 'into the near future' for transactional data (which 'only needs to be kept secret for a very short space of time'), but at least 128-bit encryption is recommended for 'long lived data' (Smart, Rijmen, Gierlichs, et al. 2014: p.12). Most current keys should be 'resized' around 2020 (*WP216*, p.29).

[65] In Canada, TJX was held not to have met PIPEDA's safeguard provisions after network intrusions detected in 2006 compromised many payment cards (PIPEDA Report of Findings #2007-389). TJX used a weak encryption protocol (WEP), failing inter alia to switch to a stronger standard (WPA) within a

book, when I refer to encryption, I mean strong encryption even if not explicitly stated, as poorly implemented encryption may be as bad as no encryption.) Hence, again, the use of expert certifications should be encouraged.

7.2.3.3.6 Nation-state decryption/cracking   Nation-states may have the resources to decrypt or crack encrypted data. Reportedly, the NSA and GCHQ have attacked Internet encryption technologies (e.g. Ball, Borger, et al. 2013). Nevertheless, as Snowden noted, 'Properly implemented algorithms backed up by truly random keys of significant length ... all require more energy to decrypt than exists in the universe' (Harding 2014). In short, the NSA did not necessarily break cryptographic algorithms, but attacked or subverted:

- *systems* used to deploy encryption (i.e. insecure implementations);
- weakly secured communication 'endpoints' (local devices), to access data before encryption or after decryption (Siddique 2013); and
- individuals/organizations – including using 'legal tools or hacking' to obtain decryption keys, 'brute computing power to break weak encryption' and/or 'forcing companies to help the [NSA] get around security systems' (Simonite 2013).[66]

In such situations, data location is irrelevant, particularly if someone is specifically targeted remotely by a determined nation-state (EEA or third country) or hacker. That does not mean that encryption is futile. Encryption, if adopted by Internet users near-ubiquitously for both storage and transmissions, is part of the longer-term solution. It should protect confidentiality if personal data are stolen or lost, and make *mass* governmental surveillance of Internet users more difficult and expensive (Schneier 2013b).[67] Certain encryption implementations have reportedly

---

reasonable period. Risks of breach were foreseeable partly because the standards organization had identified WEP's weakness. The matter was considered resolved because TJX had implemented the DPAs' recommendations, including WPA for all stores. WEP's vulnerability was published in *2001* (Fluhrer et al. 2001).

[66]   Also quoting cryptographer Jon Callas: 'If the crypto didn't work, the NSA wouldn't bother doing all of these other things ... This is what you do because you can't break the crypto'.

[67]   Google CEO Eric Schmidt: 'The solution to government surveillance is to encrypt everything' (Rubens 2014); encryption forces governments to use proper

foiled even the NSA (SPIEGEL Staff 2014) – and see 7.2.3.1 (True-Crypt). Many providers took, and are taking, steps to apply encryption as much as possible (p.278). There are initiatives to re-engineer the Internet to prevent mass spying.[68] Certain calls to ban, weaken or restrict the use of encryption (e.g. France and Germany (Jones et al. 2016)), or to require government backdoors 'only' for authorities, are misconceived, futile and dangerous, and should be resisted, as a UN Special Rapporteur (Kaye 2015), cryptography experts (Abelson et al. 2015) and others consider. Hence, encryption bans or backdoors under the UK Investigatory Powers Act and other countries' laws have been much debated (for a summary see Chase et al. (2016: para.4.2.3)). Arguments over whether and how governments should have access to encrypted data are not new (e.g. Froomkin 1995; OECD 1997; Anderson 2005) and will undoubtedly keep recurring. Personally, I support the view that laws should, on the contrary, clearly authorize end-to-end communications encryption (EDPS 2016b) and encryption of stored data for the security of everyone, as cybercriminals can exploit any backdoors.

Therefore, despite (indeed because of) nation-states' mass surveillance, customers should exercise self-help, encrypting data themselves where possible (7.2.3.1). We still lock our doors, even though burglars could pick locks and authorities could break down doors; if everyone locks their doors, it is harder for burglars and authorities to just walk in. Risks should be assessed contextually, based on the data and intended process-ing concerned, applying appropriate security measures – e.g. stronger encryption for more sensitive data, even if that degrades performance.

7.2.3.3.7 Other technical measures   Encryption is not the only tech-nical measure for controlling intelligible access to protect confidentiality, but it is the most fully developed and deployable. Other measures exist or are under development, e.g. tokenization (n.44) and information flow control (Singh et al. 2014: para.7.2). Emerging technologies like block-chain may also help to control access to personal data (Zyskind, Nathan, et al. 2015).

7.2.3.3.8 Integrity and availability   Although encryption is not the only option, by itself it (and other means to control intelligible access)

---

legal channels (Whetstone 2015). Post-Snowden, traffic encryption has increased generally (Ernesto 2014b).

[68]   Notably, developing HTTP 2.0 (Nottingham and Leiba 2015). Technically it 'doesn't require better encryption, but Mozilla and Google won't support the standard without it' (Dignan 2015).

cannot guarantee full data security. Encryption cannot protect data from loss/corruption.[69] To control access to personal data, controllers must also protect IA, not just C. Integrity may be protected notably by implementing and testing regular secure backups of data and any encryption keys. The WP29 effectively supports this view, in opining that, when a controller has no adequate backups, loss or alteration of encrypted data can affect availability and integrity, requiring breach notification to data subjects under Directive 2002/58/EC (p.279; *WP213*, secs.1, 2) – which implies that notification is unnecessary when the controller *does* have adequate backups.[70] The efficacy of security measures, and best practices, may change with scientific, technological or commercial developments. A technologically neutral approach would not specify measures such as encryption, but simply recognize 'reasonable steps' (whether legal and/or technical, etc.) to protect data's CIA,[71] or more generally to ensure continued compliance with Principles.

Having discussed logical and physical security and the role of encryption/technical measures generally, I now consider some specific cloud risks:

- unauthorized intelligible access;
- unauthorized use, disclosure or modification by someone authorized for intelligible access; and
- unauthorized intelligible access by authorities – a special case addressed separately, although the preceding issues could involve such access.

7.3 UNAUTHORIZED INTELLIGIBLE ACCESS

Prospective cloud customers are rightly concerned about providers' security against unauthorized intelligible access, but controllers' own

---

[69] Although some cryptographic applications assist integrity-checking, e.g. cryptographic authentication mechanisms like message authentication codes (*WP196*, para.3.4.3.2); for more explanation see Hon and Millard 2013b: p.19.

[70] *WP213* also stressed the importance of effective, up-to-date backups to protect integrity and availability, even with unencrypted data.

[71] See p.221. Art.17 DPD itself requires security measures 'appropriate' to the risks (changed from 'adequate', in the 1992-Proposal (COM(92)422 final, p.28)), taking into account implementation costs (p.267) – effectively involving reasonableness rather than absolute standards.

security measures are also important, given cloud's 'shared responsibility' model (p.273). One pertinent issue is: are cloud security measures better or worse than the customer's own on-premise measures?

Some studies indicate, and many consider (Dekker and Liveri 2015: p.5), that using cloud may even improve SME customers' security, as large providers can offer advanced security measures (e.g. Microsoft 2013b). A Google-commissioned independent report (Leviathan Security Group 2015a) highlighted the shortage of security expertise, which 'tends to congregate in large organizations' (Google 2015b), so that organizations, particularly SMEs, may have difficulty hiring security experts – unlike large providers (Dekker and Liveri 2015). In a recent survey, organizations considered resource/expertise shortage, not security, to be their top cloud challenge (Rightscale 2016). In another survey 51 percent of IT executives considered data security better in cloud than in their own datacentres (McKendrick 2016); indeed, security concerns are incentivizing even banks to use cloud (Munshi 2016).

7.3.1 Other Tenants

One concern is unauthorized access by cloud providers' other customers. Many cloud services involve multitenancy: different customers' applications and data-sharing hardware and software resources (1.2), separated logically through software rather than physically – e.g. in the same database, using the same hardware, but in different rows.

The WP29 considers that resource-sharing affects *integrity* (*WP196*, p.5):

> Lack of integrity caused by the sharing of resources: A cloud is made up of shared systems and infrastructures. Cloud providers process personal data emanating from a wide range of sources in terms of data subjects and organizations and it is a possibility that conflicting interests and/or different objectives might arise.

It also considers that resource-sharing poses risks to 'Isolation[72] (purpose limitation)', i.e. 'A cloud provider may use its physical control over data from different clients to link personal data' (*WP196*, p.6).

The WP29's views seem incorrect, suggesting a misunderstanding of 'integrity'.[73] Resource-sharing is irrelevant to 'integrity' in the CIA

---

[72]   Related to Germany's 'unlinkability' concept (*WP196*, fn.4).
[73]   Unless, here, the WP29 meant 'integrity' in the morality/ethics sense ('conflicting interests') rather than in the CIA sense.

sense. Furthermore, *non*-cloud processors could equally misuse and/or 'link' their different customers' data. Such 'linking' is enabled, not by resource-sharing, but rather by processors having intelligible access to their customers' data. That access (and how they handle or use accessed data) may be restricted technically and/or contractually. If services cannot scale quickly or efficiently due to insufficient resources, resource-sharing may well affect availability – but again, not integrity. 'Isolation' is also described as requiring governance of access rights/roles/privileges, hardening of hypervisors and proper management of shared resources between VMs (*WP196*, p.16). Surely those relate more to confidentiality, where resource-sharing may indeed raise risks, some of them cloud-specific.[74]

Logical segregation of data in cloud services (if 'properly managed' by providers) should be, and seems considered by some DPAs, acceptable to protect confidentiality (*Narvik 2012b* (Norway), p.15; *Moss* (Norway), p.4; *WP196*, p.16).[75] However, the effectiveness of such segregation depends not on data location, but on the strength of providers' separation-enforcing software/systems and measures taken by the controller where appropriate (OWASP 2016). Thus, the Monetary Authority of Singapore (MAS) stated in its latest outsourcing guidelines that banks should ensure that the provider has 'the ability to clearly identify and segregate customer data using strong physical or logical controls', and 'robust access controls [surviving contract termination] to protect customer

---

[74] Theoretically, IaaS co-tenants could seek to access other tenants' data by instantiating VMs co-resident with the target customer's VMs (Ristenpart et al. 2009); copying private keys (Zhang et al. 2012); or reading data remnants in hardware 'due to disk and swap data not being zeroed after use' (ContextIS 2012).

[75] Norway's DPA seems to consider access control insufficient; even though only three people had administrator rights enabling searches across all controllers' data, a processor (who used Azure to store customer data) must segregate different controllers' data physically or logically, to comply with Norwegian DPD Laws (*Securitas* (Norway)). However, the reasoning behind this view is unclear. A processor will by definition generally have access to all its customers' data. As long as only persons authorized by the processor can access that data, and the data are secured against third party access (including preventing customers, and cloud co-tenants, from accessing other customers' data), why should different customers' data have to be stored separately in cloud? In *non*-cloud situations, many processors very likely do not segregate different customers' data logically or physically, but may well use the same database, controlling access only through logical access controls. Again this may evince DPAs' stricter approach to cloud even when non-cloud systems/procedures are logically and functionally the same (cf. p.128).

information' (MAS 2016). Furthermore, as discussed above, customers may themselves prevent unauthorized intelligible access to personal data (including by co-tenants) through additional technical measures such as encryption or tokenization.

None of these issues are affected by the Restriction or data location, but rather relate to customers' and providers' technical security measures.

7.3.2 Hackers

Unauthorized hackers (whether cybercriminals or authorities) could remotely access weakly secured systems connected to the Internet, cloud based or otherwise. However, that depends on systems' security, particularly logical security, and the technical measures applied by customers and/or providers (4.5.1.2, 7.1.3) – not data location. The Restriction is irrelevant here, again.

7.4 UNAUTHORIZED USE/DISCLOSURE BY AUTHORIZED PERSONS

Art.16 DPD targets the unauthorized disclosure/use of personal data by persons authorized by the controller to have intelligible access to that data (Authorized Persons), i.e. confidentiality, but it could extend to integrity and availability (p.265). Art.17(1) requires controllers to implement appropriate technical and organizational measures (pp.18, 267) and equates 'security' (or its purpose) with preventing unauthorized or 'unlawful' processing (p.267).[76] That is broader than unauthorized access, or even CIA. Data protection 'is not limited to data security and therefore these goals are complemented with the specific data protection goals of transparency, isolation, intervenability and portability to substantiate the individual's right to data protection as enshrined in Article 8 [Charter]' (*WP196*, p.4). Accordingly, Norway's DPA assumed that an audit covered compliance with processor agreement requirements *beyond* security matters, including preventing processors from using personal data for other purposes (*Narvik 2012a* (Norway), p.6).

---

[76] 'Authorized by controllers' does *not* mean 'authorized by DPD Laws'. Controllers could authorize unlawful actions. 1992-Proposal changed 'unauthorized destruction' to 'unlawful destruction' (COM(92)422 final, p.28), and CP changed 'unauthorized' processing to 'unlawful' processing (Council 6032/94, p.4, fn.4). The GDPR's security provision no longer refers to unlawful processing, only to ensuring security 'appropriate to the risk' – p.268.

Authorized Persons may include the controller's employees, and its provider's employees. Technical security measures alone cannot, and should not be expected to, prevent them from deliberately or inadvertently using accessed personal data for illegitimate purposes. Conversely, lack of intelligible access should prevent data misuse/disclosure, although not corruption/deletion, and a controller may prevent its provider having intelligible access by encrypting data as already discussed.

The misuse of data by Authorized Persons, whether at the controller or its processor, is difficult if not impossible to control through technical measures alone, never mind to audit. Applying encryption cannot prevent such misuse, because Authorized Persons would by definition have intelligible access. Restricting data location to EEA territory cannot prevent such misuse either. It is unlikely that Authorized Persons who deliberately abuse access privileges, e.g. to breach purpose limitation or confidentiality requirements, would pay much heed to the Restriction. Confining personal data to the EEA cannot stop Authorized Persons from accessing the data remotely, whether from within or outside the EEA.

However, one essential security measure is allocating technical authorizations appropriately (7.1.3) – allowing only staff who need intelligible access to have such access, limiting their intelligible access only to the data they need for their work and not allowing them intelligible access to other data, and restricting appropriately what they can do, e.g. only read but not edit, as well as restricting their access duration. Additionally, controllers must implement appropriate organizational measures (n.16), which again are independent of data location. Indeed, human factors, whether insider breaches/errors or employees succumbing to social engineering,[77] have generally caused more security problems than technical lapses.[78]

---

[77] Attackers may access data such as customer contact lists by obtaining the user/password credentials of a provider's employee who has administrative rights or access to user information, e.g. through phishing – as happened to SaaS provider Salesforce (Krebs 2007). Security firm RSA was infiltrated through phishing emails luring recipients to open infected files (Litan 2011). Apple's support staff were 'social-engineered' to reset user passwords for SaaS service iCloud despite the attacker's inability to answer security questions, suggesting that staff did not follow organizational procedures and/or that Apple had weak procedures (Honan 2012). Accordingly, organizational measures to reduce human-related risks are vital.

[78] E.g. Ponemon (2013: p.7). Seemingly humans have always been the main security risk (ComputerWeekly 2003).

7.4.1   Controller Risks: Insider Threats

Authorized Persons may misuse their access rights to use, disclose or modify personal data without authorization, i.e. handle personal data for unauthorized purposes or in unauthorized ways.[79] Indeed, *controllers* may deliberately use personal data for purposes or in ways prohibited by DPD Laws.

It is technically possible to track and log who has accessed certain intelligible data, when, and what they did, e.g. view or modify data. Implementing such logging is an important technical measure. However, technology alone cannot monitor or restrict *why* they accessed and/or modified data, i.e. for what purposes Authorized Persons accessed personal data. Someone claiming that they accessed personal data for a particular purpose could lie. Techniques such as information flow control may restrict data flows through applications, even in cloud (Singh et al. 2014: para.7.2). However, it is difficult to prevent Authorized Persons from recording data using non-digital means, e.g. for subsequent disclosure to unauthorized recipients.[80] An employee authorized to retrieve data through an application, displayed on screen, could read displayed information over the phone, write it down, take photos of the screen, etc.: the 'confidentiality' equivalent of the 'analogue hole' well known for enabling circumvention of digital rights management technologies seeking to protect copyright. Organizational (n.16), not technical, measures are most significant here, but again cannot guarantee protection against wilful rogue insiders, e.g. Snowden in the NSA's case (Toxen 2014), or the organization's own intentional misuse/disclosure. Even with technical monitoring and logging of accesses, logs require regular checking – an organizational issue – and logging cannot prevent unauthorized *use* of data by Authorized Persons.

My point is that if controllers (or other Authorized Persons) abuse their, legitimately given, access privileges in breach of DPD Laws, that is a matter of intention and use – not data location. Technical and organizational measures may reduce these risks, e.g. by restricting the extent/duration of authorizations/privileges, but confining data location to the EEA will not, because Authorized Persons with remote access could

---

[79]   E.g. Google engineers with administrative privileges accessing personal data to taunt minors (NBC 2010). It is not only technology providers who are exposed to such insider risks; hospital employees have long snooped on celebrity patients, e.g. Parker-Pope (2008).

[80]   Access control mechanisms 'only control information release, not its propagation once released' (Myers 1999: p.1).

misuse, disclose or modify data *wherever* the data (or persons) are located. This includes disclosure to authorities (7.5). Effective jurisdiction to compel such disclosure from Authorized Persons might be gained through data being located in a particular country, but it might not (7.5.1.1), and it could equally be gained through a controller or provider incorporated in that country, even for data located elsewhere, as illustrated by Brazilian courts ordering Google to retrieve US-located data (4.5.1.2), and the ongoing battle in the *Microsoft warrant case* (p.93).

7.4.2 Processor Risks

7.4.2.1 Integrity and availability

Providers or subproviders with access to data, even if it is not intelligible access, could corrupt or destroy data, compromising availability and integrity. Outages, e.g. from technical faults, may also affect availability. However, under DPD Laws, controllers remain responsible for CIA, and should ensure data backups/operations failovers (internally, or with the same or other providers), ideally also obtaining appropriate SLAs, etc. (7.1.3).

The Restriction does not address backups/operations replication – but Art.17 implicitly does. Indeed, the Restriction may negatively affect availability/integrity, by deterring the best practice of taking multiple backups to different locations, including different countries (3.7.7.2).

7.4.2.2 Confidentiality – intelligible access?

In some situations, I argue that it should be irrelevant whether providers have intelligible access. Notably, if it is fair and lawful to publish or share personal data online using hosting providers (cloud or otherwise), then the providers should not be required to take security measures to protect confidentiality, or even to sign processor agreements, as that would add no privacy value: so one DPA has held.[81] The Restriction would add no privacy value here either, I suggest.

However, with unencrypted data not intended to be public, providers generally *do* have technical capabilities for intelligible access, indeed they often need such access for billing, support or security purposes (1.2.3, 4.5.1.2). Similarly, subproviders potentially have intelligible access if neither the controller nor the provider has applied technical measures like encryption/tokenization. In such cases, the main concerns are that (4.2, 7.1.1–7.1.2):

---

[81] Where a controller used Dropbox – p.121.

- such providers or subproviders could use or disclose data for their own (unauthorized or incompatible) purposes; and/or
- third country authorities could force such providers or subproviders to disclose intelligible data (discussed shortly).

7.4.2.3 Provider misuse – mitigation

To prevent intelligible access by providers/subproviders, and therefore their unauthorized use/disclosure, controllers may implement technical measures, notably encryption/tokenization, as already discussed. Providers may also apply encryption, to protect confidentiality of personal data against unauthorized intelligible access by third parties, including subproviders, and/or impose strict access controls to limit insider threats. Interestingly, Microsoft's 'Lockbox' technology (p.141) prevents even its own employees from accessing customer data without specific customer approval, restricting 'insider' intelligible access very tightly.

Intelligible access by providers may also be restricted structurally: Microsoft partnered with Deutsche Telekom (DT) to offer Azure, Office 365 and Dynamics CRM from two Germany-located datacentres with DT's subsidiary, T-Systems, being 'data trustee' of, and controlling access to, Microsoft customer data, while DT controls access to the infrastructure and connections are made over DT's network (although Microsoft provides operational and technical support) (Deutsche Telekom 2015). Contractually, Microsoft cannot access its customers' data unless allowed by T-Systems or the customer; technically, this is implemented through role-based access control (RalfWi 2015). The intention of course is that if Microsoft requests access to meet US authorities' requests or orders (as it may be legally compelled to do in the US), T-Systems/DT would refuse. It remains to be seen if this kind of arrangement would survive a challenge by US authorities seeking access (Ahmed and Waters 2015).

If providers have intelligible access, whether because personal data are unencrypted or they have access to the decryption keys, then controllers may (and must in any event, under DPD Art.17(3) and Art.28(3) GDPR) ensure *contractual* measures are in place: processor agreements obliging processors to 'act only on instructions from the controller' and to implement security measures. Accordingly, DPAs require controllers to identify all possible cloud subproviders (p.128)[82] and bind them under

---

[82] Datainspektionen approved 'dropbox' provider Brevo's use of Azure as compliant after, inter alia, Microsoft gave Brevo access to a list of Microsoft's subcontractors and the ability to view the current list on login to a customer

processor agreements, including confidentiality obligations (*WP196*, para.3.4.3.3). That may be difficult given the complexity of cloud supply chains,[83] particularly as this requirement applies seemingly even to subproviders without intelligible access,[84] although use of infrastructure services is closer to hardware procurement (p.128). Art.16 similarly refers to 'instructions', mainly targeting confidentiality but also potentially covering other unauthorized 'processing', i.e. affecting integrity or availability (p.265).

Many providers' standard terms entitle them to use or disclose customers' data for their own purposes (pp.126–7; p.206, particularly n.96), e.g. running content-based advertisements (p.3, n.8; p.5, n.10), or to disclose data to authorities on mere request not just court order (Hon, Millard and Walden 2013a: sec.5.4.2). Particularly upon DPAs' insistence (e.g. p.203, n.96), customers may seek contractual terms prohibiting providers from using personal data for the provider's own purposes (see p.127) except to the extent compelled by law, and requiring notification of requests/orders to providers for the customer's data unless prohibited by law (ibid.). Whether providers will agree depends on customers' bargaining power – not data location. Regulatory intervention might protect consumers or SMEs who lack bargaining power. But the enforceability against providers of any consumer-protective legislation

---

website (*Brevo 2012*, p.1). It is unclear how 'deep' down the possible subprovider chain this list goes (e.g. even datacentre providers?). 'Each Online Service has a website that lists subcontractors that are authorized to access Customer Data' (Microsoft 2014: p.10). Google lists G-Suite subprocessors (only customer/ technical support providers) at https://www.google.com/intx/en/enterprise/apps/ terms/subprocessors.html, adding (without listing them) that 'Google and its affiliates may engage third party suppliers to provide other services such as SMS aggregation, facilities management, maintenance and security services from time to time'.

[83]   5.4.2.9. Identification of all possible subprocessors would be harder still if 'subprocessor' also includes datacentre providers, suppliers of storage, networking equipment/services, payment services, etc. Nevertheless, given DPAs' views, Microsoft and Google now provide subprovider lists (n.82). Upon customer request, Microsoft supplies copies of subprocessor addresses and agreements (*Office 365* (Denmark), para.2). See further Microsoft's agreement to give prior notice before appointing new subprocessors (with early termination rights for objecting customers as a compromise) – p.202.

[84]   Because the WP29 considers that encrypted personal data remain personal data, apparently for all purposes – p.282. Cf. 7.2.3.2.

regulating cloud terms depends on effective jurisdiction over providers, not on data location.[85]

Where providers or subproviders have intelligible access, the objectives of Arts.16–17 (and their GDPR successors) can be met, and data protection laws made more technology-neutral, if laws imposed direct obligations,[86] or required contractual obligations, only on processors with intelligible access:

- not to disclose or use personal data except as the controller agrees (or as necessary to provide, bill and/or support the service) – discarding the outdated 'instructions' concept,[87] which is inappropriate for direct self-service use of IT infrastructure; and
- to take appropriate security measures, such as access controls/ authorizations and organizational measures (n.16), more particularized by GDPR Art.32(1). I argue that contractually required security measures should depend on context, e.g., if controllers or providers take backups, providers or subproviders respectively should not be required to (n.53); whereas if availability depends on a subprovider's service, then obtaining SLAs from the subprovider should be considered (although if the provider commits to adequate SLAs, its contractual liability may suffice in some circumstances).

Thus, I argue that data protection laws should require contractual obligations from processors regarding their use/disclosure/security *only* when the processors have intelligible access, irrespective of data location. The Restriction is irrelevant and unnecessary there. When providers have no intelligible access, or the personal data they host are legitimately public (7.4.2.2), then even Art.17(3) (and Art.28(3) GDPR) processor agreements should be unnecessary, as they add nothing to data protection in those situations (7.2.3.2).

---

[85] Consumer law is out of scope although consumer and data protection are often related, e.g. EDPS (2014a), Cunningham-Day (2014).

[86] GDPR would impose certain obligations directly on processors (Hon, Kosta, et al. 2014: sec.4.3) – but its approach could cause problems (Hon 2015a).

[87] 4.2, particularly p.127 on 'instructions' regarding processing purposes; 7.4.2.4 on 'instructions' regarding data deletion.

7.4.2.4 Data deletion

Another aspect of providers' or subproviders' intelligible access is data deletion, particularly following service termination. Deletion helps to prevent unauthorized intelligible access (*IT-Universitetet* (Denmark), para.2.4), and therefore unauthorized post-termination use/disclosure. Thus, one reason Datainspektionen rejected a controller's use of Google Apps was that the agreement provided insufficient information on retention/deletion of personal data after termination, raising risks of unlawful processing. In *Salems 2013* (Sweden), para.2.3, Google proposed amending its terms (n.89) so that personal data marked for deletion would be processed only if required for security and certain specified purposes. Datainspektionen considered this insufficient, because it could allow Google to continue processing data. More significantly, 'commercially reasonable period' did not indicate how long Google retained information deleted by controllers or after termination. Therefore, the controller's 'instructions' to Google must (but did not) indicate the average or maximum storage time. 'Even a relatively long maximum storage time should be acceptable' provided Google was given 'instructions' that data marked for deletion may only be processed for purposes justified for security reasons or as part of deleting that data. While that decision used 'instructions' terminology, I suggest that *contractual* restrictions on processing such data should have sufficed there (p.301). Norway's DPA accepted the controller's assessment that Google's deletion procedures were adequate for personal data, corresponding to the procedures where data were processed locally (*Narvik 2012b* (Norway), p.17). However, it recommended controller follow-up regarding a guaranteed maximum time before overwriting, and prudent procedures for used storage media disposal. Microsoft's amended terms reflect both recommendations, as do Google's (p.203).

With digital data, there are degrees of 'deletion', up to hardware destruction (Hon, Millard and Walden 2013a: sec.5.6.1).[88] Many providers do not immediately delete data, but only 'pointers' to data, overwriting the data over time,[89] as when files on local hardware are deleted. Providers deliberately may not delete all copies immediately, e.g. from

---

[88] 'Deleting' digital data is not straightforward: see ICO guidance on data deletion (p.301), which addresses locally stored data but is relevant more generally.

[89] Google Apps' terms initially provided: 'after a commercially reasonable period of time, Google will delete Customer Data by removing pointers to it on Google's active and replication servers and overwriting it over time' (Hon and Millard 2013b: sec.2.2). Google has since changed its terms to commit to

backups, to enable restoration in case of accidental or malicious deletion.[90] Deleted data will probably be overwritten eventually, as storage space is limited and providers reuse hardware for costs/efficiency reasons, restricting post-deletion 'exposure time' and risks.[91] Nevertheless, DPAs are strict on deletion, which may underlie another key change to Microsoft's cloud terms facilitating WP29 approval (p.202): obligations to delete data within a stated period after termination. For example, the WP29 requires total deletion, of all copies in all possible media, e.g. backup tapes, in all locations and 'previous versions, temporary files and even file fragments', and also log data containing personal data (*WP196*, p.12). To assess adequacy of deletion and 'whether the data are deleted in such a way that they cannot possibly be recreated from Google's servers', Google's information on deletion practices, and even an independent auditor's SAS70 Type II report (SAS70 has since been superseded), were considered insufficient (*Odense* (Denmark), para.6); therefore, it was difficult to ensure compliance with Danish DPD Laws. Separately, a processor KL used Azure briefly without a processor agreement, and accordingly was deemed a controller (*KL* (Denmark), para.3.1). This seems excessive. Many service providers use subproviders, but should not thereby become controllers. Despite Microsoft describing its deletion process, Datatilsynet required KL to seek independent third party verification that its data were 'deleted irrevocably' from Azure (*KL* (Denmark), para.3.5). It is difficult to see how such third party verification is possible.

However, is immediate total deletion of data always appropriate or necessary? With strongly encrypted data, deleting keys may be as effective as deleting data, from a technical security viewpoint. Indeed, losing a key 'could render [encrypted] data useless' and constitute accidental destruction in breach of security requirements (ICO 2012a: para.69). Even unencrypted data are overwritten over time. The DPD contemplates 'blocking' in some situations, e.g. Art.12(b) data subjects' rights to obtain 'as appropriate' rectification, erasure 'or blocking'. The WP29 recognizes that data may be 'erased or truly anonymised' as an alternative to complete deletion (*WP196*, para.3.4.1.3), and that access to data held under legal retention requirements may be 'blocked', with contractual provision for destruction, demagnetization and multiple overwriting according to 'a recognized specification' (*WP196*, p.12). The

---

deletion within a stated maximum period (p.202), but its technical procedures probably remain unchanged.

[90]   E.g. *Salems 2013* (Sweden), p.3; *Narvik 2012b* (Norway), p.7.
[91]   The data's 'security life' is also relevant – p.286.

GDPR dispenses with 'the ambiguous terminology' 'blocking'; instead, data subjects may have processing 'restricted' (Art.18). The GDPR would allow 'restriction' in fewer situations than currently (COM(2012)011 final, para.3.4.3.3). 'Restriction' is undefined, but 'automated filing systems' (undefined) should include technical restrictions to prevent further processing or amendment, e.g. 'temporarily moving' data to another system, making the data unavailable to users, or 'temporarily removing' data from websites (GDPR Rec.57). Sometimes, arguably 'restricting' may suffice instead of deletion, and should be permitted in circumstances beyond the 'right to erasure' (Hon, Kosta et al. 2014, p.43).

Some providers may have the technical ability to recreate 'deleted' data, but why require total deletion rather than, say, imposing direct data protection obligations on processors, or requiring contractual provisions (surviving service termination), not to attempt to reconstitute or use/ disclose deleted data?[92] If *contractual* processor obligations are sufficient for Art.17 security measures, why should they not suffice for deletion purposes? Alternatively, could fewer Principles be applied to 'deleted' data? The ICO's guidance on deleting personal data (ICO 2014c) introduced a concept of data 'put beyond use', perhaps similar to 'blocked' or 'restricted', where subject access rights and retention/ deletion Principles are inapplicable. 'Put beyond use' means the controller: 'is not able, or will not attempt, to use' such personal data to 'inform any decision in respect of any individual or in a manner that affects the individual in any way'; gives no other organization access to such personal data; 'surrounds' the personal data with appropriate technical and organizational security; and 'commits to permanent deletion of the information if, or when, this becomes possible'. I argue that such a technology-neutral approach should be taken to digital, indeed all, personal data.

'Deletion' needs clear definition. The 'deletion' requirement should allow for restriction or prevention of intelligible access, and should be context-appropriate, e.g., sensitive data may necessitate more secure 'deletion' (overwriting multiple times) and more trustworthy assurances regarding deletion; but overwriting once, with contractual obligations not to attempt data reconstruction, could suffice for other personal data. In short, I argue that the objectives of requiring data deletion may be met by context-appropriate technical and/or legal measures to restrict intelligible

---

[92] A variation on what Google proposed to Datainspektionen – p.299.

access to the extent reasonable in the circumstances to protect confidentiality.[93] That would seem more future-proof as technologies change. For
instance, practices for deleting data on hard drives may not reliably
delete data from solid state drives (SSDs) (Wei et al. 2011), meaning that
other methods may be needed to restrict intelligible access with SSDs;
conversely, sometimes data may be irrecoverable from SSDs even for
evidential purposes (Bell and Boddington 2010). However, equally,
providers should be more transparent regarding their storage and deletion
mechanisms, detailing the ease (or not) of retrieval of deleted data by
themselves or third parties. An issue not discussed by *WP196* is how
providers may, or should, prove that data were deleted compliantly with
contractual commitments.[94]

Finally, digital data may be deleted *remotely* via software, regardless of
data location. Controllers may more easily visit infrastructure located in
their own countries, but viewing boxes cannot verify data deletion
everywhere: destroying boxes in one datacentre cannot ensure that no
other copies of relevant data exist (also see 7.4.2.5). Therefore, the
Restriction does not assist in relation to data deletion. Independent
certifications of providers' systems and how they assure data deletion
seems the most feasible way to address this issue, and may be possible
under the GDPR (5.4.5).

7.4.2.5   Ensuring providers' compliance

Art.17(2) DPD requires controllers who use processors to 'ensure compliance' with processor security measures, including checking compliance. Its successor Art.28 GDPR seems not to specifically require
controllers to ensure processors' compliance, but undoubtedly that is
implicit despite GDPR's greater focus on processor obligations/liabilities.
DPA cloud decisions note that, while contracts can be used to ensure and
monitor processor compliance, it is difficult to monitor compliance with
multiple providers in different countries and that, therefore, data locations

---

[93]   With deleted data, integrity and availability should be irrelevant.
[94]   For a flexible cloud service 'with associated high-availability and geographic distribution', it is difficult to know 'exactly how a provider will prove
data has been destroyed everywhere to a recognized level or standard' (Ottenheimer 2012). It may be impossible for providers to assure controllers that they
have not kept copies elsewhere. What level of evidence or proof would be
appropriate in the circumstances? Perhaps providers could certify that data have
been deleted to the required degree (Hon, Millard and Walden 2013a: sec.5.6.1),
or provide contractual commitments/warranties regarding deletion, surviving
contract termination. See also *KL* (Denmark) – p.300.

must be known (p.99). For example, Datatilsynet queried whether controllers could ensure processors were implementing security measures if controllers did not know data locations (*Odense* (Denmark), para.5.3.2). However, that approach assumes that, as with access (4.5.1) and deletion (7.4.2.4), monitoring requires *physical* presence. That view disregards logical remote access, logical software controls, and the many technical tools provided in cloud for customers to monitor logical access remotely (e.g. logging tools).

Even with infrastructure located in the controller's country, physical visits can only verify physical security. Providers' logical security cannot be checked by viewing a building or boxes; that requires technical verification of source code and implementation, which is achievable without physical inspection of data locations. Physical visits can only indicate physical security, not logical data security. Anecdotally, when a customer (X) insisted on visiting a datacentre to check 'its' data, one provider told me that it simply attached labels to certain servers stating, 'X's data'. After reading the labels the customer left, satisfied. Similarly, a person responsible for compliance at a cloud customer told me that they were asked to inspect the customer's data but did not know how, so they went to the provider's datacentre and were pointed to boxes and told that they contained the customer's data.[95] How does that verify logical security?

Logs may be also viewed remotely. So again, the Restriction is not necessary there. The GDPR's emphasis on accountability, i.e. demonstrating compliance (1.5.1), and related aspects such as data protection by design and default and breach notification are in principle positive as regards ensuring compliance, but again such matters are not dependent on data location.

7.5 ACCESS BY AUTHORITIES

Having covered physical and logical security generally, and the risks of unauthorized controller or processor use or disclosure of personal data, I now discuss the risks of third country authorities' access. I cover it in this chapter because it is partly a security issue, affected by how well

---

[95] Despite physical inspections' inadequacy to verify logical security, Google agreed to allow Italy's DPA to conduct 'on-the-spot checks at Google's US headquarters to verify whether the measures being implemented are in compliance with Italian law' (Garante 2015).

controllers or providers restrict others' intelligible access. However, in many ways it is a political issue.

Access by authorities can threaten CIA and conflict with data protection obligations. Two main categories exist:

- access compelled from cloud providers, and
- direct interception/surveillance of data without providers' knowledge or cooperation.

Neither can be said to relate to the Restriction's original objective of preventing circumvention by controllers of DPD Laws. They raise a separate policy issue – protecting the personal data of EEA citizens/residents from access by third country authorities (2.2.1).

7.5.1 Compelled Access

Member States may provide exceptions or limitations to data protection law requirements, to permit governmental access to personal data for certain matters (1.5.3). Many Member States have introduced such exceptions/limitations, particularly for national security.

Art.16 DPD (p.267; 7.4) allows persons 'acting under the authority of the controller', including processors, to process personal data (including disclosing data) otherwise than as the controller instructs, if 'required to do so by law'. Art.16 does not specify which countries' laws, but this exception was intentionally broadened during the DPD's passage. In the 1992-Proposal, its wording was 'unless he is required to do so under national or Community law', e.g. for criminal investigations (COM(92)422 final, p.28). The more general 'unless he is required to do so by law' exception was subsequently added deliberately, to make DPD's text compatible with the Money Laundering Directive (Council 6648/94, p.7). It is unclear why the final DPD did not refer explicitly to 'anti-money laundering' or even 'crime detection and prevention'.

However, Art.16's GDPR replacement explicitly excludes third country laws.[96] The DPD's Mechanisms contemplated exceptions allowing third country authorities' access as required by local law, notably for national security purposes (5.3.4.3, 5.4.2.6). These illustrate lawmakers' acknowledgement that some compelled disclosures are needed, to Member State and/or third country authorities (although they should be limited to those necessary in democratic societies (*WP12*, p.21)), overriding any

---

[96] GDPR Art.29 allows such exceptions only for disclosures etc. required by 'Union or Member State law' – p.269.

contractual restrictions on disclosure; and that laws may prohibit processors from notifying controllers of requests (*WP196*, pp.13–14). However, in the post-Snowden era, the GDPR's Mechanisms are likely to restrict such disclosures more tightly, although details (new forms of SCCs etc. – 5.4.1.2) are still unknown.

Authorities can effectively compel intelligible data from providers, overriding any contractual restrictions imposed by controllers, if, but only if, both the following hold true:

- the provider has intelligible access, e.g. data are stored unencrypted or it has access to the decryption keys; and
- the authority's country has effective jurisdiction over that provider, whether based on infrastructure location[97] or incorporation, operations or assets in that country.

As regards the first, many providers have intelligible access (but not always – p.127). Hence, some authorities have shifted to seeking cloud data (Swire 2012). Post-Snowden, providers like Google have publicly increased their use of encryption (p.278). However, if providers retain the keys, authorities could still gain intelligible access with their cooperation e.g. under court order (Burton 2013). This has raised queries regarding whether such moves were mere marketing, 'security theatre' (Darrow 2013). Nevertheless, provider encryption should at least deter authorities from gaining intelligible access by *directly* tapping communications links, forcing them to obtain court orders, and should also deter intelligible access by other unauthorized persons (p.287).

Authorities having effective jurisdiction over a provider with intelligible access can seek intelligible access from providers, regardless of data location – even EEA location – because providers have the technical ability to retrieve data remotely.[98] This supports my argument that it is more important to consider which countries have effective jurisdiction

---

[97]   E.g. the DPD's equipment ground (pp.47, 52, 39) – and as occurred with SWIFT, through its using a US datacentre (3.7.1.3).

[98]   P.146, n.31; Brazil (4.5.1.2). Third countries may assert jurisdiction over providers 'located' there: 'However, customers should be aware that when they choose service providers located in third countries, the local administrative or judicial authorities may send requests to the service providers for access to the data' (CNIL 2012: pp.16–17). There, 'located' probably refers to country of establishment – ibid. p.13. Google's CEO Eric Schmidt previously opined that US corporations' non-US servers were under US intelligence jurisdiction (Meyer 2014a). See also the ongoing *Microsoft warrant case* (p.93).

over providers, than data location (except to the extent that data location gives third countries effective jurisdiction over providers – 3.9).[99] Nevertheless, the WP29 insists that 'storage' of data 'on EU territory' is 'an effective way' to facilitate DPA control over compliance (*WP227*, para.11). This may be because it considers it 'reasonably foreseeable' that third country authorities 'only seem to obtain access to data after an international transfer from a company in the EU to another company outside the EU took place' (*WP228*, p.7). However, that view fails to distinguish (again) between data location and the other company's 'location' (jurisdiction) and also ignores reports of authorities *directly* tapping communications links or hacking into systems in the EU and elsewhere (7.5.2) or being given data by EU intelligence authorities who have themselves intercepted data (p.310).

To mitigate risks of providers obtaining intelligible access, controllers should, to the fullest extent feasible, strongly encrypt data in storage and transmission (ENISA 2013: p.3; 7.2.3.3.5). Again, encryption should mitigate against authorities' attempted access, physical or logical. Where authorities can obtain only encrypted data from providers, they might still be able to 'crack' the encryption to gain intelligible access (p.286). However, whether authorities can obtain data (encrypted or unencrypted) from providers again depends on their having effective jurisdiction over the providers, not data location per se; authorities can, and do, compel providers over whom they have effective jurisdiction to retrieve data from locations outside their own countries[100] – including the EEA.

Post-Snowden, for reputational and business-preservation reasons, providers are increasingly providing more transparency regarding compelled disclosures where permitted by law, e.g. reports published by AWS, Facebook, Google, Microsoft and Twitter, which DPAs welcome (*WP215*, p.12). In terms of confidentiality, providers with intelligible access could disclose personal data upon mere request by authorities, or in their own interests – not just under legal compulsion. Here, both technical (e.g. encryption) and legal measures are relevant. Hence, controllers may restrict providers' disclosure of personal data on mere request through contractual terms: Art.17(3)'s main purpose (7.4.2.3).

As regards availability and integrity, authorities with effective jurisdiction over providers could force remote data deletion or connectivity termination *wherever* data are located. Also, authorities may directly

---

[99] Server location has 'absolutely no effect – for good or bad – on privacy', as an authority would still have jurisdiction over 'companies who own the data', irrespective of data location (Ezell et al. 2013: p.21).

[100] P.146, n.31; Brazil (4.5.1.2).

seize hardware in their territory, potentially affecting integrity and certainly availability, but providers and customers may be able to address these risks through appropriate measures (4.5.1.1, 7.5.1.1). For example, the FBI removed hosting provider DigitalOne's servers, affecting many of its customers. DigitalOne had not implemented redundancy measures whereby the removal triggered automatic disaster recovery from another facility; so, in that sense, its customers' post-seizure problems were 'down to DigitalOne' (Schwartz 2011). Yet one DigitalOne customer, Pinboard, largely maintained its availability, because it had taken its *own* measures to run a backup server elsewhere, mitigating the seizure's impact on it (Higgins 2011).

More to the point, VMs and 'nebulous temporal instances of applications divorced from physical machines' could make law enforcement action 'a game of whack-a-mole' (Lemos 2009). That statement related to fears that the FBI might broaden seizures further, causing greater collateral damage.[101] However, US authorities cannot directly seize servers in other countries, and hopefully they now appreciate better the futility of trying to stop services by seizing hardware if backups/VMs exist in other jurisdictions.

7.5.1.1 CIA, The Pirate Bay way

File-sharing service The Pirate Bay (TPB) exemplifies CIA enhancement through appropriate structuring. It is under constant threat from authorities seeking to prevent TPB users' access to copyright-infringing material. In 2012, TPB switched to IaaS to become 'more raid proof', i.e. to avoid users' confidentiality or service availability/integrity being compromised through authorities' hardware seizures, as well as to reduce operational costs and complexity, improve availability and reduce resource requirements (Ernesto 2012). TPB's solution is illustrated diagrammatically online (Hon 2014). Summarizing Ernesto (2012), Brahma (2012) and Ernesto (2014d):

- 21 VMs (p.105, n.57) run on different providers' cloud services in two countries.
- Providers are unaware that they host TPB's VMs, because of encryption.

---

[101] Had there been backups elsewhere in the USA, perhaps the FBI would have raided those locations too (Chernicoff 2011).

- All end-user communications go through TPB's own load balancer[102] – a diskless server, configured in RAM only so that, when switched off, it is difficult or impossible to recover information from it. This masks the VMs' functions.
- The TPB-owned load balancer (apparently running in one VM) and transit routers[103] are located in other (different) countries, enabling cloud providers' locations to be hidden, and helping to protect end-users' privacy.
- Communications between the load balancer and VMs are encrypted, so that providers cannot view end-users' traffic content or IP addresses.
- If one cloud service terminates, e.g. through unavailability or insolvency, to restore service TPB may 'buy' VMs from the other provider, upload VM images, and reconfigure the load balancer.
- Upon any attempted seizure, 'there are no servers to take, just a transit router. If they follow the trail to the next country and find the load balancer, there is just a disk-less server there'. If they discover the identity of the cloud provider, 'all they can get are encrypted disk-images' (Ernesto 2012).
- Even if both transit router and load balancer are seized (the 'worst case scenario'), all important data are backed up externally on VMs, reinstallable at providers anywhere.
- If the ('deeply-encrypted') servers have no communication with the load balancer for eight hours, they shut down. When rebooted, they are inaccessible without the password, without which they reboot into a deadlock.

TPB's move illustrates that appropriately designed and configured systems and procedures, using multiple cloud providers and backups, with extensive application of encryption, may be more resilient and protective of CIA than non-cloud-based systems. If country A claims jurisdiction over TPB based on its use of provider X's servers located in A, TPB may terminate the VMs in those servers (whose images are encrypted), terminate its relationship with X and switch to another provider with servers in another country. VMs may be instantiated in the other provider's servers from image backups. Communications encryption renders it difficult or impossible for A to find TPB or identify its end-users, protecting their confidentiality. Even if A obtains X's

---

[102] Device receiving end-user requests, automatically distributing traffic across multiple resources (VMs, here), to optimize workloads.
[103] Used in an efficient routing mechanism, MPLS.

cooperation, X has no intelligible access, because data and communications are encrypted.

In December 2014, authorities raided a Swedish datacentre, taking down TPB, seizing servers including TPB's 'critical' frontend load balancer (Falvinge 2014). However, TPB could 'recover quickly if a new loadbalancer with the right setup is put in place'; the VMs were not centrally hosted and continued running (Ernesto 2014a). Indeed, TPB returned online on 31 January 2015, with a restored database of 'almost everything'; perhaps service would have been restored even sooner had its load balancer not been seized (Protalinski 2015). Before that raid, TPB had never suffered more than three days' downtime (Ernesto 2014c).

Thus, supply chain complexity and multi-intermediation was positively advantageous for TPB: apart from the load balancer and transit routers, it did not own or operate any datacentres or hardware that could be stolen, seized, frozen or otherwise 'held hostage' by authorities. It did not even operate the cloud services used, renting IaaS from third parties. Whether following seizure, theft or breakdown, hardware maintenance/replacement falls to cloud providers, and need not concern their customers. In short, customers may avoid other countries' effective jurisdiction by using only third party providers, not siting their own infrastructure there (assuming they have no other connection with those countries that could give a country effective jurisdiction), ensuring encryption and backups elsewhere to preserve CIA, and thereby survive any cessation of operations or loss of data affecting specific providers and/or datacentres. Cloud's multi-intermediated supply chain may thus benefit customers by preventing certain countries from having *effective* jurisdiction over them. Using layered services (1.2.2) would distance customers still further. Microsoft's 'trustee' arrangement in Germany (7.4.2.3) illustrates another structure that seeks to avoid effective third country jurisdiction.

TPB's use of cloud illustrates the possibilities, although its solution may not suit other usages, particularly where data must be decrypted for operations. If technologies such as homomorphic encryption (7.2.3.3) become practicable, even more secure cloud computing will be feasible.

7.5.2 Authorities' Direct Access

7.5.2.1 Interception etc. – communications links

Location seems relevant when considering physical access to data-transmitting infrastructure, given US and other national authorities' direct tapping of Internet and cloud providers' internal[104] cables or Internet backbone cables – often with backbone providers' (sometimes paid) cooperation (Ball, Harding, et al. 2013; Farivar 2013), but apparently without *cloud* providers' authority or knowledge (Perlroth and Markoff 2013).[105] Unauthorized intelligible access to data transmitted over fibre-optic cables is easily gained if connections are unencrypted (Hess 2015).[106]

Obviously, authorities may more easily tap hardware sited in their own country, which might suggest that one should avoid communications using infrastructure connecting into or passing through certain countries. However, some EEA countries' intelligence agencies have been involved in sharing data with the NSA,[107] e.g. the UK GCHQ's cable-tapping Tempora programme (and data sharing with the NSA) (MacAskill et al. 2013), and mass surveillance of Internet/phone traffic by GCHQ and French, German, Spanish and Swedish intelligence agencies through cable taps and 'development of covert relationships with telecommunications companies', sometimes bypassing 'very restrictive' national interception laws (Borger 2013), then passing some data to the NSA (Landler and Schmidt 2013). Even EEA-located data may be intercepted via such taps, upon transmission over the Internet (7.5.2.1).

Some 80–90 percent of global Internet traffic crosses the USA, allegedly (Ball 2013).[108] The construction of Internet cables that do not 'touch' the USA, specifically between Brazil and Portugal, was much trumpeted (Emmott 2014). But such cables would not prevent intelligible access by US providers, e.g. emails sent to Gmail accountholders (BBC 2013). Also, cables not 'touching' the USA may still be tapped using the US's dedicated tapping submarine (AP 2005) or 'tapping points' in other countries, because other countries' authorities or telecommunications companies may also tap cables and/or cooperate with foreign authorities. Additionally, nation-states may remotely hack into 'endpoint' devices,

---

[104] I.e. connecting the provider's own datacentres, e.g. Google, Yahoo! (Gellman and Soltani 2013b).
[105] See also p.183, n.53.
[106] See p.45; WP29 (2013c: p.2).
[107] See also p.313, n.115.
[108] This statistic's source is unknown. It may be wrong – reportedly the figure was 25 percent in 2008 (Markoff 2008), and 'only a small proportion of intra-European Internet communications' in 2001 (Schmid 2001: para.3.3.1.1).

wherever located.[109] Satellite-transmitted data may be intercepted wirelessly (Dorling 2013) using appropriately sited equipment, perhaps installed on ships in international waters or drones in international airspace.[110] The end result is that potentially the NSA and other intelligence agencies have broad access to much Internet traffic, regardless of cable or hub location – i.e. even when not 'touching' US territory.

Furthermore, currently end-users cannot dictate their data's routing, e.g. to avoid cables passing through the US or UK, or to use only the Brazil–Portugal cable; Internet service providers could, if they agreed or were required by law to change their systems accordingly (3.3). However, such moves would be 'costly and difficult' and might produce undesirable results: isolation and Balkanization of the open Internet, and risks to freedom of expression through some countries seeking greater control over their citizens' Internet use (Brooks and Bajak 2013; Hon, Millard, et al. 2014).

Therefore, constraining Internet cables' endpoint locations, or requiring the use of particular routes, would be expensive yet ineffectual against nation-state interception. Accordingly, I argue that the Restriction should explicitly exclude transit, for legal certainty (3.3). Tapping data links etc. may breach international law and infringe sovereignty (Brown and Korff 2014), raising possibilities of international action. But, as with stored data, the best practical protection for transmissions is, again, for controllers and providers to employ strong encryption to prevent intelligible access to intercepted data, forcing authorities to request access through the courts. The NSA collected far fewer address books from Google, which uses secure browser transmissions by default, than from Yahoo!, which did not, suggesting that Google's encryption was effective to deter its intelligible access (Schneier 2013a).

7.5.2.2 Data location and authorities' access

EEA data location does not guarantee protection against unauthorized, perhaps illegal, access by third country (or EEA) authorities, although it could make third country access harder (Fontanella-Khan and Waters 2014). The NSA, and doubtless other third country authorities, has successfully targeted EEA-located data remotely.[111] Third countries may bribe or blackmail staff at EEA controllers/processors or datacentres, or plant undercover or 'sleeper' agents (Zetter 2014a). Brazil's initial

---

[109] E.g. AP (2013), Meyer (2014b) and Russia's hacking activities (Zetter 2014b). See also p.141, n.26.

[110] Not a fanciful possibility – 3.7.5.

[111] E.g. through hacking – n.109.

reaction to Snowden's revelations was to require providers to store locally collected data in Brazilian datacentres (Winter 2013), but 'storing data onshore will contribute almost nothing to security' because data, wherever stored, are 'highly likely to be shared across the global internet at some point', whereupon interception is possible, and 'Storing it in one place may only make it more vulnerable to attack by hackers' (Leahy 2013).[112] Ultimately, instead of forced data localization, Brazil imposed broad extraterritoriality regarding Brazilian citizens' data (Hon, Millard, et al. 2014: p.14). Similarly, with enforced EEA data localization, EEA-located data may still be intercepted when transmitted over the Internet, or hacked in situ.

Conversely, could the use of datacentres in a third country increase the risks of access by authorities there? Its authorities may seek to assert jurisdiction over those datacentre providers, but they may not always have effective jurisdiction over cloud providers who remotely use those datacentres, or (as the TPB example showed) those providers' customers, i.e. cloud customers. While datacentre providers could be compelled to change or terminate services that they provide to cloud providers, generally they cannot access customers' data held with *other* providers. If cloud customers or providers implement backups and mirror operations to datacentres in other countries (with datacentre providers who are not subject to the first country's jurisdiction), then integrity and availability may be protected, as with TPB (7.5.1.1). Confidentiality could be at risk through authorities' physical access to datacentres in their country, but physical access may not always afford intelligible access (4.5.1.1), and if authorities have effective jurisdiction to force providers to divulge details of filesystems etc., then equally, and more realistically, they could compel providers to retrieve target datasets remotely (assuming provider backdoors exist, which is not unlikely – 4.5.1.2). Remote retrieval would be much easier and quicker than attempting to physically reassemble datasets from seized hardware (p.135; p.137, n.15). In short, authorities with effective jurisdiction over providers could require them to disclose

---

[112]   This view, which I share, is taken by many security experts. Forced data localization facilitates *local* authorities' access, but 'wouldn't make things much harder for the NSA', as US authorities could attempt to force US-based organizations to disclose data 'through subpoena or court order, regardless of data location' (e.g. the *Microsoft warrant case*). Encryption could make NSA access more difficult, but strong encryption could also impede Brazilian authorities' access to data. 'It's not just about having servers in Brazil, it's about storing data on servers that are not run by US companies'. Prohibiting all use of popular US services 'would be a very high bar' (Toor 2013).

data from their systems wherever located (7.5.1), making *data* location irrelevant. In such situations, encryption or similar measures are again the best way for customers and providers to prevent or hinder authorities' intelligible access.

Finally, it must not be overlooked that forced data localization by a country may ease access its own authorities' access to that data. This may partly explain why data localization seems to be an increasing trend, e.g. in the Russian Federation (p.26).[113]

7.5.3 Authorities – the Difficult Issues

Other, perhaps more problematic, issues arise regarding authorities' access. One is the scale of indiscriminate mass data collection[114] by the NSA and EEA authorities,[115] which could well exceed what is necessary and proportionate in a democratic society (COM(2013)846 final, p.4; *WP215*, p.6).[116] Again, encryption may assist here, if adopted widely enough (p.287).

---

[113] A country may well be less restrictive regarding its own authorities' access than regarding foreign authorities' access!

[114] Particularly the wholesale tapping of communications links – 7.5.2.1. Also, disclosure orders if issued in a mass, indiscriminate, 'rubberstamped' way.

[115] E.g. Parliament resolution P7_TA(2014)0230. Denmark, the Netherlands, France, Germany, Spain and Italy all had formal agreements to provide communications data to the US (Traynor 2013). Google's Transparency Report revealed that Germany, France, India and UK made the most requests for user data, after the US (RT 2016).

[116] US authorities' powers to access private data do not exceed EU authorities' (Archer et al. 2012; Archer et al. 2013). However, non-US citizens could not benefit from US restrictions on access to US citizens' data, or challenge US laws' validity under the US Constitution (Rauhofer 2013); conversely, US citizens may challenge European laws and mass surveillance before the European Court of Human Rights, which has proved willing to rein back excessive state surveillance under Art.8 ECHR (right to private life), or before the CJEU, which invalidated the Data Retention Directive for interfering disproportionately with Charter Arts.7 and 8 (rights to privacy and data protection) in Joined cases C-293/12 and C-594/12 *Digital Rights Ireland Ltd*. Also, the DPD protects personal data regardless of data subject nationality or residence (1.5.2). The US Judicial Redress Act of 2016 extends certain protections and rights available to US citizens to citizens of designated countries (so far, the EU and most Member States) regarding data transferred to US law enforcement authorities. It does not cover 'national security' data; the Shield Ombudsman will field requests/ complaints regarding such data, transferred under the Shield or otherwise (p.168).

Another (related) issue is jurisdictional conflicts arising when controllers or processors are subject to multiple countries' jurisdictions simultaneously,[117] and processing personal data as required by one country
(e.g. disclosure to its authorities) would breach another country's laws.
Restricting 'transfers or disclosures' to authorities under third country
laws, as under the 'anti-FISA' Art.48 GDPR (p.119), would put organizations subject to multiple jurisdictions in the impossible position of
having to choose which law to break (3.7.4). The WP29 acknowledged
that 'companies may find themselves in a difficult position in deciding
whether they comply with the order to supply personal data on a large
scale or not: in either case they are likely to be in breach of European or
third country law' (*WP215*, p.7) – yet suggests that enforcement action
'should not be excluded' where controllers have 'willingly and knowingly
cooperated with intelligence services to give them access to their data'.[118]
This seems consistent with its initial, more hard-line, view that only
controllers, not processors, can disclose personal data to authorities 'upon
prior presentation of a domestic judicial authorisation/warrant or any
document justifying their need to access the data' (WP29 2013a: pp.3–4)
– although processors may equally be subject to conflicting legal
requirements.

Art.48 would affect not only US cloud providers but EEA controllers,
some of whom are effectively subject to third country jurisdiction
through having business operations abroad. Third countries where an
EEA controller has branches (or subsidiaries etc.) could require disclosure of personal data of its EEA-resident customers, threatening
otherwise to revoke its licence to operate or other penalties (p.146, n.31).
EEA controllers would be in the invidious position of having to cease
operations there, or breach DPD Laws (if the relevant DPA refuses
authorization).

The 'anti-FISA' provision's practical efficacy is doubtful (Bowden
2013: p.29). It may even be unworkable, given the daily volumes of
requirements to disclose information to foreign (particularly US) courts
and authorities (Jones 2012: p.9). Furthermore, the GDPR exempts
personal data processing for national security purposes (Art.2(2)), which

---

[117]   This already occurs intra-EEA. Personal data that are moved or replicated
to equipment in different EEA countries thereby become subject, under
Art.4(1)(c) (2.3.2), to different national laws, e.g. on security (EPOF 2011: p.3),
at different times (*WP179*, p.25) or even simultaneously.

[118]   Cf. the Canadian DPA's and ICO's (admittedly pre-Snowden) approach –
p.98; p.116, n.79 – and more nuanced recent WP29 views in *WP204* (5.4.3.3).

remains Member States' 'sole responsibility' (p.165). Thus, notwithstanding the 'anti-FISA' provision, the national security exemption could allow transfers to US authorities in the interests of national security, so Art.48 is 'at best ambiguous, at worst toothless' (DataGuidance 2013).

Long-recognized jurisdictional conflicts problems (Hague Conference on Private International Law 2010) should not be foisted on private actors; nor can DPAs resolve them (ICO 2013a: p.4). The WP29 has since recognized that compromises are necessary (5.4.3.3). These problems require resolution through countries' international agreement regarding state surveillance: its proper limits, accountability/oversight and transparency (e.g. Stepanovich and Mitnic 2015) – not through data localization. The Commission emphasized the need for a governance framework for intelligence/security services access, particularly cross-border (Commission 2013d). It acknowledged that insufficiently developed international conflict rules cause conflicts problems, particularly for inherently cross-border Internet services like cloud, and that such complexity can harm growth (COM(2014)72 final, sec.8). It also recognized the need to 'broker a more global model' while protecting 'underlying values of open multistakeholder governance of the Internet' (Commission 2014a), and to 'address jurisdictional issues on the Internet with transparent systems' (Commission 2014c). However, disquiet about surveillance was highlighted (Commission 2014a) without suggesting any specific action, except a review of national/jurisdictional conflicts 'that will suggest possible remedies'. Concerns at United Nations level regarding mass surveillance (UNGA 2014b; UNGA 2014a; Emmerson 2014), and the importance of encryption to a free society (Kaye 2015) may spur action – but that remains to be seen.

7.6 SUMMARY

Interpreting the Restriction to circumscribe the locations where EEA controllers may process personal data makes little sense for anticircumvention purposes, as this chapter has shown. If a controller controls access by maintaining appropriate security, i.e. CIA, it can comply with the Principles regardless of personal data location. With cloud, indeed the Internet, data location is less important for security than (1) whether data are (where feasible) strongly encrypted, (2) how systems are designed, including limiting provider backdoors to access customers' data/accounts, and (3) what security measures are taken, including appropriate logical access controls and authorizations/privileges, measures against hackers who could access vulnerable systems remotely wherever located, and appropriate incident detection and response measures (7.1.3). In the cloud (and Internet), where systems may be accessed remotely, logical security is as important as physical security, if not more so.

I showed (Ch.4) that physical access may not necessarily afford intelligible access to the country of infrastructure location, or to persons there. Conversely, confining data location to the EEA may not prevent a third country's access if it can compel any providers (or indeed controllers) who are effectively under its jurisdiction to retrieve EEA-located personal data remotely. Nor would it protect data against cybercriminals. To address the risks of remote unauthorized intelligible access, technical security measures (notably encryption) are more effective than restricting data location. Indeed, encouraging rather than restricting encryption is increasingly important for the protection of individuals and organizations, given the rise in cybercrime.

Thus, I argue that data protection laws should focus on the control of access to personal data, not data location. Where no unauthorized persons have intelligible access, e.g. because the data are strongly encrypted, data location should not affect confidentiality; and controllers may, and should, protect integrity and availability in more appropriate ways (notably by implementing adequate backups/failover) than by restricting data location, particularly given TBDF's ever-increasing importance and volume. DPAs consider that 'moving' personal data outside the EEA involves 'transfer', so that all possible datacentre locations must be known, but I have argued that this makes little sense without considering whether and which third countries have effective jurisdiction over a processor or subprocessor (or even controller) who has *intelligible* access, without which such jurisdiction is irrelevant.

I do not say that personal data location is irrelevant to security: only that location should not be the only or main matter, restricted regardless of who controls access. Data location is indeed relevant to control of intelligible access, in that it could enable third countries to claim jurisdiction over data (or, strictly, infrastructure/datacentre providers) 'located' there, and thereby seek disclosure of personal data or compromise data integrity/availability. However, the locations of incorporation, headquarters, offices, etc. of controllers, providers, subproviders and/or their assets or operations are at least as significant as data location to afford effective jurisdiction. Equally, the use of multiple processing locations and providers, particularly in cloud, may positively help to prevent certain countries from having effective jurisdiction over data processing. As TPB's example showed, jurisdiction based on data (strictly, infrastructure) location is not always effective to obtain intelligible access or to compromise availability or integrity, because controllers or others could structure arrangements to mitigate against such risks. I reiterate that the key issues are, not data location, but which persons have access, particularly intelligible access, regardless of locations (of data or persons), and which countries have effective jurisdiction to compel them to disclose or amend/destroy data.

Problems regarding countries' mass surveillance of individuals' private data and conflicts between jurisdictions cannot be resolved by confining personal data to the EEA (Kuner 2013a), or by laws such as the 'anti-FISA' GDPR provision, however much EU legislators may wish to clamp down on personal data exports post-Snowden. It would be a mistake to rush to the conclusion that data location requires further restriction. In this Internet age, risks from remote access outweigh risks from physical access. There are broader issues than just data protection and, given the global realities of continuous huge data flows, tightening data protection laws may simply result in many more breaches, with DPAs still lacking resources to detect or enforce breaches to the extent necessary to make the tougher restrictions fully effective – unless even more mass surveillance is introduced, of impending data exports! Ultimately, international political[119] debate and agreement are needed to resolve conflicts of laws relating to compelled data disclosure and privacy. In particular, it will be important to agree proper limits on, and oversight of, mass surveillance of the citizens of any and all countries (including Member States), and authorities' powers to override privacy rights in the name of law enforcement or national security. Agreeing how mass surveillance is best balanced against privacy rights, consistently across different countries,[120] will be a difficult challenge.[121]

---

[119] The WP29 suggests some key actions needed (*WP215*). On law enforcement (not just national security/intelligence) access and data protection, see *WP211*.

[120] E.g., how appropriate is it for the EU to demand that the US accords EU residents greater rights, regarding their surveillance by US authorities, than they have regarding their surveillance by EU authorities?

[121] On key questions that require addressing, see e.g. Smith (2015b).

8. Summary and recommendations

8.1 INTRODUCTION

The Restriction under Arts.25–6 DPD exemplifies data export controls, restricting 'transfer' of personal data 'to' third countries. Its purported aim was to prevent controllers from circumventing EU data protection laws through 'transferring' personal data outside the EEA, by prohibiting 'transfers' unless adequate data protections are maintained through using Mechanisms for adequate protection (e.g. Safe Harbour) or adequate safeguards (e.g. SCCs), except where a derogation applies (e.g. consent) (1.6.2; Ch.5). However, not only does the Restriction not achieve its aim, but also it is a barrier to EEA controllers' use of public cloud (1.2–1.3). It has become a 'Frankenrule', invoked to regulate personal data's physical location *as such*, rather than to ensure that transferred personal data are processed in compliance with substantive DPD Principles.

Therefore, I argue that the Restriction should be abolished. Laws should focus squarely on compliance with the Principles. The Restriction's legislative aims would be better achieved through control of access to intelligible personal data, with security as the enabler of such control, and holding controllers accountable regardless of personal data location.

8.2 LEGISLATIVE AIMS

The Restriction's conflation of personal data location, intelligible access and effective jurisdiction inherits assumptions embedded in pre-DPD laws and instruments (2.2). While restricting data location may serve varying policy objectives, historically countries restricted data exports on anticircumvention grounds: trying to prevent avoidance of national data protection/privacy laws through 'moving' data files outside national borders (2.2.1–2.2.2). This ground, also purportedly shared by the Restriction itself (2.3.1.2, 2.3.2), assumes that physical location of data in a particular country's territory gives it (and only it) effective jurisdiction to apply its laws to the processing of that data – and vice versa

(2.2.3–2.2.4, 2.4). Such assumptions were justifiable when low band-widths meant cross-border data movements or replication were infrequent and low-volume. However, they are now invalid (4.5–4.8).

The DPD's lawmakers almost immediately recognized that data export restrictions alone would not achieve the DPD's aims. During its legislative passage, 'block' Mechanisms were introduced to allow 'transfer' of personal data under adequate protection or adequate safeguards, accepting that measures taken by transferring controllers (and recipients), not just the laws of countries where personal data are located, play an important role in protecting personal data (2.4).

The DPD's legislative history also highlighted the difficulty of basing jurisdiction on data location. The 1990-Proposal's main jurisdictional basis was the *location* of personal data in the Community, and accordingly its version of the Restriction aimed to prevent controllers circumventing DPD Laws by 'transferring' personal data to third country *processors* (p.49). However, under both the 1992-Proposal and the final DPD, EEA-established controllers remain subject to DPD Laws even when they use third country processors.[1] Therefore, logically, the Restriction is pointless in such situations – an EEA controller cannot circumvent its subjection to EU law simply by exporting personal data. Perhaps other, unstated, policy objectives drove the Restriction's retention, and DPAs' current reliance on it to justify restricting personal data location – notably concerns, which have since come to a head, regarding non-EEA service providers' remote access to EEA citizens' personal data (p.52) and non-EEA authorities' access to their personal data.[2]

Proposals to update Convention108 would require parties to allow or disallow transfers based on whether the recipient is subject to the *jurisdiction* of another party or a non-party, rather than location of data in the relevant territories (2.2.10). I argued that jurisdiction is a better basis than data location (2.4.5, 3.8). However, the problem of recipients being increasingly subject to multiple countries' jurisdictions, including countries outside the country of data location, remains unaddressed (2.2.7, 2.4.5, 3.8).

---

[1] Pp.53, 64; 3.7.2.
[2] Pp.25, 55, 116–17, 119, 138–9, 146, 182; 3.7.1.3, 4.5.1.2, 5.3.4.3, 5.3.2, 5.3.4.3, 5.4.2.6–5.4.2.7, 7.4–7.5.

8.3 'TRANSFER' AND JURISDICTION

Even in its own terms, the Restriction is impossible to interpret and apply to the modern digital environment (Ch.3). DPAs' interpretation of 'transfer' focuses on location, i.e., physical movement of personal data to third countries (3.7). *Lindqvist*'s holding that no 'transfer' occurred upon uploading personal data to an EEA-established provider, irrespective of the data's location (3.5), illustrates the problems arising from lawmakers' failure to define 'transfer', particularly with indirect, multistage, 'pull' situations like websites; questions regarding 'making available' to all, or only known, third countries; and the issue of would-be transferors' intention to 'transfer' (3.6).

DPAs' 'location fixation' ignores the question which is far more important than data location: jurisdiction (3.7.9). Uploads of personal data to *EEA-located* servers are not considered 'transfers', seemingly regardless of recipient status (processor or controller), and regardless of whether third countries have effective jurisdiction to compel disclosure from the recipients. Conversely, transmissions to third country-located servers are always considered 'transfers', regardless of intelligible access by anyone there and even when the 'recipients' are subject to EEA or other 'adequate' jurisdiction, contrary to *Lindqvist* (p.80).[3] Yet confining personal data to EEA territory cannot protect personal data against third countries' attempts to exercise jurisdiction over personal data. Microsoft's and Google's admissions regarding forced retrieval from EEA territory under the US PATRIOT Act (p.117) and the *Microsoft warrant case* (p.93) show that third countries with effective jurisdiction over providers may seek *remote* access to their customers' data, wherever located. EEA location also cannot guarantee security, e.g. against unauthorized remote hackers, state-sponsored or otherwise. The strength of security measures depends on controllers' and (sub)providers' actions or inactions, not on data location (7.2).

---

[3] Transmissions to a harborite's non-EEA and non-US datacentres were considered 'transfers' requiring SCCs notwithstanding that, as regards any 'transferred' personal data, the relevant Member State's DPD Laws still applied to the 'transferring' controller, and the recipient-harborite was subject to 'adequate' Safe Harbour principles – *Odense* (Denmark) (p.96). Again illustrating DPAs' narrow view of Mechanisms only as ways to permit personal data 'location' in third countries, Belgian organization SWIFT's artificial subscription to Safe Harbour, to regularize its processing of personal data using US infrastructure, added nothing to data protection: it was already subject to DPD Laws (pp.89–98).

I noted that the availability of remote access and technologies such as encryption undermines the assumption that data location in a country gives it (and only it) effective jurisdiction to regulate the processing of that data (3.7.1–3.7.2). It makes little sense to consider data location without considering to what extent third countries have *effective* jurisdiction over a person with intelligible access, without which such jurisdiction is irrelevant. Given technologies like encryption, it cannot be assumed that datacentre providers (or indeed cloud (sub)providers) always have intelligible access to all data processed using their infrastructure or services. I submit that the key anticircumvention issue is whether the EEA controller can be required to, and can, comply with the Principles (e.g. through appropriate technical measures to restrict intelligible access), notwithstanding the risks associated with data location or multiple (sub)providers. If it can still comply, then the Restriction's avowed objective can be satisfied without necessarily requiring contracts 'with' (sub)providers in addition, and without imposing stricter or further requirements simply because personal data are physically 'located' in third countries or in cloud.

Thus, I argued for a more nuanced, technology-neutral approach (3.7.2), based on considering which country or countries have effective jurisdiction over persons who control access to intelligible personal data, regardless of the data's location or the means used to exercise such control (legal, organizational and/or technical). More generally, I argued that data location should not be equated with intelligible access, and instead that laws should only regulate those who control intelligible access to personal data.[4] I suggested that location of personal data in a country is relevant to privacy only if and to the extent that it gives that country jurisdiction to regulate the processing of that data (3.9). Even if that country has such jurisdiction, cloud supply chains' complexity and/or appropriate structuring of services/usage may prevent it from having *effective* jurisdiction (7.5.1.1).

Focusing on data location for its own sake may lead to absurd and/or impracticable results. Requiring controllers to know, and apply the Restriction and Mechanisms to, *all* the many possible data locations involved in cloud or Internet services would be difficult if not impossible. It also raises the question of what privacy purpose is served by knowing all such locations (3.7.3). Furthermore, data location-centricity causes problems if personal data are not 'located' within any country's territory, e.g. if servers on barges in international waters are used, because

---

[4]   1.3, 3.1, 3.7.1–3.7.2, 3.9, 4.2, 4.5.1.1, 4.5.2, 5.3.4.2, 7.2.3.2.

transfers 'to' such locations would escape the Restriction altogether (3.7.5), which would undermine the Restriction's anticircumvention aim. Again, focusing on jurisdiction over whoever controls access to intelligible personal data within such servers seems superior to considering only the data's location. The *Microsoft warrant case* (p.93) triggered proposed legislation to address these issues (p.94) based on the persons concerned, which is a better approach than data location-centricity.[5] Other problems with location-centricity include providers not necessarily knowing or controlling subproviders' data locations, particularly SME providers (3.7.6); restrictions on data locations negatively impacting on costs and data integrity/availability (3.7.7); and difficulties with verifying data location (3.7.8), where I argued that resources expended on tracking data location (3.7.8) would be better spent on improving logical and physical data security (Ch.7). Furthermore, EEA location alone cannot protect personal data; effective jurisdiction and security measures are more important in that regard (3.7.9, Ch.7).

I argued that, given the uncertainties regarding whether a 'transfer' has occurred, the difficulties with determining all relevant locations, and the possibility of data being physically located outside *any* country's territory, 'transfer' should at least be defined explicitly, and 'transit' defined and excluded (3.8–3.9). Influential sources (3.8) suggest, and some countries' laws provide (3.8), that 'transfer' connotes communication or disclosure (i.e. *intelligible* access) made with the sender's knowledge or intention. On that basis, transmitting or storing strongly encrypted personal data to or in a third country, where persons there have no intelligible access, should not constitute 'disclosure' or 'transfer'. However, issues of knowledge or intention may also be problematic. That is one reason why I recommend abolishing the Restriction, focusing instead only on substantive Principles. Supporting my argument that the focus should be on Principles, not personal data location, some DPAs stress that website publication of personal data must comply with the Principles, particularly fair processing (p.17), because otherwise, on some interpretations of *Lindqvist*, such publication might escape the Restriction altogether. The fact that DPAs felt the need to stress this shows how much the Restriction has diverted attention away from the Principles.

---

[5] Conflicts between jurisdictions could still arise if communication contents or metadata are or include EEA individuals' personal data, but such conflicts already exist; the Restriction does not prevent or resolve them.

8.4 MISMATCH BETWEEN THE RESTRICTION'S ASSUMPTIONS AND REALITY

Certain assumptions underlying the Restriction and its precursors may explain its conflation of personal data location, intelligible access and effective jurisdiction (3.7.2). However, Ch.4 showed that these assumptions are no longer valid, further undermining any justifications for the Restriction.

The Restriction embedded pre-Internet 'mainframe' models regarding control over a (single) physical file (4.4.1). Pre-Internet datasets had clear, central locations, changing location rarely. Whoever had physical access to any hardware that stored data, including the authorities of countries where the hardware was sited, had intelligible access to that data. Therefore, countries where such hardware were located had effective jurisdiction to regulate the processing of that data, and accordingly were expected to regulate that data through their laws (4.7). Thus, data export restrictions could ensure the protection of personal data and prevent any circumvention of DPD Laws – hence the focus on personal data location and the assumption that, generally, personal data would be 'transferred' through physically exporting the hardware storing that data (4.8).

Today's position is very different, with the availability of automated distributed storage and operations, high connectivity and bandwidths, near-ubiquitous remote access over the Internet, continuous multipoint data movements and data replication (4.4, 6.2) – and, of course, the availability of technological means to control intelligible access such as encryption (4.5.1.1, 7.2.3.1). Essentially, views that countries can and should regulate data 'located' in their territories are based on the assumption that countries have effective jurisdiction over persons with intelligible access to such data, treating data location as a *proxy* for intelligible access (4.6). Data export restrictions and 'border controls' over data equated data location, physical access to the data, intelligible access (4.5.1) and a country's effective jurisdiction to regulate the processing of that data. This was unsurprising given the traditional territorial basis of jurisdiction and the technologies of the time, but it has since been belied by developments (4.6–4.9).

Nowadays, physical access to data (e.g. (sub)providers' access) does not necessarily afford intelligible access to the data, because of distributed storage, possible use of proprietary filesystems, and the availability of measures like encryption (4.5.1.1). Physical security measures (locks, guards, etc.) are important for data protection, but they depend on the policies and practices of datacentre providers and their users (e.g. cloud providers), not the country of data location (4.5.1.1). True, authorities in a datacentre's country could gain physical access to seize hardware storing personal data (7.5.1) and/or tap cables directly (7.5.2). However, such risks are not unique to cloud. Risks of *remote* logical access by nation-states are greater (4.5.1.1–4.5.1.2). Countries' laws may require minimum security measures (n.22), but the security of data depends on the protective measures taken, not on the data's location (7.2; 7.5.1.1).

Similarly, in relation to logical security, risks to availability and integrity from authorities' seizures of equipment may be mitigated through implementing backups, and risks to confidentiality may be mitigated through measures such as encryption (7.2). Physical access is not necessary for intelligible access; remote access is now typical (4.5.1.2). Cloud customers access data logically, not physically; when customers seek direct, self-service access to a dataset, the relevant fragments are seamlessly retrieved from remote locations, reassembled and delivered to the customer's local device (4.5.1). Accordingly, customers may edit or delete personal data directly to satisfy data subject requests even where the data are stored in the cloud, without needing physical access to the data and without 'instructing' any cloud (sub)-providers. Physical access cannot guarantee exclusive access either, because remote access is possible (possibly concurrently by different end-users), and backups or failovers to other locations may be implemented (3.7.7.2, 4.5.1.3, 7.1.3). Thus, the physical location of infrastructure is no longer very relevant to the ability of customers and end-users to access data held within that infrastructure. However, even remote access may not afford intelligible access because security measures may be taken to restrict it, such as access controls (4.5.2).

The fact that infrastructure used to process personal data are located in a particular country is not necessarily enough to give that country effective jurisdiction to obtain intelligible access to such data, or to regulate the processing of that data. Countries may assert jurisdiction over data processing based on the location of processing infrastructure in their territories, e.g. the DPD's 'equipment' ground. However, effective jurisdiction over infrastructure providers does not necessarily afford effective jurisdiction over such providers' *customers*, their end-users, or even data processed in that infrastructure (4.6). This is because digital data may be encrypted, and are relatively easy to replicate or 'move' to different locations; and cloud often involves a complex supply chain with multiple players, many lacking enough tangible connection with the country of infrastructure location for that country's claimed jurisdiction over them to be effective (4.6, 7.5.1.1). Unauthorized logical remote access is the greater threat (4.5.1.1–4.5.1.2).

The assumption that countries' laws and regulations are the best way to protect personal data is also wrong. 'Adequate' laws alone cannot guarantee practical compliance. Continuing compliance with the Principles should be assessed for individual transfers, yet no such assessment is considered necessary for transfers to any country found 'adequate' under the DPD or the GDPR. However, I argued that third country laws, like data location, are only one relevant factor (4.7, 5.2.2.2).

Data location, physical access, intelligible access and effective jurisdiction can no longer be conflated. Technology has broken the once-inescapable link between them. Data location is but one factor, among others; it should not be an end in itself, although it is often treated as such by DPAs (3.7). EEA location does not guarantee data protection. Conversely, third country-located personal data may be adequately, indeed well, protected, e.g. through encryption. I reiterate that the true issues are control of access to personal data, particularly intelligible access, regardless of data location; and countries' effective jurisdiction over those with such control, where the main relevance of infrastructure location is that it may afford such jurisdiction – but, then again, it may not be sufficient to afford *effective* jurisdiction (4.9, 7.5.1.1).

8.5 ALLOWING TRANSFERS

Transfers were intended to be permitted based on adequate protection or adequate safeguards, under Mechanisms designed for the purpose (1.6.2). However, most Mechanisms are generally too complex, bureaucratic and unworkable to use easily in practice, because of the focus on data location instead of effective jurisdiction, some DPAs' refusal to recognize Mechanisms as sufficient to provide adequate protection or adequate safeguards, and most Mechanisms' unsuitability to modern outsourcing practices (Ch.5).

Thus, even pre-*Schrems*, some DPAs doubted Safe Harbour's efficacy to provide adequate protection, despite that being its purpose (p.163), and SCCs' adequacy is also under challenge (5.4.2.7). Many Mechanisms, designed for pre-Internet outsourcing models, are too inflexible for modern supply chains with (possibly multiple) subprocessors and continuous, dynamic data flows, as in cloud – except for large providers who control their supply chains and can secure the required subprocessor obligations (3.7.3, 5.3.4.2, 5.4.2.3, 5.4.2.9, 5.4.3.3, 5.8). SCCs are difficult and cumbersome without necessarily improving data protection, and are completely unavailable when EEA providers use non-EEA subproviders; also, SMEs lack resources to handle the numbers of SCCs often required (5.4.2). BCRs are unsuitable for public cloud, particularly layered services, only allowing transfers within a corporate group (5.4.3). Time-consuming and expensive to obtain and maintain, they are also effectively unavailable to SMEs, whether controllers or providers (5.4.3.2). Even with processor BCRs (that allow transfers within a provider's group), controllers still need DPA authorization to transfer personal data *based on* such BCRs (5.4.3.3).

Some DPAs insist on additional measures for compliance with national DPD Laws, notwithstanding the use of Mechanisms (5.3.4.1). Conversely, DPAs may require the use of Mechanisms to allow personal data to be 'located' in third countries, even when the transferors/transferees are already subject to EEA jurisdiction (as with SWIFT) or other 'adequate' jurisdiction – so that, even when using Safe Harbour, DPAs insisted on personal data being located only in the US or EEA (p.96). This underlines the Restriction's treatment as a separate 'Frankenrule' on personal data location alone, which has proved to be counterproductive, indeed positively harmful, due to controllers' wasted time and costs attempting to comply with the Restriction/Mechanisms and national DPD Laws' requirements instead of focusing on compliance with the core Principles and ensuring the sufficiency of technical security measures to protect personal data.

Particularly where controllers 'transfer' personal data to processors, I argued that the Restriction and Mechanisms are superfluous, and indeed distract from the core issue of compliance with substantive DPD Laws. I suggested that, as a normative matter, when controllers transfer personal data to processors only Art.17 DPD needs to be engaged, regardless of data location – and even Art.17 is irrelevant if the data are unintelligible to the processors or are legitimately available publicly, e.g. on websites where the processor hosts the data (p.121). While the relationship between SCCs and Art.17 agreements is unclear, I also argued that SCCs should be unnecessary if technical measures can provide continued protection regardless of personal data location (5.4.2.8). Again, if the focus were clearly on Principles such as fair processing, not personal data location, confusion regarding SCCs would not arise. Other uncertainties, e.g. whether 'onward transfer' occurs to subprocessors (5.3.4.2), would be eliminated if there were no Restriction and controllers and DPAs could simply concentrate on compliance with Art.17 DPD requirements and other Principles.

Further problems arise with the Mechanisms. Technological protections (e.g. encryption) are often disregarded when assessing the adequacy of protection (5.2.2.1–5.2.2.2),[6] or as a way to control intelligible access by the recipients or any onward transferees (5.2.2.1, 5.6–5.7). Some DPAs only consider legal protections such as rules/contracts to be sufficient, perhaps reflecting some mistrust of technology. I argued that this approach is misconceived. All appropriate means of protecting data should be given due recognition, and encouraged. Indeed, sometimes technical means can protect personal data better than contractual means (2.4.6). If you store your personal data in removable media (such as a memory stick) which you are handing to a stranger to hold for you temporarily, what would you rather do: give them the data stored in unencrypted media, asking them to sign a contract with you to keep the media securely and not view, use or disclose your data except on your instructions; or, hand them the data on encrypted media to which only you have the decryption key? Furthermore, Mechanisms' overcomplexity together with differing national approaches and requirements on Member State authorizations and the adequacy of safeguards result in uncertainties and inconsistencies all of which must weaken the normative effect of the Restriction/Mechanisms (5.2.1, 5.4, 5.4.2.5, 5.8).

The WP29's onward transfer principle, taken to its logical conclusion, could require 'adequate protection' in all countries in the possible onward chain, which is not practicable or sensible, and inconsistent with WP29's findings of adequacy where onward transfers have *not* been restricted. The WP29 considered New Zealand's lack of onward transfers restrictions not a 'major shortfall' because agencies, remaining responsible for use/disclosure in third countries, were incentivized to implement safeguards: which is exactly my argument regarding EEA controllers, who remain responsible when using processors *regardless of* data location (5.6). More fundamentally, I argued that intelligible access and jurisdiction are relevant in considering 'onward transfers', and technical protections should be recognized.[7] Yet GDPR Art.44 explicitly extends GDPR's Restriction to onward transfers, without defining them, e.g. by reference to intelligible access, or providing guidance on its practical application to onward transfers (5.6).

The GDPR's approach to adequate protection and adequate safeguards (termed 'appropriate safeguards') is retrograde because it disallows controllers' self-assessment, and seemingly even DPA authorization, of appropriate safeguards based on *technical* measures (5.4.1.2). I have

---

[6] Cf. the UK's approach of allowing controllers to self-assess adequacy based on technical protections (5.2.1).

[7] As under Canada's PIPEDA – p.218.

argued that technical means to control transfers and onward transfers (or rather, in my view, to control intelligible access) should be incentivized, not deprecated.

The GDPR's new 'compelling legitimate interests' derogation for transfers under appropriate safeguards is unlikely to be usable for cloud (and indeed many Internet) transfers (5.5.2). It assumes (erroneously) that 'repetitive' transfers cannot be adequately protected; indeed, GDPR 'hardcodes' that assumption, derived from WP29 opinions that are nearly 20 years old (5.2.2.1, 5.5.2). However, I argued that the adequacy of safeguards is more important than the repetitiveness of transfers, which alone does not make adequate protection or safeguards impossible: numerous online payments occur securely everyday using modern technologies, many 'repeated', and again I emphasize my view that the use of technical protections should be encouraged.

I argued that the simpler approach of requiring accountability, and 'reasonable' measures to ensure continued compliance (5.7), is more technologically neutral and realistic than a rule that seems to focus only on personal data location and refuses to recognize technological means of protecting personal data.

8.6 PROBLEMS OF ENFORCEMENT

Given the continuing abundance of 'transfers' (6.2), the overwhelming majority of which must be non-compliant (6.3) yet go unsanctioned (6.4), the Restriction is ineffective and pointless as a separate rule in its own right. Indeed, it is harmful because of many controllers' wasted time and costs on Mechanisms that some DPAs will not recognize as 'adequate' (5.8). Widespread disregard of the Restriction/Mechanisms (6.3.4.3) appears both to reflect and reinforce its perception as a bureaucratic rule, unrealistic in modern technological and societal environments (Ch.5).

Breaches of the Restriction are little enforced in practice, whether by data subjects (6.4.1) or DPAs (6.4.2–6.4.3). Any enforcement has focused more on any breaches of the Principles (6.4.3.1), than on the Restriction or data location per se. Similarly with any breaches of the Mechanisms (6.4.4). The Restriction and its enforcement are never likely to achieve compliance with the Principles. Even if they could, compliance with the Principles can be achieved in other, more effective, ways. I have argued that concerns regarding transborder misuse of personal data would be better addressed otherwise than by maintaining or tightening the Restriction, notably by improving cross-border DPA mutual assistance to promote compliance with and assist enforcement of national privacy/data protection laws (6.4.5). Such cooperation is developing apace, and the GDPR aims to facilitate it further. Improving DPAs' practical international cooperation seems more achievable than globally agreeing common binding standards on privacy, applicable/law jurisdiction or recognition of judgments, and makes more sense than retaining the Restriction (6.5).

8.7 ACHIEVING THE LEGISLATIVE AIMS – ACCESS AND SECURITY

The Restriction only diverts attention away from the fundamental issue, to which policymakers need to return: compliance with the core Principles. Essentially, the Principles address personal data's use, disclosure and condition (7.1.1). To control these, controllers must control *access* to personal data, particularly intelligible access; to control access to personal data, security measures (to protect confidentiality, integrity and availability, CIA) are needed, regardless of personal data location (7.1.2). Control of intelligible access protects confidentiality; control of access, even to encrypted data, protects integrity and availability (7.1.2).

Both logical and physical security are important, but they depend on the measures applied, not on data location (7.2). The efficacy of logical data segregation to protect confidentiality depends, not on data location, but on providers' systems/measures (7.3.1). Similarly, security against unauthorized remote access depends on the measures taken, not data location (7.3.2). Indeed, using multiple geographic locations positively protects integrity and availability against natural disasters (or authorities' actions) that may affect one location (3.7.7.2, 7.1.3, 7.2.2.2). Where data are unintelligible, e.g. because of encryption, the privacy risks regarding that data are much reduced, if not eliminated. Accordingly, I argued that unintelligibility should be considered in contexts *beyond* data breaches, to relax or even obviate data protection requirements – notably, the Restriction (7.2.3.2). Although *WP196* considers that encrypted (and presumably tokenized) personal data remain personal data (p.282), I argued that encrypted data should be 'personal data' only as regards those with access to *both* the encrypted data and the decryption key, i.e. those with intelligible access, rather than assuming that all (sub)providers have intelligible access. Where providers have no intelligible access to personal data, even processor agreements seem unnecessary, and knowing the data's locations (or any subproviders' identities/locations) is unnecessary to enable controllers to protect the data (7.2.3.2).

While encryption has its limitations (7.2.3.3), controllers should be encouraged to apply measures such as encryption/tokenization to the fullest extent feasible, in order to control intelligible access and prevent unauthorized use/disclosure. However, because non-experts cannot assess security measures' efficacy, the use of independent expert certifications (5.4.5) should be encouraged (5.3.4.1, 5.3.5, 5.4.5, 7.2.3.3).

The Restriction cannot prevent access to personal data. It is neither necessary nor sufficient for ensuring compliance with security measures, because physical inspection of infrastructure cannot verify *logical* security, logical security does not depend on data location, and data and logs can be viewed remotely (7.4.2.5). The Restriction cannot prevent un-authorized use/disclosure by persons authorized for intelligible access (e.g. privileged employees), including through remote access. In such situations, organizational measures are more important, e.g. limiting authorizations, imposing confidentiality obligations, contractual agree-ments, staff training, etc., but again those measures are independent of data location (7.4, 7.4.1, 7.4.2). Deletion of personal data is also important under DPD Laws, but the strength of deletion measures depends on the systems used and measures applied, not on data location (7.4.2.4).

Restricting intelligible access through technical means also helps to deter third country (indeed EEA) authorities from accessing EEA indi-viduals' personal data (7.5). Authorities may obtain access through cloud providers only if they have effective jurisdiction over providers with intelligible access (4.6, 7.5.1.1). Providers' intelligible access may be restricted through encryption etc., as already discussed. Where providers do have intelligible access, controllers should seek contractual terms forbidding providers to disclose their data except under legal compulsion – but that depends on bargaining power, not on data location (7.4.2.2– 7.4.2.3). Authorities' *effective* jurisdiction over providers may be pre-vented, in some situations, through appropriate structuring – e.g., TPB's use of cloud services in different countries, with encryption and backups (7.5.1.1), or Microsoft's trustee structure (7.4.2.3).

Confining personal data to EEA locations cannot prevent third country, indeed EEA, authorities from tapping communications links (7.5.2.1). Neither can the Restriction stop third country authorities from directly accessing EEA-located data remotely, or requiring providers to do so: EEA location alone cannot protect targeted data from remote access (7.5.2.2). However, if controllers and providers generally implement strong encryption for data, both at rest and in flight, that would help to protect confidentiality, including against interception in transit, and certainly make mass surveillance by third country or EEA authorities more difficult (7.2.3.3, 7.5.3).

8.8 RECOMMENDATIONS

As a report for Parliament noted, in this digital age surely lawmakers cannot intend to prohibit all transfers of personal data – including under personal decisions – to third countries, as 'this is undoubtedly "impractical"'; EU institutions may need to provide political guidance to DPAs and other relevant EU bodies (Chase et al. 2016: p.42). Personal data *can* be transferred while protecting privacy, if the data localization approach is abandoned. While there are some worrying moves towards deglobalization, pulling up drawbridges, physical or digital, will not solve nations' ills.

There are glimmers of hope. After *Schrems*, the WP29 called for EU–US discussions to find 'political, legal *or technical* solutions' enabling US transfers while respecting fundamental rights (WP29 2015b). Its current chair, Isabelle Falque-Pierottin (CNIL's head), reportedly said that, while 'data storage centres' in the EU might provide a short-term advantage, 'Europe cannot be a fortress. I do not much believe in regulation to keep data in Europe' (Barbière 2016). The point has been made to policymakers in the cybercrime arena that location is not 'the best way to determine jurisdiction' and 'hardly relevant in cyberspace. Data can be approached from everywhere'; alternative approaches are being discussed, including jurisdiction over providers rather than data location (Council 7323/2016), given 'loss of location' (inability to determine location, with cyber-attackers) (CoE 2016a). Vice-President Ansip pointed out that 'If individuals had more control and portability of their own data, they could choose between rival service providers … But it does depend on data being transferable between locations' (Commission 2016g). The Commission has recognized the problems with 'forcible data localization', e.g. preventing economies of scale (Commission 2016h). Even Schrems, while considering data localization the 'best solution' currently (and needed for latency reasons), thought it unappealing; avoiding US jurisdiction was 'difficult', and technical solutions probably 'the best way forward' (Baker 2016b).

Unfortunately, data localization still appears to be considered necessary for privacy; the GDPR perpetuated outdated assumptions embedded in the DPD, although the same problems arise with personal data as other data, as I have discussed at length. The ability to access data remotely, and to apply encryption or other techniques to restrict or prevent intelligible access even by those with physical access to data, means that data location, physical access, intelligible access and effective jurisdiction can no longer be conflated. It is no longer justifiable to treat data location as a proxy for intelligible access and effective jurisdiction. The focus on data location diverts attention and resources away from the true issues:

- effective jurisdiction over persons who control intelligible access to personal data – which access may be remote, and where jurisdiction may (but may *not*) be afforded by data location; and
- how conflicts may be resolved, where multiple countries have effective jurisdiction over such persons simultaneously (7.6).

All this tells us that the Restriction, and similar laws, should be abolished. We should kill the Frankenrule. Data export restrictions serve no real anticircumvention purpose. Instead, laws and regulations should centre on compliance with Principles through control of intelligible access to personal data (including via technical security measures), and accountability for personal data regardless of data location. That approach would meet the Restriction's underlying objective better, and be more technology-neutral and future-proof. It would also improve compliance by moving the spotlight back to the Principles. Resources expended on cumbersome, expensive, ineffective and unnecessary Mechanisms or data location-tracking techniques could be used to improve security instead.

That is the ideal scenario, which I hope the Commission's Art.97(1) GDPR reviews will eventually accept and adopt, at least as interpretations. However, if we must live with the Restriction, it (and other data export restrictions) should be interpreted and applied appropriately and sensibly in line with modern digital realities, involving at least the following, which I hope GDPR guidance and reviews will consider:

- clarify and consider in detail the policy objectives targeted – anticircumvention, preventing third country access, both? – and different methods available for achieving the intended objectives;
- frame 'transfer' by reference to recipients, not countries; clarify whether the issue is that the recipient is, or is not, subject to particular countries' jurisdictions;
- distinguish between 'transfer' and 'transmission': 'transfer' must require intelligible access; more generally, exclude those without intelligible access from data protection law obligations, such as

through clearly extending the E-Commerce Directive 2000/31/EC's defences for neutral intermediaries to data protection obligations;

- regarding processor use, abolish the 'instructions' requirement and prescriptive contractual requirements; instead, prohibit processors from using or disclosing personal data unless authorized by their controllers and permitted by law;
- define and exclude transit explicitly;
- the true issue is the *risk* of intelligible access by undesired persons (including non-EEA controllers; third country authorities; EEA authorities); location is only one factor, so provide guidance on risk assessment, including country risk; allow and encourage self-assessment and implementation of appropriate safeguards based on risks in particular contexts, rather than relying on 'adequate' countries' laws;
- for practicability, promulgate and recognize 'block' Mechanisms such as standard contract clauses or encryption to certain stated standards, not as the only ways to permit transfers, or as definitively 'adequate' protections or safeguards, but as 'an element' demonstrating controllers' and processors' compliance, absent contrary evidence;
- use all types of tools available; take a technologically neutral approach that encourages appropriate technical measures, not just contracts/laws, and focuses on organizational accountability and the efficacy of measures implemented rather than whether they are legal, organizational and/or technical – in particular, recognize both technical measures' effectiveness to restrict intelligible access, and contractual measures' ability to restrict processing of 'deleted' data;
- do not deprecate but rather encourage use of technical protections like strong encryption for data at rest and in transit, which will also assist against rapidly increasing threats of cybercrime; promote the development of third party expert certifications (not just on encryption, but e.g. secure deletion of digital data) to assist controllers, processors and DPAs, with authoritative bodies like ENISA specifying the required minimum standards; and
- (the most difficult issues, requiring international political agreement) seek to address the 'conflicting jurisdictions' problem, where organizations may be subject to multiple jurisdictions, to remedy current inconsistencies and contradictions and to keep improving cross-border DPA cooperation; separately, agree proper limits on authorities' collection and use of personal data, of their own as well as other countries' citizens, and effective independent oversight, transparency and remedies regarding such collection and use.

Nowadays, the Restriction is seemingly being invoked to serve policy objectives other than anticircumvention, e.g. as a bargaining chip in negotiations with third countries. But restricting data location cannot resolve conflicts between jurisdictions, or prevent mass surveillance. A bad law should never be retained to deal with problems that only international agreement can resolve.

Appendix: comparative table of key DPD and GDPR international transfers provisions

DPD	GDPR
Basic Restriction	
CHAPTER IV Transfers of personal data to third countries	CHAPTER V Transfers of personal data to third countries or international organisations
Art.25 Principles 1. The Member States shall provide that the transfer to a third country of personal data which are undergoing processing or are intended for processing after transfer may take place only if, without prejudice to compliance with the national provisions adopted pursuant to the other provisions of this Directive, the third country in question ensures an adequate level of protection.	Art.44 General principle for transfers Any transfer of personal data which are undergoing processing or are intended for processing after transfer to a third country *or to an international organisation* shall take place only if, subject to the other provisions of this Regulation, the conditions laid down in this Chapter are complied with *by the controller and processor, including for onward transfers* of personal data from the third country or an international organisation to another third country or to another international organisation. All provisions in this Chapter shall be applied in order to ensure that the level of protection of natural persons guaranteed by this Regulation is not undermined.
	Art.4 Definitions Art.4(26) 'international organisation' means an organisation and its subordinate bodies governed by public international law, or any other body which is set up by, or on the basis of, an agreement between two or more countries.

DPD	GDPR
	Rec.101 Flows of personal data to and from countries outside the Union and international organisations are necessary for the expansion of international trade and international cooperation. The increase in such flows has raised new challenges and concerns with regard to the protection of personal data. However, when personal data are transferred from the Union to controllers, processors or other recipients in third countries or to international organisations, the level of protection of natural persons ensured in the Union by this Regulation should not be undermined, including in cases of onward transfers of personal data from the third country or international organisation to controllers, processors in the same or another third country or international organisation. In any event, transfers to third countries and international organisations may only be carried out in full compliance with this Regulation. A transfer could take place only if, subject to the other provisions of this Regulation, the conditions laid down in the provisions of this Regulation relating to the transfer of personal data to third countries or international organisations are complied with by the controller or processor.
Adequate protection	
	Art.45 Transfers on the basis of an adequacy decision
Art.25(6) The Commission may find, in accordance with the procedure referred to in Article 31(2), that a third country ensures an adequate level of protection within the meaning of paragraph 2 of this Article, by reason of its domestic law or of the international commitments it has entered into, particularly upon conclusion of the negotiations referred to in paragraph 5, for the protection of the private lives and basic freedoms and rights of individuals. Member States shall take the measures necessary to comply with the Commission's decision	Art.45(1) A transfer of personal data to a third country or an international organisation may take place where the Commission has decided that the third country, *a territory or one or more specified sectors* within that third country, *or the international organisation* in question ensures an adequate level of protection. *Such a transfer shall not require any specific authorisation.*

DPD	GDPR
Art.25(2) The adequacy of the level of protection afforded by a third country shall be assessed *in the light of all the circumstances* surrounding a data transfer operation or set of data transfer operations; particular consideration shall be given to	Art.45(2) When assessing the adequacy of the level of protection, the Commission shall, *in particular*, take account of the following elements:
the *nature of the data, the purpose and duration of the proposed processing operation or operations,* the *country of origin and country of final destination,*	
the rules of law, *both general and sectoral*, in force in the third country in question and	(a) the rule of law, *respect for human rights and fundamental freedoms*, relevant legislation, both general and sectoral, including concerning public security, defence, national security and criminal law and the *access of public authorities to personal data*, as well as the *implementation* of such legislation, *data protection rules,*
the professional rules and security measures which are complied with in that country.	professional rules and security measures,
	including *rules for the onward transfer* of personal data to another third country or international organisation which are complied with in that country or international organisation, *case-law*, as well as *effective and enforceable data subject rights and effective administrative and judicial redress* for the data subjects whose personal data are being transferred;
	(b) the existence and effective functioning of one or more *independent supervisory authorities* in the third country or to which an international organisation is subject, with responsibility for ensuring and enforcing compliance with the data protection rules, including adequate enforcement powers, for assisting and advising the data subjects in exercising their rights and for cooperation with the supervisory authorities of the Member States; and
[International commitments – see Art.25(6)]	(c) the international commitments the third country or international organisation concerned has entered into, or other obligations arising from legally binding conventions or instruments as well as from its participation in multilateral or regional systems, in particular in relation to the protection of personal data.

DPD	GDPR
	Art.45(3) The Commission, after assessing the adequacy of the level of protection, may decide, by means of implementing act, that a third country, a territory or one or more specified sectors within a third country, or an international organisation ensures an adequate level of protection within the meaning of paragraph 2 of this Article. The implementing act *shall provide for a mechanism for a periodic review, at least every four years, which shall take into account all relevant developments in the third country or international organisation.* The implementing act shall *specify its territorial and sectoral application* and, where applicable, *identify the supervisory authority or authorities referred to in point (b) of paragraph 2* of this Article. The implementing act shall be adopted in accordance with the *examination procedure referred to in Article 93(2).*
	Art.45(4) The Commission shall, on an ongoing basis, *monitor developments in third countries and international organisations that could affect the functioning* of decisions adopted pursuant to paragraph 3 of this Article *and decisions adopted on the basis of Article 25(6) of Directive 95/46/EC.*
Art.25(3) The Member States and the Commission shall inform each other of cases where they consider that a third country does not ensure an adequate level of protection within the meaning of paragraph 2. Art.25(4) Where the Commission finds, under the procedure provided for in Article 31(2), that a third country does not ensure an adequate level of protection within the meaning of paragraph 2 of this Article, Member States shall take the measures necessary to prevent any transfer of data of the same type to the third country in question.	Art.45(5) The Commission *shall,* where available information reveals, in particular following the review referred to in paragraph 3 of this Article, that a third country, a territory or one or more specified sectors within a third country, or an international organisation no longer ensures an adequate level of protection within the meaning of paragraph 2 of this Article, *to the extent necessary, repeal, amend or suspend the decision* referred to in paragraph 3 of this Article by means of implementing acts *without retro-active effect.* Those implementing acts shall be adopted in accordance with the examination procedure referred to in Article 93(2). On *duly justified imperative grounds of urgency*, the Commission shall adopt *immediately applicable implementing acts* in accordance with the procedure referred to in *Article 93(3).*
Art.25(5) At the appropriate time, the Commission shall enter into negotiations with a view to remedying the situation resulting from the finding made pursuant to paragraph 4.	Art.45(6) The Commission shall enter into consultations with the third country or international organisation with a view to remedying the situation giving rise to the decision made pursuant to paragraph 5. Art.45(7) A decision pursuant to paragraph 5 of this Article is *without prejudice* to transfers of personal data to the third country, a territory or one or more specified sectors within that third country, or the international organisation in question pursuant to *Articles 46 to 49.*

DPD	GDPR
	Art.45(8) The Commission shall *publish in the Official Journal* of the European Union and on its *website* a list of the third countries, territories and specified sectors within a third country and international organisations for which it has decided that an adequate level of protection *is or is no longer* ensured.
	Art.45(9) Decisions adopted by the Commission on the basis of Article 25(6) of Directive 95/46/EC shall remain in force until amended, replaced or repealed by a Commission Decision adopted in accordance with paragraph 3 or 5 of this Article.
	Art.49(5) In the absence of an adequacy decision, Union or Member State law may, for *important reasons of public interest, expressly set limits* to the transfer of *specific categories* of personal data to a third country or an international organisation. Member States shall notify such provisions to the Commission.
	Rec.103 The Commission may decide with effect for the entire Union that a third country, a territory or specified sector within a third country, or an international organisation, offers an adequate level of data protection, thus providing legal certainty and uniformity throughout the Union as regards the third country or international organisation which is considered to provide such level of protection. In such cases, transfers of personal data to that third country or international organisation may take place without the need to obtain any further authorisation. The Commission may also decide, having given notice and a full statement setting out the reasons to the third country or international organisation, to revoke such a decision.

DPD	GDPR
	Rec.104 In line with the fundamental values on which the Union is founded, in particular the protection of human rights, the Commission should, in its assessment of the third country, or of a territory or specified sector within a third country, take into account how a particular third country respects the rule of law, access to justice as well as international human rights norms and standards and its general and sectoral law, including legislation concerning public security, defence and national security as well as public order and criminal law. The adoption of an adequacy decision with regard to a territory or a specified sector in a third country should take into account clear and objective criteria, such as specific processing activities and the scope of applicable legal standards and legislation in force in the third country. The third country should offer guarantees ensuring an adequate level of protection essentially equivalent to that ensured within the Union, in particular where personal data are processed in one or several specific sectors. In particular, the third country should ensure effective independent data protection supervision and should provide for cooperation mechanisms with the Member States' data protection authorities, and the data subjects should be provided with effective and enforceable rights and effective administrative and judicial redress.
	Rec.105 Apart from the international commitments the third country or international organisation has entered into, the Commission should take account of obligations arising from the third country's or international organisation's participation in multilateral or regional systems in particular in relation to the protection of personal data, as well as the implementation of such obligations. In particular, the third country's accession to the Council of Europe Convention of 28 January 1981 for the Protection of Individuals with regard to the Automatic Processing of Personal Data and its Additional Protocol should be taken into account. The Commission should consult the Board when assessing the level of protection in third countries or international organisations.

DPD	GDPR
	Rec. 106 The Commission should monitor the functioning of decisions on the level of protection in a third country, a territory or specified sector within a third country, or an international organisation, and monitor the functioning of decisions adopted on the basis of Article 25(6) or Article 26(4) of Directive 95/46/EC. In its adequacy decisions, the Commission should provide for a periodic review mechanism of their functioning. That periodic review should be conducted in consultation with the third country or international organisation in question and take into account all relevant developments in the third country or international organisation. For the purposes of monitoring and of carrying out the periodic reviews, the Commission should take into consideration the views and findings of the European Parliament and of the Council as well as of other relevant bodies and sources. The Commission should evaluate, within a reasonable time, the functioning of the latter decisions and report any relevant findings to the Committee within the meaning of Regulation (EU) No 182/2011 of the European Parliament and of the Council (12) as established under this Regulation, to the European Parliament and to the Council.
	Rec. 107 The Commission may recognise that a third country, a territory or a specified sector within a third country, or an international organisation no longer ensures an adequate level of data protection. Consequently the transfer of personal data to that third country or international organisation should be prohibited, unless the requirements in this Regulation relating to transfers subject to appropriate safeguards, including binding corporate rules, and derogations for specific situations are fulfilled. In that case, provision should be made for consultations between the Commission and such third countries or international organisations. The Commission should, in a timely manner, inform the third country or international organisation of the reasons and enter into consultations with it in order to remedy the situation.

DPD	GDPR
	Safeguards
Art.26(2) Without prejudice to paragraph 1, *a Member State may authorize* a transfer or a set of transfers of personal data to a third country which does not ensure an adequate level of protection within the meaning of Article 25(2), where the *controller* adduces *adequate safeguards* with respect to the protection of the privacy and fundamental rights and freedoms of individuals and as regards the exercise of the corresponding rights; such safeguards may in particular result from *appropriate contractual clauses*. Art.26(3) The Member State shall inform the Commission and the other Member States of the authorizations it grants pursuant to paragraph 2. If a Member State or the Commission objects on justified grounds involving the protection of the privacy and fundamental rights and freedoms of individuals, the Commission shall take appropriate measures in accordance with the procedure laid down in Article 31(2). Member States shall take the necessary measures to comply with the Commission's decision.	Art.46 Transfers subject to appropriate safeguards Art.46(1) In the absence of a decision pursuant to Article 45(3), a controller or processor may transfer personal data to a third country or an international organisation only if the *controller or processor has provided appropriate safeguards*, and on condition that *enforceable data subject rights and effective legal remedies for data subjects are available*. Art.46(2) The appropriate safeguards referred to in paragraph 1 may be provided for, *without requiring any specific authorisation from a supervisory authority*, by:
	(a) a legally binding and enforceable instrument between public authorities or bodies;
	(b) binding corporate rules in accordance with Article 47;

DPD	GDPR
Art.26(4) Where the Commission decides, in accordance with the procedure referred to in Article 31(2), that certain standard contractual clauses offer sufficient safeguards as required by paragraph 2, Member States shall take the necessary measures to comply with the Commission's decision.	(c) standard data protection clauses adopted by the Commission in accordance with the *examination procedure referred to in Article 93(2)*;
	(d) standard data protection clauses adopted by a supervisory authority and approved by the Commission pursuant to the *examination procedure referred to in Article 93(2)*;
	(e) an approved code of conduct pursuant to Article 40 together with *binding and enforceable commitments of the controller or processor in the third country* to apply the appropriate safeguards, including as regards data subjects' rights; or
	(f) an approved certification mechanism pursuant to Article 42 together with *binding and enforceable commitments of the controller or processor* in the third country to apply the appropriate safeguards, including as regards data subjects' rights.
[Also see Art.26(2) – Member State authorisation.]	Art.46(3) Subject to the *authorisation from the competent supervisory authority*, the appropriate safeguards referred to in paragraph 1 may also be provided for, in particular, by: (a) contractual clauses between the controller or processor and the controller, processor or the recipient of the personal data in the third country or international organisation; or (b) provisions to be inserted into administrative arrangements between public authorities or bodies which include enforceable and effective data subject rights. Art.46(4) The supervisory authority shall apply the *consistency mechanism* referred to in Article 63 in the cases referred to in paragraph 3 of this Article.
	Art.46(5) Authorisations by a Member State or supervisory authority on the basis of Article 26(2) of Directive 95/46/EC shall remain valid until amended, replaced or repealed, if necessary, by that supervisory authority. Decisions adopted by the Commission on the basis of Article 26(4) of Directive 95/46/EC shall remain in force until amended, replaced or repealed, if necessary, by a Commission Decision adopted in accordance with paragraph 2 of this Article.

DPD	GDPR
	Rec.108 In the absence of an adequacy decision, the controller or processor should take measures to compensate for the lack of data protection in a third country by way of appropriate safeguards for the data subject. Such appropriate safeguards may consist of making use of binding corporate rules, standard data protection clauses adopted by the Commission, standard data protection clauses adopted by a supervisory authority or contractual clauses authorised by a supervisory authority. Those safeguards should ensure compliance with data protection requirements and the rights of the data subjects appropriate to processing within the Union, including the availability of enforceable data subject rights and of effective legal remedies, including to obtain effective administrative or judicial redress and to claim compensation, in the Union or in a third country. They should relate in particular to compliance with the general principles relating to personal data processing, the principles of data protection by design and by default. Transfers may also be carried out by public authorities or bodies with public authorities or bodies in third countries or with international organisations with corresponding duties or functions, including on the basis of provisions to be inserted into administrative arrangements, such as a memorandum of understanding, providing for enforceable and effective rights for data subjects. Authorisation by the competent supervisory authority should be obtained when the safeguards are provided for in administrative arrangements that are not legally binding.
	Rec.109 The possibility for the controller or processor to use standard data-protection clauses adopted by the Commission or by a supervisory authority should prevent controllers or processors neither from including the standard data-protection clauses in a wider contract, such as a contract between the processor and another processor, nor from adding other clauses or additional safeguards provided that they do not contradict, directly or indirectly, the standard contractual clauses adopted by the Commission or by a supervisory authority or prejudice the fundamental rights or freedoms of the data subjects. Controllers and processors should be encouraged to provide additional safeguards via contractual commitments that supplement standard protection clauses.

DPD	GDPR
	Safeguards – BCRs
	Art.4 Definitions
	Art.4(18) 'enterprise' means a natural or legal person engaged in an economic activity, irrespective of its legal form, including partnerships or associations regularly engaged in an economic activity;
	Art.4(19) 'group of undertakings' means a controlling undertaking and its controlled undertakings;
	Art.4(20) 'binding corporate rules' means personal data protection policies which are adhered to by a controller or processor established on the territory of a Member State for transfers or a set of transfers of personal data to a controller or processor in one or more third countries within a group of undertakings, or group of enterprises engaged in a joint economic activity;
No provision in the DPD – only various WP29 opinions particularly *WP153*; *WP195*. [*WP153*; *WP195*, para.1]	Art.47 Binding corporate rules Art.47(1) The competent supervisory authority *shall* approve binding corporate rules in accordance with the consistency mechanism set out in Article 63, provided that they: (a) are legally binding and apply to and are enforced by every member concerned of the group of undertakings, *or group of enterprises engaged in a joint economic activity*, including their employees; (b) expressly confer enforceable rights on data subjects with regard to the processing of their personal data; and (c) fulfil the requirements laid down in paragraph 2.
	Art.47(2) The binding corporate rules referred to in paragraph 1 shall specify at least:
	(a) the structure and contact details of the group of undertakings, *or group of enterprises engaged in a joint economic activity* and of each of its members;
[*WP153*; *WP195*, para.4 general description of the transfers ... more precisely on: i) the nature of the data transferred ii) the purposes of the transfer/ processing iii) the data importers/exporters in the EU and outside of the EU ... (nature of data, type of data subjects, countries)]	(b) the data transfers or set of transfers, including the categories of personal data, the type of processing and its purposes, the type of data subjects affected and the identification of the third country or countries in question;
[*WP153*; *WP195*, para.1]	(c) their legally binding nature, both internally and externally;

DPD	GDPR
[*WP153*; *WP195*, para.6]	(d) the application of the general data protection principles, in particular purpose limitation, *data minimisation, limited storage periods*, data quality, *data protection by design and by default, legal basis for processing*, processing of *special categories* of personal data, measures to ensure *data security*, and the requirements in respect of *onward transfers* to bodies not bound by the binding corporate rules;
[*WP153*, paras.1, 6]	(e) the rights of data subjects in regard to processing and the means to exercise those rights, including the right not to be subject to decisions based solely on *automated processing*, including profiling in accordance with Article 22, the right to lodge a complaint with the competent supervisory authority and before the competent courts of the Member States in accordance with Article 79, and to obtain redress and, where appropriate, *compensation* for a breach of the binding corporate rules;
	(f) the acceptance by the controller or processor *established on the territory of a Member State of liability* for any breaches of the binding corporate rules by any member concerned not established in the Union; the controller or the processor shall be exempt from that liability, in whole or in part, *only if it proves that that member is not responsible* for the event giving rise to the damage;
[*WP153*; *WP195*, paras.1, 5]	(g) how the information on the binding corporate rules, in particular on the provisions referred to in points (d), (e) and (f) of this paragraph is provided to the data subjects in addition to Articles 13 and 14;
[*WP153*; *WP195*, para.2.4]	(h) the tasks of any data protection officer designated in accordance with Article 37 or any other person or entity in charge of the monitoring compliance with the binding corporate rules within the group of undertakings, or group of enterprises engaged in a joint economic activity, as well as monitoring training and complaint-handling;
[*WP153*; *WP195*, para.2]	(i) the complaint procedures;
[*WP153*; *WP195*, para.2 – network of privacy officers, audit programme]	(j) the mechanisms within the group of undertakings, or group of enterprises engaged in a joint economic activity *for ensuring the verification of compliance* with the binding corporate rules. Such mechanisms shall include data protection audits and methods for ensuring corrective actions to protect the rights of the data subject. Results of such verification should be communicated to the person or entity referred to in point (h) and to the board of the controlling undertaking of a group of undertakings, or of the group of enterprises engaged in a joint economic activity, and should be available upon request to the competent supervisory authority;

DPD	GDPR
[*WP153*; *WP195*, para.5]	(k) the mechanisms for reporting and recording changes to the rules and reporting those changes to the supervisory authority;
[*WP153*; *WP195*, paras.3, 2.3]	(l) the cooperation mechanism with the supervisory authority to ensure compliance by any member of the group of undertakings, or group of enterprises engaged in a joint economic activity, in particular by making available to the supervisory authority the results of verifications of the measures referred to in point (j);
[*WP153*; *WP195*, para.6.3 – report to DPO if a BCR group member has reason to believe that the legislation applicable to him [it] prevents the company from fulfilling its obligations under the BCRs [controller only – and has substantial effect on the guarantees provided by the rules]/[processor only – instructions from the controller]. Processor – if law enforcement request received, inform DPA for controller and BCR – see *WP228*.	(m) the mechanisms for reporting to the competent supervisory authority any *legal requirements* to which a member of the group of undertakings, or group of enterprises engaged in a joint economic activity is subject in a third country which are *likely to have a substantial adverse effect* on the guarantees provided by the binding corporate rules; and
[*WP153*; *WP195*, para.2.1]	(n) the appropriate data protection training to personnel having permanent or regular access to personal data.
	Art.47(3) The Commission may specify the format and procedures *for the exchange of information* between controllers, processors and supervisory authorities for binding corporate rules within the meaning of this Article. Those implementing acts shall be adopted in accordance with the *examination procedure* set out in Article 93(2).
	Rec.110 A group of undertakings, or a group of enterprises engaged in a joint economic activity, should be able to make use of approved binding corporate rules for its international transfers from the Union to organisations within the same group of undertakings, or group of enterprises engaged in a joint economic activity, provided that such corporate rules include all essential principles and enforceable rights to ensure appropriate safeguards for transfers or categories of transfers of personal data.

DPD	GDPR
Derogations	
Art.26 Derogations	Art.49 Derogations for specific situations
Art.26(1) By way of derogation from Article 25 and save where otherwise provided by domestic law governing particular cases, Member States shall provide that a transfer or a set of transfers of personal data to a third country which does not ensure an adequate level of protection within the meaning of Article 25(2) may take place on condition that:	Art.49(1) In the absence of an adequacy decision pursuant to Article 45(3), or of appropriate safeguards pursuant to Article 46, including binding corporate rules, a transfer or a set of transfers of personal data to a third country or an international organisation shall take place only on one of the following conditions:
(a) the data subject has given his consent unambiguously to the proposed transfer; or	(a) the data subject has *explicitly* consented to the proposed transfer, *after having been informed of the possible risks of such transfers for the data subject due to the absence of an adequacy decision and appropriate safeguards*; Art.49(3) Points (a), (b) and (c) of the first subparagraph of paragraph 1 and the second subparagraph thereof shall not apply to activities carried out by public authorities in the exercise of their public powers.
(b) the transfer is necessary for the performance of a contract between the data subject and the controller or the implementation of precontractual measures taken in response to the data subject's request; or	(b) the transfer is necessary for the performance of a contract between the data subject and the controller or the implementation of pre-contractual measures taken at the data subject's request; [Art.49(3) Points (a), (b) and (c) of the first subparagraph of paragraph 1 and the second subparagraph thereof shall not apply to activities carried out by public authorities in the exercise of their public powers.]
(c) the transfer is necessary for the conclusion or performance of a contract concluded in the interest of the data subject between the controller and a third party; or	(c) the transfer is necessary for the conclusion or performance of a contract concluded in the interest of the data subject between the controller and *another natural or legal person*; [Art.49(3) Points (a), (b) and (c) of the first subparagraph of paragraph 1 and the second subparagraph thereof shall *not* apply to activities carried out by public authorities in the exercise of their public powers.]
(d) the transfer is necessary *or legally required on important public interest grounds*,	(d) the transfer is necessary for *important reasons of public interest*; [Art.49(4) The public interest referred to in point (d) of the first subparagraph of paragraph 1 shall be *recognised in Union law or in the law of the Member State to which the controller is subject*.]

DPD	GDPR
[(d) cont.] or for the establishment, exercise or defence of legal claims; or	(e) the transfer is necessary for the establishment, exercise or defence of legal claims;
(e) the transfer is necessary in order to protect the vital interests of the data subject; or	(f) the transfer is necessary in order to protect the vital interests of the data subject *or of other persons*, where the *data subject is physically or legally incapable of giving consent*;
(f) the transfer is made from a register which according to laws or regulations is intended to provide information to the public and which is open to consultation either by the public in general or by any person who can demonstrate legitimate interest, to the extent that the conditions laid down in law for consultation are fulfilled in the particular case.	(g) the transfer is made from a register which according to *Union or Member State law* is intended to provide information to the public and which is open to consultation either by the public in general or by any person who can *demonstrate* a legitimate interest, *but only* to the extent that the conditions laid down *by Union or Member State law for consultation* are fulfilled in the particular case. [Art.49(2) A transfer pursuant to point (g) of the first subparagraph of paragraph 1 *shall not involve the entirety of the personal data or entire categories of the personal data contained in the register*. Where the register is intended for consultation by persons having a *legitimate interest*, the transfer shall be made *only at the request of those persons or if they are to be the recipients*.]
	[Art.49(1) second sub-paragraph Where a transfer could not be based on a provision in Article 45 or 46, including the provisions on binding corporate rules, and none of the derogations for a specific situation referred to in the first subparagraph of this paragraph is applicable, a transfer to a third country or an international organisation may take place only if the transfer is not repetitive, concerns only a limited number of data subjects, is necessary for the purposes of *compelling legitimate interests pursued by the controller* which are not overridden by the interests or rights and freedoms of the data subject, and the controller has assessed all the circumstances surrounding the data transfer and has on the basis of that assessment provided suitable safeguards with regard to the protection of personal data. The controller shall inform the supervisory authority of the transfer. The controller shall, in addition to providing the information referred to in Articles 13 and 14, inform the data subject of the transfer *and on the compelling legitimate interests pursued*.] Art.49(6) The controller or processor shall *document the assessment as well as the suitable safeguards* referred to in the *second subparagraph* of paragraph 1 of this Article in the records referred to in Article 30. Art.49(3) Points (a), (b) and (c) of the first subparagraph of paragraph 1 and the *second subparagraph* thereof shall not apply to activities carried out by public authorities in the exercise of their public powers.

DPD	GDPR
	Rec.111 Provisions should be made for the possibility for transfers in certain circumstances where the data subject has given his or her explicit consent, where the transfer is occasional and necessary in relation to a contract or a legal claim, regardless of whether in a judicial procedure or whether in an administrative or any out-of-court procedure, including procedures before regulatory bodies. Provision should also be made for the possibility for transfers where important grounds of public interest laid down by Union or Member State law so require or where the transfer is made from a register established by law and intended for consultation by the public or persons having a legitimate interest. In the latter case, such a transfer should not involve the entirety of the personal data or entire categories of the data contained in the register and, when the register is intended for consultation by persons having a legitimate interest, the transfer should be made only at the request of those persons or, if they are to be the recipients, taking into full account the interests and fundamental rights of the data subject.
	Rec.112 Those derogations should in particular apply to data transfers required and necessary for important reasons of public interest, for example in cases of international data exchange between competition authorities, tax or customs administrations, between financial supervisory authorities, between services competent for social security matters, or for public health, for example in the case of contact tracing for contagious diseases or in order to reduce and/or eliminate doping in sport. A transfer of personal data should also be regarded as lawful where it is necessary to protect an interest which is essential for the data subject's or another person's vital interests, including physical integrity or life, if the data subject is incapable of giving consent. In the absence of an adequacy decision, Union or Member State law may, for important reasons of public interest, expressly set limits to the transfer of specific categories of data to a third country or an international organisation. Member States should notify such provisions to the Commission. Any transfer to an international humanitarian organisation of personal data of a data subject who is physically or legally incapable of giving consent, with a view to accomplishing a task incumbent under the Geneva Conventions or to complying with international humanitarian law applicable in armed conflicts, could be considered to be necessary for an important reason of public interest or because it is in the vital interest of the data subject.

DPD	GDPR
	Rec.113 Transfers which can be qualified as not repetitive and that only concern a limited number of data subjects, could also be possible for the purposes of the compelling legitimate interests pursued by the controller, when those interests are not overridden by the interests or rights and freedoms of the data subject and when the controller has assessed all the circumstances surrounding the data transfer. The controller should give particular consideration to the nature of the personal data, the purpose and duration of the proposed processing operation or operations, as well as the situation in the country of origin, the third country and the country of final destination, and should provide suitable safeguards to protect fundamental rights and freedoms of natural persons with regard to the processing of their personal data. Such transfers should be possible only in residual cases where none of the other grounds for transfer are applicable. For scientific or historical research purposes or statistical purposes, the legitimate expectations of society for an increase of knowledge should be taken into consideration. The controller should inform the supervisory authority and the data subject about the transfer.
	Rec.114 In any case, where the Commission has taken no decision on the adequate level of data protection in a third country, the controller or processor should make use of solutions that provide data subjects with enforceable and effective rights as regards the processing of their data in the Union once those data have been transferred so that they will continue to benefit from fundamental rights and safeguards.
Comitology procedure	
Art.31	Art.93 Committee procedure
Art.31(1) The Commission shall be assisted by a committee.	Art.93(1) The Commission shall be assisted by a committee. That committee shall be a committee within the meaning of Regulation (EU) No 182/2011.
Art.31(2) Where reference is made to this Article, Articles 4 and 7 of Decision 1999/468/EC shall apply, having regard to the provisions of Article 8 thereof. The period laid down in Article 4(3) of Decision 1999/468/EC shall be set at three months.	Art.93(2) Where reference is made to this paragraph, Article 5 of Regulation (EU) No 182/2011 shall apply.

DPD	GDPR
	'Anti-FISA' provision
	Art.48 Transfers or disclosures not authorised by Union law Any judgment of a court or tribunal and any decision of an administrative authority of a third country requiring a controller or processor *to transfer or disclose* personal data may only be recognised or enforceable in any manner if based on an international agreement, such as a mutual legal assistance treaty, in force between the requesting third country and the Union or a Member State, *without prejudice to other grounds for transfer* pursuant to this Chapter.
	Rec.115 Some third countries adopt laws, regulations and other legal acts which purport to directly regulate the processing activities of natural and legal persons under the jurisdiction of the Member States. This may include judgments of courts or tribunals or decisions of administrative authorities in third countries requiring a controller or processor to transfer or disclose personal data, and which are not based on an international agreement, such as a mutual legal assistance treaty, in force between the requesting third country and the Union or a Member State. The extraterritorial application of those laws, regulations and other legal acts may be in breach of international law and may impede the attainment of the protection of natural persons ensured in the Union by this Regulation. Transfers should only be allowed where the conditions of this Regulation for a transfer to third countries are met. This may be the case, inter alia, where disclosure is necessary for an important ground of public interest recognised in Union or Member State law to which the controller is subject.
	Art.96 Relationship with previously concluded Agreements International agreements involving the transfer of personal data to third countries or international organisations which were concluded by Member States prior to 24 May 2016, and which comply with Union law as applicable prior to that date, shall remain in force until amended, replaced or revoked.

DPD	GDPR
	Rec.102 This Regulation is without prejudice to international agreements concluded between the Union and third countries regulating the transfer of personal data including appropriate safeguards for the data subjects. Member States may conclude international agreements which involve the transfer of personal data to third countries or international organisations, as far as such agreements do not affect this Regulation or any other provisions of Union law and include an appropriate level of protection for the fundamental rights of the data subjects.
Fines/DPA powers/tasks	
Art.24 Sanctions The Member States shall adopt suitable measures to ensure the full implementation of the provisions of this Directive and shall in particular lay down the sanctions to be imposed in case of infringement of the provisions adopted pursuant to this Directive.	Art.83 General conditions for imposing administrative fines Art.83(5) Infringements of the following provisions shall, in accordance with paragraph 2, be subject to administrative fines up to 20 000 000 EUR, or in the case of an undertaking, up to 4 % of the total worldwide annual turnover of the preceding financial year, whichever is higher: … (c) the transfers of personal data to a recipient in a third country or an international organisation pursuant to Articles 44 to 49; … (e) non-compliance with an order or a temporary or definitive limitation on processing or the suspension of data flows by the supervisory authority pursuant to Article 58(2) or failure to provide access in violation of Article 58(1).
	Art.57 Tasks Art.57(1) Without prejudice to other tasks set out under this Regulation, each supervisory authority shall on its territory: … (j) adopt standard contractual clauses referred to in Article 28(8) and in point (d) of Article 46(2); … (r) authorise contractual clauses and provisions referred to in Article 46(3); (s) approve binding corporate rules pursuant to Article 47; …

DPD	GDPR
	Art.58 Powers Art.58(2) Each supervisory authority shall have all of the following corrective powers: … (i) to impose an administrative fine pursuant to Article 83, in addition to, or instead of measures referred to in this paragraph, depending on the circumstances of each individual case; (j) to order the suspension of data flows to a recipient in a third country or to an international organisation. Art.58(3) Each supervisory authority shall have all of the following authorisation and advisory powers: … (g) to adopt standard data protection clauses referred to in Article 28(8) and in point (d) of Article 46(2); (h) to authorise contractual clauses referred to in point (a) of Article 46(3); (i) to authorise administrative arrangements referred to in point (b) of Article 46(3); (j) to approve binding corporate rules pursuant to Article 47.
	Art.64 Opinion of the Board Art.64(1) The Board shall issue an opinion where a competent supervisory authority intends to adopt any of the measures below. To that end, the competent supervisory authority shall communicate the draft decision to the Board, when it: … (d) aims to determine standard data protection clauses referred to in point (d) of Article 46(2) and in Article 28(8); (e) aims to authorise contractual clauses referred to in point (a) of Article 46(3); or (f) aims to approve binding corporate rules within the meaning of Article 47.

DPD	GDPR
	Art.70 Tasks of the Board Art.70(1) The Board shall ensure the consistent application of this Regulation. To that end, the Board shall, on its own initiative or, where relevant, at the request of the Commission, in particular: … (e) examine, on its own initiative, on request of one of its members or on request of the Commission, any question covering the application of this Regulation and issue guidelines, recommendations and best practices in order to encourage consistent application of this Regulation; … (i) issue guidelines, recommendations and best practices in accordance with point (e) of this paragraph for the purpose of further specifying the criteria and requirements for personal data transfers based on binding corporate rules adhered to by controllers and binding corporate rules adhered to by processors and on further necessary requirements to ensure the protection of personal data of the data subjects concerned referred to in Article 47; (j) issue guidelines, recommendations and best practices in accordance with point (e) of this paragraph for the purpose of further specifying the criteria and requirements for the personal data transfers on the basis of Article 49(1) [derogations]; … (s) provide the Commission with an opinion for the assessment of the adequacy of the level of protection in a third country or international organisation, including for the assessment whether a third country, a territory or one or more specified sectors within that third country, or an international organisation no longer ensures an adequate level of protection. To that end, the Commission shall provide the Board with all necessary documentation, including correspondence with the government of the third country, with regard to that third country, territory or specified sector, or with the international organisation… (v) promote common training programmes and facilitate personnel exchanges between the supervisory authorities and, where appropriate, with the supervisory authorities of third countries or with international organisations;…
	Art.71 Reports Art.71(1) The Board shall draw up an annual report regarding the protection of natural persons with regard to processing in the Union *and, where relevant, in third countries and international organisations*. The report shall be made public and be transmitted to the European Parliament, to the Council and to the Commission.

DPD	GDPR
	Controller and processor
	Art.28 Processor Art.28(3) Processing by a processor shall be governed by a contract or other legal act under Union or Member State law, that is binding on the processor with regard to the controller and that sets out the subject-matter and duration of the processing, the nature and purpose of the processing, the type of personal data and categories of data subjects and the obligations and rights of the controller. That contract or other legal act shall stipulate, in particular, that the processor: (a) processes the personal data only on documented instructions from the controller, *including with regard to transfers of personal data to a third country or an international organisation*, unless required to do so by Union or Member State law to which the processor is subject; in such a case, the processor shall inform the controller of that legal requirement before processing, unless that law prohibits such information on important grounds of public interest; ... Art.30 Records of processing activities Art.30(1) Each controller and, where applicable, the controller's representative, shall maintain a record of processing activities under its responsibility. That record shall contain all of the following information: ... (d) the categories of recipients to whom the personal data have been or will be disclosed including recipients in third countries or international organisations; ... (e) where applicable, transfers of personal data to a third country or an international organisation, including the identification of that third country or international organisation and, in the case of transfers referred to in the second subparagraph of Article 49(1) [compelling legitimate interests], the documentation of suitable safeguards; ... Art.30(2) Each processor and, where applicable, the processor's representative shall maintain a record of all categories of processing activities carried out on behalf of a controller, containing: ... (c) where applicable, transfers of personal data to a third country or an international organisation, including the identification of that third country or international organisation and, in the case of transfers referred to in the second subparagraph of Article 49(1) [compelling legitimate interests], the documentation of suitable safeguards; ...

DPD	GDPR
	Codes of conduct and certifications
	Art.40 Codes of conduct
	Art.40(2) Associations and other bodies representing categories of controllers or processors may prepare codes of conduct, or amend or extend such codes, for the purpose of specifying the application of this Regulation, such as with regard to: ... (j) the transfer of personal data to third countries or international organisations; ...
	Art.40(3) In addition to adherence by controllers or processors subject to this Regulation, codes of conduct approved pursuant to paragraph 5 of this Article and having general validity pursuant to paragraph 9 of this Article may also be adhered to by controllers or processors that are not subject to this Regulation pursuant to Article 3 in order to provide appropriate safeguards within the framework of personal data transfers to third countries or international organisations under the terms referred to in point (e) of Article 46(2). Such controllers or processors shall make binding and enforceable commitments, via contractual or other legally binding instruments, to apply those appropriate safeguards including with regard to the rights of data subjects.
	Art.42 Certification
	Art.42(2) In addition to adherence by controllers or processors subject to this Regulation, data protection certification mechanisms, seals or marks approved pursuant to paragraph 5 of this Article may be established for the purpose of demonstrating the existence of appropriate safeguards provided by controllers or processors that are not subject to this Regulation pursuant to Article 3 within the framework of personal data transfers to third countries or international organisations under the terms referred to in point (f) of Article 46(2). Such controllers or processors shall make binding and enforceable commitments, via contractual or other legally binding instruments, to apply those appropriate safeguards, including with regard to the rights of data subjects.
	Art.43 Certification bodies
	Art.43(8) The Commission shall be empowered to adopt delegated acts in accordance with Article 92 for the purpose of specifying the requirements to be taken into account for the data protection certification mechanisms referred to in Article 42(1).

DPD	GDPR
	Art.43(9) The Commission may adopt implementing acts laying down technical standards for certification mechanisms and data protection seals and marks, and mechanisms to promote and recognise those certification mechanisms, seals and marks. Those implementing acts shall be adopted in accordance with the examination procedure referred to in Article 93(2).
Data subject rights	
	Art.13 Information to be provided where personal data are collected from the data subject Art.13(1) Where personal data relating to a data subject are collected from the data subject, the controller shall, at the time when personal data are obtained, provide the data subject with all of the following information: … (f) where applicable, the fact that the controller intends to transfer personal data to a third country or international organisation and the existence or absence of an adequacy decision by the Commission, or in the case of transfers referred to in Article 46 or 47, or the second subparagraph of Article 49(1) [compelling legitimate interests], reference to the appropriate or suitable safeguards and the means by which to obtain a copy of them or where they have been made available.
	Art.14 Information to be provided where personal data have not been obtained from the data subject Art.14(1) Where personal data have not been obtained from the data subject, the controller shall provide the data subject with the following information: … (f) where applicable, that the controller intends to transfer personal data to a recipient in a third country or international organisation and the existence or absence of an adequacy decision by the Commission, or in the case of transfers referred to in Article 46 or 47, or the second subparagraph of Article 49(1) [compelling legitimate interests], reference to the appropriate or suitable safeguards and the means to obtain a copy of them or where they have been made available.
	Art.15 Right of access by the data subject Art.15(2) Where personal data are transferred to a third country or to an international organisation, the data subject shall have the right to be informed of the appropriate safeguards pursuant to Article 46 relating to the transfer.

DPD	GDPR
International DPA cooperation	
	Art.50 International cooperation for the protection of personal data In relation to third countries and international organisations, the Commission and supervisory authorities shall take *appropriate* steps to: (a) develop international cooperation mechanisms to facilitate the effective enforcement of legislation for the protection of personal data; (b) provide international mutual assistance in the enforcement of legislation for the protection of personal data, including through notification, complaint referral, investigative assistance and information exchange, subject to appropriate safeguards for the protection of personal data and other fundamental rights and freedoms; (c) engage relevant stakeholders in discussion and activities aimed at furthering international cooperation in the enforcement of legislation for the protection of personal data; (d) promote the exchange and documentation of personal data protection legislation and practice, including on jurisdictional conflicts with third countries.
	Rec.116 When personal data moves across borders outside the Union it may put at increased risk the ability of natural persons to exercise data protection rights in particular to protect themselves from the unlawful use or disclosure of that information. At the same time, supervisory authorities may find that they are unable to pursue complaints or conduct investigations relating to the activities outside their borders. Their efforts to work together in the cross-border context may also be hampered by insufficient preventative or remedial powers, inconsistent legal regimes, and practical obstacles like resource constraints. Therefore, there is a need to promote closer cooperation among data protection supervisory authorities to help them exchange information and carry out investigations with their international counterparts. For the purposes of developing international cooperation mechanisms to facilitate and provide international mutual assistance for the enforcement of legislation for the protection of personal data, the Commission and the supervisory authorities should exchange information and cooperate in activities related to the exercise of their powers with competent authorities in third countries, based on reciprocity and in accordance with this Regulation.

DPD	GDPR
Specific processing	
Art.9 Processing of personal data and freedom of expression Member States shall provide for exemptions or derogations from the provisions of this Chapter, Chapter IV and Chapter VI for the processing of personal data carried out solely for journalistic purposes or the purpose of artistic or literary expression only if they are necessary to reconcile the right to privacy with the rules governing freedom of expression.	Art.85 Processing and freedom of expression and information Art.85(2) For processing carried out for journalistic purposes or the purpose of academic artistic or literary expression, Member States shall provide for exemptions or derogations from Chapter II (principles), Chapter III (rights of the data subject), Chapter IV (controller and processor), *Chapter V (transfer of personal data to third countries or international organisations)*, Chapter VI (independent supervisory authorities), Chapter VII (cooperation and consistency) and Chapter IX (specific data processing situations) if they are necessary to reconcile the right to the protection of personal data with the freedom of expression and information.
	Rec.153 Member States law should reconcile the rules governing freedom of expression and information, including journalistic, academic, artistic and or literary expression with the right to the protection of personal data pursuant to this Regulation. The processing of personal data solely for journalistic purposes, or for the purposes of academic, artistic or literary expression should be subject to derogations or exemptions from certain provisions of this Regulation if necessary to reconcile the right to the protection of personal data with the right to freedom of expression and information, as enshrined in Article 11 of the Charter. This should apply in particular to the processing of personal data in the audiovisual field and in news archives and press libraries. Therefore, Member States should adopt legislative measures which lay down the exemptions and derogations necessary for the purpose of balancing those fundamental rights. Member States should adopt such exemptions and derogations on general principles, the rights of the data subject, the controller and the processor, the transfer of personal data to third countries or international organisations, the independent supervisory authorities, cooperation and consistency, and specific data-processing situations. Where such exemptions or derogations differ from one Member State to another, the law of the Member State to which the controller is subject should apply. In order to take account of the importance of the right to freedom of expression in every democratic society, it is necessary to interpret notions relating to that freedom, such as journalism, broadly.

DPD	GDPR
	Rec.48 Controllers that are part of a group of undertakings or institutions affiliated to a central body may have a legitimate interest in transmitting personal data within the group of undertakings for internal administrative purposes, including the processing of clients' or employees' personal data. *The general principles for the transfer of personal data, within a group of undertakings, to an undertaking located in a third country remain unaffected.*
	Art.88 Processing in the context of employment
	Art.88(1) Member States may, by law or by collective agreements, provide for more specific rules to ensure the protection of the rights and freedoms in respect of the processing of employees' personal data in the employment context, in particular for the purposes of the recruitment, the performance of the contract of employment, including discharge of obligations laid down by law or by collective agreements, management, planning and organisation of work, equality and diversity in the workplace, health and safety at work, protection of employer's or customer's property and for the purposes of the exercise and enjoyment, on an individual or collective basis, of rights and benefits related to employment, and for the purpose of the termination of the employment relationship.
[Unclear if this envisages international transfers, or just disclosures/transmissions]	Art.88(2)Those rules shall include suitable and specific measures to safeguard the data subject's human dignity, legitimate interests and fundamental rights, with particular regard to the transparency of processing, *the transfer of personal data within a group of undertakings, or a group of enterprises engaged in a joint economic activity* and monitoring systems at the work place.

DPD	GDPR
	Other provisions relevant to international transfers
	Art.96 Relationship with previously concluded Agreements International agreements involving the transfer of personal data to third countries or international organisations which were concluded by Member States prior to 24 May 2016, and which comply with Union law as applicable prior to that date, shall remain in force until amended, replaced or revoked.
	Art.97 Commission reports Art.97(1) By 25 May 2020 and every four years thereafter, the Commission shall submit a report on the evaluation and review of this Regulation to the European Parliament and to the Council. The reports shall be made public. Art.97(2) In the context of the evaluations and reviews referred to in paragraph 1, the Commission shall examine, in particular, the application and functioning of: (a) *Chapter V on the transfer of personal data to third countries or international organisations* with particular regard to decisions adopted pursuant to Article 45(3) of this Regulation and decisions adopted on the basis of Article 25(6) of Directive 95/46/EC; ...

DPD	GDPR
	Art.23 Restrictions 1. Union or Member State law to which the data controller or processor is subject may restrict by way of a legislative measure the scope of the obligations and rights provided for in Articles 12 to 22 and Article 34, as well as Article 5 in so far as its provisions correspond to the rights and obligations provided for in Articles 12 to 22, when such a restriction respects the essence of the fundamental rights and freedoms and is a necessary and proportionate measure in a democratic society to safeguard: (a) national security; (b) defence; (c) public security; (d) the prevention, investigation, detection or prosecution of criminal offences or the execution of criminal penalties, including the safeguarding against and the prevention of threats to public security; (e) other important objectives of general public interest of the Union or of a Member State, in particular an important economic or financial interest of the Union or of a Member State, including monetary, budgetary and taxation matters, public health and social security; (f) the protection of judicial independence and judicial proceedings; (g) the prevention, investigation, detection and prosecution of breaches of ethics for regulated professions; (h) a monitoring, inspection or regulatory function connected, even occasionally, to the exercise of official authority in the cases referred to in points (a) to (e) and (g); (i) the protection of the data subject or the rights and freedoms of others; (j) the enforcement of civil law claims. 2. In particular, any legislative measure referred to in paragraph 1 shall contain specific provisions at least, where relevant, as to:
[Unclear if this envisages international transfers, or just disclosures/transmissions]	… (d) the safeguards to prevent abuse or unlawful access or transfer; …

Note: Emphasis added.

References

451 Research, 2014. Hosting and Cloud Study 2014: Hosting and Cloud Go Mainstream – Survey Results. Available at: https://news.microsoft.com/download/presskits/cloud/docs/HostingStudy2014.pdf [accessed 26 October 2016].

Abelson, H. et al., 2015. Keys under doormats: mandating insecurity by requiring government access to all data and communications. *DSpace@MIT*. Available at: http://dspace.mit.edu/handle/1721.1/97690 [accessed 26 October 2016].

ACCA, 2012. Asia Cloud Computing Association, Cloud Readiness Index. Available at: http://www.asiacloudcomputing.org/images/stories/contents/files/CRI_2012.pdf [accessed 26 October 2016].

ACCA, 2014. Asia Cloud Computing Association, The Impact of Data Sovereignty on Cloud Computing in Asia. Available at: http://www.asiacloudcomputing.org/images/research/ACCA-DS2013_FULL.REPORT.pdf [accessed 26 October 2016].

AEPD, 2013. Agencia Española de Protección de Datos, Guía para clientes que contraten servicios de Cloud Computing. Available at: http://www.agpd.es/portalwebAGPD/canaldocumentacion/publicaciones/common/Guias/GUIA_Cloud.pdf [accessed 26 October 2016].

Ahmed, M. and Waters, R., 2015. Microsoft unveils German data plan to tackle US Internet spying. *Financial Times*. Available at: https://www.ft.com/content/540a296e-87ff-11e5-9f8c-a8d619fa707c [accessed 26 October 2016].

Air Berlin, 2011. Comments on the European Commission's Communication on a Comprehensive Approach on Data Protection in the European Union (Brussels, 4.11.2010 – COM(2010) 609 final). Available at: http://ec.europa.eu/justice/news/consulting_public/0006/contributions/organisations/air_berlin_en.pdf [accessed 26 October 2016].

Alcatel-Lucent, 2009. The European Commission's Consultation on the Legal Framework for the Fundamental Right to Protection of Personal Data. Available at: http://ec.europa.eu/justice/news/consulting_public/0003/contributions/organisations_not_registered/alcatel_lucent_en.pdf#10 [accessed 26 October 2016].

Allen & Overy, 2013. Binding Corporate Rules. Available at: http://www.allenovery.com/sitecollectiondocuments/bcrs.pdf [accessed 26 October 2016].

AmCham, 2010. AmCham EU Response to the Commission Consultation on Protection of Personal Data. Available at: http://ec.europa.eu/justice/news/consulting_public/0003/contributions/organisations/american_chamber_commerce_to_eu_en.pdf [accessed 26 October 2016].

AmCham EU, 2016. Adoption of the EU-US Privacy Shield Restores Trust to Transatlantic Data Flows. Available at: http://www.amchameu.eu/sites/default/files/press_releases/press_-_adoption_of_the_eu-us_privacy_shield_restores_trust_to_transatlantic_data_flows.pdf?platform=hootsuite [accessed 26 October 2016].

Anderson, R., 2005. The crypto wars are over! *Computer and Telecommunications Law Review*, 11(6), pp. 183–4.

Anderson, R.J., 2008. *Security Engineering: A Guide to Building Dependable Distributed Systems* 2nd edition. Tokyo, New York: John Wiley & Sons.

Angulo, J. et al., 2013. D37.1 General HCI principles and guidelines. *A4Cloud*. Available at: http://www.a4cloud.eu/sites/default/files/D37.1%20General%20HCI%20principles%20and%20guidelines.pdf [accessed 26 October 2016].

Anon, 2015. TISA Annex on Electronic Commerce. Available at: https://wikileaks.org/tisa/document/20151001_Annex-on-Electronic-Commerce/20151001_Annex-on-Electronic-Commerce.pdf [accessed 26 October 2016].

ANSI/TIA, 2005. American National Standards Institute/Telecommunications Industry Association, Telecommunications Infrastructure Standard for Data Centers ANSI/TIA-942-2005. Available at: https://global.ihs.com/doc_detail.cfm?&rid=TIA&input_doc_number=942&item_s_key=00414811&item_key_date=860905&input_doc_number=942&input_doc_title=&org_code=TIA [accessed 26 October 2016].

AP, 2005. Associated Press, New Nuclear Sub Is Said to Have Special Eavesdropping Ability. Available at: http://www.nytimes.com/2005/02/20/politics/20submarine.html [accessed 26 October 2016].

AP, 2013. Associated Press, Snowden Says US Targets Included China Cell Phones. Available at: http://www.scmp.com/news/hong-kong/article/1267265/snowden-says-us-targets-included-china-cell-phones [accessed 26 October 2016].

AP, 2014a. Associated Press, Brazil: Google Fined in Petrobras Probe. Available at: http://news.yahoo.com/brazil-google-fined-petrobras-probe-183507202.html [accessed 26 October 2016].

AP, 2014b. Associated Press, Microsoft Corporation Loses Ruling by New York Judge on Ireland Emails. Available at: http://www.cbsnews.com/news/microsoft-corporation-loses-ruling-by-new-york-judge-on-ireland-emails/ [accessed 26 October 2016].

APEC, n.d. APEC Cross-Border Privacy Enforcement Arrangement (CPEA). Available at: http://www.apec.org/Groups/Committee-on-Trade-and-Investment/Electronic-Commerce-Steering-Group/Cross-border-Privacy-Enforcement-Arrangement.aspx [accessed 26 October 2016].

APEC, 2005. APEC Privacy Framework. Available at: http://www.apec.org/Groups/Committee-on-Trade-and-Investment/~/media/Files/Groups/ECSG/05_ecsg_privacyframewk.ashx [accessed 26 October 2016].

APEC, 2009. APEC Cooperation Arrangement for Cross-Border Privacy Enforcement. Available at: http://www.apec.org/~/media/Files/Groups/ECSG/CBPR/CBPR-CrossBorderPrivacyEnforcement.pdf [accessed 26 October 2016].

APEC, 2011. APEC Cross-Border Privacy Rules System: Policies, Rules and Guidelines. Available at: http://www.apec.org/groups/committee-on-trade-and-investment/~/media/files/groups/ecsg/cbpr/cbpr-policiesrules guidelines.ashx [accessed 26 October 2016].

Appelbaum, J., Horchert, J. and Stöcker, C., 2013. Catalog reveals NSA has back doors for numerous devices. *Spiegel Online*. Available at: http://www.spiegel.de/international/world/catalog-reveals-nsa-has-back-doors-for-numerous-devices-a-940994.html [accessed 26 October 2016].

Arbeit der DSB, 2016. Zur Ungültigerklärung der Safe Harbor-Entscheidung der Europäischen Kommission durch den EuGH: Österreichische Datenschutzbehörde. Available at: http://web.archive.org/web/20160508033524/https://www.dsb.gv.at/site/6218/default.aspx [accessed 26 October 2016].

Archer, Q., Maxwell, W. and Wolf, C., 2012. A global reality: government access to data in the cloud – a comparative analysis of ten international jurisdictions. *Chronicle of Data Protection*. Available at: http://www.hldataprotection.com/uploads/file/Revised%20Government %20Access%20to%20Cloud%20Data%20Paper%20(18%20July%2012). pdf [accessed 26 October 2016].

Archer, Q., Maxwell, W. and Wolf, C., 2013. A global reality: governmental access to data in the cloud. *SCL*. Available at: http://www.scl.org/site.aspx?i=ed32952 [accessed 26 October 2016].

Austrian Bar, 2009. Consultation on the Legal Framework for the Fundamental Right to Protection of Personal Data. Available at:

http://ec.europa.eu/justice/news/consulting_public/0003/contributions/
public_authorities/austrian_bar_en.pdf [accessed 26 October 2016].

Autoriteit Persoonsgegevens (formerly CBP), 2012. Written Opinion on
the Application of the Wet bescherming persoonsgegevens [Dutch Data
Protection Act] in the Case of a Contract for Cloud Computing
Services from an American Provider. Unofficial translation. Available
at: https://autoriteitpersoonsgegevens.nl/sites/default/files/atoms/files/
dutch-dpa-written-opinion-cloud-computing-unofficial-translation.pdf
[accessed 26 October 2016].

AWS, 2014a. Amazon Web Services: Overview of Security Processes.
Available at: https://d0.awsstatic.com/whitepapers/Security/AWS%
20Security%20Whitepaper.pdf [accessed 26 October 2016].

AWS, 2014b. Announcing the AWS EU (Frankfurt) Region. Available at:
http://aws.amazon.com/about-aws/whats-new/2014/10/23/announcing-
the-aws-eu-frankfurt-region/ [accessed 26 October 2016].

AWS, 2015. AWS Customer Agreement. Available at: http://aws.amazon.
com/agreement/ [accessed 26 October 2016].

AWS, 2016. AWS Customer Agreement. Available at: http://aws.amazon.
com/agreement/ [accessed 26 October 2016].

Ax, J., 2014. RPT-UPDATE 2-U.S. judge orders Microsoft to submit
customer's emails from abroad. *Reuters*. Available at: http://www.
reuters.com/article/2014/07/31/usa-tech-warrants-idUSL2N0Q61WN20
140731 [accessed 26 October 2016].

Axciom, 2009. Response to the European Commission Consultation on
European Data Protection Legal Framework. Available at: http://ec.
europa.eu/justice/news/consulting_public/0003/contributions/organisations/
acxiom_en.pdf [accessed 26 October 2016].

Babcock, C., 2015. VMware shows off new live migration: OpenStack
options. *InformationWeek*. Available at: http://www.informationweek.
com/cloud/infrastructure-as-a-service/vmware-shows-off-new-live-
migration-openstack-options/d/d-id/1318890 [accessed 26 October
2016].

Baesman, R., 2015. Building the best place to get work done. *Dropbox
for Business Blog*. Available at: https://blogs.dropbox.com/business/
2015/06/dropbox-for-business-updates/ [accessed 26 October 2016].

Baker, J., 2016a. Privacy Shield approved by EU member states, but 4
nations abstain. *Ars Technica UK*. Available at: http://arstechnica.co.uk/
tech-policy/2016/07/privacy-shield-approved-eu-member-states-4-nations-
abstain/ [accessed 26 October 2016].

Baker, J., 2016b. Catching up with Max Schrems. *IAPP*. Available at:
https://iapp.org/news/a/catching-up-with-max-schrems/ [accessed 17
February 2017].

Baker, R.K., 2006. Offshore IT outsourcing and the 8th Data Protection Principle: legal and regulatory requirements – with reference to financial services. *International Journal of Law and Information Technology*, 14(1), pp. 1–27.

Ball, J., 2013. NSA stores metadata of millions of web users for up to a year, secret files show. *The Guardian*. Available at: http://www.theguardian.com/world/2013/sep/30/nsa-americans-metadata-year-documents [accessed 26 October 2016].

Ball, J., Borger, J. and Greenwald, G., 2013. Revealed: how US and UK spy agencies defeat Internet privacy and security. *The Guardian*. Available at: http://www.theguardian.com/world/2013/sep/05/nsa-gchq-encryption-codes-security [accessed 26 October 2016].

Ball, J., Harding, L. and Garside, J., 2013. BT and Vodafone among telecoms companies passing details to GCHQ. *The Guardian*. Available at: http://www.theguardian.com/business/2013/aug/02/telecoms-bt-vodafone-cables-gchq [accessed 26 October 2016].

Barbière, C., 2016. Better regulation agenda may hold back digital innovation. *EurActiv.com*. Available at: http://www.euractiv.com/section/digital/news/better-regulation-agenda-may-hold-back-digital-innovation/ [accessed 26 October 2016].

Barker, E., 2016. Recommendation for key management, part 1: general – SP800-57 pt.1 rev.4. *NIST*. Available at: http://dx.doi.org/10.6028/NIST.SP.800-57pt1r4 [accessed 26 October 2016].

Barker, E. and Roginsky, A., 2015. Transitions: recommendation for transitioning the use of cryptographic algorithms and key lengths – NIST.SP.800-131Ar1.pdf. *NIST*. Available at: http://dx.doi.org/10.6028/NIST.SP.800-131Ar [accessed 26 October 2016].

Barr, J., 2013. The new world of public sector IT. *AWS Official Blog*. Available at: https://aws.amazon.com/blogs/aws/the-new-world-of-public-sector-it/ [accessed 26 October 2016].

Bartock, M. et al., 2015. Trusted geolocation in the cloud: proof of concept implementation – NISTIR 7904. *NIST*. Available at: http://dx.doi.org/10.6028/NIST.IR.7904 [accessed 26 October 2016].

Bartoli, E., 2014. Data transfers in the cloud: discussion paper for the Commission's Expert Group on Cloud Computing Contracts. *Commission*. Available at: http://ec.europa.eu/justice/contract/files/expert_groups/discussion_paper_data_transfers_in_cloud.pdf [accessed 26 October 2016].

Bauer, M. et al., 2014. The costs of data localisation: friendly fire on economic recovery. *ECIPE*. Available at: http://www.ecipe.org/app/uploads/2014/12/OCC32014__1.pdf [accessed 26 October 2016].

Baumann, A., Peinado, M. and Hunt, G., 2014. Shielding applications from an untrusted cloud with Haven. In *USENIX Symposium on*

Operating Systems Design and Implementation (OSDI). usenix. Available at: https://www.usenix.org/system/files/conference/osdi14/osdi14-paper-baumann.pdf [accessed 26 October 2016].

BayLDA, 2015. 6. Tätigkeitsbericht des Bayerischen Landesamtes für Datenschutzaufsicht für die Jahre 2013 und 2014. Available at: https://www.lda.bayern.de/media/baylda_report_06.pdf [accessed 26 October 2016].

BayLDA, 2016. II Zertifizierung: Art.42 DS-GVO. Available at: https://www.lda.bayern.de/media/baylda_ds-gvo_2_certification.pdf [accessed 26 October 2016].

BBA, 2016. British Bankers' Association, BBA Response to FCA CP 15/6. Available at: https://www.bba.org.uk/policy/bba-consultation-responses/bba-response-to-fca-cp-proposed-guidance-for-firms-outsourcing-to-the-cloud-and-other-third-%C2%ADparty-it-services/ [accessed 26 October 2016].

BBC, 2013. Brazil Data Plan Aims to Keep US Spies at Bay. Available at: http://www.bbc.co.uk/news/technology-24145662 [accessed 26 October 2016].

Bell, G.B. and Boddington, R., 2010. Solid state drives: the beginning of the end for current practice in digital forensic recovery? *Journal of Digital Forensics, Security and Law*, 5(3), pp. 1–20.

Bellare, M. et al., 2009. Format-preserving encryption. In M.J. Jacobson Jr et al., eds. *Selected Areas in Cryptography*. Heidelberg: Springer, pp. 295–312. Available at: http://link.springer.com/chapter/10.1007/978-3-642-05445-7_19 [accessed 26 October 2016].

Bender, D.R., 1988. Transborder data flow: an historical review and contributions for the future. *Special Libraries*, 79(3), pp. 230–35.

Bennett, C.J., Gellman, R.M. and Raab, C.D., 1998. Application of a methodology designed to assess the adequacy of the level of protection of individuals with regard to processing personal data: test of the method on several categories of transfer. *Commission*. Available at: http://bookshop.europa.eu/en/application-of-a-methodology-designed-to-assess-the-adequacy-of-the-level-of-protection-of-individuals-with-regard-to-processing-personal-data-pbC1NA98398/downloads/C1-NA-98-398-EN-C/C1NA98398ENC_001.pdf?FileName=C1NA98398ENC_001.pdf&SKU=C1NA98398ENC_PDF&CatalogueNumber=C1-NA-98-398-EN-C [accessed 26 October 2016].

Bergkamp, L. and Dhont, J., 2000. Data protection in Europe and the Internet: an analysis of the European Community's privacy legislation in the context of the World Wide Web. *The EDI Law Review*, 7, p. 71.

Berkens, M., 2011. FBI seizes servers at Digital One in US, 'taking tens of clients sites down' when only wanting 1. *TheDomains.com*. Available at: http://www.thedomains.com/2011/06/25/fbi-seizes-servers-at-digital-one-in-us-taking-tens-of-clients-sites-down-when-only-wanting-1/ [accessed 26 October 2016].

Bernstein, D., 2014. Containers and cloud: from LXC to Docker to Kubernetes. *IEEE Cloud Computing*, 1(3), pp. 81–4.

BEUC, 2015. Data Flows in TTIP. Available at: http://www.beuc.eu/publications/beuc-x-2015-073_factsheet_data_flows_in_ttip.pdf [accessed 26 October 2016].

Bhatti, J., 2013. In wake of PRISM, German DPAs threaten to halt data transfers to non-EU countries. *Privacy & Security Law Report*, 12, p. 1329.

Bignami, F., 2004. Transgovernmental networks vs. democracy: the case of the European Information Privacy Network. *Michigan Journal of International Law*, 26(3), pp. 807–68.

Bigo, D. et al., 2012. Fighting cyber crime and protecting privacy in the cloud: study for the European Parliament's Committee on Civil Liberties, Justice and Home Affairs. *Parliament*. Available at: http://www.europarl.europa.eu/meetdocs/2009_2014/documents/libe/dv/study_cloud_/study_cloud_en.pdf [accessed 26 October 2016].

Black, J., 1987. *Rules and Regulators*. Oxford: OUP.

Block, D., 2014. Google's Audit APIs and Backupify. *The Cloud to Cloud Backup Blog*. Available at: http://blog.backupify.com/2014/07/22/googles-audit-apis-backupify/ [accessed 26 October 2016].

Blume, P., 1992. An EEC policy for data protection. *Computer/Law Journal*, 11(3), p. 399.

Blume, P., 2000. Transborder data flow: is there a solution in sight? *International Journal of Law and Information Technology*, 8(1), pp. 65–86.

Blume, P., 2013. Controller and processor: is there a risk of confusion? *International Data Privacy Law*, 3(2), pp. 140–45.

Borger, J., 2013. GCHQ and European spy agencies worked together on mass surveillance. *The Guardian*. Available at: http://www.theguardian.com/uk-news/2013/nov/01/gchq-europe-spy-agencies-mass-surveillance-snowden [accessed 26 October 2016].

Boué, T., 2013. Transatlantic data flows: shift the focus to how – not if. *BSA TechPost*. Available at: http://techpost.bsa.org/2013/09/26/transatlantic-data-flows-shift-the-focus-to-how-not-if/ [accessed 26 October 2016].

Bowden, C., 2013. The US surveillance programmes and their impact on EU citizens' fundamental rights: note for the European Parliament's

Committee on Civil Liberties, Justice and Home Affairs. *Parliament*. Available at: http://www.europarl.europa.eu/RegData/etudes/note/join/ 2013/474405/IPOL-LIBE_NT(2013)474405_EN.pdf [accessed 26 October 2016].

Bowen, P., Hash, J. and Wilson, M., 2006. Information security handbook: a guide for managers SP 800-100. *NIST*. Available at: http:// nvlpubs.nist.gov/nistpubs/Legacy/SP/nistspecialpublication800-100.pdf [accessed 26 October 2016].

Bradshaw, S., Millard, C. and Walden, I., 2013. Standard contracts for cloud services. In C. Millard, ed. *Cloud Computing Law*. Oxford: OUP.

Brahma, W., 2012. The pirate cloud. *The Pirate Bay*. Available at: http://web.archive.org/web/20131209073651/http://thepiratebay.sx/blog/ 224 [accessed 26 October 2016].

Brewster, T., 2014. Edward Snowden and the rise of cloud encryption. *Cloud Pro*. Available at: http://www.cloudpro.co.uk/cloud-essentials/ cloud-security/3931/edward-snowden-and-the-rise-of-cloud-encryption [accessed 26 October 2016].

Briat, M., 1988. Personal data and the free flow of information. In G.P.V. Vandenberghe, ed. *Freedom of Data Flows and EEC Law*. Kluwer. Cited in White (1997: [p.233]).

Bridgwater, A., 2013. Service level checklist: how to know when your provider provides stability. *Cloud Pro*. Available at: http:// www.cloudpro.co.uk/cloud-essentials/slas/3580/service-level-checklist- how-to-know-when-your-provider-provides-stability [accessed 26 October 2016].

Brill, J., 2013. At the crossroads. Keynote speech, IAPP Europe Data Protection Congress. *FTC*. Available at: https://www.ftc.gov/sites/ default/files/documents/public_statements/crossroads-keynote-address- iapp-europe-data-protection-congress/131211iappkeynote.pdf [accessed 26 October 2016].

Brooks, B. and Bajak, F., 2013. Brazil looks to break from US-centric Internet. *Yahoo News*. Available at: http://news.yahoo.com/brazil-looks- break-us-centric-internet-040702309.html [accessed 26 October 2016].

Brown, I. and Korff, D., 2014. Foreign surveillance: law and practice in a global digital environment. *European Human Rights Law Review*, (3), pp. 243–51.

Brown, I. and Marsden, C.T., 2013. *Regulating Code: Good Governance and Better Regulation in the Information Age*. Cambridge, MA: MIT Press.

Brownsdon, E., 2004. Websites and data protection: the Lindqvist case. *Privacy & Data Protection*, 4(3), pp. 3–4.

Burdon, M., Reid, J. and Low, R., 2010. Encryption safe harbours and data breach notification laws. *Computer Law & Security Review*, 26(5), pp. 520–34.

Burton, G., 2013. Google introduces encryption to Google Cloud Storage: but NSA will still have easy access. *Computing*. Available at: http://www.computing.co.uk/ctg/news/2289554/google-introduces-encryption-to-google-cloud-storage-but-nsa-will-still-have-easy-access [accessed 26 October 2016].

Buttarelli, G., 2012. Security and privacy regulatory challenges in the cloud. The 2012 European Cloud Computing – Making the Transition from Cloud-Friendly to Cloud-Active. *EDPS*. Available at: https://secure.edps.europa.eu/EDPSWEB/webdav/site/mySite/shared/Documents/EDPS/Publications/Speeches/2012/12-03-21_Cloud_computing_EN.pdf [accessed 26 October 2016].

Bygrave, L.A., 2010. Privacy and data protection in an international perspective. *Scandinavian Studies in Law*, 56, pp. 165–200.

Cabinet Office, 2015. Policy: Offshoring Information Assets Classified at OFFICIAL v1.1. Available at: https://ogsirooffshoring.zendesk.com/hc/en-us/article_attachments/202389402/Offshoring_Information_Assets_Classified_at_OFFICIAL_v1.1.pdf [accessed 26 October 2016].

CAHDATA, 2016a. Abridged Report. Available at: https://rm.coe.int/CoERMPublicCommonSearchServices/DisplayDCTMContent?documentId=09000016806b7e90 [accessed 26 October 2016].

CAHDATA, 2016b. Draft Protocol Amending the Convention for the Protection of Individuals with Regard to Automatic Processing of Personal Data (CETS No. 108). Available at: https://rm.coe.int/CoERMPublicCommonSearchServices/DisplayDCTMContent?documentId=09000016806af965 [accessed 26 October 2016].

CAHDATA, 2016c. Information Document. Available at: https://rm.coe.int/CoERMPublicCommonSearchServices/DisplayDCTMContent?documentId=09000016806a6165 [accessed 26 October 2016].

CAHDATA, 2016d. Working Document: Consolidated Version of the Modernisation Proposals of Convention 108 with Reservations. Available at: https://rm.coe.int/CoERMPublicCommonSearchServices/DisplayDCTMContent?documentId=09000016806af964 [accessed 26 October 2016].

Calder, B. et al., 2011. Windows Azure Storage: a highly available cloud storage service with strong consistency. In *Proceedings of the Twenty-Third ACM Symposium on Operating Systems Principles. ACM*, pp. 143–57. Available at: http://dl.acm.org/citation.cfm?id=2043571 [accessed 26 October 2016].

Campbell, I., 2014. Data protection laws under strain. *Irish Times.* Available at: http://www.irishtimes.com/business/data-protection-laws-under-strain-1.1836952 [accessed 26 October 2016].

Carey, P., 2010. Data protection: back to basics – part 9. *Privacy & Data Protection,* 11(1), pp. 12–15.

Carroll, M., Van Der Merwe, A. and Kotze, P., 2011. Secure cloud computing: benefits, risks and controls. In *Information Security South Africa (ISSA), 2011. IEEE,* pp. 1–9. Available at: http://ieeexplore. ieee.org/xpls/abs_all.jsp?arnumber=6027519 [accessed 26 October 2016].

Carson, A., 2016. Merck first company to win BCRs via APEC's CBPRs. *IAPP.* Available at: https://iapp.org/news/a/merck-first-company-to-win-bcrs-via-apecs-cbprs/ [accessed 26 October 2016].

Castro, D., 2013. The false promise of data nationalism. *Information Technology & Innovation Foundation.* Available at: http://www2.itif. org/2013-false-promise-data-nationalism.pdf [accessed 26 October 2016].

Cate, F., 1998. Privacy and telecommunications. *Wake Forest Law Review,* 33(1), pp. 1–50.

Catteddu, D. and Hogben, G., 2009. Cloud computing: benefits, risks and recommendations for information security. *ENISA.* Available at: http:// www.enisa.europa.eu/activities/risk-management/files/deliverables/ cloud-computing-risk-assessment/at_download/fullReport [accessed 26 October 2016].

Cave, J. et al., 2011. Does it help or hinder? Promotion of innovation on the Internet and citizens' right to privacy – study for the European Parliament's Committee on Industry, Research and Energy. *Parliament.* Available at: http://www.data-now.eu/dwnld/pdf/study.pdf [accessed 26 October 2016].

Cave, J. et al., 2012. Data protection review: impact on EU innovation and competitiveness – study for the European Parliament's Committee on Industry, Research and Energy. *Parliament.* Available at: http:// www.europarl.europa.eu/RegData/etudes/etudes/join/2012/492463/IPOL-ITRE_ET(2012)492463_EN.pdf [accessed 26 October 2016].

CBI, 2002. Confederation of British Industry, Comments on Directive 95/46 EC re Data Protection. Available at: http://ec.europa.eu/justice/ policies/privacy/docs/lawreport/paper/cbi_en.pdf [accessed 26 October 2016].

CBP, 2004. Stichting Brein: Voorafgaand onderzoek; verklaring recht-matigheid. Available at: https://cbpweb.nl/sites/default/files/downloads/ uit/z2003-1660.pdf [accessed 26 October 2016].

CBP, 2007. Publication of Personal Data on the Internet. Available at: https://cbpweb.nl/sites/default/files/downloads/mijn_privacy/en_200711 08_richtsnoeren_internet.pdf [accessed 26 October 2016].

CBP, 2013. Investigation into the Processing of Personal Data for the 'WhatsApp' Mobile Application by WhatsApp Inc. Available at: https://cbpweb.nl/sites/default/files/downloads/mijn_privacy/rap_2013-whatsapp-dutchdpa-final-findings-en.pdf [accessed 26 October 2016].

CBPRs, 2012a. Intake Questionnaire. Available at: https://cbprs.blob. core.windows.net/files/Cross%20Border%20Privacy%20Rules%20Intake %20Questionnaire.pdf [accessed 26 October 2016].

CBPRs, 2012b. Program Requirements. Available at: https://cbprs. blob.core.windows.net/files/Cross%20Border%20Privacy%20Rules% 20Program%20Requirements.pdf [accessed 26 October 2016].

Chander, A. and Lê, U.P., 2015. Data nationalism. *Emory Law Journal*, 64(3), pp. 677–739. Available at: http://law.emory.edu/elj/content/ volume-64/issue-3/articles/data-nationalism.html [accessed 26 October 2016].

Charlesworth, A., 2002. Information privacy law in the European Union: e pluribus unum or ex uno plures. *Hastings Law Journal*, 54(4), pp. 931–70.

Chase, P., David-Wilp, S. and Ridout, T., 2016. Transatlantic digital economy and data protection: state-of-play and future implications for the EU's external policies. *Parliament*. Available at: http:// www.europarl.europa.eu/RegData/etudes/STUD/2016/535006/EXPO_ STU(2016)535006_EN.pdf [accessed 26 October 2016].

Chernicoff, D., 2011. FBI throws a scare into datacenter service providers. *ZDNet*. Available at: http://www.zdnet.com/blog/datacenter/ fbi-throws-a-scare-into-datacenter-service-providers/884 [accessed 26 October 2016].

Chissick, M., 2000. The incompatibility of data protection laws and the Internet. *Electronic Business Law*, 2(10), pp. 11–12.

Christensen, L. et al., 2013. The impact of the Data Protection Regulation in the EU. *Analysis Group*. Available at: http://www.analysisgroup. com/uploadedfiles/content/insights/publishing/2013_data_protection_ reg_in_eu_christensen_rafert_etal.pdf [accessed 26 October 2016].

Cichonski, P. et al., 2012. Computer security incident handling guide SP 800-61 rev 2. *NIST*. Available at: http://nvlpubs.nist.gov/nistpubs/ SpecialPublications/NIST.SP.800-61r2.pdf [accessed 26 October 2016].

CipherCloud, 2012. Over 40% of IT Professionals Are Not Aware of the Information Commissioners Office Guidance on Cloud Computing According to Research by CipherCloud. Available at: http://www.cipher

cloud.com/company/about-ciphercloud/press-releases/40-professionals-aware-information-commissioners-office-guidance-cloud-computing-according-research-ciphercloud/ [accessed 26 October 2016].

CipherCloud, 2014. It's Clear, Confident Skies for this Bank's Chatter Cloud Deployment. Available at: http://pages.ciphercloud.com/rs/ciphercloud/images/CS-Top5CanadianBank-140110.pdf [accessed 26 October 2016].

Cisco, 2009. Cisco Response to the Consultation on the Legal Framework for the Fundamental Right to Protection of Personal Data. Available at: http://ec.europa.eu/justice/news/consulting_public/0003/contributions/organisations/cisco_en.pdf [accessed 26 October 2016].

Civic Consulting, 2012. Cloud Computing: Study for the European Parliament's Committee on Internal Market and Consumer Protection. Available at: http://www.europarl.europa.eu/document/activities/cont/201205/20120531ATT46111/20120531ATT46111EN.pdf [accessed 26 October 2016].

Clidaras, J., Stiver, D.W. and Hamburgen, W., 2009. United States patent: 7525207 – water-based data center. *US Patent and Trademark Office.* Available at: http://patft.uspto.gov/netacgi/nph-Parser?Sect2=PTO1&Sect2=HITOFF&p=1&u=/netahtml/PTO/search-bool.html&r=1&f=G&l=50&d=PALL&RefSrch=yes&Query=PN/7525207 [accessed 26 October 2016].

Cline, J., 2014. Jay Cline: U.S. takes the gold in doling out privacy fines. *Computerworld.* Available at: http://www.computerworld.com/article/2487796/data-privacy/jay-cline--u-s--takes-the-gold-in-doling-out-privacy-fines.html [accessed 26 October 2016].

Cloud Industry Forum, 2014. The Normalisation of Cloud in a Hybrid IT Market: UK Cloud Adoption Snapshot & Trends for 2015 – Paper 14. Available at: https://www.outsourcery.co.uk/media/1179/cif-paper-fourteen-the-normalisation-of-cloud-in-a-hybrid-it-market.pdf [accessed 26 October 2016].

Cluley, G., 2014. How bank hackers stole £1.25 million with a simple piece of computer hardware. *Graham Cluley.* Available at: https://grahamcluley.com/2014/04/bank-hackers-hardware/ [accessed 26 October 2016].

CNIL, 2012. Recommendations for Companies Planning to Use Cloud Computing Services. Available at: http://www.cnil.fr/fileadmin/documents/en/Recommendations_for_companies_planning_to_use_Cloud_computing_services.pdf#6 [accessed 26 October 2016].

CNIL, 2013. BCR for Processors: A New Tool to Frame International Data Transfers. Available at: http://www.cnil.fr/english/news-and-events/news/article/bcr-for-processors-a-new-tool-to-frame-international-data-transfers/ [accessed 26 October 2016].

CNIL, 2014. Reminds Cloud Computing Providers of their Obligations under Directive 95/46/EC upon its Partial Assessment of Microsoft. Available at: https://www.cnil.fr/fr/node/15673 [accessed 26 October 2016].

CNIL, 2016a. Decision No. 2016-007 of January 26, 2016 Issuing Formal Notice to Facebook Inc. and Facebook Ireland. Available at: https://www.cnil.fr/sites/default/files/atoms/files/d2016-007_med_face book-inc.-facebook-ireland-en.pdf [accessed 26 October 2016].

CNIL, 2016b. Decision No. 2016-058 of 30th June 2016 Serving a Formal Notice on Microsoft Corporation. Available at: https://www. cnil.fr/sites/default/files/atoms/files/2016-058_formal_notice_microsoft. pdf [accessed 26 October 2016].

CNIL, 2016c. Rapport d'activité 2015. Available at: https://www.cnil.fr/ sites/default/files/atoms/files/cnil-36e_rapport_annuel_2015_0.pdf [accessed 26 October 2016].

CNIL, 2016d. Safe Harbor: que doivent faire les entreprises? Available at: https://www.cnil.fr/fr/safe-harbor-que-doivent-faire-les-entreprises [accessed 26 October 2016].

CNIL et al., 2012. To Larry Page, Google. Available at: http:// ec.europa.eu/justice/data-protection/article-29/documentation/other-document/files/2012/20121016_letter_to_google_en.pdf [accessed 26 October 2016].

CoE, 1989. New Technologies: A Challenge to Privacy Protection? (1989) – Study Prepared by the Committee of Experts on Data Protection (CJ-PD) under the Authority of the European Committee on Legal Co-operation (CDCJ). Available at: http://www.coe.int/t/dghl/ standardsetting/dataprotection/Reports/NewTechnologies_1989_en.pdf [accessed 26 October 2016].

CoE, 2000a. Consultative Committee of the Convention for the Protection of Individuals with Regard to Automatic Processing of Personal Data (ETS No.108) (T-PD): Abridged Report of the 16th Meeting (Strasbourg, 6–8 June 2000). Available at: https://wcd.coe.int/ ViewDoc.jsp?Ref=CM%282000%29109&Language=lanEnglish&Site= COE&BackColorInternet=DBDCF2&BackColorIntranet=FDC864&Back ColorLogged=FDC864 [accessed 26 October 2016].

CoE, 2000b. Report of Committee on Legal Affairs and Human Rights on Draft Additional Protocol to Convention ETS 108 on Supervisory Authorities and Transborder Data Flows Doc. 8660. Available at: http://www.assembly.coe.int/nw/xml/XRef/X2H-Xref-ViewHTML.asp? FileID=8870&lang=en [accessed 26 October 2016].

CoE, 2010. Council of Europe Response to Privacy Challenges: Modernisation of Convention 108 – Position Paper. Available at: http://www.

coe.int/t/dghl/standardsetting/dataprotection/258%20Pro%20memoria%20Jerusalem%20EN.pdf [accessed 26 October 2016].

CoE, 2012. Consultative Committee of the Convention for the Protection of Individuals with Regard to Automatic Processing of Personal Data: Final Document on the Modernisation of Convention 108, T-PD(2012)04 Rev2. Available at: http://www.coe.int/t/dghl/standard setting/dataprotection/TPD_documents/T-PD_2012_04_rev2_En.pdf [accessed 26 October 2016].

CoE, 2015. Criminal Justice Access to Data in the Cloud: Challenges. Available at: http://www.coe.int/t/dghl/cooperation/economiccrime/ Source/Cybercrime/TCY/2015/T-CY(2015)10_CEG%20challenges%20 rep_sum_v8.pdf [accessed 26 October 2016].

CoE, 2016a. Criminal Justice Access to Electronic Evidence in the Cloud: Informal Summary of Issues and Options under Consideration by the Cloud Evidence Group. Available at: https://rm.coe.int/CoERM PublicCommonSearchServices/DisplayDCTMContent?documentId=09 000016805a53c8 [accessed 26 October 2016].

CoE, 2016b. Draft Explanatory Report: Convention for the Protection of Individuals with Regard to Automatic Processing of Personal Data [ETS No. 108]. Available at: http://www.coe.int/t/dghl/standard setting/dataprotection/CAHDATA/Draft%20Explanatory%20report%20 Convention%20108%20modernised%20CAHDATA_En.pdf [accessed 26 October 2016].

CoE, 2016c. Draft Modernised Convention for the Protection of Individuals with Regard to the Processing of Personal Data. Available at: http://www.coe.int/t/dghl/standardsetting/dataprotection/CAHDATA/ Consolidated%20version%20of%20the%20modernised%20convention %20108%20July%202016.pdf [accessed 26 October 2016].

Coffman, K.G. and Odlyzko, A.M., 2003. Growth of the Internet. In I. Kaminow and T. Li, eds. *Optical Fiber Telecommunications IV B: Systems and Impairments*. San Diego: Academic Press, pp. 17–56.

Commission, 2002. The Application of Commission Decision 520/ 2000/EC of 26 July 2000 Pursuant to Directive 95/46 of the European Parliament and of the Council on the Adequate Protection of Personal Data Provided by the Safe Harbour Privacy Principles and Related Frequently Asked Questions Issued by the US Department of Commerce. Available at: http://ec.europa.eu/justice/policies/privacy/docs/ adequacy/sec-2002-196/sec-2002-196_en.pdf [accessed 26 October 2016].

Commission, 2003. Analysis and Impact Study on the Implementation of Directive EC 95/46 in Member States (Technical Annex to First Report). Available at: http://ec.europa.eu/justice/policies/privacy/docs/lawreport/consultation/technical-annex_en.pdf [accessed 26 October 2016].

Commission, 2005a. Data Protection: Commission Approves New Standard Clauses for Data Transfers to Non-EU Countries. Available at: http://europa.eu/rapid/press-release_IP-05-12_en.htm [accessed 26 October 2016].

Commission, 2005b. Standard Contractual Clauses for the Transfer of Personal Data to Third Countries: Frequently Asked Questions – MEMO/05/3. Available at: http://europa.eu/rapid/press-release_MEMO-05-3_en.htm [accessed 26 October 2016].

Commission, 2007. Notifications Pursuant to Article 26(3) of Directive 95/46/EC [unpublished].

Commission, 2009. Frequently Asked Questions Relating to Transfers of Personal Data from the EU/EEA to Third Countries. Available at: http://ec.europa.eu/justice/policies/privacy/docs/international_transfers_faq/international_transfers_faq.pdf [accessed 26 October 2016].

Commission, 2010a. Data Protection: Commission Requests UK to Strengthen Powers of National Data Protection Authority, as Required by EU Law. Available at: http://europa.eu/rapid/press-release_IP-10-811_en.htm [accessed 26 October 2016].

Commission, 2010b. Summary of Replies to the Public Consultation about the Future Legal Framework for Protecting Personal Data. Available at: http://ec.europa.eu/justice/news/consulting_public/0003/summary_replies_en.pdf [accessed 26 October 2016].

Commission, 2012a. 2011 Report on the Application of the EU Charter of Fundamental Rights. Available at: http://ec.europa.eu/justice/fundamental-rights/files/charter_report_en.pdf#41 [accessed 26 October 2016].

Commission, 2012b. Background Information. Available at: http://ec.europa.eu/justice/policies/privacy/thridcountries/background-info_en.htm [accessed 26 October 2016].

Commission, 2012c. Supplementary Evidence from the European Commission Following the Evidence Session on 11 September 2012 (to UK House of Commons Justice Committee for its Report on the EU Data Protection Framework Proposals). Available at: http://www.publications.parliament.uk/pa/cm201213/cmselect/cmjust/572/572we14.htm [accessed 26 October 2016].

Commission, 2012d. Unleashing the Potential of Cloud Computing in Europe COM(2012)529 final. Available at: http://eur-lex.europa.eu/

LexUriServ/LexUriServ.do?uri=COM:2012:0529:FIN:EN:PDF [accessed 26 October 2016].

Commission, 2013a. Impact Assessment Report on the Future of EU-US Trade Relations Accompanying the Document Recommendation for a Council Decision Authorising the Opening of Negotiations on a Comprehensive Trade and Investment Agreement, Called the Transatlantic Trade and Investment Partnership, between the European Union and the United States of America. Available at: http://trade. ec.europa.eu/doclib/docs/2013/march/tradoc_150759.pdf [accessed 26 October 2016].

Commission, 2013b. Notifications under Article 26(3) of Directive 95/46/EC (cut-off date: 31.05.2007) [unpublished].

Commission, 2013c. Notifying Member State/Number of Notifications/ Destination Country: Period 1/06–31/12/2007 [unpublished].

Commission, 2013d. What Does the Commission Mean by Secure Cloud Computing Services in Europe? MEMO/13/898. Available at: http:// europa.eu/rapid/press-release_MEMO-13-898_en.htm [accessed 26 October 2016].

Commission, 2014a. Commission to Pursue Role as Honest Broker in Future Global Negotiations on Internet Governance. Available at: http://europa.eu/rapid/press-release_IP-14-142_en.htm [accessed 26 October 2016].

Commission, 2014b. Notifying Member State/Number of Notifications/ Destination Country: Period 1/01/2008–31/12/2008 [unpublished].

Commission, 2014c. The Internet Needs Better Governance, Starting Now. Available at: http://europa.eu/rapid/press-release_SPEECH-14-333_en.htm [accessed 26 October 2016].

Commission, 2015a. Answer to a Written Question: Protection of Personal Data in TTIP and TiSA – E-011094/2015. Available at: http:// www.europarl.europa.eu/sides/getAllAnswers.do?reference=E-2015-01 1094&language=EN [accessed 26 October 2016].

Commission, 2015b. Communication on the Transfer of Personal Data from the EU to the United States of America under Directive 95/46/EC following the Judgment by the Court of Justice in Case C-362/14 (Schrems) COM(2015)566 Final. Available at: http://ec.europa.eu/ justice/data-protection/international-transfers/adequacy/files/eu-us_data_ flows_communication_final.pdf [accessed 26 October 2016].

Commission, 2015c. Outcome of the Workshop: Workshop 'Facilitating Cross Border Data Flow in Europe – on Data Location Restrictions'. Available at: http://ec.europa.eu/newsroom/dae/document.cfm?doc_id= 9326 [accessed 26 October 2016].

Commission, 2016a. Article 31 Committee Summary Record 4 July 2016. Available at: http://ec.europa.eu/transparency/regcomitology/

index.cfm?do=search.documentdetail&3JYTfuHLKeOtXKZPkkxKm/j
5eqPtq890AOhWko1oT2kn/Qhs71dMAJ5dvcXCvNIj   [accessed   26
October 2016].

Commission, 2016b. Background to the Public Consultation on the
Evaluations and Review of the ePrivacy Directive. Available at: http://
ec.europa.eu/newsroom/dae/document.cfm?action=display&doc_id=15
039 [accessed 26 October 2016].

Commission, 2016c. Client and Supplier Countries of the EU28 in
Merchandise Trade (Value %) (2015, Excluding Intra-EU Trade).
Available   at: http://trade.ec.europa.eu/doclib/docs/2006/september/
tradoc_122530.pdf [accessed 26 October 2016].

Commission, 2016d. European Commission Launches EU-U.S. Privacy
Shield: Stronger Protection for Transatlantic Data Flows. Available at:
http://europa.eu/rapid/press-release_IP-16-2461_en.htm   [accessed   26
October 2016].

Commission, 2016e. Inception Impact Assessment: European Free Flow
of Data Initiative within the Digital Single Market. Available at:
http://ec.europa.eu/smart-regulation/roadmaps/docs/2016_cnect_001_
free_flow_data_en.pdf [accessed 26 October 2016].

Commission, 2016f. Overview on Binding Corporate Rules. Available
at: http://ec.europa.eu/justice/data-protection/international-transfers/
binding-corporate-rules/index_en.htm [accessed 26 October 2016].

Commission, 2016g. Speech by Vice-President Ansip at the Consumer
Summit 2016, Brussels, 'Consumers matter: making the most of data
and the digital world'. Available at: http://europa.eu/rapid/press-
release_SPEECH-16-3467_fr.htm [accessed 26 October 2016].

Commission, 2016h. Speech by Vice-President Ansip at the Digital
Assembly 2016 in Bratislava, Slovakia: 'Europe should not be afraid of
data'. Available at: http://europa.eu/rapid/press-release_SPEECH-16-
3219_en.htm [accessed 26 October 2016].

Commission, 2016i. What Is Mutual Recognition? Available at: http://ec.
europa.eu/justice/data-protection/international-transfers/binding-corporate-
rules/mutual_recognition/index_en.htm [accessed 26 October 2016].

ComputerWeekly, 2003. Human Error Causes Most Security Breaches.
Available   at: http://www.computerweekly.com/news/2240050011/
Human-error-causes-most-security-breaches   [accessed   26   October
2016].

Conference of Data Protection Commissioners (DSK), 2015. DSK Pos-
ition   Paper.   Available   at: http://www.bfdi.bund.de/SharedDocs/
Publikationen/EU/Art29Gruppe/Safe-Harbor_Positionspapier-DSK_
Engl.pdf?__blob=publicationFile&v=1 [accessed 26 October 2016].

Connolly, C., 2008. The US Safe Harbor: fact or fiction? *Galexia*.
Available   at: http://www.galexia.com/public/research/assets/safe_

harbor_fact_or_fiction_2008/safe_harbor_fact_or_fiction.pdf [accessed 26 October 2016].

Connolly, C., 2013. EU/US Safe Harbor: effectiveness of the framework in relation to national security surveillance. Speaking/background notes for an appearance before the Committee on Civil Liberties, Justice and Home Affairs (the LIBE Committee) inquiry on 'Electronic mass surveillance of EU citizens', Strasbourg, 7 October 2013. Available at: http://www.europarl.europa.eu/document/activities/cont/201310/201310 08ATT72504/20131008ATT72504EN.pdf [accessed 26 October 2016].

Constantin, L., 2011. Google admits handing over European user data to US intelligence agencies. *Softpedia.* Available at: http://news.softpedia.com/news/Google-Admits-Handing-over-European-User-Data-to-US-Intelligence-Agencies-215740.shtml [accessed 26 October 2016].

Constantin, L., 2015. Europol and security vendors disrupt massive Ramnit botnet. *PCWorld.* Available at: http://www.pcworld.com/article/2889092/europol-and-security-vendors-disrupt-massive-ramnit-botnet.html [accessed 26 October 2016].

ContextIS, 2012. Dirty Disks Raise New Questions about Cloud Security. Available at: http://www.contextis.com/resources/blog/dirty-disks-raise-new-questions-about-cloud/ [accessed 26 October 2016].

Copyright Task Force, 2011. WS1 on Improvement of Regulation 45/2001 in the Context of the Review of the Data Protection Directive. Available at: http://ec.europa.eu/justice/news/consulting_public/0006/contributions/public_authorities/task_force_copyright_en.pdf [accessed 26 October 2016].

Corbett, J.C. et al., 2013. Spanner: Google's globally distributed database. *ACM Transactions on Computer Systems (TOCS)*, 31(3), p. 8.

CPNI, 2010. Centre for the Protection of National Infrastructure, Protection of Data Centres: CPNI Viewpoint 02/2010. Available at: http://www.cpni.gov.uk/Documents/Publications/2010/2010006-VP_data_centre.pdf [accessed 26 October 2016].

CPVP, 2008. Control and Recommendation Procedure Initiated with Respect to the Company SWIFT SCRL. Available at: http://www.privacycommission.be/sites/privacycommission/files/documents/swift_decision_en_09_12_2008.pdf [accessed 26 October 2016].

Cunningham-Day, J., 2014. The evolving relationship between DP and consumer protection laws. *Privacy Laws & Business United Kingdom Newsletter*, 76(Nov), pp. 5–7.

Darrow, B., 2013. Google adds server-side encryption to cloud storage. *Gigaom.* Available at: https://gigaom.com/2013/08/15/google-adds-server-side-encryption-to-cloud-storage/ [accessed 26 October 2016].

Data Protection Commissioner, 1999. The Eighth Data Protection Principle and Transborder Dataflows v.1. Available at: https://www.igt.

hscic.gov.uk/Knowledgebase/Kb/Information%20Commissioner/IC_The %20Eighth%20Data%20Protection%20Principle%20and%20Transborder %20Flows.pdf [accessed 26 October 2016].

Data Protection Commissioner of Ireland, 2012. Data Protection 'in the Cloud'. Available at: http://www.dataprotection.ie/viewdoc.asp?Doc ID=1221 [accessed 26 October 2016].

Data Protection Commissioner of Ireland, 2016. Statement by the Office of the Data Protection Commissioner in Respect of Application for Declaratory Relief in the Irish High Court and Referral to the CJEU. Available at: https://www.dataprotection.ie/docs/25-05-2016-Statement-by-this-Office-in-respect-of-application-for-Declaratory-Relief-in-the-Irish-High-Court-and-Referral-to-the-CJEU/1570.htm [accessed 26 October 2016].

Data Protection Registrar, 1994. Tenth Report of the Data Protection Registrar. London: HMSO.

DataGuidance, 2013. PRISM Debate Breathes New Life into 'Anti-FISA' Clause. Available at: http://www.dataguidance.com/dataguidance_privacy_this_week.asp?id=2120 [accessed 21 March 2015].

Datainspektionen, n.d. Transfer of Personal Data to a Third Country. Available at: http://www.datainspektionen.se/in-english/in-focus-transfer-of-personal-data/#3 [accessed 26 October 2016].

Datainspektionen, 2011. Cloud Services and the Personal Data Act. Available at: http://www.datainspektionen.se/in-english/cloud-services/ [accessed 26 October 2016].

Datainspektionen, 2014. Förvaltningsrätten ger Datainspektionen rätt om molntjänst. Available at: http://www.datainspektionen.se/press/nyheter/2014/forvaltningsratten-ger-datainspektionen-ratt-om-molntjanst/ [accessed 26 October 2016].

Datatilsynet, 2012. Use of Cloud Computing Services. Available at: https://www.datatilsynet.no/English/Publications/cloud-computing/ [accessed 26 October 2016].

Davidson, J. et al., 1999. *Goode: Consumer Credit Law and Practice.* R. Goode, ed. London: LexisNexis, Butterworths Law.

Dean, J. and Ghemawat, S., 2008. MapReduce: simplified data processing on large clusters. *Communications of the ACM*, 51(1), pp. 107–13.

Dekker, M. et al., 2013. Auditing security measures: an overview of schemes for auditing security measures. *ENISA.* Available at: https://www.enisa.europa.eu/publications/schemes-for-auditing-security-measures/at_download/fullReport [accessed 26 October 2016].

Dekker, M.A.C. and Liveri, D., 2015. Cloud security guide for SMEs: cloud computing security risks and opportunities for SMEs. *ENISA.* Available at: http://www.enisa.europa.eu/activities/Resilience-and-CIIP/

cloud-computing/security-for-smes/cloud-security-guide-for-smes/at_
download/fullReport [accessed 26 October 2016].

Determann, L., 2013. Data privacy in the cloud: myths and facts. *Privacy Laws & Business International Newsletter*, 121(Feb), pp. 17–22.

Deutsche Telekom, 2015. Deutsche Telekom to Act as Data Trustee for Microsoft Cloud in Germany. Available at: https://www.telekom.com/en/media/media-information/archive/deutsche-telekom-to-act-as-data-trustee-for-microsoft-cloud-in-germany-362074 [accessed 26 October 2016].

Dhont, J. et al., 2004. Safe Harbour decision implementation study. Universität Namur, Bericht für die Europäische Kommission, Generaldirektion Binnenmarkt und Dienstleistungen. *Commission*. Available at: http://ec.europa.eu/justice/policies/privacy/docs/studies/safe-harbour-2004_en.pdf [accessed 26 October 2016].

DIGITALEUROPE, 2009. Response to European Commission Consultation on the Legal Framework for the Fundamental Right to Protection of Personal Data. Available at: http://ec.europa.eu/justice/news/consulting_public/0003/contributions/organisations/digital_europe_en.pdf [accessed 26 October 2016].

Dignan, L., 2015. HTTP 2.0 wins approval: road to better encryption? *ZDNet*. Available at: http://www.zdnet.com/article/http-2-0-wins-approval-road-to-better-encryption/ [accessed 26 October 2016].

DoC, 2000. US Department of Commerce, Safe Harbor Privacy Principles. Available at: https://build.export.gov/main/safeharbor/eu/eg_main_018475 [accessed 26 October 2016].

DoC, 2013. US Department of Commerce, Clarifications Regarding the US-EU Safe Harbor Framework and Cloud Computing. Available at: https://build.export.gov/build/idcplg?IdcService=DOWNLOAD_PUBLIC_FILE&RevisionSelectionMethod=Latest&dDocName=eg_main_092416 [accessed 26 October 2016].

Dorling, P., 2013. New Snowden leaks reveal US, Australia's Asian allies. *The Age*. Available at: http://www.theage.com.au/technology/technology-news/new-snowden-leaks-reveal-us-australias-asian-allies-20131124-2y3mh.html [accessed 26 October 2016].

Dropbox, 2011. Dropbox: How Secure Is Dropbox? Available at: https://www.dropbox.com/help/27/en [accessed 26 October 2016].

Dulay, D., 2013. Out with the old: stronger certificates with Google Internet Authority G2. *Google Online Security Blog*. Available at: http://googleonlinesecurity.blogspot.co.uk/2013/11/out-with-old-stronger-certificates-with.html [accessed 26 October 2016].

Durie, R., 2000. An overview of the Data Protection Act 1998. *Computer and Telecommunications Law Review*, 6(4), pp. 88–93.

Düsseldorfer Kreis, 2010. Decision by the Supreme Supervisory Authorities for Data Protection in the Nonpublic Sector on 28/29 April 2010 in Hannover: Examination of the Data Importer's Self-Certification According to the Safe-Harbor-Agreement by the Company Exporting Data. Available at: http://www.datenschutz-berlin.de/attachments/710/Resolution_DuesseldorfCircle_28_04_2010EN.pdf [accessed 26 October 2016].

ECIPE, 2013. European Centre for International Political Economy, The Economic Importance of Getting Data Protection Right: Protecting Privacy, Transmitting Data, Moving Commerce. Available at: https://www.uschamber.com/sites/default/files/legacy/reports/020508_Economic Importance_Final_Revised_lr.pdf [accessed 26 October 2016].

EDPS, 2007a. Co-operation or Consultation under Articles 24(b) Respectively 46(d) of Regulation (EC) 45/2001 Concerning the Publication of Personal Data on the Internet and the Applicability or not of Article 9 of the Regulation. Available at: http://www.edps.europa.eu/EDPSWEB/webdav/shared/Documents/Supervision/Adminmeasures/2007/07-02-13 _Commission_personaldata_internet_EN.pdf [accessed 26 October 2016].

EDPS, 2007b. Opinion of the European Data Protection Supervisor on the Communication from the Commission to the European Parliament and the Council on the Follow-up of the Work Programme for Better Implementation of the Data Protection Directive (2007/C 255/01). Available at: https://secure.edps.europa.eu/EDPSWEB/webdav/site/my Site/shared/Documents/Consultation/Opinions/2007/07-07-25_Dir95- 46_EN.pdf [accessed 26 October 2016].

EDPS, 2010. Data Protection and Cloud Computing under EU law. Available at: https://secure.edps.europa.eu/EDPSWEB/webdav/shared/Documents/EDPS/Publications/Speeches/2010/10-04-13_Speech_Cloud_ Computing_EN.pdf [accessed 26 October 2016].

EDPS, 2011. Opinion of the European Data Protection Supervisor on the Communication from the Commission to the European Parliament, the Council, the Economic and Social Committee and the Committee of the Regions: 'A Comprehensive Approach on Personal Data Protection in the European Union'. Available at: http://eur-lex.europa.eu/LexUri Serv/LexUriServ.do?uri=CELEX:52011XX0622(01):EN:NOT [accessed 26 October 2016].

EDPS, 2012a. Opinion of the European Data Protection Supervisor on the Data Protection Reform Package. Available at: https://secure. edps.europa.eu/EDPSWEB/webdav/site/mySite/shared/Documents/Consultation/Opinions/2012/12-03-07_EDPS_Reform_package_EN. pdf [accessed 26 October 2016].

EDPS, 2012b. Opinion on the Commission's Communication on 'Unleashing the Potential of Cloud Computing in Europe'. Available at: https://secure.edps.europa.eu/EDPSWEB/webdav/site/mySite/shared/ Documents/Consultation/Opinions/2012/12-11-16_Cloud_Computing_ EN.pdf [accessed 26 October 2016].

EDPS, 2014a. Privacy and Competitiveness in the Age of Big Data: The Interplay between Data Protection, Competition Law and Consumer Protection in the Digital Economy – Preliminary Opinion. Available at: https://secure.edps.europa.eu/EDPSWEB/webdav/site/mySite/shared/ Documents/Consultation/Opinions/2014/14-03-26_competitition_law_ big_data_EN.pdf [accessed 26 October 2016].

EDPS, 2014b. The Transfer of Personal Data to Third Countries and International Organisations by EU Institutions and Bodies. Available at: https://secure.edps.europa.eu/EDPSWEB/webdav/site/mySite/shared/ Documents/Supervision/Papers/14-07-14_transfer_third_countries_EN. pdf [accessed 26 October 2016].

EDPS, 2016a. Opinion on the EU-U.S. Privacy Shield Draft Adequacy Decision. Available at: https://secure.edps.europa.eu/EDPSWEB/ webdav/site/mySite/shared/Documents/Consultation/Opinions/2016/16-05-30_Privacy_Shield_EN.pdf [accessed 26 October 2016].

EDPS, 2016b. Preliminary EDPS Opinion on the Review of the ePrivacy Directive (2002/58/EC). Available at: https://secure.edps.europa. eu/EDPSWEB/webdav/site/mySite/shared/Documents/Consultation/ Opinions/2016/16-07-22_Opinion_ePrivacy_EN.pdf [accessed 26 October 2016].

EDRi et al., 2016. Proceed with Caution: Flexibilities in the General Data Protection Regulation. Available at: https://edri.org/files/GDPR_ analysis/EDRi_analysis_gdpr_flexibilities.pdf [accessed 26 October 2016].

EESC, 2012. Opinion of the European Economic and Social Committee on the 'Proposal for a Regulation of the European Parliament and of the Council on the protection of individuals with regard to the process of personal data and on the free movement of such data (General Data Protection Regulation)'. *Official Journal of the European Union*, C229(21 July 2012), pp.90–97.

Efrati, A., 2013. How Google Transfers Data to NSA. *Digits (WSJ)*. Available at: http://blogs.wsj.com/digits/2013/06/11/how-google-transfers-data-to-nsa/ [accessed 26 October 2016].

Emmerson, B., 2014. Report of the Special Rapporteur on the Promotion and Protection of Human Rights and Fundamental Freedoms while Countering Terrorism UN Doc A/69/397. *United Nations*. Available at: http://docbox.un.org/DocBox/docbox.nsf/GetFile?OpenAgent&DS=A/ 69/397&Lang=E&Type=PDF [accessed 26 October 2016].

Emmott, R., 2014. Brazil, Europe Plan Undersea Cable to Skirt U.S. Spying. *Reuters*. Available at: http://www.reuters.com/article/2014/02/24/us-eu-brazil-idUSBREA1N0PL20140224 [accessed 26 October 2016].

ENISA, 2013. Securing Data in Cyber Space: ENISA Comments Following Recent Large-Scale Data Compromise Activity. Available at: http://www.enisa.europa.eu/publications/flash-notes/securing-data-in-cyber-space/at_download/file [accessed 26 October 2016].

ENISA, 2015. SME Cloud Security Tool. Available at: http://www.enisa.europa.eu/activities/Resilience-and-CIIP/cloud-computing/security-for-smes/sme-guide-tool [accessed 26 October 2016].

EPOF, 2011. European Privacy Officers Forum, Comments on the Review of the European Data Protection Framework. Available at: http://ec.europa.eu/justice/news/consulting_public/0006/contributions/not_registered/epof_en.pdf [accessed 26 October 2016].

Ernesto, 2012. Pirate Bay moves to the cloud, becomes raid-proof. *TorrentFreak*. Available at: http://torrentfreak.com/pirate-bay-moves-to-the-cloud-becomes-raid-proof-121017/ [accessed 26 October 2016].

Ernesto, 2014a. Can The Pirate Bay make a comeback? *TorrentFreak*. Available at: https://torrentfreak.com/can-pirate-bay-make-comeback-141210/ [accessed 26 October 2016].

Ernesto, 2014b. Encrypted Internet traffic surges in a year, research shows. *TorrentFreak*. Available at: http://torrentfreak.com/encrypted-internet-traffic-surges-140514/ [accessed 26 October 2016].

Ernesto, 2014c. Pirate Bay responds to the raid, copies and the future. *TorrentFreak*. Available at: https://torrentfreak.com/pirate-bay-crew-responds-to-the-raid-copies-and-the-future-141215/ [accessed 26 October 2016].

Ernesto, 2014d. The Pirate Bay runs on 21 'raid-proof' virtual machines. *TorrentFreak*. Available at: http://torrentfreak.com/the-pirate-bay-runs-on-21-raid-proof-virtual-machines-140921/ [accessed 26 October 2016].

Ernesto, 2015. Pirate Bay responds to Cloudflare and moderation concerns. *TorrentFreak*. Available at: http://torrentfreak.com/pirate-bay-will-ditch-cloudflare-asks-users-moderate-150203/ [accessed 26 October 2016].

Essers, L., 2013. Skype, Microsoft cleared in Luxembourg NSA investigation. *PCWorld*. Available at: http://www.pcworld.com/article/2064540/skype-microsoft-cleared-in-luxembourg-nsa-investigation.html [accessed 26 October 2016].

Estonian Ministry of Economic Affairs and Communication and Microsoft, 2015. Implementation of the Virtual Data Embassy Solution. Available at: http://download.microsoft.com/download/5/5/B/55B89

687-C789-43DE-A5B1-89D9CE6BCF71/Implementation%20of%20the %20Virtual%20Data%20Embassy%20Solution%20Summary%20Report. pdf [accessed 26 October 2016].

Ezell, S., 2015. Opinion: why privacy alarmists are wrong about data rules in big trade deals. *Christian Science Monitor*. Available at: http://www.csmonitor.com/World/Passcode/Passcode-Voices/2015/ 0715/Opinion-Why-privacy-alarmists-are-wrong-about-data-rules-in-big-trade-deals [accessed 26 October 2016].

Ezell, S.J., Atkinson, R.D. and Wein, M.A., 2013. Localization barriers to trade: threat to the global innovation economy. *Information Technology & Innovation Foundation*. Available at: http://www2.itif.org/2013-localization-barriers-to-trade.pdf [accessed 26 October 2016].

Facebook, 2016. Messenger Starts Testing End-to-End Encryption with Secret Conversations. Available at: http://newsroom.fb.com/news/ 2016/07/messenger-starts-testing-end-to-end-encryption-with-secret-conversations/ [accessed 26 October 2016].

Falvinge, R., 2014. 'How to learn absolutely nothing in fifteen years,' by the copyright industry. *TorrentFreak*. Available at: http://torrent freak.com/how-to-learn-absolutely-nothing-in-fifteen-years-by-the-copy right-industry-141214/ [accessed 26 October 2016].

Farivar, C., 2013. Seven telcos named as providing fiber optic cable access to UK spies. *Ars Technica*. Available at: http://arstechnica.com/ tech-policy/2013/08/seven-telcos-named-as-providing-fiber-optic-cable-access-to-uk-spies/ [accessed 26 October 2016].

Federal Office for Information Security (Germany), 2016. Cloud Computing Compliance Controls Catalogue (C5). Available at: https:// www.bsi.bund.de/SharedDocs/Downloads/EN/BSI/CloudComputing/ ComplianceControlsCatalogue/ComplianceControlsCatalogue.pdf?__ blob=publicationFile&v=3 [accessed 26 October 2016].

Ferracane, M.E., 2015. A race against time: new data protection rules in the Internet era. *ECIPE*. Available at: http://ecipe.org/blog/a-race-against-time-new-data-protection-rules-in-the-internet-era/ [accessed 26 October 2016].

Ferraiolo, D.F. and Kuhn, D.R., 1992. Role-based access controls. In *15th National Computer Security Conference. arXiv*, pp. 554–63. Available at: http://arxiv.org/abs/0903.2171 [accessed 26 October 2016].

Financial Conduct Authority, 2016. FG 16/5: Guidance for Firms Outsourcing to the 'Cloud' and Other Third-Party IT Services. Available at: http://www.fca.org.uk/static/fca/article-type/news/fg16-5.pdf [accessed 26 October 2016].

Financial Services Authority, 2010. FSA Fines Zurich Insurance £2,275,000 Following the Loss of 46,000 Policy Holders' Personal

Details. Available at: http://www.fsa.gov.uk/library/communication/pr/2010/134.shtml [accessed 26 October 2016].

Finley, K., 2012. Microsoft cloud floats to China (without Microsoft). *WIRED*. Available at: https://www.wired.com/2012/11/azure-goes-to-china/ [accessed 26 October 2016].

Finnegan, M., 2015. Microsoft and AWS set sights on the UK: but will AWS and Microsoft's UK data centres resolve data sovereignty concerns? *ComputerworldUK*. Available at: http://www.computerworld uk.com/cloud-computing/will-aws-microsofts-uk-data-centres-resolve-data-sovereignty-concerns-3629408/ [accessed 26 October 2016].

Fluhrer, S., Mantin, I. and Shamir, A., 2001. Weaknesses in the key scheduling algorithm of RC4. In *Selected Areas in Cryptography*. Berlin, Heidelberg: Springer, pp. 1–24. Available at: http://link.springer.com/chapter/10.1007/3-540-45537-X_1 [accessed 26 October 2016].

Fontanella-Khan, J. and Waters, R., 2014. Microsoft to shield foreign users' data. *Financial Times*. Available at: http://www.ft.com/cms/s/0/e14ddf70-8390-11e3-aa65-00144feab7de.html?siteedition=uk [accessed 26 October 2016].

FRA, 2010. Data Protection in the European Union: The Role of National Data Protection Authorities – Strengthening the Fundamental Rights Architecture in the EU II. Available at: http://fra.europa.eu/en/publication/2012/data-protection-european-union-role-national-data-protection-authorities [accessed 26 October 2016].

FRA, 2012. Annual Report 2012: Fundamental Rights – Challenges and Achievements in 2012. Available at: http://fra.europa.eu/sites/default/files/annual-report-2012-chapter-3_en.pdf [accessed 26 October 2016].

FRA, 2014. Access to Data Protection Remedies in EU Member States. Available at: http://fra.europa.eu/sites/default/files/fra-2014-access-data-protection-remedies_en_0.pdf [accessed 26 October 2016].

FRA, 2015. Surveillance by Intelligence Services: Fundamental Rights Safeguards and Remedies in the EU – Mapping Member States' Legal Frameworks. Available at: http://fra.europa.eu/sites/default/files/fra_uploads/fra-2015-surveillance-intelligence-services_en.pdf [accessed 26 October 2016].

FRA and CoE, 2014. Handbook on European Data Protection Law. Available at: http://fra.europa.eu/sites/default/files/fra-2014-handbook-data-protection-law-2nd-ed_en.pdf [accessed 26 October 2016].

Froomkin, A.M., 1995. The metaphor is the key: cryptography, the clipper chip, and the constitution. *University of Pennsylvania Law Review*, 143(3), pp. 709–897.

FTC, 2011a. FTC Settlement Bans Online U.S. Electronics Retailer from Deceiving Consumers with Foreign Website Names. Available at:

https://www.ftc.gov/news-events/press-releases/2011/06/ftc-settlement-bans-online-us-electronics-retailer-deceiving [accessed 26 October 2016].

FTC, 2011b. In the Matter of Google, Inc. (102 3136). Available at: https://www.ftc.gov/enforcement/cases-proceedings/102-3136/google-inc-matter [accessed 26 October 2016].

FTC, 2012a. In the Matter of Facebook, Inc. (092 3184). Available at: https://www.ftc.gov/enforcement/cases-proceedings/092-3184/facebook-inc [accessed 26 October 2016].

FTC, 2012b. In the Matter of Myspace LLC (102 3058). Available at: https://www.ftc.gov/enforcement/cases-proceedings/102-3058/myspace-llc-matter [accessed 26 October 2016].

FTC, 2014. FTC Signs Memorandum of Understanding with UK Privacy Enforcement Agency. Available at: http://www.ftc.gov/news-events/press-releases/2014/03/ftc-signs-memorandum-understanding-uk-privacy-enforcement-agency [accessed 26 October 2016].

FTC, 2015. In the Matter of TES Franchising, LLC. Available at: https://www.ftc.gov/enforcement/cases-proceedings/152-3015/tes-franchising-llc-matter [accessed 26 October 2016].

FTC, 2016a. FTC Approves Final Order in Vipvape APEC Cross Border Privacy Rule Case. Available at: https://www.ftc.gov/news-events/press-releases/2016/06/ftc-approves-final-order-vipvape-apec-cross-border-privacy-rule [accessed 26 October 2016].

FTC, 2016b. FTC Issues Warning Letters to Companies Claiming APEC Cross-Border Privacy Certification. Available at: https://www.ftc.gov/news-events/press-releases/2016/07/ftc-issues-warning-letters-companies-claiming-apec-cross-border [accessed 26 October 2016].

Gallagher, S., 2015. Microsoft's Office 365 'lockbox' gives customers last word on data access. *Ars Technica*. Available at: http://arstechnica.com/information-technology/2015/04/microsofts-office-365-lockbox-gives-customers-last-word-on-data-access/ [accessed 26 October 2016].

Gallup, 2008a. Data Protection in the European Union: Citizens' Perceptions Analytical Report – Flash Eurobarometer #225. Available at: http://ec.europa.eu/public_opinion/flash/fl_225_en.pdf [accessed 26 October 2016].

Gallup, 2008b. Data Protection in the European Union: Data Controllers' Perceptions – Analytical Report (Flash Eurobarometer 226). Available at: http://ec.europa.eu/public_opinion/flash/fl_226_en.pdf [accessed 26 October 2016].

Garante, 2012. Cloud Computing: How to Protect your Data without Falling from a Cloud. Available at: http://www.garanteprivacy.it/web/

guest/home/docweb/-/docweb-display/docweb/1906181 [accessed 26 October 2016].

Garante, 2015. Google to Comply with the Privacy Measures Set Forth by the Italian DPA: Verification Protocol Approved by the DPA. Available at: http://garanteprivacy.it/web/guest/home/docweb/-/docweb-display/docweb/3740585 [accessed 26 October 2016].

Garcia, F.J., 2004. Bodil Lindqvist: a Swedish churchgoer's violation of the European Union's Data Protection Directive should be a warning to US legislators. *Fordham Intellectual Property, Media & Entertainment Law Journal*, 15(4), pp. 1205–44.

Gardner, S., 2016. EU certificate may be U.S. data transfer alternative. *Bloomberg BNA*. Available at: http://www.bna.com/eu-certificate-may-n73014446298/ [accessed 26 October 2016].

Gartner, 2013. Cloud Encryption Gateways. Available at: http://www.gartner.com/it-glossary/cloud-encryption-gateways/ [accessed 26 October 2016].

GDV, 2009. Gesamtverband der Deutschen Versicherungswirtschaft e. V., Position Paper: Consultation on the Legal Framework for the Fundamental Right to Protection of Personal Data. Available at: http://ec.europa.eu/justice/news/consulting_public/0003/contributions/organisations/german_insurance_association_en.pdf [accessed 26 October 2016].

Gellman, B. and Soltani, A., 2013a. NSA collects millions of e-mail address books globally. *The Washington Post*. Available at: http://www.washingtonpost.com/world/national-security/nsa-collects-millions-of-e-mail-address-books-globally/2013/10/14/8e58b5be-34f9-11e3-80c6-7e6dd8d22d8f_story.html [accessed 26 October 2016].

Gellman, B. and Soltani, A., 2013b. NSA infiltrates links to Yahoo, Google data centers worldwide, Snowden documents say. *The Washington Post*. Available at: http://www.washingtonpost.com/world/national-security/nsa-infiltrates-links-to-yahoo-google-data-centers-worldwide-snowden-documents-say/2013/10/30/e51d661e-4166-11e3-8b74-d89d714ca4dd_story.html [accessed 26 October 2016].

Georgiadis, C.K. et al., 2001. Flexible team-based access control using contexts. In *Proceedings of the Sixth ACM Symposium on Access Control Models and Technologies. ACM*, pp. 21–7. Available at: http://dl.acm.org/citation.cfm?id=373259 [accessed 26 October 2016].

German Conference of Federal and State Data Protection Commissioners, 2013. Conference of Data Protection Commissioners Says that Intelligence Services Constitute a Massive Threat to Data Traffic between Germany and Countries outside Europe. Available at: http://www.bfdi.bund.de/SharedDocs/Publikationen/Entschliessungssammlung/ErgaenzendeDokumente/PMDSK_SafeHarbor_Eng.pdf?__blob=publicationFile [accessed 26 October 2016].

Ghemawat, S., Gobioff, H. and Leung, S.-T., 2003. The Google file system. In *ACM SIGOPS Operating Systems Review*, 37(5), 29–43. Available at: http://dl.acm.org/citation.cfm?id=945450 [accessed 26 October 2016].

Giannakouris, K. and Smihily, M., 2014. Cloud computing: statistics on the use by enterprises. *Eurostat*. Available at: http://ec.europa.eu/eurostat/statistics-explained/index.php/Cloud_computing_-_statistics_on_the_use_by_enterprises [accessed 26 October 2016].

Gibbs, S., 2014. Swedish police raid sinks The Pirate Bay. *The Guardian*. Available at: http://www.theguardian.com/technology/2014/dec/10/swedish-police-raid-pirate-bay [accessed 26 October 2016].

Gidda, M., 2013. Edward Snowden and the NSA files: timeline. *The Guardian*. Available at: http://www.theguardian.com/world/2013/jun/23/edward-snowden-nsa-files-timeline [accessed 26 October 2016].

Gondree, M. and Peterson, Z.N.J., 2013. Geolocation of data in the cloud. In *Proceedings of the Third ACM Conference on Data and Application Security and Privacy. ACM*, pp. 25–36. Available at: http://doi.acm.org/10.1145/2435349.2435353 [accessed 26 October 2016].

Google, n.d. Compliance Amendments for G Suite: Model Contract Clauses. Available at: https://support.google.com/a/answer/2888485 [accessed 26 October 2016].

Google, 2011. Security Whitepaper: Google Apps Messaging and Collaboration Products. Available at: http://static.googleusercontent.com/media/www.google.com/en//a/help/intl/en-GB/admins/pdf/ds_gsa_apps_whitepaper_0207.pdf [accessed 26 October 2016].

Google, 2012. Data Center Locations. Available at: http://www.google.co.uk/about/datacenters/inside/locations/ [accessed 26 October 2016].

Google, 2014. Data Processing Amendment to Google Apps Agreement. Available at: https://www.google.com/intx/en/work/apps/terms/dpa_terms.html [accessed 26 October 2016].

Google, 2015a. Google Compute Engine Service Level Agreement (SLA). Available at: https://cloud.google.com/compute/sla [accessed 26 October 2016].

Google, 2015b. The Impacts of Data Localization on Cybersecurity. Available at: http://googlepublicpolicy.blogspot.com/2015/02/the-impacts-of-data-localization-on.html [accessed 26 October 2016].

Goulart, K., 2014. Survey: for cloud computing use, business needs trump cost savings as top driver. *SearchCIO*. Available at: http://searchcio.techtarget.com/news/2240212159/Survey-For-cloud-computing-use-business-needs-trump-cost-savings-as-top-driver [accessed 26 October 2016].

Gould, J., 2013. SafeGov conversation with PerspecSys CEO David Canellos. *SafeGov.* Available at: http://web.archive.org/web/2016 0809081338/http://www.safegov.org/2013/2/14/safegov-conversation-with-perspecsys-ceo-david-canellos [accessed 26 October 2016].

GPEN, 2016. About the Network. Available at: https://www.privacy enforcement.net/about_the_network [accessed 26 October 2016].

Grant, H. and Crowther, H., 2016. How effective are fines in enforcing privacy? In D. Wright and P.D. Hert, eds. *Enforcing Privacy.* Law, Governance and Technology Series. Cham, Switzerland: Springer International Publishing, pp. 287–305. Available at: http://link.springer.com/chapter/10.1007/978-3-319-25047-2_13 [accessed 26 October 2016].

Graux, H., 2014. Establishing a trusted cloud Europe: a policy vision document by the steering board of the European Cloud Partnership. *Commission.* Available at: http://ec.europa.eu/information_society/newsroom/cf/dae/document.cfm?doc_id=4935 [accessed 26 October 2016].

Graux, H., 2016. Code of conduct for cloud service providers: state of play, open issues and next steps. *Commission.* Available at: http://ec.europa.eu/newsroom/dae/document.cfm?action=display&doc_id=16751 [accessed 26 October 2016].

Greenleaf, G., 2011a. Do not dismiss 'adequacy': European standards entrenched. *Privacy Laws & Business International Newsletter,* 114(Dec), pp. 16–18.

Greenleaf, G., 2011b. Global data privacy in a networked world. *SSRN.* Available at: http://papers.ssrn.com/abstract=1954296 [accessed 26 October 2016].

Greenleaf, G., 2012. The influence of European data privacy standards outside Europe: implications for globalization of Convention 108. *International Data Privacy Law,* 2(2), pp. 68–92.

Greenwald, G. and MacAskill, E., 2013. NSA Prism program taps in to user data of Apple, Google and others. *The Guardian.* Available at: http://www.theguardian.com/world/2013/jun/06/us-tech-giants-nsa-data [accessed 26 October 2016].

Gruber, A., 2016. Safe-Harbor-Sünder: Datenschützer verhängt Bußgelder. *Spiegel Online.* Available at: http://www.spiegel.de/netz welt/netzpolitik/safe-harbor-suender-hamburgs-oberster-datenschuetzer-verhaengt-bussgelder-a-1096091.html [accessed 26 October 2016].

GTISC and GTRI, 2013. Georgia Tech Information Security Center and Georgia Tech Research Institute, Emerging Cyber Threats Report 2014. Available at: http://www.gtsecuritysummit.com/2014Report.pdf [accessed 26 October 2016].

Gunasekara, G., 2007. The 'final' privacy frontier? Regulating transborder data flows. *International Journal of Law and Information Technology*, 15(3), pp. 362–93.

Gupta, A., 2016. Scaling to exabytes and beyond. *Dropbox Tech Blog*. Available at: https://blogs.dropbox.com/tech/2016/03/magic-pocket-infrastructure/ [accessed 26 October 2016].

Hague Conference on Private International Law, 2010. Cross-Border Data Flows and Protection of Privacy. Available at: http://www.hcch.net/upload/wop/genaff2010pd13e.pdf [accessed 26 October 2016].

Hakim, D., 2013. Europe aims to regulate the cloud. *The New York Times*. Available at: http://www.nytimes.com/2013/10/07/business/international/europe-aims-to-regulate-the-cloud.html [accessed 26 October 2016].

Halabi, S., 2000. *Internet Routing Architectures* 2nd edition. Indianapolis, IN: Cisco Press.

Hansen, T., 2016. Dropbox is growing in Europe. *Dropbox Business Blog*. Available at: https://blogs.dropbox.com/business/2016/02/dropbox-is-growing-in-europe/ [accessed 26 October 2016].

Harding, L., 2014. Edward Snowden: US government spied on human rights workers. *The Guardian*. Available at: http://www.theguardian.com/world/2014/apr/08/edwards-snowden-us-government-spied-human-rights-workers [accessed 26 October 2016].

Harris, E.C., 2006. Personal data privacy tradeoffs and how a Swedish church lady, Austrian public radio employees, and transatlantic air carriers show that Europe does not have the answers. *American University International Law Review*, 22(5), pp. 745–800.

Harris Poll and Ovum, 2015. 2015 Vormetric Insider Threat Report. Available at: http://enterprise-encryption.vormetric.com/rs/vormetric/images/CW_GlobalReport_2015_Insider_threat_Vormetric_Single_Pages_010915.pdf [accessed 26 October 2016].

Harrison, J., 2014. EU data protection authorities endorse Microsoft's cloud computing agreement. *SCL*. Available at: http://www.scl.org/site.aspx?i=ed36831 [accessed 26 October 2016].

Hawes, J., 2014. Russia's latest Internet law proposal: anti-NSA, or pro-FSB? *Naked Security*. Available at: https://nakedsecurity.sophos.com/2014/07/04/russias-latest-internet-law-proposal-anti-nsa-or-pro-fsb/ [accessed 26 October 2016].

Henderson, H., 2009. *Encyclopedia of Computer Science and Technology*. New York: Infobase Publishing.

Henderson, J., 2014. SCL event report: international data transfers. *SCL*. Available at: http://www.scl.org/site.aspx?i=ne39783 [accessed 26 October 2016].

Hess, K., 2015. Infamous hacker Kevin Mitnick sniffs fiber, reads email. *ZDNet*. Available at: http://www.zdnet.com/article/infamous-hacker-kevin-mitnick-sniffs-fiber-reads-email/ [accessed 26 October 2016].

Higgins, A., 2011. FBI Siezes [sic] 3 server racks from datacenter taking popular blogs and bookmarking sites offline. *Before It's News*. Available at: http://beforeitsnews.com/alternative/2011/06/fbi-siezes-3-server-racks-from-datacenter-taking-popular-blogs-and-bookmarking-sites-offline-740486.html [accessed 26 October 2016].

HmbBfDI, 2016. Unzulässige Datenübermittlungen in die USA. Available at: https://www.datenschutz-hamburg.de/news/detail/article/unzulaessige-datenuebermittlungen-in-die-usa.html [accessed 26 October 2016].

Hoffmann-Andrews, J., 2013. Forward secrecy at Twitter. *Twitter Engineering Blog*. Available at: https://blog.twitter.com/2013/forward-secrecy-at-twitter-0 [accessed 26 October 2016].

Hölzle, U., 2012. Google's data centers: an inside look. *Official Google Blog*. Available at: http://googleblog.blogspot.com/2012/10/googles-data-centers-inside-look.html [accessed 26 October 2016].

Home Office, 1996. Consultation paper on the EC Data Protection Directive. *Journal of Information, Law & Technology*, (1). Available at: http://www2.warwick.ac.uk/fac/soc/law/elj/jilt/1996_1/special/consultation/.

Hon, W.K., 2014. Cloud computing: geography or technology – virtualisation and control. *SCL*. Available at: https://www.scl.org/site.aspx?i=ed35439 [accessed 26 October 2016].

Hon, W.K., 2015a. GDPR & cloud providers [slides]. *Cloudscape*. Available at: http://admin.cloudscapeseries.eu/Repository/document/PresentationCSVII/KuanHon_GDPRCloud%20Providers.pdf [accessed 26 October 2016].

Hon, W.K., 2015b. Open season on service providers? The General Data Protection Regulation cometh … . *SCL*. Available at: http://www.scl.org/site.aspx?i=ed43376 [accessed 26 October 2016].

Hon, W.K., 2016a. Article 31 Committee flowchart: Privacy Shield. *Kuan0.com*. Available at: http://blog.kuan0.com/2016/05/article-31-committee-flowchart-privacy.html [accessed 26 October 2016].

Hon, W.K., 2016b. Article 93(2) GDPR comitology: flowchart. *Kuan0.com*. Available at: http://blog.kuan0.com/2016/05/article-932-gdpr-comitology-flowchart.html [accessed 26 October 2016].

Hon, W.K., 2016c. GDPR's extra-territoriality means trouble for cloud computing. *Privacy Laws & Business International Newsletter*, 140, pp. 25–8.

Hon, W.K., 2016d. International transfers under GDPR: key changes. *Privacy Laws & Business International Newsletter*, 141, pp. 7–11.

Hon, W.K., 2016e. More detail on workings of GDPR certification schemes necessary to prompt business take-up, says expert. *Out-Law*. Available at: http://www.out-law.com/en/articles/2016/october/more-detail-on-workings-of-gdpr-certification-schemes-necessary-to-prompt-business-take-up-says-expert/ [accessed 26 October 2016].

Hon, W.K., 2016f. Privacy Shield: history, key links. *Kuan0.com*. Available at: http://blog.kuan0.com/2016/09/privacy-shield-history-key-links.html [accessed 26 October 2016].

Hon, W.K., 2016g. Update E-Commerce Directive to address imbalance in GDPR liabilities for infrastructure cloud providers, says expert. *Out-Law*. Available at: http://www.out-law.com/en/articles/2016/september/update-e-commerce-directive-to-address-imbalance-in-gdpr-liabilities-for-infrastructure-cloud-providers-says-expert/ [accessed 26 October 2016].

Hon, W.K. and Millard, C., 2012. Data export in cloud computing: how can personal data be transferred outside the EEA? The Cloud of Unknowing, Part 4. *SCRIPTed*, 9(1), p. 25.

Hon, W.K. and Millard, C., 2013a. Cloud technologies and services. In C. Millard, ed. *Cloud Computing Law*. Oxford: OUP.

Hon, W.K. and Millard, C., 2013b. Control, security, and risk in the cloud. In C. Millard, ed. *Cloud Computing Law*. Oxford: OUP.

Hon, W.K. and Millard, C., 2013c. How do restrictions on international data transfers work in clouds? In C. Millard, ed. *Cloud Computing Law*. Oxford: OUP.

Hon, W.K. and Millard, C., 2016. Use by banks of cloud computing: an empirical study. *SSRN*. Available at: https://papers.ssrn.com/abstract=2856431 [accessed 26 October 2016].

Hon, W.K., Millard, C. and Hörnle, J., 2013. Which law(s) apply to personal data in clouds? In C. Millard, ed. *Cloud Computing Law*. Oxford: OUP.

Hon, W.K., Millard, C. and Walden, I., 2013a. Negotiated contracts for cloud services. In C. Millard, ed. *Cloud Computing Law*. Oxford: OUP.

Hon, W.K., Millard, C. and Walden, I., 2013b. What is regulated as personal data in clouds? In C. Millard, ed. *Cloud Computing Law*. Oxford: OUP.

Hon, W.K., Millard, C. and Walden, I., 2013c. Who is responsible for personal data in clouds? In C. Millard, ed. *Cloud Computing Law*. Oxford: OUP.

Hon, W.K., Kosta, E., Millard, C., et al., 2014. Cloud accountability: the likely impact of the proposed EU Data Protection Regulation. *SSRN*. Available at: http://papers.ssrn.com/abstract=2405971 [accessed 26 October 2016].

Hon, W.K., Millard, C., Reed, C., et al., 2014. Policy, legal and regulatory implications of a Europe-only cloud. *SSRN*. Available at: http://papers.ssrn.com/abstract=2527951 [accessed 26 October 2016].

Hon, W.K., Millard C., Singh, J., et al., 2016. Policy, legal and regulatory implications of a Europe-only cloud. *International Journal of Law andInformation Technology*, 24(3), pp. 251–78.

Honan, M., 2012. How Apple and Amazon security flaws led to my epic hacking. *WIRED*. Available at: http://www.wired.com/2012/08/apple-amazon-mat-honan-hacking/all/ [accessed 26 October 2016].

Hoskins, M., 2014. Pointless data protection practices. *Data Protector*. Available at: http://dataprotector.blogspot.co.uk/2014/06/pointless-data-protection-practices.html [accessed 26 October 2016].

Hoyle, C., 1992. Legal aspects of transborder data flow. *Computer Law & Security Report*, 8(4), pp. 166–72.

Hu, V.C. et al., 2014. Guide to attribute based access control (ABAC) definition and considerations, SP 800-162. *NIST*. Available at: http://csrc.nist.gov/publications/drafts/800-162/sp800_162_draft.pdf [accessed 26 October 2016].

IAPP, 2010. Data Protection Authorities: 2010 Global Benchmarking Survey. Available at: https://www.privacyassociation.org/media/pdf/knowledge_center/IAPP_DPA2010_GlobalBenchmarking_Survey.pdf [accessed 26 October 2016].

IAPP, 2011. Data Protection Authorities: 2011 Global Survey. Available at: https://www.privacyassociation.org/media/pdf/knowledge_center/DPA11_Survey_final.pdf [accessed 26 October 2016].

IAPP, 2013. International Data Transfers: Reviewing the Options [presentations and meeting held under the Chatham House Rule]. London.

IAPP and EY, 2016. Annual Privacy Governance Report 2016. Available at: https://iapp.org/media/pdf/resource_center/IAPP-2016-GOVERNANCE-SURVEY-FINAL2.pdf [accessed 26 October 2016].

IBM, 2014. IBM Cyber Security Intelligence Index: Schwachstelle Mensch. Available at: https://www-03.ibm.com/press/de/de/press release/44264.wss [accessed 26 October 2016].

ICC, 2004. ICC Report on Binding Corporate Rules for International Transfers of Personal Data. Available at: http://www.iccwbo.org/Data/Documents/Digital-Economy/ICC-report-on-Binding-Corporate-Rules/ [accessed 26 October 2016].

ICC, 2009. ICC Response to the European Commission Consultation on the Legal Framework for the Fundamental Right to Protection of Personal Data. Available at: http://ec.europa.eu/justice/news/consulting_public/0003/contributions/organisations_not_registered/international_chamber_of_commerce_icc_en.pdf [accessed 26 October 2016].

ICC, 2012. Cross-Border Law Enforcement Access to Company Data: Current Issues under Data Protection and Privacy Law 373/507. Available at: http://www.iccwbo.org/Data/Policies/2012/Cross-border-law-enforcement-access-to-company-data-current-issues-under-data-protection-and-privacy-law/ [accessed 26 October 2016].

ICO, 2010. The Eighth Data Protection Principle and International Data Transfers v4. Available at: https://ico.org.uk/media/for-organisations/documents/1566/international_transfers_legal_guidance.pdf [accessed 26 October 2016].

ICO, 2012a. Guidance on the Use of Cloud Computing. Available at: http://www.ico.org.uk/for_organisations/data_protection/topic_guides/online/~/media/documents/library/Data_Protection/Practical_application/cloud_computing_guidance_for_organisations.ashx [accessed 26 October 2016].

ICO, 2012b. ICO Cloud Event 27 February 2012: Summary of Key Points. Available at: http://webarchive.nationalarchives.gov.uk/2013 0402163358/http://www.ico.gov.uk/news/current_topics/cloud_event_summary_2012.aspx [accessed 26 October 2016].

ICO, 2012c. Information Commissioner's Office: Initial Analysis of the European Commission's Proposals for a Revised Data Protection Legislative Framework. Available at: http://webarchive. nationalarchives.gov.uk/20130102190125/http://www.ico.gov.uk/news/~/media/documents/library/Data_Protection/Research_and_reports/ico_initial_analysis_of_revised_eu_dp_legislative_proposals.ashx [accessed 26 October 2016].

ICO, 2013a. ICO Views on the European Parliament LIBE Committee's Approach to the Draft General Data Protection Regulation and Draft Directive on Data Protection in Criminal Justice and Law Enforcement. Available at: http://webarchive.nationalarchives.gov. uk/20140603200757/http://www.ico.org.uk/news/blog/2013/~/media/documents/library/Data_Protection/Research_and_reports/ico-views-european-parliament-libe-committee-19122013.pdf [accessed 26 October 2016].

ICO, 2013b. Proposed New EU General Data Protection Regulation: Article-by-Article Analysis Paper. Available at: https://ico.org.uk/media/about-the-ico/documents/1042564/ico-proposed-dp-regulation-analysis-paper-20130212.pdf [accessed 26 October 2016].

ICO, 2014a. Corporate Plan Targets Better Data Protection Results. Available at: https://ico.org.uk/about-the-ico/news-and-events/news-and-blogs/2014/03/corporate-plan-targets-better-data-protection-results/ [accessed 26 October 2016].

ICO, 2014b. Data Controllers and Data Processors: What the Difference Is and What the Governance Implications Are Version 1.0. Available at: https://ico.org.uk/media/for-organisations/documents/1546/data-controllers-and-data-processors-dp-guidance.pdf [accessed 26 October 2016].

ICO, 2014c. Deleting Personal Data Version 1.1. Available at: https://ico.org.uk/media/for-organisations/documents/1475/deleting_personal_data.pdf [accessed 26 October 2016].

ICO, 2014d. Review of the Impact of ICO Civil Monetary Penalties. Available at: https://ico.org.uk/media/1042346/review-of-the-impact-of-ico-civil-monetary-penalties.pdf [accessed 26 October 2016].

ICO, 2015a. Assessing Adequacy: International Data Transfers. Available at: https://ico.org.uk/media/1529/assessing_adequacy_international_data_transfers.pdf [accessed 26 October 2016].

ICO, 2015b. Data Protection Rights: What the Public Want and What the Public Want from Data Protection Authorities – V1, Available at: https://ico.org.uk/media/about-the-ico/documents/1431717/data-protection-rights-what-the-public-want-and-what-the-public-want-from-data-protection-authorities.pdf [accessed 26 October 2016].

ICO, 2015c. ICO Response to ECJ Ruling on Personal Data to US Safe Harbor. Available at: https://ico.org.uk/about-the-ico/news-and-events/news-and-blogs/2015/10/ico-response-to-ecj-ruling-on-personal-data-to-us-safe-harbor/ [accessed 26 October 2016].

ICO, 2016a. Privacy Regulators Study Finds Internet of Things Short-falls. Available at: https://ico.org.uk/about-the-ico/news-and-events/news-and-blogs/2016/09/privacy-regulators-study-finds-internet-of-things-shortfalls/ [accessed 26 October 2016].

ICO, 2016b. The Guide to Data Protection. Available at: https://ico.org.uk/media/for-organisations/guide-to-data-protection-2-6.pdf [accessed 26 October 2016].

IDC, 2014. Uptake of Cloud in Europe: Follow-up of IDC Study on Quantitative Estimates of the Demand for Cloud Computing in Europe and the Likely Barriers to Take-up (Final Report of the Study 'SMART 2013/0043: Uptake of Cloud in Europe'). Available at: http://ec.europa.eu/digital-agenda/en/news/final-report-study-smart-20130043-uptake-cloud-europe [accessed 26 October 2016].

IEEE, 2000. Institute of Electrical and Electronics Engineers, IEEE Standard Specifications for Public-Key Cryptography 1363-2000. Available at: http://ieeexplore.ieee.org/xpls/abs_all.jsp?arnumber=891000 [accessed 26 October 2016].

Information Commissioner (Slovenia), 2012. Personal Data Protection & Cloud Computing. Available at: https://www.ip-rs.si/fileadmin/user_upload/Pdf/smernice/Cloud_computing_and_data_protection_-_ENG_final.pdf [accessed 26 October 2016].

Ingram, M., 2013. Snowden maintains the NSA has direct access to company servers, which means someone is lying. *Gigaom.* Available at: https://gigaom.com/2013/07/09/snowden-maintains-the-nsa-has-direct-access-to-company-servers-which-means-someone-is-lying/ [accessed 26 October 2016].

Institute of Customer Service, 2016. Reaction to Parliamentary Inquiry on Cyber-Security Breaches. Available at: https://www.institute ofcustomerservice.com/media-centre/press-releases/article/reaction-to-parliamentary-inquiry-on-cyber-security-breaches [accessed 26 October 2016].

Intel, 2009. Intel Corporation Response to European Commission Public Consultation on the Legal Framework for the Fundamental Right to Protection of Personal Data. Available at: http://ec.europa.eu/justice/news/consulting_public/0003/contributions/organisations/intel_corporation_en.pdf [accessed 26 October 2016].

Intel, 2015. Intel Corporate Privacy Rules Deed Poll v4.1. Available at: http://www.intel.co.uk/content/dam/www/public/us/en/documents/corporate-information/corporate-privacy-rules-deed-poll.pdf [accessed 26 October 2016].

International Conference of Data Protection and Privacy Commissioners, 2009. International Standards on the Protection of Personal Data and Privacy: The Madrid Resolution. Available at: https://icdppc.org/wp-content/uploads/2015/02/The-Madrid-Resolution.pdf [accessed 26 October 2016].

International Conference of Data Protection and Privacy Commissioners, 2012. Resolution on Cloud Computing. Available at: https://icdppc.org/wp-content/uploads/2015/02/Resolution-on-Cloud-Computing.pdf [accessed 26 October 2016].

International Conference of Data Protection and Privacy Commissioners, 2014. Resolution on Enforcement Cooperation. Available at: https://icdppc.org/wp-content/uploads/2015/02/ResolutionInternational-cooperation.pdf [accessed 26 October 2016].

International Conference of Data Protection and Privacy Commissioners, 2016. Resolution on International Enforcement Cooperation. Available at: https://icdppc.org/wp-content/uploads/2015/02/7._resolution_on_international_enforcement_cooperation.pdf [accessed 26 October 2016].

IPC, 2012. Information and Privacy Commissioner of Ontario, Reviewing the Licensing Automation System of the Ministry of Natural Resources: A Special Investigation Report [PC12-39]. Available at: https://www.ipc.on.ca/wp-content/uploads/2016/08/Reviewing-the-Licensing-Automation-System-of-the-Ministry-of-Natural-Resources-A-Special-Investigation-Report-PC12-39.pdf [accessed 26 October 2016].

IPPC, 2009. International Pharmaceutical Privacy Consortium, Comments in Response to the Consultation on the Legal Framework for the Fundamental Right to Protection of Personal Data. Available at: http://ec.europa.eu/justice/news/consulting_public/0003/contributions/organisations_not_registered/international_pharmaceutical_privacy_consortium_en.pdf [accessed 26 October 2016].

Irion, K., 2012. Government cloud computing and national data sovereignty. *SSRN*. Available at: http://papers.ssrn.com/abstract=1935859 [accessed 26 October 2016].

ISO/IEC, 1993. International Organization for Standardization/International Electrotechnical Commission, ISO/IEC 2382-1:1993: Information Technology – Vocabulary – Part 1: Fundamental Terms. Available at: http://www.iso.org/iso/catalogue_detail.htm?csnumber=7229 [accessed 26 October 2016].

ISO/IEC, 2014a. International Organization for Standardization/International Electrotechnical Commission, ISO/IEC 17788:201: Information Technology – Cloud Computing – Overview and Vocabulary. Available at: http://standards.iso.org/ittf/PubliclyAvailableStandards/c060544_ISO_IEC_17788_2014.zip [accessed 26 October 2016].

ISO/IEC, 2014b. International Organization for Standardization/International Electrotechnical Commission, ISO/IEC 27018:2014: Information Technology – Security Techniques – Code of Practice for Protection of Personally Identifiable Information (PII) in Public Clouds Acting as PII Processors. Available at: http://www.iso.org/iso/home/store/catalogue_tc/catalogue_detail.htm?csnumber=61498 [accessed 26 October 2016].

Jäger, H.A. et al., 2013. Sealed cloud: a novel approach to safeguard against insider attacks. In *Open Identity Summit 2013. Springer Link*, pp. 187–97. Available at: http://link.springer.com/chapter/10.1007/978-3-319-12718-7_2 [accessed 26 October 2016].

Jansen, W. and Grance, T., 2011. Guidelines on security and privacy in public cloud computing SP 800-144. *NIST*. Available at: http://nvlpubs.nist.gov/nistpubs/Legacy/SP/nistspecialpublication800-144.pdf [accessed 26 October 2016].

Jensen, M. et al., 2009. On technical security issues in cloud computing. In *IEEE International Conference on Cloud Computing, 2009. CLOUD'09. IEEE*, pp. 109–16. Available at: http://ieeexplore.ieee.org/xpls/abs_all.jsp?arnumber=5284165 [accessed 26 October 2016].

Johnston, C., 2014. All sent and received e-mails in Gmail will be analyzed, says Google. *Ars Technica*. Available at: http://arstechnica.com/business/2014/04/google-adds-to-tos-yes-we-scan-all-your-e-mails/ [accessed 26 October 2016].

Jones, R., 2012. Extra territoriality and international transfers under the draft Regulation. *Privacy & Data Protection*, 12(3), pp. 6–9.

Jones, S., Robinson, D. and Chazan, G., 2016. EU spymasters lobby for change in encryption law. *Financial Times*. Available at: https://www.ft.com/content/08fe566e-679e-11e6-ae5b-a7cc5dd5a28c [accessed 26 October 2016].

Kamarinou, D., 2013. International transfers of personal data and corporate compliance under Directive 95/46/EC, the draft Regulation and the international community: part 1. *Communications Law*, 18(2), pp. 49–55.

Kaye, D., 2015. Report of the Special Rapporteur on the promotion and protection of the right to freedom of opinion and expression UN Doc A/HRC/29/32. *United Nations*. Available at: http://www.un.org/ga/search/view_doc.asp?symbol=A/HRC/29/32 [accessed 26 October 2016].

Kelly, S.M., 2014. Microsoft updates privacy policy after accessing blogger's Hotmail. *Mashable*. Available at: http://mashable.com/2014/03/21/microsoft-privacy-hotmail/ [accessed 26 October 2016].

Kerr, O., 2014. Judge upholds warrant for Microsoft e-mail on foreign server. *The Washington Post*. Available at: http://www.washingtonpost.com/news/volokh-conspiracy/wp/2014/07/31/judge-upholds-warrant-for-microsoft-e-mail-on-foreign-server/ [accessed 26 October 2016].

King, L., 2011. Vodafone in network outage following datacentre break-in. *Computerworld UK*. Available at: http://www.computerworlduk.com/news/mobile-wireless/3262920/vodafone-in-network-outage-following-datacentre-break-in/ [accessed 26 October 2016].

King, N.J. and Raja, V.T., 2013. What do they really know about me in the cloud? A comparative law perspective on protecting privacy and security of sensitive consumer data. *American Business Law Journal*, 50(2), pp. 413–82.

Kirby, M., 2011. The history, achievement and future of the 1980 OECD guidelines on privacy. *International Data Privacy Law*, 1(1), pp. 6–14.

Kiss, J., 2014. Snowden: Dropbox is hostile to privacy, unlike 'zero knowledge' Spideroak. *The Guardian*. Available at: https://www.theguardian.com/technology/2014/jul/17/edward-snowden-dropbox-privacy-spideroak [accessed 26 October 2016].

Koman, R., 2006. Google will turn over information to Brazil. *ZDNet*. Available at: http://www.zdnet.com/article/google-will-turn-over-information-to-brazil/ [accessed 26 October 2016].

Kommerskollegium, 2014. No Transfer, No Trade: The Importance of Cross-Border Data Transfers for Companies Based in Sweden. Available at: http://www.kommers.se/Documents/dokumentarkiv/publikationer/2014/No_Transfer_No_Trade_webb.pdf [accessed 26 October 2016].

Kommerskollegium, 2015. No Transfer, No Production: A Report on Cross-Border Data Transfers, Global Value Chains, and the Production of Goods. Available at: https://ec.europa.eu/futurium/en/system/files/ged/publ-no-transfer-no-production.pdf [accessed 26 October 2016].

Konarski, X. et al., 2012. Reforming the Data Protection Package: Study for the European Parliament's Committee on Internal Market and Consumer Protection. *Parliament*. Available at: http://www.europarl.europa.eu/document/activities/cont/201209/20120928ATT52488/20120928ATT52488EN.pdf [accessed 26 October 2016].

Konferenz der Datenschutzbeauftragten des Bundes und der Länder & Düsseldorfer Kreises, 2014. Orientierungshilfe: Cloud Computing Version 2.0. Available at: https://www.datenschutz-bayern.de/technik/orient/oh_cloud.pdf [accessed 26 October 2016].

Korff, D., 1998. Existing case-law on compliance with data protection laws and principles in the member states of European Union: annex to the annual report 1998 (XV D-5047-98) of the working party established by article 29 of Directive 95-46-EC. *Commission*. Available at: http://bookshop.europa.eu/bg/existing-case-law-on-compliance-with-data-protection-laws-and-principles-in-the-member-states-of-the-european-union-pbC11398960/downloads/C1-13-98-960-EN-C/C11398960ENC_001.pdf;pgid=y8dIS7GUWMdSR0EAlMEUUsWb00001NlDENTl;sid=DbrM8gKOPVTM8VBCFq5SVWCrQNnSgAVdC2k=?FileName=C11398960ENC_001.pdf&SKU=C11398960ENC_PDF&CatalogueNumber=C1-13-98-960-EN-C [accessed 26 October 2016].

Korff, D., 2002a. Comparative summary of national laws (EC study on implementation of Data Protection Directive (study contract ETD/2001/B5-3001/A/49)). *Commission*. Available at: http://ec.europa.eu/justice/policies/privacy/docs/lawreport/consultation/univessex-comparative study_en.pdf [accessed 26 October 2016].

Korff, D., 2002b. EC study on implementation of Data Protection Directive 95/46/EC. *SSRN*. Available at: http://papers.ssrn.com/abstract=1287667 [accessed 26 October 2016].

Korff, D., 2010. Comparative study on different approaches to new privacy challenges in particular in the light of technological developments: Working Paper No.2 – Data protection laws in the EU: the difficulties in meeting the challenges posed by global social and technical developments. *Commission*. Available at: http://ec.europa.

eu/justice/policies/privacy/docs/studies/new_privacy_challenges/final_report_working_paper_2_en.pdf [accessed 26 October 2016].

Korff, D. and Brown, I., 2010. Data protection laws in the EU: the difficulties in meeting the challenges posed by global social and technical developments. *Commission*. Available at: http://ec.europa.eu/justice/policies/privacy/docs/studies/new_privacy_challenges/final_report_working_paper_2_en.pdf [accessed 26 October 2016].

KPMG, 2011. The Cloud: Changing the Business Ecosystem. Available at: https://www.kpmg.com/IN/en/IssuesAndInsights/Thought Leadership/The_Cloud_Changing_the_Business_Ecosystem.pdf [accessed 26 October 2016].

Kraus, J.L., 1993. On the regulation of personal data flows in Europe and the United States. *Columbia Business Law Review*, (1), pp. 59–88.

Krebs, B., 2007. Security fix: Salesforce.com acknowledges data loss. *The Washington Post*. Available at: http://voices.washingtonpost.com/securityfix/2007/11/salesforcecom_acknowledges_dat.html [accessed 26 October 2016].

Kroes, N., 2013. Data isn't a four-letter word. *Commission*. Available at: http://europa.eu/rapid/press-release_SPEECH-13-1059_en.htm?locale=en [accessed 26 October 2016].

Kumar, V. and Dani, R., 2015. Announcing Customer Lockbox for Office 365. *Office Blogs*. Available at: https://blogs.office.com/2015/04/21/announcing-customer-lockbox-for-office-365/ [accessed 26 October 2016].

Kuner, C., 2007a. *European Data Protection Law: Corporate Compliance and Regulation* 2nd edition. Oxford; New York: OUP.

Kuner, C., 2007b. Internet update 1.0, European data protection law: corporate compliance and regulation. *Oxford University Press*. Available at: http://global.oup.com/booksites/content/9780199283859/updates/040920071 [accessed 26 October 2016].

Kuner, C., 2008. Internet update 2.0, European data protection law: corporate compliance and regulation. *Oxford University Press*. Available at: http://global.oup.com/booksites/content/9780199283859/updates/1704200814 [accessed 26 October 2016].

Kuner, C., 2009. Onward transfers of personal data under the U.S. Safe Harbor Framework. *Privacy & Security Law Report*, 8(33). Available at: http://www.wsgr.com/attorneys/BIOS/PDFs/kuner-0809.pdf [accessed 26 October 2016].

Kuner, C., 2010. Data protection law and international jurisdiction on the Internet (part 2). *International Journal of Law and Information Technology*, 18(3), pp. 227–47.

Kuner, C., 2011. *Regulation of Transborder Data Flows under Data Protection and Privacy Law*, Paris: Organisation for Economic

Co-operation and Development. Available at: http://www.oecd-ilibrary.org/content/workingpaper/5kg0s2fk315f-en [accessed 26 October 2016].

Kuner, C., 2013a. Requiring local storage of Internet data will not protect privacy. *OUPblog*. Available at: http://blog.oup.com/2013/12/data-security-privacy-storage-law/ [accessed 26 October 2016].

Kuner, C., 2013b. *Transborder Data Flows and Data Privacy Law*. Oxford: OUP.

Kuner, C. et al., 2013. The extraterritoriality of data privacy laws: an explosive issue yet to detonate. *International Data Privacy Law*, 3(3), pp. 147–8.

Kupczyk, D., 2014. Draft ad hoc contractual clauses for EU data processor to non-EU sub-processor: consensus at last? *Privacy & Data Protection*, 14(7), pp. 9–12.

Kusnetzky, D., 2014. Monitoring SaaS applications: the customer's responsbility [sic]. *ZDNet*. Available at: http://www.zdnet.com/article/monitoring-saas-applications-the-customers-responsbility/ [accessed 26 October 2016].

Lacor, P., 2016. Making European infrastructure available to our customers. *Dropbox Business Blog*. Available at: https://blogs.dropbox.com/business/2016/09/making-european-infrastructure-available-to-our-customers/ [accessed 26 October 2016].

Landler, M. and Schmidt, M.S., 2013. Spying known at top levels, officials say. *The New York Times*. Available at: http://www.nytimes.com/2013/10/30/world/officials-say-white-house-knew-of-spying.html [accessed 26 October 2016].

Laoutaris, N. et al., 2009. Delay tolerant bulk data transfers on the Internet. In *Proceedings of the Eleventh International Joint Conference on Measurement and Modeling of Computer Systems*. ACM, pp. 229–38. Available at: http://doi.acm.org/10.1145/1555349.1555376 [accessed 26 October 2016].

Leahy, J., 2013. Brazil sparks furore over Internet privacy bill. *Financial Times*. Available at: http://www.ft.com/cms/s/5cd5b638-487a-11e3-8237-00144feabdc0.html [accessed 26 October 2016].

Leloup, D., 2016. Mis en demeure par la CNIL, Facebook a formellement adressé sa réponse. *Le Monde.fr*. Available at: http://www.lemonde.fr/pixels/article/2016/08/10/mis-en-demeure-par-la-cnil-facebook-a-formellement-adresse-sa-reponse_4980771_4408996.html [accessed 26 October 2016].

Lemos, R., 2009. When the FBI raids a data center: a rare danger. *CIO*. Available at: http://www.cio.com/article/490340/When_the_FBI_Raids_a_Data_Center_A_Rare_Danger [accessed 26 October 2016].

LeSieur, F., 2012. Regulating cross-border data flows and privacy in the networked digital environment and global knowledge economy. *International Data Privacy Law*, 2(2), pp. 93–104.

Lessig, L., 2006. *Code: And Other Laws of Cyberspace, Version 2.0.* Revised edition. New York: Basic Books.

Leuthner, C., 2016. Don't rely on Safe Harbor: proceedings in Germany – and the new EU-US Privacy Shield is unveiled. *datonomy*. Available at: http://datonomy.eu/2016/03/01/dont-rely-on-safe-harbor-proceedings-in-germany-and-the-new-eu-us-privacy-shield-is-unveiled/ [accessed 26 October 2016].

Leviathan Security Group, 2015a. Analysis of Cloud vs. Local Storage: Capabilities, Opportunities, Challenges. Available at: https://static1.squarespace.com/static/556340ece4b0869396f21099/t/559dada7e4b069728afca39b/1436396967533/Value+of+Cloud+Security+-+Scarcity.pdf [accessed 26 October 2016].

Leviathan Security Group, 2015b. Comparison of Availability between Local and Cloud Storage. Available at: https://static1.squarespace.com/static/556340ece4b0869396f21099/t/559dad9ae4b069728afca34a/1436396954508/Value+of+Cloud+Security+-+Availability.pdf [accessed 26 October 2016].

Leviathan Security Group, 2015c. Value of Cloud Security: Vulnerability. Available at: http://www.leviathansecurity.com/wp-content/uploads/Value-of-Cloud-Security-Vulnerability.pdf [accessed 26 October 2016].

Leyden, J., 2010. Brazilian banker's crypto baffles FBI. *The Register*. Available at: http://www.theregister.co.uk/2010/06/28/brazil_banker_crypto_lock_out/ [accessed 26 October 2016].

Lillington, K., 2015. Oracle keeps European data within its EU-based data centres. *The Irish Times*. Available at: http://www.irishtimes.com/business/technology/oracle-keeps-european-data-within-its-eu-based-data-centres-1.2408505 [accessed 26 October 2016].

Litan, A., 2011. RSA SecurID attack details unveiled: lessons learned. *Gartner*. Available at: http://blogs.gartner.com/avivah-litan/2011/04/01/rsa-securid-attack-details-unveiled-they-should-have-known-better/ [accessed 26 October 2016].

Lloyd, I.J., 1996. An outline of the European Data Protection Directive. *Journal of Information, Law & Technology*, 1. Available at: http://www2.warwick.ac.uk/fac/soc/law/elj/jilt/1996_1/special/lloyd.

Lomas, N., 2016. Facebook ordered to stop tracking non-users in France. *TechCrunch*. Available at: http://social.techcrunch.com/2016/02/09/facebook-ordered-to-stop-tracking-non-users-in-france/ [accessed 26 October 2016].

London Economics, 2013. Implications of the European Commission's Proposal for a General Data Protection Regulation for Business: Final

Report to the Information Commissioner's Office. Available at: https://ico.org.uk/media/about-the-ico/documents/1042341/implications-european-commissions-proposal-general-data-protection-regulation-for-business.pdf [accessed 26 October 2016].

Lowans, B., MacDonald, N. and Casper, C., 2012. *Five Cloud Data Residency Issues That Must Not Be Ignored*. Stamford, CT: Gartner.

MacAskill, E. et al., 2013. GCHQ taps fibre-optic cables for secret access to world's communications. *The Guardian*. Available at: http://www.theguardian.com/uk/2013/jun/21/gchq-cables-secret-world-communications-nsa [accessed 26 October 2016].

MacIver, K., 2013. The geopolitics of government cloud. *diginomica*. Available at: http://diginomica.com/2013/06/03/the-geopolitics-of-government-cloud/ [accessed 26 October 2016].

Mahmoodi, T., 2011. Energy efficient protocols in self-aware networks [slides]. *Stanford University*. Available at: http://netseminar.stanford.edu/past_seminars/seminars/12_13_11.pdf [accessed 26 October 2016].

Maier, B., 2010. How has the law attempted to tackle the borderless nature of the Internet? *International Journal of Law and Information Technology*, 18(2), pp. 142–75.

MainStrat, 2009. Comparative Study on the Situation in the 27 Member States as Regards the Law Applicable to Non-Contractual Obligations Arising out of Violations of Privacy and Rights Relating to Personality, JLS/2007/C4/028, Final Report. Available at: http://ec.europa.eu/justice/civil/files/study_privacy_en.pdf [accessed 26 October 2016].

Makulilo, A.B., 2012. Privacy and data protection in Africa: a state of the art. *International Data Privacy Law*, 2(3), pp. 163–78.

Malcolm, W., 2012. Overseas or cross-border transfers of personal data. In R. Jay, *Data Protection Law & Practice*. London: Sweet & Maxwell.

Marchini, R. et al., 2007. Legitimising cross-border data flows by the 'self-assessment' method: different approaches throughout Europe. In J. Kuper, ed. *International Data Transfers: Data Protection Special Report*. London: BNA, pp. 6–28. Available at: http://www.dechert.com/files/Publication/2ebd5e8e-ccd4-46f6-8488-2abe6e7d0f26/Presentation/PublicationAttachment/830295f9-ac1b-4021-9b87-3f504b9a9203/IDT0607_marchini.pdf [accessed 26 October 2016].

Margolis, D. et al., 2016. SMTP strict transport security. *IETF*. Available at: https://tools.ietf.org/id/draft-margolis-smtp-sts-00.html [accessed 26 October 2016].

Markoff, J., 2008. Internet traffic begins to bypass the U.S. *The New York Times*. Available at: http://www.nytimes.com/2008/08/30/business/30pipes.html [accessed 26 October 2016].

MAS, 2016. Monetary Authority of Singapore, Guidelines on Outsourcing. Available at: http://www.mas.gov.sg/~/media/MAS/Regulations%20and%20Financial%20Stability/Regulatory%20and%20Supervisory%20Framework/Risk%20Management/Outsourcing%20Guidelines_Jul%202016.pdf [accessed 26 October 2016].

McGinn, F., 2011. FBI LulzSec server takedown fails. *Examiner.com*. Available at: http://www.examiner.com/article/fbi-lulzsec-server-takedown-fails [accessed 25 March 2015].

McKendrick, J., 2016. Shift: public cloud considered more secure than corporate data centers. *ZDNet*. Available at: http://www.zdnet.com/article/shift-public-cloud-more-secure-than-corporate-data-centers/ [accessed 26 October 2016].

McKenty, J., 2013. Three signs it's time to get off Amazon's cloud. *WIRED*. Available at: http://www.wired.com/insights/2013/09/three-signs-its-time-to-get-off-amazons-cloud/ [accessed 26 October 2016].

Mell, P. and Grance, T., 2011. The NIST definition of cloud computing SP800-145. *NIST*. Available at: http://nvlpubs.nist.gov/nistpubs/Legacy/SP/nistspecialpublication800-145.pdf [accessed 26 October 2016].

Merkel, D., 2014. Docker: lightweight Linux containers for consistent development and deployment. *Linux Journal*, 2014(239), p. 2.

Meyer, D., 2013. Heroku comes to Europe, but data protection issues remain. *Gigaom*. Available at: https://gigaom.com/2013/04/25/heroku-comes-to-europe-but-data-protection-issues-remain/ [accessed 26 October 2016].

Meyer, D., 2014a. Microsoft says it will let users choose where data is stored, but things aren't that simple. *Gigaom*. Available at: http://gigaom.com/2014/01/23/microsoft-says-it-will-let-users-choose-where-data-is-stored-but-things-arent-that-simple/ [accessed 26 October 2016].

Meyer, D., 2014b. NSA and GCHQ spoofed LinkedIn to hack Belgian cryptography professor. *Gigaom*. Available at: https://gigaom.com/2014/02/01/nsa-and-gchq-hacked-belgian-cryptographer-report/ [accessed 26 October 2016].

Meyer, D., 2016. German DPA attacks U.S. Commerce Dept. over Safe Harbor. *IAPP*. Available at: https://iapp.org/news/a/german-dpa-attacks-u-s-commerce-dept-over-safe-harbor/ [accessed 26 October 2016].

Microsoft, n.d. Azure Datacenters. Available at: http://azuredatacentermap.azurewebsites.net/ [accessed 26 October 2016].

Microsoft, 2009. Microsoft Response to the Commission Consultation on the Legal Framework for the Fundamental Right to Protection of Personal Data. Available at: http://ec.europa.eu/justice/news/consulting_public/0003/contributions/organisations/microsoft_corporation_en.pdf [accessed 26 October 2016].

Microsoft, 2013a. Microsoft Security Advisory 2880823: Deprecation of SHA-1 Hashing Algorithm for Microsoft Root Certificate Program. Available at: https://technet.microsoft.com/library/security/2880823 [accessed 26 October 2016].

Microsoft, 2013b. Small and Midsize Businesses Cloud Trust Study: U.S. Study Results. Available at: https://news.microsoft.com/download/presskits/security/docs/TwCJune13US.pdf [accessed 26 October 2016].

Microsoft, 2014. Microsoft Online Services Terms. Available at: http://www.microsoftvolumelicensing.com/Downloader.aspx?DocumentId= 7703 [accessed 26 October 2016].

Millard, C. and Carolina, R., 1995. Commercial transactions on the global information infrastructure: a European perspective. *John Marshall Journal of Computer & Information Law*, 14(2), pp. 269–302.

Miller, R., 2014. Bitcoin exchange blames data center provider for $100,000 theft. *Data Center Knowledge*. Available at: http://www.datacenterknowledge.com/archives/2014/03/20/bitcoin-exchange-blames-data-center-provider-100000-theft/ [accessed 26 October 2016].

Ministry of Justice, 2011. Letter to Dr Pounder FS50290504. Available at: http://amberhawk.typepad.com/files/uk-deficiency-details_may-2011.pdf [accessed 26 October 2016].

Ministry of Justice, 2012. Call for Evidence on EU Data Protection Proposals Regulation COM(2012)11 and Directive COM(2012)10. Available at: https://consult.justice.gov.uk/digital-communications/data-protection-proposals-cfe/supporting_documents/eudataprotection proposalscallforevidence.pdf [accessed 26 October 2016].

Minoli, D., 2004. *A Networking Approach to Grid Computing* 1st edition. Hoboken, NJ: Wiley-Blackwell.

Mizroch, A., 2014. For location-tracking startup, a data-privacy odyssey. *Digits*. Available at: http://blogs.wsj.com/digits/2014/11/04/for-location-tracking-startup-a-data-privacy-odyssey/ [accessed 26 October 2016].

Mlot, S., 2016. Facebook to open first data center in Ireland. *PCMAG*. Available at: http://www.pcmag.com/article2/0,2817,2498365,00.asp [accessed 26 October 2016].

Moerel, L., 2012a. *Binding Corporate Rules: Corporate Self-Regulation of Global Data Transfers*. Oxford: OUP.

Moerel, L., 2012b. Case study report: data protection – executive summary (HiiL Constitutional Foundations of Transnational Private Regulation research project). *Hague Institute for the Internationalisation of Law*. Available at: http://www.hiil.org/data/site management/media/Data%20Protection%20Case%20Study%20Executive %20Summary.pdf [accessed 26 October 2016].

Moiny, J.-P., 2012. Memorandum on introducing the concept of jurisdiction into Article 1 of Convention T-PD(2012)10. *CoE.* Available at: http://www.coe.int/t/dghl/standardsetting/dataprotection/TPD_documents/T-PD(2012)10%20E%20-%20Memorandum%20on%20introducing%20the%20conc%20%20of%20jurisdiction%20(J-PH%20Moiny)%20(final).pdf [accessed 26 October 2016].

Mosch, M., 2011. User-controlled data sovereignty in the cloud. In *Proceedings of the PhD Symposium at the 9th IEEE European Conference on Web Services (ECOWS 2011). IEEE.* Available at: http://www.rn.inf.tu-dresden.de/uploads/Publikationen/ecows2011mosch.pdf [accessed 26 October 2016].

Munshi, N., 2016. Data security concerns force banks up into the cloud. *Financial Times.* Available at: https://www.ft.com/content/e4667fe2-7522-11e6-bf48-b372cdb1043a [accessed 26 October 2016].

Munson, L., 2014. Whatsapp now provides end-to-end encryption by default for messages. *Naked Security.* Available at: https://nakedsecurity.sophos.com/2014/11/19/whatsapp-now-provides-end-to-end-encryption-by-default-for-messages/ [accessed 26 October 2016].

Murray, A., 2006. *The Regulation of Cyberspace: Control in the Online Environment.* London, UK: Routledge-Cavendish.

Myers, A., 2016. FTC enforcement of the U.S.-EU Safe Harbor Framework. *International Association of Privacy Professionals.* Available at: https://iapp.org/media/pdf/resource_center/IAPP_FTC_SH-enforcement.pdf [accessed 26 October 2016].

Myers, A.C., 1999. JFlow: practical mostly-static information flow control. In *Proceedings of the 26th ACM SIGPLAN-SIGACT symposium on Principles of programming languages. ACM,* pp. 228–41. Available at: http://dl.acm.org/citation.cfm?id=292561 [accessed 26 October 2016].

Nakashima, E., 2016. Justice Dept. asks court to review decision on Microsoft emails held in Ireland. *Washington Post.* Available at: https://www.washingtonpost.com/world/national-security/justice-department-appeals-court-decision-on-access-to-microsoft-emails-held-in-ireland/2016/10/14/1a1ac910-920e-11e6-a6a3-d50061aa9fae_story.html [accessed 26 October 2016].

Naydenov, R. et al., 2015. Secure use of cloud computing in the finance sector: good practices and recommendations. *ENISA.* Available at: https://www.enisa.europa.eu/publications/cloud-in-finance/at_download/fullReport [accessed 26 October 2016].

NBC, 2010. Google Had at Least Two Creepy Stalker Engineers. *NBC News.* Available at: http://technolog-discuss.nbcnews.com/_news/2010/09/15/5116575-google-had-at-least-two-creepy-stalker-engineers [accessed 26 October 2016].

Netskope, 2016. EMEA Cloud Report. Available at: https://resources. netskope.com/h/i/285920664-september-2016-emea-cloud-report [accessed 26 October 2016].

Nielsen, N., 2015. EU data chiefs failed to report US privacy complaints. *euobserver*. Available at: https://euobserver.com/connected/130792 [accessed 26 October 2016].

NIST, 2004. Standards for Security Categorization of Federal Information and Information Systems (FIPS 199). Available at: http://csrc. nist.gov/publications/fips/fips199/FIPS-PUB-199-final.pdf [accessed 26 October 2016].

NIST, 2016. Attribute Based Access Control. Available at: https:// nccoe.nist.gov/sites/default/files/library/fact-sheets/abac-fact-sheet.pdf [accessed 26 October 2016].

Nottingham, M. and Leiba, B., 2015. HTTP/2 approved. *IETF Blog*. Available at: http://www.ietf.org/blog/2015/02/http2-approved/ [accessed 26 October 2016].

OECD, 1997. OECD Guidelines for Cryptography Policy. Available at: http://www.oecd.org/internet/ieconomy/guidelinesforcryptography policy.htm [accessed 26 October 2016].

OECD, 2006. Report on the Cross-Border Enforcement of Privacy Laws. Available at: http://www.oecd.org/internet/ieconomy/37558845.pdf [accessed 26 October 2016].

OECD, 2007. OECD Recommendation on Cross-Border Co-operation in the Enforcement of Laws Protecting Privacy. Available at: http:// www.oecd.org/sti/ieconomy/38770483.pdf [accessed 26 October 2016].

OECD, 2011. Report on the Implementation of the OECD Recommendation on Cross-Border Co-operation in the Enforcement of Laws Protecting Privacy. Available at: http://www.oecd-ilibrary.org/content/ workingpaper/5kgdpm9wg9xs-en [accessed 26 October 2016].

Office of the United States Trade Representative, 2014. 2014 Section 1377 Review on Compliance with Telecommunications Trade Agreements. Available at: http://www.ustr.gov/sites/default/files/2013-14% 20-1377Report-final.pdf [accessed 26 October 2016].

Office of the United States Trade Representative, 2016. The 2016 National Trade Estimate Report. Available at: https://ustr.gov/sites/ default/files/2016-NTE-Report-FINAL.pdf [accessed 26 October 2016].

OPC, 2006. PIPEDA Review Discussion Document. Available at: https:// www.priv.gc.ca/media/1312/pipeda_review_060718_e.pdf [accessed 26 October 2016].

OPC, 2009. Guidelines for Processing Personal Data across Borders. Available at: https://www.priv.gc.ca/en/privacy-topics/personal-information-transferred-across-borders/gl_dab_090127/ [accessed 26 October 2016].

OPC, 2012. Interpretation Bulletin: Accountability. Available at: https://www.priv.gc.ca/en/privacy-topics/privacy-laws-in-canada/the-personal-information-protection-and-electronic-documents-act-pipeda/pipeda-compliance-help/pipeda-interpretation-bulletins/interpretations_02_acc/ [accessed 26 October 2016].

OPC, 2013a. An Update on Our Internet Privacy Sweep. Available at: http://blog.priv.gc.ca/index.php/2013/09/20/an-update-on-our-internet-privacy-sweep/ [accessed 26 October 2016].

OPC, 2013b. Initial Results from Our Internet Privacy Sweep: The Good, the Bad, and the Ugly. Available at: http://blog.priv.gc.ca/index.php/2013/08/13/initial-results-from-our-internet-privacy-sweep-the-good-the-bad-and-the-ugly/ [accessed 26 October 2016].

OPC, 2014. Global Privacy Enforcement Network Targets Apps in Second Online Sweep. Available at: https://www.priv.gc.ca/en/opc-news/news-and-announcements/2014/nr-c_140506/ [accessed 26 October 2016].

O'Quinn, J.C., 1998. None of your business: world data flows, electronic commerce, and the European privacy directive. *Harvard Journal of Law & Technology*, 12(3), pp. 683–702.

Orange, 2009. Contribution of Orange/France Telecom Group to the Consultation on the Legal Framework for the Fundamental Right to Protection of Personal Data. Available at: http://ec.europa.eu/justice/news/consulting_public/0003/contributions/organisations/orange_en.pdf [accessed 26 October 2016].

Osborne, C., 2015. How to send encrypted messages to iOS, Android devices for free. *ZDNet*. Available at: http://www.zdnet.com/article/how-to-send-encrypted-messages-to-ios-android-devices-for-free/ [accessed 26 October 2016].

Ottenheimer, D., 2012. Developing a cloud SLA: key security and compliance issues. *SearchCloudSecurity*. Available at: http://searchcloudsecurity.techtarget.com/tip/Developing-a-cloud-SLA-Key-security-and-compliance-issues [accessed 26 October 2016].

OWASP, 2016. Open Web Application Security Project, Cloud-10 Multi Tenancy and Physical Security. Available at: https://www.owasp.org/index.php/Cloud-10_Multi_Tenancy_and_Physical_Security [accessed 26 October 2016].

Palazzolo, J. and Ovide, S., 2014. U.S. judge rules Microsoft must produce emails held abroad. *Wall Street Journal*. Available at: http://

www.wsj.com/articles/u-s-judge-rules-microsoft-must-produce-emails-held-abroad-1406826302 [accessed 26 October 2016].

Palekar, N.S., 2007. Privacy protection: when is adequate actually adequate. *Duke Journal of Comparative & International Law*, 18(2), pp. 549–76.

Parker-Pope, T., 2008. More celebrity snooping by hospital workers. *Well (New York Times)*. Available at: http://well.blogs.nytimes.com/2008/04/03/more-celebrity-snooping-by-hospital-workers/ [accessed 26 October 2016].

PCI SSC, 2011. PCI Security Standards Council, Information Supplement: PCI DSS Tokenization Guidelines. Available at: https://www.pcisecuritystandards.org/documents/Tokenization_Guidelines_Info_Supplement.pdf [accessed 26 October 2016].

PCPD, 2014. Guidance on Personal Data Protection in Cross-Border Data Transfer. Available at: http://www.pcpd.org.hk/english/resources_centre/publications/guidance/files/GN_crossborder_e.pdf [accessed 26 October 2016].

PDPC, 2014. Advisory Guidelines on Key Concepts in the Personal Data Protection Act. Available at: https://www.pdpc.gov.sg/docs/default-source/annual-seminar-2014-pr/key-concepts.pdf?sfvrsn=0 [accessed 26 October 2016].

Pearce, G. and Platten, N., 1998. Achieving personal data protection in the European Union. *Journal of Common Market Studies*, 36(4), pp. 529–47.

Pearce, R., 2013. Business booms for cloud encryption provider after PRISM revelations. *TechWorld*. Available at: http://www.techworld.com.au/article/524404/business_booms_cloud_encryption_provider_after_prism_revelations/ [accessed 26 October 2016].

Perlroth, N. and Markoff, J., 2013. N.S.A. may have hit Internet companies at a weak spot. *The New York Times*. Available at: http://www.nytimes.com/2013/11/26/technology/a-peephole-for-the-nsa.html [accessed 26 October 2016].

Perspecsys, 2013. Gartner Report Highlights Enterprise Need for Security Solutions to Assist with Data Access, Compliance & Security in the Cloud. Available at: https://promotedstories.com/story/177282 [accessed 26 October 2016].

Pinsent Masons, 2015. More German Regulators Oppose Model Clauses for EU-US Data Transfers. Available at: http://www.out-law.com/en/articles/2015/october/more-german-regulators-oppose-model-clauses-for-eu-us-data-transfers/ [accessed 26 October 2016].

Pohlmann, K.C., 1989. *The Compact Disc: A Handbook of Theory and Use*. Madison, WI: A-R Editions, Inc.

Poitras, L. et al., 2013. Attacks from America: NSA spied on European Union offices. *Spiegel Online*. Available at: http://www.spiegel. de/international/europe/nsa-spied-on-european-union-offices-a-908590. html [accessed 26 October 2016].

Ponemon, 2013. 2013 Cost of Data Breach Study: Global Analysis. Available at: http://www.ponemon.org/local/upload/file/2013%20 Report%20GLOBAL%20CODB%20FINAL%205-2.pdf [accessed 26 October 2016].

Poullet, Y., Louveaux, S. and Asinari, M.V.P., 2001. Data protection and privacy in global networks: a European approach. *EDI Law Review*, 8(2/3), pp. 147–96.

du Preez, D., 2014. UBS CTO: outsourcing is dying and data regulation is stifling global services. *diginomica*. Available at: http:// diginomica.com/2014/04/01/ubs-cto-outsourcing-dying-data-regulation- stifling-global-services/ [accessed 26 October 2016].

Protalinski, E., 2015. The Pirate Bay is back online after almost two months. *VentureBeat*. Available at: http://venturebeat.com/2015/01/31/ the-pirate-bay-is-back-online-after-almost-two-months/ [accessed 26 October 2016].

Quan, D.M. et al., 2012. Energy efficient resource allocation strategy for cloud data centres. In E. Gelenbe, R. Lent and G. Sakellari, eds. *Computer and Information Sciences II*. London: Springer, pp. 133–41. Available at: http://link.springer.com/chapter/10.1007/978-1-4471- 2155-8_16 [accessed 26 October 2016].

Rackspace, 2009. International Transfer of Data. Available at: http://ec.europa.eu/justice/news/consulting_public/0003/contributions/ organisations_not_registered/rackspace_us_inc_en.pdf [accessed 26 October 2016].

RalfWi, 2015. Microsoft Cloud in Germany. Available at: https://blogs. technet.microsoft.com/ralfwi/2015/12/08/microsoft-cloud-in-germany/ [accessed 26 October 2016].

Rambøll Management, 2005. Economic Evaluation of the Data Protec- tion Directive 95/46/EC. Available at: http://ec.europa.eu/justice/ policies/privacy/docs/studies/economic_evaluation_en.pdf [accessed 26 October 2016].

Rashid, F.Y., 2011. Rustock botnet size nearly halved since server takedown: Microsoft. *eWeek*. Available at: http://www.eweek.com/c/a/ IT-Infrastructure/Rustock-Botnet-Size-Nearly-Halved-Since-Server- Takedown-Microsoft-711751 [accessed 26 October 2016].

Rauhofer, J., 2013. Governmental access to cloud data: a response. *SCL*. Available at: http://www.scl.org/site.aspx?i=ed32967 [accessed 26 October 2016].

Reding, V., 2013. Women and the Web: why data protection and diversity belong together. *Commission*. Available at: http://europa.eu/rapid/press-release_SPEECH-13-637_en.htm [accessed 26 October 2016].

Reed, C., 2007. The law of unintended consequences: embedded business models in IT regulation. *JILT*. Available at: http://go.warwick.ac.uk/jilt/2007_2/reed/.

Reed, C., 2012. *Making Laws for Cyberspace*. Oxford: OUP.

Reid, P., 2004. 'Regulating' online data privacy. *SCRIPT-ed*, 1(3), pp. 488–504.

Reidenberg, J.R., 1997. Lex informatica: the formulation of information policy rules through technology. *Texas Law Review*, 76(3), pp. 553–94.

Reidenberg, J.R., 2002. International issues: international data transfers, applicable law and jurisdiction. *Commission*. Available at: http://ec.europa.eu/justice/policies/privacy/docs/lawreport/reidenberg_en.pdf [accessed 26 October 2016].

Reidenberg, J.R. and Schwartz, P.M., 1998. On-line services and data protection and privacy: regulatory responses volume II – annex to the annual report 1998 (XV D/5047/98) of the working party established by article 29 of Directive 95/46/EC. *Commission*. Available at: http://ec.europa.eu/justice/data-protection/document/studies/files/19981201_dp_law_online_regulatory_en.pdf [accessed 26 October 2016].

Renfro, S., 2013. Secure browsing by default. *Facebook Engineering*. Available at: https://www.facebook.com/notes/facebook-engineering/secure-browsing-by-defa%20ult/10151590414803920?_fb_noscript=1 [accessed 26 October 2016].

Reynolds, M., 2016. 'Land is so yesterday': e-residents and 'digital embassies' could replace country borders. *WIRED UK*. Available at: http://www.wired.co.uk/article/taavi-kotka-estonian-government [accessed 26 October 2016].

Rheinland-Pfälzische Landesdatenschutzbeauftragte, 2015a. Folgerungen des Landesbeauftragten für den Datenschutz und die Informationsfreiheit Rheinland-Pfalz aus dem Urteil des EuGH vom 6. Oktober 2015 (C-362/14) 'Safe Harbor'. Available at: https://www.datenschutz.rlp.de/de/aktuell/2015/images/20151026_Folgerungen_des_LfDI_RLP_zum_EuGH-Urteil_Safe_Harbor.pdf [accessed 26 October 2016].

Rheinland-Pfälzische Landesdatenschutzbeauftragte, 2015b. Noch ein langer Weg bis zum 'sicheren Hafen' – aber die Richtung stimmt! Available at: https://www.datenschutz.rlp.de/de/presseartikel.php?pm=pm2015122201 [accessed 26 October 2016].

Rightscale, 2016. 2016 State of the Cloud Report. Available at: http://assets.rightscale.com/uploads/pdfs/RightScale-2016-State-of-the-Cloud-Report.pdf [accessed 26 October 2016].

Ring, T., 2013. Eurocloud all hot air. *SC Magazine UK*. Available at: http://www.scmagazineuk.com/euro-cloud-all-hot-air/article/317292/ [accessed 26 October 2016].

Ring, T., 2014. WhatsApp flaw leaves users open to spying. *SC Magazine UK*. Available at: http://www.scmagazineuk.com/whatsapp-flaw-leaves-users-open-to-spying/article/343647/?DCMP=EMC-SCUK_Newswire [accessed 26 October 2016].

Ristenpart, T. et al., 2009. Hey, you, get off of my cloud: exploring information leakage in third-party compute clouds. In *Proceedings of the 16th ACM Conference on Computer and Communications Security. ACM*, pp. 199–212. Available at: http://doi.acm.org/10.1145/1653662.1653687 [accessed 26 October 2016].

Roberts, P.F., 2014. In wake of Snowden, U.S. cloud providers face calls to wall off data. *ITWorld*. Available at: http://www.itworld.com/security/402153/wake-snowden-us-cloud-providers-face-calls-wall-data [accessed 26 October 2016].

Robinson, N. et al., 2009. Review of the European Data Protection Directive. *RAND Cambridge*. Available at: http://www.rand.org/content/dam/rand/pubs/technical_reports/2009/RAND_TR710.pdf [accessed 26 October 2016].

Robinson, P., 1986. Legal issues raised by transborder data flow. *Canada-United States Law Journal*, 11, pp. 295–316.

RT, 2016. US, Germany, France Top Google Transparency Report User Data Requests. Available at: https://www.rt.com/news/362711-top-google-user-data-requests/ [accessed 26 October 2016].

Rubens, P., 2014. 2014: The year of encryption. *BBC*. Available at: http://www.bbc.co.uk/news/business-25670315 [accessed 26 October 2016].

Ryan, P.S., Falvey, S. and Merchant, R., 2013. When the cloud goes local: the global problem with data localization. *Computer*, 46(12), pp. 54–9.

Salesforce, 2015. Privacy and Data Protection Questions and Answers for Salesforce Customers: European Court of Justice's Decision Regarding the EU-US Safe Harbor Framework. Available at: http://www.salesforce.com/company/privacy/data-processing-addendum-faq.jsp [accessed 26 October 2016].

Sanger, D.E. and Shanker, T., 2014. N.S.A. devises radio pathway into computers. *The New York Times*. Available at: http://www.nytimes.com/2014/01/15/us/nsa-effort-pries-open-computers-not-connected-to-internet.html [accessed 26 October 2016].

Sargsyan, T., 2016. Data localization and the role of infrastructure for surveillance, privacy, and security. *International Journal of Communication*, 10, pp. 2221–37.

Scahill, J. and Begley, J., 2015. The great SIM heist: how spies stole the keys to the encryption castle. *The Intercept*. Available at: https://first look.org/theintercept/2015/02/19/great-sim-heist/ [accessed 26 October 2016].

Schmid, G., 2001. Report on the existence of a global system for the interception of private and commercial communications (ECHELON interception system): Temporary Committee on the ECHELON Interception System – A5-0264/2001. *Parliament*. Available at: http://www.europarl.europa.eu/sides/getDoc.do?type=REPORT&reference=A5-2001-0264&format=XML&language=EN [accessed 26 October 2016].

Schneier, B., 1999. Crypto-Gram: February 15, 1999. *Crypto-Gram Newsletter*. Available at: http://www.schneier.com/crypto-gram-9902.html#snakeoil [accessed 26 October 2016].

Schneier, B., 2013a. NSA harvesting contact lists. *Schneier on Security*. Available at: https://www.schneier.com/blog/archives/2013/10/nsa_harvesting.html [accessed 26 October 2016].

Schneier, B., 2013b. NSA surveillance: a guide to staying secure. *The Guardian*. Available at: http://www.theguardian.com/world/2013/sep/05/nsa-how-to-remain-secure-surveillance [accessed 26 October 2016].

Schuster, F. et al., 2015. VC3: Trustworthy data analytics in the cloud using SGX. In *2015 IEEE Symposium on Security and Privacy. IEEE*, pp. 38–54. Available at: http://ieeexplore.ieee.org/lpdocs/epic03/wrapper.htm?arnumber=7163017 [accessed 26 October 2016].

Schwartz, M.J., 2011. Are you ready for an FBI server takedown? *Network Computing*. Available at: http://www.networkcomputing.com/government/are-you-ready-fbi-server-takedown/1418400854 [accessed 26 October 2016].

Schwartz, P.M., 2009. Managing global data privacy: cross-border information flows in a networked environment. *The Privacy Projects*. Available at: http://theprivacyprojects.org/wp-content/uploads/2009/08/The-Privacy-Projects-Paul-Schwartz-Global-Data-Flows-20093.pdf [accessed 26 October 2016].

Schwartz, P.M. and Solove, D.J., 2013. Reconciling personal information in the United States and European Union. *SSRN*. Available at: http://papers.ssrn.com/abstract=2271442 [accessed 26 October 2016].

Shelley, M., 1831. *Frankenstein: or, The Modern Prometheus*. London: Henry Colburn & Richard Bentley.

Shih, G. and Carsten, P., 2014. Apple begins storing users' personal data on servers in China. *Reuters*. Available at: http://www.reuters.com/article/us-apple-data-china-idUSKBN0GF0N720140815 [accessed 26 October 2016].

Siddique, H., 2013. Edward Snowden's live Q&A: eight things we learned. *The Guardian*. Available at: http://www.theguardian.com/world/2013/jun/18/edward-snowden-live-q-and-a-eight-things [accessed 26 October 2016].

Simitis, S., 1994. From the market to the polis: the EU Directive on the Protection of Personal Data. *Iowa Law Review*, 80(3), pp. 445–70.

Simonite, T., 2013. NSA leak leaves crypto-math intact but highlights known workarounds. *MIT Technology Review*. Available at: http://www.technologyreview.com/news/519171/nsa-leak-leaves-crypto-math-intact-but-highlights-known-workarounds/ [accessed 26 October 2016].

Simorjay, F., 2016. Shared responsibilities for cloud computing. *Microsoft*. Available at: https://gallery.technet.microsoft.com/Shared-Responsibilities-81d0ff91/file/153019/1/Shared%20responsibilities%20for%20cloud%20computing.pdf [accessed 26 October 2016].

Singapore, Parliament 2012, *Debates*, vol.89, session 1 pt.2, 15 October, 3:56pm. Available at http://sprs.parl.gov.sg/search/report.jsp?current PubID=00078007-WA [accessed 26 October 2016].

Singel, R., 2011. Dropbox lied to users about data security, complaint to FTC alleges. *WIRED*. Available at: http://www.wired.com/2011/05/dropbox-ftc [accessed 26 October 2016].

Singh, J. et al., 2014. Regional clouds: technical considerations. *University of Cambridge, Computer Laboratory*. Available at: http://www.cl.cam.ac.uk/techreports/UCAM-CL-TR-863.pdf [accessed 26 October 2016].

Smart, N.P. and Vercauteren, F., 2010. Fully homomorphic encryption with relatively small key and ciphertext sizes. In P.Q. Nguyen and D. Pointcheval, eds. *Public Key Cryptography–PKC 2010*. Berlin, Heidelberg: Springer, pp. 420–43. Available at: http://link.springer.com/chapter/10.1007/978-3-642-13013-7_25 [accessed 26 October 2016].

Smart, N.P., Rijmen, V., Gierlichs, B., et al., 2014. Algorithms, key size and parameters report: 2014. *ENISA*. Available at: http://www.enisa.europa.eu/activities/identity-and-trust/library/deliverables/algorithms-key-size-and-parameters-report-2014/ [accessed 26 October 2016].

Smart, N.P., Rijmen, V., Stam, M., et al., 2014. Study on cryptographic protocols. *ENISA*. Available at: http://www.enisa.europa.eu/activities/identity-and-trust/library/deliverables/study-on-cryptographic-protocols/at_download/fullReport [accessed 26 October 2016].

Smith, B., 2012. Why cloud customers can't ignore model clauses, especially now. *Microsoft on the Issues*. Available at: http://blogs.microsoft.com/on-the-issues/2012/07/05/why-cloud-customers-cant-ignore-model-clauses-especially-now/ [accessed 26 October 2016].

Smith, B., 2013. Protecting customer data from government snooping. *The Official Microsoft Blog*. Available at: http://blogs.microsoft.com/blog/2013/12/04/protecting-customer-data-from-government-snooping/ [accessed 26 October 2016].

Smith, B., 2015a. A message to our customers about EU–US Safe Harbor. *Microsoft on the Issues*. Available at: http://blogs.microsoft.com/on-the-issues/2015/10/06/a-message-to-our-customers-about-eu-us-safe-harbor/ [accessed 26 October 2016].

Smith, B., 2015b. Safety, privacy and the Internet paradox: solutions at hand and the need for new trans-Atlantic rules. *Microsoft*. Available at: http://mseu.blob.core.windows.net/eumedia/2015/01/Brad-Smith-Brussels-January-20-2015.pdf [accessed 26 October 2016].

Smolaks, M., 2013. Amazon takes its cloud to China. *TechWeekEurope*. Available at: http://www.techweekeurope.co.uk/news/amazon-takes-cloud-china-134330 [accessed 26 October 2016].

Soghoian, C., 2011. How Dropbox sacrifices user privacy for cost savings. *slight paranoia*. Available at: http://paranoia.dubfire.net/2011/04/how-dropbox-sacrifices-user-privacy-for.html [accessed 26 October 2016].

Sophos, 2014. New Sophos research reveals attitudes and understanding of data protection across Europe. Available at: http://www.sophos.com/en-us/press-office/press-releases/2014/10/attitudes-and-understanding-of-data-protection-across-europe.aspx [accessed 26 October 2016].

SPIEGEL Staff, 2013. Inside TAO: documents reveal top NSA hacking unit. Available at: http://www.spiegel.de/international/world/the-nsa-uses-powerful-toolbox-in-effort-to-spy-on-global-networks-a-940969-3.html [accessed 26 October 2016].

SPIEGEL Staff, 2014. Inside the NSA's war on Internet security. Available at: http://www.spiegel.de/international/germany/inside-the-nsa-s-war-on-internet-security-a-1010361.html [accessed 26 October 2016].

Stackpole, T., 2013. The world's most notorious micronation has the secret to protecting your data from the NSA. *Mother Jones*. Available at: http://www.motherjones.com/politics/2013/08/sealand-havenco-data-haven-pirate [accessed 26 October 2016].

Stepanovich, A. and Mitnic, D., 2015. Universal implementation guide for the international principles on the application of human rights to communications surveillance. *AccessNow*. Available at: https://necessaryandproportionate.org/files/2016/04/01/implementation_guide_international_principles_2015.pdf [accessed 26 October 2016].

Stine, K. et al., 2008. *Volume I Revision 1, Volume I: Guide for Mapping Types of Information and Information Systems to Security Categories (SP 800-60)*. Gaithersburg, MD: NIST.

Stupp, C., 2016. European Commission paralysed over data flows in TiSA trade deal. *EurActiv.com*. Available at: http://www.euractiv.com/section/trade-society/news/european-commission-paralysed-over-data-flows-in-tisa-trade-deal/ [accessed 26 October 2016].

Sullivan, B., 2016. Cloud is cheaper in the US than in Europe. *TechWeek-Europe UK*. Available at: http://www.techweekeurope.co.uk/cloud/cloud-management/cloud-cheaper-us-than-europe-187169 [accessed 26 October 2016].

Svantesson, D.J.B., 2011. The regulation of cross-border data flows. *International Data Privacy Law*, 1(3), pp. 180–98.

Svantesson, D.J.B., 2012. Data protection in cloud computing: the Swedish perspective. *Computer Law & Security Review*, 28(4), pp. 476–80.

Swain, B., Pohlman, M. and Posey, L., 2011. Cloud Security Alliance GRC Stack training. *Cloud Security Alliance*. Available at: https://downloads.cloudsecurityalliance.org/initiatives/grc/CSA_GRC_Stack_Training.pdf [accessed 26 October 2016].

Swire, P., 2012. From real-time intercepts to stored records: why encryption drives the government to seek access to the cloud. *International Data Privacy Law*, 2(4), pp. 200–206.

Swire, P.P., 1998. Of elephants, mice, and privacy: international choice of law and the Internet. *International Lawyer (ABA)*, 32(4), pp. 991–1026.

Swire, P.P., 2004. Elephants and mice revisited: law and choice of law on the Internet. *University of Pennsylvania Law Review*, 153(6), pp. 1975–2002.

Swire, P.P. and Litan, R.E., 1998. *None of Your Business: World Data Flows, Electronic Commerce, and the European Privacy Directive*. Washington, DC: Brookings Institution Press.

Synergy Research Group, 2016. Amazon Leads; Microsoft, IBM & Google Chase; Others Trail. Available at: https://www.srgresearch.com/articles/amazon-leads-microsoft-ibm-google-chase-others-trail [accessed 26 October 2016].

Taieb, S. and Cohen, B., 2013. European Parliament Committee report to recommend suspension of EU-U.S. Safe Harbor. *Hogan Lovells Chronicle of Data Protection*. Available at: http://www.hldataprotection.com/2013/10/articles/consumer-privacy/eu-inquiry-on-electronic-mass-surveillance-highlights-disenchantment-with-eu-us-data-sharing-programs/ [accessed 26 October 2016].

Tene, O., 2011a. For privacy, European Commission must be innovative. *Center for Democracy & Technology*. Available at: https://cdt.org/blog/for-privacy-european-commission-must-be-innovative/ [accessed 26 October 2016].

Tene, O., 2011b. Privacy: the new generations. *International Data Privacy Law*, 1(1), pp. 15–27.

de Terwangne, C. and Louveaux, S., 1997. Data protection and online networks. *Computer Law & Security Review*, 13(4), pp. 234–46.

The Radicati Group, Inc., 2012. Email Statistics Report, 2012–2016 (Executive Summary). Available at: http://www.radicati.com/wp/wp-content/uploads/2012/04/Email-Statistics-Report-2012-2016-Executive-Summary.pdf [accessed 26 October 2016].

Thomlinson, M., 2014. Microsoft announces Brussels Transparency Center at Munich Security Conference. *Microsoft on the Issues.* Available at: http://blogs.microsoft.com/on-the-issues/2014/01/31/microsoft-announces-brussels-transparency-center-at-munich-security-conference/ [accessed 26 October 2016].

Timberg, C., 2013. Google encrypts data amid backlash against NSA spying. *The Washington Post.* Available at: http://www.washington post.com/business/technology/google-encrypts-data-amid-backlash-against-nsa-spying/2013/09/06/9acc3c20-1722-11e3-a2ec-b47e45e6 f8ef_story.html [accessed 26 October 2016].

TNS Opinion & Social, 2011. Attitudes on Data Protection and Electronic Identity in the European Union. Report (Special Eurobarometer 359). Available at: http://ec.europa.eu/public_opinion/archives/ebs/ebs_359_en.pdf [accessed 26 October 2016].

Toor, A., 2013. Cutting the cord: Brazil's bold plan to combat the NSA. *The Verge.* Available at: http://www.theverge.com/2013/9/25/4769534/brazil-to-build-internet-cable-to-avoid-us-nsa-spying [accessed 26 October 2016].

Toxen, B., 2014. The NSA and Snowden: securing the all-seeing eye. *Communications of the ACM,* 57(5), pp. 44–51.

Travis, A., 2016. UK security agencies unlawfully collected data for 17 years, court rules. *The Guardian.* Available at: https://www.the guardian.com/world/2016/oct/17/uk-security-agencies-unlawfully-collected-data-for-decade [accessed 26 October 2016].

Traynor, I., 2013. Key US-EU trade pact under threat after more NSA spying allegations. *The Guardian.* Available at: http://www.theguardian.com/world/2013/jun/30/nsa-spying-europe-claims-us-eu-trade [accessed 26 October 2016].

Trustwave, 2014. 2014 Trustwave Global Security Report. *Trustwave.* Available at: http://web.archive.org/web/20140827221356/http://www2.trustwave.com/rs/trustwave/images/2014_Trustwave_Global_Security_Report.pdf [accessed 26 October 2016].

Tung, L., 2013. Should Europe's schools adopt a code banning cloud companies from data mining? *ZDNet.* Available at: http://www.zdnet.com/should-europes-schools-adopt-a-code-banning-cloud-companies-from-data-mining-7000021036/ [accessed 26 October 2016].

Umhoefer, C. and Malafosse, J.B., 2015. France: CNIL contacting data controllers following Safe Harbor invalidation. *Privacy Matters*. Available at: http://blogs.dlapiper.com/privacymatters/france-cnil-contacting-data-controllers-following-safe-harbor-invalidation/ [accessed 26 October 2016].

UN, 1982. United Nations, Transnational Corporations and Transborder Data Flows: A Technical Paper. Available at: http://web.archive.org/web/20070630131921/http://unctc.unctad.org/data/e82iia4a.pdf [accessed 26 October 2016].

UNGA, 2014a. United Nations General Assembly, Resolution on Protection of Human Rights and Fundamental Freedoms while Countering Terrorism (18 December 2013) UN Doc A/RES/68/178. Available at: https://documents-dds-ny.un.org/doc/UNDOC/GEN/N13/450/13/PDF/N13450
13.pdf [accessed 26 October 2016].

UNGA, 2014b. United Nations General Assembly, Resolution on the Right to Privacy in the Digital Age (18 December 2013) UN Doc A/RES/68/167. Available at: http://www.un.org/ga/search/view_doc.asp?symbol=A/RES/68/167 [accessed 26 October 2016].

UOOU, 2013. Úřad pro ochranu osobních údajů, K právní ochraně osobních údajů při jejich předávání vrámci cloudových služeb. Available at: https://www.uoou.cz/VismoOnline_ActionScripts/File.ashx?id_org=200144&id_dokumenty=6582 [accessed 26 October 2016].

US DDTC, 2014a. US Department of State, Directorate of Defense Trade Controls, Clarification of Recent Press Release on Tokenization and Cloud Computing. Available at: http://www.pmddtc.state.gov/documents/Tokenization_clarification_statement_DDTC.pdf [accessed 26 October 2016].

US DDTC, 2014b. US Department of State, Directorate of Defense Trade Controls, The Use of Specified Methods of Tokenization to Secure ITAR-Controlled Data in Connection with Cloud Computing. Available at: http://perspecsys.com/wp-content/uploads/DDTC-Response-to-Perspecsys.pdf [accessed 26 October 2016].

US International Trade Administration, 2015. United States, APEC Economies Endorse Privacy Recognition in Support of Processors in Global Data Value Chain. Available at: https://blog.trade.gov/2015/10/26/united-states-apec-economies-endorse-privacy-recognition-in-support-of-processors-in-global-data-value-chain/ [accessed 26 October 2016].

US State Department, 2012. Five Myths Regarding Privacy and Law Enforcement. Available at: http://photos.state.gov/libraries/useu/2317

71/PDFs/Five%20Myths%20Regarding%20Privacy%20and%20Law%20Enforcement_October%209_2012_pdf.pdf [accessed 26 October 2016].

Van Eecke, P., 2015. Meeting European data protection and security requirements with CipherCloud solutions. White Paper. *Ciphercloud.* Available at: http://pages.ciphercloud.com/rs/830-ILB-474/images/meeting-european-data-protection-and-security-requirements-with-cipher cloud-solutions.pdf [accessed 26 October 2016].

Van Hoboken, J., Arnbak, A. and Van Eijk, N., 2012. Cloud computing in higher education and research institutions and the USA Patriot Act. *SSRN.* Available at: http://papers.ssrn.com/abstract=2181534 [accessed 26 October 2016].

Vassilaki, I., 1993. An empirical survey of cases concerning the transborder flow of personal data. *Computer Law & Security Report*, 9(1), pp. 33–7.

Venkatraman, A., 2014. VMware opens cloud datacentre in London for European IaaS customers. *ComputerWeekly.com.* Available at: http://www.computerweekly.com/news/2240225126/VMware-opens-cloud-datacentre-in-London-for-European-IaaS-customers [accessed 26 October 2016].

Verizon, 2010. Response to European Commission Communication on 'a Comprehensive Strategy on Data Protection in the European Union'. Available at: http://ec.europa.eu/justice/news/consulting_public/0006/contributions/not_registered/verizon_en.pdf [accessed 26 October 2016].

Verizon, 2014. 2014 Data Breach Investigations Report. Available at: http://www.verizonenterprise.com/resources/reports/rp_Verizon-DBIR-2014_en_xg.pdf [accessed 26 October 2016].

Vincens, L., 2012. Keeping your feet on the ground while your head's in 'the cloud'. *Privacy Laws & Business International Newsletter*, 118(Jul), pp. 24–6.

Vodafone, 2011. A Comprehensive Approach on Personal Data Protection in the European Union European Commission Communication COM(2010) 609: Vodafone's Response. Available at: http://ec.europa.eu/justice/news/consulting_public/0006/contributions/organisations/vodafone_en.pdf [accessed 26 October 2016].

VON Europe, 2011. Comments on the Commission's Data Protection Communication. Available at: http://ec.europa.eu/justice/news/consulting_public/0006/contributions/organisations/von_en.pdf [accessed 26 October 2016].

Vrijschrift Foundation, 2016. CETA Will Undermine Protection of Personal Data. Available at: https://www.vrijschrift.org/serendipity/

index.php?/archives/204-CETA-will-undermine-protection-of-personal-data.html [accessed 26 October 2016].

Walden, I., 2013. Law enforcement access to data in clouds. In C. Millard, ed. *Cloud Computing Law*. Oxford: OUP.

Wandall, H. and Cooper, D., 2016. How to align APEC and EU cross-border transfer rules. *Law360*. Available at: https://www.cov.com/-/media/files/corporate/publications/2016/04/how_to_align_apec_and_eu_cross_border_transfer_rules.pdf [accessed 26 October 2016].

Weber, R.H., 2013. Transborder data transfers: concepts, regulatory approaches and new legislative initiatives. *International Data Privacy Law*, 3(2), pp. 117–30.

WEF, 2011. World Economic Forum, Personal Data: The Emergence of a New Asset Class. Available at: http://www3.weforum.org/docs/WEF_ITTC_PersonalDataNewAsset_Report_2011.pdf [accessed 26 October 2016].

Wei, M.Y.C. et al., 2011. Reliably erasing data from flash-based solid state drives. In *FAST '11, 9th Usenix Conference on File and Storage Technologies*. usenix, pp. 105–18. Available at: http://static.usenix.org/legacy/events/fast11/tech/full_papers/Wei.pdf [accessed 26 October 2016].

Weichert, D.T., 2011. Cloud computing and data privacy. *Unabhängiges Landeszentrum für Datenschutz*. Available at: https://www.datenschutzzentrum.de/cloud-computing/20100617-cloud-computing-and-data-privacy.pdf [accessed 26 October 2016].

Weis, S., Morris, Z. and Millican, J., 2015. Securing email communications from Facebook. *Facebook*. Available at: https://www.facebook.com/notes/protect-the-graph/securing-email-communications-from-facebook/1611941762379302?_fb_noscript=1 [accessed 26 October 2016].

Whetstone, R., 2015. Privacy, security, surveillance: getting it right is important. *Google Europe Blog*. Available at: http://googlepolicyeurope.blogspot.com/2015/02/privacy-security-surveillance-getting.html [accessed 26 October 2016].

White, A., 1997. Control of transborder data flow: reactions to the European Data Protection Directive. *International Journal of Law and Information Technology*, 5(2), pp. 230–47.

White, T., 2009. *Hadoop: The Definitive Guide* 1st edition. Sebastopol, CA: O'Reilly Media, Inc.

Whittaker, Z., 2011. Microsoft admits Patriot Act can access EU-based cloud data. *ZDNet*. Available at: http://www.zdnet.com/blog/igeneration/microsoft-admits-patriot-act-can-access-eu-based-cloud-data/11225 [accessed 26 October 2016].

Winstead, B.K., 2011. Data residency and legal questions about the cloud. *Exchange and Outlook Blog*. Available at: http://

windowsitpro.com/blog/data-residency-and-legal-questions-about-cloud [accessed 26 October 2016].

Winter, B., 2013. Brazil's Rousseff targets Internet companies after NSA spying. *Reuters*. Available at: http://www.reuters.com/article/2013/09/12/net-us-usa-security-snowden-brazil-idUSBRE98B14R20130912 [accessed 26 October 2016].

Wojtan, B., 2011. The new EU Model Clauses: one step forward, two steps back? *International Data Privacy Law*, 1(1), pp. 76–80.

Wood, S., 2016. Safe Harbor: calmer waters on the horizon. *ICO Blog*. Available at: https://iconewsblog.wordpress.com/2016/02/11/safe-harbor-calmer-waters-on-the-horizon/ [accessed 26 October 2016].

Woollacott, E., 2015. Leaked TISA documents reveal privacy threat. *Forbes*. Available at: http://www.forbes.com/sites/emmawoollacott/2015/06/04/leaked-tisa-documents-reveal-privacy-threat/ [accessed 26 October 2016].

WP29, 2003. Sixth Annual Report on the Situation Regarding the Protection of Individuals with Regard to the Processing of Personal Data and Privacy in the European Union and in Third Countries Covering the Year 2001. Available at: http://ec.europa.eu/justice/policies/privacy/docs/wpdocs/2003/2003-6th-annualreport_en.pdf [accessed 26 October 2016].

WP29, 2004. Seventh Report on the Situation Regarding the Protection of Individuals with Regard to the Processing of Personal Data and Privacy in the European Union and in Third Countries Covering the Years 2002 and 2003. Available at: http://ec.europa.eu/justice/policies/privacy/docs/wpdocs/2004/7th_report_prot_individs_en.pdf [accessed 26 October 2016].

WP29, 2005. Eighth Annual Report on the Situation Regarding the Protection of Individuals with Regard to the Processing of Personal Data in the European Union and in Third Countries Covering the Year 2004. Available at: http://ec.europa.eu/justice/policies/privacy/docs/wpdocs/2005/8th_annual_report_en.pdf [accessed 26 October 2016].

WP29, 2006. Ninth Annual Report on the Situation Regarding the Protection of Individuals with Regard to the Processing of Personal Data and Privacy in the European Union and in Third Countries Covering the Year 2005. Available at: http://ec.europa.eu/justice/policies/privacy/docs/wpdocs/2006/9th_annual_report_en.pdf [accessed 26 October 2016].

WP29, 2007. Tenth Annual Report on the Situation Regarding the Protection of Individuals with Regard to the Processing of Personal Data and Privacy in the European Union and in Third Countries Covering the Year 2006. Available at: http://ec.europa.eu/justice/

policies/privacy/docs/wpdocs/2007/10th_annual_report_en.pdf [accessed 26 October 2016].

WP29, 2008. Eleventh Annual Report on the Situation Regarding the Protection of Individuals with Regard to the Processing of Personal Data and Privacy in the European Union and in Third Countries Covering the Year 2007. Available at: http://ec.europa.eu/justice/ policies/privacy/docs/wpdocs/2008/11th_annual_report_en.pdf [accessed 26 October 2016].

WP29, 2011. Fourteenth Annual Report of the Article 29 Working Party on Data Protection. Available at: http://ec.europa.eu/justice/data-protection/article-29/documentation/annual-report/files/2011/14th_annual_ report_en.pdf [accessed 26 October 2016].

WP29, 2013a. Letter to Alexander Seger, Council of Europe: Article 29 Working Party's Comments on the Issue of Direct Access by Third Countries' Law Enforcement Authorities to Data Stored in Other Jurisdiction, as Proposed in the Draft Elements for an Additional Protocol to the Budapest Convention on Cybercrime. Available at: http://ec.europa.eu/justice/data-protection/article-29/documentation/other-document/files/2013/20131205_wp29_letter_to_cybercrime_committee. pdf [accessed 26 October 2016].

WP29, 2013b. Letter to FedEE on Binding Corporate Rules. Available at: http://ec.europa.eu/justice/data-protection/article-29/documentation/ other-document/files/2013/20131008_bcr_fedee_en.pdf [accessed 26 October 2016].

WP29, 2013c. Letter to Viviane Reding on PRISM. Available at: http:// ec.europa.eu/justice/data-protection/article-29/documentation/other-document/files/2013/20130813_letter_to_vp_reding_final_en.pdf [accessed 26 October 2016].

WP29, 2014a. Article 29 Data Protection Working Party 96th Plenary Meeting. Available at: http://ec.europa.eu/justice/data-protection/ article-29/press-material/press-release/art29_press_material/2014/2014 0612_wp29_press_release_96th_plenary.pdf [accessed 26 October 2016].

WP29, 2014b. Fifteenth Annual Report. Available at: http://ec.europa.eu/ justice/data-protection/article-29/documentation/annual-report/files/2013/ 15th_annual_report_en.pdf [accessed 26 October 2016].

WP29, 2014c. Letter to Commissioner Reding on Actions to Restore Trust in Data Flows between the EU and the US. Available at: http://ec.europa.eu/justice/data-protection/article-29/documentation/other-document/files/2014/20140410_wp29_to_ec_on_sh_recommendations. pdf [accessed 26 October 2016].

WP29, 2014d. Letter to Dorothee Belz, Microsoft, on a New Version of the "Enterprise Enrollment Addendum Microsoft Online Services Data

Processing Agreement" and Its Annex 1 "Standard Contractual Clauses (Processors)". Available at: http://ec.europa.eu/justice/data-protection/article-29/documentation/other-document/files/2014/20140402_microsoft.pdf [accessed 26 October 2016].

WP29, 2015a. Sixteenth Annual Report. Available at: http://ec.europa.eu/justice/data-protection/article-29/documentation/annual-report/files/2014/16th_annual_report_en.pdf [accessed 26 October 2016].

WP29, 2015b. Statement. Available at: http://ec.europa.eu/justice/data-protection/article-29/press-material/press-release/art29_press_material/2015/20151016_wp29_statement_on_schrems_judgement.pdf [accessed 26 October 2016].

WP29, 2016. Statement on the Decision of the European Commission on the EU-U.S. Privacy Shield. Available at: http://ec.europa.eu/justice/data-protection/article-29/press-material/press-release/art29_press_material/2016/20160726_wp29_wp_statement_eu_us_privacy_shield_en.pdf [accessed 26 October 2016].

WTO, 1999. World Trade Organization, Work Programme on Electronic Commerce: Progress Report to the General Council. Available at: http://docsonline.wto.org/imrd/directdoc.asp?DDFDocuments/t/S/L/74.doc [accessed 26 October 2016].

Wubben, M., Schermer, B.W. and Teterissa, D., 2012. Legal aspects of the Digital Single Market: current framework, barriers and developments. Ministry of Economic Affairs, Agriculture and Innovation of the Netherlands. *Considerati*. Available at: http://considerati.com/wp-content/uploads/2013/08/Legal_aspects_of_Digital_Single_Market1.pdf [accessed 26 October 2016].

Zenium, 2015. Research Reveals Data Center Sector Still Rocked by Natural Disasters. Available at: https://www.zeniumdatacenters.com/research-reveals-data-center-sector-still-rocked-by-natural-disasters/ [accessed 26 October 2016].

Zetter, K., 2012. FBI uses 'sledgehammer' to seize e-mail server in search for bomb threat evidence. *WIRED*. Available at: http://www.wired.com/threatlevel/2012/04/fbi-seizes-server/ [accessed 26 October 2016].

Zetter, K., 2014a. NSA may have undercover operatives in foreign companies. *WIRED*. Available at: http://www.wired.com/2014/10/nsa-may-undercover-operatives-foreign-companies-new-documents-show/ [accessed 26 October 2016].

Zetter, K., 2014b. Russian 'Sandworm' hack has been spying on foreign governments for years. *WIRED*. Available at: http://www.wired.com/2014/10/russian-sandworm-hack-isight/ [accessed 26 October 2016].

Zhang, Y. et al., 2012. Cross-VM side channels and their use to extract private keys. In *Proceedings of the 2012 ACM Conference on Computer and Communications Security. ACM*, pp. 305–16. Available at: http://doi.acm.org/10.1145/2382196.2382230 [accessed 26 October 2016].

Ziadeh, A., 2015. A cloud lockbox to keep data secure. *GCN*. Available at: https://gcn.com/articles/2015/05/29/vc3-cloud-lockbox.aspx [accessed 26 October 2016].

Zinser, A., 2002. International data transfer out of the European Union: the adequate level of data protection according to article 25 of the European Data Protection Directive. *John Marshall Journal of Computer and Information Law*, 21(4), pp. 547–66.

Zyskind, G., Nathan, O. et al, 2015. Decentralizing privacy: using blockchain to protect personal data. In *Security and Privacy Workshops (SPW), 2015 IEEE. IEEE*, pp. 180–84. Available at: http://ieeexplore.ieee.org/xpls/abs_all.jsp?arnumber=7163223 [accessed 26 October 2016].

Zyskind, G., Nathan, O. and Pentland, A., 2015. Enigma: decentralized computation platform with guaranteed privacy. *arXiv preprint arXiv:1506.03471*. Available at: http://arxiv.org/abs/1506.03471 [accessed 26 October 2016].

Index